on the
MOVE

To Nat, Ben, and Nina

on the
MOVE

A Chronology of Advances in Transportation

Leonard C. Bruno

 Gale Research Inc. Detroit • Washington, DC • London

Gale Research Inc. Staff

Lawrence W. Baker, *Senior Developmental Editor*
Peg Bessette, Carol DeKane Nagel, Rita Skirpan, *Contributing Editors*

Mary Beth Trimper, *Production Assistant*
Evi Seoud, *Assistant Production Manager*
Mary Kelley, *Production Assistant*

Benita L. Spight, *Data Entry Supervisor*
Gwendolyn S. Tucker, *Data Entry Leader*
Virgil L. Burton III, Mary Daniels, Beverly Jendrowski, *Data Entry Associates*

Cynthia Baldwin, *Art Director*
Barbara J. Yarrow, *Graphic Services Supervisor*
Tracey Rowens, *Cover Designer*
Bernadette M. Gornie, *Page Designer*
Willie F. Mathis, *Camera Operator*

The Graphix Group, *Typesetting*

Library of Congress Cataloging-in-Publication Data

Bruno, Leonard C.
    On the move : a chronology of advances in transportation / edited [i.e. compiled] by Leonard C. Bruno.
        p. cm.
    Includes index
    ISBN 0-8103-8396-9 : $29.95
    1. Transportation—History. I. Title.

TA1015.B78 1990
629.04—dc20

92-10926
CIP

Contents

Foreword

The story of transportation is at one with the long history of mankind. It is nearly impossible to conjure an image of early mankind, no matter how primitive, that does not involve people moving themselves and their goods about in the best way they knew how.

This long and ancient history is often neglected since, in most of our own lifetimes, the advances made in transportation have been so spectacular. In this century alone, mankind has revolutionized travel on land, air, space, and water. Twenty years after the Wright Brothers first flew, I was born. By then, flying had already been a factor in the First World War and was becoming a more common, if not commonplace, phenomenon. With the passage of another twenty years, aviation had become a major, determining factor in a second international conflict. The postwar world saw flight begin to finally come into its own with the development of regular, routine travel by air. It also laid the foundation for mankind's beginning exploration of the upper atmosphere and, eventually, outer space.

In nearly all other areas of transportation there have been similarly spectacular leaps of accomplishment during this short time. Using speed as one indicator of progress, we see the land speed record exceed 600 mph, high speed trains carry passengers at about 160 mph, powerboats exceed 300 mph, and hydrofoils skim at about 120 mph. In the more eye-catching areas of air and space, greater speeds are achieved. Since 1947 when I became the first person to exceed the speed of sound (flying at Mach 1.06 or about 700 mph), similar rocket research aircraft like the *X-15* have achieved speeds over 4500 mph, and in 1974, a Lockheed *SR-71A* took less than two hours to fly from New York to London, averaging about 2000 mph. The fastest speed at which humans have ever travelled was achieved during the Apollo 10 moon mission when the Command Module went 24,791 mph. And today's Space Shuttle regularly reaches speeds of about 17,600 mph on each mission.

Yet speed is but one factor in the overall story of transportation, and it was not always the most important. In mankind's long and sometimes precarious existence, the goal of travel or transport was simply to get where you were going, or arrive alive and in one piece. Once it became somewhat assured that a person could do just that, the luxuries of comfort and speed became desirable. Such a long-range perspective or way of viewing things is especially useful for placing current events in their proper context, but it is sometimes not achievable since we often lack the simple facts of what happened when and in what order. This simple requirement, a chronology of events in the history of transportation, is exactly what is offered in this ambitious reference book. *On the Move* offers information to the serious researcher as well as the interested browser, and contains the nuts-and-bolts of transportation history needed by both. It was executed in the broadest manner and leaves no area or field unexamined. It therefore includes—besides the obvious automobile, airplane, boat, and spacecraft accomplishments—many important but often neglected subjects like bridges, roads, canals, and such specialized vehicles as carts, helicopters, submarines, bicycles, and even roller skates. In addition to corporate and biographical information, there are entries on altogether unexpected things like escalators and elevators. The breadth of its coverage is surpassed only by the fact that each and every entry is given as specific a date as possible and then placed in its proper chronological position. Such an arrangement gives the reader an unprecedented synoptic view of mankind's not-always-steady but always fascinating progress in transportation. Finally, a unique timeline of five hundred major events compresses this history into another useful way of looking at this information, and the two annotated bibliographies are especially helpful to readers wanting to know even more.

One idea the reader should take away, whether browsing or using this book in depth, is that transportation is a uniquely human endeavor whose importance is surpassed only by its inherent fascination.

Chuck Yeager
Brig. Gen., USAF, Ret.

Preface

Movement is all around us. So it has been since life began, for it seems obvious that to be alive is to move. Even the deep-rooted tree or the sessile coral show many types of subtle movement. Animals move, sometimes with purpose, as when they migrate, but only mankind transports. A person may run, walk, pedal, drive, fly or hover, his means limited only by his technology and his ingenuity. Today he can move at supersonic speeds while sitting. He can hurtle on tracks beneath mountains, skim the ocean's surface, quietly rise to the top of skyscrapers, or scream through outer space at 25,000 mph. Transportation—the act or process of transporting—is, therefore, a word usually reserved for people.

On the Move is a history of transportation—or man moving—told chronologically. Without the ordered, factual progression that chronology provides, history—or organized, related, and interpreted information—would not be possible. A chronology places events in the sequence in which they occurred. Its importance can be better appreciated by attempting to write history without the certainty of which event was prior to another. Historical cause and effect would be reduced to speculation, and nothing could be argued with any certitude. Knowledge of the time when something happened and, therefore, of what came before and after it is really the skeleton upon which the flesh of history is placed. Neither is fully useful without the other.

Scope

This chronology of transportation attempts to be as broad in range and scope as possible but interprets transportation strictly as people moving. Therefore, if a tunnel were built to move only water, it is not included. If it were used to move people, as pedestrians or as passengers in cars or trains, then it is included.

Aside from the inclusion of several significant military aircraft, *On the Move* focuses mostly on civilian or non-military modes and means of transportation. Also, this book is not primarily a chronicling of important "firsts" in any fields, although a significant number of entries in every area note the first time something occurred. In trying to be broad in scope, this work takes note of the non-technological as well, such as any influential books that were published, laws passed, organizations founded, people born, as well as related important discoveries and inventions.

Qualifications of the Data

Because of the breadth of the meaning of transportation employed and the book's goal of comprehensiveness, there must necessarily be some qualifications stated. First, the information offered is only as good as the source material from which it was derived. These sources are detailed in two annotated bibliographies—one for young adults and one for adults—found at the back of the volume. They are, for the most part, excellent works conscientiously and accurately written. Sometimes, however, two or more authoritative sources can be found describing the same event, with each differing by as much as 100 years. Dates that must be estimated are indicated in *On the Move* by the "circa" symbol (c.) preceding the year.

Second, history is a story that is constantly being rewritten. New information can result in a revision of "facts" or sometimes even in a major reinterpretation. From a strictly chronological standpoint, many examples of recent discoveries (such as carbon dating techniques) place in question the correctness of a very early date that everyone had heretofore agreed on and accepted. Conversely, other new information may suggest that many fairly recent events are actually much older than believed. Added to this are differing versions of what time periods such well-known epochs as the Stone Age or Iron Age should span. All of this is to say that the record of history upon which we all draw is an imperfect and changing one—especially for the older dates. And it will probably always be so. Nonetheless, our rough approximations are necessary and useful, and are the best we have so far. Other dating problems that may result in inconsistencies occur with projects of long duration. For example, the Panama Canal entry could have been placed in the year 1904, when construction began, or in 1914, when it was completed.

Finally, the "first" of anything is not as clear-cut a demarcation as it might appear. With an aircraft, for example, the entry given might be the date of its first roll-out, its first test flight, or its first operational or commercial flight. These and other qualifiers and exceptions that affect why one date is given over another are almost too numerous to mention. One date is absolute however. The book's cutoff date is December 31, 1991.

Special Features

On the Move contains a timeline of some 500 selected transportation events placed in order by year. More information about an individual event can be found in the chronological entry for that event in the text. Assorted entries are "pulled out" in the outside margins throughout the book for added highlighting. If an entry cannot be located by a quick browse, the index will indicate its exact page location. Nearly 150 line drawings and photographs add visual interest to the text. There are two annotated bibliographies, each aimed at a different audience. One contains the more general or popularly written books and might be considered appropriate to the high school, or young adult, level. The other offers lengthier, more comprehensive works geared to the adult reader.

Acknowledgments

I am indebted to a number of blameless, friendly, and very helpful people. First is Lawrence W. Baker, Senior Developmental Editor at Gale Research Inc. A more supportive and sympathetic editor cannot be found. Our work together seemed always effortless and was characterized by mutual respect and good humor. David E. Salamie, Senior Editor in New Publication Development at Gale, is responsible for both the idea for the book and the selection of the author. I thank him for both wise choices.

My wife, Jane, was quick to convince me that this book could actually be written in the time allotted, and then she backed me up by allowing me to work on it, guilt-free, during family time. Her schedule became more grueling than mine, but love can handle anything it seems. My three children are thanked by my dedicating this book to them. They deserve even more. My hardworking colleague, Michelle B. Cadoree, was the one who showed me how actually to do the book, by sharing some of her complete mastery of the personal computer, and by setting up a program that would allow me to accomplish a great deal in a short time. She is also responsible for both inputting much of the book as well as for the very large, useful index. I cannot thank her enough. My friend, Michael Adelman, came to our aid in time of crisis by lending his computing hardware with absolutely no strings attached. With his generous gift, we were able to increase our output considerably and to work all hours if necessary. He is a true friend indeed. Finally, about one-third of the photographs were taken by a very accomplished professional, J. Rudolph Vetter, who delivers even more than he promises.

Although *On the Move* is a chronology and not a history, it is nonetheless as subjective and as interpretive as any narrative history. While facts may be facts, other considerations may make for qualitative and quantitative differences or discrepancies. This book is the product of one person's research, and while it may benefit from the continuity such singular selection affords, it is also subject to all the known vagaries and effects of subjectivity. Obviously, a great deal had to be left out, and what one person deselects easily, another might never exclude.

The author has therefore consciously and scrupulously sought to be as objective and fair as possible, but no doubt an entry may seem spurious or ephemeral to some reader, who may also search fruitlessly for something which he or she considers to be extremely significant. Although this may be inevitable when a book is selective and not comprehensive, the author has certainly tried to include every identifiable, significant transportation accomplishment. Exclusion of a major event is only by omission, and the author would be grateful to be made aware of any such errors, as well as any factual mistakes. Comments and suggestions can be sent to: Editor, *On the Move*, Gale Research Inc., 835 Penobscot Bldg., Detroit, MI 48226.

Leonard C. Bruno

Photo Credits

Photographs and line drawings appearing in *On the Move* were received from the following sources (page numbers are also noted):

The American Railway. New York: Charles Scribner's Sons, 1897.
108

American Public Transit Association
110, 145, 174, 194, 223, 257, 282

Amtrak
361

Automotive Hall of Fame, Inc.
cover (wheel), 132, 146, 165, 171, 227, 274

Beesley, Lawrence. *The Loss of the SS. Titanic*. Boston: Houghton Mifflin Company, 1912.
181 (left)

Bruel, François-Louis. *Histoire Aéronautique*. 1909.
cover (balloon), 38, 59, 60

Byrn, Edward W. *The Progress of Invention in the Nineteenth Century*. New York: Munn & Co., 1900.
71, 83, 114, 117, 136

Chevrolet Motor Division
263 (left)

Clarkson, Thomas. *The History of the Rise, Progress, and Accomplishment of the Abolition of the African Slave-Trade*. London: Longman, Hurst, Rees and Orme, 1808. Volume II.
64

Embassy of Japan
352

Federal Aviation Administration
165, 213, 222 (both), 230, 233, 251, 313, 315, 321, 331, 355, 351, 357

Federal Highway Administration
33, 39 (bottom), 41, 45, 53, 54, 55, 66, 67, 79 (both), 81, 84, 91, 104, 106, 107, 116, 129, 137, 143

Feldhaus, F. M. *Ruhmesblätter der Technik*. Leipzig: Friedrich Brandstetter, 1910.
131

Geitel, Max. *Der Siegeslauf der Technik*. Stuttgart: Union Deutsche Verlagsgefellschaft, 1908-1909. Volume I.
154

Geitel, Max. *Der Siegeslauf der Technik*. Stuttgart: Union Deutsche Verlagsgefellschaft, 1908-1909. Volume III.
163

Ginzrot, Johann C. *Die Wagen und Fahrwerke der Griechen und Römer*. München: J. Lentner, 1817. Volume 1.
9

Library of Congress
cover (steamer), 19, 27, 37, 82, 94, 99, 102, 121, 123, 130, 134, 138, 161, 162, 179, 181 (right), 195, 196, 197, 203, 212, 226 (right), 229, 237, 258, 263 (right), 329 (bottom)

National Aeronautics and Space Administration
cover (space shuttle), 64, 113, 144, 171, 184, 199, 201, 206, 208, 221, 226 (left), 232, 234, 242, 244, 259, 267, 269, 279, 283, 287, 289, 290, 306, 314, 316, 317, 323, 324, 328, 329 (top), 343, 346, 353

Northrop Corporation
363

Smithsonian Institution
   176, 178, 262
Spears, John R. *The Story of the American Merchant Marine.* New York: The Macmillan Company, 1915.
   186
Stratton, Ezra. *The World on Wheels.* New York: The Author, 1878.
   6 (both)
U.S. Coast Guard
   49, 158, 205, 215, 330, 334
U.S. Department of Transportation, Maritime Administration
   63, 101, 340
U.S. Maritime Commission
   238
Veranzio, Fausto. *Machinae Novae.* Venice: c. 1615.
   40
Williams, Henry S. *The Conquest of Space and Time.* New York: The Goodhue Company, 1911.
   169
Zonca, Vittorio. *Novo Teatro di Machine.* Padua: P. Bertelli. 1607.
   39 (top)

History of Transportation

From the earliest times of pre-history, mankind has sought an easier, more efficient way of getting himself and his goods from one place to another. On land, primitive man moved about first on foot, with women carrying most of the goods and children. Even then it seems, the male role of hunter and defender necessarily relegated the female to a support function of bearing both children and burdens. Although there is no way to be certain of the exact order of invention, sleds made first of flat pieces of wood or stone were used to drag larger loads, and when animals began to be domesticated, dogs and then onagers (asses) were lashed to these sleds and made to pull them.

Water travel during pre-history evolved in much the same obvious and common-sense way, with a person wading or swimming across a narrow stream or using a log as a float to hold on to or even to sit on. Bundles of reeds or logs lashed together probably formed the first rafts, and the first real boats were the dug-out or burned-out log canoe. Primitive man could be fairly ingenious in attempting to get across bodies of water, and it is known that he used inflated animal skins as floats and also built slab and rope bridges.

By about 4000 B.C., the wheel was probably invented and the horse had been tamed. Most believe the wheel was invented in the Sumer region of Mesopotamia and eventually spread to Egypt and the Far East. The tripartite wheel, or the wooden wheel made of three connected, solid sections, came first, and was followed by the stronger and lighter spoked wheel of the Middle East. The Greeks improved the design by inventing the strong, cross-bar wheel. With the wheel and the small but strong horse, land transportation advanced from the primitive, plodding ox-cart to the sophisticated chariots of Egypt.

As Rome developed into world power, it raised road-building to a very high standard, connecting its empire with large, durable, well-drained roads made of smooth stone blocks. The Romans also seemed to develop a specialized, horse-drawn vehicle for nearly every purpose. Some of their aqueducts and bridges survive even today, and their stone arch bridges were major achievements—both in science and art. It was also during this early period that the Chinese built a land route across Asia and began their canal system.

Near the beginning of this second time period (around 300 B.C.), the Egyptians became the first pioneers of water travel, tailoring their reed boats to suit the demands of the Nile River. These were propelled both by oars and sails and steered by oars at the rear. These early ships eventually were developed by the Phoenicians, Greeks, and Romans. All were carvel-built, meaning their planks ran front-to-back, butted edge-to-edge, and the boat's strength came from its frame and keel. This type would come to dominate Mediterranean ship design for some time. Around 1300 B.C., Phoenician merchant ships were sailing in the open sea, using oars and sails. Nearly 1000 years later, Greek "biremes," using a double-bank of oars pulled by slaves, was a common sight, and by 200 A.D., high, wide-decked Roman cargo ships with a central square sail were common. About this time, the wholly new lateen or triangular sail was introduced by the Arabs on their traditional dhows, which also used the first stern rudder. These would be later adopted in Europe and would provide added maneuverability.

With the fall of Rome and the disorder that ensued, most advances took place in the far north. Here the first horse collar appeared, enabling a draft animal to pull with its shoulder and not be choked by pulling with its less-strong neck. Viking ships of the ninth century A.D. attained their distinctive shape and design and were all clinker-built or lap-jointed and then caulked. They were driven by oars and a single, central sail.

During the later medieval times, beginning around 1100 A.D., all existing road systems were nearly deteriorated, and both draft animals and wheeled vehicles had a rough time travelling. In France, an early form of wagon suspension was developed using leather straps, and larger, stronger horses began to be bred. Bridge-building was begun anew after centuries of neglect, and it was during this period that the first London Bridge was built. In Italy, the Ponte Vecchio pioneered the use of the beautiful and functional segmental arch.

By the end of the 14th century, canals in Italy were using locks to transport barges to different ground levels. Also, by about 1400 A.D., European ships had two masts, a lateen sail, and a stern rudder. And their captains now had the compass. Thus the ocean voyages of great discovery would begin to take place.

Land travel in the next three centuries developed slowly, but increasingly, more and different types of coaches were built in Europe. In the 17th century, a well-to-do individual had his own private coach, and stagecoaches were available for public use. In larger cities like London and Paris, hackney carriages could be hired like today's taxis. Toward the end of the century, such travel became much more comfortable as metal springs replaced the old leather strap suspension systems. In Germany during the 16th century, the first wooden-track rail systems began to be used for small trucks or cars carrying coal from the mines.

Ocean travel during this time was characterized first by the three-masted ship with a lateen sail and then by four-masted, larger versions with high forecastles. At the end of this period, warships were highly decorated, had three decks, and could carry as many as 100 guns or cannons. Among the smaller vessels seen then was the Dutch yacht, a small, agile, single-masted vessel. Among the important bridges built were the beautiful Santa Trinitata Bridge in Florence, Italy with its new arch, the single-arched Rialto in Venice, Italy, and the Pont Notre Dame and Pont Neuf in Paris, France. The first Eddystone Lighthouse was also built during the late 17th century on Eddystone Rock in the open sea of the English Channel, 14 miles off Plymouth, England.

During the 18th century, major developments in transportation would begin to change forever the age-old ways of doing things and getting around. First, road systems were improved greatly by Frenchman Pierre Tresaguet and Englishman Thomas Telford, both of whom brought science and engineering to the laying of a new road. Wooden rails and the beginnings of iron rails were still used only for transporting cargo or goods, but horses were now pulling these rail-cars. Major canal systems, like Bridgewater Canal in England, were constructed, and the first bridge made of iron was built near Coalbrookdale, England in 1777. Private carriages were becoming lighter and sleeker, with better suspension systems, and mail began to be carried by stagecoaches in England in 1784. As steam power became a safer, more viable system, it was applied in France in 1769 by Nicholas Cugnot who created the first self-propelled vehicle. This three-wheeled carriage, with its large steam boiler sitting in front, can in many ways be regarded as the predecessor of both the automobile and the locomotive.

Steam was also applied tentatively to propelling boats for the first time during this century, and small river steamers appeared in England, France, and America. It was also at this time that mankind made its first successful balloon flight, and the science and practice of aeronautics began in earnest. In 1783, the Montgolfier brothers sent two willing aeronauts floating over Paris in their hot-air balloon. Two years later, hydrogen was first used in balloons, and longer flights became possible. Ballooning spread rapidly to nearly every major country, including the United States, and work began immediately on how to propel and control a balloon once it was airborne.

The 19th century saw both an elaboration of many earlier discoveries and the creation of many other pre-modern transportation systems and methods. Wheeled transportation witnessed an incredible number of major advances. Scotsman John Macadam greatly improved on Telford's road-building techniques, and his system became universally accepted and applied. Running over these excellent new roads were the first steam-powered carriages or omnibuses beginning in the 1830s. This form of intra-city public transportation was supplemented and often replaced, first by the mule or horse-drawn tram or trolley which ran on rails around mid-century, and then by cable cars and electric-powered trolleys.

Extended rail travel began with Richard Trevithick's 1804 invention of the steam-powered locomotive on rails, and in 1825, the first public railway opened in England. Locomotive technology rapidly progressed to a single, large locomotive having eight driving wheels, and by 1869, the huge American continent was spanned by railroad tracks. Massive railroad bridges began to appear, like the Forth Bridge in Scotland, and railways were sometimes raised above ground or elevated in large, congested cities, or sunk underground, creating the first underground rail systems or subways. Canal systems, like the Erie Canal, came to life, flourished, and declined badly in the face of rail competition—all within this one century. Construction also started on major ship canals, like the Suez and Panama Canals.

Steam propulsion on water came into its own during this time, with Robert Fulton's practical successes. Propulsion methods for large ships evolved from paddle wheels to screw propellers driven by steam, and in 1897, the steam turbine proved to be the way of the future. Also on the seas, the American clipper had a brief heyday, as its sleek, sharp bows and many sails made it capable of speedy and profitable voyages. Back on land, the foot-propelled hobby-horse evolved into the velocipede bicycle with front wheel cranks, and it in turn changed by 1885 into the recognizable, chain-driven, safety bicycle. Finally, progress in the air was made first theoretically, with the work of George Cayley, and then actually, as powered airships or dirigibles were developed and flown.

Our own century witnessed even greater, more prolific and revolutionary advances in transportation. Following the fin-de-siècle invention by Karl Benz and Gottlieb Daimler of the gas-powered automobile, Henry Ford's assembly-line-produced Model T made the motor car available to large numbers of people. The car would seemingly come to transform everything it touched. It required that old roads be improved and new roads be built where none existed. It led eventually to the European Autostrada and Autobahn and the U.S. interstate highway system; to traffic laws and courts, uniform street signs, and massive corporations and industries; and at one time, to 50,000 annual road-related deaths in the United States alone. The automobile offered mobility and maybe even opportunity to everyone, and it became an integral part of every culture, especially for America.

Certainly as spectacular, if not as ubiquitous, was the development of practical, powered flight. Once the Wright brothers understood and mastered the technical details of what makes a heavier-than-air vehicle get off the ground and fly about under control, the aeronautical industry began to develop almost naturally. The gas-powered airplane was further developed during World War I, and each subsequent hurdle, barrier, and record seemed to fall successively. The first commercial jet airline flew in 1952 and led eventually to the 747s, European Airbuses, and supersonic transport of today. Air travel and automobiles caused the decline of most railroad systems, despite electrification and diesel traction, but Japan's speedy "Bullet-Train" has proven to be a successful inter-city model. The giant ocean liners also rose and fell during this time, as did the huge passenger airships, like the *Graf Zeppelin* and *Hindenburg*. Many smaller, more specialized transportation systems developed, like helicopters, hydrofoils, hovercraft, nuclear submarines, refrigerated ships, motorcycles, long distance buses, and supertankers.

Mankind also launched himself into space in 1961 and walked on the Moon in 1969. Over two decades later, space travel is by no means routine, but the U.S. Space Shuttle has achieved the technical goal of a reusable space transportation system.

It would appear that this century, more than any other, can be viewed properly as the transportation century. Getting about—quickly, safely, comfortably, and on time—has become crucial to the way the modern world is run and organized. It also appears that such will be the case in the next century and probably thereafter. Mankind, it seems, will always be on the move.

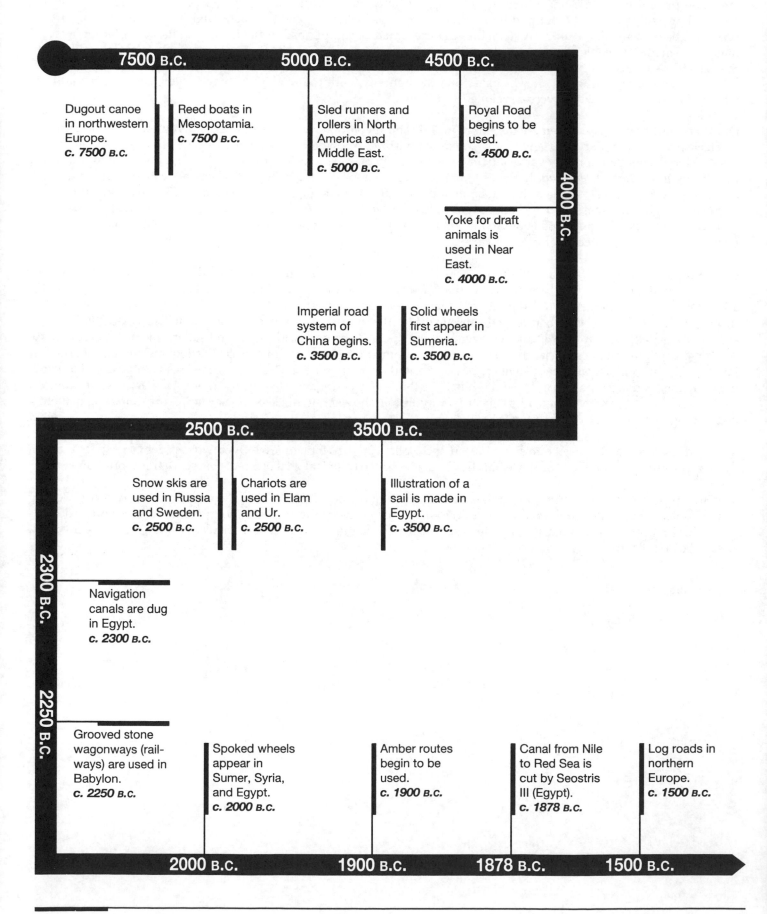

7500 B.C.

5000 B.C.

4500 B.C.

Dugout canoe in northwestern Europe.
c. 7500 B.C.

Reed boats in Mesopotamia.
c. 7500 B.C.

Sled runners and rollers in North America and Middle East.
c. 5000 B.C.

Royal Road begins to be used.
c. 4500 B.C.

4000 B.C.

Yoke for draft animals is used in Near East.
c. 4000 B.C.

Imperial road system of China begins.
c. 3500 B.C.

Solid wheels first appear in Sumeria.
c. 3500 B.C.

2500 B.C.

3500 B.C.

Snow skis are used in Russia and Sweden.
c. 2500 B.C.

Chariots are used in Elam and Ur.
c. 2500 B.C.

Illustration of a sail is made in Egypt.
c. 3500 B.C.

2300 B.C.

Navigation canals are dug in Egypt.
c. 2300 B.C.

2250 B.C.

Grooved stone wagonways (railways) are used in Babylon.
c. 2250 B.C.

Spoked wheels appear in Sumer, Syria, and Egypt.
c. 2000 B.C.

Amber routes begin to be used.
c. 1900 B.C.

Canal from Nile to Red Sea is cut by Seostris III (Egypt).
c. 1878 B.C.

Log roads in northern Europe.
c. 1500 B.C.

2000 B.C.

1900 B.C.

1878 B.C.

1500 B.C.

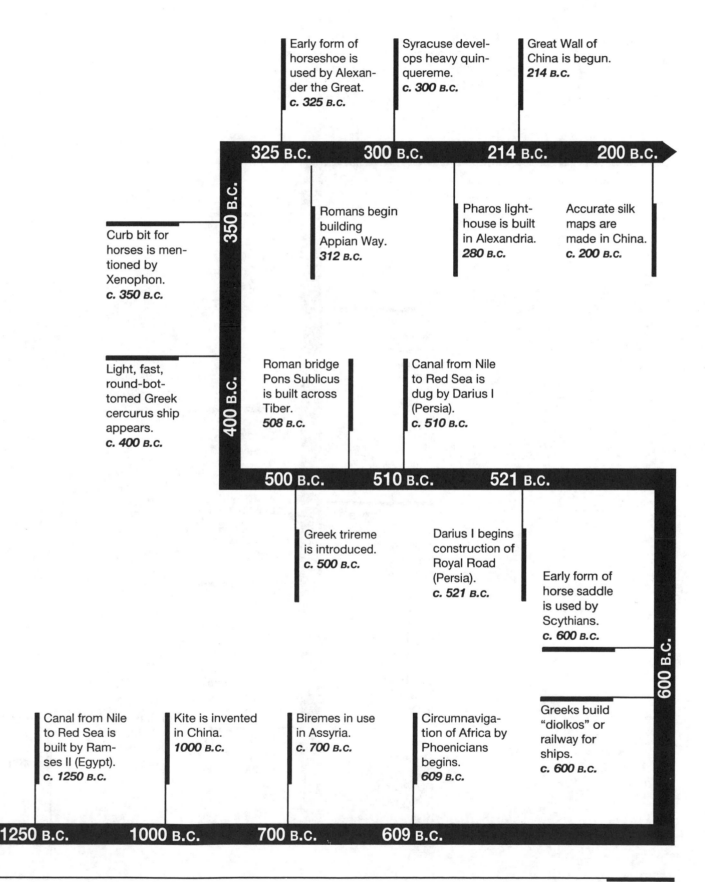

Early form of horseshoe is used by Alexander the Great.
c. 325 B.C.

Syracuse develops heavy quinquereme.
c. 300 B.C.

Great Wall of China is begun.
214 B.C.

325 B.C.   300 B.C.   214 B.C.   200 B.C.

350 B.C.

Curb bit for horses is mentioned by Xenophon.
c. 350 B.C.

Romans begin building Appian Way.
312 B.C.

Pharos lighthouse is built in Alexandria.
280 B.C.

Accurate silk maps are made in China.
c. 200 B.C.

400 B.C.

Light, fast, round-bottomed Greek cercurus ship appears.
c. 400 B.C.

Roman bridge Pons Sublicus is built across Tiber.
508 B.C.

Canal from Nile to Red Sea is dug by Darius I (Persia).
c. 510 B.C.

500 B.C.   510 B.C.   521 B.C.

Greek trireme is introduced.
c. 500 B.C.

Darius I begins construction of Royal Road (Persia).
c. 521 B.C.

Early form of horse saddle is used by Scythians.
c. 600 B.C.

600 B.C.

Canal from Nile to Red Sea is built by Ramses II (Egypt).
c. 1250 B.C.

Kite is invented in China.
1000 B.C.

Biremes in use in Assyria.
c. 700 B.C.

Circumnavigation of Africa by Phoenicians begins.
609 B.C.

Greeks build "diolkos" or railway for ships.
c. 600 B.C.

1250 B.C.   1000 B.C.   700 B.C.   609 B.C.

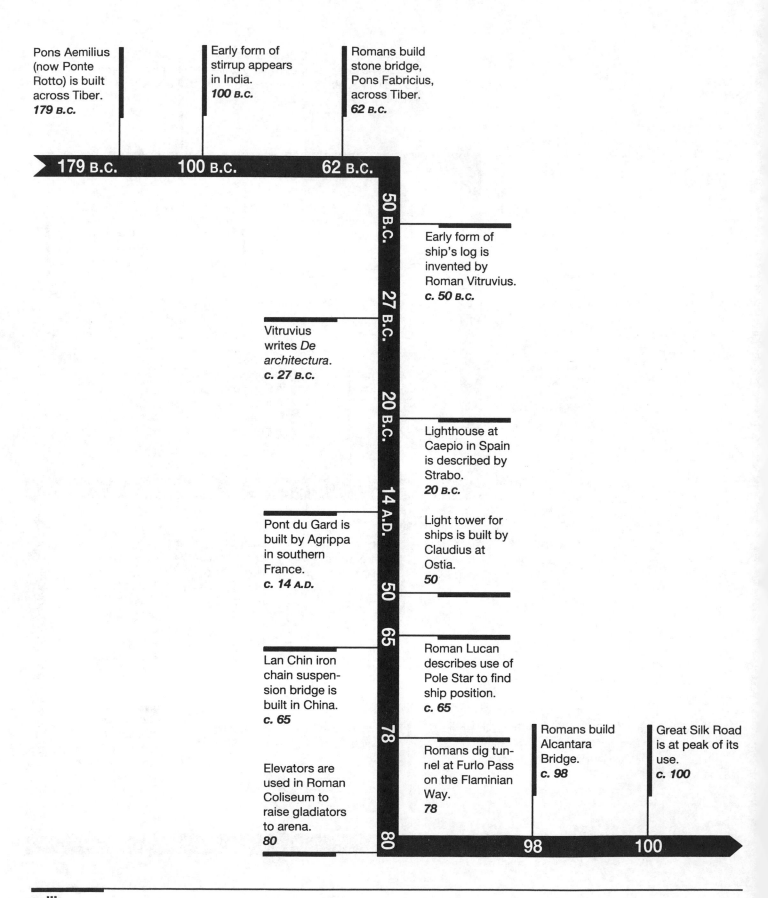

Pons Aemilius (now Ponte Rotto) is built across Tiber.
179 B.C.

Early form of stirrup appears in India.
100 B.C.

Romans build stone bridge, Pons Fabricius, across Tiber.
62 B.C.

179 B.C. **100 B.C.** **62 B.C.**

50 B.C.

Early form of ship's log is invented by Roman Vitruvius.
c. 50 B.C.

27 B.C.

Vitruvius writes *De architectura*.
c. 27 B.C.

20 B.C.

Lighthouse at Caepio in Spain is described by Strabo.
20 B.C.

14 A.D.

Pont du Gard is built by Agrippa in southern France.
c. 14 A.D.

Light tower for ships is built by Claudius at Ostia.
50

50

65

Lan Chin iron chain suspension bridge is built in China.
c. 65

Roman Lucan describes use of Pole Star to find ship position.
c. 65

78

Romans build Alcantara Bridge.
c. 98

Great Silk Road is at peak of its use.
c. 100

Elevators are used in Roman Coliseum to raise gladiators to arena.
80

Romans dig tunnel at Furlo Pass on the Flaminian Way.
78

80

98 **100**

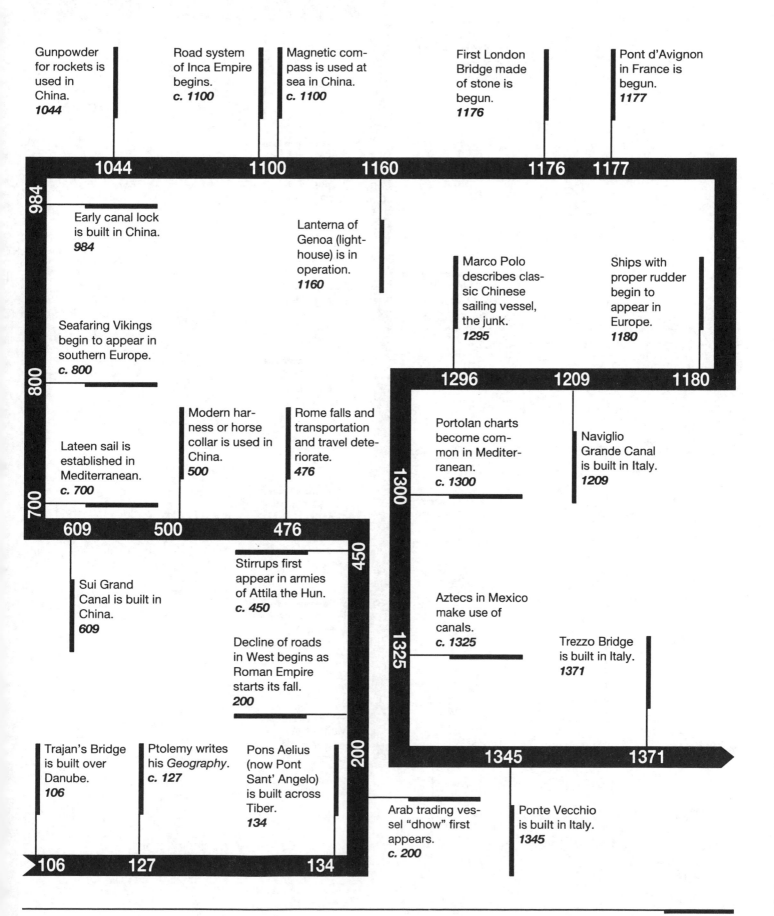

Gunpowder for rockets is used in China.
1044

Road system of Inca Empire begins.
c. 1100

Magnetic compass is used at sea in China.
c. 1100

First London Bridge made of stone is begun.
1176

Pont d'Avignon in France is begun.
1177

1044 **1100** **1160** **1176** **1177**

984

Early canal lock is built in China.
984

Lanterna of Genoa (lighthouse) is in operation.
1160

Marco Polo describes classic Chinese sailing vessel, the junk.
1295

Ships with proper rudder begin to appear in Europe.
1180

Seafaring Vikings begin to appear in southern Europe.
c. 800

800

1296 **1209** **1180**

Lateen sail is established in Mediterranean.
c. 700

Modern harness or horse collar is used in China.
500

Rome falls and transportation and travel deteriorate.
476

Portolan charts become common in Mediterranean.
c. 1300

Naviglio Grande Canal is built in Italy.
1209

700

1300

609 **500** **476**

Sui Grand Canal is built in China.
609

450

Stirrups first appear in armies of Attila the Hun.
c. 450

Aztecs in Mexico make use of canals.
c. 1325

Trezzo Bridge is built in Italy.
1371

Decline of roads in West begins as Roman Empire starts its fall.
200

1325

200

Trajan's Bridge is built over Danube.
106

Ptolemy writes his *Geography*.
c. 127

Pons Aelius (now Pont Sant' Angelo) is built across Tiber.
134

1345 **1371**

Arab trading vessel "dhow" first appears.
c. 200

Ponte Vecchio is built in Italy.
1345

106 **127** **134**

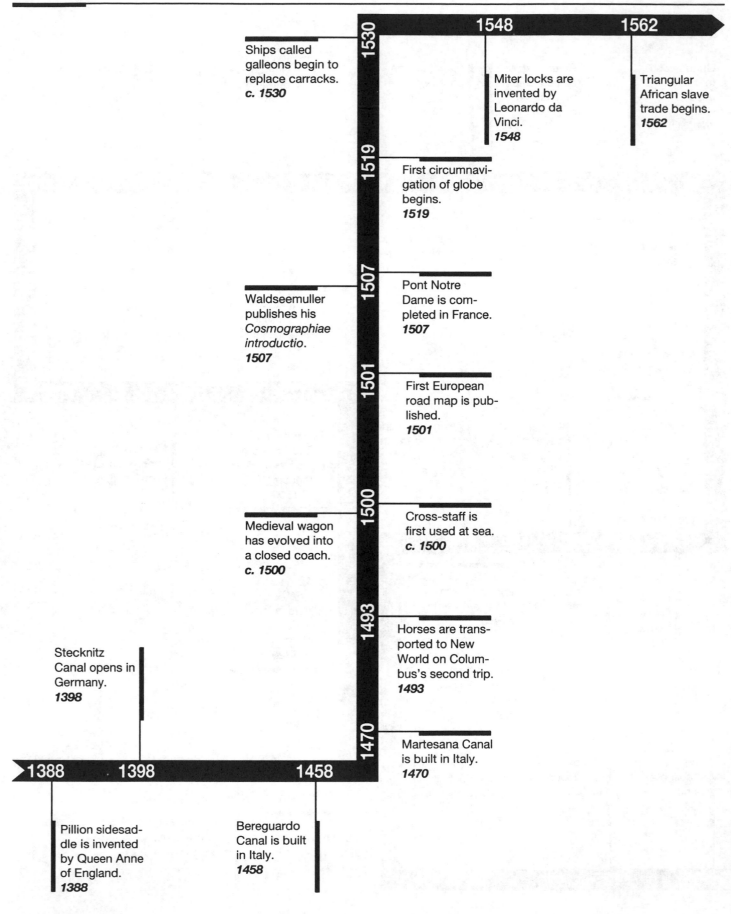

1530

1548

1562

Ships called
galleons begin to
replace carracks.
c. 1530

Miter locks are
invented by
Leonardo da
Vinci.
1548

Triangular
African slave
trade begins.
1562

1519

First circumnavi-
gation of globe
begins.
1519

1507

Waldseemuller
publishes his
*Cosmographiae
introductio.*
1507

Pont Notre
Dame is com-
pleted in France.
1507

1501

First European
road map is pub-
lished.
1501

1500

Medieval wagon
has evolved into
a closed coach.
c. 1500

Cross-staff is
first used at sea.
c. 1500

1493

Horses are trans-
ported to New
World on Colum-
bus's second trip.
1493

1470

Martesana Canal
is built in Italy.
1470

Stecknitz
Canal opens in
Germany.
1398

1388

1398

1458

Pillion sidesad-
dle is invented
by Queen Anne
of England.
1388

Bereguardo
Canal is built
in Italy.
1458

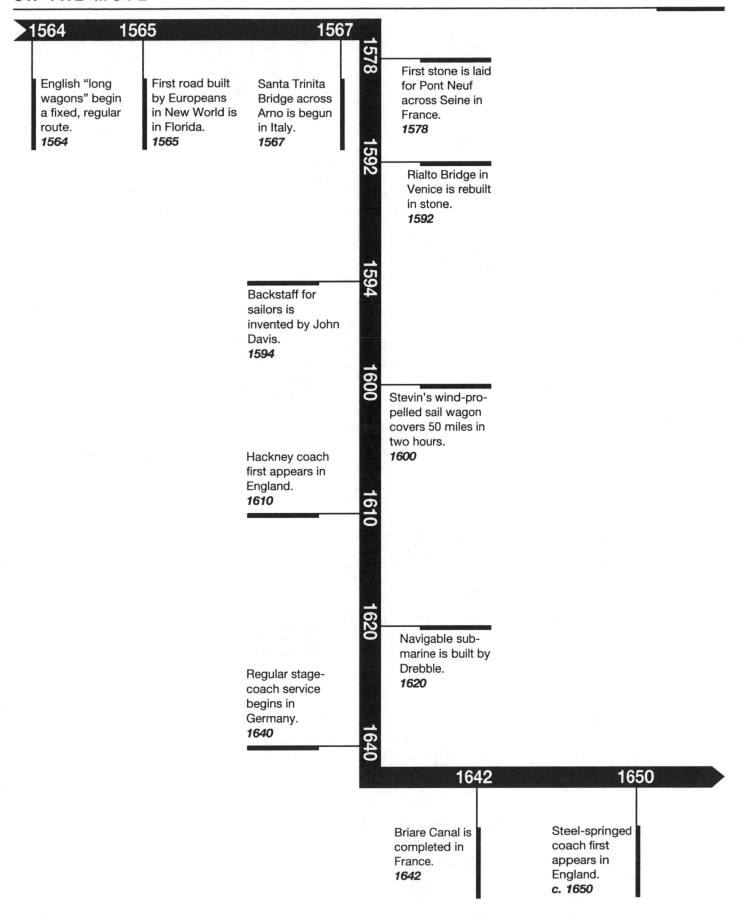

1564

1565

1567

1578

English "long wagons" begin a fixed, regular route.
1564

First road built by Europeans in New World is in Florida.
1565

Santa Trinita Bridge across Arno is begun in Italy.
1567

First stone is laid for Pont Neuf across Seine in France.
1578

1592

Rialto Bridge in Venice is rebuilt in stone.
1592

1594

Backstaff for sailors is invented by John Davis.
1594

1600

Stevin's wind-propelled sail wagon covers 50 miles in two hours.
1600

Hackney coach first appears in England.
1610

1610

1620

Navigable submarine is built by Drebble.
1620

Regular stagecoach service begins in Germany.
1640

1640

1642

1650

Briare Canal is completed in France.
1642

Steel-springed coach first appears in England.
c. 1650

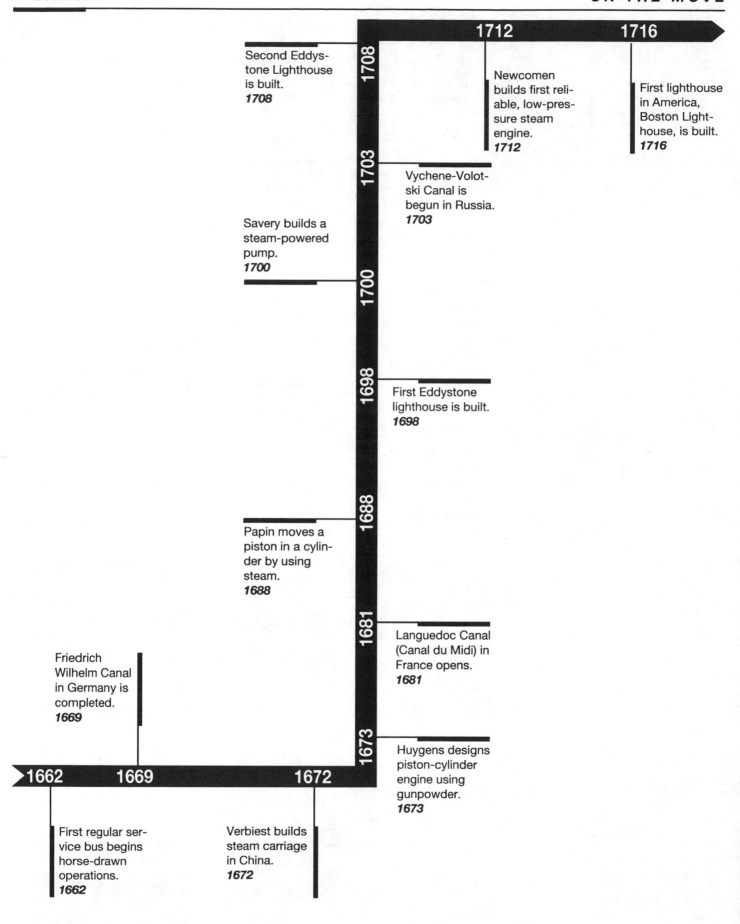

1712   **1716**

Second Eddys-
tone Lighthouse
is built.
1708

1708

Newcomen
builds first reli-
able, low-pres-
sure steam
engine.
1712

First lighthouse
in America,
Boston Light-
house, is built.
1716

1703

Vychene-Volot-
ski Canal is
begun in Russia.
1703

Savery builds a
steam-powered
pump.
1700

1700

1698

First Eddystone
lighthouse is built.
1698

1688

Papin moves a
piston in a cylin-
der by using
steam.
1688

1681

Languedoc Canal
(Canal du Midi) in
France opens.
1681

Friedrich
Wilhelm Canal
in Germany is
completed.
1669

1673

1662   **1669**   **1672**

Huygens designs
piston-cylinder
engine using
gunpowder.
1673

First regular ser-
vice bus begins
horse-drawn
operations.
1662

Verbiest builds
steam carriage
in China.
1672

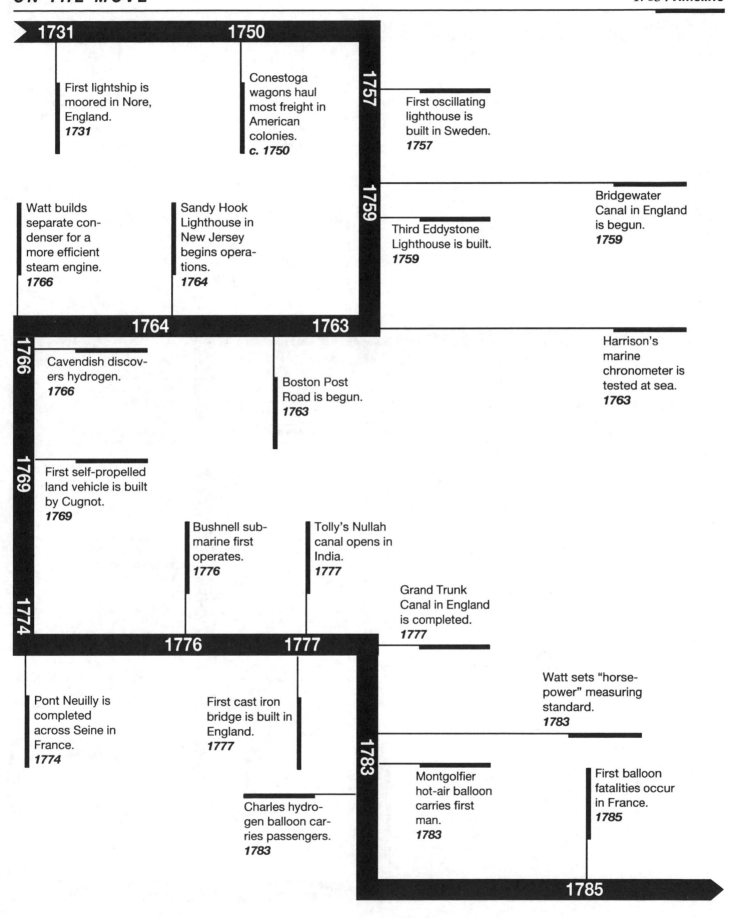

1731

First lightship is moored in Nore, England.
1731

1750

Conestoga wagons haul most freight in American colonies.
c. 1750

1757

First oscillating lighthouse is built in Sweden.
1757

1759

Watt builds separate condenser for a more efficient steam engine.
1766

Sandy Hook Lighthouse in New Jersey begins operations.
1764

Third Eddystone Lighthouse is built.
1759

Bridgewater Canal in England is begun.
1759

1764

1763

Cavendish discovers hydrogen.
1766

Boston Post Road is begun.
1763

Harrison's marine chronometer is tested at sea.
1763

1766

1769

First self-propelled land vehicle is built by Cugnot.
1769

Bushnell submarine first operates.
1776

Tolly's Nullah canal opens in India.
1777

Grand Trunk Canal in England is completed.
1777

1774

1776

1777

Pont Neuilly is completed across Seine in France.
1774

First cast iron bridge is built in England.
1777

1783

Watt sets "horsepower" measuring standard.
1783

Charles hydrogen balloon carries passengers.
1783

Montgolfier hot-air balloon carries first man.
1783

First balloon fatalities occur in France.
1785

1785

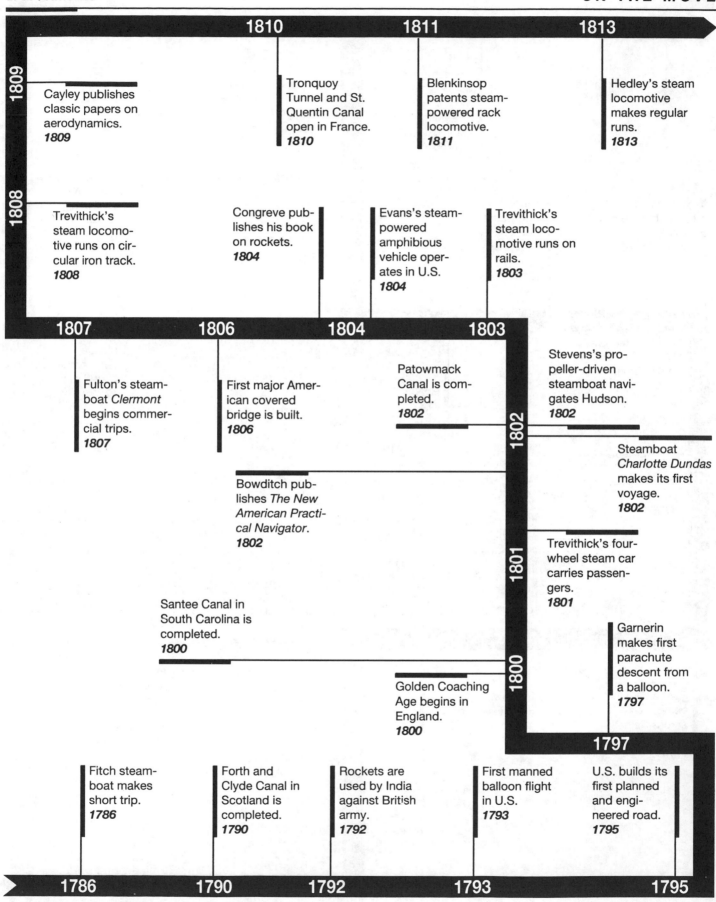

1810

1811

1813

1809

Cayley publishes classic papers on aerodynamics.
1809

Tronquoy Tunnel and St. Quentin Canal open in France.
1810

Blenkinsop patents steam-powered rack locomotive.
1811

Hedley's steam locomotive makes regular runs.
1813

1808

Trevithick's steam locomotive runs on circular iron track.
1808

Congreve publishes his book on rockets.
1804

Evans's steam-powered amphibious vehicle operates in U.S.
1804

Trevithick's steam locomotive runs on rails.
1803

1807   **1806**   **1804**   **1803**

Fulton's steamboat *Clermont* begins commercial trips.
1807

First major American covered bridge is built.
1806

Patowmack Canal is completed.
1802

Stevens's propeller-driven steamboat navigates Hudson.
1802

1802

Steamboat *Charlotte Dundas* makes its first voyage.
1802

Bowditch publishes *The New American Practical Navigator*.
1802

Trevithick's four-wheel steam car carries passengers.
1801

1801

Santee Canal in South Carolina is completed.
1800

Garnerin makes first parachute descent from a balloon.
1797

1800

Golden Coaching Age begins in England.
1800

1797

Fitch steamboat makes short trip.
1786

Forth and Clyde Canal in Scotland is completed.
1790

Rockets are used by India against British army.
1792

First manned balloon flight in U.S.
1793

U.S. builds its first planned and engineered road.
1795

1786   **1790**   **1792**   **1793**   **1795**

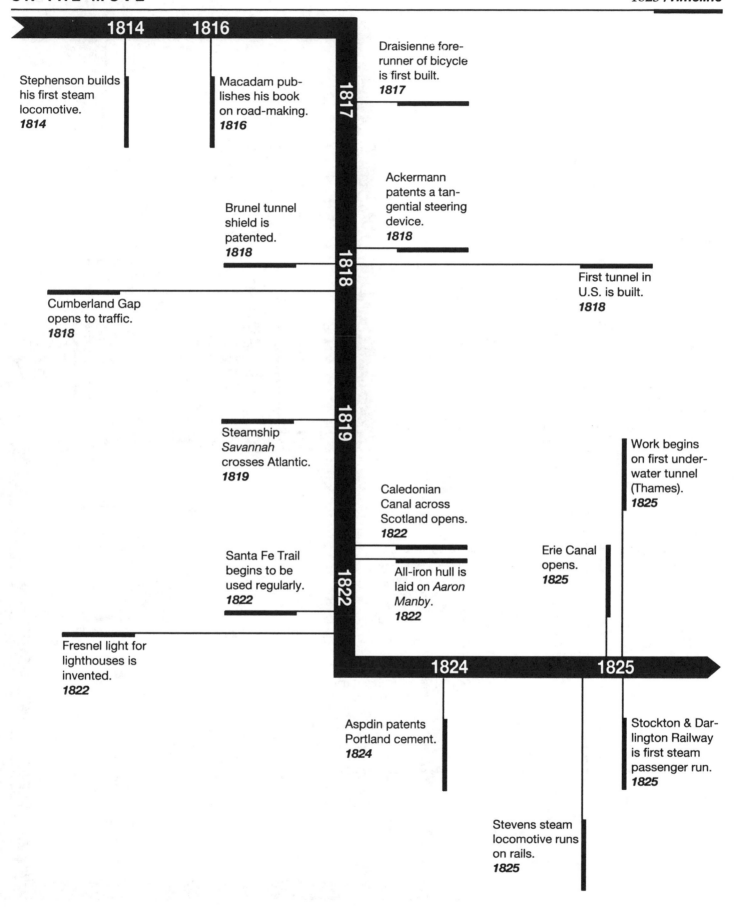

1814

1816

Stephenson builds
his first steam
locomotive.
1814

Macadam pub-
lishes his book
on road-making.
1816

Draisienne fore-
runner of bicycle
is first built.
1817

1817

Brunel tunnel
shield is
patented.
1818

Ackermann
patents a tan-
gential steering
device.
1818

1818

First tunnel in
U.S. is built.
1818

Cumberland Gap
opens to traffic.
1818

1819

Steamship
Savannah
crosses Atlantic.
1819

Work begins
on first under-
water tunnel
(Thames).
1825

Caledonian
Canal across
Scotland opens.
1822

Santa Fe Trail
begins to be
used regularly.
1822

1822

All-iron hull is
laid on *Aaron
Manby*.
1822

Erie Canal
opens.
1825

Fresnel light for
lighthouses is
invented.
1822

1824

1825

Aspdin patents
Portland cement.
1824

Stockton & Dar-
lington Railway
is first steam
passenger run.
1825

Stevens steam
locomotive runs
on rails.
1825

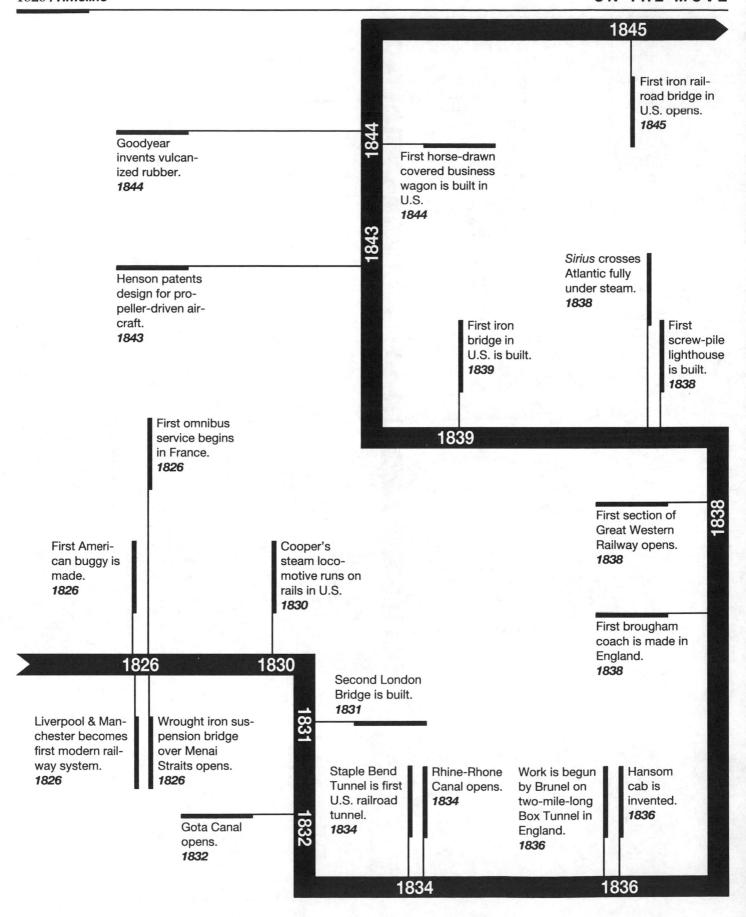

1845

First iron rail-road bridge in U.S. opens.
1845

Goodyear invents vulcanized rubber.
1844

1844

First horse-drawn covered business wagon is built in U.S.
1844

1843

Henson patents design for propeller-driven aircraft.
1843

Sirius crosses Atlantic fully under steam.
1838

First iron bridge in U.S. is built.
1839

First screw-pile lighthouse is built.
1838

1839

First omnibus service begins in France.
1826

1838

First section of Great Western Railway opens.
1838

First American buggy is made.
1826

Cooper's steam locomotive runs on rails in U.S.
1830

First brougham coach is made in England.
1838

1826   **1830**

Second London Bridge is built.
1831

1831

Liverpool & Manchester becomes first modern railway system.
1826

Wrought iron suspension bridge over Menai Straits opens.
1826

Staple Bend Tunnel is first U.S. railroad tunnel.
1834

Rhine-Rhone Canal opens.
1834

Work is begun by Brunel on two-mile-long Box Tunnel in England.
1836

Hansom cab is invented.
1836

1832

Gota Canal opens.
1832

1834   **1836**

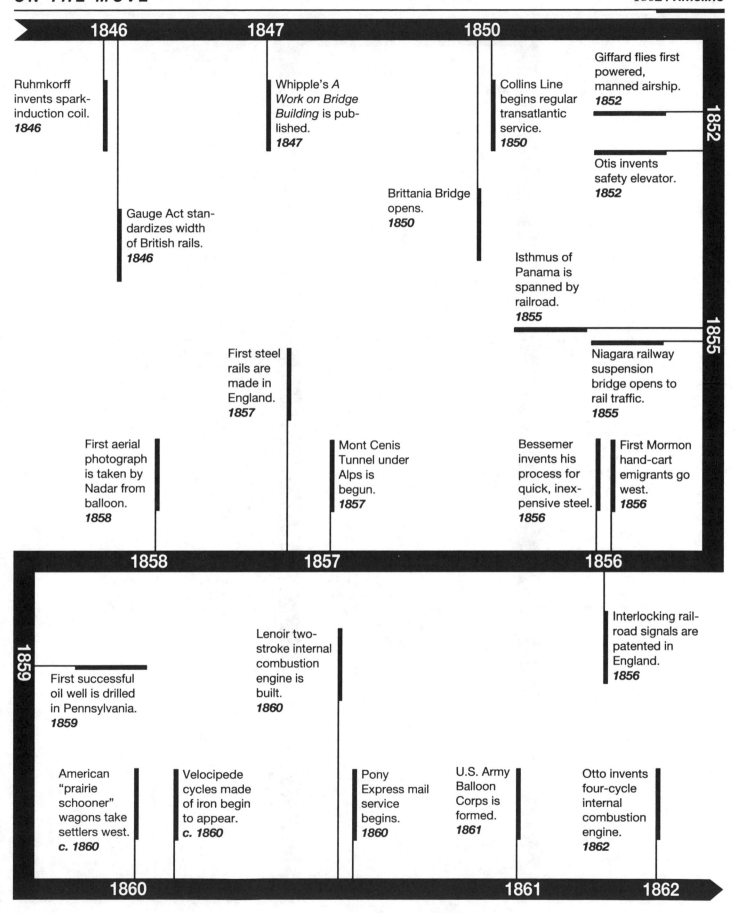

1846

Ruhmkorff invents spark-induction coil.
1846

Gauge Act standardizes width of British rails.
1846

1847

Whipple's *A Work on Bridge Building* is published.
1847

1850

Collins Line begins regular transatlantic service.
1850

Brittania Bridge opens.
1850

Giffard flies first powered, manned airship.
1852

Otis invents safety elevator.
1852

Isthmus of Panama is spanned by railroad.
1855

1852

1855

Niagara railway suspension bridge opens to rail traffic.
1855

First steel rails are made in England.
1857

First aerial photograph is taken by Nadar from balloon.
1858

Mont Cenis Tunnel under Alps is begun.
1857

Bessemer invents his process for quick, inexpensive steel.
1856

First Mormon hand-cart emigrants go west.
1856

1858

1857

1856

Interlocking railroad signals are patented in England.
1856

1859

First successful oil well is drilled in Pennsylvania.
1859

Lenoir two-stroke internal combustion engine is built.
1860

American "prairie schooner" wagons take settlers west.
c. 1860

Velocipede cycles made of iron begin to appear.
c. 1860

Pony Express mail service begins.
1860

U.S. Army Balloon Corps is formed.
1861

Otto invents four-cycle internal combustion engine.
1862

1860

1861

1862

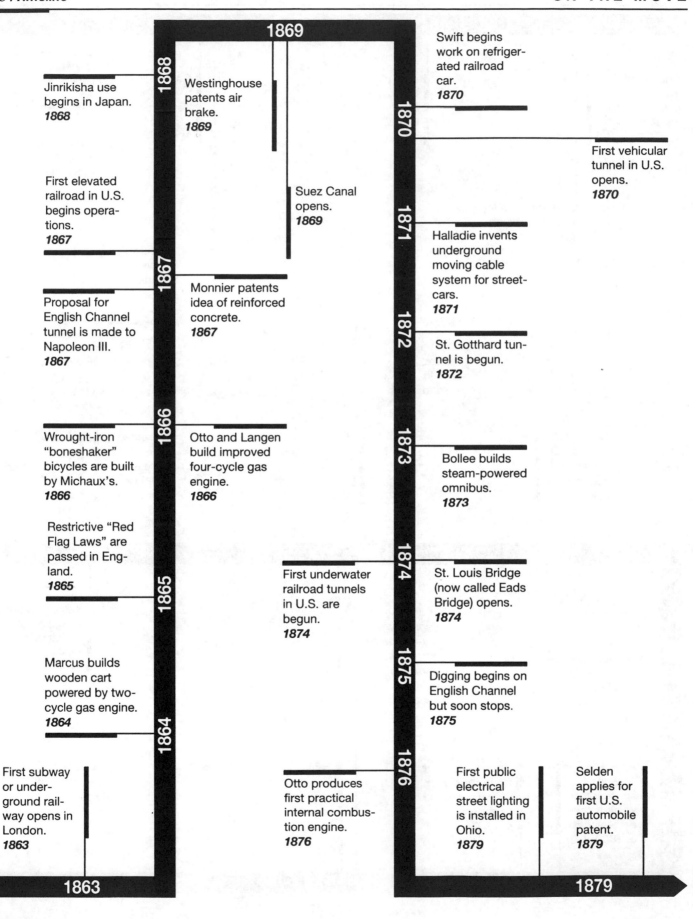

1869

Jinrikisha use
begins in Japan.
1868

Westinghouse
patents air
brake.
1869

Swift begins
work on refriger-
ated railroad
car.
1870

First elevated
railroad in U.S.
begins opera-
tions.
1867

Suez Canal
opens.
1869

First vehicular
tunnel in U.S.
opens.
1870

Proposal for
English Channel
tunnel is made to
Napoleon III.
1867

Monnier patents
idea of reinforced
concrete.
1867

Halladie invents
underground
moving cable
system for street-
cars.
1871

St. Gotthard tun-
nel is begun.
1872

Wrought-iron
"boneshaker"
bicycles are built
by Michaux's.
1866

Otto and Langen
build improved
four-cycle gas
engine.
1866

Bollee builds
steam-powered
omnibus.
1873

Restrictive "Red
Flag Laws" are
passed in Eng-
land.
1865

First underwater
railroad tunnels
in U.S. are
begun.
1874

St. Louis Bridge
(now called Eads
Bridge) opens.
1874

Marcus builds
wooden cart
powered by two-
cycle gas engine.
1864

Digging begins on
English Channel
but soon stops.
1875

First subway
or under-
ground rail-
way opens in
London.
1863

Otto produces
first practical
internal combus-
tion engine.
1876

First public
electrical
street lighting
is installed in
Ohio.
1879

Selden
applies for
first U.S.
automobile
patent.
1879

1863

1879

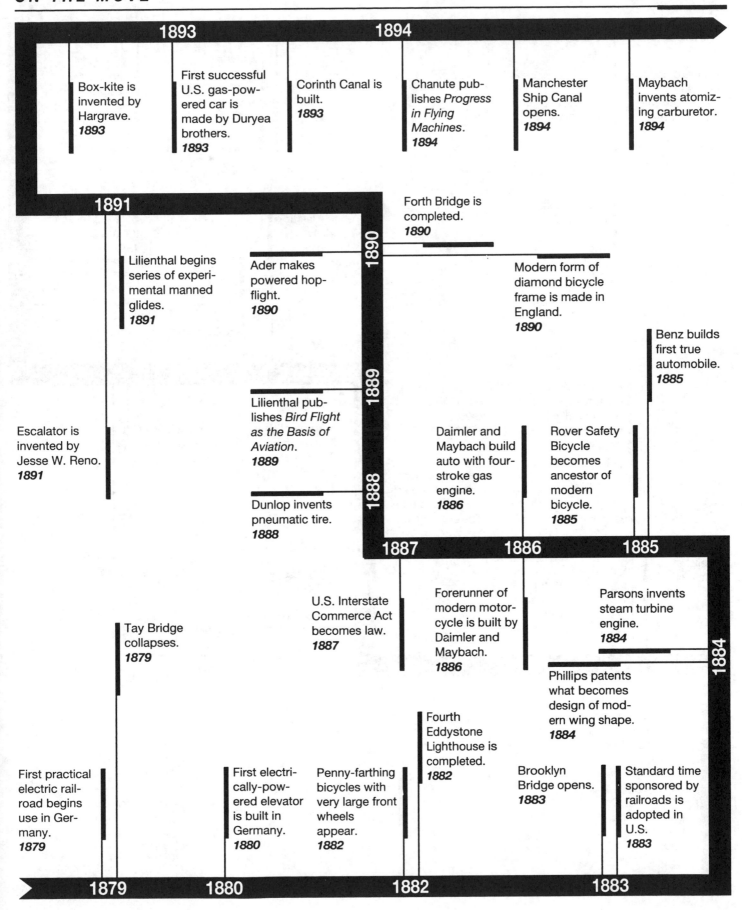

1893

Box-kite is invented by Hargrave.
1893

First successful U.S. gas-powered car is made by Duryea brothers.
1893

1894

Corinth Canal is built.
1893

Chanute publishes *Progress in Flying Machines.*
1894

Manchester Ship Canal opens.
1894

Maybach invents atomizing carburetor.
1894

1891

Lilienthal begins series of experimental manned glides.
1891

Escalator is invented by Jesse W. Reno.
1891

1890

Ader makes powered hop-flight.
1890

Forth Bridge is completed.
1890

Modern form of diamond bicycle frame is made in England.
1890

1889

Lilienthal publishes *Bird Flight as the Basis of Aviation.*
1889

1888

Dunlop invents pneumatic tire.
1888

Daimler and Maybach build auto with four-stroke gas engine.
1886

Rover Safety Bicycle becomes ancestor of modern bicycle.
1885

Benz builds first true automobile.
1885

1887

1886

1885

U.S. Interstate Commerce Act becomes law.
1887

Forerunner of modern motorcycle is built by Daimler and Maybach.
1886

Parsons invents steam turbine engine.
1884

1884

Phillips patents what becomes design of modern wing shape.
1884

Tay Bridge collapses.
1879

Fourth Eddystone Lighthouse is completed.
1882

First practical electric railroad begins use in Germany.
1879

First electrically-powered elevator is built in Germany.
1880

Penny-farthing bicycles with very large front wheels appear.
1882

Brooklyn Bridge opens.
1883

Standard time sponsored by railroads is adopted in U.S.
1883

1879   **1880**   **1882**   **1883**

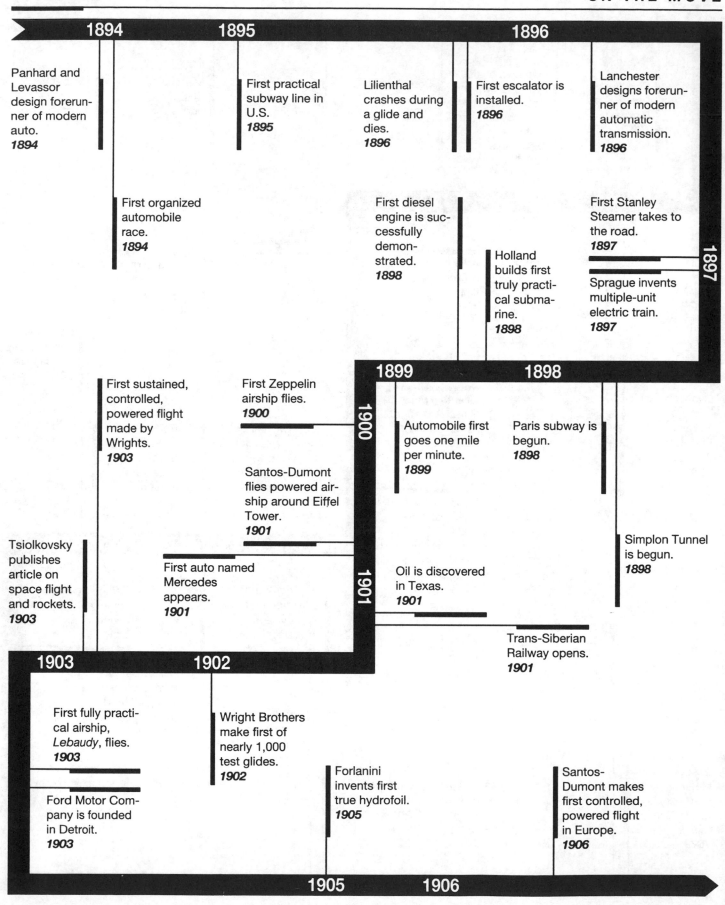

1894

1895

1896

Panhard and
Levassor
design forerun-
ner of modern
auto.
1894

First practical
subway line in
U.S.
1895

Lilienthal
crashes during
a glide and
dies.
1896

First escalator is
installed.
1896

Lanchester
designs forerun-
ner of modern
automatic
transmission.
1896

First organized
automobile
race.
1894

First diesel
engine is suc-
cessfully
demon-
strated.
1898

Holland
builds first
truly practi-
cal subma-
rine.
1898

First Stanley
Steamer takes to
the road.
1897

Sprague invents
multiple-unit
electric train.
1897

1897

First sustained,
controlled,
powered flight
made by
Wrights.
1903

First Zeppelin
airship flies.
1900

1899

1898

1900

Automobile first
goes one mile
per minute.
1899

Paris subway is
begun.
1898

Santos-Dumont
flies powered air-
ship around Eiffel
Tower.
1901

Tsiolkovsky
publishes
article on
space flight
and rockets.
1903

First auto named
Mercedes
appears.
1901

Oil is discovered
in Texas.
1901

1901

Simplon Tunnel
is begun.
1898

Trans-Siberian
Railway opens.
1901

1903

1902

First fully practi-
cal airship,
Lebaudy, flies.
1903

Wright Brothers
make first of
nearly 1,000
test glides.
1902

Forlanini
invents first
true hydrofoil.
1905

Santos-
Dumont makes
first controlled,
powered flight
in Europe.
1906

Ford Motor Com-
pany is founded
in Detroit.
1903

1905

1906

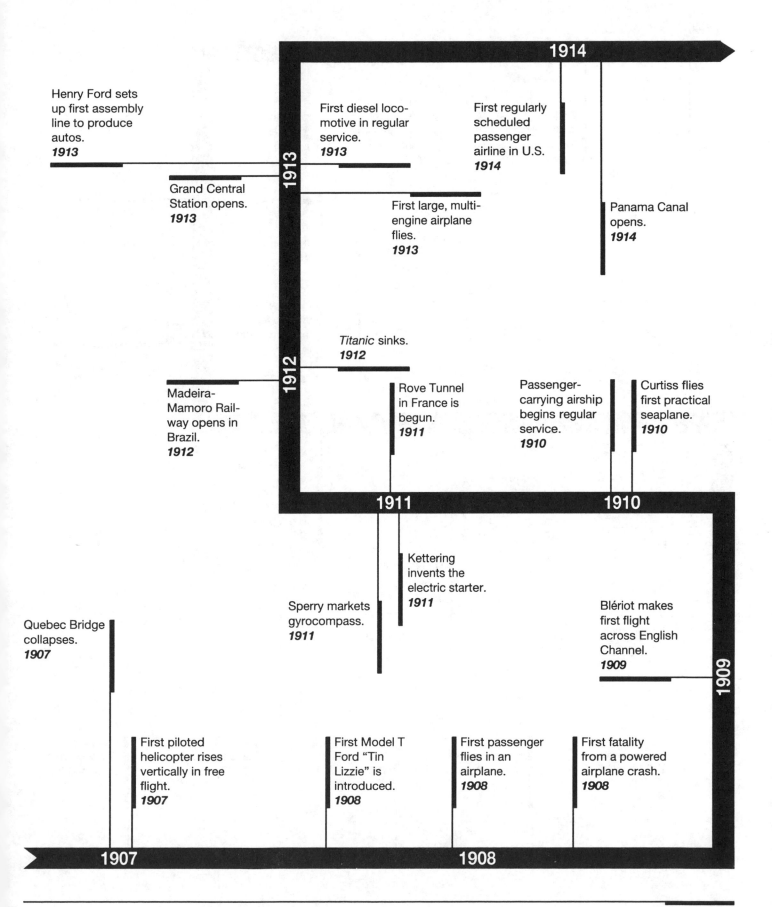

1914

Henry Ford sets up first assembly line to produce autos.
1913

First diesel loco-motive in regular service.
1913

First regularly scheduled passenger airline in U.S.
1914

1913

Grand Central Station opens.
1913

First large, multi-engine airplane flies.
1913

Panama Canal opens.
1914

Titanic sinks.
1912

1912

Madeira-Mamoro Rail-way opens in Brazil.
1912

Rove Tunnel in France is begun.
1911

Passenger-carrying airship begins regular service.
1910

Curtiss flies first practical seaplane.
1910

1911

1910

Kettering invents the electric starter.
1911

Sperry markets gyrocompass.
1911

Blériot makes first flight across English Channel.
1909

Quebec Bridge collapses.
1907

1909

First piloted helicopter rises vertically in free flight.
1907

First Model T Ford "Tin Lizzie" is introduced.
1908

First passenger flies in an airplane.
1908

First fatality from a powered airplane crash.
1908

1907

1908

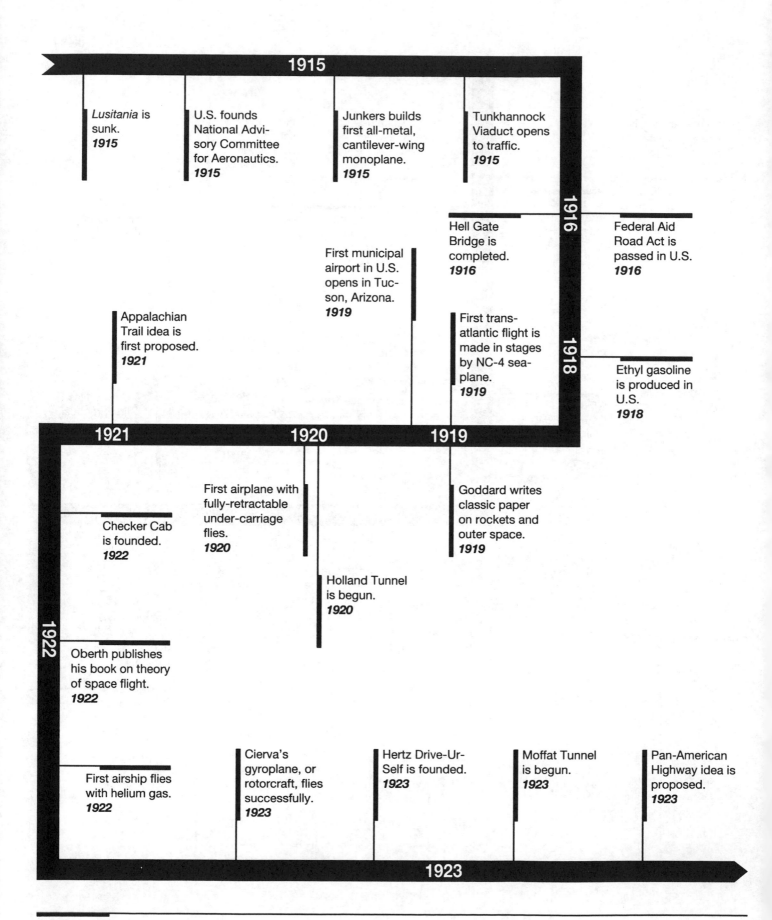

1915

Lusitania is sunk.
1915

U.S. founds National Advisory Committee for Aeronautics.
1915

Junkers builds first all-metal, cantilever-wing monoplane.
1915

Tunkhannock Viaduct opens to traffic.
1915

1916

Hell Gate Bridge is completed.
1916

Federal Aid Road Act is passed in U.S.
1916

First municipal airport in U.S. opens in Tucson, Arizona.
1919

1918

First transatlantic flight is made in stages by NC-4 seaplane.
1919

Ethyl gasoline is produced in U.S.
1918

Appalachian Trail idea is first proposed.
1921

1921

1920

1919

First airplane with fully-retractable under-carriage flies.
1920

Goddard writes classic paper on rockets and outer space.
1919

Checker Cab is founded.
1922

Holland Tunnel is begun.
1920

1922

Oberth publishes his book on theory of space flight.
1922

First airship flies with helium gas.
1922

Cierva's gyroplane, or rotorcraft, flies successfully.
1923

Hertz Drive-Ur-Self is founded.
1923

Moffat Tunnel is begun.
1923

Pan-American Highway idea is proposed.
1923

1923

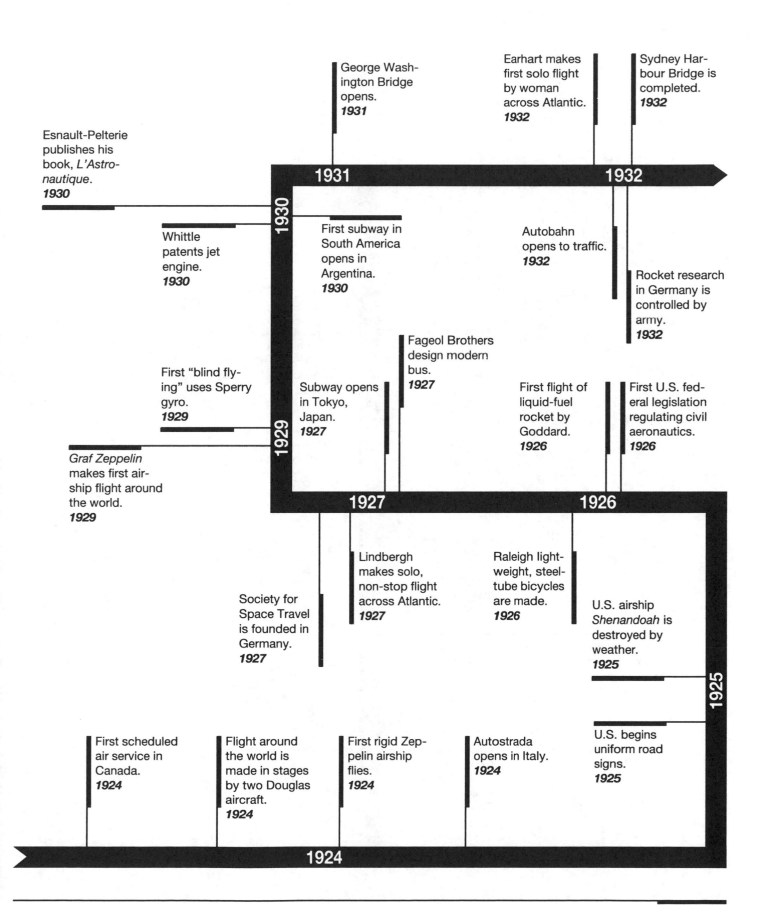

Esnault-Pelterie publishes his book, *L'Astro-nautique.*
1930

George Wash-ington Bridge opens.
1931

Earhart makes first solo flight by woman across Atlantic.
1932

Sydney Har-bour Bridge is completed.
1932

1931

1932

1930

Whittle patents jet engine.
1930

First subway in South America opens in Argentina.
1930

Autobahn opens to traffic.
1932

Rocket research in Germany is controlled by army.
1932

First "blind fly-ing" uses Sperry gyro.
1929

Fageol Brothers design modern bus.
1927

First flight of liquid-fuel rocket by Goddard.
1926

First U.S. fed-eral legislation regulating civil aeronautics.
1926

1929

Subway opens in Tokyo, Japan.
1927

Graf Zeppelin makes first air-ship flight around the world.
1929

1927

1926

Lindbergh makes solo, non-stop flight across Atlantic.
1927

Raleigh light-weight, steel-tube bicycles are made.
1926

U.S. airship *Shenandoah* is destroyed by weather.
1925

Society for Space Travel is founded in Germany.
1927

1925

First scheduled air service in Canada.
1924

Flight around the world is made in stages by two Douglas aircraft.
1924

First rigid Zep-pelin airship flies.
1924

Autostrada opens in Italy.
1924

U.S. begins uniform road signs.
1925

1924

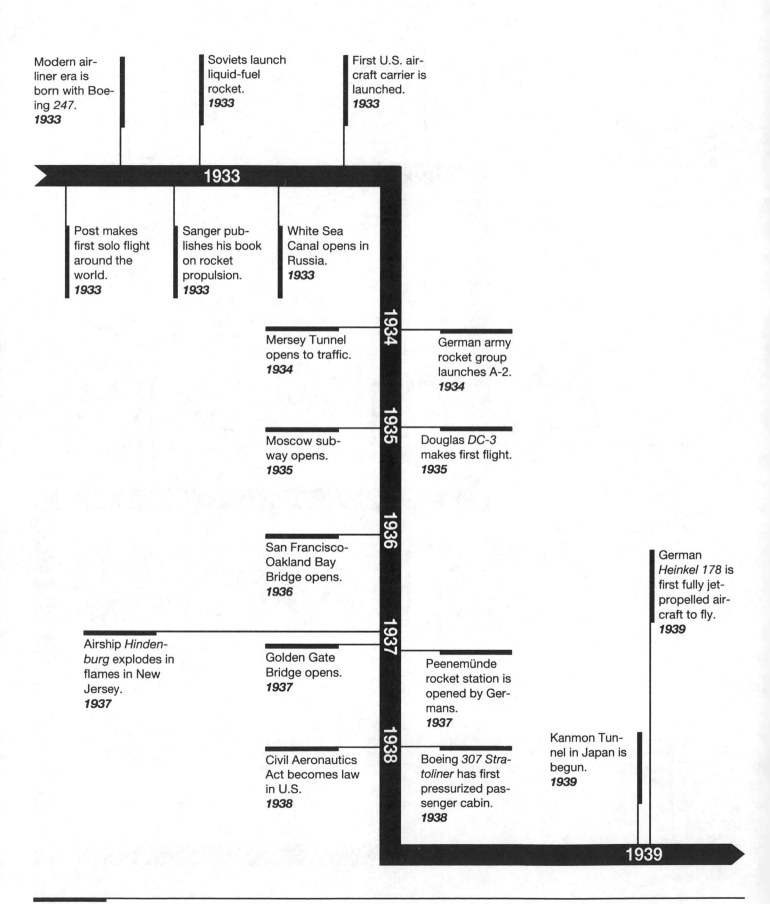

Modern air-
liner era is
born with Boe-
ing *247*.
1933

Soviets launch
liquid-fuel
rocket.
1933

First U.S. air-
craft carrier is
launched.
1933

1933

Post makes
first solo flight
around the
world.
1933

Sanger pub-
lishes his book
on rocket
propulsion.
1933

White Sea
Canal opens in
Russia.
1933

1934

Mersey Tunnel
opens to traffic.
1934

German army
rocket group
launches A-2.
1934

1935

Moscow sub-
way opens.
1935

Douglas *DC-3*
makes first flight.
1935

1936

San Francisco-
Oakland Bay
Bridge opens.
1936

German
Heinkel 178 is
first fully jet-
propelled air-
craft to fly.
1939

1937

Airship *Hinden-
burg* explodes in
flames in New
Jersey.
1937

Golden Gate
Bridge opens.
1937

Peenemünde
rocket station is
opened by Ger-
mans.
1937

Kanmon Tun-
nel in Japan is
begun.
1939

1938

Civil Aeronautics
Act becomes law
in U.S.
1938

Boeing *307 Stra-
toliner* has first
pressurized pas-
senger cabin.
1938

1939

First piloted aircraft breaks the speed of sound.
1947

Bathyscaphe is invented by Piccard.
1948

New York's Idlewild Airport is dedicated.
1948

Von Braun and rocket staff move to Huntsville, Alabama.
1950

Sailplane crosses English Channel.
1950

1947

1948

1950

International Civil Aviation Organization is formed.
1947

Goodrich makes first U.S. tubeless tires.
1948

First International Astronautical Congress is held.
1950

First automatic elevators are installed.
1950

Michelin markets first radial tire.
1948

International Air Transport Association is formed.
1945

1945

1951

U.S. captures Peenemünde rockets and scientists.
1945

U.S. enacts Federal-Aid Highway Act of 1944.
1944

Scuba gear is developed by Cousteau and Gagnan.
1943

U.S. completes test launches of captured German V-2 rockets.
1951

New Jersey Turnpike opens to traffic.
1951

1944

1943

First jet airliner for commercial passenger service.
1952

U.S. rocket plane *MX-324* flies.
1944

Peenemünde rocket group launches V-2.
1942

1942

Douglas *DC-4* is first four-engine airliner.
1942

1952

Blunt nose principle for spacecraft reentry is proposed by Allen.
1952

Volga-Don Canal opens.
1952

Sikorsky builds and flies first true helicopter.
1940

Tacoma Narrows Bridge collapses.
1940

First Los Angeles freeway is dedicated.
1940

1940

Prototype of Boeing *B-52* makes first flight.
1952

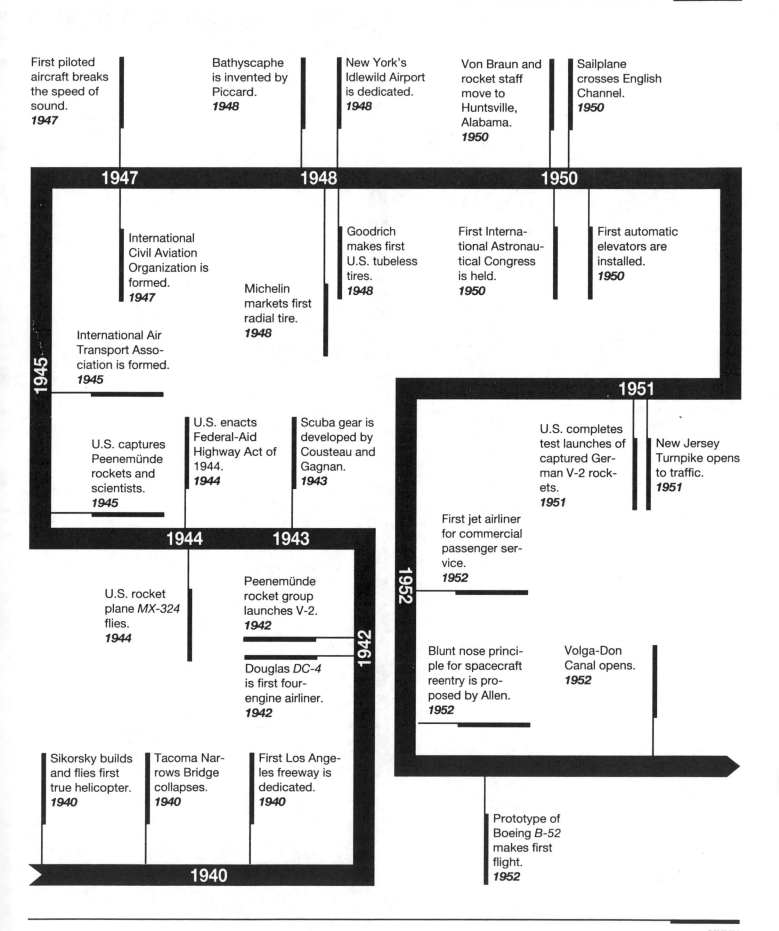

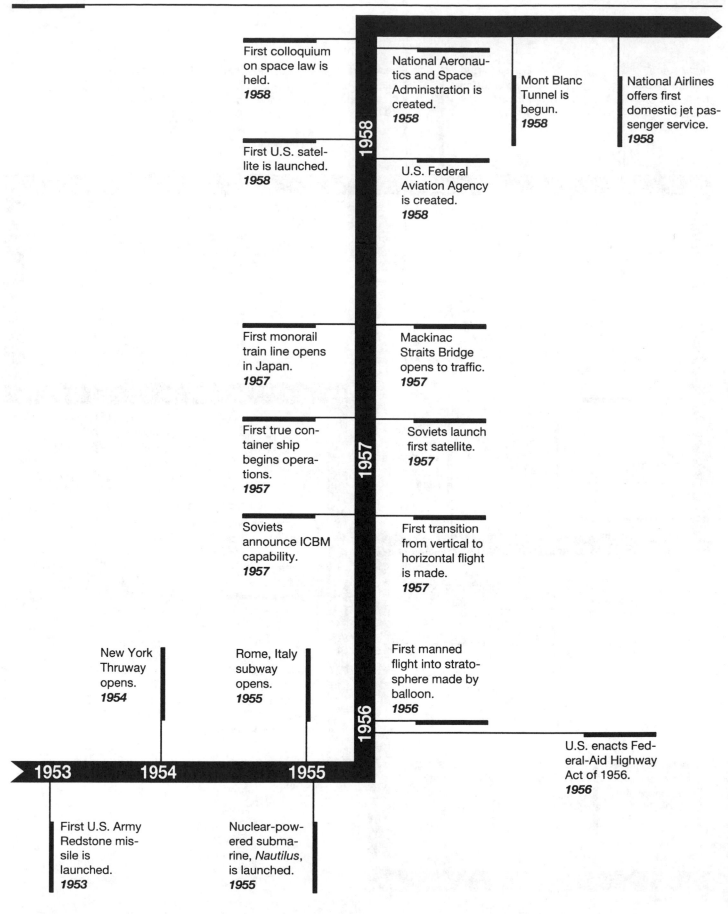

First colloquium on space law is held.
1958

National Aeronautics and Space Administration is created.
1958

Mont Blanc Tunnel is begun.
1958

National Airlines offers first domestic jet passenger service.
1958

First U.S. satellite is launched.
1958

U.S. Federal Aviation Agency is created.
1958

1958

First monorail train line opens in Japan.
1957

Mackinac Straits Bridge opens to traffic.
1957

First true container ship begins operations.
1957

Soviets launch first satellite.
1957

1957

Soviets announce ICBM capability.
1957

First transition from vertical to horizontal flight is made.
1957

New York Thruway opens.
1954

Rome, Italy subway opens.
1955

First manned flight into stratosphere made by balloon.
1956

1956

1953   **1954**   **1955**

U.S. enacts Federal-Aid Highway Act of 1956.
1956

First U.S. Army Redstone missile is launched.
1953

Nuclear-powered submarine, *Nautilus*, is launched.
1955

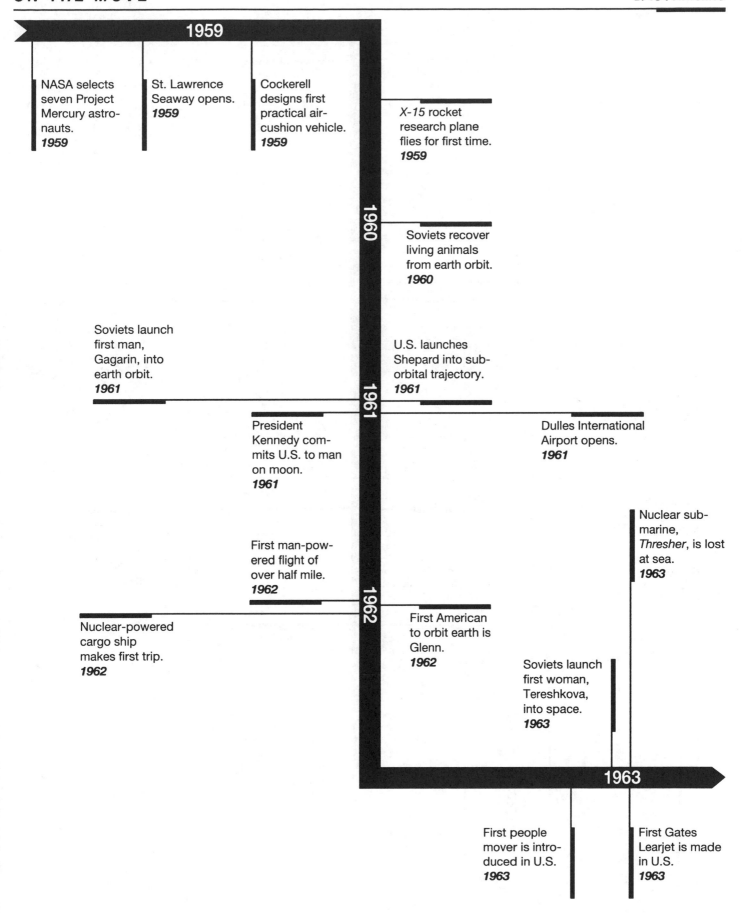

1959

NASA selects seven Project Mercury astronauts.
1959

St. Lawrence Seaway opens.
1959

Cockerell designs first practical air-cushion vehicle.
1959

X-15 rocket research plane flies for first time.
1959

Soviets recover living animals from earth orbit.
1960

1960

Soviets launch first man, Gagarin, into earth orbit.
1961

U.S. launches Shepard into sub-orbital trajectory.
1961

1961

President Kennedy commits U.S. to man on moon.
1961

Dulles International Airport opens.
1961

Nuclear submarine, *Thresher*, is lost at sea.
1963

First man-powered flight of over half mile.
1962

1962

Nuclear-powered cargo ship makes first trip.
1962

First American to orbit earth is Glenn.
1962

Soviets launch first woman, Tereshkova, into space.
1963

1963

First people mover is introduced in U.S.
1963

First Gates Learjet is made in U.S.
1963

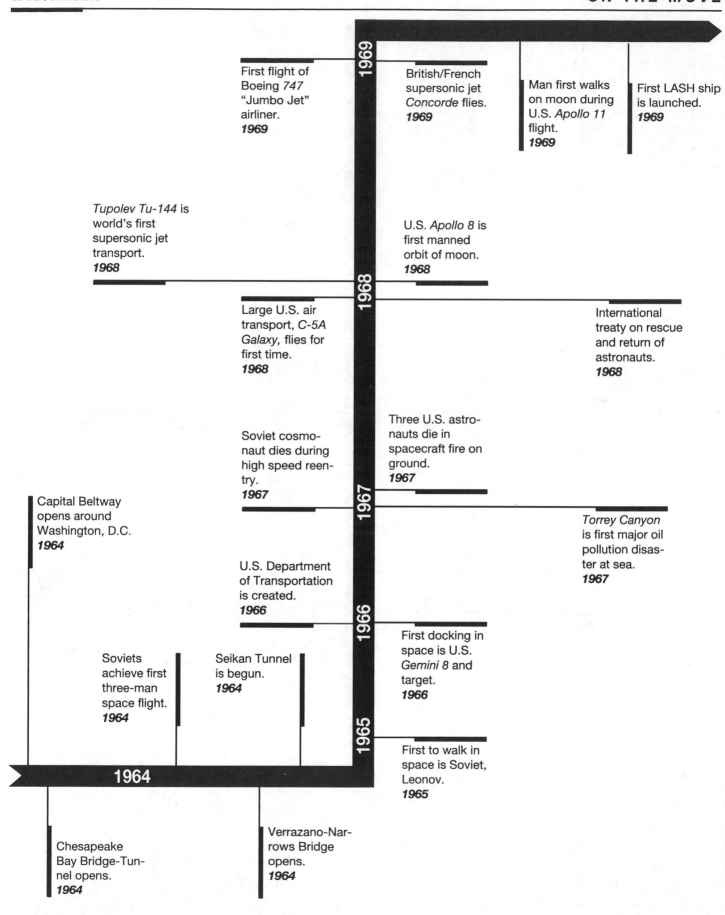

First flight of
Boeing *747*
"Jumbo Jet"
airliner.
1969

British/French
supersonic jet
Concorde flies.
1969

Man first walks
on moon during
U.S. *Apollo 11*
flight.
1969

First LASH ship
is launched.
1969

1969

Tupolev Tu-144 is
world's first
supersonic jet
transport.
1968

U.S. *Apollo 8* is
first manned
orbit of moon.
1968

1968

Large U.S. air
transport, *C-5A
Galaxy,* flies for
first time.
1968

International
treaty on rescue
and return of
astronauts.
1968

Soviet cosmo-
naut dies during
high speed reen-
try.
1967

Three U.S. astro-
nauts die in
spacecraft fire on
ground.
1967

1967

Capital Beltway
opens around
Washington, D.C.
1964

Torrey Canyon
is first major oil
pollution disas-
ter at sea.
1967

U.S. Department
of Transportation
is created.
1966

1966

First docking in
space is U.S.
Gemini 8 and
target.
1966

Soviets
achieve first
three-man
space flight.
1964

Seikan Tunnel
is begun.
1964

1965

First to walk in
space is Soviet,
Leonov.
1965

1964

Chesapeake
Bay Bridge-Tun-
nel opens.
1964

Verrazano-Nar-
rows Bridge
opens.
1964

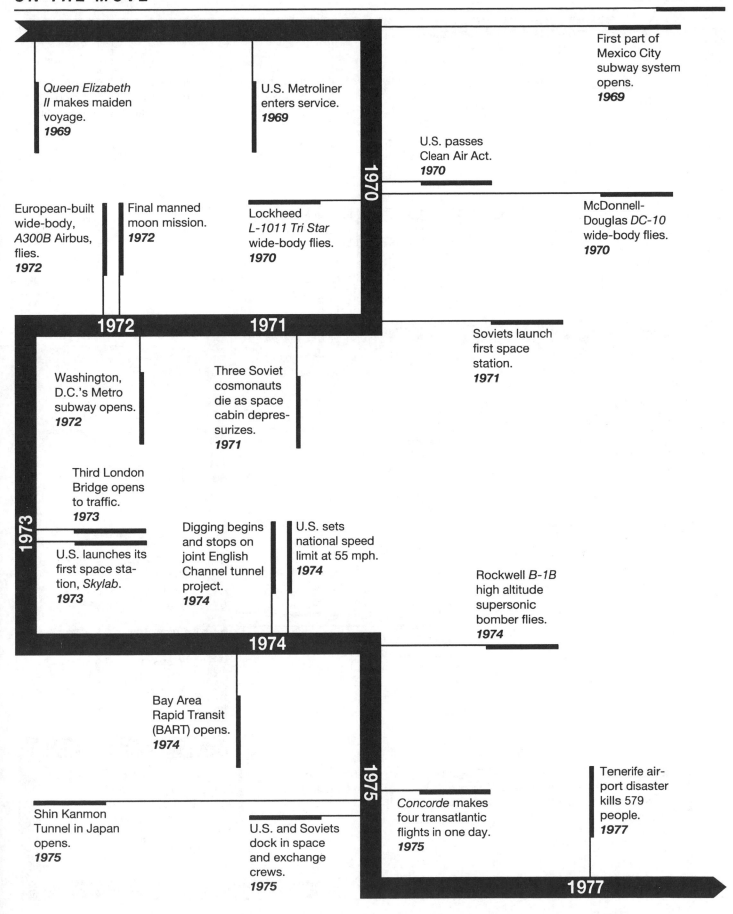

First part of Mexico City subway system opens. *1969*

Queen Elizabeth II makes maiden voyage. *1969*

U.S. Metroliner enters service. *1969*

U.S. passes Clean Air Act. *1970*

1970

European-built wide-body, *A300B* Airbus, flies. *1972*

Final manned moon mission. *1972*

Lockheed *L-1011 Tri Star* wide-body flies. *1970*

McDonnell-Douglas *DC-10* wide-body flies. *1970*

1972　**1971**

Washington, D.C.'s Metro subway opens. *1972*

Three Soviet cosmonauts die as space cabin depressurizes. *1971*

Soviets launch first space station. *1971*

Third London Bridge opens to traffic. *1973*

1973

U.S. launches its first space station, *Skylab*. *1973*

Digging begins and stops on joint English Channel tunnel project. *1974*

U.S. sets national speed limit at 55 mph. *1974*

Rockwell *B-1B* high altitude supersonic bomber flies. *1974*

1974

Bay Area Rapid Transit (BART) opens. *1974*

1975

Tenerife airport disaster kills 579 people. *1977*

Shin Kanmon Tunnel in Japan opens. *1975*

U.S. and Soviets dock in space and exchange crews. *1975*

Concorde makes four transatlantic flights in one day. *1975*

1977

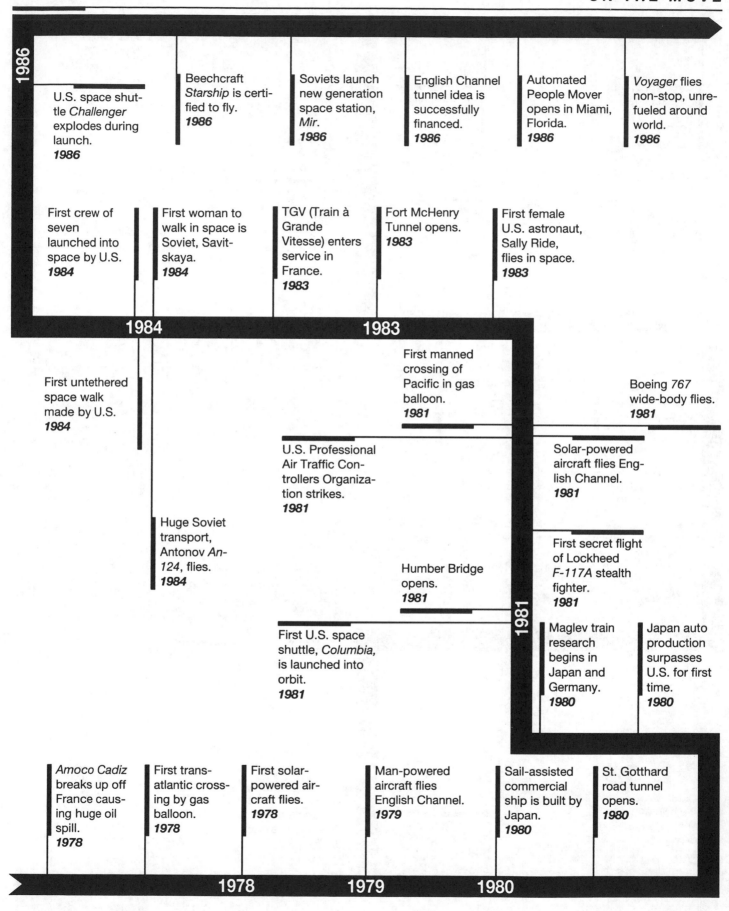

1986

U.S. space shuttle *Challenger* explodes during launch.
1986

Beechcraft *Starship* is certified to fly.
1986

Soviets launch new generation space station, *Mir*.
1986

English Channel tunnel idea is successfully financed.
1986

Automated People Mover opens in Miami, Florida.
1986

Voyager flies non-stop, unrefueled around world.
1986

First crew of seven launched into space by U.S.
1984

First woman to walk in space is Soviet, Savitskaya.
1984

TGV (Train à Grande Vitesse) enters service in France.
1983

Fort McHenry Tunnel opens.
1983

First female U.S. astronaut, Sally Ride, flies in space.
1983

1984

1983

First untethered space walk made by U.S.
1984

First manned crossing of Pacific in gas balloon.
1981

Boeing *767* wide-body flies.
1981

U.S. Professional Air Traffic Controllers Organization strikes.
1981

Solar-powered aircraft flies English Channel.
1981

Huge Soviet transport, Antonov *An-124*, flies.
1984

Humber Bridge opens.
1981

First secret flight of Lockheed *F-117A* stealth fighter.
1981

1981

Maglev train research begins in Japan and Germany.
1980

Japan auto production surpasses U.S. for first time.
1980

First U.S. space shuttle, *Columbia*, is launched into orbit.
1981

Amoco Cadiz breaks up off France causing huge oil spill.
1978

First transatlantic crossing by gas balloon.
1978

First solar-powered aircraft flies.
1978

Man-powered aircraft flies English Channel.
1979

Sail-assisted commercial ship is built by Japan.
1980

St. Gotthard road tunnel opens.
1980

1978   **1979**   **1980**

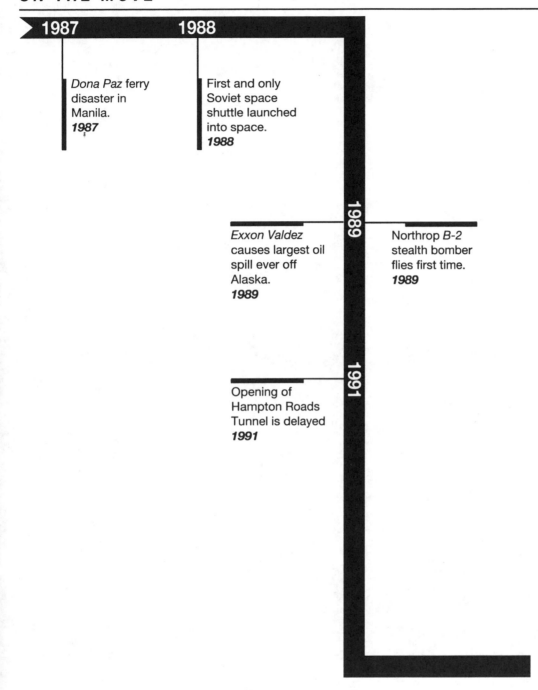

1987

1988

Dona Paz ferry disaster in Manila.
1987

First and only Soviet space shuttle launched into space.
1988

1989

Exxon Valdez causes largest oil spill ever off Alaska.
1989

Northrop *B-2* stealth bomber flies first time.
1989

1991

Opening of Hampton Roads Tunnel is delayed
1991

Key to Symbols

Four symbols, or icons, are used throughout *On the Move* as easy identifiers to the four forms of transportation covered here—Air, Land, Space, and Water.

Air

Land

Space

Water

The icons are meant to *represent* the transportation mode only, not to be a perfect match. For instance, the train represents *all* land events discussed, not just those relating to the railroad industry.

on the
MOVE

c. 30,000 B.C. Aborigines are believed to have reached Australia aboard some sort of seagoing craft.

c. 28,000—22,000 B.C. Earliest known image of animals that are eventually domesticated and used for transportation and other purposes are drawings discovered in 1940 in the Lascaux cave in Dordogne, France. These wall paintings are carbon dated to the earliest phase of the Old Stone Age (32,000—10,000 B.C.). It is speculated that primitive man made these drawings of oxen, horse, deer, and other animals over a long period of time and that they may have served as a place for performing hunting and magical rites. (See c. 12,000 B.C.)

c. 12,000 B.C. Domestication of animals by man begins as the dog is the first animal to be tamed. Fossil remains of dogs dated to this period are found with those of humans in caves near Kirkuk (northern Iraq). By 10,000 B.C., goats are domesticated and by 6,000 B.C., man has tamed the onager (wild ass) and the wild ox. These large animals are strong enough to pull a litter, sled, and eventually a wheeled cart.

c. 10,000 B.C. Despite the lack of archaeological evidence, many believe that the earliest seaborne trade so far identified—the carrying of obsidian (a black, natural glass of volcanic origin) from the Island of Melos to mainland Greece—is conducted in log boats. When a hollowed-out log is softened by soaking it in hot water, its sides can be forced apart to give a wider, more stable craft. This process also gives the ends "sheer" or a sweeping up-curve.

c. 7500 B.C. Reed boats are developed in Mesopotamia and Egypt, while in northwestern Europe, dugout canoes are being used.

c. 7500 B.C. Wooden paddle dated to this time is uncovered from a peat bog at Star Carr in Yorkshire, England, suggesting that it was used to propel a dugout canoe. (See c. 6300 B.C.)

c. 6300 B.C. Remains of a dugout canoe dated to this time are found in Pesse, The Netherlands. This crude boat has been hacked out hollow with flint tools.

c. 6000 B.C. Ancestor of the sled is the simple Y-shaped tree bough which evolves into a travois. This method of transporting things involves two poles tied together, with the inverted V resting on the back of a man or animal. Between the poles is slung a wooden or net frame. The North American Indians of recent times used the travois tied to their horses.

c. 5000 B.C. Archaeological evidence suggests that reindeer are used to pull sleds in northern Europe. Heavy weights can be moved easily when friction is reduced.

c. 5000 B.C.

Reindeer pull sleds

c. 5000 B.C. The sled or sledge is in common use in northern Europe, North America, Egypt, Assyria, and the Middle East. Originally, it is a simple rectangular platform that can be pulled or pushed. It can be dragged over most any surface and is later improved by the addition of runners. A four-wheeled wagon can be thought of as simply a sled on wheels. After this time, but before 3500 B.C., it is thought that rollers made from logs are used as the first wheels.

c. 5000 B.C. Earliest known ship illustration dates from this period and is found at Hierakonpolis in Egypt. Although crude, it is distinctly a ship built from papyrus (a marsh plant) with a steering oar worked from the port (left) side. It also shows a type of covered shelter built in and two paddles.

c. 4500 B.C. Oldest long-distance highway, later called the Royal Road by sixth century B.C. Persians, begins to be regularly used. It takes foot travelers on a 1,755-mile journey, beginning in Susa, the ancient city of Elam (now in Iran), all the way to the Turkish ports of Ephesus and Smyrna. Sennacherib, King of Assyria (705—681 B.C.), leaves a memorial in his capital city of Ninevah inscribed, "Royal Road. Let No Man Decrease It." His instructions are that anyone whose property encroaches the 78-foot-wide main street of the city should be put to death. (See 521 B.C.)

c. 4000 B.C. The yoke is used possibly for the first time in the Near East. It is a wooden bar or frame that rests on the shoulders (withers) of draft animals and is tied to the neck or horns to assure that they pull together. Besides the wheel, the yoke represents the most important prehistoric technical invention for transport, since it enables the pulling power of animals to be more fully exploited.

c. 4000 B.C. Archaeological research reveals that overland travel in these prehistoric times is far more extensive than believed. Flint implements of the Ertboll culture (now in Denmark) are transported over rough roads, not only to Norway but into the interior of Germany.

c. 3500 B.C. With the invention of the wheel at the dawn of the Bronze Age, there arose the need for hard surfaces capable of supporting concentrated loads. Pavement may have been laid in India and a cobble surface (small stones) may have been laid in Assyria. The first wheeled vehicles are believed to have appeared in Sumer (now Iraq) at this time.

c. 3500 B.C. The ass, a beast of burden smaller than the horse, proves an excellent draft animal. It is used for transporting goods by this date and is in regular service on the caravan routes stretching from eastern Europe and North Africa to India and China well before 3000 B.C. As time passes, other animals are similarly used—the ox, reindeer, elephant, yak, buffalo, llama, and camel. The horse is a relative newcomer, having been introduced to Egypt by the Hyksos about 1675 B.C. and to Babylonia by the Kassites about 1500 B.C.

c. 3500 B.C. Imperial road system of China begins to be developed. Radiating from the cities of Sianfu, Nanking, and Ch'eng-tu, it totals about 2,000 miles (3,200 kilometers). Many are wide and well-built, and some are surfaced with stone, although generally they are not well-maintained. They differ from western roads in their marked crookedness.

c. 3500 B.C. Earliest illustration of a sail dates from this period. It is painted on the outside of a funerary vase found near Luxor, Egypt. The sail is fixed to a single mast and there is a shelter aft (toward the rear).

3400 B.C. Egyptians raid the coast of Syria in seagoing wooden ships. Hulls are constructed by pegging together overlapping lengths of cedar wood with wooden nails driven in holes. When the wood swells, the planks become firmly held together. These ships have no keel or center beam and so are held together tightly with ropes wrapped around the hull. They also have one square sail that can be used only with a following wind and oars and paddlers for use without a sail.

c. 3250 B.C. Indus civilization in Sindh, Baluchistan, and the Punjab (which flourished about 3250—2750 B.C.) paved the roads of its cities with burned bricks cemented with bitumen (a tar-like substance). Great attention is paid to drainage, as the nearby houses have drain pipes that carry water to a street drain located in the center of the street. It is two to four feet (about one meter) deep and is covered with slabs of bricks.

c. 3100 B.C. Earliest bridge on record is believed to have been built on the River Nile by Menes (fl. c. 3100 B.C.), the first king of unified Egypt. No details of the bridge are known.

c. 3000 B.C. Wheels discovered in royal tombs at Kish in the Tigris-Euphrates Valley are estimated to be of this period, and therefore are the oldest actual wheels extant.

c. 3000 B.C. An alabaster relief of this period found in Sumer (ancient Babylonia) shows two bearers transporting a large vessel hanging from a pole they each are bearing on their shoulders. This is a variation of the yoke used on animals.

c. 3000 B.C. Slide-car, a type of improved and more permanent travois, is used to carry objects. It has two poles or shafts that are usually attached to an animal's side with its other ends dragging along the ground. The poles are kept apart by crossbars and the burden is carried on them.

c. 3000 B.C. Egyptian King Cheops, who reigned from about 2900 to 2877 B.C., is said to have built a solid trackway for hauling the huge limestone blocks used to erect the Great Pyramids. This idea is attributed to the later Greek historian, Herodotus (c. 484—425 B.C.).

c. 3000 B.C. The earliest known wheeled vehicle in India is assigned to this period. It is a cart that looks like a three-spoked, bent ladder on wheels.

c. 3000 B.C. A road is built on the island of Crete during the Minoan civilization (from 3000 to 1000 B.C.), extending from Gortyna on the south coast over the mountains to Knossos on the north coast. Constructed of layers of stone, it is about 12 feet (3.6 meters) wide and the central portion consists of two basalt slabs two inches (50 millimeters) thick. The center of the road appears to have been used for foot traffic and the edges for animals and carts. Drainage is provided by a crown throughout its length and gutters in some sections. There are also guard houses at frequent intervals.

c. 3000 B.C. Four-wheeled wagons dating back this far have been found in the "Queen's Grave" at the site of the city of Ur. This is the city of ancient Sumer in Babylonia, now part of Iraq.

c. 3000 B.C. Anchors are known to be used by both the Chinese and Egyptians, although they are only heavy stones or weighted bags thrown overboard from ships. Around 600 B.C., it is believed that the first single-palm grapnel (claw) made of metal is used.

2613 B.C. Egyptian Pharaoh Sneferu (c. 2613—c. 2494 B.C.), a great shipbuilder, founds the Fourth Dynasty and brings 40 ships filled with cedar wood from Byblos in Phoenicia to Egypt. The existing "invoice" documenting this transaction can be considered the oldest "shipping document" known. Since Egypt has few large trees, it must import its wood or use papyrus for boats.

2600 B.C. In building their largest pyramid, the Egyptians use some form of hoist to raise both men and materials. The Great Pyramid stands over 500 feet high and many of the building blocks weigh over 200,000 pounds.

c. 2600 B.C. Egyptian Pharaoh Cheops, also known as Khufu (fl. 26th century B.C.), dies, and in his Great Pyramid tomb at Giza are placed parts of a wooden boat, 160 feet (48.8 meters) long and 20 feet (6.1 meters) wide. It contains room for twenty rowers who are distinctly not paddlers.

c. 2500 B.C. On a piece of a sacrificial plaque made of limestone found in the city of Ur (now in Iraq) and dated before this time, a chariot is shown whose wheel is made of three pieces of wood. The center wheel piece is plum-shaped, with crescent-shaped pieces on either side.

c. 2500 B.C. One of the earliest recorded passenger chariots is used by the warriors of Elam (the Biblical name of a country in what is now southwestern Iran). Its wheels are made in three pieces, held together by copper. It is pulled by wild asses called onagers and driven in a standing position. Another version shows the driver sitting.

2500 B.C. Domesticated elephants are represented on seals from the Indus Valley (India) civilization dating to this period. They are used as beasts of burden as well as for riding. The Indian "howdah" or "houdah" is a seat or a covered pavilion placed on the elephant's back in which the rider sits. With the post-World War II passing of the old, princely order of society in India, howdahs become used primarily for ceremonial processions.

c. 2500 B.C. Detailed carved relief from the pyramid of Egyptian Pharaoh Sahure (second king of the fifth dynasty of Egypt) shows eight of his ships returning from a raid on the Syrian coast carrying prisoners.

c. 2500 B.C. Egyptian hieroglyph of this period (the sixth Egyptian dynasty) signifying a swimmer is found in modern times. This hieroglyph (ancient picture writing) which stands for the word swimming, shows a person doing what is recognizable as the crawl stroke (a speed swimming style consisting of alternating overarm strokes plus a kick). This indicates that by at least this time in Egypt, the more natural and easier breaststroke had already evolved into the crawl.

c. 2500 B.C. Remains of early snow skis dating to this period are found in two separate places, indicating that they are used for transportation over snow. Skis are found buried in the Altai Mountains in Khasakstan, Russia as well as in a peat bog at Hoting in Angermanland, Sweden. The Swedish Hoting ski is more of a snowshoe-like design.

c. 2400 B.C. Ship illustrations of this period show design changes in Egyptian ship construction. Several stout ropes are seen running from bow to stern (front to back). These are added to raise both ends of the ship which tend to sag as the boats become longer. As boats continue to grow even more in size, additional fore-and-aft braces are added. They are similar to the fore-and-aft strengtheners seen even today on the shallow-draught Mississippi river boats.

c. 2300 B.C. Bridles (strap-like headgear an animal wears so it can be controlled) and bits made of horn or bone (the hard part of a bridle held in the animal's mouth) are introduced in Mesopotamia. Oxen are guided by a rope threaded through their nose or by a cord attached to a ring through their nose.

2300 B.C. Early clay map of this period is found at Nuzi, in northern Iraq. It shows mountains, rivers, and settlements and gives dimensions of cultivated areas of land.

c. 2300 B.C. Navigation canals are ordered built by Pepi I, Egyptian king of the sixth dynasty (c. 2345—2181 B.C.), to bypass the rapids near Aswan. They are dug by the governor of Upper Egypt, Uni, who leaves an inscription there, saying he dug three canals in one year.

c. 2250 B.C. Principle of a railway, as a track that guides vehicles along it, is known and used in Babylonian times. They build grooved stone wagonways, about five feet (1500 millimeters) apart. Remains of these can still be found, as can those later used by the Greeks.

c. 2180 B.C. First known tunnel of any importance used to transport men and goods is built under the Euphrates River by the Babylonians in Mesopotamia. After diverting the river from its usual bed

to a temporary channel, they dig a 3,000-foot long tunnel, 12 feet wide and 15 feet high, under the river bed and line it with bricks and asphalt. The river is then let back to follow its natural course.

c. 2024 B.C. With the fall of the Third Dynasty of Ur, the Sumerians disappear from the scene. Sumer (the southern part of ancient Babylonia, now part of southern Iraq) is today considered the location for the first civilizations of the world, and the Sumerians were undoubtedly the first to use the wheeled vehicle.

c. 2000 B.C. Most wheels of this period are no longer simply solid pieces of a log (cut cross-wise and thus easily breakable as well as heavy and often wobbly), but are made in the form of tripartite disks. They consist of three planks carved to fit segments of a circle and held together by crosspieces, with a raised area in the middle of the center plank forming a hub around the axle. Spoked wheels also appear about this time on chariots in Syria and Egypt.

c. 2000 B.C. Unique "rut" roads are built on the island of Malta. They consist of two V-shaped grooves about 4.5 feet (1.35 meters) apart cut into the coral sandstone of the island. The roads are apparently traversed by carts, drawn by human power, with the wheels running in the grooves.

c. 2000 B.C. Prehistoric rock drawing at the Los Buitres near Penalsordo, Spain shows an H-shaped slide-car with wheels and a ladder-shaped chassis. The image is drawn as if seen from above.

c. 2000 B.C. Egyptian wall paintings of this period show a sled with runners being towed by two oxen. The sled is carrying a hearse containing a mummy to a tomb.

c. 2000 B.C. Evidence indicates that wheeled vehicles have been in use in China even before the Hsia dynasty (before 2000 B.C.).

c. 2000 B.C. Earliest known pictorial representation of a person skiing is found in a rock carving in Rodoy, Norway. The stylized figure has very long skis, the front ends of which curve up dramatically.

2000 B.C. Seagoing, sail-driven commercial and naval vessels begin to become more common in the

Mediterranean. They are both sizeable and sophisticated. In Crete, the Minoans develop ships using a log keel (long center beam) with ribs and planking on the sides joined at the stem and stern.

c. 2000 B.C. Andean peoples of early Peru are known to have migrated across the Pacific Ocean in balsa wood rafts.

c. 2000 B.C. Horses are tamed by the nomads in the steppes of what is now Iran. Although not as strong as an ox and difficult to harness, they prove well-suited to pulling a light, wheeled vehicle that becomes the chariot. Eventually, horses are sufficiently trained to allow men to ride on their backs.

c. 1900 B.C. Earliest roads in Europe, called the "Amber Routes," begin to be made and used at first by Etruscan and Greek traders to transport amber and tin from north of Europe to the Mediterranean and Adriatic. Four separate routes have been identified. It is these busy roads that bring the civilized peoples of the Mediterranean—the Etruscans and the Greeks—into contact with the north European tribes they describe as "barbarians."

c. 1878 B.C. Precursor of the modern-day Suez Canal is built by Sesostris III (12th dynasty king of Egypt who rules from 1878 to 1843 B.C.). He cuts a canal through the First Nile Cataract at Elephantine (modern Aswan) to the Red Sea. Egyptian commercial interests lead them to have fleets in both the Mediterranean and the Red Sea, and this connecting canal becomes both a military and economic necessity.

c. 1850 B.C. Rowing-boats are recorded as being on the Nile River during the reign of Pharaoh Sesostris III, king of Egypt from 1878 to 1843 B.C. With the Nile's prevailing winds coming northwest or against its flow, a boat can row downstream easily with the current and use its sail to return.

c. 1700 B.C. In China, a wheeled chariot and two horses are buried in the grave of a prominent member of the Shan Dynasty (1766—1123 B.C.). The chariot remains and horse skeletons are unearthed in modern times and tell much about this particular mode of transportation in China.

1530 B.C. In the Pacific Ocean region, a thriving civilization based on its ability to move upon the sea exists. A migration eastward by boat reaches Hawaii.

c. 1500 B.C. Evidence indicates that log roads were built extensively in northern Europe (modern Netherlands, Germany, Poland, Latvia, Sweden, and Russia) to carry traffic across wet and swampy areas. They are built by laying two or three strings of logs in the direction of the road on a bed of branches and boughs up to 20 feet (6 meters) wide and covering them with transverse logs 9 to 12 feet (2.7 to 3.6 meters) long laid side by side. In the best roads, every fifth or sixth log is fastened to the underlying subsoil with pegs. They are maintained by covering with sand and gravel or sod.

c. 1500 B.C. Wheels on the Egyptian war chariots have six spokes. The wooden wheels are made of shaped sections that are lashed together with rawhide passed through slots on the sides. Drivers guide their horses with reins attached to a bit which is held in the horse's mouth by a leather bridle. The horse-drawn chariot had been introduced into Egypt about 100 years earlier by their Hyksos conquerors.

1500 B.C. Egyptian Queen Hatshepsut (c. 1540—c. 1481 B.C.) sends her ships from the port of Suez sailing south to find the legendary land of Punt. Since they return after a year with gold, incense, ivory, and spices, it is believed that they reached either India via the open sea or Ethiopia and East Africa by sailing along the coasts.

c. 1500 B.C. Phoenicians emerge as a powerful trading nation based mainly on ships. They build their craft from the famous cedar trees of Lebanon and use planks of wood held together by wooden toggles (crosspiece). This differs from Egyptian construction methods. They also depend mainly on sails rather than oars for propulsion. They do not know the rudder but steer by using a long oar on the port (left) side. These early merchant ships are broad and short, so as to carry more cargo, and are called "round ships" as opposed to the "long ships" which are used for war. Unlike the Egyptians who generally sail the calm Nile River, the Phoenicians are explorers of the open sea.

c. 1500 B.C. Series of great masonry piers are unearthed at Knossos in Crete and are believed to have been part of viaduct carrying a road over a ravine.

c. 1400 B.C. ■ Primitive sled-wagon depicted on walls at Luxor in Thebes shows logs used as a type of wheel.

This city in ancient Crete, capital of the legendary King Minos, is the center of a sophisticated Bronze Age culture that dominates the Aegean at this time. This site is excavated in 1900 by English archaeologist Arthur Evans (1851—1941), who unearths the city.

1352 B.C.

Chariots buried with King Tut

1352 B.C. When Egyptian King Tutankhamen (reigned 1361—1352 B.C.) dies, among the treasures he is buried with are his chariots. When the intact tomb is discovered in 1922 by British archaeologist Howard Carter (1873—1939), among the items found are the working parts of five dismantled chariots, one of which is inlayed with semi-precious stones and stained glass. Each entire vehicle—its carriage body, the pole, wheels, and all the small parts—is made of wood.

C. 1350 B.C. First images of men riding horses and controlling them with bridles are found in the tomb of Egyptian Pharaoh Horemhab (reigned c. 1348—c. 1320 B.C.). His tomb is discovered near Memphis, Egypt in 1975.

C. 1250 B.C. One of the more famous canals of antiquity is built by Egyptian King Rameses II the Great (1304—1237 B.C.). It links the Nile River near Cairo to the northern part of the Bitter Lakes, with access from there to the Red Sea.

1198 B.C. Fleet of Egyptian Pharaoh Rameses III (ruled 1198—1166 B.C.) defeats the combined fleets of the Libyans, Syrians, and Philistines at Pelusium. Using both their own ships and those of the Phoenicians, the Egyptians have their oarsmen sitting behind solid bulwarks, safe from spears and arrows.

1180 B.C. In Trojan War between early Greeks and the people of Troy, vessels used in battle are later described by Greek epic poet Homer (fl. 8th century B.C.) in the *Iliad* and the *Odyssey*. These ships have one bank of oars and a single, square sail on one mast.

c. 1175 B.C. ■ Bas-relief on temple at Aboo-simbel in Nubia shows Rameses III standing in his ornamental chariot.

1003 B.C. Ancient Chinese character for the word "bridge" is said to date from this time. A two-part character, the left side stands for "wood" and the right side for "lofty."

1000 B.C. The kite is invented in China. As the true ancestor of the airplane, it can be considered the earliest type of heavier-than-air device to fly, since the propulsion is supplied by the pull on the tow line and the lift is supplied by the kite being tilted or inclined to the wind. It is really a tethered glider and will play an important role in the history of flying.

1000 B.C. Phoenicians are the most accomplished seamen of this time and become virtual masters of the Mediterranean. While most seafaring is confined to daylight, Phoenician astronomy results in star maps that enable their navigators to travel by sea at night. They use the pole-star as their northerly bearing.

1000 B.C. Use of camels for labor as pack animals appears in Mesopotamia. It is believed that camels have been used for some time before this as beasts of burden as well as for riding. The camel is physiologically the best desert transport animal. It can go for long periods without much food or water, can carry heavy loads, and does not need roads or paths. Although nomadism is today disappearing, it is still a way of life in the Sahara, and the camel is an integral part of that culture.

c. 1000 B.C. Small boats made by covering a light frame with stout hide or a kind of cloth first appear about this time in Asia. These often take the form of the coracle in India called a "quffa" which looks like a large basket without a lid. They also can be the small, light, skin-covered craft that becomes the Celtic wicker coracle.

c. 1000 B.C. "Clapper" bridges of Dartmoor, England are believed to have been built at this time. These simple examples of a beam bridge—still found in the English countryside—are made of flat stone slabs sitting atop stone piers and spanning small rivers and streams. Some disagree that these bridges are of this early period, since most of the waters they span are easily fordable. These experts argue that the clappers were built no earlier than the late Middle Ages. Simple slab bridges like these are not found only in England today but in Spain as well. There is also evidence that they were built in Babylon, Egypt, and China.

c. 859 B.C. Assyrian bas-reliefs (slightly raised wall sculpture) of King Ashurnasirpal III (king from 883 to 859 B.C.) show his soldiers swimming across a river using inflated goat skins. Although this is the earliest known depiction of this form of water transport, the use of inflated animal skins has been going on for quite some time, and it is not an unusual eastern practice.

800 B.C. Liege-lords of China begin fending off invasions of barbaric tribes whose foot soldiers are combatted by Chinese chariots.

c. 783 B.C. Bridge across the Euphrates River at Babylon is described by Greek historian Herodotus (c. 484—c. 425) as having been built by Nitocris, Queen of Babylon. It has stone piers connected with wooden platforms which are removed at night to prevent anyone from entering the city.

776 B.C. With the introduction of the Greek Olympic games, organized and regular chariot racing begins. These are low-wheeled vehicles with metal bodies large enough for only one standing driver who could lean against the padded dashboard with his knees. Many Greeks become passionate about chariot racing, and Greek writer Aristophanes has one of his characters in the *Clouds* complain about his son, saying, "He rides, he drives, he dreams of horses…"

776 B.C.

Chariot racing begins

c. 750 B.C. In two epic Greek poems, the *Iliad* and the *Odyssey*, ascribed to the Ionian called Homer, there are references to and descriptions of the war chariots of the day. Both also contain information on other vehicles and roads. The *Iliad* tells how Priam went to Achilles in an ox-drawn wagon to beg for the body of Hector, and that this was a new and wonderful vehicle with a wicker roof.

c. 705 B.C. Assyrian King Sennacherib (d. 681 B.C.) is known to have ridden in a chariot with spoked wheels. He stands well ahead of the wheels, with the horses taking part of his weight. The Egyptians' chariots have the driver and passengers stand over the axle, with their whole weight on the wheels—a much better method.

c. 700 B.C. Related tribes of migrating peoples called Scythians take possession of the steppes in the northern regions of the tributaries of the Black Sea, transporting their homes with them. These nomads live in what might be called two-wheeled covered wagons that are round or hemispherical and are pulled by oxen.

c. 700 B.C. First serious road builders are probably the Mesopotamians who develop a travel route from the Babylonian Empire west and southwest to Egypt. Processional roads in which burnt brick and stone are laid in bituminous (tar-like) mortar connect the temples and palaces of the ancient cities of Assur, Babylon, and Tall al-Asmar.

c. 700 B.C. In Greece, the chariot ceases to be used in warfare and becomes useful only as a carriage for getting around and for racing and hunting. Their chariots are well-made, very light, and strong. Their wheels are low to prevent easy tipping and are spoked. They use two, three, or four horses at once.

c. 700 B.C. Aqueducts to carry water are built by Sennacherib (d. 681 B.C.), king of Assyria, to bring water into the city of Ninevah, and by Hezekiah (reigned c. 715—c. 686 B.C.), king of Judah, to supply Jerusalem with water. Although these structures are used to transport water, they are early evidence of bridge-building.

681 B.C. First recorded illustration of a bireme—a ship with two banks of rowers—is found in the ruins of Sennacherib's (d. 681 B.C.) palace in Assyria that date to this period. Wall reliefs also show a Phoenician ship with a detachable ram-bow. This weapon is designed to ram and penetrate the hull of an enemy ship and to snap off, leaving the ramming ship watertight and free to maneuver.

c. 668 B.C. Ashurbanipal, last of the great kings of Assyria (reigned 668—628 B.C.), assembles at Nineveh the first systematically organized library in the Near East, the remains of which are excavated in 1845. The reliefs discovered show the transportation of huge statues, loaded carts, sleds, and many other chariots as well as different types of vehicles of the period. The King's chariot has an umbrella-shaped sunshade under which he stands.

621 B.C. Earliest Roman bridge about which a record exists is the "Pons Sublicus," or Bridge of Piles, that figures in the legendary feats of Roman hero Horatius Cocles. This wooden bridge is generally believed to be the first of eight bridges over the Tiber River at Rome. Horatius and two companions are said to have held off Lars Porsena and his Etruscan army at the bridge in 508 B.C., giving the Romans time to cut it down and prevent an invasion of the city. It is believed built this year by Ancus Martius traditionally the fourth king of Rome, from 642 to 617 B.C.

609 B.C. First circumnavigation of Africa is begun by the order of Egyptian Pharaoh Necho II (ruled 610—595 B.C.). He commissions a Phoenician fleet and

orders its captains to sail from Suez indefinitely, always keeping land within sight on the starboard (right) side. Four years later, the fleet arrives in Alexandria, having gone completely around Africa and returned to the Mediterranean via the Straits of Gibraltar.

c. 600 B.C. Early form of saddles are used by the Scythians, one of the great horse peoples of all time. Their saddles are made of leather and felt and are two cushions well-stuffed with deer hair, joined by straps. The cushions are placed on top of a felt saddlecloth called a "numnah," which is elaborately embroidered. This cloth doubles as a blanket at night for the nomadic riders. The Argentine gaucho uses a saddle today that in its essentials differs little from those of the Scythians.

c. 600 B.C. Greek fighting ship of this time is the galley—a long, low, sleek vessel that is lightly built and propelled by oars. The Greeks use paid freeman and not slaves as oarsmen. The later biremes and triremes (two and three banks of oars) are versions of the galley.

600 B.C. Greek merchant ships of this period resemble a Phoenician bireme (two sets of oars) and carry a gang-plank. The use of this plank that can be let down onto a beach or promontory indicates that they regularly traded not only at the major ports but at those without cargo-handling facilities as well. Since the planks have roped-in sides, it is assumed that their major trade was in livestock.

c. 600 B.C. Earliest known map of the world is a Babylonian clay tablet of this period which shows the earth as a flat disk surrounded by ocean and islands. (See c. 510 B.C.)

600 B.C. Railway for ships, a "diolkos" or "portage way" in Greek, is built by Greek tyrant Periander (d. 586 B.C.). Running across the Isthmus of Corinth, it consists of wheeled cradles running in grooves cut in a paved causeway. Small warships or empty cargo vessels are then wheeled overland between Kenchreai and Lechaion. This is done in lieu of building a canal.

c. 558 B.C. Greek historian Xenophon (431—350 B.C.), writing about Persian King Cyrus II (c. 590—c. 529 B.C.), credits the Persians with the invention of the "mower," a war chariot with sharp blades mounted on its wheels.

536 B.C. Pontoon bridge across the Euphrates River is built out of stuffed skins used as floats by Cyrus II, King of the Persians (c. 590—c. 529 B.C.) who sends his army across.

521 B.C. Persian King Darius I (d. 485 B.C.) comes to power and builds a great overland artery connecting east and west over the ancient route called the Royal Road. Darius builds it solely for use by the State—for its trade, communications, and military interests. Its route is as straight as possible, does not always lead to the major centers or cities, and is thus not useful to invaders.

510 B.C. Canal is dug by Darius I the Great, of Persia (550—486 B.C.), from the Nile River to the Red Sea. In 1886 during the excavation for the Suez Canal, a stela (stone pillar with writing on it) is discovered with an inscription by Darius which says, "I ordered this canal to be dug from the river called the Nile which flows in Egypt to the sea which goes from Persia."

c. 510 B.C. Early realistic map of the world is drawn by Greek historian and travel writer Hecataeus of Miletus. His map shows the land portion of the world as a circle surrounded by water. Within the circle's middle, he places the Mediterranean Sea, with Europe to its north, Africa to its south, and Asia to its west.

510 B.C. Pontoon bridge of boats is built across the Danube River by Darius I, king of Persia (550—486 B.C.), who sends his army across during the Scythian campaign. (See 493 B.C.)

c. 500 B.C. Carthaginians (North Africa) are said to have built stone-paved highways along the southern shore of the Mediterranean Sea.

c. 500 B.C. The well-known seal of Persian King Darius I (550—486 B.C.) shows him standing in his chariot placing an arrow in his bow to shoot at a lion-like beast. Within his lifetime, the seals are changed to show him riding horseback.

c. 500 B.C. First set of laws governing conduct at sea, the *Lex Rhodia,* is adopted by most of the maritime nations. Named after Rhodes, the capital and island in the Mediterranean, it becomes the original basis for all subsequent maritime jurisprudence. As the island of Rhodes is placed at a cross-roads in the Mediterranean and its people are ancient seafarers, the sensible laws they

evolve to assure order at sea become well-known and eventually accepted.

c. 500 B.C. Guild system is organized by shipowners in the city of Byzantium, later renamed Constantinople. They join together to lay down codes of conduct governing sailors and to rationalize the chartering of their ships. Ships are often chartered for a single trip or expedition by groups of merchants, and some system of accountability at sea and in port is necessary.

Fig. 2.

c. 500 B.C. ■ Ancient Plaustrum or two-wheeled farm carts attributed to Eastern Nomads during this time.

c. 500 B.C. Greek trireme, with three banks of oars, is introduced. It is known that many such vessels are used in the Battle of Salamis. (See 480 B.C.)

c. 500 B.C. Etruscans build a stone arch bridge at Bieda, north of Rome. Its arch spans 7.2 meters and is built of wedge-shaped stone blocks fitted together with mortar. Many believe the Etruscans, the ancestors or at least predecessors of the Romans, to have invented the arch bridge.

c. 500 B.C.

Stone arch bridge built

493 B.C. Pontoon bridge of boats is built across the Bosporus River by Darius I, king of Persia (550—486 B.C.). The temporary, floating bridge is constructed at a place where the river is 3,000 feet wide and is used by his armies in their invasion of Thrace. Pontoon bridges are subsequently used by military leaders from Xerxes I of Persia (c. 519—465 B.C.) and Alexander the Great (356—323 B.C.), to today's modern generals.

480 B.C. Greece defeats Persia in the Battle of Salamis. The superior numbers of the Persian fleet, led by Xerxes I (c. 519—465 B.C.), become entangled in the narrow strait and are cut to pieces by the Greek triremes.

480 B.C. Carthaginian expedition led by Hanno (fl. fifth century B.C.) sails around the west coast of Africa.

480 B.C. Xerxes I of Persia (c. 519—465 B.C.), intending to attack Greece, cuts a 4,000-meter canal on the Isthmus of Mount Athos after crossing the Hellespont River using a bridge of boats. Greek historian Herodotus (c. 484—c. 420 B.C.) comments that, since Xerxes could have hauled his ships across the isthmus with less effort than it took to dig this canal, "I conclude that he dug the canal out of a desire for ostentation." It is not known if Xerxes ever does lead his ships through the canal.

c. 450 B.C. Greek historian Herodotus (c. 484—c. 420 B.C.) describes a Persian "harmanaxa" or woman's wagon. It is the earliest four-wheeled vehicle known to be used as a carriage. It is believed that the Chaldeans used four-wheeled chariots as early as 2000 B.C. This vehicle has a rectangular, box-like body with curtains and a canopy, and is usually pulled by two horses. At first used only by women and older people, it is used in the later days of the Persian Empire by elegant young men who are ridiculed by their elders.

414 B.C. Greek historian Thucydides (c. 460—c. 400 B.C.) describes the use of divers at the siege of the island of Sphacteria and later at the siege of Syracuse. He does not tell what kind of devices, if any, the soldiers use to remain underwater.

411 B.C. Bridge is built spanning the strait at Chalcis connecting the island of Euboea and mainland Greece. Erected during the Second Peloponnesian War (431—404 B.C.), it has heavy piers and abutments connected with wooden planks or stone lintels dowled together.

c. 400 B.C. Greek Archytas of Tarentum (flourished c. 400—345 B.C.), also called Archytas the Pythagorean, is said to have made a wooden pigeon or dove that appeared to fly. It was probably propelled by a jet of steam, on some form of "whirling arm."

c. 400 B.C. Earliest and simplest Roman vehicle is the "plaustrum," the standard form of farmer's ox cart, described as a platform on solid wheels.

c. 400 B.C. First saddle built on a wooden frame is used by the Sarmatians, a tribe of skilled horsemen who overcome the Scythians in what is now southern Russia. It is purposely built higher in the back to give the infantry rider a brace when he collides with his foe.

c. 400 B.C. The wheelbarrow, a one-wheeled cart with two handles, is known to exist in China at least as early as this period. With its single wheel so far in front, it acts as a fulcrum and allows heavy weights to be easily lifted and transported by what is essentially the lever action of the person lifting and pushing it. Although a seemingly simple invention, it does not reach Europe for several hundred years.

c. 400 B.C. The "cercurus" type of ship first appears in Greek waters. This light, fast, round-bottomed boat becomes the standard cargo carrier of the time. Its mast carries a large, square sail and it is aided by a single bank of 20 oars. It is also used for military purposes.

c. 400 B.C. Inflatable skins used as boats are described by Greek historian Xenophon (b. 431 B.C.) in his book, *Anabasis*. He tells that his soldiers cross the Euphrates to get needed provisions by stitching their skin tents together. (See c. 859 B.C.)

c. 350 B.C. Greek historian Xenophon (431—350 B.C.) mentions a curb bit in his writings. This jointed device that fits in a horse's mouth can put extremely heavy and painful pressure on a horse's jaw, and gives the rider more control since the levered system acts as a fulcrum. The rider could easily break an animal's jaw with this terrible device.

332 B.C. Alexander III the Great (356—323 B.C.), king of Macedonia, is said to have gone below the surface of the water using some sort of glass barrel.

c. 325 B.C. Alexander III the Great (356—323 B.C.), king of Macedonia and military genius, is reported to have used "boots" or "sandals" on his horses' feet to protect them in rough terrain. These are an early form of horseshoes. (See c. 50 B.C.)

324 B.C. First sea voyage to be recorded in detail is that of Greek explorer Pytheas (fl. 330 B.C.). Leaving what is now Marseilles, France, he sails through the Straits of Gibraltar, visits Brittany, and crosses the North Sea to Scandinavia.

312 B.C. Construction begins on the "Via Appia," or Appian Way, under the direction of Roman censor and dictator Appius Claudius, or Caecus (the Blind). One of 29 great military roads or "viae militares" that radiated from Rome, it follows the Mediterranean coast south to Capua, then turns eastward to Beneventum where it divides into two, both of which reach Brundisium (Brundisi). From there it traverses the Adriatic coast to Hydruntum, totalling 410 miles (660 kilometers) from Rome. Probably the most famous road of all time, it embodies the heights reached by the Romans, who were the first scientific road builders. (See 300 B.C. for construction details)

312 B.C. Romans build their first aqueduct, the Aqua Appia, and become the most prolific tunnel builders among the ancients. They eventually build 11 aqueducts to bring water to Rome, each having several miles of underground tunnels. In 537 A.D., the invading Goths attempt to sneak into the city using the Aqua Virgo as an underground passage. Roman General Belisarius had already blocked this passage and successfully defended Rome.

c. 300 B.C. A network of well-built roads exists in northern and western India. The rulers of the Maurya Empire, which stretches from the Indus to the Brahmaputra and from the Himalayas to the Vindhya Range, recognize that the unity of their empire depends on the quality of their Great Royal Road.

300 B.C. Rome adopts as a standard the four-course road construction methods used to build the Appian Way. First, two parallel trenches about 40 feet (12 meters) apart are dug to indicate direction as well as the nature of the subsoil. The foundation is then covered with a light bedding of sand or mortar on which four courses are built: (1) a "statumen" layer of large flat stones 10 to 24 inches (250—600 millimeters) thick; (2) a "rudus" course of smaller stones mixed with lime about nine inches (225 millimeters) thick; (3) the "nucleus" layer, about one foot (300 millimeters) thick, consisting of small gravel and coarse sand mixed with hot lime; and (4) a "summa crusta" on top, made of flint-like lava about six inches (150 millimeters) deep. The road varies in thickness from three to five feet (0.9 to 1.5 meters) and is about 36 feet (10.5 meters) wide. It has a two-way center lane, heavily crowned, that is 15.5 feet (4.7 meters) wide and flanked by curbs. This is paralled by one-way side lanes 7.75 feet (2.3 meters) wide. Roman roads are invariably as straight as possible since their primary purpose is to serve the military in marching its regimented legions. Because of its road system, Rome was able, at the height of its greatest geographic extension (from Scotland to Egypt), to control its empire with a mere thirty legions (180,000 regular troops).

c. 300 B.C. Gears or toothed wheels are known to appear in Egypt. The discovery is made that one wheel can be made to turn another wheel at right angles to it if a series of pegs are fixed perpendicular to the wheel's rim. This discovery was elaborated on by Greek mathematician Archimedes (c. 287—212 B.C.), the later medieval clockmakers, and Italian engineer/artist Leonardo da Vinci (1452—1519). When the ability to make precisely-cut metal teeth was achieved during the Industrial Revolution, the gear became a vital and necessary part of all mechanisms, transportation included.

c. 300 B.C.
Gears appear in Egypt

288 B.C. Sailing ship discovered in 1964 in the waters off Kyrenia, Cyprus is carbon-dated to this year. It is a 60-foot (18.3-meter) cargo ship carrying almonds and wine. The hull is lined with lead, which is fixed to the timber by bronze tacks. It had a crew of four.

280 B.C. First recorded lighthouse, the famous Pharos of Alexandria, is built. Ptolemy II Philadelphus of Egypt (308—246 B.C.) erects a 400-foot (121.9-meter) marble tower, on top of which a fire is kept burning to indicate the position of Alexandria to ships.

280 B.C.
First known lighthouse built

c. 265 B.C. Gigantic ship, the *Syracusa*, is built by Achias at Corinth for Gerone II of Syracuse, who presents it to Ptolemy II Philadelphus of Egypt (308—246 B.C.). This massive ship is said to be able to carry an army of 4000 troops. It is propelled by 20 banks of oars and four masts, and is in fact, a massive, double quinquereme (with

10 banks of oars on each side). Although armed with eight siege catapults on its deck, it is never used in battle.

264 B.C. Punic Wars between Rome and Carthage begin. The Roman fleet consists mainly of triremes (three banks of oars) built and manned by Greeks. The superior Carthaginian fleet has many large quinqueremes (five banks of oars). Within four years, the Romans catch up, building 100 quinqueremes and 20 large triremes.

260 B.C.

Romans win first sea battle

260 B.C. Rome fights its first sea battle and wins convincingly against Carthage. Roman tactics are similar to those on land. They ram or hook an enemy vessel, drop the gangplank, and have their fierce legionaries stream aboard.

241 B.C. Rome becomes master of the Mediterranean by defeating Carthage in the sea battle of Egadian. Carthage is no longer a sea power.

236 B.C. Greek mathematician Archimedes (c. 287—212 B.C.) develops a hoist or lifting device operated by ropes and pulleys. As later described by Roman architect Vitruvius (c. 70—c. 25 B.C.), these hoisting devices are operated by ropes and pulleys in which the hoisting ropes are coiled around a winding drum by a capstan (a vertical drum that can be rotated, and around which a cable or rope is turned) and levers.

215 B.C. Ling Ch'u Canal in Kuangsi, China is dug.

214 B.C.

Work on Great Wall of China begins

214 B.C. Great Wall of China, one of the largest construction projects ever carried out, is effectively begun when Emperor Shih Huang-ti (259—210 B.C.) connects a number of existing defensive walls into a single, continuous system fortified by watchtowers. The wall, which eventually runs about 4,000 miles (6,400 kilometers) and is 15 to 39 feet (4.5 to 12 meters) high and up to 32 feet (9.75 meters) wide in some places, also serves as a fortfied roadway along which troops may be moved swiftly. Shih Huang-ti founds the Ch'in Dynasty and first unifies China as it is known today. The dynasty is maintained by his military who control the regions through a network of roads built to standard dimensions for chariots. Often the roads have ruts for the wheeled chariots to follow like a railway. The Great Wall is constructed of masonry and earth and faced with brick on its eastern sides. It is substantially rebuilt in the 15th and 16th centuries.

206 B.C. Rigid saddles without stirrups first appear in China during the Han dynasty (206 B.C.—220 A.D.).

c. 200 B.C. The western Celts are the only people still using chariots for military purposes. As described much later by Julius Caesar, they are used tactically only for approaching the enemy at high speed and for creating a shocking psychological effect.

c. 200 B.C. Earliest maps found in China are two silk maps found in Hunan province in the tomb of a prime minister's son dated to this period. Both maps are accurate and show that cartography is well advanced in China at this time.

190 B.C. Rome defeats the Syrian fleet, and for the next hundred years the Mediterranean is known as a "Roman Lake." Trade flourishes under these peaceful conditions.

179 B.C. Second of eight Roman bridges across the Tiber River, Pons Aemilius, is begun. Believed to be the first stone-arch bridge over the Tiber, its arches span 24 meters and its piers are 7.8 meters thick. This highly ornamented bridge is completed in 142 B.C. Damaged by floods more than once, it is rebuilt several times and the standing remains of one arch can still be seen today as part of the Ponte Rotto (Rotto meaning "broken").

133 B.C. Canal in China is dug that covers the 90 miles from the Han capital of Ch'ang-an to the Yellow River.

109 B.C. Third of eight Roman bridges across the Tiber River, the Pons Milvius, is built. Crossing the river about one-and-one-half mile outside of Rome, it has seven spans totaling 413 feet. One of the major Roman roads, the Flaminian Way, crosses over this stone bridge, which is known today as Pont Molle. Some of the original structure can still be seen.

101 B.C. Fossa Mariana, a canal from Arles to the Mediterranean, is built by Roman general Gaius Marius (c. 157—86 B.C.). Used at first for military purposes, it has later commercial uses.

100 B.C. Early form of the stirrup appears in India as a sling for the big toe. This is obviously only useful in warmer climates where the riders can go barefoot. (See 450)

c. 100 B.C. Romans build a navigation canal that runs for 26 kilometers across the Pontine marshes near Rome and parallels the Appian Way. There is passenger service on this canal and travelers often sleep overnight on their boats.

81 B.C. Emperor of Japan decrees that each Japanese province must build a ship. It is from this date that real development and advances in Japanese shipbuilding begin.

71 B.C. A form of "chatty raft" of this period is later described by Roman historian Lucius Annius Florus (fl. late first century A.D.), in his book, *Epitome*. This form of water transport is believed to have originated with the Etruscans who came to Italy from Asia Minor, and is essentially a raft constructed of jars. Florus tells how Spartacus (d. 71 B.C.) and his insurgents crossed the Straits of Messina on rafts built of round-bottomed jars lashed together. Such rafts are widely used in India and called "chatty" after the name of the brittle, unglazed pot.

70 B.C. Roman Consul Gnaeus Pompeius Magnus (106—48 B.C.) sends 500 biremes with no sails to destroy the pirates off the Algerian coast who threaten trade. These ships are very fast, canoe-like, low-profile vessels, and have no problem surprising and destroying the pirate ships.

62 B.C. Fourth of eight Roman bridges crossing the Tiber River, the Pons Fabricius, is built. Named after its Roman builder, Lucius Fabricius, this stone bridge is the best preserved of the Roman bridges and is known today as Ponte Quattro Capi after the four-headed statue of the Roman herald of the gods and guardian of streets and boundaries, Mercury. A curious Roman administrative principle concerning bridge-building is that the builders are held responsible for their stability for 40 years time, after which they are repaid the deposit required of them. (See 46 B.C.)

55 B.C. Julius Caesar builds a temporary bridge across the Rhine River. In his war commentaries, *De Bello Gallico*, Caesar says he builds a wooden trestle bridge in ten days. Supported by wooden, sloping piles driven into the river bottom, it spans probably more than

1,000 feet. After the bridge serves Caesar's purposes, his army tears it down.

55 B.C. Julius Caesar (100—44 B.C.) invades Britain. In his detailed reports of British craft, he makes it quite clear that they use the advanced shipbuilding techniques of the Scandinavians, and that the Romans have a difficult time fighting these very strong, very high vessels.

c. 50 B.C. Horseshoes are mentioned in the writings of Roman poet Catullus (c. 84—c. 54 B.C.). These U-shaped metal plates that protect a horse's hooves from wear on hard surfaces are apparently a Roman invention. Since a hoof is very dense and insensitive (like a fingernail), it is feasible to attach the plate or shoe by nailing.

c. 50 B.C. Staunches are known to be in use for both canal and river navigation in China. These dam-like systems are used in conjunction with flashes or sudden releases of water which help a boat through the shallows.

c. 50 B.C. Earliest known attempt to determine either the speed of a ship or its distance covered (known in English as the "log") is made by Roman architect/engineer Marcus Vitruvius Pollio (c. 75—c. 25 B.C.). Vitruvius uses a water wheel fixed to the hull of a ship which carries a drum filled with pebbles. Each time the wheel revolves, one pebble falls into a box to be counted, and from this an estimate of the distance travelled can be made.

46 B.C. Fifth of eight Roman bridges crossing the Tiber River, Pons Cestius, is built by Lucius Cestius, governor of Rome. This stone bridge connects one side of the island of Aesculapius or San Bartolommeo to the river bank, while the Pons Fabricius connects the other side. The island divides the Tiber into two channels. (See 62 B.C.)

44 B.C. In the year of Julius Caesar's assassination, there are a number of Roman vehicles in use, some very different, and each with a special purpose. A chariot called a "currus" is the standard way for a man of means to get about. A standing driver handles the horses or mules while the passenger stands on the tailboard. The "carpentum" is a small, box-like, two-wheeled wagon used mainly by the clergy and a few women (who needed the consent of the Senate). People in a hurry can travel in

c. 50 B.C.
Romans invent horseshoes

a "cisium" or mail cart. Later in the empire, a "raeda" is a common vehicle—a kind of open round tub on wheels that holds up to six passengers—as is a "birotum," or chariot, in which the driver is seated. Finally, there is the "letica," or litter, in which a man of influence is carried on the shoulders of four bearers, usually in a covered and curtained couch.

37 B.C. Romans tunnel under Posilipo, a volcanic ridge near Naples. Called today the Grotta di Sejano, this tunnel road is about 3,000 feet long and is built by Roman General Marcus Agrippa (63—12 B.C.) for use by the Imperial Villa. A second tunnel, called today the Grotta di Posilipo, is later built by Emperor Claudius (41—54 A.D.). It is about the same length but is intended for use by ordinary people.

c. 27 B.C. Handbook for Roman architects, *De architectura*, is written by Roman engineer and architect Marcus Vitruvius Pollio (c. 75—c. 25 B.C.), known as Vitruvius. Composed of ten books or sections, it contains valuable details of Roman bridge-building. It is first printed in book form and made available to a larger audience sometime between 1483 and 1490, when a Latin version is printed in Rome, Italy. It has rightly been called the Bible of architectural theory.

20 B.C. Pharos or lighthouse at Caepio in Spain is described by Greek geographer Strabo (c. 63 B.C.—19 A.D.) as standing on a rock surrounded by the sea and resembling the famous Pharos of Alexandria.

12 B.C. Fossa Drusiana, a navigation canal dug by Marcus Livius Drusus (38—9 B.C.), is built from the Rhine to the North Sea. Using this canal, he is able to move his troops very quickly.

c. 14 A.D. Pont du Gard, a superior example of Roman aqueduct-building at its best, is built in southern France. Believed to have been ordered built by Agrippa (63—12 B.C.), the son-in-law of Augustus (63 B.C.—14 A.D.), this magnificent, three-tiered structure over the river Gard has gigantic dimensions. Its first tier has six huge arches each spanning from 50 to 80 feet, the second tier has a row of 11 arches, and the third row, which carries the water, consists of 35 smaller arches. It is more than 160 feet above the river. In 1743 the middle tier is widened to make a road and the aqueduct serves as a bridge as well.

50 Light tower at Ostia, the chief port at Rome, is built by Emperor Claudius (10 B.C.—54 A.D.) on the bank of the Tiber River. As the power and influence of Rome increases, the number of operating lighthouses it erects reaches at least 30 by the time of its decline around the year 400.

50 Wooden floats or wooden swimming blocks are depicted on the western gateway of the Buddhist shrine at Sanchi, India built this year. This water scene shows Indian fishermen using a simple log to support themselves and move about in the water. This reflects what is probably one of the oldest methods of getting across a body of water. It requires nothing but a log.

c. 65 First evidence of the use of star altitudes to discover position as opposed to merely direction is found in the writings of Roman poet Lucan (39—65). He says, "We do not follow any of the restless stars which move in the sky, for they deceive poor sailors. We follow no stars but one, that does not dip into the waves, the never-setting Axis, brightest star in the twin Bears. This it

is that guides our ships." This must be a reference to the bright Pole Star which moves little in the sky and whose altitude above the horizon is nearly constant. It is an extremely convenient navigational marker since its altitude is approximately the same as the observer's latitude.

c. 65 Lan Chin bridge is built over the Lantshang River in the Yunnan Province of China. It is described as a 250-foot (76-meter) suspension bridge with iron chains and a timber deck.

70 Pien Canal in Honan, China is built by engineer Wang Ching. It connects the grain-growing area west of Xinyang to the Huaihe and Hongze Lakes.

75 Archaeological and historical evidence indicates that by this time India used several methods of road construction. These include brick pavement, the stone slab pavement, and a type of concrete used as either a foundation course or as an actual road surface. They also know the principles of grouting (filling crevices) with gypsum, lime, or bituminous mortar.

78 Romans dig a tunnel at Furlo Pass on the Flaminian Way by order of Emperor Vespasian (9—79 A.D.). One of the principal highways of the empire, this road runs northeast from Rome. The tunnel is 120 feet long, 17 feet wide, and 14 feet high. It still exists today.

80 Large, crude elevators are used in the Roman Coliseum to raise gladiators and wild animals from the basement area to the level of the arena. Known as the Flavian Amphitheater, the Coliseum is begun by Emperor Vespasian (9—79 A.D.) and completed by his son, Emperor Titus (39—81 A.D.).

80 A.D.

Elevators used at Roman Coliseum

98 Roman orator and historian Cornelius Tacitus (c. 56—c. 120) travels to what is now Sweden and describes in his book *Germania* the "Viking" ships he finds. These, he says, are "long, narrow, and light; equally curved fore and aft." The Vikings will not change this shape for a thousand years.

c. 98 Romans build Puente Alcantara (Al Kantara is Arabic for bridge) over the Tagus River near the border of Spain and Portugal. Built by Caius Julius Lacer for the Emperor Trajan (53—117), its great stone arches span the gorges of the river 170 ftee below. It is founded on solid rock and has mighty granite piers 30 feet square that stand even today.

100 Rigid saddles without stirrups first appear in the West in Roman Gaul, probably introduced by the "barbarians" from the East.

c. 100 Great Silk Road, an 8,000-mile route between Cathay (China) and Hispania (Spain), is at the peak of its use. This circuitous trade and caravan route between today's cities of Cadiz, Spain and Shanghai, China (via Rome, across the Adriatic to Istanbul, through Turkey and then Asia) sends the spices, condiments, and jewels of the East westward and gold and silver eastward. It also is the site for any cross-cultural contact that occurs. Altogether, it covers 8,000 miles (12,800 kilometers) and is still in use at the time of Marco Polo's travels (c. 1270—1290 A.D.).

c. 100 Details of the construction of Roman aqueducts (bridges that transport water over a long distance) are written in a manuscript by Roman engineer Sextus Julius Frontinus (first century A.D.). This treatise becomes popularly available when it is first published as *De aquaeductibus urbis Romanae* in Rome, Italy in book form between 1483 and 1490. Frontinus not only gives details and dimensions of Rome's nine aqueducts, but also very detailed information on its complex water supply and distribution system. The great tiered and arched aqueducts still standing in Segovia, Spain and in France are evidence of Roman bridge-building, despite the fact that they are built to carry only water.

106 First bridge spanning the Danube River, Trajan's Bridge, is built by Apollodorus of Damascus (d. 130) for the Roman Emperor Trajan (53—117) who uses timber arches atop masonry piers to span the half-

mile river east of the Iron Gate Rapids (now part of Romania). Its 170-foot (52-meter) spans are the longest built for over 1000 years. It is memorialized on the still-surviving Trajan's Column in Rome which depicts its construction in bas-relief (a sculpture slightly raised from the surface it is carved on).

c. 127 Greek astronomer Claudius Ptolemy (c. 100—c. 165) writes his *Geography*, a treatise on mathematical geography that is also a collection of maps. Discovered by the West in the 15th century, it is published and becomes the ultimate authority on geographic matters. Despite its many errors, it is the first successful attempt at scientific geography, and Ptolemy's definition of geography as map-making still holds true today. He said it "is a representation in pictures of the whole known world together with the phenomena which are contained therein."

134 Sixth of eight Roman bridges crossing the Tiber River, Pons Aelius, is completed by Emperor Hadrian (76—138). Now called the Ponte Sant' Angelo, there are originally seven arches over the river, with the roadway 34 feet wide. The extensive foundings, which last even today, are made of masonry and are built while the river is partially diverted. Hadrian builds it to connect the Campus Martius (a sports field called the Field of Mars) with the Mausoleum—his future tomb which is now known as Castle St. Angelo. This famous bridge is later adorned with ten colossal statues of angels made by 17th century artist/architect Gian Lorenzo Bernini (1598—1680) and later installed by Pope Clement IX (1649—1721).

160 Greek satirist Lucian of Samosata (125—190) writes what is probably the first example in literature of the notion of spaceflight. In his *Vera historia (True History)*, he describes a sailing vessel that is carried to an inhabited moon by a great wind. His second book, *Icaromenippus*, owes much to the Daedelus myth, for its hero flies on bird's wings to the moon and other planets.

166 Direct commerce with China begins from the port of Antioch on the Mediterranean Sea. It lasts for only two centuries, when the eastern carrying trade is taken over by the Persians, Arabs, and Abyssinians. Direct trade is not renewed until the 13th century.

200 Decline of roads in the West begins as the Roman empire starts to fall apart. Road networks are not maintained, and as they fall into disrepair, transport wagons give way to pack trains which can negotiate the deteriorating roads. Commerce and contact is reduced and travel becomes more difficult.

c. 200 Seventh of eight Roman bridges built across the Tiber River, Pons Janiculensis, is built. Crossing the river with four semicircular arches, there are steps at either end that lead down from the street to the river. Now called Ponte Sisto, it was extensively rebuilt in 1474 under Pope Sixtus IV (1414—1484).

c. 200 Traditional Arab trading vessel called a "dhow" first appears. It is equipped with fore-and-aft sails of the triangular, lateen type which allow it to sail across the direction of the wind as well as with it. Supposedly modeled on the shape of a whale, it is an efficient and speedy vessel. The name dhow is neither an Arabic nor a European word, and its origins are unknown.

233 The triumphal procession of Roman Emperor Marcus Aurelius Severus Alexander (b. c. 208) is led by the Emperor's cart being drawn by elephants. This is unusual, even for the Romans.

348 Double slipways are known and used in Chinese canals. These enable a canal to change levels without losing water. A dam is built across the canal with inclined ramps on each side. Boats are then hauled up and over by ox-powered capstans (a cable winding around a spindle-mounted drum that the oxen rotate), and lowered back into the canal on the other side.

c. 350 Nydam boat dated to this time is discovered buried in Schleswig (part of Germany and Denmark) and dug up in 1863. It is 76 feet long, made of oak, and has identical ends. There is no indication of a mast, and it is propelled by 14 oars on each side. It is clinker-built as opposed to the carvel style of the south. Clinker-built ships are made to weather high seas and are typically northern boats. Their external planks are lap-jointed. Carvel-built ships are typically southern and their planks are placed edge-to-edge, making for a smooth surface.

350 Shanyang Canal in Chiangsu, China is built.

c. 399 Chinese Buddhist monk Fa Hsian (fl. 399—414) journeys through India and writes in his diary of crossing the Indus River "by a suspension bridge of ropes."

404 In Japan, the Association of Wheeled Vehicles, a hereditary occupational guild, is mentioned in the manuscript *Nihon Shoki*. This is the fifth year of the reign of Emperor Richu.

438 Theodosian Code, the earliest collection of existing laws, is issued by Theodosius II (b. 401), Roman Emperor of the east. Among its regulations, weight limits for roads are specified for every type of vehicle that uses the road system. These weight limits are fixed at a very low level in order to better protect the road, and punishments were unusually severe for offenders: exile for free citizens and mine servitude for the slaves.

438 A.D. Roman emperor issues road laws

c. 450 Stirrups first appear as used by the Mongolian armies of Attila the Hun (king of the Huns from 434 to 453). The great advantage provided by this hanging sling or ring into which a horserider can put his feet is that it provides him with a more comfortable, secure ride. In terms of combat, however, it revolutionizes infantry tactics and is the technological basis for shock combat. With the lateral support provided by the stirrup, the horse and rider become one. The rider can use his hands to do battle and can deliver a fearsome blow that has the entire weight of the horse and rider behind it. With his feet securely held, the rider will not himself be knocked off by such a blow.

c. 450 A.D. Stirrups first appear

476 Rome "falls" as the young Emperor Romulus Augustulus (b. c. 461) abdicates and transfers the seat of the empire from the west to the east at Constantinople. The progressive deterioration of the famous Roman road system continues, and by the end of this century the barbarians have virtually wiped out the imperial system of travel and transportation.

476 In this first year of the Merovingian dynasty (the Frankish Empire centered in Gaul which lasted from 476 to 751), travel and transportation is almost solely by ox-drawn wagons. These vehicles do not need engineered and well-maintained roads, but can travel on ordinary earth tracks. During these three centuries, which mark the transition from antiquity to the Middle Ages, the Roman road system has virtually fallen apart.

484 St. Brendan (c. 484—578), adopted by Irish sailors as their patron saint, is born at Tralee in Ireland. He is later immortalized as the hero of a legendary Christian tale of sea adventure, *Navigatio Brendani (The Voyage of Brendan)*, in which he makes astonishing sailing voyages across the Atlantic.

500 Modern harness or horse collar is depicted in frescoes in Kansu, China. This device, which goes over an animal's head and neck and sits on its shoulders, is a vast improvement over the neck strap. The neck strap presses on the animal's windpipe and jugular, and its pulling power is greatly impaired. The much more mechanically efficient collar does not interfere with the animal's breathing or blood circulation, and it can throw all its weight into pulling—this time with its shoulders and not with its neck. The first modern harness is introduced into Europe from Asia and appears in Europe about 800.

500 As roads are torn up for other use and barriers erected for protection, trade vanishes under the emphasis on localism. Wheel travel begins to disappear and people walk and use pack animals. Carts are restricted to farms and local travel. Robbers multiply and safe, reliable transportation and communication becomes a thing of the past.

555 Byzantine historian Procopius (b. c. 290) describes in his writings a race of gliding Finns called "Skridfinns," to distinguish them from Finns who do not glide or ski on snow. He does not describe their skis.

600 Population of Rome, once a city teeming with nearly one million people, shrinks to fifty thousand, and transportation to and from that city continues to decline.

603 Emergence of the Italian city-state system begins as Pisa becomes an autonomous city republic and builds its own naval fleet for war and commerce. Others will follow, creating their own navies.

609 Sui Grand Canal is built by Chinese Emperor Sui Yang Ti (569—618). It begins near Hangzhou and runs north across the Yangtse and Yellow rivers to Beijing. Its primary purpose is to carry grain junks from

central China to Beijing. It also carries many passengers. Over the centuries, it is improved and extended many times. Along its banks runs an Imperial road planted with elms and willow trees. Like China's Great Wall, it has been built in sections over many centuries and is, today, certainly the oldest canal that is still a working waterway.

672 Byzantines destroy the invading Mohammedan fleet using "Greek fire." This mixture of naphtha, sulphur, and saltpetre burns furiously when used with a bellows. Many ships also catch fire from the water surface itself, since this material burns while floating.

700 Arab seamen on the Red Sea and Indian Ocean use the "karmal," a hand-size rectangular board with a knotted cord attached to its center, to find their ship's latitude. They hold the appropriate knot in their teeth and use the pole star to determine whether the boat is too far north or south to reach the desired port.

c. 700 Lateen or triangular sail becomes established in the Mediterranean. Its evolution and use is pioneered by the Arabs. As a "loose-footed" sail or one with great flexibility of movement, it can be adjusted quickly to a large variety of angles to better catch the wind. In a sea with no trade winds like the Mediterranean, such a sail proves ideal.

716 Nilometer is invented by the Egyptians who install this measuring device at Cairo. It is basically a stone pillar that stands in a well and measures the rise and fall of the Nile River. It is marked in cubits (one cubit equals 22 inches or 55.8 centimeters).

c. 730 Charles Martel (c. 688—741), leader of the Frankish kingdom, learns of the stirrup from Byzantium, and gives them to his lords on the condition that they fight for him. This is in part responsible for the feudal regimes based on homage and service that soon emerge throughout Europe. (See 450)

800 Skis are mentioned in written accounts as being used by the Chinese during the T'ang Dynasty.

c. 800 Seafaring Vikings begin to appear in southern Europe. First called Northmen or Norsemen and later Vikings, these explorers and adventurers dominate the northern waters and eventually sail southward, raiding coastal towns. Their well-built ships are made of wood and very strong. Viewed from the side, their bow

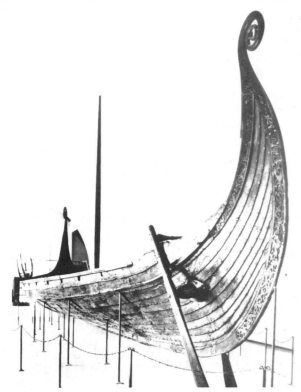

800 ■ Oseberg Viking ship excavated in 1904.

and stern are identical. They also have overlapping planks which are nailed (clinker-built), and they use both oars and a sail.

839 City of Amalfi rebels against the Lombards and declares itself a city republic. This seaport near Naples, Italy will become a local sea power and will formulate in 1010 the Amalfian Code. This series of 66 articles regulating maritime law and custom is widely applied and influences later maritime law.

840 Venice declares itself a city republic. Having been a crossroads of east and west since it was founded by refugees from Attila in the fifth century, Venice is naturally very commercially-oriented, and begins a ship-building program that will make it an important maritime power in the Mediterranean. Each year, the city demonstrates its dependence on the sea when its Doge or leader symbolically marries the city to the sea by casting a gold ring into the waters.

897 *Cottonian Manuscript*, a document written during the lifetime of Alfred the Great (849—899), king of the West Saxons, describes the new fleet he creates to ward off the Viking raids. These very large ships are twice the size of his normal vessels, having 40 or even 60

oars on one side. With a deep draught, they are powerful, steady ships.

927 The Japanese book *Engishiki* describes how the "koshiguruma" is built. Its name means literally "waist vehicle," and it is drawn by men pulling a waist-high bar. It also describes ox-drawn carriages.

984 First canal lock for which there is clear evidence is built by Chinese engineer Ch'iao Wei-Yo on the Grand Canal. A lock is a chamber enclosed at either end by movable gates and placed between two stretches of water which vary in height from each other. Water is then admitted through sluices to raise the boat, or water is drained through sluices to lower the boat to the proper new canal level. Compared to stauches and flash-locks, a lock saves water and is safer to use. Although the lock is apparently invented in China, it is little-used there, and its later development occurs mainly in the west.

984 A.D.
First canal lock built

994 In England, Saxons build a timber bridge across the Thames River in London.

c. 1000 Arnulf, archbishop of Milan (fl. 970—974), mentions in his work, *Gesta Mediolanensium*, a vehicle called a "carroccio." It is a platform on four wheels with a long pole or staff in its middle, from which is flown an army's standard (flag). This flag-carrier vehicle allows the standard to be flown high enough for all to see yet still be as mobile as the army.

c. 1000 Whiffletree, a horizontal transverse bar that joins the harnesses of two animals, first appears in Europe. Also called a whippletree, this crossbar device helps to equalize the pull of draft animals.

c. 1000 Evidence indicates that Leif Eriksson (c. 980—c. 1025), son of Erik the Red, sails with a crew of 35 from Greenland to what is probably northern Newfoundland. Many speculate that subsequent Viking expeditions eventually land on mainland America.

c. 1000 *Sagas* of the Norwegian Vikings describe several Viking kings as being superb skiers. The Vikings even have a god and goddess of skiing, Uller and Skada.

c. 1010 A monk, Eilmer of Malmesbury (c. 980—1066), also called Oliver of Malmesbury, attempts to fly with wings attached to his hands and feet. He jumps from the top of Malmesbury Abbey in Great Britain, and breaks both legs.

1010 Persian poet Ferdowsi (c. 935—c. 1020) finishes his huge (60,000-verse) epic poem, *Shah-nameh (Book of Kings)*, which includes the retelling of many ancient legends about man's attempts to fly into space.

1044 First known recipe for making black powder (gunpowder) is given by Chinese Wu Ching Tsao Yao in his book *Collection of the Most Important Military Techniques*. Gunpowder may have been in use in China as early as the seventh century. The Chinese use the explosive properties of this substance (six parts saltpetre, three parts sulphur, one part charcoal) for both celebration (firecrackers) and war. They create all manner of fiery projectiles for flame throwers, grenades, bomblets and cannon (bamboo fire-tubes). The rocket is thus invented in China and is first used as a form of artillery.

1066 Following the Norman invasion of England, the hammock-wagon is introduced to the Saxons. An open, four-wheeled wagon bearing a hammock strung between two poles, it is used especially by armies to move wounded soldiers. When first used by the Romans, it was called the "carruca nutans" or swinging carriage.

1066 Bayeaux Tapestry, a medieval embroidery depicting the Norman Conquest of England, reveals horsemanship details of the Norman knights. As knights become more heavily armored, their horses are bred to be larger and stronger. Their saddles are larger and deeper and they use stirrups (footholds). Such mounted soldiers prove too much for the Saxon infantry who are shattered by massed cavalry charges.

1066 Ships play a large part in the Norman invasion and conquest of England, as Harold II of England (c. 1020—1066) disperses his excellent navy as soon as autumn arrives, believing that William, Duke of Normandy (c. 1028—1087), will wait until spring to invade. William has not yet invaded because of a lack of vessels to carry his troops, but he quickly builds many and "borrows" others, so that on this day he has 400 large and 1,000 small craft. The Bayeux Tapestry shows some details of William's fleet.

1076 Turks enter Syria and capture Jerusalem from their fellow Moslems. This spurs Christians in the West to begin the first crusade and they recapture the Holy City in 1099. The long, cross-country journeys of the knights and their followers focuses attention on the demands of long-distance travel and the need for new bridges and better roads.

1095 First crusade is launched. This series of military expeditions organized by the Christian west against the Muslim powers that hold the holy lands results in eastern horses being imported to Europe. These swifter and more agile horses are first used for reconnaissance and later for racing.

1097 First Crusade begins, requiring a massive fleet of ships to take the western armies to reconquer the Holy Land. Venice and Genoa each contribute 200 galleys (a large, low ship propelled by oars and sails), Pisa donates 120, and Barcelona and Marseilles also supply scores of galleys.

c. 1100 Japanese books *Chojugiga, Ban Dainagon Ekotoba*, and *Senmen Koshakyo* all contain illustrations of vehicles of the time.

c. 1100 Road system of the Inca empire in South America begins as the Incas establish themselves at Cuzco (Peru) and start two parallel roadways extending from what is now Quito, Ecuador to points south of Cuzco, Peru. One goes along the coast about 2,250 miles (3,600 kilometers) and another follows the Andes for about 1,650 miles (2,640 kilometers). Their roads resemble those of ancient China, being about 25 feet (7.5 meters) wide with stone surfaces held together by asphalt-like materials. As the Incas did not have the wheel, their road traffic consists entirely of people on foot and pack animals (llamas). They have both a swift courier system by foot as well as a visual signalling system that uses manned watchtowers. They also build suspension bridges with wool or fiber cables.

c. 1100 Roman system of transport waterways is revived in northern Italy, while in England, Henry I (1069—1135) begins the same.

c. 1100 Earliest known use of a magnetic compass at sea by the Chinese occurs.

1135 Henry I of England (1069—1135) orders all highways to be made broad enough for two wagons to pass or for sixteen soldiers to march abreast. Political authorities and central governments are beginning again to assume responsibility for roads and even attempt to protect travelers from the numerous highwaymen who rob them.

1143 Portugal declares its independence from Spain and immediately begins its own shipbuilding industry, recognizing that a large, powerful fleet for commerce and warfare is the key to becoming a power in the Mediterranean world.

1147 The Second Crusade, unlike the first in that it lacks any real transport fleet, fails miserably.

1148 One of the earliest examples of a typical medieval sluice or movable gate for canal passage is built at Het Gein and Otterspoor on the Nieuwe Rijn Canal in Holland. It is of the lifting-gate variety.

c. 1150 English engineer and priest Peter of Colechurch (c. 1150—1205) is born in England. He is the first to believe that a stone bridge across the Thames River at London should replace the wooden ones that have steadily fallen apart. His famed London Bridge, completed in 1209 four years after his death, is built with an immense supporting structure that acts almost as a dam. It is supported by 19 boat-shaped artificial islands for piers. Its 20 arches make the bridge 926 feet (282 meters) long and 26 feet wide.

1156 Frederick I of Germany (c. 1123—1190) allows travelers to carry swords for protection against highway thieves.

1157 First medieval lighthouse is built by the Pisans at Meloria in Italy. The poet Petrarch (1304—1374) writes of this tower about 1350, and Leonardo da Vinci (1452—1519) includes it in his detailed maps of the area.

1160 Lanterna of Genoa, one of the most celebrated of all Italian lighthouses, exists at least as early as this year as proven by shipping records. Its keepers make signals on the tower's top by burning straw, pitch, and tar. The present tower, which was built to replace an earlier version, was for a time the charge of Antonio Colombo, an uncle of Christopher Columbus (1451—1506).

1162 In Turkey, the "Saracen of Constantinople" attempts to fly with sail-like wings made of a large stiffened cloak. He fell straight down from the high tower and was killed.

1170 Rival sea powers of Venice and Byzantium begin to wage an inconclusive war. Venetian ships of this period are known to have an overall length of 117 feet (35.6 meters), a beam of 12 feet (3.7 meters), and a depth of 6.6 feet (2 meters). They are propelled mainly by oars, with 54 on each side. Each oar measures 26 feet (7.9 meters) and is set on an outrigger one yard (0.9 meters) away from the hull.

1176 First London bridge made of stone is begun under the direction of Peter of Colechurch (1150—1205). Completed in 1209 after his death, it is a design of 19 pointed arches and a drawbridge. Although the arched passways under the bridge are intended to be broad, the piers are built very wide and close together, narrowing a 900 feet-wide tidal estuary into a waterway of about 250 feet. Guiding a boat through the arch openings is hazardous, and a saying—"London Bridge is made for wise men to go over and fools to go under"—becomes popular. Its fame rests primarily on the houses and shops built on its roadway, the rents from which are intended, with tolls, to pay for its upkeep. They spill onto the narrow road, and project and overhang its sides. Accidents are frequent and fires common. Despite all its problems and its lack of skillful engineering or aesthetic charm, it is the only bridge across the River Thames for more than five centuries.

1176 A.D.
Construction of London Bridge begins

1177 Pont d'Avignon, one of the first bridges to be built in France after the fall of the Roman Empire and the first great medieval bridge, is begun by a French priest named Benezet (c. 1165—c. 1184). Legend tells how Benezet has a vision and takes as his life's mission the building of a bridge across the Rhone River. It has a graceful, original design of four arches, each resting on piers some 25 feet thick. A typical medieval stone structure, it has a chapel built on it. Benezet dies during the project which is completed in 1187, and he is eventually sainted as the patron of bridges. Three arched spans still jut pointlessly into the river today, making for the odd sight of a bridge that does not connect to the other side.

1180 Ships with proper rudders begin to appear in Europe. Before the rudder—which is a flat piece of wood attached upright to a ship's stern (rear part) so that it can be turned, causing the ship's front to turn in the same direction—ships used steering oars from the starboard (right) side. It is not known who invents the rudder.

1184 Philip II of France (1165—1223) orders the street in front of the Louvre—his palace and castle—to be paved with large, irregular stones to overcome its terrible stench. Transportation and travel are a secondary concern. He later changes the name of his city from Lutetia (the dirty) to Paris (the beautiful).

1187 Earliest documented reference of the use of a compass in Europe is made in a treatise titled, *De utensilibus (On Instruments).* Written by English scholar Alexander Neckham (1157—1217), it mentions a needle carried on board ship that shows mariners their course when the Polestar is hidden by clouds.

1190 Popular German poem "Salman and Morolf" tells of a war hero who uses a diving boat made of leather to sabotage enemy boats. It is supplied with air via a long tube.

1190 May Third Crusade begins as Richard I of England (1157—1199), known as Richard the Lion Hearted, sets sail for the port of Acre (now Israel) with a fleet of over 600 ships. Encountering there a magnificent three-masted Turkish vessel carrying some 1,500 troops, the Crusaders send wave after wave of galleys at the huge ship, boarding it and being repelled. Finally, with successive rammings, the vessel heels over and the troops continue to fight standing on the ship's sinking side. The Turks refuse to be rescued and fight while drowning. Only 42 are saved. Three days later, Acre falls to the Crusaders.

1194 Lighthouse is built to guide ships through the Straits of Messina, between southern Italy and northeastern Sicily.

c. 1200 With the growth of towns and the revival of fairs, traffic and travelers increase, and the practice begins of paying tolls as a charitable duty to pay for road and bridge upkeep. Paying for part of a bridge or stretch of road becomes a kind of penance for sin. Bridges are also dedicated to saints, and travelers are encouraged to make offerings at bridgehead shrines to ensure a safe crossing.

c. 1200 As nobles and monks travel greater distances on horseback between widely separated agricultural tracts of land, they become increasingly aware of the importance of good roads. The managers of the feudal system thus compel its serfs to repair roads and bridges as one of the three duties, or "trinoda necessitas," required by their lords.

1200 Richard I, king of England (1157—1199), known as the Lion Hearted, contributes his *Rules of Oleron* to the law of the sea. His code of maritime conduct attempts to update the *Lex Rhodia,* to regulate commercial ventures, and to provide for the safety of both ships and sailors. (**See c. 500** B.C.)

c. 1200 As cargo ships are adapted into fighting ships, "castles" are added as fighting platforms forming a kind of protective cage-work. Built originally as temporary structures, they become a permanent feature by the end of the 15th century. The forecastle becomes known as the foc'sle, and the aftercastle becomes the poop.

1200 Sverrir (1149—1202), king of Norway, equips his army scouts with skis and sends them to reconnoiter the Swedish enemy. Later, during the Norwegian Civil War, soldiers on skis take the king's infant son to safety over the mountains in the dead of winter.

1202 First lighthouse in northern Europe is claimed to be the Falsterbo Light built by the city of Lubeck, Germany at the eastern entrance to the Baltic. It is built to benefit the fishing fleet.

1203 Oldest known hoist still in existence is installed in the Abbey of Mont St. Michel on the coast of France. The load is raised by winding a rope around a large drum, with a donkey on a treadmill supplying the pulling power.

1209 Naviglio Grande Canal is built in Italy, connecting Lake Maggiore with the outskirts of Milan. Constructed initially as an irrigation canal, it is later brought into the city first by means of a sluice-gate and then with a lock so that marble from the quarries near Lake Maggiore could be hauled into Milan to build the new cathedral. (See 1438)

1214 Mongolian warrior-ruler Genghis Khan (c. 1162—1227) captures the city of Peking, China. By 1259, his followers control Asia from Siberia to the Persian Gulf. This unification of Asia overthrows restrictive Turkish control of the Great Silk Road trade route and opens China to European merchants.

c. 1225 Soldiers in the army of Mongolian warrior-ruler Genghis Khan (c. 1162—1227) carry watertight skin bags which can be inflated and used as a float to cross rivers. This small, easily-carried device is a standard piece of equipment of his Mongol armies.

1232 Chinese repel Mongols laying siege to the town of Kai-fung-fu with "arrows of flaming fire." Many interpret this to mean rockets are used and thus point to this date as the earliest evidence of their invention and use.

1232 Earliest documented reference to the use of a compass by Arab sailors is found in a collection of Persian anecdotes written this year. It describes a fish-shaped iron leaf used as a compass.

1242 Earliest positively-identified representation of a stern rudder appears on the seal of the town of Elbing, Germany. The seal shows a standing sailor with his hand on the rudder, guiding a single-masted fishing boat. (See 1180)

1242 Compass is described by an Arabian writer as a magnetized needle that floats on water by means of a splinter of wood or a reed. It is used as a directional aid in the Syrian seas.

1247 English scholar Roger Bacon (c. 1219—c. 1292) writes the formula for black powder (gunpowder) in a letter, indicating that knowledge of its existence has migrated to the West from China, probably via the Arabs. Bacon says, "thou wilt call up thunder and destruction, if thou know the art."

c. 1250 Roger Bacon (c. 1219—c. 1292), an English monk and scholar, writes his *De Mirabili Potestate Artis et Naturae* (not published until 1542), in which he describes a way to fly using hollow globes of copper filled with "aetherial air" which would float in the atmosphere. He also writes about a flying boat or carriage whose flapping wings are moved by turning a crank handle. He actually builds no machines.

c. 1250 Roger Bacon (c. 1219—c. 1292) prophesies the coming of horseless carriages, saying in his *Epistola de secretis operibus* that "cars can be made so that without animals they will move with unbelievable rapidity... ."

c. 1250 First known tide tables are drawn up by the monks of St. Albans to determine the height of the Thames River at London Bridge. The monks are able to calculate the rise and fall of the river based on the cycle and phases of the moon.

c. 1250 A.D.

Tide tables first used

c. 1250 English monk and scholar Roger Bacon (c. 1219—c. 1292) predicts in his writings "a vessel which, being almost or wholly submerged, would run through the water against waves and wind" with great speed.

1252 First bridge is built across the Grand Canal in Venice, Italy. This wooden bridge is the first in a succession of various types of bridges across the Canal, including pontoon, timber, and even a type of drawbridge. It is paid for by a toll charge that gives the bridge its name—Money Bridge. When a more permanent bridge is desired in the 16th century, the city decides that a stone bridge with shops be built at the narrowest point of the canal, the Rialto. (See 1592)

1255 City state of Venice makes its own laws of the sea. As a dominant and very prosperous sea power, Venice creates new laws that fix the size of ships and regulate the amount of port dues each must pay. It also creates new standards of measurement pertinent to maritime commerce.

1266 Roger Bacon (c. 1219—c. 1292) writes of a round rather than flat earth, and prophesies that, "it is possible that great ships and seagoing vessels shall be made which can be guided by one man and will move with greater swiftness than if they were full of oarsmen."

1269 August First treatise written on the magnetic compass is the *Epistola de magnete* by French crusader and scholar Petrus Peregrinus de Maricourt. He writes this letter during the siege of Lucera in Italy, and in it he not only gives the first detailed description of the compass as an instrument of navigation, but he also describes a new kind of pivoted compass.

1274 A.D.

English pay tolls

1274 A traverse toll or charge for "pavage" is instituted in London, England on animals pulling loads on its main street. This system transfers the cost of street paving from local property owners to the actual users of the road.

1274 Deer hunting while on skis is forbidden in Norway. Such an edict underscores how widespread skiing is at this time.

c. 1275 Welsh longbow is introduced by English King Edward I (1239—1307). An experienced archer using this six-foot-long bow can shoot a rider at 400 yards and penetrate his armor at close range. This weapon is dreaded by knights who adapt by wearing even heavier, full-body armor, which leads to breeding even larger horses. Armor for horses is used as well.

1280 Syrian military historian al-Hasan al-Rammah gives instructions for making gunpowder and rockets called "Chinese arrows" in his work *The Book of Fighting on Horseback and with War Engines.*

1281 First European attempt to reach India by sailing west is made as two ships under the command of Vivaldi brothers Ugolino and Vadino (both fl. late 13th century) leave Genoa, Italy. They pass Gibraltar and put ashore briefly on the Atlantic coast of Morocco, after which they are never seen again. The mystery of their fate remains unsolved.

1285 England passes its first road act during the reign of Edward I (1239—1307). Created to discourage highway robbers, it states "that highways leading from one market town to another shall be enlarged, where as woods, hedges or dykes be, so that there be neither dyke, tree, nor bush, whereby a man may lurk to do hurt, within 200 foot on one side and 200 foot on the other side of the way." It further provides "that when any highway is worn deep and incommodious that another shall be laid out alongside."

1292 Philip IV (1268—1314), king of France, begins construction of a naval base at Rouen. His large shipyard facility can work on 17 ships at a time, both building and repairing. In three years, it turns out 50 ships. He uses his fleet to wage war with England and Flanders.

1293 Northern branch of the old Grand Canal in China is completed. This section of this ancient waterway system runs 700 miles, from Huaian to Beijing.

1295 Classic Chinese sailing vessel, the junk, is described by Italian adventurer Marco Polo (1254—1324) upon his return to Venice from China. The origins of these ships are very old, and the term describes some 70 different types. Essentially, they are flat-bottom ships with a high stern (end) and forward-thrusting bows and have one to five masts. The junk is probably the first ship to have a central stern rudder (to steer) and is considered the most aerodynamically efficient of all the large ocean-going sailing ships.

c. 1300 Growing traffic on medieval roads necessitates some form of regulation, and the *Sachsen-und Schwabenspiegel* is passed. This is a German book of laws that details the rules of the road. It contains such specifics as the widths of various types of roads.

c. 1300 In Western Europe, Marcus Graecus describes in his book, *Liber ignium ad comburendos hostes (Book of Fire to Destroy the Enemy),* many devices that sound like rockets.

c. 1300 Evidence that the compass is known to mariners in northern Europe is found in the *Hauksbok,* the last edition of the *Landnamabok (Book of Settlements).* This Scandinavian document tells about a "lodestone" that sailors use on the high seas.

1300 Hanseatic League, one of the most famous of the many commercial alliances that are formed in northern Europe, rationalizes ship design. Their ships are built primarily for trade and rely solely on sails for propulsion, carrying no oars. Their hull design also incorporates a straight stem with a fitted rudder.

c. 1300 First accurate coastal sailing charts, known as "portolan charts," become common in the Mediterranean. They are graphic documents that also contain written descriptions. The oldest surviving chart, the Pisan Chart, dates from this time. After a while, the companion text is dropped and they function more as real maps. All are oriented with north at the top, and may have been used in conjunction with early forms of the compass. The compass revolutionizes map-making, for it is now possible to both make a map and use it based on information obtained by direct observation using a scientific instrument.

1312 August Venetian Senate decrees that a light be kept burning every night on the tower of St. Nicholas for the benefit of passing ships.

1319 First use of a ship-mounted cannon is made by the Genoese navy.

1323 A chapel is privately built at St. Catherine's on the Isle of Wight, England, on the condition that the priest say daily masses for the donor's family and keep a fire burning at night for passing ships.

c. 1325 Earliest known illustration of a pull-string type of helicopter model is found in a Flemish manuscript in the Royal Library at Copenhagen, Denmark. This toy, called a "moulinet a noix" by the French, is a direct ancestor of the helicopter.

c. 1325 Aztec civilization of Mexico makes heavy use of canals. Its capital, Tenochtitlan, is built on islands in Lake Texcoco, parts of which the Aztecs fill in to create more islands. Canals are built to connect them much as Venice is today. The city and its canals are destroyed by the conquering Spaniards in 1521.

1326 Small handgun first appears and influences road travel. Since it becomes standard practice to carry a gun under the left arm (since most people are right-handed), road travelers now all stay to the right in order to keep approaching strangers on their left or potentially, at gunpoint. In this year, the Council of Florence (Italy) appoints two officials to make them handguns. This is also the year of the earliest illustration of a gun as found in an English manuscript, *De nobilitatibus sapientis et prudentiis regum,* written for the English King Edward III (1312—1377) by Walter de Milemete.

1326—1327 First known illustration in the Western world of any kind of aircraft dropping a bomb. This picture shows a windsock type of kite with wings that is being flown by three soldiers over a city under siege. A round, fused bomb with fins hangs from the kite.

This unfinished drawing is seen in Walter de Milimate's manuscript *De Nobilitatibus* in the library of Christ Church in Oxford, England.

c. 1330 Japanese word "fuguruma," the name of a two-wheeled, roofed vehicle used indoors to carry books, appears in the *Tsurezuregusa (Essays on Idleness).*

1342 An important innovation in coaches and carriages—the suspension of the carriage body on ropes or chains—is first described by a chronicler of Elizabeth, Dowager Queen of Hungary's visit to her son, Andrew, King of Naples. Making the body somewhat independent of the vehicle's frame lessened to a great degree the sometimes torturous and bone-racking experience the passenger felt in a carriage.

1345 Ponte Vecchio, the medieval Italian bridge over the Arno River in Florence, is rebuilt as it is known today. The Romans first have a bridge at this site. A later one built in 1177 is destroyed by a catastrophic flood in 1333 which sweeps away every bridge in Florence. This new bridge is designed by Florentine artist Taddeo Gaddi (c. 1300—c. 1366) who takes advantage of the nearly-dry summertime condition of the Arno to build very deep, solid foundations. The bridge has three segmental, very flat arches—the first of its kind. A segmental arch is smaller than a semicircle and its ends thrust or push not straight down but sideways. Stress and pressure on such an arch is crucial, and although Gaddi has no mathematics adequate to figure this problem, he somehow gets it right. Butcher shops are first built on the bridge, but Grand Duke Cosimo I (1519—1574) orders out "these vile arts" nearly 200 years later, and the goldsmiths, silversmiths, and jewelers move in, adding onto its sides for the colorful, picturesque disorder we see today. This bridge is the only one in Florence left standing by the retreating Germans during World War II.

c. 1350 Oldest known illustration of a railway of any kind is in a window in the Minster of Freiburg in Breisgau, Germany. It was presented by a mine owner and it shows a miner pushing a cart-like vehicle along a row of tracks.

1350 Islands forming New Zealand are colonized by inhabitants of Tahiti whose ships compose the Maori Great Fleet. The Maoris overcome the local tribes and establish a flourishing colony.

c. 1364 French King Charles V (1338—1380) orders the provost of the city of Paris to compel by force all of its citizens to help in the repair of its roads and bridges, most of which are in wretched condition.

1368 Edward III of England (1312—1377) begins the practice of discrimination against foreign ships, as his Navigation Laws prescribe that only English vessels may carry wine into his kingdom. Other nations follow suit and retaliate, beginning a discriminatory trade pattern in Europe.

1370 By this time, Asia has been converted to Islam and the silk road trade routes between east and west are severed once again.

c. 1370 Drawings of this time reveal that many ships are adopting both the square sails of the north and the triangular (lateen) sails of the south. This begins the merging of the two types of ships to form the "carrack"—a three-masted, carvel-built (flush planking) ship that will become the prototype for the western European ocean-going ship.

1371 Longest single span masonry bridge ever built in Europe is the Trezzo Bridge built over the Adda River at Trezzo in the Duchy of Milan. Using Taddeo Gaddi's (c. 1300—c. 1366) new segmental arch which is particularly useful for long span bridges, a bridge with a single, long granite arch (236 feet) is built. A segmental arch (which is smaller than a semicircle) can be long without being very high. This is unlike the typical Roman semicircular arch which is half as high as it is wide. This is so because the span is its diameter and the height is its radius (and therefore half the diameter). A bridge with a single span can be easily destroyed however, and the Trezzo is brought down around 1410.

1372 Street travel in the larger cities presents sanitary problems. Parisian housewives are permitted to throw filth from their windows onto the street below if they first shout three times, "Gare l'eau," or "Take care of the water!"

1373 First lock for canal navigation in Europe is built at Vreeswijk in The Netherlands where a canal from Utrecht enters the river Lek. It consists of two sluicegates, one behind the other, enclosing a basin or chamber and forming what is essentially a lock. (See 984)

1379 In Italy, the Paduans use rockets during the siege of Chiogga to attack the town of Mestre, near Venice. This is later documented by Italian scholar Ludovico A. Muratori (1672—1750), writing in 1728, who first uses the Italian form, "rocchetta."

1388 Sidesaddle is invented by Queen Anne of England (1366—1394) (wife of Richard II). Since it was considered scandalous for a woman to straddle a horse as a man would, the queen's new saddle allowed a woman to sit with both legs on the same side of the horse. Prior to this, whenever women rode horses, they usually rode behind a man, sitting on "pillions" which were little side-seats placed directly behind the man's saddle. The inventive queen basically adapted stirrups to the pillion and did away with the man and his saddle.

c. 1391 English poet Geoffrey Chaucer (c. 1342—1400) writes his *Tretis of the astrolabie*. Written by Chaucer for his son to show him how to use the astrolabe to conduct simple astronomical calculations, it also contains a reference to compass cards, indicating that they are well known in his day. This commonsense innovation mounts the compass needle on a card which shows the points or directions of the compass. Eventually, the card has 32 points with north at the top.

1398 July First summit-level canal in Europe, the Stecknitz Canal in Germany, opens. Its locks are used for the first time to overcome differences in land as well as differences in water levels. A summit-level canal is a canal that goes over a watershed or the high point between two rivers that flow down opposite sides of a mountain or hill. The highest section of the canal is higher than either of the rivers, and pumps must be used to bring water there.

c. 1400 Flemish historian and poet Jean Froissart (c. 1333—c. 1401) suggests in his *Chronicles* that the accuracy of military rockets can be improved if they are launched from inside a tube which would stabilize the flight path and better control the angle of ascent.

c. 1400 New type of sailing ship, the "Danzig Ship," first appears in north European waters. The strengthened hull has become more streamline and a crow's nest is added to the mast. It is still single-masted and has a single square sail. Also by now, the Venetians are using two-masted ships with lateen sails.

c. 1400 ■ Early 20th-century Chinese junk made after the same traditional design used before Columbus sailed to New World.

1411 In England, Bishop Stafford grants an indulgence (forgiveness or payment for sins committed) to people willing to help repair the roads from Plymouth to Smathpolemille.

1413 Lock for canal navigation is built at Gouda, The Netherlands by Jan van Rhijnsburch. It has a triple set of gates. (See 984)

1417 King of England orders the streets of London paved because they are "very foul and full of pits and sloughs, very perilous, and noisome, as well for the King's subjects on horseback, as on foot, and with carriages."

c. 1420 First illustration of a jet-propelled aircraft. In a manuscript titled *Metrologum de Pisce Cane et Volucre*, the Italian engineer Giovanni da Fontana (c. 1395—c. 1455) shows a picture of his model bird being propelled through the air by something coming from its tail. He states that it flies about 100 feet each time.

1420 Italian Giovanni da Fontana (fl. 1410—1420) describes and illustrates in his sketchbook, *Bellicorum instrumentorum (Book of Instruments of War)*, a number of rocket-propelled military devices for air, sea, and ground. It is not known if any of his designs were ever built and used.

1420 Footbridge with a light deck suspended from iron chains is described as in use to cross the Brahmaputra River in Tibet.

1420 Portuguese school of navigation is founded by Prince Henry the Navigator (1394—1460). Although he makes no voyages of discovery himself, Henry is a patron of geographers and mapmakers and organizes and encourages a number of exploratory voyages down the African coast and out into the Atlantic.

1430 Prince Henry the Navigator (1394—1460) helps Portugal become a great sea power. This innovative leader encourages the design and construction of new types of ships, and actually experiments with several new designs. His enlightened study of the field of navigation leads to the voyages of discovery that create an overseas Portuguese empire.

1438 First lock for canal navigation in Italy is built by Italian engineers Filippo da Modena and Fioravante da Bologna. They bring two staunches (gates or dams) between Via Arena and Naviglio Grande closer together to reduce water consumption and thereby create a lock. (See 1209)

1450 First European illustration of a conventional flat, or plane-like surface kite is made in Vienna, Austria. This suggests that this type of kite had been in use for some time and probably came from the East. It will soon become more popular than the old European winged windsock type of kite.

c. 1450 As improvements are made in the quality of coaches used by European nobility, they become more aware of the need for better roads. Many public-spirited people leave money in their wills to be used for road construction and repair. It is still the rare central authority that regularly takes care of roads.

c. 1450 As the number of toll roads increases, traffic begins to move more and more by water, and canals and channels are improved.

1452 Special military ski troops are formed in Sweden. In later conflicts, Swedish soldiers will go to war equipped with either skis or snowshoes.

1458 First European lateral canal (one paralleling a river) to have its steep gradient controlled by locks, the Bereguardo Canal in northern Italy is built by Italian engineer Bertola da Novate (c. 1410—1475). This canal is only 12 miles long but has a difference of 80 feet in height from one end to the other. Bertola uses 18 locks to get boats up and down the canal.

c. 1460 An illustration of a helicopter model is seen at Le Mans, France, in the hand of the Christ Child in a painting of the Madonna and Child. This sophisticated model which rotates by a pull on wound string is obviously the development of a long line of such models.

1470 Martesana Canal is built by Italian Bertola da Novate (c. 1410—1475), the leading canal engineer of his time. It connects Milan with the River Trezzo and uses only two locks in 24 miles. The great masonry wall separating the canal from the river in its first five miles can still be seen today much as it was when first built.

1470 Painting of a ship with three wind-bearing sails is made by a Dutch artist, "W. A."

c. 1474 Some type of mechanical insect or fly made of iron is made in Nuremberg, Germany by Johannes Mueller (1436—1476), also called Regiomontanus. This is thought to be a kind of glider model.

1482 Leonardo da Vinci (1452—1519), multi-talented Italian artist and scientist, is appointed "painter and engineer of the duke" by Ludovico Sforza (1452—1508), Duke of Milan, and is responsible for the maintenance of public buildings and the upkeep of canals. He keeps this position until the duke falls from power in 1499 and Leonardo leaves Milan. While in Milan, he invents the miter lock for the Naviglio Grande Canal. This is a canal gate angled into the downward force of the stream. The gate consists of two pieces, one hinged at each side of the lock, which meet at an angle when closed. Miter gates are stronger than the vertical-lift gates they will replace and are still in use today.

1484 First to adapt an astronomer's astrolabe for use at sea is German navigator and geographer Martin Behaim (c. 1436—c. 1507). This ancient astronomical device, probably of Greek origin, can now be used by mariners to measure the altitude of the sun, moon, and stars and thus find a latitude bearing. In its simple form, the mariner's astrolabe consists of a graduated circular disk with a movable sighting device.

1485 First printed book on engineering and architecture, *De re aedificatoria (Ten Books on Architecture)*, by Italian scholar Leone Battiste Alberti (1404—1472), is published. Among his many subjects is a description of the principle of the lock or double-gate canal lock. (See 984)

1487 First known English ship with four masts is the *Regent* built by Henry VII (1457—1509) of England. This huge ship mounts 141 small cannons.

1492 August 3 Italian navigator Christopher Columbus (1451—1506) departs from the port of Palos, Spain to discover a direct route to the Indies. He commands a fleet of three ships, the largest of which, the *Santa Maria*, he sails on himself. Little is known about his ship, but Columbus does write later that, "only smaller ships are desirable for voyages of discovery, for the ship I took with me on my first voyage was cumbersome and, because of this, was lost in the harbor at Navidad." Together with the other two, the *Nina* and the *Pinta*, he sets foot on the island of San Salvador in the Bahamas on October 12, 1492. This first encounter of the old world with the new will open the way for the exploration, exploitation, and colonization of the Americas.

1493 First horses from Europe are transported to the New World by Christopher Columbus (1451—1506) on his second voyage. He disembarks them at Hispaniola (San Domingo).

1494 Papal Bull (decree) is issued by Pope Alexander VI (1431—1503) dividing the new world between Spain and Portugal. Dividing line is a north-south line drawn 100 leagues (345 miles) west of the Azores and Cape Verde Islands. West of the line is Spanish; east is Portuguese.

1497 Vasco da Gama (1460—1524) leaves Portugal with a fleet of three ships and sails around the tip of

Africa, eventually reaching the southwest coast of India. He returns to Lisbon over two years later.

1497 May 2 Giovanni Caboto (c. 1450—c. 1499), Italian explorer living in England and known as John Cabot, and his son leave Bristol in the *Mathew,* a three-masted trading ship with a crew of 18. Sailing in a northwesterly direction, the ship reaches land on June 24. Cabot believes he has reached the northeast coast of Asia, but he has landed either at southern Labrador, Newfoundland, or Cape Breton Island.

c. 1498 Giovanni Battista Danti (c. 1477—1517) conducts some trial glides over Lake Trasimeno in Perugia, Italy using feathered wings on a structure of iron bars. (See 1503)

1499 Florentine explorer Amerigo Vespucci (1454—1512) makes his first voyage across the Atlantic. He believes that the recently-discovered land mass is not part of Asia but a new continent. After making several voyages for the kings of Portugal and Spain, he is famous enough to be mistaken by German mapmaker Martin Waldseemueller (c. 1470—c. 1521) as the discoverer of the new world. Waldseemueller thus names the new continent after him, calling it "America." (See 1507)

1499 A.D.
Vespucci sails the Atlantic

c. 1500 First international mail-coach is founded in Germany by the von Taxis brothers, Franz and Joseph, who are appointed postmaster generals by Maximilian I (1493-1519).

c. 1500 Many 16th-century woodcuts for books of the time show that the medieval wagon has by now evolved into a coach. Usually, a simple tarpaulin awning over the ribbed body transformed an open wagon into a closed passenger-carrying coach. These can be seen in Jorg Wickram's (c. 1505—c. 1560) drawings for his 1555 book *Rollwagenbuchlein* and in Jost Amman's (1539—1591) 1572 woodcuts.

c. 1500 Cross-staff is first used at sea by seamen to determine the altitude of celestial bodies (and thus find their own latitude). Based on the principle of the ancient Arab "kamal," it is a long wooden shaft with a movable crosspiece set at right angles to it. Holding one end of it to his eye, the navigator slides the cross along until the horizon is in line with the lower end of the cross and the celestial object with the upper end. The staff is marked with a graduated scale on which the position of the crosspiece gives the altitude of the body being observed. (See 1594)

c. 1500 Italian artist and scientist Leonardo da Vinci (1452—1519) sketches what is essentially all the equipment a diver would need to remain underwater and move about. A wineskin holds the air he breathes from a surface tube and he uses a mask with a glass window. The diver carries a bag of sand to remain below.

1501 First European road map is published by Erhard Etzlaub (d. 1532) of Nuremberg. This German map depicts western and central Europe, indicating the main pilgrim routes to Rome.

1501 First holes cut into the hulls of ships to accommodate its cannons on the lower deck are made by a Brest, France shipbuilder named Descharges. The same thing is done later by James Baker, shipwright to Henry VIII of England (1491—1547). This fundamentally changes the role of a ship from being a platform for men and guns to being itself a weapons system.

1503 Giovanni Battista Danti (c. 1477—1517) is seriously injured after attempting a flight across the city square from a tower in Perugia, Italy. He crashes onto a roof of St. Mary's Church, which saves his life.

1504 Longest time to complete a bridge is taken by the builders of the Karlsbrucke bridge over the Moldau at Prague, Czechoslovakia. Begun in 1357 by Hapsburg emperor Karl IV, it is interrupted by politics, religion, war, and economics, and is not finished until 1504. It uses 16 stone arch spans to cross the nearly 2000-foot-wide river. It stands as the longest entirely-over-water bridge in Europe, since the longer Pont d'Avignon rests partly on an island.

1505 Leonardo da Vinci (1452—1519), multi-talented genius born in Florence, Italy, turns to a scientific investigation of the problems of flight by studying birds and bats and produces his *Sul volo degli uccelli*. Most of his aeronautical notes and drawings are lost, but surviving documents show his designs and experiments dealing with flapping-wing aircraft (ornithopters). He also sketches, almost as an afterthought, the world's first parachute.

1505 A.D.

da Vinci sketches first parachute

1507 German mapmaker Martin Waldseemueller (c.1470—c. 1521) publishes his book *Cosmographiae introductio,* which contains a world map showing for the first time a new continent named "America." Unaware of Columbus's earlier voyage, he says, "I do not see why anyone should object to its being called after Americus the discoverer, a man of natural wisdom, Land of Americus or America, since both Europe and Asia have derived their names from women."

1507 First stone arch bridge in Paris, France, the Pont Notre Dame, is completed. Following the collapse of the wooden bridge on this spot over the Seine, French King Louis XII (1462—1515) chooses an Italian priest, Giovanni Giocondo (c. 1433—1515), to build a more durable and lasting structure. The innovative Giocondo builds a stone bridge with six arches, and introduces a new design called "corne de vache" or cow's horn, which allows him to broaden the deck of the bridge considerably without using any additional material or larger piers.

1507 September John Damian (fl. 1500), an Italian adventurer living in Scotland, attempts to fly from the walls of Stirling Castle, Scotland, on wings made of chicken feathers and is injured.

1509 English King Henry VII (1457—1509) expends 2,000 pounds sterling toward new roads between Windsor and Canterbury. They are to be ditched on both sides, crowned in the center, and covered with gravel wide enough for two carts to pass.

1512 August 12

Cannons first used in sea battle

1512 August 12 First sea battle in which cannons are used to sink another vessel rather than to kill its crew takes place at the Battle of Brest between the French and the English. Fighting ships are now built with cannon mounted within their hulls so that they can be fired through unlidded ports. As two huge ships, the *Regent* and the *Cordelier,* fire broadsides directly at each other, *Cordelier* explodes, taking the *Regent* with her. The crews of both ships—1,600 men—are killed in the explosions. This so stuns the rest of both fleets that they call off the battle by mutual consent. From now on, however, ships will try to blow each other out of the water.

1516 Italian Renaissance poet and playwright Ludovico Ariosto (1474—1533) first publishes his romantic epic, *Orlando furioso.* His hero, Astolpho, travels to the moon by a chariot driven by Saint John the Evangelist. It is believed that much of this influential poem was inspired by Lucian of Samosata's *Vera historia* which was translated into Latin in 1475.

1518 First recorded fire engine is built for the city of Augsburg, Germany by goldsmith Anthony Blatner. Indications are that it is a wheeled carriage with a lever-operated pump.

1518 November 30 Italian bridge builder and architect Andrea di Pietro Palladio (1508—1580) is born in Padua, Italy. His fully illustrated book, *I Quattro Libri dell'Architettura (Four Books on Architecture),* published in 1570, is still unsurpassed as a textbook on classical design. His outstanding building achievement is his bridge over the Cismone River in Bassano, Italy. It is built without any supports in the water, since Palladio uses a version of the old Roman truss (a structural form of support based on a triangle) to span the entire 100 feet (30 meters).

c. 1519 One of the oldest railroad illustrations in a book appears in *Der Urssprung gemeynner Berckrecht,* published in Strasbourg, France by Johann Haselberg (fl. 1515—1538). The illustration contained in this book on German mining laws shows a miner pushing a small wagon or truck along a wooden railway.

1519 September 20 First known circumnavigation of the globe is made as Ferdinand Magellan (1480—1521) leaves Cadiz, Spain with a fleet of five ships and 265 men. The voyagers endure many hardships—scurvy, mutiny and executions, near-starvation—and Magellan is killed on April 27, 1521 in a skirmish with natives of the Philippines. The crews continue on and eventually return to Spain, having gone completely around the globe. It is one of Magellan's captains, Juan Sebastian de Elcano (c. 1476—1526), who along with the 19 survivors, actually circumnavigates the globe.

1526 First European to take African slaves to the Americas, Spanish explorer Lucas Vasquez de Ayllon (c. 1475—1526), lands on the coast of South Carolina with about 500 colonists and 100 slaves. Most of the company dies of fever and the colony is abandoned. (See 1562)

1530 In England, the Statute of Bridges is passed which places responsibility for repair of decaying bridges on local shire and town inhabitants.

c. 1530 Ships known as "galleons" come to replace the traditional carrack. This name represents a variety of ships that are usually four-masted and with a longer, lower hull. They are faster, more weatherly, and hold their course better than the old carrack. (See c. 1370)

1532 Writings of Roman military expert Flavius Vegetius Renatus (who flourished during the fourth century A.D. and was called Vegetius), are published with illustrations in Paris, France. His work, *De re militari*, contains an image of a diver standing under water with his head encased in a leather bag which is shaped to fit tightly around his head and shoulders. The top part of the bag tapers into a tube which extends to the surface.

1532 British admiral John Hawkins (1532—1595) is born in London, England. An innovative and far-sighted naval architect, he is best known for rebuilding Britain's fleet which eventually withstands the Spanish Armada in 1588. He replaces its older galleons with newly-designed ships that, while carrying fewer but heavier guns, are still faster and more maneuverable. He also institutes Britain's African slave trade.

1533 Pedro Sancho, secretary to Spanish Captain Francisco Pizarro (c. 1478—1541), describes an Inca suspension bridge made of interwoven hemp and wood. It is likely that such sagging, trembling, but very effective and useful suspended foot bridges had been in use for thousands of years in South America before this account. In the Inca Empire, these bridges are part of an organized administrative communication system which links the Inca cities by mountain roads that criss-cross the Andes Mountains. All Inca transport is by foot or pack animal, since they never invented the wheel.

1536 Denis Bolori (d. 1536), an Italian clockmaker in Troyes, France, is said to have flown or glided from a cathedral tower for about a mile using wings flapped by a spring mechanism. He is killed when his craft crashes after breaking a spring.

1536 King Henry VIII (1491—1547) grants a charter to the Guild of the Blessed Trinity to build two light towers in Shields, England, and to keep "a perpetual light" nightly on each. The Guild is also empowered to levy tolls on passing ships.

1538 April 6 Hernando De Soto (c. 1500—1542) sets sail from San Lucar, Spain for America with a fleet of nine vessels that contain over 200 horses. After landing in what is now Tampa Bay, Florida, he and his men proceed inland and cross the Mississippi River. After encountering hostile Indians, disease, and other difficulties, the band loses or abandons all of its horses—leading many to speculate that these animals may have been the ancestors of the wild horses of the western plains.

c. 1539 Vessels that sound more like kayaks than submarines are described by Olaus Magnus (1490—1558), bishop of Uppsala, who describes seeing them during his visit to Scandinavia. He says that pirates use these leather vessels to prey on other ships by attacking them from under the water.

1539 ■ Coming of the horse to the new world.

1540 In London, England, street paving at this time consists of cobblestones flanking a central open gutter. Other English cities have gutters on either side of the paving.

1540 June 20 Joao Torto, in Viseu, Portugal, builds two pairs of cloth-covered wings, an upper and lower, which are connected by iron hoops. While preparing to jump from the town's cathedral to the nearby St. Mathew's fields, he is killed when the elaborate helmet he is wearing slips over his eyes and he falls onto a roof.

1543 Polish astronomer Nicolaus Copernicus (1473—1543) publishes his *De revolutionibus orbium coelestium* (*On the Revolutions of the Heavenly Orbs*) which places the sun, rather than the earth, at the center of the universe. This correct and revolutionary theory will substantially change man's picture of the solar system and his place in it. No spaceflight progress could ever be made as long as men believed that the sun moved around a stationary earth.

1545 A.D.

Universal joint invented

1545 Universal joint is invented by Italian mathematician and physician Girolamo Cardano (1501—1576). Later called the cardan, this joint allows for the relative angular movement of two shafts whose geometric axes converge at a single point. This joint becomes essential for automobiles which use it to link two turning shafts whose positions may vary in relation to each other. Cardano's invention is included in his work, *De subtilitate rerum*, published in 1545.

1545 July 19 English warship *Mary Rose* is lost off Portsmouth, England. Having been keeled over by a severe and very sudden gust of wind with its lower gun ports open, it sinks quickly. Nearly all of its crew and soldiers, totalling 270, are killed. In 1968, the wreck of the *Mary Rose* is discovered, and the remains of its hull are raised in 1982 for restoration.

1546 The concept of a central road-repair authority finds its first actual expression in a weakly-enforced act passed during the reign of English King Henry VIII (1491—1547).

1546 First printed tide tables are published by the Breton Brouscon in the *Nautical Almanac*.

1548 Miter locks invented by Leonardo da Vinci (1452—1519) for canal navigation are adopted Italian engineer Giacomo da Vignola (1507—1573), who builds three such locks each 100 feet long near Bologna, Italy. (See 1482)

c. 1550 An unknown Italian, wearing wings possibly of cloth, jumps from a tower in Tour de Nesles, in Paris, France, and breaks his neck. According to the poet Augie Gailliard, who wrote of the event, he dropped "like a pig" close to the base of the tower.

1550 Federico Grisone, one of the great riding masters, publishes his book on horsemanship, *Gli Ordine di Cavalcare*, in Naples, Italy. Among the many pieces of equipment detailed here are the cruel and appalling devices used to "break" a horse and maintain the rider's domination.

1550 Lighthouse in the Bosporous Strait, between Europe and Asia, is described as an octagonal tower, 120 steps high with a glass lantern nine feet high and 12 feet in diameter lit by a large copper pan of oil containing 20 floating wicks.

1550 Earliest known locks for canal navigation in France are built on the rivers near Bourges.

1552 First guide to roads is published in Paris by Charles Estienne (1504—1564). It is titled *La guide des chemins de France*.

1555 English Parliament passes the basic Act that sets standards for road improvement which remains until 1835. It makes certain duties compulsory and issues regulations for road travel and construction. It further states that "every parish shall annually elect two surveyors of highways" responsible for the upkeep of roads.

1555 First English-built coach is built by Walter Rippon for the Earl of Rutland. Nine years later he builds one for Queen Elizabeth I. (1533—1603)

1555 Snow skis are described and illustrated in a travel and history book, *Historia de gentibus septentrionalibus*, by Swedish cleric Olaus Magnus (1490—1557). He says they are "flat boards curved in front like bows," and that one is the length of the skier, and the other a foot shorter. Different sized skis are used for the next two centuries at least, with the long ski providing the glide and the shorter one, called the "andor," giving the push.

1556 Some of the best and most accurate illustrations of 16th-century mining rail wagons and railways are printed in Georg Agricola's (1494—1555) *De re metallica (On Metals)*. Published in Basel, Switzerland, this classic work on all aspects of mining and metallurgy is the product of Agricola's lifetime study. It took him 20 years to write the book and another five to have it printed.

1560 While there are about 500 coaches in use on the continent, in London, England there are only two. English roads are fairly comfortable for horseback riders but almost unbearable for wheeled vehicles making long trips.

1561 Most important canal in Belgium at this time, the Willebroek Canal, is completed. Built by Jean de Locquenghien (1518—1574), it gives Brussels a connection with the sea by way of Antwerp. It is also called the Brussels Canal.

1562 English Queen Elizabeth I (1533—1603) increases the annual number of days of road repair work required of each citizen from four days to six.

1562 Slave trade begins as English naval officer John Hawkins (1532—1595) ships a cargo of slaves from Guinea, in West Africa, to the Spanish West Indies. This eventually develops into the triangular slave trade. First, ships leave England for the Atlantic coast of Africa bearing goods which are traded for African slaves. The second or middle voyage shuttles its human cargo—under horrible conditions in which an estimated 20 percent die—to the West Indies or to one of the American colonies. They are delivered to their "owners," and the third part of the voyage begins as the ships sail homeward with goods produced on American plantations.

1563 First ship built in North America to cross the Atlantic Ocean is built by French Huguenots who settled on Parris Island, South Carolina but who are struggling to survive and decide to return to France. They build a light sailing ship, using bedding and even shirts for sails, and eventually reach the French shoreline where they are rescued by English sailors.

1564 Road conditions in England are sufficiently improved so that "wains" or carrier wagons begin a regular, fixed route, going about 10 to 15 miles a day. They are soon expanded and transformed into the famous "long wagons"—large, covered vehicles carrying 20 or more passengers and baggage.

1565 First road built by Europeans in the New World joins the crude, wooden fort at St. Augustine (on the northeast coast of Florida) with Fort Caroline (San Mateo), some 40 miles away.

1566 Earliest known lock for canal navigation in England is built by Englishman John Trew as part of the Exeter Canal. It is only 3 feet deep and 16 feet wide and has vertically rising gates.

1567 First miter gates in Holland are used on locks at Spaarndam. (See 1498)

1567 Santa Trinita bridge across the Arno River in Florence, Italy is ordered built by Grand Duke

Cosimo I (1519—1574). It is designed by innovative and influential Italian sculptor/architect Bartolommeo Ammannati (1511—1592), who designs the first "basket-handled" arch. His new design is an ellipse, an even flatter arch than the Ponte Vecchio, and he thus avoids having to build any steeply inclined approaches to the bridge. Built of stone, it is blown up by the retreating Germans only two days before their request for an armistice to World War II. It is rebuilt in 1957 exactly as it was—including its four famous statues—using original materials and pieces recovered from the river.

1569 Flemish cartographer Gerard Mercator (1512—1594) publishes his map of the world for which he invents a cylindrical projection technique. He represents the globe as a cylinder and plots the earth's parallels and meridians, thus solving the age-old problem of how to depict a spherical surface on flat paper.

1570 Italian architect Andrea Palladio (1508—1580) describes the use of the truss (a structural form of support based on a triangle) for bridges in his book, *I Quattro Libri dell'Architettura*. Published in Venice, Italy, this work becomes one of the most influential Western architectural treatises, espousing the classic ideals of harmony, order, and mathematical proportionality. His adaptation of the well-known truss to bridges (it had been used to support roofs) will lead to the construction of many covered bridges in Switzerland, Germany, and colonial America. (See 1797)

1571 October 7 Greatest galley battle ever fought takes place between the Turkish fleet and the combined Christian fleet at Lepanto, off the western coast of Greece. In a battle that rages from dawn to midnight, the Turks are eventually massacred. The western fleet consists of over 200 ships rowed by 43,000 oarsmen and manned by 12,000 seamen and 28,000 soldiers. The Turkish fleet is even larger. This battle shows the value of the Venetian "galleasse," a light, extremely fast ship that combines the maneuverability of oars with the wind-assisted speed of a masted ship. This is also the last naval action fought between galleys manned by oarsmen.

1574 Common Log or English Log is first reported as used on board ship to tell its speed. It consists of a wooden board, weighted at its base to keep it upright in the water, with a line attached which is cast from the ship and let out for a certain amount of time (usually 30 seconds). The amount of line reeled back in is used as part of an equation to obtain the ship's speed.

1574 Snowshoes are described by Swiss professor Josias Simmler (1530—1576) in his book *De Alpibus commentarius*. He recommends their use by pilgrims and merchants who must make the trek across the mountain passes.

1578 A.D.

Submarine
first
described

1578 English mathematician William Bourne (d. 1583) publishes the first detailed description of a submarine in his book *Inventions or Devices*. Although he offers no illustrations, his text describing a submarine is remarkably detailed. He never builds his own model, but his writing serves to not only inspire later inventors, but also to tell them exactly how to go about building a submersible that will work. (See 1747)

1578 May 31 First stone is ceremoniously placed for what will be the Pont Neuf, the new bridge crossing the Seine in Paris, France and connecting the Ile de la Cité with the left and right banks. Designed by Jacques Androuet du Cerceau (c. 1520—c. 1585), its two separate arms have the flat arches of the Ponte Vecchio and the cow's horn of the Pont Notre Dame. Interrupted by wars, it is finally completed in 1605 and becomes, after the Pont Neuf, the second great Renaissance bridge of Paris.

1579 Description of a submersible is given by Johannes Taisnier (b. 1509) who tells in his book, *A Very Necessarie and Profitable Booke Concerning Navigation*, how he witnessed two Greeks descending below the water in Toledo, Spain. He describes "a very large kettle" in which they descend via ropes.

1584 Lighthouse is begun on the Islet of Cordouan, a great reef in the Bay of Biscay near the city of Bordeaux, France. Ordered by King Henry III (1551—1589) and designed by French engineer/architect Louis de Foix, the barrel-shaped building is one of the most elaborate lighthouses ever built. Its four stories make it part palace, part fort, part cathedral, and part functioning lighthouse. It is an elaborately ornamented structure for such a hostile place, and it has a domed ceiling with mosaics as well as sculptures, arches, and gilt-work. Completion takes 26 years. It survives today, rebuilt in a more functional style.

1585 Robert Norman (born c. 1560), English manufacturer of compasses, publishes his book *The Newe Attractive*. This book begins the serious, scientific theorizing about magnetism and the action of compasses. It leads to William Gilbert's (1544—1603) famous work. (See 1600)

1586 Hammocks are first used on a ship as beds for sailors by English naval officer John Hawkins (1532—1595). On one of his trips to the West Indies, Hawkins sees natives sleeping in hanging beds slung from trees which they call "hammacoes." Prior to their being adopted by the British Navy, sailors simply slept on the wooden deck. They remain in use until the late 18th century.

1588 July 21 One of the world's greatest sea battles begins as 54 English ships first engage the invading Spanish Armada off Plymouth Sound. In a nine-day battle that goes up the Channel, into the North Sea, and around Scotland, the British prove victorious, starting their rise as a maritime power and Spain's fall. The very slow, high-sided Spanish "galleons" prove easy targets for the lower-slung, faster and harder-to-hit English ships.

1589 Giovanni Della Porta (1535—1615), an Italian, publishes his *Magia Universalis* which contains a description of an eastern or flat kite he calls *The Flying Dragon*. His description is to serve as the basis for most of what is written about kites for the next hundred years.

1592 Rialto Bridge over the Grand Canal in Venice, Italy is rebuilt in stone. Famous as one of the world's most pictured bridges, it is built by Antonio da Ponte (1512—c. 1595) whose design wins a competition. His bridge is a single, low circular arch of 88 feet, above which is a peaked, covered arcade. It is 75 feet wide and has a center road for pedestrian traffic that is lined with shops and sidewalks. The central problem of this bridge is its foundation, since Venice is a city of many islands formed in soft alluvial ground (clay, silt, sand, or gravel that is deposited by running water). Da Ponte solves this problem by driving as many as 6,000 piles of birch-alder beneath each abutment. Rialto is today preeminent among Venice's over 300 bridges—without which this network of islands would never exist.

1592 First ironclad warships are built and used by Korean admiral Yi Sun-shin in repelling the invasion of Japanese military ruler Toyotomi Hideyoshi (1537—1598). The Korean "tortoise ships" are low-

1590 ■ Rialto Bridge, Venice, Italy, seen in the 20th century.

decked, armed galleys covered by an iron-plated dome. This use of iron on a ship appears to be a solitary incident. Such armored ships do not appear in the West until the 19th century.

1594 Backstaff is invented by British navigator John Davis (c. 1550—1605). The disadvantage of having to look directly into the sun to find its altitude with a cross-staff is overcome with Davis's invention. With the backstaff, the observer stands with his back to the sun and relies on the shadow cast by the movable arm rather than on direct sighting.

c. 1595 Fausto Veranzio (1551—1617) publishes in Venice, Italy his book, *Machina Novae*, which shows an illustration of a sheet or sail type of parachute. As Leonardo da Vinci's parachute sketch is not to be discovered until the late 19th century, Veranzio's is the first parachute that the world came to know. His parachute obviously derives from a ship's sail, and the picture of it in his book shows it being used to escape from a building.

1596 Underwater diving box is described and shown in a mechanical picture-book written by Italian Buonaiuto Lorini (fl. 1600). In his *Delle Fortificationi*, he describes the submersible as being rectangular, with square glass windows. It is held together by strong iron bands and is ballasted by lead. He also shows a plan for what he calls a "diving apparatus" which has a diver's head in a tube. There is no evidence that these are ever built.

1599 First carriage with glass windows appears in Paris, France. The wealthy traveller who did not want to stay in a dirty or unsafe inn could now spend the night inside his coach, changing into night-clothes and sleeping in bedding taken along.

1599 Reference to a submersible of some kind is made in a book by Francesco de' Marchi (b. 1506) called *Architettura militare*. This writer states that over 50 years before his time an Italian, Guglielmo de Lorena, was able to stay underwater for over one hour in what he describes as some sort of diving bell. He says the apparatus was lowered in a sling, but he does not give many more details.

c. 1600 Paolo Giudotti (c. 1560—1629) is said to have flown or glided about 1000 feet (c. 300 meters) in Lucca, Italy, using wings made of whalebone and covered with feathers. He falls through a roof when his arms grow tired, and breaks his leg.

1599 A.D.

Glass windows used on carriages

1600 ■ Simon Stevin's sail-propelled cart with front wheels that can be used to steer.

c. 1600 Giovanni Francesco Sagredo (1571—1620) is said to have worn wings based on those of a falcon and to have thrown himself from a height and landed many yards from his starting point in Venice, Italy.

1600 A.D.

Wind-propelled wagon built

1600 First land vehicle that does not use muscle power of any sort as the source of its power is built by Belgian-Dutch mathematician Simon Stevin (1548—1620). His wind-propelled "zeylwagen," or sail wagon, is built of wood and canvas and is a kind of two-masted ship on wheels that is also steerable. It is said to have covered 50 miles from The Hague in only two hours.

c. 1600 Flanged wooden wheels are used on wagonways in England. They are ribbed or rimmed and cut with their grain going parallel to the axle for strength.

c. 1600 In some parts of Europe, especially Germany, suspended coaches had made riding so comfortable, that for the first time pleasure-driving (or riding) began to be taken up by the wealthy. One official saw a threat, saying that "the manly virtues, dignity, courage, honor and loyalty of the German nation were impaired, as carriage-driving was equal to idling and indolence."

1600 English physician and physicist William Gilbert (1544—1603) publishes his *De Magnete*. This pioneering work in the study of magnetism and the compass lays the foundation for the modern knowledge of both. Using the new, experimental methods of his time, Gilbert dismisses many old wive's tales about magnetism and the compass and offers a sound theoretical basis for both phenomena which lead to further technical improvements.

1600 December 31 East India Company is founded in England. Receiving its charter from Queen Elizabeth I (1533—1603), this commercial, and later political, organization is formed to take part in the East Indian spice trade. This powerful monopoly builds and owns the ships it sends on voyages, and operates as an extension of the state. Eight other European nations set up similar East India companies to compete, and the British model survives until 1873. During its time, it builds some of the finest ships ever seen.

1603 Between this year and 1610, 11 locks for canal navigation are built in Sweden as part of the job of canalizing the river Eskilstuna between Lakes Hjalmar and Malar.

1603 October Earliest recorded railway in Britain begins construction. This two mile (3 kilometers) long line is made of wood planks over which wagons with flanged (built with a rim or rib for guiding) wheels are drawn by horses. It transfers coal taken from the pits.

1605 In England, "long wagons" carrying passengers and goods between English cities travel day and night, changing horses every 12 to 16 miles. It is from these relay points or stops called stages that the name stagecoach originates.

1607 As the Englishmen land in the New World at Jamestown, Virginia, they soon discover the vehicle preferred by the Indian is the canoe. In smooth waters, the dugout canoe is most favored. Capt. John Smith (1580—1631) described how it is made, saying, "Their fishing is much in boats. These they make of one tree by burning and scratching away the coals with stones and shells, till they have made it in the form of a trough." For the rough waters of the Chesapeake Bay, Capt. Smith also described their light bark canoes, "made of barks of trees,

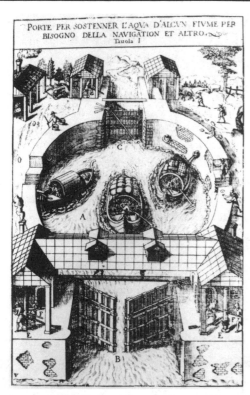

PORTE PER SOSTENNER L'AQVA D'ALCVN FIVME PER BISOGNO DELLA NAVIGATION ET ALTRO.
Tauola I

1607 ■ Early mitre lock based on Leonardo da Vinci's work.

1607 ■ American Indian hollow-out canoe.

sewed with bark and well luted with gum," which were quicker to build than the dugout and easier to handle.

1608 Telescope is invented by Dutch eyeglass-maker Hans Lippershey (c. 1570—c. 1619), who puts two convex lenses together, magnifying the image. Once perfected, the telescope becomes a standard instrument on all ships at sea.

1608 First American-made cargo to be shipped to a foreign country consists of pitch, tar, soap, ashes, and glass. It is sent from Jamestown to that colony's sponsors in England.

1609 German astronomer and mathematician Johannes Kepler (1571—1630) publishes *Astronomia nova (New Astronomy)* which contains his laws of planetary motion. His three great laws—that planets orbit the sun in ellipses, not circles; that lines drawn from the sun to a planet will sweep over equal areas in equal periods of time; and that the period of any planet's orbit is related to its distance from the sun—mark the beginning of scientific understanding about movement in and through outer space.

1610 The hackney coach, a four-wheeled coach drawn by two horses and seating six people, first appears in England. The number of these vehicles increases so rapidly, that the noise and congestion on the narrow London streets force authorities to introduce special regulations for their control.

1611 First American bridge built by English settlers is located at "James Towne" island, Virginia. Not a real bridge in the sense of connecting two sides of a body of water, it is more of a wharf about 200 feet long that extends from the bank of the James River to the nearby, deeper channel.

1612 Great Sauk Trail or Potawatomi Trail is discovered in America by the French. An overland route connecting New France (Canada) and the Mississippi River Valley, it is named for the Sac Indians who with the Fox Indians used this path in their travels from eastern Canada to the far northwest. It branches at the "place of the strait" (in French, "place du detroit"—now Detroit) and runs west between the Checagou (Chicago) and Illinois Rivers, considered the strategic key to the American continent.

1613 Illustrations of a diver recovering a cannon from the ocean floor are included in a book by Diego Ufano titled *Tratado dela artilleria*. The picture shows the diver wearing a hood from which a long tube extends to the surface.

1616 First description in Europe of a suspension bridge is published by Croatian bishop Fausto Veranzio (b. 1551). In his *Machinae novae*, published in

1609 A.D.

Kepler publishes laws of planetary motion

1611 A.D.

First American bridge built

Venice, he describes a portable suspension bridge with a horizontal floor connected to cables by vertical hangers. The cables or chains are anchored half-way up a tower on each side. Veranzio is believed to have been influenced by Leonardo da Vinci (1452—1519), in that he was a good friend of Giovanni Ambrogio Mazenta (1565—1635), Leonardo's biographer and keeper of the great man's notebooks. It is not known if any of his designs are ever built.

1615 ■ Early parachute design by Veranzio.

1617 August

One-way streets appear

1617 August One-way streets for traffic control are ordered in London, England, as an Act of Common Council transforms 17 narrow, congested streets into one–way avenues.

1618 First illustration of a "standard" (plane-surface) diamond-shaped kite with tail, appears in an engraving by the Dutchman, Crispin van de Passe (c. 1565—1637).

1619 An English patent is granted to Thomas Wildgosse for "drawing carts without horses." The mechanism is not described, but historians believe it to be some kind of gear worked by the hands of the person seated in the vehicle.

c. 1620 English philosopher and statesman Francis Bacon (1561—1626) writes of what are supposedly underwater vehicles he calls "diving kettles." There is no evidence, however, to back up his statement, which says, "We have heard it said that they have invented another machine, like a little ship, by the aid of which man can travel below water for a considerable distance."

1620 First navigable submarine is invented by Cornelis Drebbel (1572—1633), Dutch engraver and glassworker living in England. His "diving boat" is made of wood and propelled by oars and sealed against water by a covering of greased leather. His vessel travels under the Thames River at a depth of 12 to 15 ftee (about 4 meters) from Westminster to Greenwich. Air is supplied to the boat by two tubes which use floats to keep one end above water.

1620 September 6 A British ship, the *Mayflower*, leaves Plymouth, England carrying 73 men and 29 women. Two months later, it lands near Cape Cod, Massachusetts and begins the real colonization of the new world. Little is known about the ship, but it is believed to weigh 180 tons and have three masts. It is fairly old, having participated in the Spanish Armada engagement. (See 1588).

c. 1622 In Flanders, the 44-mile-long canal linking Bruges, Passchendaele, Nieuport, and Dunkirk is completed.

1625 Streets in Pemaquid, Bristol Township, Maine are paved at least as early as this year. Pemaquid was the center of the most prolific fishing grounds along the North American coast, and later excavations indicate the town had paved streets above the high water mark that led down to the water.

1625 A patent by Englishman Edward Knapp for suspending coach and carriage bodies on steel springs is issued. These promise to make coach travel a much more comfortable experience.

1628 August 10 Newly-built Swedish ship, the *Wasa*, first enters the waters off Stockholm. A magnificent ship, fully equipped and manned with a crew of 433 sailors, it keels over severely after being hit by a strong wind gust, and sinks quickly when its open gun ports let in the sea. It sits at the bottom until discovered in 1956. Five years later it is raised and preserved—a fully-

1625 ■ Early paved streets in Maine.

loaded ship that offers the 20th century an opportunity to study all aspects of early 17th century shipbuilding and everyday life.

c. 1630 First bridge in English colonies may have been the pile-and-beam bridge known as Cradock Bridge built over the Mystick River in Medford, Massachusetts. (See 1634)

1630 November 9 First ferry route in America is established in Massachusetts. Ferry operators on the Charles River between Boston and Charleston charge one penny for each passenger and for each 100 pounds of cargo.

1632 September First highway legislation in North America is passed by the Legislature of the British Colony of Virginia. It provides that "highways shall be layd out in such convenient places as are requisite according as the Governor and Council or the commissioners for the monthlie corts shall appoynt, or according as the parishioners of every parish shall agree."

1634 The first illustration of a diamond-shaped kite in an English-language book is in John Bate's *The Mysteryes of Nature and Art* published in London, England.

1634 Johannes Kepler's (1571—1630) *Somnium (Dream)* is published four years after his death. An unusual work of early science fiction, this story of a voy-

age to the moon is written by a man of science who probably knows there is no real atmosphere between the earth and the moon. Kepler therefore does not use winged transportation but rather resorts to supernatural demons who transport humans through the rarified air by giving them a protective potion. He describes the moon using the latest astronomical knowledge but he inhabits it with creatures who live underground. This is a strange but influential work.

1634 First bridge in English colonies may have been built by Israel Stoughton (d. c. 1645) who is granted permission by the Court of the Massachusetts Bay Colony to build a mill and a bridge on the Neponset River at Dorchester, Massachusetts. It is not known if this bridge is ever built. (See c. 1630)

1636 Pilgrims in New England learn of the existence of several Indian trails connecting the Massachusetts Bay Colony with the first white settlement along the Connecticut River. After learning of these trails from Indians who come to Boston to sell their corn, the settlers rename them and begin using them.

1638 Travel to the moon is the subject of fictional works by English bishops Francis Godwin (1562—1633) and John Wilkins (1614—1672). Godwin's book, *The Man in the Moone,* is published in London this year, and Wilkins' book, *The Discovery of a New World,* is published in 1640.

1639 Transportation by ox-drawn carts is introduced into Edo, Japan.

1640 Regular stagecoach service in Germany is begun by the Taxis family. Beginning only with the Hildesheim and Bremen route via Hanover, it soon develops into many connected routes of coaches. Stages also make their first appearance in England, and in France in 1647, 43 towns are connected to Paris by public coach routes.

1642 Briare Canal in France, linking the Loire and the Seine rivers, is completed. Begun in 1604 under King Henry IV (1553—1610), it is stopped when the king is assassinated in 1610. Work resumes in 1637, and when finished, this important canal includes 40 locks with a

1638 A.D.

Moon travel mentioned in fiction

1640 A.D.

Stage-coach service begins

unique staircase of six locks in a row to allow boats to go up and down a 65-foot fall. It serves as a model for the later and even more ambitious French effort, the Languedoc Canal. (See 1681)

(See 1681)

1644 A.D.

New England shipbuilding industry begins

1644 Early colonial sailing ship, the *Trial,* is built in Boston, Massachusetts, marking the beginning of New England's substantial shipbuilding industry.

1646 First side ponds for use in canal navigation are built as part of a canal lock at Boesinghe in Flanders. Side ponds are an important development since they allow some water to be run off from a lock into ponds beside the lock to be saved and used again.

1647 Tito Livio Burattini (born in Venice, c. 1615) builds a working model of a flying machine which is said to have made several successful indoor flights in Krakow, Poland. His model sounds like a complex flapping ornithopter worked with springs, having four pairs of wings in tandem and a tail unit.

1648 John Wilkins (1614—1672), English bishop of Chester, summarizes much of the submersible knowledge of his time along with some fanciful ideas of his own in his book, *Mathematicall Magick.*

1649 French physician M. Richard makes a carriage that is propelled by passengers. This simple method has a man standing in back of the carriage working levers with his feet, much as a person would today work a paddle boat while seated.

1649 Johann Hautsch of Germany builds a man-powered carriage. This elaborately designed chariot is propelled by men pedalling while concealed inside. This vehicle can move a stately 2 mph and is purchased by the Crown Prince of Sweden.

c. 1650 Evliya Celebi (1611—1683), with wings like an eagle's attached to his arms, leaps from the Galata Tower in Scutari, Turkey, and is said to have flown or glided several miles.

c. 1650 By this time, in England, the four-horse coach is no longer a rarity but is part of every rich man's property. Coaches have become more than a means of transport and now signal a sign of rank and status both in England and the Continent.

1650 In Japan, a "daihachiguruma," meaning literally an eight-man cart, is used for the first time.

c. 1650 The steel-springed coach first appears in England. This technical breakthrough does much to ensure a smoother, sway-free coach ride.

c. 1650 Local governments in New England exercise the power of local taxation for the repair and construction of highways.

c. 1650 The continuous sound of the post-horn is heard for the first time. This horn is blown, playing the same six-note tune, by stagecoaches in Europe who are warning every other vehicle that they have the right-of-way. Other coaches, like the extra mail, the express mail, and the ordinary mail coach have their own, distinctive tune, as well as an alarm signal. Stagecoaches got their name by going "in stages" to their destination, using fresh horses at each stage.

1650 Polish artillery expert Kasimierrz Siemienowicz (d. after 1651), publishes *Artis magnae artilleriae pars prima (The Great Art of Artillery, First Part),* in Amsterdam. This highly creative and original book offers rocket ideas and methods that mark the beginning of a modern, experimental approach to rocket propulsion. It contains sketches of a multiple rocket or a rocket with "stages." It is exactly this suggestion—that the emptied stage be jettisoned once used in order to reduce weight—that 20th-century staged rockets come to use. His book also proposes adding fins to the rocket for stability. This volume is soon translated into every major language and becomes the bible of rocketry for two centuries.

1652 Dutch doctor Jan van Riebeeck (1619—1677) is sent to Cape Town (South Africa) to establish a settlement there whose purpose is to grow vegetables. The degenerative disease scurvy is known to be minimized by proper diet (it is caused by a deficiency of Vitamin C), so the Dutch plan to have all their ships call at Cape Town to stock up on fresh vegetables for their return journey home.

1654 First toll bridge in North America may have been the bridge Richard Thurby is licensed by the Essex County, Massachusetts court to build over Newbury River in Rowley. The Court orders a toll for horses, cows, and oxen and a lesser charge for hogs, sheep, and goats. People may pass free.

1654 First fire engine in the United States is made by iron maker Joseph Jencks, of Lynn, Massachusetts for the town of Boston. It is little more than a portable pump worked by shifts of men at its handles. Its cistern or reservoir is kept full by a bucket brigade.

c. 1655 Rum is first issued as an official ration to British sailors. By 1740, the rum is first diluted with water, and thereafter reduced until finally abolished in 1970.

1656 Travel beyond the earth is the subject of *Histoire comique des états et empires de la lune* (*Comic History of the States and Empires of the Moon*), written by French satirist and dramatist Savinien Cyrano de Bergerac (1619—1655). Published posthumously, as is his *Histoire comique des états et empires du soleil* (*Comic History of the States and Empires of the Sun*) in 1662, these works blend much of the science of the time with his parodying of other, similar works. One of the propulsive devices he allows his characters to use to fly through space is a system of firecrackers tied around their flying machine.

c. 1660 Allard, a tightrope walker, attempts to fly at St. Germain in France, before King Louis XIV, and is seriously injured.

1660 Sport of yachting is introduced into England as the Dutch present Charles II (1630—1685) at his restoration to the English throne with a small pleasure vessel they call a "jacht." This is a small, fast, single-masted boat usually used for scouting when speed is important. (See October 1, 1661)

1660 British Navy abolishes the rank of "Generals-at-Sea" and replaces it with Admirals. From now on, the commander of a vessel must excel in seamanship and not simply in military tactics. Modern specialization at sea begins.

1660 French engineer Hubert Gautier (1660—1737) is born in Nimes, France. It is Gautier who first recognizes the importance of applying scientific techniques to the planning, execution, and testing of engineering projects. He is also the author of two classic handbooks, *Traité de la construction des chemins* (*Treatise on the Construction of Roads*), 1715, and *Traité des ponts* (*Treatise on Bridges*), 1716.

1661 October 1 First recorded yacht race in England takes place when King Charles II (1630—1685) in his yacht, *Katherine,* races the Duke of York in the yacht *Anne.* (See 1660)

1662 English Parliament passes an act further regulating road construction. Traffic has so increased that mandatory citizen labor alone is unable to keep up, so tolls are resorted to as a matter of national policy to pay for road repairs.

1662 "Great Bridge" over the Charles River in Cambridge, Massachusetts is built. Although little is known about this bridge, which serves as the only crossing for 130 years, it is believed that its superstructure is composed of hewn timbers. A contemporary refers to "the old piers or supports being cribs of logs filled with stones and sunk in the river."

1662 March 18 First bus begins operations in France. This scheduled service operates horse-drawn vehicles that seat eight and are known as "carrosses à cinq solz." Owned by a company formed under Royal Patent by French scientist and philosopher Blaise Pascal (1623—1662) and his friend and financial backer, the Duc de Roannez, the service runs between Porte de Saint-Antoine and the Porte du Luxembourg, and leaves on time whether full or empty.

1662 December 22 First modern catamaran, a boat with two hulls, is the *Experiment,* built in Dublin, Ireland by William Petty. It proves especially seaworthy and wins several yacht races. The word catamaran comes from the Tamil language of South India and means literally "tied logs." It is therefore also used to describe a variety of primitive rafts, floats, or balance boards.

1663 Robert Hooke (1635—1703) presents to the Royal Society of London a plan for a machine with which one could walk on water or land with "the swiftness of a crane." The patent he takes out is for a single-wheeled vehicle which is supposed to have been propelled by the movement of a rider situated inside the wheel itself.

1662
Dec. 22

First
catamaran
built

1664 In a book called *Technica curiosa* which summarizes the technical achievements of his time, priest Gaspar Schott (1608—1666) tells of a portable diving bell. It is not known if anyone uses it with success.

c. 1665 Robert Hooke (1635—1703), talented physicist and inventor of Oxford, England, builds model birds powered by "springs and wings." These resemble a model ornithopter, which Hooke later writes, "rais'd and sustain'd it self in the Air." First mention of these is in *The Posthumous Works of Robert Hooke*, published in 1705.

1666 After the Great Fire of 1666 that burns out the heart of the city of London, English coaches are made wider because the new streets are widened.

1666 First known canal tunnel is begun in southwestern France. Called the Malpas Tunnel, it is on the Languedoc Canal (Canal de Midi) and connects the Mediterranean Sea and the Atlantic Ocean. It is 540 feet long and is completed in 1681. It is also the first tunnel for which gunpowder is used to break rocks.

1667 Administration of roads, bridges, and ferries in French Canada is established as the first "grand voyer" is appointed. This is the name for the superintendent of roads and bridges who, very early, administers a system of responsibility for the maintenance of old roads and the building of new ones.

1669 Important German canal, the Friedrich Wilhelm Canal in Germany, is completed. This 15-mile-long waterway is a summit-level canal that carries much Silesian trade to Berlin and later to Hamburg. (See July 1398)

1670 In Italy, Jesuit priest Francesco de Lana de Terzi (1631—1687) publishes his *Prodromo; Overo, Saggio di Alcune Invenzioni Nuovo Premesso All'arte Maestra*, in Brescia, Italy, in which his design for a "Flying Ship" appears. This is literally a boat or ship to be raised by four copper vacuum spheres. This would not have worked, since the spheres would have been crushed by atmospheric pressure. His influential book also contains his descriptions of air-raids and airborne invasions, anticipating what would come in modern times.

1670 Walking on water is described by Englishman Thomas Hill (fl. 1590) in his book, *Natural and Artificial Conclusions*, published in 1670. In it, Hill says, "Take two little Timbrels, and bind them under the soles of thy feet, and at thy stave's end fasten another; and with these thou may'st walk on water…" It is not known if Hill succeeds in walking with Timbrels (a small drum or tambourine).

1671 Johann Scheffer (1621—1679) publishes in Frankfurt, Germany his encyclopedic study of wheeled transport called *De re vehiculari veterum (On Ancient Vehicles)*. It surveys the vehicles of ancient Greece and Rome.

1672 Steam cart or carriage is built in China by the Belgian Jesuit missionary priest Ferdinand Verbiest (d. 1688). Built for the Emperor Khang-hi, this small, mechanical experiment is self-propelled but not at all practical. It is basically a small steam boiler sitting atop four wheels while a fifth steering wheel extends out on a lever.

1672 Court records for this year show that John Smith of Hadley, Massachusetts is directed by authorities "to fell a tree across Swift River for a foot bridge, if any such be at hand." Bridges having decks composed of one or two tree trunks are sometimes described as "foot and walkit" structures.

c. 1673 Charles Bernouin is said to have flown or glided from a tower using wings described as a "well-tensioned sail." He later breaks his neck and dies attempting to fly at Frankfurt-am-Main, Germany.

1673 Dutch physicist and astronomer Christian Huygens (1629—1695) describes and designs the first piston-and-cylinder or explosion engine using gunpowder. This is the first internal combustion engine. Using gunpowder is too dangerous however, and the next improvement will be to move the piston up and down in the cylinder using steam and then cooling.

1673 January 22 First post rider takes the colonial mails from New York to the major cities of New England.

1675 English roads are improved to the point that stagecoaches can operate both summer and winter.

c. 1675 Birch bark canoe used by the Algonquin Indians in Canada is described by Frenchman N. Denys in a letter. He gives a detailed account of how

1673 ■ First Colonial post rider.

these canoes are made and describes their virtues. They combine speed and carrying capacity with extreme lightness, so they could easily be "portaged" or carried around unnavigable sections. They are also strong enough to withstand a trip through rapids. While the French eventually learn to handle these canoes as well as the Indians, they seldom try to build them themselves.

1675 Royal Observatory at Greenwich, England is founded by King Charles II (1630—1685). Because of its authority and prestige, Greenwich becomes the place used by navigators and mapmakers for the prime meridian. A meridian is an imaginary north-south line drawn between the earth's poles and through a particular spot. With the 18th-century adoption of Greenwich as the spot from which everyone would measure longitude, a standard was agreed upon and everyone was, in a sense, speaking the same navigational language.

1678 A French locksmith named Besnier attempts to fly at Sable, France. His hinged wings, which he flaps alternately using his arms and legs, are made of taffeta cloth stretched over a frame. He apparently is able to glide across a wide river, and his flight becomes one of the most widely illustrated in history.

1678 French priest Jean de Hautefeuille (1647—1724) suggests a piston-and-cylinder engine using gunpowder. This is based on the principle that a vacuum is produced in a cylinder when gunpowder is exploded. The creation of a vacuum moves the piston inside the cylinder. His attempts to use this method to work the

water pumps in the Gardens of Versailles are not successful.

1680 *De Motu Animalium*, by Giovanni Alphonso Borelli (1606—1679), professor of mathematics at Messina, and later Pisa, in Italy, is published posthumously in Rome. In it, he proves conclusively that human anatomy and musculature—as compared to a bird's—is completely inadequate to lift a man off the ground. This explanation remains true until the 1980s when, with modern knowledge of aerodynamics and modern ultra-light materials, human-powered flights will become possible.

1680 English scientist and mathematician Isaac Newton (1642—1727) designs a machine that is moved by the jet action of steam escaping through a hole in the boiler. Although it is more of a concrete expression of the reaction principle stated by Newton—"To every action there is always an equal and opposite reaction"—than it is a true vehicle design, it still represents one of the first major studies of the potential of using steam as a source of power.

1680 Detailed drawings for underwater travel are included by Italian physicist Giovanni Alfonso Borelli (1608-1679) in his book *De motu animalium (On the Motion of Animals)*. Among his plans are a sealed boat propelled by oars from the inside, and a man-sized diving bell—neither of which would have worked. However, other plans for a breathing system, while complicated, do have the possibility of working and could be considered a forerunner of the modern aqualung.

1680 First ship of any size to be built and launched onto one the five Great Lakes separating the United States and Canada is sent onto Lake Ontario by French explorer Robert La Salle (1643—1687). La Salle later explores the Mississippi River to the Gulf of Mexico, and dies at the hands of mutineers.

1681 First recorded use of the English word "railway." Although the British use railway and railroad interchangeably, the Americans will use only "railroad."

1681 Theory of breathing underwater is advanced by French priest Jean de Hautefeuille (1647—1724), who writes a short book, *L'Art de respirer sous l'eau (The Art of Breathing Underwater)*. Although he understands the

1680 A.D.

Steam-powered machine designed

critical role of pressure when trying to pump air to a diver, his attempts to build a working device do not succeed.

1681 May Languedoc Canal in France, also known as the Canal du Midi, opens and links the city of Toulouse with the Mediterranean. This 150-mile (241-kilometer) waterway takes 15 years to finish and is considered by many to be the greatest feat of civil engineering between Roman times and the 19th century. The canal has 100 locks, ascends 206 feet, and then descends 620 feet to the Mediterranean. There are also three long aqueducts and a 180-yard (165-meter) long tunnel. It is the pioneer and model of the modern European canal.

c. 1682 A pyrotechnics workshop or rocket works is established in Moscow during the reign of Tsar Peter I the Great of Russia (1672—1725) to make signal illuminating rockets for the Russian Army.

1685 Ancestor of the modern pneumatic caisson— the compressed air chamber used under water to build bridge foundations on top of solid rock—is used on the construction of the Pont Royal across the Seine in Paris, France. Ordered built by King Louis XIV (1638—1715) and thus its name, it is a stone bridge of five low arches designed by French architect Jules Hardouin Mansart (1646—1708). François Romain, a cleric/engineer, is called in from Holland to help with the foundations, and he devises the open caisson method. In this, he sinks a barge of loaded gravel, leaving a space in the center from which water is pumped. The piles are then driven and the masonry foundation laid inside this dry chamber. Romain calls it his "caisse" method.

1686 Bernard Le Bovier de Fontenelle (1657—1757), French scientist and man of letters, publishes his most famous work, *Entretiens sur la pluralité des mondes (Discourses on the Plurality of Worlds).* Among his speculations on other planets, Fontenelle reasons by analogy that advances in transport systems are all that is needed for man to visit other planets (which he claims are inhabited). He writes: "The art of flying has just been born; it will improve until one day we will go to the Moon."

1687 English scientist, astronomer, and mathematician Isaac Newton (1642—1727) publishes his scientific classic, *Philosophia naturalis principia mathematica (Mathematical Principles of Natural Philosophy).* This work explains in precise mathematical terms almost every motion in the universe, from an apple falling to the orbit of a planet, and tells how everything is subject to what he calls his law of universal gravitation. With knowledge of his third law of motion, "for every action there is an equal and opposite reaction," spaceflight becomes theoretically possible, since this is the principle of the (reaction) rocket.

1688 Denis Papin (1647—1712), French physicist and assistant to Christian Huygens (1629—1695), builds the first engine to move a piston in a cylinder by using the power of steam.

1689 First written reference to skis in the literature of continental Europe is made by German Johann Weichard von Valvasor (1641—1693) in his Austrian travel book, *Die Ehre des Herzogtums Krain.* He describes the "rare invention," saying, "These little boards are bent and turned up, and in the middle there is fixed a leather strap into which the feet are placed."

1689 March 6 English astronomer Edmund Halley (1656—1742) writes a paper entitled, "A Method of Walking under Water." Between this time and 1691, he writes four more papers which describe his invention of a diving bell and a diving helmet. Halley then builds both devices and uses them himself under water. His bell and helmet both receive air from the surface via barrels lowered from the surface. His divers are able to maneuver on the bottom well enough for him to set up a company to salvage wrecks. Halley's apparatus are far in advance of anything done to date.

1690 Walking on water is described by German historian Johann Christoph Wagenseil (1633—1705) of Nuremberg in his writings. He tells of his invention called "the Hydrapsis, or Water-Shield: A Machine by the Help of Which a Person May Walk upon the Water without Fear of Sinking."

1693 March 24 English instrument maker John Harrison (1693—1776) is born in Foulby, Yorkshire. Beginning in 1728, this self-taught mechanic builds a series of five clocks that provide the British Navy with the first reliable marine chronometer. This device begins the modern era of ship navigation, as it makes possible the simple and accurate determination of longitude at sea (north/south location).

1695 In England, a law is passed to prevent road users from dashing past toll areas. It empowers local authorities to block roads at toll houses with a turn-pike or turnpole. This familiar device is mounted on a vertical pivot and is swung clear after the toll is paid.

1695 Humphrey Mackworth (1657—1727) applies sails to coal wagons that move on rails or tracks at Neath, South Wales.

1697 Oldest stone arch bridge still in service on a modern U.S. highway is first built. The Frankford Avenue Bridge spanning the Pennypack Creek in Philadelphia, Pennsylvania, often called the Pennypack Bridge, is a three-span stone bridge that is widened for a trolley route in 1893. It is used by automobiles even today.

1698 First sea voyage undertaken for solely scientific purposes begins its two-year expedition. British astronomer Edmund Halley (1656—1742) commands the war sloop *Paramour Pink* on its mission "to observe variations in compass readings in the South Atlantic and to determine accurate latitudes and longitudes of his port of call."

1698 Russian tsar and emperor Peter I the Great (1672—1725) tours European shipyards and returns to his homeland to create a new Russian navy. He later adopts a policy of securing access to the Baltic and the Black Seas.

1698 First American colonial road map for public use is printed in *Tulley's Almanac* in Boston, Massachusetts. The almanac also gives a list of towns and their distances from Boston.

1698 November 14 First Eddystone Lighthouse is built and is the first to be exposed to the full force of the sea. Designed by English engineer Henry Winstanley (1644—1703), it marks the dangerous submerged reef 14 miles (22.5 kilometers) southwest of Plymouth, England. Built of timber and draped with iron hoisting gear as well as balconies, cornices, flagpoles and many odd ornamental gadgets, it is destroyed by a violent storm on November 26, 1703. Winstanley dies in his creation. Its value is immediately recognized however, and another is built in 1708. (See 1708)

1700 British engineer Thomas Savery (c. 1650—1715) builds a pistonless, steam-powered engine that pumps water.

1700 It takes a week for a coach to travel from London to York, England.

c. 1700 French King Louis XIV (1638—1715) rides in an opulent coach that contains many new features. The rear part of the carriage is suspended and the front part has low wheels with a revolving axle that enables it to turn.

1700 White settlers begin to follow the Iroquois or Mohawk Trail, a beaten path that is the most direct route between the Hudson River and Lake Erie. This trail precisely follows the best topography and was used by generations of Indians who also employed swift runners who could carry messages from the present sites of Albany to Buffalo in three days.

1700 London, England has about 600 hackney carriages which are available for hire by those who can pay. The city of Paris, France has about half that number for hire.

c. 1700 By this time, the center of most nations' maritime interests has shifted from the Mediterranean to the Atlantic. Technologically, the sail has totally replaced the oar in boats of any size.

1703 Englishman David Russen (fl. 1705) publishes his fictional work, *Iter Lunare: or Voyage to the Moon*. In it, he proposes that a man might be sent to the moon if a large enough spring catapult were used from the top of a high mountain.

1703 Dutch jurist Cornelis van Bynkershoek (1673—1743) publishes his main work on international law, *De dominio maris (On the Dominion of the Seas)*. His opinion that a country's sovereignty should extend three miles (5.6 kilometers) from its coast is eventually adopted by most countries. He sets three miles as the limit, since that is the farthest the most powerful cannon of his time can reach. This law remains observed until after World War II when many nations extend their coastal waters to 50 miles (92.6 kilometers) or more.

1703 Worst storm losses ever in the English Channel occur as England loses about 150 merchant vessels and 13 warships. Many are wrecked on the dangerous line of shoals called Goodwin Sands, long a graveyard for ships.

1703 Russian Tsar Peter I the Great (1672—1725) begins the construction of the Vychene-Volotski Canal to join the Neva River to one of the tributaries of the Volga River. Although the first Russian canals were dug in the 15th century, Peter attempts to use the newer methods he observed on his trip through Western Europe. This canal is completed in 1709.

1705 Daniel Defoe (1660—1731), the great English novelist, publishes one of his lesser known works, *The Consolidator*, dealing with travel to the moon. He describes the engine of his spacecraft in terms that closely resemble real rocket propulsion.

1708 Second Eddystone Lighthouse is built by English engineer John Rudyerd. Made of laminated timber on top of a tall, smooth masonry base, it stands until it is destroyed by fire in 1755. It is firmly anchored to the reef with iron rods driven deep in the rock. (See 1759)

1709 Bartolomeu Lourenco de Gusmao (1686—1724), a Brazilian Jesuit priest at Lisbon, Portugal, constructs and probably tests with some success a model glider version of his *Passarola*. This small model in the shape of a bird is covered by a hood or cloth parachute which probably catches the wind when aloft. Illustrations of his model are first published during this year and eventually become one of the most widely published aeronautical images in history.

1712 British engineer Thomas Newcomen (1663—1729) builds the first reliable, safe steam engine. Low pressure steam is used to vertically raise a piston.

1713 A.D.

First American schooner built

1713 First American schooner-type ship (a sailing craft with both fore and aft sails, and with two to four masts) is built by American Andrew Robinson in Gloucester, Massachusetts.

1714 Emmanuel Swedenborg (1688—1772) of Sweden suggests an aircraft design that looks like a carriage fixed below a large canopy. He plans to propel it with flappers worked by a spiral spring. His plans are published two years later in his book *Daedalus Hyperboreas*.

1715 French engineer Hubert Gautier (1660—1737) publishes his *Traité de la construction des chemins (Treatise on the Construction of Roads)* in Paris. This is the second, enlarged edition of his first version published in Toulouse in 1693. In it, Gautier describes the history of the French road system from the Roman era to his time.

c. 1716 Wrought iron strips are placed on top of wooden rails in England to prevent wear. This prolongs the life of the mine wagonways and is, in a way, a precursor of the solid iron rail.

1716 French engineer Pierre Tresaguet (1716—1794) is born in France. It was Tresaguet who first introduced modern road-building ideas to France and the rest of the world. His rational system and methods of improved road construction influenced John Loudon McAdam (1756—1836) and were later adopted in England by Thomas Telford (1757—1834).

1716 English engineer James Brindley (1716—1772) is born in Tunstead, Derbyshire. Self-educated, Brindley designs a network of shipping canals which serves as England's major industrial transportation system until the emergence of railroads in the early 19th century.

1716 First company of elite ski troops is formed in Norway, and regular ski drills become part of their maneuvers. These soldiers are credited with being the first to use a leather strap around their heel besides the toestrap, to keep their skis from falling off when skiing downhill.

1716 First book devoted solely to bridges is written by French engineer Hubert Gautier (1660—1737). His book, *Traité des ponts (Treatise on Bridges)* calls for the application of scientific principles to bridge-building. It is published in Paris.

1716 February 1 Corps des Ingenieurs des Ponts et Chaussees (Bridges and Highways Corps) is formed in Paris, France during the very early reign of the child-king, Louis XV (1710—1774). It is the first civil department or governmental organization founded for the scientific advancement of bridgebuilding. Plans of all roads, bridges, and canals in central France must be approved by this body of engineers. Its first head is Jacques Gabriel (1667—1742). (See 1747)

1716 September 14 First lighthouse in America, Boston Lighthouse, is built on Little Brewster Island in Boston Harbor, Massachusetts. Early settlers had built warning bonfires on this same spot. This and most other early American lighthouses have simple oil lamps which do not use glass chimneys, mirrors, or lenses.

1716 ■ Boston Lighthouse as seen in the 20th century.

1719 First fog warning signal, a cannon, is set up at Boston Lighthouse. Since Boston Harbor is often foggy, the lighthouse keeper, John Hayes, takes to firing a cannon at intervals, "to answer ships in a Fog."

1721 New Orleans beacon is built at Fort Boulaye in the Mississippi delta by Adrien de Pauger to offer ships a known landmark. It is not known if the 62-foot-high beacon is lighted or not.

1721 May 25 First marine and fire insurance company in America is opened in Philadelphia, Pennsylvania by John Copson.

1724 June 8 English engineer John Smeaton (1724—1792) is born in Austhorpe, Yorkshire. A pioneer in the field of civil engineering, Smeaton plans harbors, canals, dams, bridges, and drainage works. He wins lasting fame for his Eddystone Lighthouse that survives 120 years of storms.

c. 1725 One-horse open sleighs are common in the northern American colonies in winter when everyone travels on runners. They resemble a squarish, high-backed bench, and are built to be simple and sturdy. Besides a fur skin or blanket across their laps, travellers often ride with their feet on heated bricks or on a tin foot-warmer filled with hot coals.

1725 September 25 Military engineer Nicolas-Joseph Cugnot (1725—1804) is born in Poid, France. Best known for building the first self-propelled road vehicle in 1769, Cugnot built his huge, strange-looking steam-powered tricycle to pull the army's heavy guns. Although in no way a practical vehicle, it does prove the viability of steam-powered traction and is, in some ways, the very first automobile.

1726 German engineer Jacob Leupold (1674—1727) publishes his *Theatrum pontificale; oder Schau-Platz der Brucken und Brucken-Baues*. After Gautier's 1714 book, this is the next major treatment of bridges and bridge-building. It is one part of ten volumes by Leupold dealing with all aspects of mechanical engineering. It is perhaps the most comprehensive of all the early bridge books.

1727 First recorded mention of the use of two ski poles with disks at the ends is made by Johann Gerhard Scheller in his book, *Reise-Beschreibung von lappland und Bothnien*.

1728 English Parliament passes an act making the destruction of toll houses punishable by three months in jail or public whipping. Opposition to toll roads by people who believe road passage should be free continues with some rioting, and Parliament increases the penalty to death in 1735.

1729 First recorded use of "check rails" on railway curves. Later used on bridges and viaducts to prevent derailments, these second rails stop the outer wheel flange from mounting the running rail.

1729 Cast iron flanged (rimmed or ribbed) wheels for rail wagons are made in Coalbrookdale, England. Although brittle, cast iron is a very hard metal, and certainly a durable improvement over wooden rail wheels.

1730 British mathematician John Hadley (1682—1744) invents the reflecting nautical quadrant. This navigational device measures the altitude of the Sun or a star above the horizon and helps find geographical position at sea. It becomes an invaluable navigational tool and is soon widely used on all ships. It later evolves into the sextant.

1731 A.D.

First fire engine built

1731 First efficient fire engine in America, built in England, becomes part of the Union Fire Company of Philadelphia, headed by Benjamin Franklin (1706—1790). This hand-operated mobile pump replaces the old-fashioned bucket brigade.

1731 First lightship is moored in Nore, England, close to the Thames estuary—one of the busiest waterways in the world. It is a result of the private initiative of two Englishmen, Robert Hamblin and David Avery. The light provided by the anchored ship proves beneficial to the coastal establishment which gladly pays for its upkeep. It is not until after 1800 that lightships are established in other countries.

1733 Book on horsemanship is published in Paris, France by François Robichon de la Guerinière (d. 1751). His *Ecole de Cavalerie* explains how to train a horse without it being forced into submission. This represents a more humane philosophy of "dressage" or schooling of a horse.

1733 First military ski manual is written by Captain Jens Emmahusen of Trondheim, Norway.

c. 1733 First perambulator or baby carriage is built in England by William Kent (c. 1686—1748) for the third Duke of Devonshire. This vehicle has four wheels, two 21-inch wheels in the rear and two 16-inch wheels in the front. Its body is in the shape of a scallop shell and its hood folds close. The design indicates that it is intended to be pulled by a dog. (See 1850)

1734 A.D.

First use of metal in bridge

1734 First recorded use in the West of metal in a suspension structure is the chain bridge built near Glorywitz, Prussia by the Army of the Palatinate of Saxony.

1736 Transylvanian writer and historian Peter Apor (1676—1752) gives meticulously detailed descriptions of the many vehicles of his time in his book *Metamorphosis Transylvaniae*, published in Budapest, Hungary.

1736 English clockmaker Jonathan Hulls (b. 1699) takes out a patent for a stern-wheel tugboat powered by a Newcomen atmospheric steam engine. There is no evidence that Hulls ever builds his boat, but he does publish a book in 1737 called *A Description and Draught of a New-Invented Machine for Carrying Vessels or Ships out of, or Into Any Harbour.*

1736 January 19 Scottish engineer James Watt (1736—1819) is born in Greenock, Renfrew. Commonly believed to be the inventor of the steam engine, he actually developed the condensor which made existing engines much more efficient. He steadily improved his steam engine which soon became a prime mover for both industry and transportation. A versatile genius, he also defined "horsepower" as 550-foot-pounds per seconds, a value still used today.

1740 Ventilation system for ships is invented by English botanist Stephen Hales (1677—1761). He installs his system, which uses a forced draft provided by a bellows, on the ship *Sorbay*. It is later adapted to ventilate mines and large buildings like prisons.

1740 First lighthouse in Canada is the tower built at the French stronghold of Louisburg on Cape Breton Island, Nova Scotia. It is 75 feet tall and has an oil lamp.

1740 England passes a law attempting to reform its scandalous methods of recruiting sailors. Until this law, any male, English or foreign, can be impressed into the Navy. There is no appeal against the press-gangs of the Royal Navy. This law actually reforms little, since first, it states that only British subjects 18 to 55 can be taken away to serve, and second, even that restriction generally goes unobserved. Press-gangs are eventually abolished altogether in 1815.

1740 August 26 Joseph-Michel Montgolfier (1740—1810), pioneer hot-air balloonist, is born in Annonany, France. Achieved, along with his brother, Jacques-Etienne, the world's first public demonstration of a hot-air balloon on June 4, 1783, as well as the first manned, untethered balloon flight on November 21, 1783. While Joseph-Michel took the lead in the 1782 experiments on the lifting power of heated air, his brother came to share in both the work and the achievements. Together, they began the age of flight.

1741 English Parliament begins the practice of weighing stations for wagons and loads. Reasoning that the heavier the load, the more damage is done to the road, it devises a complicated scale of overweight charges.

1742 The Marquis de Bacqueville (c. 1680—1760) attempts to fly across the River Seine in Paris with wings attached to both his arms and legs. After leaping from a riverside house, he crashes onto a barge and breaks his legs.

1742 David Bushnell (1742—1824), American inventor and pioneer of the submarine, is born in Saybrook, Connecticut. The Yale-educated Bushnell builds a one-man vessel, the *Turtle*, which is the first submersible to attack an enemy ship, as it attempts unsuccessfully to sink a British ship in New York harbor during the U.S. Revolutionary War. He eventually commands the U.S. Army Corps of Engineers at West Point and later practices medicine.

1743 January 21 American inventor John Fitch (1743—1798) is born in Windsor, Connecticut. After working as a clockmaker and surveyor, he turns to steam navigation and builds his first steamboat in 1786. By 1790, he begins the first regular steamboat service, carrying passengers and freight on the Delaware River. It proves a commercial failure however, and Fitch commits suicide.

1745 Earliest description of an Eskimo kayak is written by Hans Egede (1686—1758) in his book, *A Description of Greenland*. This one-man, mostly-enclosed, light and narrow-framed boat has sharp ends and is covered with the skin of the bearded seal. The kayak reached this form many centuries before this account, and it is perfectly suited to the rigors of the arctic wastes where life depends upon the success of seal hunting in waters full of ice-floes.

1745 First summit-level canal in Britain is built by Thomas Steers (1672—1750). It runs from Newry in Northern Ireland to Lough Neagh, bringing coal from the Tyrone coal mines over the canal and then by sea to Dublin.

1745 January 6 Jacques-Etienne Montgolfier (1745—1799), pioneer hot-air balloonist, is born in

Annonany, France. Achieved, along with his brother, Joseph-Michel, the world's first public demonstration of a hot-air balloon on June 4, 1783, as well as the first manned, untethered balloon flight on November 21, 1783. After Joseph-Michel discovered the lifting power of heated air, Jacques-Etienne joined him in 1782 in applying it experimentally. Together, they were flight pioneers.

1746 Wooden lighthouse is built by the town of Nantucket, Massachusetts on Brant Point, on the western side of the entrance to Nantucket Harbor. It burns down more than once, and is also wrecked by storms. Entering the harbor is very dangerous at night, so the lighthouse is regularly rebuilt.

1747 First officially recognized college of road engineering, the Ecole des Ponts et Chaussées (School of Bridges and Highways), is founded in Paris, France. The organizer of the school is named Trudaine, and its first teacher and director is the brilliant, young Jean-Rodolphe Perronet (1708—1794).

1747 Submarine is built by English carpenter Nathaniel Symons using ideas offered by William Bourne (d. 1583) nearly two centuries earlier. He builds a boat in two sections joined with leather which, from the inside, he can control the water ballast and go under and come up again. His boat does not have any means of propulsion, however. (See 1578)

1748 Jacques Vaucanson (1709—1782), French engineer who builds all manner of automatons and becomes famous for his mechanization of silk weaving, drives a carriage propelled by clockwork springs in front of King Louis XV.

1749 Alexander Wilson, professor of history at Glasgow University, Scotland, uses a kite for scientific research as he measures the temperature of clouds at 3,000 feet using a thermometer attached to a train of several paper kites. He predates Benjamin Franklin (1706—1790), who conducts his own electrical experiments using kites in 1752.

1749 Beavertail Lighthouse is built by the Colony of Rhode Island on the south end of Conanicut Island at the entrance to Narragansett Bay. Built of rubble-stone and 64 feet high, it benefits the town of Newport, making it a more secure harbor for the profitable triangular slave trade (rum to Africa for slaves, slaves to

1749 A.D.

Kite first used in scientific research

the south or the West Indies for molasses, molasses to Newport for its rum factories).

1749 Englishman John Lethbridge describes in the September issue of *The Gentleman's Magazine* "a machine to recover wrecks at sea." It resembles a large, wide pipe enclosed at both ends. It is lowered and maneuvered by a suspension chain and has holes for the diver's arms. Lethbridge claims to have used this device for three years.

c. 1750 Daleme springs for carriages are introduced in France. With these, the carriage body is still suspended on straps, but steel springs are inserted between the straps and the body. Although it removes the jolt felt from potholes, it has a sway ressembling that of a boat. Eighteenth-century carriages are becoming more elegant, light, and more finely shaped.

1750 A regular stage-wagon service runs from Philadelphia, Pennsylvania to New York via Trenton and Brunswick. It is a covered vehicle with no springs, and is fitted with rigid wooden benches for passengers. By the time of the Revolution, a passenger could travel by stage from Philadelphia to the Paulus Hook (now Jersey City) ferry in two days, where stages were available for the journey to New York and Boston.

c. 1750 A.D.

Conestoga wagons haul freight

c. 1750 In colonial America, Conestoga wagons haul most of the freight. They travel only by day and do not change their six, heavy horses. Its hoops, strong hemp cover, and dory-shape foster a legend that it was first built by a ship carpenter. A very high body makes fording streams easier. It is known that they originated in Lancaster County, Pennsylvania.

c. 1750 Bath chair is invented by Englishman James Heath. This three-wheel conveyance is originally intended for use by ladies and invalids, and for nearly the next three-quarters of a century it rivals and then replaces the sedan chair. The hooded chair can be pushed from behind and is steered by the occupant who controls it with a long, curved rod attached to the small pivoting front wheel. It is especially popular at British seaside resorts.

1751 Pennsylvania Road becomes the most important sunrise-to-sunset pathway connecting the eastern colonies with the west territories. Like most early American roads, it was transformed from an old Indian trail and fur trader's path into a larger thorough-

fare. Beginning in 1792, it is surfaced with broken stone and gravel, and its "turnpiking" or stone surfacing is completed in 1820. (See 1794)

1753 First decree by the British Parliament related to the creation of a railroad is issued concerning a rail mining line that runs between Middleton and Leeds.

1753 July 4 Jean-Pierre-François Blanchard (1753—1809) is born in Les Andelys, France. A pioneer balloonist, he made his first ascent in Paris on March 2, 1784. Along with John Jeffries, an American, he made the first aerial crossing of the English Channel (Dover, England to Calais, France) on January 7, 1785. He made the first balloon flight over the North American continent on January 9, 1793. He died at The Hague some days after experiencing a heart attack while flying his balloon.

1753 October 31 British Army Maj. George Washington (1732—1799) and woodsman Christopher Gist (c. 1706—1759) set out on a perilous round-trip mission from Virginia deep into Ohio Country before the outbreak of the French and Indian War (1754—1763) that involves them using horses both overland and through rivers, canoes, a hastily-made log raft, and finally, walking on foot. Both men survive this dead-of-winter trek during which their ability to use any and all means of transportation to keep moving is severely tested.

1754 Mikhail Vasilyevitch Lomonosov (1711—1765), a Russian scientist, is said to have built and flown a model helicopter with a twin contra-rotating rotor.

1754 British General Edward Braddock's (1695—1755) failure to capture Fort Duquesne and expel the French from the Ohio Valley is blamed mostly on the lack of a good road. Braddock attempts to cut a road through 120 miles of forest that is wide enough for his long train of covered wagons. Progress through the wilderness is painfully slow—from two to five miles a day—and Braddock is eventually killed as his weary and sick troops are ambushed and defeated.

1754 British Parliament decrees that no large-wheeled vehicle can travel on a turnpike road unless its wheels are at least nine inches wide. The exception is for vehicles drawn by four or less horses. It is believed that large, heavy vehicles with narrow wheels are mainly responsible for road deterioration.

1755 ■ Braddock's Road hacked out of the thick woods of Pennsylvania.

1755 Streetcar is invented by Englishman John Outram. Built as a vehicle for public transport, it runs on cast iron rails and is pulled by two horses. However, it is not put to use in the city, where it eventually will be most used.

1755 Colony of Georgia builds a brick tower on Tybee Island at the mouth of the Savannah River. It apparently serves as an unlighted beacon until it is lighted in 1791.

1755 September 13 American inventor Oliver Evans (1755—1819) is born in Newport, Delaware. The broadly-talented Evans automates part of his mill before becoming a pioneer in the use of high-pressure steam. In 1802, his amphibious steam tractor moves on both land and water under its own power—the first self-powered vehicle in America.

1756 In England, an Act is passed authorizing the removal of houses from the Old London Bridge and directing that after they are torn down, all carriage traffic on the new road will keep to the left side. This left-side vehicular rule is peculiar to England and runs counter to that of the continent's right-side practice. It is speculated that England's left-handed custom developed from it being so influenced by its history and tradition of knighthood. In their horseback fights and mock battles, knights traveled to the left while keeping the reins in the left hand, allowing their free right hand to wield their weapons. (See 1904 British Motor Car Order)

1756 September 21 Scottish engineer John Loudon Macadam (1756—1836) is born in Ayrshire, Scotland. Inventor of the macadam method of road surfacing, his rational system of building roads gave England a transportation system adequate to the needs of a growing industrial power. Macadam emigrated to New York at 14 years of age to work for his prosperous uncle, but returned to Scotland in 1783 after supporting the Crown during the American Revolution.

1757 First oscillating lighthouse light is built by Swedish inventor Jonas Norberg (1711—1783), sometimes known as Johan Nordquist. In order to distinguish the Swedish lighthouse at Korso from a nearby light, he builds a mechanism that turns the light horizontally, giving the effect of a flashing signal. (See February 15, 1781)

1757 August 9 Scottish engineer Thomas Telford (1757—1834) is born near Westerkirk, Dumfries. An extremely versatile engineer, he is known for his many bridges and highways that run through England, Scotland, and Wales. As a pioneer in iron bridge construction, he built the first successful long-span suspension bridge across the Menai Strait in Wales.

1758 June 9 First railway authorized by a governmental body is the Middleton Railway leading into Leeds. The British Parliament authorizes this colliery or coal line and calls it a "wagonway." (See August 12, 1812)

1759 Snow skis are described as being seen in Canada for the first time, being used at an ice carnival.

1759 First entirely artificial major navigation canal in Great Britain, the Bridgewater Canal, is begun to be dug. This engineering masterpiece designed by English engineer James Brindley (1716—1772) is completed in 1761. Covering ten miles (16 kilometers), it is a gravity-flow canal (with no locks) which so facilitates the transportation of coal to Manchester that the price of coal is cut in half.

1759 Third Eddystone Lighthouse off Plymouth, England is built by English engineer John Smeaton (1724—1792). Made out of interlocking stone blocks, this

1757 A.D.

First oscillating lighthouse built

new design revolutionizes lighthouse and tower design, and stands firm until erosion forces its replacement in 1882. (See 1882)

1760 The Tobacco-Rolling Road flourishes in Virginia. Tobacco is transported from inland Virginia to the Potomac River in hogsheads rolled along the ground. These are wooden casks full of tobacco that are rolled for about one hundred miles. The road or trail taken by the rollers often follows the high ground to avoid soaking the casks which could damage the tobacco.

1760 ■ American slaves roll hogheads of tobacco on the Tobacco-Rolling Road in Virginia.

c. 1760 As England increases its foreign trade, the importance of an efficient transportation system for its interior (away from its seaports) becomes apparent. Economist Adam Smith (1723—1790) states, "Good roads, canals and navigable rivers, by diminishing the expense of carriage, put the remote parts of the country nearly on a level with these in the neighborhood of a town…"

1760 First book in English treating bridge design and construction is published in London, England. Written by English architect, Stephen Riou, it is titled *Short Principles for the Architecture of Stone Bridges.*

1760 A.D.

First known roller skates

1760 First roller skates are attributed to Belgian instrument-maker Joseph Merlin, who wears them while playing a violin. In 1823, Englishman Robert J. Tyers patents a pair with five small wheels arranged in a line. These are similar to today's rollerblades which simulate an ice-skating stroke. In 1863, the traditional four-wheel skates are introduced by American James L. Plimpton. (See 1863)

1761 First pile-trestle bridge in colonial America is Sewall's Bridge built in York, Maine. This well-documented bridge built by Samuel Sewall across the York River is 270 feet long and 25 feet wide. Tree trunks are driven deep as piles which support the trestles or wooden legs.

1761 Lighthouse made of masonry is built at the rocky entrance to New London by the Colony of Connecticut. It is 64 feet high and has a diameter of 24 ftee. Its light consists of three lamps which require annually 800 gallons of "strained Sperm Ceti Oil."

1761 June 7 English engineer John Rennie (1761—1821) is born in Phantassie, Scotland. His best known works are two masonry bridges, the Waterloo Bridge (1817) and the new London Bridge (1831). The latter replaces the Colechurch bridge and is 690 feet (210 meters) long with five semi-elliptical arches and narrow piers. Rennie also builds canals, docks, harbors, and coastal facilities.

1762 American engineer James Finley (1762—1828) is born in Philadelphia, Pennsylvania. He builds the first metal suspension bridge in the United States. This 1801 bridge across Jacob's Creek on the road between Uniontown and Greensburgh, is 70 feet (21 meters) long, 12½ feet (3.8 meters) wide with a wooden deck supported by iron chains suspended from two towers. It collapses in 1825.

1763 Boston Post Road is begun. Completed in 1792, it connects Boston and New York. When the impoverished new nation is unable to build new roads via taxes, the solution is found in turnpike companies chartered by the State and financed and operated by private citizens. The Boston Post Road is the most famous of these, but the earliest one completed was the Little River Turnpike, in Virginia, authorized in 1785.

1763 Modern era of ship navigation begins when British instrument maker John Harrison (1693—1776) sends his "marine chronometer" off on a sea voyage to Barbados to be tested. Longitude at sea could be determined if a sailor had a clock that would run accurately at sea, for he could keep it at Greenwich, England time, calculate the difference between it and local time, and astronomically establish his longitude. Such a clock seemed impossible until Harrison. His ingenious device proved not only able to withstand the sway of the ship, but to compensate for changes in temperature as well. He eventually receives the £20,000 reward offered by the British government to the inventor of such an important instrument.

1763 American William Henry builds a paddle boat powered by a Watts-type steam engine. It does not work very well.

1764 Melchior Bauer (b. 1733) designs but does not try to fly an airplane consisting of a four-wheeled car for the pilot attached to a large fixed-wing above. It is to be manually propelled by means of a rocking system of flappers.

1764 Founder of modern road technology, French civil engineer Pierre-Marie-Jerome Tresaguet (1716—1794) becomes engineer of bridges and roads at Limoges. He later becomes inspector general of roads and bridges of France and replaces the thick Roman road design with an original and economical design based on two principles: a firm, well-drained foundation, and a surface impervious to water. His roads have three layers. The foundation is of large, heavy stones set on a cambered (arched or curved) footing. Above this comes the "base course" of somewhat smaller stones. Finally, the surface is composed of small graded stones and the entire road is held in place by strong curbstones on either side. Aside from his actual technical achievements, Tresaguet is credited with first introducing the notion that road building is susceptible to the methods of experimental science.

1764 June 11 Oldest original lighthouse still standing and in use in the United States, the Sandy Hook Lighthouse in New Jersey, begins operations. This 103-foot-high tower has a seven-foot-high lantern and seven-foot thick walls. Its builders strive to make it the best on the continent.

1765 England's first road engineer, John Metcalf (1717—1810), applies the same methods originated by Frenchman Pierre-Marie-Jerome Tresaguet (1716—1794) to three miles of road between Harrowgate and Boroughbridge. Although blind, Metcalf builds such

good roads he is given other contracts and eventually builds 180 miles of roads in Yorkshire.

1765 November 14 American inventor Robert Fulton (1765—1815) is born in Little Britain (now Fulton), Pennsylvania. Beginning as a gunsmith and portrait painter, Fulton turns to designing ships, submarines, torpedoes, and canals. His paddle-wheel *Clermont* becomes the first commercially-successful steam-powered vessel. It is Fulton who makes steamships run profitably and who eventually transforms navigation at sea.

1766 Henry Cavendish (1731—1810), British physicist and chemist, discovers an inflammable gas produced by the action of acids on metals which 20 years later is named hydrogen by Antoine Lavoisier. Cavendish finds this new gas unusually light with only one fourteenth the density of air. In 1793, he and James Watt discover simultaneously the composition of water and show how it may be decomposed to produce hydrogen. Once hydrogen can be produced quickly and easily for balloons, its advantages in sustaining flight are realized to be far greater than hot-air, and after the Montgolfiers, hydrogen balloons become the preferred choice.

1766 ■ "Flying Machine" stage wagon makes passenger runs between Philadelphia and New York.

1766 Scottish engineer James Watt (1736—1819) greatly improves the efficiency of the steam engine by building a separate condensor. This keeps the cylinder at a steady high temperature. He patents this in 1769 and later invents the first double-acting steam engine and several other steam engine refinements. A reliable power source for locomotion is now available.

1765
Nov. 14

Robert Fulton born

1766 A.D.

Hydrogen discovered

1766 First canal tunnel in England, the Harecastle Tunnel on the Trent and Mersey Canal (first known as the Grand Trunk Canal), is begun. It is built by James Brindley (1716—1772) and is over a mile-and- a-half long when finished in 1777.

1767 Cast iron bars are used on top of wooden rails in Coalbrookdale, England to protect the rails from wear.

1767 Cape Henlopen Lighthouse, on the south side of the entrance to Delaware Bay, is completed. It is put out of action during the Revolutionary War, but repaired in 1784. In 1926 it is destroyed in a storm.

1767 May 30 Construction begins on the Charleston Lighthouse on Morris Island, South Carolina. This stone tower is the first built in the south.

1768 In France, Alexis J. Paucton (1732—1798) suggests in his book, *Theorie de la Vis Archimede*, a man-carrying and man-powered helicopter with two helical-screws or propellers. Although this is never built by him, it ranks as the first suggestion of horizontal or sideways propulsion using an airscrew or propeller.

1768 British naval architect Frederik Chapman (1721—1808) publishes his treatise on ship-building, *Architectura navalis mercatoria*. It is Chapman who pioneers a more scientific approach to ship construction, as he is the first to use scale models of new ship designs. He tests their performance in a specially-built tank.

1768 Earliest documented evidence of a design for an iceboat is published in the book *Architectura Navalis Mercatoria* by Swede Frederik H. Chapman (1721—1808). This design shows a typical sailboat with a cross plank under the hull near the bow, a runner at each end, and a sharp iron shoe or blade at the stern (rear) on the bottom of what would be the rudder. (See 1790)

1768 Plymouth Lighthouse is built on Gurnet Point in Plymouth, Massachusetts. It is distinguished from other American lighthouses by its unique system of double, horizontal lights.

1769 With the founding of a Spanish mission at San Diego de Alcala, the most southerly of 21 missions and forts is built along a 700-mile route paralleling the Pacific Coast. Stretching from Sonoma, just above today's San Francisco, to San Diego, this revered California road, which the Franciscans walk on foot, becomes known as "El Camino Real of the Padres."

1769 First self-propelled vehicle is designed by Nicholas-Joseph Cugnot (1725—1804) whose steam-fueled car or truck is built for transporting the French Army's cannons. Commissioned by the minister of war and built at the Paris Arsenal, this huge, three-wheeled vehicle is able to go about 2.5 mph (4 km/h) but has to stop every 15 minutes for its boiler to be refilled. It is the first such vehicle built for actual, practical use and not for experimentation, although it proves nearly impossible to steer.

1769 April 25 Engineer Marc I. Brunel (1769—1849) is born in Hacqueville, France. A prolific inventor who worked both in the United States and England, Brunel patented in 1818 the tunnelling shield which solved the historic problem of underwater tunnelling. His 1843 tunnel under the Thames River is a major engineering accomplishment.

1770 October 10 American engineer Benjamin Wright (1770—1842) is born in Wethersfield, Connecticut. Wright is chief engineer, along with surveyor James Geddes, in the construction of the Erie Canal—America's first major engineering project. He works on other American canals and uses his expertise in overland construction and as a surveyor to become one of the country's first railroad engineers.

1771 Nicholas-Joseph Cugnot (1725—1804) builds his second full-size steam vehicle. It is designed to carry as much as four to five tons. It is said to have run into a low stone wall during one of its trials and is thus involved in the world's first motor car accident. When the French government loses interest in the project, Cugnot puts it aside.

1771 Portsmouth Harbor Lighthouse is built at Fort William and Mary on the point in Newcastle, New Hampshire.

1771 April 13 British engineer Richard Trevithick (1771—1833) is born in Illogan, Cornwall. Having designed a high pressure steam engine that was simpler, cheaper, lighter, and more efficient than James Watt's low-pressure engines, Trevithick applied his engine to move a steam carriage in 1801, and has a strong claim as the inventor of the modern railroad engine. He left England for Peru in 1816 to work as a mining engineer and returned penniless in 1827. He was an inventive genius whose output of new ideas outpaced his ability to see them through.

1772 Canon Pierre Desforges (born c. 1723) builds his winged "voiture volante" in Estampes, France. It consists of a wicker gondola with manually operated flapping wings and an overhead cloth canopy. This device is launched from the 100-foot Tour Guinette at Estampes, and falls directly to the ground. He suffers only minor injuries.

1772 American statesman and scientist Benjamin Franklin (1706—1790) outlines his plans for an eastern U.S. canal system. Writing to the mayor of Philadelphia about his plans, he says, "Rivers are ungovernable things, especially in Hilly Countries...," but "canals are quiet and very manageable."

1772 Frenchman named Freminet attempts unsuccessfully to design and test a self-contained underwater breathing device.

1772 May 20 Military rocket pioneer William Congreve (1772—1828) is born in London, England. An artillery officer in the British army, Congreve made improvements to the design of black-powder rockets and helped stabilize them for use as effective military weapons. He based his rockets on those used by India against the British in 1792 and 1799 at Seringapatam. His rockets were used by the British in Europe and America, and his work stimulated many other European countries to form rocket corps.

1773 December 27 George Cayley (1773—1857) is born in Scarborough, Yorkshire, England. Pioneer of early aviation regarded by many as the father of flight. After studying birds, he discarded the notion of movable wings and turned to what would become the modern airplane by designing fixed wings, a fuselage, and a tail unit with rudders for control. He also founded the science of aerodynamics. His glider took his coachman on the first manned glider flight in 1853. Among his several correct predictions are the internal combustion engine which he said would power airplanes someday. A true theoretical genius far ahead of his time.

1774 Pont de Neuilly is completed across the Seine north of Paris, France. Built by French civil engineer Jean Rudolphe Perronet (1708—1794), this stone arch bridge embodies his revolutionary discovery that the sideways thrust of a series of elliptical (flat) arches is passed along to the abutments at the ends of the bridge. This enables him to design the stone arch in its ultimate, very flat, form and to make the supporting piers very slender. His five elliptical arches spanning a total of 766 feet are supported by piers only 3.9 meters wide (taking up less than one ninth of the width of the river). If typical Roman arches are used, they would take up one quarter the width. Perronet's revolutionary design stands the test of time, and is replaced in 1956 by a larger, modern bridge.

1774 June English wheelwright named Day disappears in his submersible boat in 100 feet of water at Plymouth harbor. Having been successful staying below in his craft at a depth of 30 feet, Day is unaware of the extreme difference in pressure at 100 feet, and neither he nor his wooden submersible is ever seen again.

1775 From this date on, especially in large English towns, roads are good enough to maintain a thriving coach business. The average life of the poor stage horse, however, is only six years.

1775 Frenchman Guillaume de La Follie (c. 1733—1780) publishes *Le philosophe sans Pretention (The Unassuming Philosopher)*, which hints at the modern science fiction novel in its use of realistic means of propulsion through space. La Follie has a traveller from Mercury arrive on earth who uses an electrically-powered chariot to fly through space. La Follie's work reflects recent advances in electrical knowledge.

1775 March 10 American frontiersman Daniel Boone (1734—1820) departs from Watauga, Tennessee with a group of well-armed men and blazes a trail that becomes known as the Wilderness Road. On April 1, he begins erecting a fort at what will become Boonesborough, Kentucky. By 1790, over 90 percent of Kentucky's population of 75,000 had used this road to get there.

1775 March 10 Daniel Boone blazes a trail

1776 Joseph Priestley's (1733—1804) book, *Experiments on Different Kinds of Air* (1774), is first translated into French. It is read by Joseph-Michel Montgolfier who is inspired to begin experiments with various gases and the properties of heated air.

1776 A "flying coach" pulled by horses covers the distance from London, England to Edinburgh, Scotland in four days.

1776 George Washington (1732—1799), commander of American forces in the Revolutionary War, orders General Israel Putnam (1718—1790) to build a floating bridge across the Schuylkill River in case he has to evacuate his position in New Jersey. The bridge is built but never needed because of the Continental Army's victory at Trenton.

1776 September 7

First operational submarine used

1776 September 7 First operational submarine is operated by American Ezra Lee under New York Harbor. Invented by American David Bushnell (1742—1824), this unique turtle-shaped vessel is intended to be propelled under water by an operator who hand-turns its propeller. The *Turtle* is made of oak and covered with tar, and submerges by taking on water. The air supply lasts about 30 minutes, and it surfaces by pumping out the water. Lee tries to screw a mine into the hull of a British man-of-war, but cannot do it. Despite this failure, General George Washington (1732—1799) gives Bushnell a revolutionary wartime commission in the engineers.

1776 October

First U.S. naval action takes place

1776 October First naval action by the newly-formed United States of America takes place on Lake Champlain. A makeshift fleet put together and commanded by American Benedict Arnold (1741—1801) is defeated by British General Guy Carleton (1724—1808).

1777 First cast iron bridge opens in Coalbrookdale, England. Built by two English ironmasters, Abraham Darby III (1750—1791) and John Wilkinson (1728—1808), this bridge crossing the Severn River consists of a single 140-foot semicircular arch made up of five arched ribs. Just as stone replaced wood in bridge construction, iron will replace stone as both a stronger and more adaptable material. This historic bridge still stands today.

1777 Eighteen-mile long canal, called Tolly's Nullah, opens in Calcutta, India. It becomes part of the Calcutta and Eastern Canals, a system of navigable channels stretching about 1,130 miles.

1777 Grand Trunk Canal in England is completed. Known later as the Trent and Mersey Canal, it provides the first east-west waterway connection across England and makes possible the export of British goods to European markets.

1777 May 20 First iron boat, an unnamed pleasure craft, is launched on the River Foss in Yorkshire, England. Apart from the facts that it can hold 15 passengers and is light enough to be carried by two men, nothing is known of its builder. The known facts are recorded in an issue of the journal *Gentleman's Magazine*. (See July 6, 1787)

1778 Railway is introduced by Englishman William Wilkinson (c. 1744—1808), who builds a line at Indret on the Loire River to serve a munitions factory.

1778 January 20 English explorer and navigator James Cook (1728—1779) first lands at Waimea, Kauai Island, Hawaii and sees natives using several forms of surfboards. He observes surfboards of all shapes and sizes, which they ride prone, kneeling, and even standing up. This is evidence of an ancient surfing tradition in the Pacific that may date as far back as three or four thousand years. Surfing is called "he'e nalu" by the Hawaiians, which means literally, "wave sliding." Cook also witnessed Tahitians surfing the year before.

c. 1780 Indian ruler Hyder Ali, prince of Mysore (c. 1722—1782), uses iron-cased rockets with ten-foot (three-meter) balancing sticks against British East India troops. His rockets weigh 6 to 12 pounds (2.7 to 5.4 kilograms) and travel up to 1½ miles (2.4 kilograms). (See 1792)

1781 Tiberius Cavallo (1749—1809), Italian scientist living in England, first demonstrates the lifting properties of hydrogen gas as he fills soap bubbles with hydrogen and releases them. Later experiments attempting to fly bladders filled with hydrogen are not successful.

1781 Jean-Pierre Blanchard (1753—1809), builds his full-size "vaisseau volant" in Saint Germain, France. It looks like a huge, tented houseboat, and is to be lifted and propelled by manually operated flappers on rods. It does not leave the ground.

1781 Karl Friedrich Meerwein (1737—1810), architect to the Prince of Baden, tests in Gliessen, Germany what could be called a glider-ornithopter. Calculating that 126 square feet of wing surface would keep him aloft, he apparently makes a short glide, probably with some flapping. Meerwein lies face down beneath the aircraft's wings, as the Wright Brothers later would do in their glider experiments. He describes his work in his 1784 pamphlet *L'Art de Voler à la Maniere des Oiseaux*.

1781 February 15 First revolving lighthouse light is installed by Swede Jonas Norberg (1711—1783) in the Carlsten Lighthouse near Marstrand in Sweden. It emits flashes at regular intervals using an arrangement of oil lamps and reflectors attached to a vertical axis and rotated by clockwork. Its system of giving strong and weak flashes at regular intervals proves to be more noticeable for ships at sea than a steady strong flash. Revolving lights will become standard.

1781 June 9 British engineer George Stephenson (1781—1848) is born in Wylam, Northumberland. The self-educated Stephenson is generally credited with establishing the steam railroad which dominated inland transportation for almost a century. He built the first practical steam locomotive, the first general freight and passenger railroad, and, with his son, designed many tracks and bridges for his trains.

1782 Lighthouse illumination is revolutionized as Swiss inventor Aimé Argand (1755—1803) builds an oil lamp whose circular wick and glass chimney give a brilliant flame. Combined with the parabolic reflectors coming into use—hundreds of mirror fragments set in a curved plaster of Paris mould—lighthouses can now produce a beam of very high intensity from a relatively small light source.

1782 November After observing that warmed or hot air rises, Joseph-Michel Montgolfier (1740—1810) in Avignon, France, devises a means of inflating a silk container by holding it over a fire. He then makes a small, three-to-four cubic foot (0.08-to-0.1-cubic meter), oblong-shaped balloon that ascends after he inflates and releases it. He notifies his brother Etienne in Annonay, and together they work on building a large balloon.

1783 Sebastian Lenormand, a French physician, experiments with a parachute in Montpelier, France, by jumping from a tree with two parasols. Later in the year, he descends from the tower of the Montpelier Observatory using a conical parachute 14 feet in diameter.

1783 Scottish engineer James Watt (1736—1819) tests a working horse and decides it can raise a 150-pound weight about four feet a second. He thus translates

1783 ■ 18th-century French print satirizes "tower jumpers."

"horsepower" into a standard of 550 foot-pounds per second. This unit of measurement is still in use today. In the metric system, this unit is named for Watt, and one horsepower equals 746 watts.

1783 Early steam-propelled boat is a large clinker-built vessel built by the Marquis Claude de Jouffroy d'Abbans (1751—1832) of France. The engine of his steamboat, the *Pyroscaphe*, turns a pair of small paddle wheels. His boat moves on the River Saone for about 15 minutes before breaking down.

1783 June 4 In Annonay France, the Montgolfier brothers, Joseph-Michel (1740—1810) and Jacques-Etienne (1745—1799), give the first public demonstration of their hot-air balloon by sending up a large model made of linen lined with paper. The balloon is 30 feet (nine meters) in diameter when inflated and open at the bottom so it can be filled with hot air from a ground fire. It rises about 6,000 feet (2,000 meters) and stays up for 10 minutes. The brothers use the lifting power of air, but have no idea why it happens (that hot air expands and becomes lighter in density).

1783 June 4

First hot-air balloon demonstrated

1783 August 27 The French government issues a proclamation to its citizens "On the Ascent of Balloons or Globes in the Air, so that alarm be not occasioned to the people." It announces the earlier Montgolfier flight and tells the people that, "Anyone who shall see in the sky such a globe ... should be aware that, far from being an alarming phenomenon, it is only a machine that cannot possibly cause any harm, and which will some day prove useful to the wants of society."

1783 August 27 French physics professor Jacques-Alexandre-Cesar Charles (1746—1823) sends up from the Champ de Mars in Paris a small (13 feet in diameter) balloon filled with hydrogen gas (which is lighter than air) rather than hot air. He solves the Montgolfiers' problem of air leaking out with the help of Charles (c. 1760—1820) and M. N. Robert (1758—1820), who coat the silk bag with a kind of varnish or elastic gum. It flies free as high as 3,000 feet (c. 1,000 meters) for 15 miles (c. 24 kilometers) to Gonesse where terrified farmers attack and destroy it. This type of hydrogen balloon, which is closed at the bottom to contain the gas, becomes known as a "Charliere."

1783 ■ J. A. C. Charles and the first hydrogen balloon.

1783 September 19 In Versailles, France, before the court of King Louis XVI, the Montgolfiers send up their hot-air balloon carrying a sheep, a rooster, and a duck in a wicker basket hung below. This is the first aerial voyage of living creatures in history. They float free for about eight minutes and land safely about two miles (three kilometers) away. These early flights are short, since the air in the balloon is not kept hot and the balloon slowly descends as the air cools.

1783 October Joseph-Michel Montgolfier (1740—1810) first suggests the idea of a jet-propelled balloon. From the beginning, balloonists are concerned with trying to steer or guide a balloon, and Montgolfier believes rightly that if hot-air were expelled it would move the balloon.

1783 October 15 First man to ascend in a tethered balloon is French scientist Jean François Pilatre de Rozier (1756—1785). His hot-air Montgolfier balloon ascends to 84 feet (26 meters)—the length of the rope. Because of unknown dangers, the honor of being the first human to ascend nearly goes to two criminals, as proposed by King Louis XVI. But Pilatre de Rozier argues successfully that such men do not deserve this glory, and he volunteers instead.

1783 November 21 The first free or untethered human flight takes place when the young scientist Jean François Pilatre de Rozier (1756—1785) and the Marquis François Laurent d'Arlandes (1742—1809) fly as high as 500 feet and travel five miles (8 kilometers), floating for about 25 minutes across Paris in a large, brightly-painted Montgolfier hot-air balloon. Benjamin Franklin (1706-1790) is among the spectators, and he later writes of the balloon as a momentous new invention.

1783 December 1 J. A. C. Charles (1746—1823) and one of the Robert brothers make the first manned trip in a hydrogen balloon, going 27 miles (c. 43 kilometers) from Paris to Nesle, France. A crowd of 400,000 watch them leave from the Tuileries Gardens. After landing, Charles goes up again by himself, achieving the first solo balloon flight. But when the balloon shoots up to over 9,000 feet, Charles becomes so terrified that he never flies again. Modern ballooning derives many of its features from Charles, who fits his balloon with a valve, a suspended basket or car, ballast or weight for stability and control, and a barometer to act as an altimeter (to determine altitude).

1784 Englishman John Palmer suggests to the postmaster-general that the mail be carried on the regular stagecoach runs instead of by boys on horses. On August 2, 1784, a passenger coach takes the mail from Bristol to London, beginning what eventually becomes a routine, regular mail service in England.

1784 William Murdock (1754—1839), Scottish inventor and an associate of James Watt (1736—1819), builds a small, three-wheel, non-passenger-carrying steam-powered wagon which he tests successfully but which gets away from him after dark and terrifies the locals.

1784 Whaling is established in Nova Scotia as several families loyal to the British Crown leave the United States and settle in Halifax. Within a year, they build a fleet of four ships and form a new industry. The Cunard family is one of these, and one of their sons, Samuel Cunard (1787—1865), founds the first regular Atlantic steamship line.

1784 State of Massachusetts builds a wooden lighthouse at Great Point on the northeast extremity of Nantucket Island.

1784 January 19 The largest hot-air balloon ever made, called *Le Flesselle* by the Montgolfier brothers, makes an ascent from Lyons, France with seven aboard. The balloon's capacity is 700,000 cubic feet (c. 23,000 cubic meters) and it goes up to 3,000 feet (1,000 meters). This is the only time one of the Montgolfiers (Joseph-Michel) ever flies in a balloon. Flesselle is the name of the Governor of Lyons.

1784 February 25 The first manned balloon ascent outside of France takes place in Italy, when Paul Andreani (c. 1760—1820) goes up with two brothers, Agostino and Carlo Gerli (c. 1750—c. 1800), in a hot-air, Montgolfier balloon from the grounds of his villa at Moncuco near Milan.

1784 April 28 The airscrew or propeller is revived or re-invented for the model helicopter as a means of forward propulsion by the French scientists Launoy and Bienvenu, who present it to the French Academie des Sciences. It consists of two twin-blade propellers at the top and bottom of a short pole, each rotating in the opposite direction, and operated by a wound bowstring.

It is this device that George Cayley (1773—1857) will copy in 1796 and which will lead eventually to the development of the modern helicopter.

1784 May 20 First women to ascend in a tethered balloon are the Marchioness de Montalembert, the Countess de Montalembert, the Countess de Podenas, and Mademoiselle de Ligarde whose Montgolfier balloon lifts to the length of the restraining rope.

1784 June 4 First woman to make a free balloon flight is Madame Thible of Lyons, who ascends from her city with a man named Fleurant as pilot in the hot-air balloon called *Le Gustave*. Gustave III, King of Sweden, after whom the balloon is named, is among the spectators. Mme. Thible and Fleurant sing opera to each other as they ascend. The balloon lands two miles away.

1784 June 4
First woman flies in balloon

1784 June 24 First manned tethered balloon ascent in the United States is made by 13 year old volunteer, Edward Warren, who flies in American, Peter Carnes's (1749—1794), hot-air balloon in Baltimore, Maryland.

1784 ■ Peter Carnes in the first U.S. balloon flight.

1784 July 7 First manned balloon trip in Austria is made in Vienna by an Austrian, J.G. Stuver, in a hydrogen balloon.

1784 July 11 French priest Abbé Miolan (c. 1760—c. 1820) and engraver Janinet build a hot-air balloon they believe can be propelled by hot-air escaping from their shuttered port-holes around the balloon. They do not realize that the pressure of escaping air will be too little to actually move the balloon in a certain direction. They never can test their idea since the balloon fails to take off and is destroyed by the disappointed crowd.

1784 September 15 First manned balloon trip in England is made by the Italian, Vincenzo Lunardi (1759—1806), secretary to the Neapolitan Ambassador in London. The Prince of Wales watches as Lunardi ascends in a hydrogen balloon from London, taking with him a pigeon, a cat, a dog, and provisions which include a bottle of wine, as well as two oars. He lands once, takes off again, and finally completes his 24-mile (c. 38 kilometers) journey in over two hours.

1784 October 4 First balloon ascent in England by a native Briton is made by an Oxford confectioner, James Sadler (1751—1828), in a hot-air Montgolfier balloon at Oxford.

1784 October 16 Frenchman Jean-Pierre Blanchard (1753—1809) makes the first in-the-air attempt to propel his balloon by means of an airscrew (propeller). Called a "moulinet," it is hand-operated and does not work. Blanchard flies from Chelsea, London, and takes his patron, Dr. John Sheldon, along as a passenger.

1784 November 30 First scientific observations from above the earth are made by Jean-Pierre Blanchard (1753—1809) and his wealthy expatriate American patron, Dr. John Jeffries (1744—1819). They ascend from London in a hydrogen balloon.

1785 A.D.

Dirigible designed

1785 Jean-Baptiste Marie Meusnier (1754—1793), a lieutenant in the French Corps of Military Engineers, designs but does not build what is essentially a modern dirigible airship (or a powered blimp). His remarkably prophetic airship foreshadows many modern features, including its elongated-oval shape, interior balloonet or balloon within a balloon to preserve its shape, a car slung by rigging beneath it, and three propellers. Meusnier cannot get the financial backing to build his dirigible, but his detailed plans inspire those who follow. He is later killed in battle.

1785 January 7 The English Channel is crossed for the first time by air as Jean-Pierre Blanchard (1753—1809) and John Jeffries (1744—1819) fly their hydrogen balloon from Dover, England to a forest near Calais, France. In a nightmarish, two-hour crossing, during which the balloon is at times hitting waves, the men are forced to throw everything they have overboard, to the point where they even discard their pants to lighten the load.

1785 March 26 Parisian aristocrat Sophie la Roche reports that in what she calls "the pilgrimage of the coaches," about 1,800 vehicles take part in the customary drive to the Longchamp convent during Holy Week.

1785 May 9 English engineer Joseph Bramah (1748—1814) takes out a patent for propelling a ship through the water by "a wheel with inclined fans or wings." His design has a propeller under water which is turned by a steam engine. It is not known if he ever builds this system.

1785 June 3 Jean-Pierre Blanchard (1753—1809) experiments with a parachute, releasing a silk parachute 20 feet in diameter loaded with weights over England. Later, he drops dogs attached to parachutes from his balloon.

1785 June 15 First balloon fatalities occur as Jean Francois Pilatre de Rozier (1756—1785) and Pierre-Ange de Romain (d. 1785) are killed near Boulogne while attempting a France-to-England crossing of the Channel. Rozier has built his own version of a combination hydrogen/hot-air balloon (one was atop the other), and 25 minutes after taking off, the balloon catches fire and crashes. Rozier had made history, along with the Marquis d'Arlandes, as the first to fly less than two years before. He is now the first to die.

1785 July 12 First manned balloon ascent in Holland is made by Jean-Pierre Blanchard (1753—1809) at the Hague.

1785 October 3 First manned balloon ascent in Germany is made by Jean-Pierre Blanchard (1753—1809) in Frankfurt-am-Main.

1785 November 20 First manned balloon ascent in Belgium is made by Jean-Pierre Blanchard (1753—1809) in Ghent.

1786 ■ Restored U.S.F. *Constellation* in Baltimore Harbor in 1979.

1786 First national institution formed for specific purpose of lighthouse management, the Board of Trustees, is established in Scotland. After 1798, the board becomes the Commissioners for Northern Lighthouses, and builds several new structures.

1786 Steam-propelled boat is demonstrated before George Washington (1732—1799) by its inventor, James Rumsey (1743—1792). His boat uses the principle that if water is forced out of a vessel's stern at high speed, the reaction will propel the boat forward. (See December 1787)

1786 July First successful American steamboat makes a short trip on the Delaware River. Built by American John Fitch (1743—1798), this small vessel is a barge with a steam engine which operates, through linking beams, six vertical oars or paddles on each side. (See 1787)

1787 Iron flanged (rimmed) rails or "plates" are introduced in England by John Carr. These L-shaped rails are laid on top of wooden planks and eventually replace the cast iron bars.

1787 American inventor Oliver Evans (1755—1819) secures the right to use Maryland roads for a proposed steam carriage. (See October 17, 1789)

1787 American inventor John Fitch (1743—1798) builds an improved version of his steamboat and this 50-foot stern-wheeler makes a run on the Delaware River in Philadelphia, Pennsylvania. (See 1790)

1787 July 6 English engineer John Wilkinson (1728—1808) pioneers the use of iron on ships, as he launches the first of his 70-foot (21.3-meter) long iron barges. Although not made completely of iron, his river barges are used to transport cannons on the Severn River. Wilkinson contributes to many new applications of iron, and it is said he becomes so obsessed with finding new uses for it, that he builds himself an iron coffin.

1787 December First boat powered by a water-jet system makes its first run on the Potomac River. Designed by American inventor James Rumsey (1743—1792), the 18-foot (5.5-meter) boat runs against a current with two tons on board. The system takes in water through brass valve cocks and shoots it out from the stern using steam pressure.

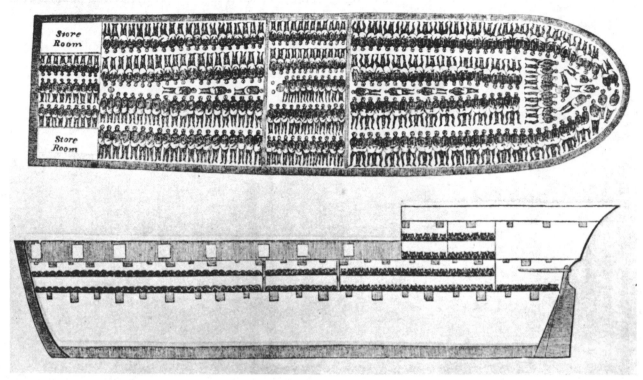

1786 ■ Method of transporting and stowing slaves on British ship *Brookes*.

1788 First use of guiding lights in the United States is made when the State of Massachusetts builds the Newburyport Harbor Lights. These two small lighthouses on Plum Island at the entrance to the Merrimac River are built so that ships that keep the two lights in line (so they appear as one) will pass safely over the Newbury bar.

1788 January 18 Transportation—meaning banishment to a penal colony—begins in Australia with the arrival of the first English convicts. Transportation or deportation has long been a punishment imposed by British law, but with the Americas no longer willing to receive them (the United States being independent), the British send the first 800 convicts to Australia. By 1841, they will have sent 80,000. Free settlers will not be allowed to travel to Australia until 1793.

1789 A.D.

First road map book published

1789 First known book of road maps published in the United States is compiled by Christopher Colles (1738—1816). His book is entitled *A Survey of the Roads of the United States of America.*

1789 The lifeboat is invented following a British design contest for a "life saving boat." After a ves-sel founders on the River Tyne during a storm and its crew dies in plain sight of hundreds of sightseers, the public calls for such a boat. The winning design is offered by Henry Greathead (1757—1816).

1789 April 28 English Capt. William Bligh (1754—1817) and 18 sailors are set adrift in the middle of the Pacific Ocean in a 16-foot (4.9-meter) boat by *Bounty* mutineers. Using his knowledge of the Pacific winds, he is able to bring his small, open craft safely to Timor in the Dutch East Indies—a distance of 3,600 miles (5,793 kilometers) by sea—with seven of his men dead. He returns to England in 1790 and sails on the Pacific again. The drama of one of the most famous mutinies of all time overshadows Captain Bligh's amazing open-boat accomplishment.

1789 August 7 Act of Congress creates the U.S. Lighthouse Establishment as an administrative unit of the federal government. By this act, the new federal government undertakes the upkeep of all lighthouses and other seamarks formerly run by the colonies.

1789 October 17 American inventor Oliver Evans (1755—1819) takes out the first American patent on a self-propelled road vehicle. The patent is issued by the State of Maryland.

1790 In England, a road harrow and drag is invented by John Harriot to smooth roadbeds.

1790 Nathan Read of Massachusetts obtains a patent for a four-wheeled, steam vehicle.

1790 Forth and Clyde Canal in Scotland is completed. This canal was suggested as early as 1724 by the author of *Robinson Crusoe*, Daniel Defoe (1660—1731). It is one of the first canal routes in Europe whose boats offer sleeping accommodations for overnight travel.

1790 First commercial canal in the United States opens. It runs along the James River for seven miles, from Richmond to Westham, Virginia.

1790 First iceboat in America is built by Oliver Booth in Poughkeepsie, New York. His boat is a plain rectangular box with a runner at each corner and a sail attached to a front mast. Booth sails on the frozen Hudson River with his iceboat.

1790 First regular steamboat service begins during the summer as American inventor John Fitch (1743—1798) operates a one-boat line between Pennsylvania and New Jersey. During its brief summer run, his steamboat totals between 2,000 and 3,000 miles, and reaches speeds as high as 7—8 mph. The service does not make a profit however, and Fitch never has a chance to try again.

1791 Lighthouse on Portland Head at the entrance to Portland Harbor, Maine is completed. This 80-foot tower is the first lighthouse built by the new nation, and is the oldest U.S. lighthouse still in operation.

1791 First lighthouse built by the new U.S. Lighthouse Establishment, the octagonal sandstone tower at Cape Henry, Virginia, is lighted. It is 72 feet tall and has eight lamps, each containing eight quarts of oil.

1791 February Earliest statewide transportation plan in U.S. history is drawn up by The Society for Promoting the Improvement of Roads and Inland Navigation of Pennsylvania. Although not adopted by the state legislature, this bold plan proposed a Board of Commissioners be created with power to decide the locations of principal roads and which ones should be improved at public cost. Because of the plan however, the state did allow the granting of charters to private turnpike companies. (See 1795)

1791 October 31 John Barber receives a patent in England for an internal combustion engine that has all the elements of a modern gas turbine. It is not known if he ever builds a workable engine.

1792 Rockets are used by the Indian army of Prince Tippoo Sahib of Mysore (1753—1799) against the British Army in India (Hyder Ali's son). Made of iron casings lashed to bamboo canes and weighing no more than two to three pounds, they terrify the British and produce heavy casualties, but do not win the battle. In 1799, the same Tippoo uses rockets against the British again, but is killed. English artillery expert William Congreve (1772—1828) is now assigned the task of producing a working rocket for the British. (See 1804)

1792 A.D.

India uses military rockets against British army

1792 Earliest definitive history of British canals, *A General History of Inland Navigation, Foreign and Domestic*, by John Phillips, is published in England.

1792 First ambulance is designed by Napoleon's (1769—1821) personal surgeon, Baron Dominique Jean Larrey (1766—1842). His horse-drawn "flying ambulances" are mounted on springs to prevent further injuring the wounded by jarring them over rough ground in carts.

1792 A.D.

Ambulance designed

1792 One of the earliest American wooden truss bridges is reportedly built by Enoch Hale (1753—1837) in Bellows Falls, Vermont. It has a truss arch (a structural form of support based on a triangle) and its two 175-foot spans each rests on an island. It is also possible that a similar truss arch bridge was built even earlier in Norwich, Connecticut by John Bliss. (See 1797)

1792 April 9 State of Pennsylvania incorporates right-hand rule of the road in an Act concerning the construction of the first road between Philadelphia and Lancaster. (See April 9, 1804)

1792 April 9

Right-hand rule of the road enacted

1793 U.S. President George Washington (1732—1799) approves a contract for a floating beacon for the Delaware River at a cost of $264.

1793 January 9 First manned free balloon ascent in America is made by Frenchman Jean-Pierre Blanchard (1753—1809) in Philadelphia. Ascending in a hydrogen balloon from the yard of old Walnut Street Prison, he flies 46 minutes and lands in Gloucester County, New Jersey.

1794 The lack of a good road and the resultant high cost of wagon transportation is a major factor in the Whiskey Rebellion that takes place in eastern Pennsylvania during the early years of U.S. history. Road conditions forced farmers to convert their heavy, bulky grain into the lighter, cheaper-to-carry liquid form of whiskey. Federal troops were later required to put down a rebellion against the excise tax which the government levied on their whiskey output.

1794 A.D.

Ball bearing patented

1794 Patent is granted in England to Philip Vaughn for a radial ball bearing to be used in conjunction with a vehicle axle. Vaughn's specifications are too exacting for the machine tools of his time, and widespread use of ball bearings does not take place until the 1860s, when they become used by bicycle makers. Modern ball bearings are hardened steel balls that roll easily and translate a sliding action into a rolling action.

1794

March 29

French form air force

1794 March 29 First "air force," called the "Aerostiers" or Aerostatic Corps of the Artillery Service, is formed in France.

1794 May 7 English varnish maker Robert Street patents an explosion engine in England. His pumping engine runs on vaporized turpentine and is really a hand-operated, power-assisted water pump in which an explosion throws up the piston and gravity returns it.

1794 June 2 First military use of a balloon is made by J. M. J. Coutelle (1748—1835) and N. J. Conte of the French army's "Aerostiers" at Mauberge, France when they observe enemy positions from their captive balloon. Later, on June 26, aerial reconnaissance is also effectively made against the Austrians at the Battle of Fleurus and again the following year at the seige of Mainz in Germany.

1794 July 15 English inventor William Lyttleton takes out a patent for a screw propeller of three blades which is rotated by hand-power or by a steam engine. It has a copper screw.

1795 First engineered and planned road built in the United States, the privately built toll turnpike

from Philadelphia to Lancaster, Pennsylvania, is completed. Its 62-mile (100 kilometers) length has nine tollgates and costs $465,000. Surfaced with broken stone and gravel, it is the first macadam road in the United States, as well as the best built and most important U.S. road of this time. It is also the first major U.S. road to be built by a chartered turnpike company. This method of allowing a private firm to build a road and then charge tolls for its use is the only way many debt-burdened states can have roads built.

1795 ■ Lancaster Pike becomes the first well-built, long-distance American road.

1795 First rails laid in United States are put down in Boston, Massachusetts for a horse-drawn system. Throughout the United States, a number of horse-powered wooden railways are built for industrial purposes.

1795 Cast iron is used to build the trough of the Pontcysyllte Aqueduct which carries boats on the Ellesmere Canal in Shropshire, England. Designed by British engineer Thomas Telford (1757—1834), the 1,007-foot span has a trough built of wedge-shaped sections which bolt together. The wedges then build up to form arches that rest on masonry piers. The aqueduct opens in 1805 and is still in operation.

1795 November 17 Little Falls Canal on the Mohawk River in New York is opened. It takes two years to build this canal, half of which is cut through solid rock. Five locks carry boats through a fall of 40 feet.

1796 Englishman George Cayley (1773—1857), influenced by the model helicopter made by Launoy

1797 ■ Zane's Trace becomes a popular alternative land trail to the Ohio River.

and Bienvenu in 1784, makes his own model of two bow-string-propelled, opposite-rotating rotors, each composed of corks stuck with four feathers. This idea of a wing held rigid marks a crucial breakaway from the ornithopter concept of flapping, and is a direct influence on all later helicopter development. He later publishes his ideas in 1809.

1796 Englishman named Parker patents a "Roman" true hydraulic cement made from natural cement rock, calcined and ground to powder. The real prototype of modern cement is later produced by Joseph Aspdin (1779—1855). (See 1824)

1796 May 17 U.S. Congress recognizes how heavily traveled the old Indian trail between the Ohio River and Wheeling, West Virginia is, and authorizes that a 226-mile post road be built.

1797 First recorded use of flanged (rimmed or ribbed) wheels in eastern Europe is at the Oraviga Mines in the Banat, Hungary. They are made of wood.

1797 First American patent granted for a bridge design is awarded to American portrait painter Charles Wilson Peale (1741—1827). Although he never builds a bridge, he does publish in this year his book, *An Essay on Building Wooden Bridges*.

1797 Montauk Point Lighthouse, near the edge of a high cliff at the east end of Long Island, New York, is built.

1797 American millwright Timothy Palmer (1751—1821) patents a truss arch bridge design that closely resembles that of 16th century architect Andrea

Palladio (1508—1580). As a self-taught carpenter and architect, Palmer built a bridge over the Merrimack River near Newburyport, Massachusetts in 1792 that becomes the prototype for American truss bridges. The sturdy triangular truss shapes begin to replace the less-stable trestle-type. Palmer goes on to build several important American bridges. (See 1806)

1797 October 22 The modern parachute is born as Andre-Jacques Garnerin (1770—1823) makes the first human parachute descent from the air from a hydrogen balloon in Paris. The parachute is of the ribbed parasol-type with a diameter of nearly 40 feet (12 meters) when fully opened. Garnerin jumps from a height of 2,300 feet (700 meters) and lands safely, although he swings wildly back and forth while descending.

1798 October 16 French showman Pierre Tetu-Brissy achieves the dubious distinction of making the first balloon ascent on horseback. Tetu-Brissy sits on his horse which stands on an oblong platform hung beneath a hydrogen balloon.

1799 First design for a modern airplane or one with rigid or fixed main wings (not flapping), a tail-unit with a rudder (for side-to-side control), and an elevator (for up-and-down control), is made in England by George Cayley (1773—1857).

c. 1799 At the end of the 18th century, 700 miles of canals had been dug in Great Britain, and these canals are linked to rivers that, altogether, give Britain a total of 2,000 miles of navigable waters. This extensive river and canal transport capability will play a major role in the coming-to-be of Britain's Industrial Revolution.

1797 October 22

First parachute descent

1800 English era known as the "Golden Coaching Age" begins and lasts about 30 years. As France is involved with civil warfare, England is entering its own industrial revolution and becoming a wealthy and dominant world power. During these years, it develops an extensive road system, dotted with comfortable inns and teeming with coaches and carriages. Technical improvements on coaches continue.

1800 English engineer George Medhurst (1759—1827) patents an explosive (gunpowder) engine and proposes to apply this to a carriage. Although he builds neither the engine nor the carriage, his drawings represent one of the earliest designs of an internal combustion reciprocating piston crank engine.

1800 First suggestion for a tunnel under the English Channel is made by French engineer Albert Mathieu. His plan is to build one tunnel atop another, with the upper a paved road for horse-drawn vehicles. Oil lamps would serve for lighting. The lower tunnel would be used for drainage. (See 1865)

1800 The staggering size of Britain's shipping power is seen in the number of registered ships in that country. By this first year of the new century, England has 20,983 registered vessels.

1800 Santee Canal in South Carolina is completed. Built by Swedish engineer Christian Senf, it connects the Santee River with the headwaters of the Cooper River which flows into Charleston Harbor. Senf uses slave labor to build this 22-mile-long canal which has 12 locks and 8 aqueducts. It is a major engineering feat for the new country.

c. 1800 Standard British canal vehicle, the "monkey boat," is built by Englishman Thomas Monk (1765—1843). This characteristically narrow boat is only seven feet wide in the beam, but can be as long as 70 feet. They become home to many families, all of whom operate the boat and live on it as well.

1800 September Cayuga trestle bridge, spanning one-and-one-quarter miles over Cayuga Lake in New York, is built. Wide enough to allow three wagons to pass side by side, it costs the Manhattan Company of New York $150,000 to build.

1800 September 28 First fireboat in the United States is stationed on the East River in New York City. Built in England and imported at a price of $4,000, it is a flat-bottom boat with a pointed bow, and is rowed by 12 men. It uses a hand-operated pump.

1800
Sept. 28
First fireboat used in U.S.

1800 December 29 American inventor Charles Goodyear (1800—1860) is born in New Haven, Connecticut. After long experiments seeking to find a way to make rubber strong yet pliable over a range of temperatures, Goodyear got lucky and discovered by accident the process for vulcanizing rubber. Although he is unable to make anything of his business ventures and dies bankrupt and alone, it is his process that eventually makes possible the commercial use of rubber, primarily to make automobile tires.

1801 First passenger-carrying vehicle is the four-wheel steam car built in England by Cornish engineer Richard Trevithick (1771—1833). It carries several people, with a combined weight of over one ton, as the driver sits in front and steers two small front wheels. The passengers ride high and comfortably inside a coach-like body.

1801 First metal suspension bridge in the United States is built by James Finley over Jacob's Creek in Uniontown, Pennsylvania. It is also the first suspension bridge in the world with a rigid, level deck suitable for vehicular traffic. It spans 70 feet (21 meters) and is 12_ feet (3.8 meters) wide. It collapses in 1825.

1801 May 21 First public goods railway line, the Surrey Iron Railway, is incorporated by British Parliament. This horse-operated railway is for freight transport only and not for passengers. It opens for business on July 26, 1803.

1802 A.D.

Catskill Turnpike opens

1802 Catskill Turnpike, a 95-mile U.S. road westward from Catskill, New York to Wattle's Ferry on the Susquehanna River, opens for travel. This route is one of the three main paths connecting New England with the Great Lakes region.

1802 First mechanical ship's log is patented by Englishman Edward Massey. It consists of a small rectangular box containing a rotating wheel. The mechanism is towed astern (at the rear), hauled in and read, and reset at each change of course. A log indicates a ship's speed and distance covered. (See 1878)

1802 A.D.

First propeller- driven boat built

1802 First propeller-driven boat is built by American inventor John Stevens (1749—1838), who fits his 18-foot (5.5-meter) row boat with a high-pressure, multitubular boiler driven by twin-screw propellers. He navigates his boat, the *Little Juliana,* on the Hudson River until 1806.

1802 Although a steamboat is used on the Forth and Clyde Canal in Scotland to pull boats, its use there and elsewhere on canals will be discontinued for fear of damaging the canal's banks. Since they go faster, they necessarily make bigger waves which erode the canal's earthen banks. Modern canals will eventually protect their sides with stone or concrete. (See March 1802)

1802 Patowmack Canal, started in 1785, is completed. Built to improve navigation on the Potomac River, this pioneering enterprise cuts canals around the five main falls of the river, using masonry locks, each 90 feet by 14 feet. Inspired by President George Washington (1732—1799) and built by American James Rumsey

(1743—1792), it opens 220 miles of river to navigation from the tidewater and is the first major river project undertaken by the new nation.

1802 Best navigation book of its time, *The New American Practical Navigator,* by American mathematician and seaman Nathaniel Bowditch (1773—1838), is published. His accurate book on the science of navigation at sea gains international recognition and goes through 60 editions.

1802 March First large, successful steamboat, the *Charlotte Dundas,* makes its first voyage. Built by William Symington (1763—1831) on the River Clyde in Scotland on orders from Lord Dundas, governor of the Forth and Clyde Canal, who wants to replace the horses that tow the barges up and down the canal, this ship tows two 70-ton barges up the river for 19.5 miles (31.4 kilometers) at an average speed of 3.5 mph (5.6 km/h). After making steady runs up and down the river for nearly a month, it is taken out of service because the wash from its paddle wheel damages the banks of the canal.

1802 September 21 The Frenchman Andre-Jacques Garnerin (1770—1823) makes the first parachute descent in England, jumping from a balloon over London.

1803 First steam locomotive is built by Englishman Richard Trevithick (1771—1833), although there is no evidence that it runs at this time. It has a single horizontal cylinder mounted inside the boiler. It has flat wheels designed to run on rails but may have proved too heavy for them. (See February 22, 1804)

1803 Richard Trevithick (1771—1833), in conjunction with his cousin, Andrew Vivian, redesigns and patents his reliable and controllable "Celebrated London Carriage." It is capable of moving 10 mph (16 km/h). Trevithick eventually scraps the car and sells its engine to power a mill after he is unable to interest anyone in investing in it.

1803 Natchez Trace, a U.S. route extending from Nashville, Tennessee to Natchez, the capital of Mississippi Territory, is opened officially by the U.S. government. Having existed first as an Indian trail, it becomes the overland route, through some 460 miles of forest and Indian lands, used by the flatboat crews which floated their goods down the Ohio and Mississippi rivers but could not pole upstream.

1803 Road-building in the U.S. midwest is greatly stimulated by an act that allots it five percent of the net proceeds of the sale of public lands in Ohio. This act takes effect at the time Ohio is granted statehood.

1803 July 31 American engineer John Ericcson (1803—1889) is born in Langban Shyttan in Varmland, Sweden. Designer of the ironclad Union ship, *Monitor*, and pioneer of screw (propeller) propulsion, he is on the forefront of many advanced and innovative ideas concerning ship design and propulsion.

1804 First flight of a model airplane of modern design. George Cayley's (1773—1857) five-foot-long model glider has fixed wings and a tail-unit with stabilizing and control surfaces.

1804 Englishman Obadiah Elliot invents the elliptical spring for horse-drawn coaches. A marked improvement over the C-spring, it does away with suspension devices and straps since it fits directly between the bottom of the coach and the axles. This design change revolutionizes the manufacture of coaches.

1804 Oliver Evans (1755—1819), American mechanic born in Delaware, produces an amphibious steam-powered dredge called the *Orukter Amphibolos*. He drives it one-and-one-half miles (two kilometers) through the streets of Philadelphia and into the Schuylkill River under its own power. More than a self-propelled vehicle, it looks like a flat-bottomed boat with wheels and is a 20-ton working dredge, equipped with chain buckets, digging devices, and paddles to move it through the water. Since he drove this device on land, it is the first powered road vehicle to operate in the United States.

1804 William Congreve (1772—1828) publishes in England *A Concise Account on the Origin and Progress of the Rocket System*. This important book lays down some of the fundamentals of rocket engineering, and stresses the advantages of a rocket, which imparts no dangerous recoil, over a conventional cannon, which does. He says this lack of any recoil means they are especially effective for use on ships.

1804 Largest American canal to date, the Middlesex Canal in Massachusetts, opens. This 27-mile-long canal joins Boston Harbor with the Merrimack River at Lowell. It takes 14 years to complete its 7 aqueducts, 50 bridges, and 20 locks. With its low freight costs and high volume of traffic, it demonstrates the practicality of canal transportation in the new nation.

1804 February 22 English inventor Richard Trevithick (1771—1833) builds a second steam locomotive and demonstrates in a trial run that it can pull a load far heavier than any horse can. His new locomotive pulls 10 tons of iron and 5 wagons carrying 70 men for a distance of 9.5 miles (15 kilometers) at nearly 5 mph (8 km/h). Trevithick's steam locomotive has a single boiler and uses dangerous but powerful high-pressure steam.

1804
February 22

Steam locomotive outpulls horse

1804 ■ Richard Trevithick's locomotive.

1804 April 9 First U.S. state law prescribing right-hand travel for all public highways is passed by the New York State legislature.

1804 June 29 First railway to convey fare-paying passengers is the Oystrermouth Railway in England. It is drawn by horses and later even by sails.

1804 September 16 American engineer and inventor Squire Whipple (1804—1888) is born in Hardwick, Massachusetts. He is not only the first to build an iron bridge using scientific principles, but also publishes the first book to offer a theoretical understanding of bridge construction. His book, *A Work on Bridge Building*, is first published in 1847. Seven of his bridges survive today.

1805 First discovery that a slightly curved wing gives better lift and stability is made in England by George Cayley (1773—1857), who incorporates his findings in a model.

1805 A third steam locomotive is built according to Richard Trevithick's (1771—1833) design, but at five tons it weighs too much for the rails. It is the first locomotiive to have flanged (rimmed or ribbed) wheels.

1805 William Congreve (1772—1828) builds a practical war rocket at the Woolwich Arsenal in London and is officially encouraged to continue. After a year's work, he produces a six-pound (2.7 kilogram) rocket payload that can travel about 6,000 feet (1,830 meters). This is twice as far as Indian rockets.

**1805
October 21**

**Battle of
Trafalgar
fought**

1805 October 21 Last large-scale battle fought completely under sail is the Battle of Trafalgar. British admiral Horatio Nelson (1758—1805) defeats the combined French-Spanish fleet, smashing French naval power and establishing England as ruler of the seas for the next century. Nelson dies by a sharpshooter's musket ball as the victory is completed.

1806 Isaac de Rivaz (1752—1828) of Saint Gingolph, Switzerland builds the first vehicle powered by an internal combustion engine. His four-wheel wagon has a single, vertical cylinder that is powered by hydrogen carried in a tank over the rear wheels. De Rivaz reasons correctly that a controlled explosion inside an open-top cylinder would power the vehicle's axles, and his car does run slowly although it stalls frequently. He builds a similar, improved version in 1813.

1806 Beaufort Scale is proposed by British Commander Francis Beaufort (1774—1857). Used to measure wind intensity, this scale (from 0 to 12) makes possible the standardization of sailing records. It is adopted by all navies in 1854 and by the international meteorological community in 1874. (See 1921)

1806 A.D.

**First
American
covered
bridge built**

1806 First major American covered bridge is Timothy Palmer's (1751—1821) Permanent Bridge over the Schuykill River in Philadelphia, Pennsylvania. Palmer's 550-foot, three-arch bridge uses his now-popular trussed arches (a structural form of support based on a triangle). Following a suggestion by Judge Richard Peters (1744—1828) that a covering would make the bridge even more permanent, Palmer not only covers the bridge but

adds siding as well, completely enclosing the bridge. It is destroyed by fire in 1875.

1806 January 30 Trenton Bridge, a large covered bridge spanning the Delaware River, opens to traffic. The five-ribbed, wooden-truss arch bridge becomes the funnel through which east coast traffic can connect Brunswick, Maine to Savannah, Georgia.

1806 March 29 U.S. President Thomas Jefferson (1743—1826) approves a Congressional act that directs him to appoint three commissioners to lay out and build a road from the head of navigation on the Potomac River at Cumberland, Maryland to a point on the Ohio River. Although resisted by the seaport cities who thought that a government-financed road might hurt their interests in competing for the western trade, those who saw the need to strengthen and unify the country east-to-west prevailed. (See 1818)

1806 April 9 Isambard K. Brunel (1806—1859), British engineer and son of Marc I. Brunel, is born in Portsmouth. Beginning his training as a teenager with his father who was building the Thames Tunnel, Brunel later designs the *Great Western*, the first steamship to make regular Atlantic crossings, as well as the vessel that laid the Atlantic telegraph cable of 1866. Early in his career he worked on railroads, bridges, and tunnels.

1806 June 12 American engineer John Roebling (1806—1869) is born in Muhlhausen, Prussia (now Germany). One of the few real genius bridge builders, Roebling develops and makes the steel-wire cable that makes long-span suspension bridges possible. His major projects include the Niagara Falls suspension bridge and the Brooklyn Bridge crossing New York City's East River. He dies while supervising the Brooklyn Bridge and his son finishes the project.

1806 October 8 First modern European rockets are used in wartime, as the British Navy fires Congreve rockets against the French in the city of Boulogne. Each 32-pound, iron-case rocket is attached to a 15-foot guiding stick and has a range of 3,000 yards. Over 2,000 rockets bombard the French in about half an hour. Modern rocketry begins.

1807 American Silas Whitney operates a horse-drawn and gravity wooden tramway on Beacon Hill in Boston, Massachusetts.

1807 August First practical, rĕliable steamboat begins trials on the Hudson River. Built by American inventor Robert Fulton (1765—1815), the 150-foot *Clermont* steams from New York to Albany in 32 hours, compared to the four days required by a sailing sloop. The steam engine has a single vertical cylinder which, through cranks and gears, drives two 15-foot (4.6-meter) paddlewheels, one on each side of the hull. Commercial trips start in September, and prove so successful that Fulton builds another steamboat.

1807 August 4 First night ascent in a balloon is made by Andre-Jacques Garnerin (1770—1823) in Paris, France.

1807 September 2—5 The city of Copenhagen, Denmark is partially destroyed as waves of Congreve rockets fired by the British Navy put the city aflame. The siege of Copenhagen proves conclusively that the rocket is a valuable military weapon.

1808 Following the rocket attack on Copenhagen, Denmark by the British, the Royal Danish Academy of Science and Letters calls for the scientific study of the mathematical principles involved in rocketry, as well as a study of propellant.

1808 Underwater salvage work is described in detail by C. Antoine Brize-Fradin (b. 1767) in his book, *La chimie pneumatique appliquée aux travaux sous l'eau*. Brize-Fradin adapts the diving bell ideas of Edmund Halley (1656—1742) and also invents a backpack system that can be considered an early version of the modern aqualung.

1808 April 4 Albert Gallatin (1761—1849), U.S. Secretary of the Treasury, presents a report to the Senate "respecting roads and canals." After making the first national inventory of transportation resources, it urges the federal government to finance a national transportation system of roads and canals, arguing that "No other single operation, within the power of the Government, can more effectually tend to strengthen and perpetuate that union…" The report becomes the model for later national transportation policies.

1808 October British inventor Richard Trevithick (1771—1833) creates a sensation in London when he operates a small, eight-ton locomotive, called *Catch Me Who Can*, on a circular iron track built behind a high fence.

For one shilling, the public is able to watch or ride at 12 mph. His machine suffers a derailment and Trevithick gives up his steam rail idea, not having funds for repairs.

1809 Jacob Degen (1756—1848), a Swiss clockmaker, tests in Vienna, Austria a wing-flapping device (ornithopter) supported aloft by a balloon. His exploits are widely reported in the press and read in England by George Cayley (1773—1857) who thought that Degen might have flown using his own muscle power. Degen's adventures are the direct inspiration for Cayley to publish his classic triple paper, *On Aerial Navigation*.

1809 First steamboat in British North America is built in Montreal for Canadian merchant John Molson (1764—1836). Called the *Accomodation*, it uses its 6-hp engine to make its first trip to Quebec. In the next few years, Molson launches several new and larger steamboats on the Montreal-to-Quebec St. Lawrence River line. In 1826, Canadian John Torrance forms a company that builds powerful steamboats and challenges Molson's line. Other companies are soon formed and steamboat travel on the St. Lawrence becomes commonplace.

1809 First steamboat used at sea is built by American inventor John Stevens (1749—1838). His 100-foot (30-meter) steamship, the *Phoenix*, makes a coast-hugging sea voyage.

1809—1810 Englishman George Cayley (1773—1857) publishes a three-part paper, *On Aerial Navigation*, in Nicholson's *Journal of Natural Philosophy, Chemistry and the Arts*, which will lay the foundations of modern aerodynamics. The articles appear in November 1809, February 1810, and March 1810 and suggest many principles and features that will become part of a modern airplane: streamlined design, wheels under the plane to gain take-off speed, and an engine to propel the aircraft.

1809 August 19 First Canadian steamboat, the *Accommodation*, is launched on the St. Lawrence River. Built in Montreal by Canadian brewer John Molson (1763—1836) and his two British partners, John Bruce and John Jackson, it has a single vertical steam cylinder and piston and can carry 20 passengers and a crew of six.

1810 First recorded mono (single-track) railway opens. It is patented by Englishman Henry Palmer and carries freight.

1809—1810 A.D.

Important paper on aerodynamics written

c. 1810 French General and Emperor Napoleon I (1769—1821) writes a letter to his wife, Marie-Louise, in which he mentions a crude elevator or lift. Probably a reference to the "flying chair" invented by a Parisien, Villayer, it consists of a counter-weighted chair attached to a rope, that is free to move up and down in a shaft.

1810 A.D.

French tunnel scares boatmen

1810 Tronquoy Tunnel opens on the St. Quentin Canal in France. As the first wide tunnel in which timber and stone arches are used to prevent the soft ground from collapsing, it so terrifies boatmen that no one will use it. Authorities eventually have to give free canal dues forever to the first boat to go through. Others naturally follow.

1810 St. Quentin Canal in northern France opens. This 58-mile-long canal has a 3.5 mile tunnel and links the North Sea and the Scheldt and Lys systems with the English Channel via the Somme, as well as with Paris and Le Havre via the Oise and Seine rivers.

1810 What may be the oldest existing covered bridges in the United States are built this year. One is the Dellville Bridge, an arch-truss over Sherman's Creek in Wheatfield, Pennsylvania, and the other is the Halpin Bridge over Muddy Brook in Middlebury, Vermont.

1810 September 4 American naval architect Donald MacKay (1810—1880) is born in Nova Scotia. After emigrating to New York in 1827 and working as apprentice to a ship's carpenter, he owns his own shipyard by 1845. There he proceeds to design and build a series of clipper ships that are the fastest of their day. By 1855, the demand for clipper ships is down, and he begins building iron ships.

1811 First steam-powered ferry, the *Juliana*, built by American inventor John Stevens (1749—1838), begins regular service on the Connecticut River.

1811 A.D.

Underwater gear described in book

1811 Underwater gear to be worn by a man is described by Friedrich von Drieberg (1780—1856) in his book, *Memoire sur une nouvelle machine à plonger, appelée Triton*. Drieberg's ingenious device, which he calls "Triton," is strapped to the diver's back and head. His crownlike hat is connected to a set of bellows on his back, which is worked by his head movements. The bellows are connected to his mouth and to tubes which rise to the surface. To operate, the diver moves his head, which sends down air from overhead and which also compresses it so it can be inhaled.

1811 February 1 Bell Rock Lighthouse in Scotland turns on its light for the first time. Designed and built by Scottish engineer Robert Stevenson (1772—1850), this 100-foot-high lighthouse takes five years to build. It is perched atop Inchcape Rock, a sunken reef in the North Sea which lies directly in the shipping track and is submerged by 11 feet of water during high tide. This open-sea lighthouse has a base that is 42 feet wide. It still stands today.

1811 April 10 Englishman John Blenkinsop (1783—1831) obtains a patent for a steam locomotive that is propelled by a toothed wheel engaging a rack on one of the rails. He uses this design believing that a locomotive with smooth wheels cannot get enough traction to move. (See August 12, 1812)

1811 May 31 Joseph Berblinger, a tailor in Ulm, Germany and one of the last of the tower jumpers, attempts to fly or glide in his city using a Degen-type ornithopter, but without the supporting balloon. King Friedrich of Wurttemberg witnesses the event and sees Berblinger crash unhurt into the Danube River.

1811 August 3 American inventor Elisha Graves Otis (1811—1861) is born in Halifax, Vermont. In 1852, Otis invented the first elevator with an adequate safety guard. This device would keep any lift from falling even if the rope or cable holding it were severed. In 1856, the first safety elevator for passenger service was installed in a New York store, and his business began. Otis's elevators were even more important to the development of skyscrapers than structural steel, since such tall buildings would have been impractical if their occupants had no easy and rapid means of going up and down them.

1811 September First steamboat to sail down the Mississippi River is a Fulton-built vessel, the *New Orleans*, owned by American Nicholas J. Roosevelt (1767—1854). The journey experiences a sighted comet, an earthquake, a small fire on-board, Roosevelt's wife giving birth, and the ship's captain marrying Roosevelt's maid when they arrive at Natchez. The ship runs afterwards between New Orleans and Natchez, becoming the first steamboat to go up-river. It is wrecked in 1815.

1812 First armored steam warship is built by American inventor Robert Fulton (1765—1815). This single-paddle wheel steamboat called the *Demologos* is designed to protect New York harbor. Fulton places its single wheel in the middle of the hull where he feels it will be less vulnerable to attack.

1812 First broad contract for the maintenance of lighthouses is made by an Act of the U.S. Congress which authorizes the secretary of the treasury to purchase a patent by Winslow Lewis for a "reflecting and magnifying lantern."

1812 First British passenger steamboat, Scotsman Henry Bell's (1767—1830) *Comet,* inaugurates a successful ferry service between Glasgow, Greenock, and Helensburgh, Scotland. It is smaller than Fulton's boat but it has a better engine. Two years later, Bell is running five ferries on the Thames River in London.

1812 August 12 First commercial use of steam locomotives occurs in England by Matthew Murray. Built by John Blenkinsop (1783—1831), this locomotive's four wheels are propelled by a toothed wheel which engages in a rack on the side of one rail. It weighs about five tons.

1813 English engineer William Hedley (1779—1843) builds a small smooth-wheeled steam locomotive called *Puffing Billy* that makes regular hauling runs on the Wylam Wagonway. This disproves the common notion that smooth wheels could not get traction on the iron track.

1813 Large-scale coach manufacturing in the United States can be traced to the firm of Lewis Downing in Concord, New Hampshire, whose coaches win great fame. Compared to European coaches, they seem inelegant, but they are typically American—practical, light, and durable.

1813 William Moore, an English mathematician at Woolrich Royal Academy, publishes a sophisticated work, *A Treatise on the Motion of Rockets,* which applies Newton's laws of motion to reactive flight and forsees many of the specifics of thrust, propellant, and temperature that will have to be known before rocketry becomes a science. His work, however, is ignored by the European community.

1813 First steam passenger service in Canada begins. The 140-foot (42.7-meter) long *Swiftsure* runs a ferry service on the St. Lawrence River.

1813 June The British Army officially forms the Rocket Brigade. It first goes into action against Napoleon's army at the Battle of Gohrde on September 16, 1813. This is the first modern military rocket unit. Soon Austria, Russia, France, Italy, Sweden, Denmark and other nations add rocket brigades to their inventory of weapons.

1814 British Navy navigator Matthew Flinders (1774—1814) publishes his *Voyage to Terra Australis.* This contains, besides an account of his voyage to Australia, his opinion that compass deviation or error can often be attributed to much of the iron used in the ship itself. Awareness and recognition of compass deviance is important if it is to be corrected.

1814 July 25 Self-taught British engineer George Stephenson (1781—1848) builds his first locomotive which makes its first successful run. He makes improvements on existing designs and goes into business building locomotives. (See September 27, 1825)

1814 July 25
First locomotive built

1814 September 13—14 Francis Scott Key (1779—1843), American lawyer and composer of the U.S. National Anthem, "The Star-Spangled Banner," witnesses the British shelling of Fort McHenry during the War of 1812. His composition immortalizes the spectacle as well as the words "rocket's red glare," which refer to the Congreve rockets fired from the British sloop *Erebus.* Most of the 32-pound rockets fall short of the fort.

1814 Sept. 13—14 "...rocket's red glare..."

1815 M. Bozek of Prague, Czechoslovakia builds a full-size steam vehicle that moves somewhat under its own power, although it ultimately fails due to the "inadequacy of its steam boiler."

1815 February 6 First railroad charter in the United States is granted to John Stevens (1749—1838) of Hoboken by the New Jersey Legislature. It authorizes the construction of a rail line between the Delaware and Raritan rivers, near Trenton and New Brunswick. (See February 1825)

1815 November 21 Washington City Canal, a two-and-one-quarter-mile run from the Potomac River across the city to the Anacostia River, officially opens. In 1833 it is linked to the Chesapeake and Ohio Canal, but it is not profitable enough to pay for its own upkeep. It deteriorates steadily, and by the 1870s, brick sewers are built and it is covered over to form streets. Today's Constitution Avenue, from the foot of Capitol Hill to 17th Street N.W., is built on top of the Tiber Creek portion of the canal.

1816 Englishman George Cayley (1773—1857) publishes his ideas and designs for a streamlined airship that look remarkably like those that would first fly at the turn of the century.

1816 A.D.

New style roads advocated

1816 In England, a committee studying how to improve roads asks the advice of Scottish engineer John Loudon Macadam (1756—1836) and he puts his ideas into a book, *Remarks on the Present System of Road-Making*. Macadam's theories are contrary to existing practice, for he advocates using coarsely cut stones that will bond together by pressure from heavy carriage wheels. The common practice of using small round stones and gravel results in ruts where the wheels force stones out. Macadam's system produces a road that becomes increasingly packed hard by regular use, and is generally adopted.

1816 Thomas Telford (1757—1834), Scottish civil engineer and famed bridge builder, builds the Carlisle-Glasgow road, considered equal in quality to those of John Loudon McAdam (1756—1836), his rival. He places great emphasis on maintaining a level roadway and building a stone surface capable of carrying the heaviest of loads. His roads have two courses or layers.

1816 Entirely new design for river steamers is created by American steamboat captain Henry M. Shreve (1785—1851). His new design has a flat, shallow hull, a high-pressure steam engine placed on the main deck instead of in the hold, and a second deck. His new boat, *Washington*, makes the trip from Pittsburgh to New Orleans and then to Louisville, and establishes the definitive Mississippi River steamboat type.

1816 England begins to manufacture and export steam engines made for ships.

1816 First suspension bridge to use wire cables is built across the Schuykill River at Philadelphia, Pennsylvania. Following the collapse of the rebuilt Schuykill Falls chain bridge on January 17, 1816, the owner of the factory across the river, Josiah White, has an 18-inch-wide suspension bridge quickly built for his workers. One end is anchored to a tree and the other to the factory itself. Workers pay one penny to cross, to pay the $125 construction costs, and go to work directly through a second-story window. It eventually collapses under the weight of a winter snow.

1816—1817 Two Swiss gunsmiths living in London, England, Samuel John Pauly and Durs Egg, make the first serious attempt to build a dirigible (powered) airship. Their ingenious fish-shaped craft is abandoned when Pauly dies. It will later influence Zeppelin in Germany.

1816 February 5 First U.S. State Board of Public Works is created by the Virginia General Assembly. This institutionalizes the state's concern and responsibility for public roads, and other states soon create their own agencies.

1816 March 17 First steamboat to cross the English Channel is the 63-foot (19.2-meter) British steamer, *Majory*. When it makes the trip however, its name is *Elise*, since it had been bought by a French firm. The short trip takes an uncomfortable 17 hours as it fights a stiff southerly gale.

1816 July First steamboat in Sweden, the *Stockholms-Haxan* or the "Witch of Stockholm," conducts its first trials on Lake Malar. Its four-hp engine propels it to a speed of four knots.

1816 August 27 The pirate fleet and base at Algiers are bombarded and destroyed by the British Navy using Congreve rockets.

1817 Forerunner of the bicycle is patented by German Baron Carl von Drais de Sauerbraun (1785—1851). Called a "Laufmaschine" or a "running machine," it is little more than a curved beam set above two wooden wheels. The front wheel is steerable and the vehicle scoots along as the rider pushes off the ground with his feet. The vehicle becomes all the vogue for a while in Paris and London, and is called a "Draisienne" in French and a hobby horse in England. (See 1819)

1817 English inventor Richard Trevithick (1777—1833) begins driving a pilot tunnel under the Thames River in London. After five years of little success—his three-by-five-foot tunnel collapses at 1,000 feet—the project is abandoned but a money prize is offered for a workable plan. (See February 1825)

1817 British House of Commons committee begins investigations into the many steamboat explosions occurring, which result in regulations requiring standards and inspections for engines on ships.

1817 First major lighthouse in Australia is a 76-foot high tower erected at the entrance to Sydney Harbor, then named Port Jackson. Above the tower is a 15-foot-high lantern with a parabolic reflector and oil lamps.

1818 Rudolph Ackermann (d. 1834) patents in England a tangential steering device orginated in Munich by German mechanic George Lankensperger. This system, which prevents the entire vehicle from reacting to every bump in the road, has the front wheels on a rigid axle with pivoted ends. It is the first to use the modern principle of rounding corners.

1818 First tunnel of any kind in the United States is a canal tunnel on the Schuylkill Navigation in Pennsylvania. Built by three brothers named Fudge and completed in 1821, it is 450 feet long, 18 feet high, and 20 feet wide. About 1860, the tunnel's roof is cut through, known as "daylighting" a tunnel. It no longer exists.

1818 French-born engineer Marc Isambard Brunel (1769—1849) invents and patents the first tunnel shield and revolutionizes the way tunnels are dug. Inspired by the teredo—a worm that bores into wood and lines its way with a deposit that makes a hard shell—Brunel describes his device as a casing or cell that can be forced ahead of the work being done. This is the forerunner of the modern circular shield.

1818 Cumberland Gap, also known as the National Pike, opens for traffic between Cumberland, Maryland and Wheeling, West Virginia. By 1838, it is extended to Springfield, Ohio and part of the way to Vandalia, Illinois. It is the first important road to be built with federal funds, costing nearly $7 million over the years.

1818 First lighthouses on the Great Lakes are established in Buffalo, New York, at the junction of Buffalo Creek and Lake Erie, and in Erie, Pennsylvania, on Presque Isle at the entrance of Presque Bay.

1818 September 27 First Italian steamboat is Pietro Andriel's 128-foot- (39-meter-) long *Ferdinando I*. Made of wood and using a British engine, it can accommodate 50 passengers plus another 16 in private cabins.

1818 December 22 Patent is applied for by Denis Johnson of London, England, for what he calls a "pedestrian curricle," but which quickly becomes better known as the "dandy horse" or "hobby horse." It is essentially an improved version of the German Baron Carl von Drais de Sauerbraun's (1785—1851) wooden "running machine"—the precursor of the bicycle—but the patent makes no mention of von Drais de Sauerbraun or his earlier invention.

1818 Dec. 22 "Hobby horse" patent sought

1819 First steamboat with two engines, the British ship *Talbot*, is built. It has one for each of its paddles.

1819 May 22 First steamship to cross the Atlantic Ocean, the *Savannah*, leaves Savannah, Georgia for Liverpool, England. Built as a wooden sailing ship, it has a steam engine added as auxiliary power for use when there is insufficient wind. It arrives in England on June 20, during which time it uses its engine for a total of only 80 hours. When spotted off the coast of Ireland, a ship is sent to its rescue since it was believed to be on fire, but the Irish coastguard cannot catch up with the "burning" vessel.

1819 May 22 First steamship crosses Atlantic

1819 July 6 First woman to die while ballooning is the widow of Jean-Pierre Blanchard, Marie-Madeleine (1780—1819). During her 67th ascent, her hydrogen balloon catches fire at Tivoli Gardens in Paris, and she falls from the car onto a roof below.

1820 General Jackson's Military Road opens for traffic, connecting Nashville, Tennessee with New Orleans, Louisiana. General Andrew Jackson (1767—1845), who later became U.S. president, clears timber for a width of 40 feet throughout the over 500-mile length of road. This road sustains the infant manufacturing industries born in the far south when the British blockaded the seaports during the War of 1812.

1820 English cleric William Cecil (1792—1882) builds an internal combustion engine that uses hydrogen gas. He demonstrates his working engine to the Cambridge Philosophical Society.

1820 First lightship in the United States is stationed in Chesapeake Bay, off Craney Island, at the entrance to the Elizabeth River near Norfolk, Virginia. A lightship is an anchored vessel with a light on it.

1820 First lighthouse on the Mississippi River is built at the mouth of the river on Franks Island.

1820 There are an estimated 250 major lighthouses built and functioning throughout the world at this date.

1820 A.D.

First lighthouse fog bells used

1820 First fog bells are used in a U.S. lighthouse located on West Quoddy Head, Maine.

c. 1820 Earliest functional open underwater helmet is used for underwater salvage operations by brothers Charles and John Deane. It is connected to the surface via an air line and has separate openings for air intake and exhaust.

1820 May 23 American engineer James B. Eads (1820—1887) is born in Lawrenceburg, Indiana. His contributions to boat and bridge-building were many and significant, but his most important was the development of pneumatic caissons. His caissons were submersible chambers filled with compressed air which enabled workmen to sink the foundations of a bridge below the river bottom and onto the supporting bedrock. His St. Louis bridge across the Mississippi River has three steel arches spanning more than 1,500 feet. The bridge, which opened in 1874, still stands and is now named the Eads Bridge.

1821 Julius Griffiths of England patents a steam carriage which is built for him by famous mechanic Joseph Bramah (1748—1814). He builds a large line of passenger-carrying coaches.

1821 A.D.

Steamboat begins first regular run

1821 First steamboat to operate a regular, scheduled run across the English Channel, the *Rob Roy,* begins service. The French are so impressed that they buy the vessel, rename it *Henri Quatre,* and use it to carry mail on the Calais-Dover run.

1821 July Ground is broken for the Lachine Canal on the St. Lawrence River. This first major canal in

Canada is completed in 1825 and runs about 8.5 miles. It has a depth of five feet and contains six locks. Navigation of the river is now extended across Lake St. Louis to the mouth of the Ottawa.

1821 July 19 Coal-gas is first used for inflating balloons by Charles Green (1785—1870) in London, England. This ascent is part of the coronation festivities of George IV. Gas from ordinary coal is not only cheaper than hydrogen and available in most towns, but fills the balloon faster and is less affected by temperature changes, allowing balloons to stay aloft longer.

1821 October 22 First steamship to cross the Atlantic east-to-west, the British *Rising Star,* leaves Gravesend, England. It eventually steams and sails (since its engine is used in an auxiliary manner) down the coast of South America and around Cape Horn, becoming the first steamer to enter the Pacific Ocean. It is not known how much its steam engine is actually used.

1821 December 5 Earliest known fatality in a railroad accident occurs when British carpenter David Brook is walking home in a blinding storm and fails to hear or see a coal train.

1822 The Santa Fe Trail, the first of the pioneer roads connecting the U.S. frontier near the Mississippi River with the far West, begins to be used regularly. Used from earliest times as a trail west, it became a wilderness road and then is gradually widened. Its most dangerous part is the 58-mile stretch of desert, 3,000 feet above sea level, between the ford of the Arkansas River and the lower spring of the Cimarron River, since there is no drinking water available on this parched area.

1822 First all-iron ship's hull is laid on the *Aaron Manby* at Staffordshire, England. The 120-foot (36.6-meter) steamer is built primarily to persuade people that iron-hulled ships will not sink, and this year becomes the first iron-hulled, paddle-steamer to cross the English Channel. It goes between 8 and 9 knots. Ships with iron hulls will become popular in tropical waters, as they prove resistant to the wood-destroying water-beetle.

1822 Pencil-like beam of light ideal for lighthouses is first produced by French physicist Augustin Fresnel (1788—1827), whose work on the nature of light leads

1822 ■ Santa Fe Trail becomes the first road to connect the Mississippi River with the Far West.

to new lenses. His prism system, which replaces the older method of mirrors, results in all light coming from the source being refracted into a horizontal beam. This revolutionizes the effectiveness of lighthouses.

1822 Caledonian Canal across Scotland is first opened. Built by British engineer Thomas Telford (1757-1834), this 60.5-mile-long canal consists of 22 miles of artificial waterways connecting a chain of freshwater lakes. It has 29 locks.

1822 January 12 Belgian-French inventor Jean Joseph Etienne Lenoir (1822—1900) is born in Mussy-la-Ville, Belgium. Self-educated and versatile, he designs and builds in 1860 the first internal combustion engine that works. It runs on coal gas, has three cycles, and overall is not very efficient. He hitches it to an old horse cart in 1862 and slowly drives his horseless carriage through the Vincennes forest near Paris. About 25 years later, such an engine will run on gasoline and the age of the automobile will begin.

1823 First macadam road in the United States is laid over the Boonesborough Turnpike Road between Hagerstown and Boonsboro, Maryland. Construction follows the details given by John Loudon Macadam (1756—1836) in his book. The road is compacted not by use, which would take too much time, but by a two-to-three-ton cast-iron roller. (See 1816)

1823 U.S. Congress passes the Rivers and Harbors Act of 1823. This legislation recognizes that many of the nation's transportation issues and problems are interstate in character and it lays the foundation for national or federal involvement and the expenditure of funds.

1823 First steamship in Holland, the *Nederlander,* enters service.

1823 February First significant federal land grant to a state for the construction of a road is made when the U.S. Congress grants Ohio a 120-foot right-of-way for a public road from the lower rapids of the Miami River of Lake Erie to the western boundary of the Western Reserve.

1824 Timothy Burstall and John Hill build a steam coach in England. It weighs over seven tons and its speed is a maximum 4 mph (6.5 km/h).

1824 English bricklayer Joseph Aspdin (1779—1855) patents what he calls Portland cement, a material produced from a synthetic mixture of limestone and clay. He calls it Portland because of its resemblance

1824 A.D.

Portland cement patented

1823 ■ First American Macadam Road is laid between Hagerstown and Boonsboro, Maryland.

when set to Portland stone. Cement is used to make mortar and concrete, and becomes a widely used and essential material for roads and bridges.

1824 W. H. James produces his first steam carriage in England. Reflecting the common belief that passengers could not be carried safely on the same chassis as the engine, James places them in a separate car behind, attached as a trailer.

1824 March 2 Landmark U.S. Supreme Court decision frees U.S. rivers from monopoly control. Court rules in *Gibbons v. Ogden* that the monopoly granted by the State of New York to steamboat operator Thomas Gibbons violates the interstate commerce clause in the U.S. Constitution. This decision opens all U.S. waterways to any and all steamboats that comply with safety regulations.

c. 1825 George Pocock, an English kite experimenter, sends up his daughter, Martha, as the first woman to fly beneath a kite.

1825 Two American steam carriages appear. One is by T. W. Walker, in Edgar County, Illinois and one in Springfield, Massachusetts by Thomas Blanchard. Blanchard secures an official endorsement from the Massachsetts legislature but still cannot find buyers.

1825 Oldest existing tunnel in the United States is begun. Called the Union Tunnel, it is near Lebanon, Pennsylvania and is 720 feet long. It is finished in 1827.

1825 Englishman William James designs a compressed air self-contained underwater breathing device, but there is no proof that it is ever used under water.

1825 A.D.

Russia builds its first canal

1825 First canal is built by Russia as part of its new, major canal system. This first canal is dug just to bring stone from the Volga River to Moscow by boat to erect a church. In 1937, the Moscow Canal links the upper Volga and the Moskva River at Moscow. It is 80 miles long and has 11 locks.

1825 February First steam locomotive to run on rails in the United States is built by John Stevens (1749—1838), an inventive New Jersey farmer. Stevens builds a half-mile circular track in his backyard in Hoboken and experiments with his new machine. Stevens is

one of the first to be convinced that railroads and not canals are the overland transport systems of the future for America.

1825 February Work is begun on the first underwater tunnel by Marc Isambard Brunel (1769—1849) and his son Isambard Kingdom Brunel (1806—1859). Building this tunnel under the Thames River in London is beset by money problems, accidents, delays, and a May 1827 disaster when the river actually breaks through the shield. Work is suspended for seven years, but the tunnel is finally completed in March 1843. It remains a pedestrian tunnel and tourist attraction until 1865 when it is taken over for a railroad line. It is now part of the London underground railway system. This tunnel assumes a special importance because, first, it proves that tunnels can be driven through any type of ground and, second, because it introduces the transportation tunnel into the urban environment as a solution to traffic congestion.

1825 September 27 First steam-hauled public passenger train ceremonially opens the Stockton & Darlington Railway in England. One of George Stephenson's (1781—1848) improved locomotives called *Locomotion* steams 21 miles (34 kilometers) with a load of 69 tons in tow, 12 wagons with goods, and 21 wagons carrying nearly 600 excited passengers sitting on wooden benches. For the first time in history, land transportation is possible at a rate faster than any horse can run. This historic line quickly turns a profit and news of its success spreads around the world. Stephenson's locomotives begin a transportation revolution throughout the world.

1825 October 26 Erie Canal, stretching more than 350 miles from Buffalo on Lake Erie to the Hudson River at Albany, New York, officially opens. This first great American engineering work is organized by DeWitt Clinton (1769—1828), mayor of New York, and built by American engineer James Geddes (1763—1838). It has 82 locks, takes eight years to build, and costs $7 million. When finished, it connects by boat the Atlantic Ocean to the Great Lakes, and is instrumental in making New York the most important U.S. port. It also is the route most settlers take to open up the midwest. Aside from the trade and goods it carries, there are fast passenger boats, 75 feet long and only 11 feet wide, with dining rooms and sleeping quarters. The Erie Canal proves a better bargain for the merchant, since one horse on a macadam road can haul two tons, but the same single horse pulling a barge

1825 ■ Erie Canal idealized.

pet valve vaporizes the liquid fuel and is an early version of a carburetor.

1826 First steamship involved in a naval engagement is the armed Greek vessel, the *Karteria*. It engages and sinks seven Turkish sailing ships.

1826 Wrought iron suspension bridge across the Menai Straits in Wales opens. This highly original and very successful design by British engineer Thomas Telford (1757—1834) uses 80 chains made of wrought iron tie bars hanging from tall stone towers to carry a two-lane, wooden roadway. The towers are 46 meters high and the bridge spans 174 meters. It replaces a ferry and permanently links London to Holyhead. The great iron bridge is built very high so as not to impede shipping. It is completely rebuilt in 1940.

1826 Descriptions of skis and skiing methods are contained in Englishman Arthur De Capell Broke's (1791—1858) book, *A Winter in Lapland and Sweden*. He tells of the Norwegian skis being of unequal length and "hollowed in the center of the underside to prevent lateral slip." He also describes how the poles are used.

1826 May 5 First modern railway system (in that it is operated entirely by steam locomotives) is incoporated. It is with this line—the Liverpool & Manchester Railway—that the railway becomes established as a means of regular public transport that rivals and finally passes the coach and canal companies. The engineer is George Stephenson (1781—1848). The entire railway opens on September 15, 1830. It has double tracks and operates passenger trains on a timetable. It still runs today.

1826 May 5
First modern railway incorporated

1826 October 7 American Gridley Bryant's Granite Railway opens in Quincy, Massachusetts. Bryant uses the line to transport granite used to build the Bunker Hill Monument. The three mile long, broad-gauge railroad is horse-drawn.

1827 Northwestern Turnpike, eventually connecting Winchester, Virginia with Parkersburg on the Ohio River, is authorized by the Virginia General Assembly. The stone-covered road is Virginia's bid for the lucrative Ohio River trade and reaches Parkersburg in 1838.

1827 First public motor vehicle is operated by British builder and businessman Goldsworthy Gurney (1793—1875). His large steam-powered coaches regu-

on the canal can haul 50 tons. The Canal is unrivalled until the 1850s when railroads begin to compete.

1826 First "omnibus" begins service in Nantes, France. This horse-drawn stage becomes popular once it allows passengers with tickets to change coaches at certain junctions. The name for the service is believed to have come either from the individual named Omnes who started the Nantes service, or possibly after the Latin adjective "omnis" meaning "for all."

1826 Samuel Brown (d. c. 1849) of Brompton, London, patents a "gas-vacuum" engine working on alcohol and air and adapts it to a road vehicle. It is an internal combustion engine that works without an internal explosion. The burning and cooling of alcohol creates a vacuum that opens a valve and causes a large piston to move. His carriage climbs a hill, but its twin cylinder engine gives only 4 hp and is outperformed by steam carriages.

1826 First American "buggy" is made. This is the most typical American horse-drawn carriage and best known. Modeled after a German wagon design, it owed its extreme lightness to its frame and wheels being made of hickory wood. It has four small wheels and elliptical springs, front and rear, mounted at right angles to the front.

1826 Samuel Morey (1762—1843) patents in New Hampshire a two-cylinder poppet valve gas engine that is water-cooled and has some compression. His pop-

1827 ■ Velocipede or "Hobby Horse."

larly carry as many as six paying passengers inside and twelve sitting outside on a route between London and Bath. They also run four times daily between Gloucester and Cheltenham, a distance of nine miles.

1827 American George Tucker (1775—1861) publishes *A Voyage to the Moon* under the pseudonym Joseph Atterlay. He describes imaginatively a metal called "lunarium" that allows his spacecraft loaded with scientific equipment to get to the moon by means of its anti-gravity qualities. Novelists continue to seek more credible or scientific means of propulsion through space to satisfy their better educated readers.

1827 Water-powered turbine is built by French engineer Benoit Fourneyron (1802—1867). This is the precursor of the later steam and gas turbines. A turbine is any machine that converts the energy in a moving stream of fluid into mechanical energy. It does this by passing the stream through a system of fixed and moving fin-like blades which are then rotated. Fourneyron gets the idea from his teacher at the Ecole de Saint-Etienne, who first used the word "turbine" and who is known now only as Burdin.

1827 First book on bridge construction printed in the United States is a translation of M. I. Sganzin's (1750—1837) *An Elementary Course of Civil Engineering*. It is translated from the French by Joseph M. Sganzin (1750-1837) and published in Boston, Massachusetts.

1827 January 8 George Pocock successfully demonstrates his "char-volant," a kite-drawn carriage, on the road between Bristol and Marlborough in England. Pocock harnesses two very large kites to a horseless carriage and is pulled along at 20 mph. In the same year, he also publishes *The Aeropleustic Art, or Navigation in the Air by the Use of Kites or Bouyant Sails*.

1827 February 28 First railroad in Maryland is granted its charter. Its first stone is laid on Independence Day, 1828.

1827 April First steamship to cross the Atlantic fully under power—as opposed to using sails and steam—is the Dutch ship, *Curacao*. Its trip from Rotterdam, Netherlands to the West Indies lasts 22 days.

1827 September 7 First railroad in the Austrian Empire opens with a run in what is now Czechoslovakia. It operates with horses instead of steam.

1827 October 20 Last sea battle fought wholly under sail is the Battle of Navarino Harbor, off the coast of Greece. A combined British-French-Russian fleet defeats a Turkish-Egyptian combine, thus ensuring the independence of Greece.

1828 First vehicle to incorporate a differential in its transmission is a steam carriage built by Frenchman Marcel Pecquer. This advanced vehicle also has a driving wheel geared to the rear axle, spring suspension, and a competent steering arrangement. (See 1833)

1828 First successful use of planet gearing is made in Paris. This device for transmitting power from one rotating shaft to one or more others through small gears that mesh with the outer teeth of the larger gear will become an important factor in the development of automobiles. Only with such a device can the turning power of an engine be transmitted to the wheels.

1828 Russian theorist Alexander D. Zasyadko (1779—1837) designs and builds solid rockets that are used during the Russo-Turkish war.

1828 July 4 Failed Chesapeake and Ohio Canal begins to be dug. Inspired initially by President George Washington's (1732—1799) dream of linking the Potomac River with the Great Lakes, it takes 22 years and $14 million to reach Cumberland, Maryland, just short of the Alleghanies, when money and effort finally give out. It is used for a short time to transport coal from Cumberland mines to Washington, but never pays its way and is soon abandoned.

1828 October Delaware and Hudson Canal opens. Running 107 miles southwest from Kingston on the Hudson River to Port Jarvis on the Delaware River then to Honesdale, Pennsylvania, this canal carries coal from the mines of Pennsylvania.

1828 October 1 First railroad in France opens between St. Etienne and Andrezieux and is horse-drawn. Steam is introduced in 1844.

1829 Welland Canal, a Canadian project linking Lake Erie to Lake Ontario, opens. It copes with the 326-foot (98-meter) rise of the Niagara River by a system of 40 locks, and makes navigation possible to Lake Michigan and Chicago, Illinois.

1829 Largest pier, Southend Pier in Essex, England, is begun. This wooden pier is extended in 1846 from 1,800 feet to 1.25 miles. In 1886 it is almost entirely rebuilt and extended to almost 7,000 feet. Builders in the 19th century create these extended walkways into the sea to enable visitors to reach the healthier ocean air. They also have a more practical function, enabling pleasure boats to connect with seaside resorts without having to use rowboats or ferries.

1829 First major engineered structure on an American railroad, the Carrollton Viaduct over Gwynns Falls in Baltimore, Maryland, is built. This two-span, granite-block bridge is still in use today.

1829 August 29 British steam locomotive called the *Stourbridge Lion* purchased by the Delaware & Hudson (D&H) Canal Company to transport coal, makes its first run in the United States. It proves much too heavy for the track, however, which regularly crumbles under its weight. Horatio Allen (1802—1890) is the engineer. D&H gives up on steam.

1829 October 6 Competitive trials are held in England by the Liverpool & Manchester railway to determine the best locomotive available. George Stephenson's (1781—1848) *Rocket* wins the money prize easily and establishes itself as the first locomotive to combine the fundamentals which would serve steam rail traction for the rest of its days: separate cylinders driving the wheels via short connecting rods which uses steam more efficiently; and a boiler with an internal nest of longitudinal fire tubes that was served by an external water-jacketed firebox.

1829 ■ George Stephenson's "Rocket" locomotive.

1829 October 17 Delaware and Chesapeake Canal officially opens. This canal across the isthmus of the peninsula from the Delaware River to the Chesapeake Bay runs 19 miles. Boats travelling from Philadelphia, Pennsylvania to Baltimore, Maryland cut 300 miles off what would be a 400-mile trip.

1830 Idea of using compressed air while building tunnels is first patented by Englishman Lord Cochrane (1779—1854). Compressed air is air reduced in volume by being put under pressure. When a tunnel is being driven through porous soil or under water, if the air in the tunnel is compressed, its pressure becomes greater than that of the water outside the tunnel, and the

1829 October 17 Delaware and Chesapeake Canal opens

1830 ■ Peter Cooper's locomotive "Tom Thumb" races and defeats a horse-drawn rail coach.

water is kept out. Workers must stay in a lock when entering or leaving compressed air, and the pressure is gradually adjusted upwards or downwards.

1830 Railroad spikes with a hooked head for holding flat-bottomed rails to the ties (or sleepers) are designed by American Robert L. Stevens (1787—1856). (See 1840)

1830 Federal funding for the Maysville Turnpike, a stone-surfaced road through the Blue Grass region of Kentucky, is vetoed by President Andrew Jackson (1767—1845). Although eventually completed by the state in 1835, the road issue established the national policy of not funding roads of strictly local (not interstate) benefit.

1830 A.D.

Train carries mail

1830 Mail is first carried by train on the Liverpool & Manchester Railway in Britain.

1830 English mail coach is at the peak of its capabilities in terms of stability, lightness, and speed. A journey of 175 miles takes only 18 hours.

c. 1830 First caravan to provide elaborate living accommodations is the horse-drawn vehicle built in France for circus owner Antoine Franconi. This house on wheels has a kitchen, dining room, and bedroom. The word caravan is derived from the Persian "karwan," meaning "a company of travellers." (See 1897)

1830 Canal mileage in the United States totals 1,277 miles compared to only 73 miles of railroad. Ten years later, there are 3,326 miles of canals and 2,828 miles of railroad. By 1850, there are 3,698 miles of canals and 9,021 miles of railroads. Railroads will soon put most American canals out of business.

1830 May 4 First railroad tunnel to be used for passenger traffic, the Tyler Hill Tunnel, opens for traffic. Part of the Canterbury & Whitstable Railway in England, it is 838 yards (766 meters) long. Passenger traffic ends in 1931 and the line closes completely in 1952.

1830 May 24 First section of the Baltimore & Ohio Railroad (B&O) opens between Ellicott's Mills and Baltimore, Maryland. This becomes the first common-carrier railroad in the United States. It begins as a horse-drawn service.

1830 August 28 American philanthropist Peter Cooper (1791—1883), convinced that steam is the future of the railroad, builds a crude, little locomotive called *Tom Thumb* with which he pulls Baltimore & Ohio (B&O) Railroad directors down a track. These men are so impressed they organize a trial contest to find the best locomotive. (See 1831)

1830 September 9 Charles F. Durant (1805—1873), America's first great balloonist, makes his first U. S. ascent at Castle Garden, New York. He stays in the air for two hours, landing at South Amboy, New Jersey. His skill and enthusiasm inspire a passion for ballooning in America.

1830 September 15 Fatal railroad accident occurs at the grand opening of the Liverpool & Manchester Railway. William Huskisson, British member of Parliament, is accidently struck by George Stephenson's (1781—1848) steam locomotive while speaking to the Duke of Wellington.

1830 September 15 First modern railway line, the Liverpool & Manchester Railway, opens for business. (See May 5, 1826)

1831 First fixed tandem-wing (arranged one behind the other) airplane is designed by Thomas Walker, an English portrait painter. In the second edition of his *Treatise upon the Art of Flying by Mechanical Means* (first published in 1810), Walker adds this new design, which is never built, but which will almost certainly influence D. S. Brown, and through him, Samuel P. Langley (1834—1906) and Louis Bleriot (1872—1936).

1831 Austrian automobile pioneer Siegfried Markus (1831—1899) is born. His early work building a number of experimental internal combustion-powered vehicles, lead some to call him and not Karl Benz (1844—1929) the inventor of the first automobile.

1831 First railroad tunnel in the Western Hemisphere, the Staple Bend Tunnel, is begun near Jamestown, Pennsylvania. It is part of a railroad/canal transportation route that runs from Philadelphia to Pittsburgh. When completed in 1833 for a cost of $37,500, it is 900 feet long, 19 feet high, and 20 feet wide. It still stands but has not been used since 1852.

1831 First locomotive headlight is a pine-knot fire on an open platform car used in South Carolina. For the next 20 years, candles and whale oil are used in reflector lamps at the front of the trains. In 1859, kerosene and gas lamps appear, and electricity is introduced in 1881. Figure-8 oscillating headlights first appear in 1936, and sealed-beams in 1946.

1831 Select Committee of British Commons holds hearings to review the progress of mechanical transport. It decides that steam carriages are not harmful to roads and that extremely high tolls levied against them (and not against horse-drawn coaches) should be reduced. Power vehicles, however, continue to be discriminated against for the next 60 years.

1831 Baltimore & Ohio Railroad (B&O) sponsors a competition to test the practical potential of steam locomotives. The contest is won by Pennsylvania watchmaker Phineas Davis, who enters a vertical-boiler four-wheeler. Although his locomotive is an evolutionary dead-end, it convinces B&O to eliminate horses and convert entirely to steam. It does this by 1835.

1831 First known honeymoon railroad trip in the United States is made by Mr. and Mrs. Henry L. Pierson of Ramapo, New York on the South Carolina Canal & Railroad Company train.

1831 First practical electric motor is invented by American physicist Joseph Henry (1797—1878), who publishes a paper describing it. The significance of his accomplishment, which was to devise a way to turn a wheel when an electric current is applied, cannot be overemphasized. Its applicability to transportation was realized and applied early on. Electric motors could be any size; they would work even if the electricity came from miles away or from a portable battery; and they could be started and stopped at will.

1831 Morris Canal in New Jersey opens, running from Phillipsburg on the Delaware River eastward to Newark Bay in Newark, New Jersey. It uses inclined planes instead of locks, so that when a barge enters a gate, it settles onto a boat cradle or trolley on tracks as the water drains out. It then either rolls down the track or is hauled up to the next level. After this canal is abandoned in 1923, its old bed at Newark is used for a subway line in 1935.

1831 January 15 First regular steam railroad in the United States, the South Carolina Railroad, opens. It uses a steam locomotive designed by American Horatio Allen (1802—1890). After six months of successful service on the six-mile (ten kilometers) track in Charleston, the boiler explodes and puts the line out of business.

1831 August 1 London Bridge is replaced and the new bridge is officially opened by King William IV (1765—1837). Designed by John Rennie (1761—1821) and built by his son, John (1794—1874), it is a stone bridge of contemporary design, with only five elliptical arches and narrow piers that allow traffic and the river to flow though much easier than the old bridge which was more of a dam. The bridge stands until 1971 when it is sold, taken down in pieces, and re-erected for tourists in Lake Havasu, Arizona.

1831 August 9 First steam train in New York State runs from Albany to Schenectady. It is pulled

1831 A.D.
Electric motor invented

1831 August 1
New London Bridge opens

by Mohawk & Hudson Railroad's first locomotive called the *DeWitt Clinton.*

1831 November U.S. mail is carried for the first time by rail in South Carolina by the South Carolina Canal & Railroad Company.

1831 November 12 British-built locomotive called *John Bull* enters service at Bordentown, New Jersey. Isaac Dripps, an American machinist, adds a "pilot" and a four-wheel truck assembly that guides it over sharp curves.

1832 Walter Hancock of Stratford, England designs and builds for the London and Paddington Steam Carriage Company a passenger-carrying steam-powered vehicle far ahead of its time. Called the Hancock "Enterprise," it is the first to depart from using the frame of horse-drawn stage coaches. Built very functionally, it looks very much like an early trolley car with a salon-like interior equipped with shades and windows. It also uses high-pressure steam, one of the first to do so.

1832 A.D.

First urban streetcar built

1832 First urban streetcar in the United States is built by American wagon builder John Stephenson and goes into use in New York between Upper Manhattan and Harlem. This 30-passenger, stagecoach-on-rails is pulled by horses and operates for only three years. Similar horsecar services are started in Boston and Cambridge, Massachusetts (1856) and Philadelphia, Pennsylvania (1858). By 1859, the lines were running in Cincinnati, Ohio, Chicago, Illinois, and Pittsburgh, Pennsylvania.

1832 Gota Canal, connecting the Baltic and North seas in Sweden, is completed. Regarded by many as a white elephant, this canal is built by English engineer Thomas Telford (1757—1834), far wider than most existing canals, and it requires 63 locks to move boats through its 120 miles (192 kilometers). It takes 22 years to finish and costs six times Telford's original estimate. Many feel it delayed the construction of a Swedish railroad system some 30 years.

1832 British inventor Robert Wilson (1803—1882) is awarded a silver medal by the Scottish Society of Arts for his design of a screw propeller for ships. It is not tested in water trials.

1832 French engineer Pierre Louis Frederic Sauvage (1785—1857) designs and patents his idea for a screw propeller for ships. His design is tested and found wanting, and Sauvage ends up bankrupt.

1832 Frenchman Condert is considered the earliest successful compressed-air diver to use a self-contained underwater breathing device. He later drowns when he cannot disengage himself from his weights.

1832 Coal-carrying canal, the Canal de Charleroi àBrussels, opens operating in Belgium from Brussels south to Charleroi.

1832 February 18 Octave Chanute (1832—1910), first great historian of aviation, is born in Paris, France. Brought to the United States when young, Chanute was a civil engineer before turning to aviation. In 1894 he published *Progress in Flying Machines*, which summarized the entire history and progress of aviation to that time and became a bible for the Wright Brothers. He later served them as confidant and encourager.

1832 June 10 German engineer and inventor Nikolaus A. Otto (1832—1891) is born in Holzhausen. After Lenoir built the first internal combustion engine in 1860, later research by others indicated that such an engine would be most efficient with four movements or cycles of the piston in the cylinder. Otto was the first to build such a four-stroke engine, which he patented in 1877. By 1890, Otto engines were the only ones used, and they made possible both the automobile and powered flight.

1833 Richard Roberts of Manchester, England applies differential gearing to a steam carriage which solves the problem of turning corners. It works by insuring that when the car goes around a corner, the wheel on the inside of the bend—which travels a shorter distance than the outer wheel—rotates slower. (See 1828)

1833 In England, Maceroni & Squire use a high pressure boiler in a steam carriage. They run a successful line of passenger coaches.

1833 First known vessel to be built in the new clipper ship style, the American *Ann McKim*, is launched at Fells Point, Baltimore, Maryland. "Clipper" ships do not have one particular design, but are the faster, bigger sailing ships that are built to "clip" days off a voyage, and thus be able to compete with steamships. Their two major design developments are the bow change from a blunt "U" to a sharp "V," and their iron hulls covered on top by wood and below water by copper sheathing.

1833 Ohio and Erie Canal, running 308 miles from Portsmouth on the Ohio River northward to Cleveland on Lake Erie, opens. This canal gives Ohio farmers an opportunity to reach the markets of the South, and transforms the city of Cleveland, doubling its population in five years.

1833 "Cowcatcher" for locomotives is invented by American Isaac Dripps and first used on the Camden & Amboy Railroad. In its original design attached to the front of the train, its projecting prongs impale any animal standing on the tracks. It is then modified and the prongs are replaced by a set of heavy, angled bars that pushes the animal out of the way.

1833 May 11 An ocean liner headed for Quebec, Canada from England strikes an iceberg in the North Atlantic and sinks, killing 215 poeple.

1833 June 6 First president of the United States to ride on a railroad train is Andrew Jackson (1767—1845). He rides on a line between Ellicott Mills and Baltimore, Maryland.

1833 November 9 First U.S. railroad passenger deaths occur on the Camden & Amboy line between Spotswood and Hightstown, New Jersey. Two people die and 12 passengers are injured as a broken axle causes the car to overturn. One of the injured is Cornelius Vanderbilt (1794—1877), later the railroad "King" of America.

1834 First railroad tunnel in United States, the Staple Bend Tunnel, is built four miles east of Johnstown, Pennsylvania. Linking the 36-mile Johnstown-to-Holidaysburg route, it is 901 feet long, 20 feet wide, and 19 feet high. It costs $37,000 to build.

1834 Rhine-Rhone Canal opens. This 217-mile-long canal provides a direct north-south water route, connecting the Saone River with the Rhine. By modern standards, it is a narrow, shallow canal.

1834 Delaware and Raritan Canal, running 45 miles from Bordentown on the Delaware River to New Brunswick on the Raritan River in New Jersey, opens. Nearly a century later, its abandoned bed is used to build part of a modern highway for automobiles.

1834 Pennsylvania Canal, as much a railroad as a canal, opens. Connecting Philadelphia and Pittsburgh, it uses nearly every mode of transportation known at the time. On this 394-mile, four-day trip, canalboats are pulled by horses and steam-powered cables, are carried in sections on rail cars, go up and down inclined planes powered by stationary steam engines, and float down river. This astonishing system accomplishes the task of crossing the Alleghany Mountains. Not surprisingly, the costs of running this route are very high, and railroads eventually put it out of business.

1834 March 17 German automobile pioneer Gottlieb Willhelm Daimler (1834—1900) is born in Schorndorf, Wurttemberg. Trained as an engineer, he works for and greatly helps Nikolaus A. Otto (1832—1891), the inventor of the four-stroke internal combustion engine, from 1872 to 1882. Unable to convince Otto to try to use his engine to power a vehicle, Daimler leaves and forms his own company with another ex-Otto employee, Wilhelm Maybach (1846—1929). Together, they develop a light gas engine that powers their 1886 car. This is the direct ancestor of the modern car. Daimler and Benz never worked together, and their businesses are joined long after Daimler dies.

1834 August 17 The French Count Lennox builds his airship *L'Aigle* in Paris, France. It is to be propelled by eight manually-operated oars and paddlewheels. When being inflated for the first time it escapes from its net and bursts, and is destroyed by the disappointed crowd. Its one unique feature is a basket on a winch to raise or lower passengers.

1834 August 22 Samuel Pierpont Langley (1834—1906), aviation pioneer, astronomer, and physicist, is born in Roxbury, Massachusetts. In August 1903, his unmanned, one-quarter-size model airplane became the first gas-powered, heavier-than-air machine to fly, even tentatively. His later manned, full-scale, powered attempts to fly when catapulted from a house-boat were not successful. He overemphasized his power source while not understanding the importance of design and control.

1834 December 17 First railroad in Ireland opens between Dublin and Kingstown (now Dun Laoghaire).

1835 First locomotive built on continental Europe is constructed for the Brussels-Malines line by Englishman John Cockerill (1790-1840) who works for the Belgian Seraing ironworks.

1835 Steam-powered elevator called the "teagle" is used in an English factory to lift freight. It consists of a cage that is counter-balanced and hoisted by ropes.

1835 Highway Act is passed in England and abolishes the 300-year-old system of statute labor which required citizens to repair roads. This new law authorizes taxes for road repair and empowers parishes to be divided into districts employing a competent surveyor to direct road improvement.

1835 Vermont blacksmith Thomas Davenport makes an experimental electric railway in model size. The type of his motor is not known.

1835 Edgar Allen Poe (1809—1849), American poet and short story writer, publishes *Lunar Discoveries* in which his hero travels to the moon in a balloon. Poe characteristically dooms his character, making him unable to return to earth.

1835 A.D.

Canada–U.S. railroad construction begins

1835 Construction begins on a railroad in Canada that will facilitate travel from Montreal to the United States. After a charter is granted to the Champlain and St. Lawrence Railroad Company in 1832, it builds a railway of wood faced with iron strips and imports a steam engine from England. In 1848, the St. Lawrence and Atlantic Railway begins a line that will connect Montreal to Portland, Maine.

1835 April 8 Richard Clayton, an American citizen born in England in 1811, makes a hydrogen balloon flight of 350 miles (560 kilometers) from Cincinnati, Ohio to Monroe County, Virginia in nine-and-one-half hours. This extremely long flight draws an enormous public response to ballooning.

1835 May 5 First railroad in Belgium opens from Brussels to Malines. It uses George Stephenson's (1781—1848) locomotives and is the first to be conceived as part of a planned national system.

1835 August 24 First train to enter Washington, D.C. comes from Baltimore, Maryland and is witnessed by President Andrew Jackson (1767—1845).

1835 December 7 First railroad in Germany, the Ludwigsbahn, opens from Nuremberg to Furth. It uses a Stephenson locomotive.

1836 English "hansom" carriage is invented by Joseph A. Hansom (1803—1882). This hired carriage is a light, open two-seater that is driven from a highly elevated box placed behind the passengers, with whom the driver can communicate via a hole. They replace the former hackneys.

1836 First two locomotives to be equipped with whistles are built in Lowell, Massachusetts under the supervision of George Washington Whistler. One goes into service at Jamaica, Long Island and the other at Wilmington, Delaware. Whistles are used to give early notice of a train's approach.

1836 First railroad snow plow is used successfully on the Utica & Schenectady Railroad.

1836 Work is begun by British engineer Isambard K. Brunel (1806—1859) on the Box Tunnel, part of the Great Western Railway in England. Completed in 1841, it is nearly two miles long and costs the lives of 100 men to build it. It is the longest tunnel in Europe until Mont Cenis in France in 1871.

1836 British inventor Francis Pettit Smith (1808—1874) successfully tests a steam-driver screw propeller on a small model on the Paddington Canal in London.

1836 Swedish-born American inventor John Ericcson (1803—1889) patents a double screw propeller for ships which is successfully tested on a ship in England.

1836 February 5 Henry R. Campbell of Philadelphia, Pennsylvania patents an eight-wheeled engine which becomes well-known as the American type. Built by James Brooks of Philadelphia, this eight-wheel type is more copied in England than America.

1836 April First railroad car ferry, the *Susquehanna*, opens for business on the Susquehanna River between Havre de Grace and Perryville, Maryland. In the winter of 1854, this river freezes so solid that tracks are simply laid across the ice connecting the two lines. Between January 15 and February 24, 1,378 railroad cars are hauled across.

1836 April 20 First narrow-gauge public railroad, the Festiniog Railway in Wales, opens. Narrow-gauge is any track less than standard gauge (4 feet, 8.5 inches or 1,435 millimeters). This track is 1 foot, 11.5 inches (600 millimeters). It is horse-drawn.

1836 July 4 Illinois and Michigan Canal, running from Chicago on Lake Michigan to LaSalle on the Illinois River, begins excavation. Completed in 1848, this 96-mile-long canal transforms the obscure little town of Chicago (population about 4,000) into one of the wealthiest and most populated U.S. cities. As a man-made link between the Great Lakes and the Mississippi River, this canal enables a boat to travel from the Gulf of Mexico to Lake Michigan.

1836 July 21 First steam railroad in Canada, the Champlain & St. Lawrence Railroad, opens between Laprairie and St. John. It uses a Stephenson locomotive.

1836 September 18 First specifically-built trailer for horses is used by British racehorse owner George Bentinck (1802—1848). Built by British coach-builders named Herring on Bentinck's orders, it is a horse-drawn van with a padded interior. Until this innovation, racehorses slowly walked the distances between tracks. Bentinck gets good odds and bets heavily on his horse named Ellis, who no one thinks can get to the Yorkshire track on time since it is kept at Sussex. Ellis arrives fresh and wins by two lengths.

1836 October 9 First railroad in Russia opens from Pavlovsk to Tsarskoe Selo as part of the St. Petersburg & Pavlovsk Railroad. It begins with horses and switches to a locomotive by Stephenson.

1836 November 7—8 Ballooning gains in respectability and seriousness as Charles Green (1785—1870) and passengers Robert Holland and Monck Mason fly in Green's *Vauxhall Balloon* from Vauxhall Gardens in London to Weilburg, Nassau in Germany, 480 miles (c. 770 kilometers) in 18 hours. On this balloon voyage the trail-rope (a long rope lowered before landing to slow down its descent and regulate its height) is first used by Green, following a suggestion by Thomas Baldwin in his book *Airopaidia*, published in 1786.

1837 Robert Davidson builds a five-ton, non-rechargeable electric car in Scotland.

c. 1837 American Thomas Davenport tries out his rotary armature electric motor. This non-rechargeable electric car runs a distance on a short track.

1837 First railroad sleeping car, a remodeled day coach, begins service between Harrisburg and Chambersburg, Pennsylvania. It is designed by Philip Berlin, manager of the Cumberland Valley Railroad.

1837 April 10 Earliest known aeronautical experiment in Canada is conducted by Canadian schoolteacher John Rae. He successfully launches a paper balloon able to carry weight. Its lift is provided by the heating of its blackened surface by the sun.

1837 May 9 Steamboat *Ben Sherrod* catches fire and burns on the river below Natchez, Mississippi, killing 175 people.

1837 July 4 First trunk railway in Britain (one which connects two other systems or lines) opens. The Grand Junction Railway connects the London & Birmingham and the Liverpool & Manchester lines.

1837 July 24 Robert Cocking (1776—1837), a 61-year-old painter and amateur scientist, is killed in Lee Green, London. His Cayley-inspired, ribbed and canopied parachute from which he hangs in a basket, tears apart upon release from below a balloon. He could be said to be the first man to be killed on a heavier-than-air machine.

1837 August 22 First contract is made for the carrying of mail by steamship. The British government contracts with P & O (Peninsular and Oriental Steam Navigation Co.) to carry the mail to Spain and Portugal.

1838 William Barnett of Brighton, England builds a double-acting cylinder engine that uses either alcohol or coal-gas. His practical contributions are, first, his pressurizing the combustible mixture and, second, his use of a flame ignition system. It is not known if he ever puts it on a carriage.

1838 First brougham coach is made in England by Robinson and Cook for Lord Brougham, then Lord Chancellor. This ancestor of many 19th-century coaches has several innovations, one of which is its extremely low-slung center body which is sunk deep enough to permit easy entrance from ground level.

1838 Largest locomotive driving wheels ever built are the 10-foot (3.05-meter) diameter wheels fitted to three broad-gauge engines built for the Great Western Railway.

1838 Infant railroad industry in England grows to the extent that, after a period of adjustment, stagecoaches actually do more business bringing people to and from train stations.

1838 Third class rail passengers are first carried on British trains. Third class consists of open wagons without seats.

1838 Jump coil is made by American Charles G. Page (1812–1868) and is used in his non-rechargeable electric car which goes 19 mph (31 km/h). A heavily wound coil is found to dramatically boost a current. In modern engines, it is these thousands of windings of copper wire that boost a car battery's 12 volts to the 14,000 volts required for the spark plug to ignite the fuel. (See 1846)

1838 A.D.

U.S. links railroads to mail service

1838 United States decides all railroads will also be post or mail routes, linking the future of its mail delivery policy to its future transportation planning.

1838 Steam locomotive is first introduced in Nova Scotia on a short coal line at Pictou. The coal industry and not passenger service takes priority.

1838 Fog bell operated by the tide is installed at the Whitehead Lighthouse in Maine. This "perpetual fog bell" is operated by tidal motion which winds up a weight that then drives the striking mechanism.

1838 First screw-pile lighthouse is erected on Maplin Sound at the mouth of the Thames River in London. Invented by Englishman Alexander Mitchell, it sits atop piles that are twisted into a sand or coral bottom like a screw into a piece of wood. These small, sturdy structures become standard replacements for lightships in the United States after the Civil War (1861—1865). (See October 28, 1850)

1838 First sizeable seagoing vessel to be driven by a screw propeller is the 237-ton *Archimedes*, designed by British engineer Francis Pettit Smith (1808—1874). It has a single 7-foot (2.13-meter) propeller which is later replaced by a two-bladed screw. It reaches a speed of 10 knots.

1838 First all-metal bridge in United States, a modest cast-iron arch designed by Richard Delafield, is completed. Its 80-foot span crosses Dunlap's Creek at Brownsville, Pennsylvania and carries the National Road. This historic bridge still survives.

1838 January Washington, D.C. and New York are finally linked by a chain of railroads, with ferry service across major rivers and stagecoaches between stations in principal cities.

1838 January 6 First railroad in Austria opens from Vienna to Florisdorf and Deutsch Wagram.

1838 April 4 First Atlantic crossing entirely under steam begins as British steamship *Sirius* leaves Cork harbor for New York. It is loaded down with 40 passengers, 20 tons of water, and 450 tons of coal. The 1834 invention by Englishman Samuel Hall (1781—1863) of surface condensors that use fresh water instead of sea water means that boilers do not have to be cleaned out every four days, though they do require that a ship carry a huge supply of fresh water. It arrives in New York on April 23 with its coal supply virtually exhausted, covering 2,961 miles with an average speed of 6.7 knots.

1838 April 8 British steamship *Great Western* leaves Bristol bound for New York. The first steamship built specifically for transatlantic crossings, it is designed by talented British engineer Isambard K. Brunel (1806—1859). It arrives in New York on April 23, only four hours after the *Sirius* does, but makes the trip in over three fewer days. It becomes the first steamer to regularly cross the Atlantic, until it stops near the end of 1846.

1838 June 4 First section of the Great Western Railway, from London to Bristol, opens. This is significant, for it is laid out to the extremely broad gauge of seven feet (2,134 millimeters) by the great British civil engineer, Isambard Kingdom Brunel (1806—1859). This line will be one of the protagonists in the "Battle of the Gauges" waged between Brunel's and George Stephen-

1839 ■ First U.S. iron bridge is built over Dunlap's Creek in Brownsville, Pennsylvania.

son's (1781—1848) ideas about what track width should become the national standard. (See August 18, 1846)

1838 July 7 A bill passed by the U.S. Congress is signed by President Martin Van Buren (1782—1862) making every railroad a postal route.

1838 July 8 Ferdinand Graf von Zeppelin (1838—1917) is born in Baden, Germany. The first large-scale builder and pioneer of rigid dirigible balloons (powered airships). He made his first balloon ascent in St. Paul, Minnesota serving as a volunteer and observer for the Union Army in the U.S. Civil War (1861—1865). His *LZ-1*, the first of the "zeppelins," made its initial flight on July 2, 1900. They later flew bombing missions during World War I and served as transatlantic passenger airships during the interwar period.

1839 Electric telegraph is first used on a railroad in England, the Great Western Railway. Installed by William Fothergill-Cooke (1806—1879) and Charles Wheatstone (1802—1875), it works well and in 1845, is responsible for the arrest at Paddington Station of a murderer who had boarded a train at Slough. This incident galvanizes public opinion in favor of the telegraph.

1839 Electric-powered carriage is built and driven by Robert Anderson of Aberdeen, Scotland. It is powered by a primitive chemical battery motor that provides power for only five minutes, after which the chemicals have to be replenished. It is no match for steam vehicles and soon is abandoned.

1839 First step in the development of the bicycle from the wooden hobby horse to a mechanically-moved, two-wheeled vehicle is made by Scottish blacksmith Kirkpatrick Macmillan. He appears to be the first to discover that two wheels placed in line could be balanced and could be propelled by treadles and cranks fitted to one of the axles. He allows his machine to be copied and makes no attempt to market it. (See 1842)

1839 First iron bridge in the United States is completed over Dunlap's Creek, along the present Main Street in Brownsville, Pennsylvania. It is on the route of the National Pike leading to Bridgeport, Connecticut. The cast-iron arch is 80 feet long and has a macadam surface and wrought-iron railings.

1839 First state railroad commission is established in Rhode Island.

1839 One of the earliest tugboats, the steam-powered *Robert F. Stockton*, is fitted with a double-screw propeller and successfully tows four coal barges in England.

1839 First paddleboat to be propelled by an electric motor is designed and built by a Russian physicist named Jacobi. Using a large engine powered by electro-magnets—first with a Daniell galvanic battery and later a Grove battery—it paddles up the Neva River near St. Petersburg at about 2 mph (3 km/ph). Since the batteries use zinc plates dissolved in acid, the engine emits toxic, nitrous gases, making continued use impossible.

1839 First practical "closed" helmet and diving dress is developed by Augustus Siebe (1788—1872). The closed helmet is sealed to the diver's watertight suit and is weighted to counteract its air-filled buoyancy. A

1839 A.D.

First electric motor-powered paddleboat designed and built

hand-cranked pump at the surface supplies air via a hose. Siebe's design remains unchanged until World War II.

1839 Mittelland Canal in Germany is completed. This nearly 300-mile-long canal lies at the heart of the German canal system and connects with many other canals. It allows the Rhine River to have a mouth in Germany because it joins the Rhine-Herne Canal in the south.

1839 March 4

First U.S. long distance railway express opens

1839 March 4 First U.S. long distance railway express service opens between Boston, Massachusetts and New York. It is started by a former railroad conductor, William F. Harnden (1812—1845).

1839 April 27 John Wise (1808—1879), an American, introduces the balloon ripping-panel, a glued section that the pilot can pull open for quick emptying of the balloon after landing. This prevents the balloon from being dragged along the ground.

1839 September 24 First railroad in The Netherlands opens between Amsterdam and Haarlem.

1839 October United States is the second government to offer mail contracts to steamship companies that will carry the mail overseas. In 1846, the government contracts with Edward Mills's Ocean Steam Navigation Co. to carry the mail across the Atlantic.

1839 October 4 First railroad in Italy opens between Naples and Portici.

1839 November 14 First railroad trip by royalty is made by British Prince Albert and his brother, Ernest. They travel from Slough to London. Queen Victoria (1819—1901) first travels by train on June 13, 1842. The visibility of such prominent individuals on trains has a great deal to do with the public's acceptance of this new form of transportation.

1840 Englishman Charles Green (1785—1870) designs and builds a model of a spherical balloon held aloft by a clockwork-driven propeller, with a trail-rope fitted with floats, to fly across the Atlantic ocean.

1840 A.D.

Railroad signals introduced

1840 Railroad disc-and-crossbar signals are introduced on the Great Western Railway in England. The disc and crossbar are at right angles to each other, so when the crossbar faces the train, it means "stop." When turned 90 degrees the disc means "line clear."

1840 Frank Hills' steam coach travels from London to Hastings and back without mechanical trouble—first time 100 miles (160 kilometers) is covered by a powered vehicle. Forty years would pass before this feat is surpassed. (See 1841)

1840 First patent for a machine that makes railroad spikes is issued to Henry Burden of Troy, New York.

1840 Regular transatlantic steamer service is begun by the British and North American Royal Mail Steam Packet company (it later becomes the Cunard Steamship Company).

1840 Skiing as a sport begins as Norwegian Sondre Norheim (1825—1895) makes the first recognized ski jump. He discovers that by landing on sloping and not flat ground, he can jump farther than anyone before him. (See 1860)

1840 February 5 Scottish inventor John Boyd Dunlop (1840—1921) is born in Dreghorn, Ayrshire. A veterinary surgeon, Dunlop invents the pneumatic (air-filled) rubber tire while trying to give his son a more comfortable tricycle ride. He is so successful, he founds his own company within three years. Although his pneumatic tire is invented as an improvement for the bicycle, it arrived just as the automobile was coming on the scene, and so contributed to its success as well.

1840 August 10 First manned balloon flight in Canada is made by American Louis A. Lauriat, whose balloon flies 21 miles in New Brunswick.

1841 Frank Hills's steam carriage goes 25 mph and covers 128 miles in one day over heavy roads in England. (See 1840)

1841 First farm tractor or steam "cart horse" is made by William Worby of England.

1841 North American Indian "bull boat" is first described by American artist and author George Catlin (1796—1872) in his *Letters and Notes on the Manners, Customs, and Condition of the North American Indians*. He tells of it holding three people and being "made in the form of a large tub, of a buffalo skin stretched on a frame of willow boughs." It is not known for how long the Plains Indians had been using this form of boat.

1841 First U.S. lighthouse to use a Fresnel lens is the Navesink Lighthouse (New Jersey) which imports one from France. A Fresnel lens gives a much-improved, pencil-like beam of light.

1841 American inventor John Holland (1841—1914) is born in Ireland. After emigrating to the United States in 1873, Holland designs and builds what is generally recognized as the first fully practical submarine. He builds many versions and models, many of which pioneer features that eventually become standard on modern submarines. His company becomes the Electric Boat Company, which is still in business today.

1841 First street lighting by electric lamps is accomplished experimentally in Paris by two Frenchmen, Deleuil and Archereau. (See 1857)

1841 February 4 Clement Ader (1841—1926), engineer and inventor, born in Muret, France. An aviation enthusiast from his youth, Ader constructed in 1890 a steam-powered, bat-winged monoplane which made a take-off but not a sustained flight on October 9 of that year. His short, hop-flight was the first demonstration that a full-scale machine that was heavier than air could get off the ground.

1841 September British lighthouse on the north end of Sunderland pier is moved in its entirety to the far end of the new eastern extension of the pier (over 500 feet) without interrupting the illumination from the tower. The lighthouse is re-erected without one crack.

1842 In England, W. H. Phillips successfully flies a model helicopter driven by jets of steam from the rotor tips. Steam is produced by burning coal, saltpetre and gypsum.

c. 1842 Frenchman Alexandre Lefebvre, builds and rides a version of Macmillan's two-wheeled, foot-pedalled vehicle. He moves to California and continues to make them. By now, the French name "velocipede" has come to be applied to two-wheelers that have some means of mechanically transmitted leg power. (See 1839)

1842 January 24 First reigning monarch to travel by train is Frederick William IV (1795—1861) of Prussia.

1842 May 8 First major train disaster occurs in France when the main axle on the first locomotive of a Versailles-Paris express breaks without warning. Several coaches pile into the engines and many passengers are unable to escape because their compartment doors are locked. Fifty-three people die in the fiery crash, and locked doors are barred from now on.

1843 Oregon Trail, the first overland wagon road to the Pacific coast, begins to be heavily used by settlers. The thousands of emigrants who swarm to Oregon solidify the eventual U.S. claim to the Northwest country.

1843 Early skiing competition is held in Tromso, Norway. The event features a cross-country ski race as well as downhill and jumping.

1843 March Tunnel under the Thames River in London, England is completed. (See February 1825).

1843 March 28 William Samuel Henson (1805—1888) receives the patent, and publishes in London, his design for an *Aerial Steam Carriage*. This is the first reasoned, formulated, and detailed design for a propeller-driven aircraft. Because this monoplane design receives world-wide publicity, it can be said to have greatly influenced the basic configuration of the modern airplane.

1843 April George Cayley (1773—1857), at the age of 70, publishes his design for a convertiplane. It has four helicopter rotors to make it rise vertically and two propellers for forward propulsion.

1844 First covered business wagon in the United States is built by Ezra M. Stratton in New York. A flat, spring wagon with a fixed hood and pulled by a single horse, it protected the business's merchandise and remained basically unchanged into the early years of the 20th century. Stratton uses his wagon to deliver bottled soda water.

1844 Stuart Perry (1814—1890), a New York businessman and part-time inventor, patents air and water cooled engines and his tube ignition.

1844 French automobile pioneer Emile Levassor (1844—1897) is born. He and his partner, Rene Panhard (1841—1908), develop the classic or conventional design for the automobile. Their car has the engine in the front under a hood, driven by a pedal-controlled clutch and a longitudinal shaft to the gearbox. Levassor is also a successful racer who dies after being thrown from his car in the Paris-Bordeaux Race.

1844 A.D.

Inflatable raft invented

1844 First artificially-made inflatable boat is made by English sailor Peter A. Halkett. It is essentially a one-man raft that can be inflated by a nozzle. Called a "Gutta Percha" boat, it uses India rubber to air-proof an inflatable canvas raft. It proves successful and is taken on several Arctic expeditions.

1844 May 24 Electric telegraph is introduced in the United States when American inventor Samuel F. B. Morse (1791—1872) builds a telegraph line—paid for by the U.S. Congress—along the forty-mile stretch of Baltimore & Ohio (B&O) Railroad. (See September 22, 1851)

1844 June 15 First railroad in Switzerland opens from Basel to St. Ludwig (St. Louis, France). (See August 9, 1847)

1844 June 15

Goodyear patents "vulcanizing" rubber

1844 June 15 American inventor Charles Goodyear (1800—1860) patents "vulcanizing" rubber. While experimenting on how to prevent rubber from becoming stiff in the cold and soft and sticky in hot weather, Goodyear accidentally drops some India rubber mixed with sulfur on a hot stove and discovers it becomes dry and flexible in either temperature. Although he wins his patent case in 1852, he eventually dies heavily in debt. His name and discovery live today in the major use of rubber to make automobile tires.

1844 November 25 German automobile pioneer Karl F. Benz (1844—1929) is born in Karlsruhe. After studying engineering, he builds two-stroke gas engines of his own design in 1880 and decides to use them to power a vehicle. He is generally acknowledged as being the first to build a gas-powered automobile in 1885. His original design of a belt-driven, horseless carriage sells well however, and he is reluctant to depart from that design. He therefore has little effect on the further development of the automobile.

1845 Robert W. Thomson (1822—1873) of England makes a patent specification of the principle of the pneumatic (air-filled) tire. Made of canvas with leather treads around the inner tube, it gives a comfortable ride but presents Thomson with so many manufacturing problems that he drops the idea. He later loses a long court battle with John B. Dunlop (1840—1921) over who first invented it. (See 1888)

1845 First hydraulic elevator is invented by English engineer William G. A. Armstrong (1810—1900). This lifting device is essentially a water-powered mechanism.

1845 Miami and Erie Canal, connecting the Ohio River at Cincinnati with Lake Erie at Toledo is completed. It takes so long to finish this canal (20 years), that by the time it is completed it is unable to compete with the emerging railroad system.

1845 European newspapers tell of two young men, one Swede and one Norwegian, who are able to run over water using "the gear called 'skies,' by aid of which the inhabitants of the Northern regions traverse the snow-filled valleys and ravines without sinking."

1845 April The short era of the steam paddleship comes to an end as the British Admiralty stages a "tug-of-war" between a paddle wheel ship and one with a screw propeller. The two steam-powered sister ships pull against each other in a calm sea, and the screw-propelled *Rattler* tows the paddle-wheel *Alecto* away at about 2.5 knots. Aside from this power disparity, paddle wheels have other disadvantages besides their vulnerability to damage: the wheels come out of the water, which complicates steering, when the ship rolls severely, and because they operate close to the surface of the water, they are susceptible to excessive slippage when loaded and under full power.

c. 1840 ■ Canal boy leads a mule who tows a barge on an American canal.

1845 May 4 First iron railroad bridge in the United States opens on the Reading Railroad near Manayunk, Pennsylvania.

1845 July 26 First propeller-driven steam liner to cross the Atlantic, the *Great Britain,* leaves Liverpool, England for New York. Built by British engineer Isambard K. Brunel (1806—1859), it is also the first large, ocean-going ship to be made of iron. The largest ship in the world when built, it is 322 feet (98 meters) long and is constructed of overlapping iron plates. Designed to accommodate 360 passengers, it takes only 60 on this slow but pioneering voyage. It takes 14 days and 21 hours to reach New York.

1846 John Wise (1808—1879), during the Mexican-American War (1846—1848), offers to drop "aerial torpedoes" over Vera Cruz from a tethered balloon flown down wind over the city. The military authorities decline his offer.

1846 Heinrich D. Ruhmkorff (1803—1877), German technician living in Paris, improves the spark-induction coil to the point that for many years, his name is used synonymously with "induction."

1846 American automobile pioneer George B. Selden (1846—1932) is born. Selden was not technically-inclined but was, rather, an attorney who was astute enough to realize that one day, an internal combustion engine would be used to power a four-wheel vehicle. In 1877, Selden applied for a patent for a carriage (yet unbuilt) powered by a Bratton-type two-stroke gas engine. He delayed getting the definitive patent until someone actually had built such a vehicle, and then he went to court. Following his court victory in 1903, he sold his rights to a syndicate and received 1.25% royalty on every car sold in the United States. Henry Ford (1863—1947) refused to pay the syndicate and finally broke Selden's patent hold in court in 1911.

1846 "Railway mania" in England peaks as speculation in new railroad companies soars. Since new companies promise high dividends, and shares can be acquired for only a small deposit, many investors buy more shares than they can afford, expecting to sell them immediately and make a profit. The crash of 1847 ruins many an investor, but the boom that precedes it brings much needed capital to an emerging industry.

1846 Englishman William Hale (1797—1870) sells his patented invention of a spin-stabilized rocket to the U.S. Army Ordnance Department. Hale's ideas are a practical improvement, since the addition of angled fins to the rear of the rocket makes them able to be stabilized by spinning and thus more accurate. It also does away with the long, cumbersome guide stick.

1846 Englishman Thomas R. Crampton (1816—1888) makes the first major improvement to George Stephenson's (1781—1848) locomotive and creates a much more stable vehicle. Crampton overcomes Stephenson's problem of the boiler overhanging too far forward in relation to the wheel axles. By shifting one driving axle behind the firebox, he leaves only two axles under the cylindrical body of the boiler, creating a more stable locomotive.

1846—1848 The United States makes limited use of American-made, Hale rockets during the Mexican War of 1846—1848.

1846—1848 A.D.

U.S. uses Hale rockets in war

1846 February 9 German automobile pioneer Wilhelm Maybach (1846—1929) is born in Lowenstein. Along with Gottfried Daimler (1834—1900), he works for Nikolaus A. Otto (1832—1891), the inventor of the four-stroke internal combustion engine. He and Daimler later form their own company, devoted to building an automobile, which they produce in 1886. It is Maybach who is responsible for many of the technical advances achieved by the company.

1846 April 13 Pennsylvania Railroad Company is incorporated.

1846 July 15 First railroad in Hungary opens between Pest and Vacz.

1846 July 18 First plank road in the United States opens to traffic in Syracuse, New York. Introduced to the United States from Canada where 500 miles were laid between 1834 and 1850, it was claimed to be superior to macadam roads, and cheaper. Since no provision for drainage was made, rain eventually percolated through the wooden seams, softened the soil, became trapped, and finally floated the boards off the road.

1846 July 18

First U.S. plank road opens

1846 August 18 Gauge Act of 1846 settles the "Battle of the Gauges" and standardizes the width of British rail lines at 4 feet, 8½ inches (1,435 millimeters). Brunel's wider gauge, 7 feet, ¼ inches (2,140 millimeters), is majestic and promises better stability but Stephenson's winning narrower gauge is cheaper to build and much of it already exists. This gauge eventually becomes the international standard, although wider and narrower lines still exist.

1846 October 6 American engineer George Westinghouse (1846—1914) is born in Central Bridge, New York. His interest in railroads led to his first major invention, the air brake, patented in 1869. This eventually became widely accepted and in 1893 was made compulsory on all U.S. trains. He also devised new railroad signalling systems and later became the person chiefly responsible for the adoption of alternating current for electric power transmission in the United States.

1847 W. S. Henson (1805—1888) attempts to test fly in England his steam-driven model airplane, based on his *Aerial Steam Carriage* of 1843. This propeller-driven model with a wing-span of 20 feet, cannot keep itself in the air after leaving its ramp. Henson gives up and emigrates to the United States.

1847 American Moses G. Farmer (1820—1893) builds an experimental, non-rechargeable electric car for two passengers.

1847 First scientifically-based rules for bridge construction are offered by American engineer and inventor Squire Whipple (1804—1888) in his book, *A Work on Bridge Building*. Whipple's book is the first serious attempt to replace rule-of-thumb methods with a theoretical means of calculating stresses and strains.

1847 First U.S. government appropriation of funds is made for helping shipwreck victims. An item is added to the lighthouse appropriation bill that provides for "furnishing the lighthouses on the Atlantic coast with means of rendering assistance to shipwrecked mariners." For the first time, U.S. lighthouse staff are expected to do more than give warning.

1847 April

First double-decker bus built

1847 April First double-decker bus is built by Adams and Co. of London, England. These horse-drawn vehicles can accommodate 14 upper-deck passengers sitting back-to-back on the roof.

1847 June 2 First U.S. steamship to cross the Atlantic, the *Washington,* leaves from New York. It is a wooden paddle-steamer.

1847 June 26 First railroad in modern Denmark opens from Copenhagen to Roskilde.

1847 July 6 Richard Gypson, with Henry Coxwell (1819—1900) and two other passengers, makes a safe balloon descent over London after it bursts. While plummeting down, Coxwell cuts the neck-line (the cord used to keep the balloon tied at the bottom), which allows the inner envelope to float up into the top of the net and act as a parachute. This procedure soon becomes standard life-saving practice when a balloon bursts.

1847 August 9 First railroad wholly within Switzerland opens between Zurich and Baden.

1848 John Stringfellow (1799—1883), Henson's friend and collaborator, carries on in England and builds his own steam-driven model monoplane. It has curved wings spanning ten-and-one-half feet and a tail. It is launched from an overhead wire in a shed, and whether it ever really maintains a level or rising flight path is a matter of controversy, although there is no evidence that it did.

1848 The sedan chair, one of the oldest forms of transport, is last publicly offered for hire in the West in Edinburgh, Scotland. This portable, often covered, chair is designed to carry one person and is borne on poles by two men.

1848 Sailing ships from Ireland carry hundreds of thousands of Irish emigrants to Canada and the United States as a result of the Irish potato famine. It is estimated that 25,000 die on their way as a result of "ship fever," a generic term for dysentery, cholera, and typhoid fever.

1848 First concrete boats are made by Frenchman Joseph Louis Lambot, who plasters a sand-cement mortar over a boat frame of iron bars and mesh.

1848 May 23 Otto Lilienthal (1848—1896), key figure in the history of flying, is born in Anklam, Germany. He became the first man to fly (glide) with both regularity and control. Regarded by many as the inspirer and father of modern aviation, his experiments on constantly-improved hang-gliders focused on giving him insight into the problem of control—eventually mastered by the Wright Brothers who regarded his 1899 book as their bible. He was killed in a crash on August 9, 1896.

1848 October 28 First railroad in Spain opens between Barcelona and Mataro.

1848 November 3 First railroad in South America opens between Georgetown and Plaisance, British Guyana.

1849 First train ferry is designed by Thomas Grainger who ferries rail cars across the Firth of Forth, Scotland.

1849 Steam hammers are first used to drive and sink bridge piles in the construction of the Tyne railway bridge at Newcastle, England. Built by British engineer Robert Stephenson (1803—1859), it spans 1,873 feet and carries three tracks of the Northeastern Railway. The new hammer is able to sink a 10-meter-long pile in four to five minutes. This is compared to the very slow traditional method of using horses to turn a capstan to raise the hammer each time.

1849 First suspension bridge to surpass a span of 1,000 feet, the Wheeling Suspension Bridge, opens. Built by American engineer Charles Ellet, Jr. (1810—1862), it crosses the Ohio River at Wheeling, West Virginia and links the National Road from Cumberland, Maryland to the West. The very long deck is suspended by iron wire cables from two stone towers. It serves well until May 17, 1854 when the entire suspended portion collapses during a severe storm. Ellet rebuilds the bridge which stands, after several overhauls, even today.

1849 June First balloon bombing raid is carried out during the Seige of Venice, as 200 unmanned hot-air balloons are sent against Venice by the Austrians. Each carries a small bomb and a timing fuse. Unpredictable winds make this experiment a failure.

1849 September The Alps are crossed by air for the first time, from Marseilles, France to Stubini near Turin, Italy, by French balloonist, Francisque Arban (1815—1849). A month later on October 7, he is lost over the Mediterranean after an ascent from Barcelona, Spain.

c. 1850 Commercial elevators are first introduced in America by Henry Waterman of New York. He develops a steam-operated platform hoist using ropes and a cage. Elevators remain dangerously unsafe if the rope breaks.

1850 Japanese writer Mitsukuri Genpo completes his translation, *Suijosen Setsuryaku*, a European handbook on steamboats. It is commissioned to be translated by the Satsuma clan.

c. 1850 Nineteenth-century coaches develop features and design indicative of their nationality. Thus the English coach is characteristically flat-roofed and has straight sidewalls; the typical French coach has a slightly convex roof and curved sidewalls; and the German coach has roof and sidewalls that are strongly curved.

c. 1850 The large, thriving city of London, England has no more than 10,000 people commuting to it by rail, but as many as 244,000 commute by foot or horse-drawn omnibus.

1850 U.S. Congress passes a land grant act which provides the basis for the eventual spanning of the continent by several railroad networks. This stimulus to the construction of railroads promotes economic growth and fosters greater political and social cohesion in the United States.

1850 New speed record for sailing ships, 13 days from Boston Light to the Equator, is set by American Donald MacKay's (1810—1880) clipper ship, the *Staghound*. This very long, slim clipper ship has a hollow bow for cargo and a radically streamlined hull.

c. 1850 First and only hinged ship, the *Connector*, is built in England. This unusual ship is built in three sections with hinged or articulated joints that allow it to be split up into three to load or discharge cargo. Essentially a variation of the barge train used on inland waterways, it is designed to ride easier in rough seas because the ship's sections will undulate with the waves. However, sideways rolling will easily tear the sections apart, and the ship is never tried at sea.

c. 1850 A.D.

Only hinged ship built

1850 Britannia Bridge opens over the Menai Straits in Wales. Built by British engineer Robert Stephenson (1803—1859), the son of George Stephenson (1781—1848), this railway bridge is made of two huge rectangular wrought-iron tubes supported on masonry piers. The two main spans are each 138 meters long and sag no more than one-and-a-half centimeters when a full loaded train passes over them. This bridge demonstrates conclusively the great tensile strength of wrought iron and is the forerunner of scores of railroad bridges.

1850 A.D.

Baby carriages first built

1850 First regular manufacture of perambulators (baby carriages) begins in England as two rival British firms start producing a new type carriage. Previous to these hand-pushed, three-wheel designs, all perambulators had been pulled. These new carriages only accommodate children old enough to sit up. Those made for infants do not appear until 1876.

1850 A.D.

Iron buoys introduced in U.S.

1850 Iron buoys are introduced in the United States, as one of the first is anchored at Little Egg Harbor, New Jersey.

1850 January 1 First U.S. lighthouse to be built in a location directly exposed to the open sea, the Minot's Ledge Lighthouse, is completed. This 75-foot-high wrought-iron skeleton warns ships southeast of Boston, Massachusetts of the submerged jagged rocks that have claimed so many victims. It is destroyed by a severe storm on April 17, 1851, which kills its two keepers.

1850 January 29 Lawrence Hargrave (1850—1915), Australian aviation pioneer, born at London, England. An emigre to Australia, Hargrave is best known for his invention of the box-kite—a design whose inherent stability and strong lifting power were to be used by early builders of gliders, whether they were aware of him or not. His later designs for a powered airplane lacked a good power source and never flew.

1850 April 27

First transatlantic steamship service begins

1850 April 27 Collins Line inaugurates its regular transatlantic service between Britain and the United States. Its four steamships are built as a response to the British Cunard Line's dominance of the transatlantic trade. The Collins steamers are the biggest and fastest ships afloat and establish new standards of design. But two sinkings and the Cunard Line's decision to build the *Persia*, a huge, iron-hulled steamer, puts the Collins Line out of business.

1850 May Englishman Hugh Bell ascends in his balloon equipped with a man-powered propeller. Called the *Locomotive Balloon*, it cannot be propelled and drifts for 30 miles (48 kilometers).

1850 June 29 The French savants, J. A. Barral (1819—1884) and A. J. Bixio (1808—1865), make the first of their balloon ascents in Paris, France to conduct scientific observations. In the same year, they ascend above the clouds to 23,000 feet while investigating the atmosphere.

1850 September 20 First federal railroad land-grant act is signed by U.S. President Millard Fillmore (1800—1874). These land-grants or loans to railroad companies by the U.S. government stimulate the construction of more lines.

1850 September 28 First systematic coloring and numbering of all buoys is provided for by an act of the U.S. Congress. The act prescribes that "buoys should be colored and numbered so that in entering from seaward red buoys with even numbers should be on the starboard or right hand; black buoys with odd numbers on the port or left hand; buoys with red and black horizontal stripes should indicate shoals with channel on either side; and buoys in channel ways should be colored with black and white perpendicular stripes." As harbor traffic increases in the United States, the old, informal system of basically no system will no longer do, and standardization becomes imperative.

1850 October 28 First lighthouse in the United States to be erected as a screw-pile structure, the Brandywine Shoal Lighthouse, is built in Delaware Bay. (See 1838)

1850 November Pierre Jullien (1816—1876), a French clockmaker, successfully flies his 23-foot-long model airship. This prophetically-streamlined airship model is filled with gas and is propelled by two clockwork-driven propellers. Two years later he builds a 164-foot-long airship that influences Henri Giffard (1825—1888), although it is never tested.

1851 American Charles G. Page (1812—1868) builds a non-rechargeable electric car that goes 19 mph (31 km/h).

1851 Steel wheels for locomotives are first produced by German industrialist Alfred Krupp (1812—1887). Steel proves to outlast iron wheels nearly five times longer.

1851 Hoosac Tunnel on the Boston & Maine Railroad is begun. Its construction is so plagued by technical problems, incompetence, and corruption that it takes 24 years and an estimated $20 million to complete.

c. 1850 ■ One of the first trains over the Alleghany Mountains.

When opened in 1875, it is over four miles (7,562 meters) long. It is one of the earliest projects in the United States to use both compressed-air drilling and nitroglycerine for tunnelling.

1851 As road quality in major cities continues to improve, the city of Paris builds macadamized roads and covers them with asphalt.

1851 Submersible vehicle built by American Lodner D. Philips (1825—1869) makes a manned dive beneath Lake Michigan. His submarine has a cylindrical body with cone-shaped ends and is driven by a hand-operated propeller system. After many successful dives, Philips dies in his underwater vehicle.

1851 First major iron truss bridge, the Newark Dyke Bridge, is built over the Trent River in England. Designed by English engineer James Warren, the iron truss bridge spans 240 feet. A truss is a structural form of support based on a triangle. Warren uses both cast iron and wrought iron in his truss, with the more expensive wrought iron used only where tensile strength is needed. For parts under compression and not tension, he uses the cheaper cast iron.

1851 First mechanical fog warning signal is installed in a U.S. lighthouse. Both an air fog whistle and an air trumpet or reed horn are tested experimentally at the Beavertail Lighthouse at the entrance to Narragansett Bay in Rhode Island. The air compressor is operated by a horse rather than any sort of engine.

1851 July 1 First refrigerator-type railroad car in the United States begins service when eight tons of butter are carried to Boston, Massachusetts from Ogdensburg, New York. The butter is carried in a wooden boxcar insulated with sawdust and packed with ice. (See January 16, 1868)

1851 August 16 First international railway link on the North American continent opens between Laprairie, Quebec and Rouses Point, New York. By this international agreement, the first of its kind in the world, rolling stock of foreign ownership are permitted free entry into either Canada or the United States.

1851 September 22 First recorded use of a telegraph for train dispatching occurs on the New York & Erie Railroad in Turner (now Harriman), New York.

1851 November 1 Train service begins on the Nikolaev Railway between Moscow and St. Petersburg, Russia.

1851 December 25 First railroad in Chile opens.

1852 The Société Aérostatique et Météorologique de France, the first aeronautical society in the world, is founded. Its originator is Jules-François Dupuis-Delcourt (1802—1864).

1852 First "safety" elevator is invented by an American, Elisha Graves Otis (1811—1861). Otis designs a safety brake that will keep an elevator from falling even if the cable holding it is completely cut. His first safety guard consists of a used wagon spring on top of the hoist platform and a ratchet bar attached to the guide rails. If the cable snaps, the tension would be released from the spring and each end would immediately catch the ratchet, locking the platform in place and preventing a fall. (See September 20, 1853)

1852 French engineer Emile Loubat invents the system of placing horse-drawn streetcar rails

Margin notes

1851 August 16

First international railway begins

1851 November 1

Russian train service begins

1852 A.D.

Safety elevator invented

within the street pavement itself, making them flush with the street and posing much less of an obstacle to coach and wagon traffic. He installs these sunken street rails on the Sixth Avenue line in New York this same year. By 1860, horse-drawn railcars on these new rails are rapidly replacing the omnibuses or coaches, since the former is a much more efficient use of horsepower. A team of horses can pull vehicles of two tons or more with up to 50 passengers on rails. This is double the weight and number of a horse-drawn omnibus.

1852 A.D.

Wells Fargo founded

1852 Wells, Fargo & Co., a major American banking and transportation business, is founded by Henry Wells (1805—1878), William G. Fargo (1818—1881), and associates. It links New York with San Francisco, California by sea via an overland route over the Isthmus of Panama. It later expands its transportation services to the entire West Coast, and eventually operates throughout the world.

1852 First lighthouse on the dangerous stretch of reefs between Cape Florida and Key West, Florida, the Carysfort Reef Lighthouse, begins operations.

1852 British Captain John R. Ward carefully studies and experiments with all known types of lifejackets and concludes that the cork belt is the best, although the most expensive. It is made of many segments of cork that are strung together and then sewn to a stout linen or canvas belt.

1852 January 3 Wooden mail ship, the *Amazon*, catches fire on its maiden voyage, killing 37 of the 161 passengers and 68 crew members. As a result, the British government requires all future mail ships to have iron hulls and be propeller-driven.

1852

February 23

British steamer sinks

1852 February 23 British 1,400-ton paddlewheel steamer *Birkenhead*, carrying troops and civilians from England to South Africa, runs aground. As the ship sinks, the officers help civilians into the few lifeboats, and then stand "at parade" even as the ship breaks up. Over 200 people are saved, and of the 420 who die, nearly every one is a soldier. Rudyard Kipling (1865—1936) memorializes this heroism in his poem, *The Birken'ead Drill*. Historians later note that the soldiers who died were green recruits who had no notion of what was actually happening.

1852 September 24 First powered, manned airship is flown by its builder, the French engineer, Henri Giffard (1825—1888). Powered by a steam engine and propeller, the airship flies at about 5 mph and covers 17 miles (c. 27 kilometers) from Paris to near Trappes, France. This craft marks the beginning of the practical airship.

1852 September 25 Englishman George Cayley (1773—1857) publishes an illustrated article in *Mechanics Magazine* which describes a glider he calls a "governable parachute."

1852 December 9 First locomotive west of the Mississippi River, the *Pacific*, runs from St. Louis to Cheltenham, Missouri—about five miles.

1853 Englishman George Cayley (1773—1857) builds his third full-size airplane and tests it in Yorkshire, England by persuading a driver or coachman to make a glide as passenger.

1853 Michel Loup, a Frenchman, designs but does not build a large, fixed-wing aircraft with propellers set into the wings.

1853 New York architect James Renwick (1818—1895) produces the first terra cotta in the United States and proposes its use as paving material for roads. Terra cotta is a fired clay used for architectural purposes such as roofing and facing. It is more commonly used for statuettes and vases. Renwick is a professor of natural philosophy and experimental chemistry at Columbia University who also designs the Smithsonian Institution and St. Patrick's Cathedral in New York City.

1853 J. K. Fisher of New York builds a steam carriage which runs 15 mph and remains operating for two years.

1853 English engineer James H. Nasmyth (1808—1890) builds an 80-foot long vessel that is semi-submersible. Driven by a single propeller steam engine, it rides just under water with only a small dome and a smoke stack jutting above the surface. Built with military purposes in mind, the boat is called an "anti-invasion floating mortar" by Nasmyth.

1853 ■ American clipper ship *Shooting Star*.

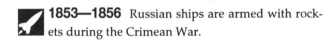

1853—1856 Russian ships are armed with rockets during the Crimean War.

1853 January 1 First practical steam-powered fire engine in the United States is tested by its inventor, Alexander B. Latta, in Cincinnati, Ohio. Powered by a steam boiler, it weighs five tons and can shoot a stream of water 240 feet. It runs on three wheels, with the front wheel able to pivot. Four horses are used to supplement its engine's pulling power.

1853 January 10 Earliest known instance of meals being served on a train in the United States occurs as the Baltimore & Ohio (B&O) runs two special trains from Baltimore, Maryland to Wheeling, West Virginia and engages a caterer to provide food.

1853 January 24 An all-rail route is completed linking Chicago, Illinois with several eastern cities, although many changes of cars are necessary.

1853 April 18 First railroad in India, the Great Indian Peninsula, opens between Bombay and Thana.

1853 May 6 One of the first major U.S. train accidents occurs as a New York and New Haven Railway passenger train runs through an open drawbridge and plummets into the Norwalk River, killing 46 people.

1853 June A railroad in Connecticut equips one of its passenger trains with vestibules. These enclosed yet flexible connections between cars allow passengers to walk from one car into another on a moving train.

1853 September 20 Elisha Graves Otis (1811—1861) demonstrates his safety elevator at the New York City Crystal Palace Exhibition. Standing on the hoist platform in the main area of Exhibition Hall, Otis repeatedly orders the support rope cut, and his safety mechanism works every time. *The New York Tribune* writes, "At last a safe lift had been made that the public could trust." Otis's Union Elevator Works founds the elevator industry.

1854 Steam locomotive is first introduced into Japan. U.S. Commodore Matthew Perry's fleet brings a miniature steam locomotive which it operates in Yokohama and Edo. At the same time, The Netherlands presents Japan with its first paddle-wheel steamboat.

1853 Sept. 20

Elevator industry begins

1853 ■ Currier print of a typical American open sleigh.

1854 "Night seat" rail coaches go into service between Philadelphia, Pennsylvania and Baltimore, Maryland. These cars are equipped with luxurious, adjustable, reclining-seats.

1854 First lighthouse on the U.S. Pacific coast, Alcatraz Lighthouse, is completed. Located on an island in San Francisco Bay, it is built against the prison and former fortress of Alcatraz.

1854 Submarine is built by German Wilhelm Bauer, who names his short, stubby vessel the *Brandtaucher*. It moves under water by a treadmill-powered propeller, and Bauer uses it during a German-Danish naval encounter to frighten Denmark's fleet. His vessel sinks soon after, but he and his crew escape.

1854 First recorded ski race in the United States is held in Sierra County, California. The straight downhill event is run by skiers using 15-foot skis.

1854 March Crimean War (1854—1856) breaks out. This conflict between Turkey and Russia, in which Great Britain and France are allies of Turkey, convinces most governments that future ships must be both fully powered and armor-plated.

1854 March First true prototype of the modern ocean steamship, the *City of Glasgow*, leaves Liverpool, England for New York and disappears without a trace. This 227-foot- (69-meter-) long ship with a two-bladed propeller carries 480 people, passengers and crew. It is assumed that the ship hits an iceberg.

1854 April 30 First railroad in Brazil opens from Maua, at the end of the Bay of Rio to the foot of the Petropolis Serra.

1854 May 15 First transalpine railroad opens over the Semmering Pass (Austria to Yugoslavia). After the Brenner Pass Line opens on August 24, 1867, these are the only main lines which cross the Alps without a major tunnel.

1854 May 18 First public railroad in Australia to carry passengers and goods, the Port Elliot & Goolwa Railway, opens. It uses horses and not steam.

1854 June 27 Louis-Charles Letur is killed when his pedal-operated parachute glider is dragged into trees before it is released from a balloon.

1854 August 17 First steamship to be fitted with a compound engine, the *Brandon*, leaves Southampton, England for New York. The compound principle for steam engines—using high and low pressure cylinders—uses the same steam twice and cuts coal consumption in half. This breakthrough reduces one of steam's major disadvantages on long voyages—that ships had to either carry enormous loads of coal or stop somewhere to refuel.

1854 September 1 First railroad in Norway opens between Christiania (now Oslo) and Eidsvoll.

1854 September 12 First steam railroad in Australia opens from Melbourne to Port Melbourne.

1854 September 27 Lavishly built American steam ocean liner the *Atlantic* is rammed in a fog by French steamer *Vesta*, and sinks in four hours. As many as 322 are believed killed.

1855 First recorded use of the word "caboose" to describe the last car on an American freight train is made on the Buffalo, Corning & New York Railroad. Its rooftop cupola appears to have been introduced in 1863 by American freight conductor, T. B. Watson.

1855 Japanese begin making their own steam engines for ships.

1855 Isthmus of Panama is spanned by railroad.

1855 Alfred Drake of Philadelphia patents an incandescent metal as an ignition method for gaseous mixtures. Drake had displayed this "hot-tube" igniter as early as 1843. It is a thimble-like piece of cast iron projecting into a recess of the cylinder wall and is kept red hot by a flame. It becomes a popular device.

1855 First self-propelled steam-powered fire engine in the United States is patented by A. B. Latta.

1855 The Vanderbilt Line begins operations in the North Atlantic. Founded by American entrepreneur Cornelius "Commodore" Vanderbilt (1794—1877), this freight and passenger steamship line undercuts its competition and drives them from the market. By 1862, Vanderbilt sells his steamships and turns his attention to railroads.

1855 February Susan Morningstar, first female railroad employee in the United States, is hired to help clean the Baltimore & Ohio (B&O) terminal in Baltimore, Maryland.

1855 February 1 First special postal train begins service in England between London and Bristol. It is operated by the Great Western Railway.

1855 March 6 First train to cross a span sustained by wire cables goes over the Niagara Bridge, the first successful railway suspension bridge in the world. Designed and built by American engineer John A. Roebling (1806—1869), it has a span of 821 feet at a height of 245 feet above the rapids. The two decks are suspended from four cables which rest atop two masonry towers. It is replaced by an arch bridge in 1896.

1855 September Special horse-and-buggy flatcar rail services become a popular form of long-distance transportation for U.S. farmers en route to the markets of Nova Scotia. The horses and buggies are tied down to the flatcars.

1856 French automobile pioneer Albert de Dion (1856—1946) is born. A privileged young man who becomes famous as a gambler and a duellist, he believes in the future of automobiles and so joins with his brother-in-law, Georges Bouton, to build their first practical gas-powered tricycle in 1895. They continue to develop the car, and are the largest auto maker in the world for some

time. De Dion also founds the daily publication *L'Auto* and is a prime mover in the Automobile Club de France.

1856 Richard Dudgeon of New York builds his first steam carriage. It is eventually destroyed in the Crystal Palace Fire in London, but he builds a duplicate in 1860 which runs very well. It is not as comfortable as many of the European models, since the passengers must sit around the steaming boiler.

1856 Interlocking signals for railroad operation are patented by Englishman John Saxby (1821—1913). Soon to become universal, they ensure the coordination of all points and signals on a line and prevent conflicting signals from being given.

1856 English metallurgist Henry Bessemer (1813—1898) announces his discovery of what becomes known as the "Bessemer process," a quick, inexpensive way of making steel. Up to this time, steel was made by an extremely costly method of first making cast iron, converting it into wrought iron, and then adding carbon. Steel was desirable since it has the hardness of cast iron and the toughness of wrought iron. Bessemer found that ready-made steel could be made without the wrought iron step by blasting the fired iron with air and stopping at just the right time. The availability of affordable steel begins the era of large-scale transportation ventures, like giant ocean liners and huge suspension bridges. It will also become an integral new material for automobiles and aircraft.

1856 Italian priest and physicist Eugenio Barsanti (1821—1864) and Italian engineer Felice Matteucci (1808—1887) obtain a British patent for a three-stroke cycle, internal combustion engine which omits the compression cycle. It does not go into production, as Barsanti dies soon after.

1856 First of the Mormon hand-cart emigrants make their way on a 1,400-mile journey west from the Missouri River to their promised land of Salt Lake City, Utah. Lacking money to buy large wagons and oxen or horses, the emigrants from England, Wales, Denmark and other European countries follow the plan of their leader, Brigham Young (1801—1877), and pull their belongings and supplies along by hand on two-wheel carts. The first three caravans reach their destination safely, but the fourth and fifth are caught in the snow, and 135 out of 150 persons die. 1860 is the last year these

1856 A.D.
Steel-making process advances

1856 A.D.
Mormon hand-cart journey to Salt Lake City begins

1856 ■ Destitute Mormon immigrants from Europe pull their hand-carts from Iowa to Salt Lake City.

strange and sadly desperate experiments in transportation are conducted.

1856 First lighthouse in Newfoundland is a cylindrical, cast-iron tower built on the edge of a cliff at Cape Race, 87 feet above the sea.

1856 A.D.

Mail delivered on skis

1856 "Snowshoe Thompson" begins delivering mail on skis in California. Born Jon Thompson (b. 1827) in Telemark, Norway, he regularly carries the mail 90 miles (145 kilometers) from Placerville to Carson Valley, California, using a pair of 12-foot (4-meter) skis and a single, large ski pole.

1856 Germany begins a steamship service in the North Atlantic.

1856 January First railroad in Africa opens between Alexandria to Cairo, Egypt. It runs 130 miles (210 kilometers).

1856 February 22

First U.S. west coast railroad opens

1856 February 22 First railroad on the U.S. west coast opens between Sacramento and Folsom, California.

1856 April 21 First railroad bridge to span the Mississippi River opens in Davenport, Iowa. After it is partially burned on May 6 following a steamboat collision, it is rebuilt and reopened on September 8, 1856.

1856 July 17 An excursion train filled with students collides in Philadelphia, Pennsylvania with an inbound train sent incorrectly down the same track. In the ensuing fire, 66 children are killed. The engineer of the inbound train becomes so distraught he poisons himself.

1856 September 8 First Canadians to fly in a balloon are A. E. Kierzkowski, A. X. Rambau, and David S. Ramsey. They are passengers in Frenchman Eugene Godard's balloon.

1856 October 28 First railroad in Portugal opens between Lisbon and Carregado.

1856 December 1 First railroad in Sweden opens between Gothenburg and Jonsered, and from Malmo to Lund.

1856 December 2 First railroad sleeping-car patents are issued to American T. T. Woodruff.

c. 1857—1858 Felix Du Temple (1823—1890), a French naval officer, successfully flies and safely lands his model airplane. It has swept-forward wings and is powered by clockwork.

1857 Jean-Marie Le Bris (1808—1872), a French sea-captain, builds and tests at Trefeuntee, France his full-size glider, whose design he bases on the albatross. He crashes and breaks a leg after one short glide. His launch method is to gain lift by being pulled along on a cart.

1857 American engineer Frank J. Sprague (1857—1934) is born. As the man who probably contributed most to the development of electric rapid transit systems, Sprague built the first successful trolley line in 1888 and developed electric trolley cars. His major contribution was his system of motors that permits either unified control of an entire train from the lead car or independent operation of individual cars. He also helped develop the electric elevator.

1857 U.S. government experiments with camels, purchasing 75 camels from Egypt and Arabia to be used by the army in the western deserts. American mule drivers prove incapable of understanding the camel's temperament and habits and treat them roughly, making them balky and uncooperative. Further attempts to organize camel caravans bring about incipient mutiny, and the experiment in desert transportation is abandoned. Some camels are simply turned loose and others are kept in forts or sold to menageries.

1857 First railroad shipment of refrigerated meat is made out of Chicago, Illinois.

1857 First of the long tunnels under the Alps in Europe, the Mont Cenis Tunnel, is begun. Intended to connect France and Italy, the tunnel is first dug through hard rock with hand tools. After Italian engineer Germain Sommeillier invented the rock drill operated by compressed air, work speeds up tremendously and it is completed in 1871. It is a double-track tunnel, eight miles long and one mile below the summit of the mountain.

1857 First steel rails (for railroad tracks) are made by Englishman Robert Forester Mushet (1811—1891). He lays them as an experiment on a heavily used line at Derby Station on the Midland Railway. Steel is a superior form of iron.

1857 Venice, Italy is linked to the cities of Europe as the Milan-Venice Railway is completed. The vital connection is a 3.5-kilometer bridge begun in 1846.

1857 Upper Ganges Canal in India is completed. Built for navigation as well as irrigation, it extends 300 miles, ending at Cawnpore. It is carried over the Solani River by a 900-foot long, 170-foot wide aqueduct.

1857 First street to be lit permanently by electricity is La Rue Imperiale in Lyons, France. The lights are installed by two Frenchmen, Lacassagne and Thiers.

1857 First steam whistle fog horn in the United States is installed in the Beavertail Lighthouse in Rhode Island.

1857 March 23 First passenger elevator is installed in the retail store of E. V. Haughwout & Company in New York. Built by the Otis Company, it is powered by steam and is capable of lifting 1,000 pounds at 40 feet per minute. This building is five stories high.

1857 August 30 First railroad in Argentina opens between Parque and Floresta.

1857 September 12 Ship powered by side-wheels and sails named the *Central America* leaves Cuba for New York and sails into a hurricane. The crew of 101 men and 474 other passengers are battered for two days, and the dying ship drifts off the coast of South Carolina. Although another ship, the *Marine*, comes to its aid, rough seas prevent any transfer of passengers, and the *Marine* watches as the *Central America* goes down, killing 423 people.

1857 September 17 Konstantin Eduardovich Tsiolkovsky (1857—1935), pioneer in spaceflight theory and rocket design, is born in Russia. Mostly self-taught and nearly deaf, this genius is hailed by many as the father of space travel, since he discovers the principles of spaceflight. He was the first to state in concrete mathematical terms how to fly successfully into space and the first to describe the actual physical means of how to do it. His life's work detailed nearly every aspect associated with space travel, and he foresaw and influenced many of the things that actually came to be. He never once tested or even built a working model of one of his rockets, and labored in near-poverty and obscurity for most of his life.

1857 Sept. 17 Russian space pioneer born

1857 November 23 Last wooden-hulled ship specifically designed for transatlantic service, the *Adriatic*, goes into service. This American vessel makes only one Atlantic voyage.

1858 American named Blake invents a steam-powered "stone-breaker" that provides four to six cubic yards of crushed stone an hour. Roadmakers and engineers now have access to a sufficient supply of irregular stones for their road surfaces. Until now, stones were broken by hand.

1858 Pierre-Constant Hugon (b. 1814) of France patents a non-compression, double-acting gas engine and builds one after Jean Joseph Etienne Lenoir (1822—1900) in 1860. He later abandons his work.

1858 Reports are made of a man named Ochoner who goes up the Rhine River while standing erect on what are called "podoscaphs." He propels himself upriver by paddling with a long pole flattened at the ends.

c. 1858—1859 Francis Herbert Wenham (1824—1908), an English marine engineer, begins a prolonged study of wings, and offers the correct idea that most of a wing's lift comes from it front edge. He argues that a long, narrow wing would give the most lift. He tests models as well as full-size gliders, on which he lays prone. He later publishes a paper documenting his findings. (See 1866)

c. 1858—1859 A.D. Engineer studies wings

1858 ■ Butterfield's Overland Mail becomes the first overland mail service between the Mississippi River and the Pacific coast.

1858
March 18

Father of diesel engines born

1858 March 18 German engineer Rudolph Christian Karl Diesel (1858—1913) is born in Paris, France. A brilliant scholar at the Munich Polytechnic, Diesel will always be known for the compression-ignition internal combustion engine named after him. His powerful, efficient engines still power more than half the world's tonnage of ships, and a large number of locomotives were diesel driven. Diesel engines are now used in buses, tractors, trucks, and even some cars.

1858 March 29 First manned hydrogen balloon ascent in Australia is made as two Australians named Dean and Brown fly at Melbourne.

1858 August 23 First serious passenger train runaway occurs on the Oxford, Worcester & Wolverhampton Railway in England when part of a heavy passenger train breaks away and runs backwards into a following passenger train. Fourteen people are killed.

1858 September 2 Samuel King (1828—1914) introduces the dragline in America, following Thomas Baldwin's suggestion in 1786 and Charles Green's (1785—1870) first use of it in 1836. It is a long rope attached to the basket which helps to stabilize altitude by dragging on the ground when the balloon is flying very low. (See 1836)

1858 September 15 First overland mail service between the Mississippi River and the Pacific coast is provided by the "Butterfield Overland Mail" stagecoaches. This successful system makes a one-way trip from St. Louis to San Francisco in less than 24 days. The coaches carry nine people on three inside seats and as many as ten on top with the driver.

1858 October First aerial photograph is taken by the famous French photographer, Nadar, whose real name is Felix Tournachon (1820—1910). He photographs the city of Paris from his captive balloon.

1859 First storage battery is invented by French physicist Gaston Plante (1834-1889). Until his device, batteries that produced electricity as the result of a chemical reaction had to be discarded when the chemical reaction was completed. When Plante found a way to reverse that chemical reaction (via lead plates immersed in sulfuric acid) and produce an electric current (or recharge the battery), he invented a way of storing electricity. His batteries will prove essential to the later development of the automobile.

1859 ■ Peak of the golden era of Mississippi River steamboats.

1859 In England, the London General Omnibus Company Ltd. reports carrying 39 million riders annually. Although not a real urban mass transit system (since its rates are too high for the poorer classes), it does contribute to the growth of new middle class residential areas only one to two miles outside the city's center. Despite its success, the coaches will soon be replaced by a rail system.

1859 Horse-drawn tramcar or railcar is first introduced into England by American George F. Train (1829—1904). All Europe eventually switches from omnibuses (horse-drawn coaches) to horse-drawn streetcars on rails.

1859 First iron-clad ship, the French *La Gloire*, is launched. Built with a conventional wooden hull, this armed warship is covered from a point six feet (1.8 meters) under the water line to its main deck with iron plating to a thickness of 4.5 inches (114.3 millimeters). Many consider this to be the first true battleship.

1859 February 3 Hugo Junkers (1859—1935), born in Rheydt, Germany. Pioneer aircraft designer and early proponent of the monoplane as well as the all-

metal aircraft. In 1910, he patented his "flying wing" concept of having the entire aircraft (engine and passengers) contained within one single airfoil or wing. His J-1 Blechesel monoplane was the first all-metal airplane to fly. His company later played an important role for World War II German airpower.

1859 July 2 Two American balloonists, John Wise (1808—1879) and John La Mountain (1830—1878), fly in their balloon from St. Louis, Missouri to Henderson, New York. They make the 809-mile (c. 1300 kilometers) trip in 20 hours.

1859 July 2
Balloonists fly 809 miles

1859 August 27 First successful oil well is drilled just outside the city limits of Titusville, Pennsylvania by Edwin L. Drake (1819—1880). The success of this well and the growing demand for petroleum products leads to exploration and drilling elsewhere. The beginning of the oil and gas industry coincides with the invention of the internal combustion engine (1860).

1859 September 1 First Pullman railroad sleeping car begins service on an overnight trip between Bloomington, Minnesota and Chicago, Illinois. The first Pullman conductor is Jonathan L. Barnes. Invented by

1859 ■ Interior of an early Pullman railroad car.

George M. Pullman (1831—1897), a former cabinet maker, this is only a beginning experiment. (See 1864)

1859 October 8 Canadian named Hickock walks on top of the River Don wearing four-foot- (1.2-meter-) long shoes made of tin.

1860 A.D.

Gas engine invented

1860 Etienne Lenoir (1822—1900) invents the gas engine in France. Its lighter-weight descendant will drive the first sustained, powered flight by the Wrights 43 years later.

1860 First practical gas engine or internal combustion engine is a two-stroke gas engine built and patented by Jean Joseph Etienne Lenoir (1822—1900) of Belgium. Having experimented with several fuels, he finally settles on coal gas and uses an electric spark from a Ruhmkorff induction coil for ignition. Two years later, he installs his new engine in a high riding carriage. His success spurs other inventors to examine the possibilities of the internal combustion engine instead of steam. (See 1862)

c. 1860 "Velocipede" tricycles and quadricycles made of iron begin to appear in England. One of the best known is a quadricycle (four-wheel) made by Eng-

lishman Willard Sawyer. It has a treadle-drive directly attached to a cranked wrought-iron axle.

c. 1860 American "covered wagon" called the "prairie schooner" takes settlers to the far west. Similar to a Conestoga wagon, these wagons carry people as well as freight. They have a flat, box body instead of the tipped-up, boat-shaped design of the Conestoga, and the wooden sides are not nearly as tall. These wagons carry a family's entire possessions, and only those settlers who are unable to walk may ride. They are the main means of westward migration for many years.

1860 Russian Konstantin I. Konstantinov (1817—1871), director of St. Petersburg Rocket Manufacturing Plant, tests a rocket with an effective range of five kilometers.

1860 First partly self-contained diving system is invented by Frenchmen Benoit Rouquayrol (1826—1875), Auguste Denayrouze (1837—1883), and Louis Denayrouze (1848—1910). This advanced diving system has a "demand valve" for breathing as does today's scuba gear. The system is not totally free from some dependence on the surface. By 1875 however, their improved device is fully independent.

1860 Modern ski design is created by Sondre Norheim (1825—1895) of Telemark, Norway who designs three novel faetures: his skis are "waisted" or made narrower under the bindings for better control; they are shorter, less than eight feet (2.5 meters); and they have a heel strap of twisted willow in addition to the toe strap. With this new equipment, Norheim creates his novel turns, the "Telemark" and the "Christiana." Within a few years, skis are no longer made of unequal length.

1860 First ships to be specifically fitted and used as floating hospitals are the British sail-rigged steamships *Melbourne* and *Mauritius*.

1860 April 3 Pony Express, the first rapid overland mail service to the Pacific coast, officially opens. Connecting St. Joseph, Missouri with Sacramento, California, the trips average ten days, about half the time of the Butterfield stage line. Regularly changing horses and riders, the pony riders cover 250 miles in a 24-hour period compared with a coach's 100—125 miles. Although famous and colorful, the system is a financial diaster and is put out of business by the completion of the transcontinental telegraph system. (See September 15, 1858)

1860 June 17 Largest ship of its time, the *Great Eastern*, leaves Southampton on its maiden voyage. Built by British engineer Isambard K. Brunel (1806—1859) on an outlandishly large scale, this 340-foot- (103.6-meter-) long steamship is driven by both propeller and paddles. It can accommodate a crew of 400 with room for 800 first class, 2,000 second class, and 1,200 third class passengers. On this first voyage, it carries only 40 passengers, and in its 11 transatlantic trips, it never breaks even. Most ports are too shallow for it and most docks too small. It is used from 1864 to 1866 to lay transatlantic cable, since its vast holds are capable of carrying over 1,000 miles (1,600 kilometers) of cable at a time.

1860 June 26 First railroad in South Africa opens between Durban and the Point (Natal).

1861 Balloons are begun to be used for reconnaissance by both Union and Confederate sides in the American Civil War. The Union's Thaddeus S. C. Lowe (1832—1913), appointed chief balloonist to the Army of the Potomac by President Abraham Lincoln, makes the most flights, and conveys valuable information from his tethered balloon to the ground by an electric wire attached to his balloon.

1861 The idea of driving the front wheel of a velocipede or bicycle directly by cranks or pedals on the axle is attributed to Pierre Michaux and his son Ernest (b. 1841) and their employee, Pierre Lallement. They set up shop in the Champs Elysées in Paris and begin manufacturing. (See 1866)

1861 American automobile pioneer Charles Duryea (1861—1938) is born. He and his brother Frank (1869—1967) build the first practical American car that leads to the creation of the first car manufacturing company in the United States. Their initial 1893 vehicle leads to the formation of the Duryea Motor Wagon Company of Peoria, Illinois. The early Duryea cars had many advanced features but were not commercially successful.

1861 During the first Japanese mission to Europe, the delegation led by Takenouchi Yasunori rides its first train at Suez, Egypt.

1861 First ski club is founded in Kiandra, Australia. It is ironic that the first ski organization should not be in Norway or even in the Alps, yet Norwegian laborers have been emigrating to Australia, New Zealand, Canada, and the United States, and taking their skis with them. Norway forms its own ski club this year also.

1861 March 8 First military engagement between ironclad ships occurs in Norfolk, Virginia during the American Civil War (1861—1865). After the Confederate ironclad, the *Merrimac*, destroys two Union ships, it is confronted by the Union ironclad, the *Monitor*. After a battle of nearly fours hours during which both are hit with explosive shells over 20 times, neither vessel is put out of action. The conclusion reached by most after this battle is that contemporary armor is superior to contemporary weapons.

1861 April 20 Thaddeus S. C. Lowe (1832—1913), American inventor and balloonist, makes a balloon trip from Cincinnati, Ohio to the South Carolina coast in nine hours.

1861 May 13 First railroad opens in what is now Pakistan, from Karachi City to Kotri.

1861 October 1 First American Army Balloon Corps is formed under the command of Thaddeus S. C. Lowe (1832—1913), Chief Aeronaut of the Union Army during the U. S. Civil War. The Corps eventually has a complement of 50 men and seven balloons.

1861 November First ship used as an aircraft-carrier is a converted coal-barge named *G.W. Parke Curtis*. This boat serves as a mother-ship on the Potomac River for Thaddeus S. C. Lowe's (1832—1913) Union Army observation balloon *Washington*.

1862 Gabriel de La Landelle, a Frenchman, coins the word "aviation," as well as "aviateur" in 1863.

1862 Aerial reconnaissance by camera is conducted for the first time as Thaddeus S. C. Lowe (1832—1913) produces panoramic photographs of Confederate military positions around Richmond, Virginia taken from his balloon during the American Civil War.

1862 First railroad tunnel in Australia, the Elphinstone Tunnel, opens on the Victorian Government

*1861
March 8
First military
battle
between
ironclad
ships*

*1862 A.D.
First aerial
reconnais-
sance
conducted*

Railways Bendigo Line northwest of Melbourne. It is 418 yards (382 meters) long and is still in use.

1862 Mullan Road, a 624-mile wagon road from Fort Beaton in Dakota Territory to Wallula in Washington Territory, opens. It follows an old trail used so long by Indians to hunt for buffalo that their travel had worn a path a foot deep in places. It is not macadamized.

1862 German inventor Nikolaus A. Otto (1832—1891) experiments with the four-cycle system on his four-cylinder engine. The four cycles or movements of the piston create four efficient actions inside the cylinder: *induction* of the fuel-air mixture (as piston descends); *compression* or squeezing of the mixture (as the piston rises); *ignition* or *power stroke* (as the expanding gases drive the piston down again); and *exhaust* of the hot gases (as the rising piston pushes them out the now-open valve). This cycle will become the basis of the internal combustion engine. When a modern engine is running, every cylinder goes through the same sequence of events, or cycle, hundreds of times a minute.

c. 1860 ■ Mule-drawn rail car.

1862 First traffic islands designed as a pedestrian safety zone are built in Liverpool, England at the suggestion of John Hastings.

1862 Precursor of the modern submarine is built by a Spanish inventor named Monturiol. His vessel, the *El Ictineo,* is far ahead of its time and incorporates many features associated with a modern submarine. It has a double hull and ballast tanks between the hulls which can be pumped out by compressed air. Its steam engine can run even when submerged and a special chemical plant produces oxygen.

1862 January 16 Alphonse Beau de Rochas (1815—1893) of France suggests and patents a four-cycle engine, but never builds it. He never pays the patent fees, so it is never published. In 1886, this document is used in court to break the monopoly held by Gasmotoren-Fabrik Deutz as the world's sole supplier of Nikolaus Otto's new engine. It shows priority of design (on paper), even though it was never built.

1862 March 31 First locomotive in the Pacific Northwest, the Oregon Pony, arrives in Portland, Oregon.

1862 May Jean Joseph Etienne Lenoir (1822—1900), inventor of the first practical internal combustion engine, builds an experimental gas-powered, wood-frame vehicle which he drives around Paris at about 2 mph (3 km/h) over short distances.

1862 May 31 Information obtained from Thaddeus S. C. Lowe's (1832—1913) balloon observations saves Union forces from defeat at the Battle of Fair Oaks, Virginia during the U. S. Civil War. Union General George McClellan is warned by Lowe of Confederate General Albert Johnston's approaching troops.

1862 July 1 President Abraham Lincoln (1809—1865) signs a bill authorizing construction of a line of railroads from the Missouri River to the Pacific Coast. This bill also incorporates the Union Pacific Company and subsidizes it with federal money, enabling it to build a line from Nebraska to Utah. There it meets the Central Pacific and forms the transcontinental railroad.

1862 September 5 Henry Tracy Coxwell (1819—1900) and British meteorologist, James Glaisher (1809—1903) make an extremely high altitude ascent from Wolverhampton, England. Both men are nearly killed when they lose consciousness, but Coxwell manages to open the release valve with his teeth (his hands being too numb) before blacking out, and the balloon slowly descends. Glaisher later claims they reached 36,000 feet (c. 11,000 meters), but most experts now think the men may have soared as high as 24,000 feet. Today, pilots don their oxygen masks at 15,000 feet.

1863 Nadar (1820—1910) founds Société d'Aviation as well as the periodical *L'Aéronaute* two years later. This will become one of the world's leading aeronautical journals.

1863 Jules Verne (1828—1905) publishes his first aeronautical novel, *Five Weeks in a Balloon*, in France. This work and his many later books will both fire the imagination and prepare many a mind for the reality of aeronautics to come.

1863 British automobile pioneer Frederick Henry Royce (1863—1933) is born. A self-taught, brilliant engineer, he builds a twin cylinder car in 1904 that achieves new levels of quality, reliability, and quiet. His car so impresses aristocrat Charles Stewart Rolls (1877—1910) that he joins with Royce to form Rolls-Royce Ltd. in 1906 to produce high-quality luxury cars.

1863 First railroad dining cars are introduced on the Philadelphia to Baltimore run.

1863 First viable railroad labor union, the Brotherhood of the Footboard, is organized.

1863 First steel rails (for railroad tracks) in the United States are laid by the Pennsylvania Railroad at Altoona and Pittsburgh, Pennsylvania. Steel is a superior form of iron.

1863 Largest 19th century submarine, the French-made *Le Plongeur*, is launched. Built by Frenchmen named Brun and Bourgeois, it is a 140-foot-long iron submersible whose 80-hp engine runs on compressed air which it carries in bottles in large quantity. Its extreme length and flatness cause it to plummet downwards at a steep angle when submerging, and it never succeeds as a useful, controllable underwater vehicle, despite its many advances.

1863 During American Civil War (1861—1865), Confederate forces build small, steam-powered iron-clad submarines, all of which are named *David*. Meant to navigate just at the surface with a hatch open to get air for its boiler, the submarine nearly sinks on every run. It is not successful. (See 1864)

1863 Breakthrough in roller skate design is made by American James L. Plimpton, whose "rocking action" skate touches off a roller skating craze. His new design, which he patents this year, is the first to allow the skater to turn while keeping all his wheels on the skating surface. Plimpton inserts a rubber cushion between the wood plate and the axles which allows the skate to turn in the direction to which foot pressure is applied. Skaters no longer are restricted to skating only in a straight line.

1863 January 10 First underground city passenger railroad or subway, London, England's Metropolitan Railway, opens to traffic. It runs between Farringdon Street and Bishop's Road, Paddington. Begun in 1860, it is built by the cut-and-cover method. Despite sulfurous fumes from steam locomotives burning coke, the subway vents the smoke through ventilators and open-roofed sections and proves a popular success.

1863 January 10

First subway opens

1863 July 30 American automobile pioneer Henry Ford (1863—1947) is born in Greenfield Village, Michigan. The son of an immigrant farmer, Ford has no technical training but does have a natural mechanical sense. Having made a crude car in 1896, he keeps improving it, and leaves the employ of the Edison Co. to later set up his own car-making business. After James S. Couzens (1872—1936) designs the Model T for Ford Motor Company, Ford decides to forego any other models and increase production of the Model T, unchanged, year after year at a steadily reducing price. He is able to do this by his pioneering use of the "assembly line," begun in 1908, in which he brings the parts to the workers who each have one task. This plan is wildly successful and Ford becomes a legend.

1863 July 30

Henry Ford born

1863 July 31 Gustave de Ponton d'Amecourt (1825—1888), a French Viscount, designs and demonstrates in Paris his steam-powered, contra-rotating blade, model helicopter. It does not successfully fly.

1863 December 1 First steam-operated railroad in New Zealand opens between Christchurch and Ferrymead.

1864 Prolific Austrian inventor Siegfried Markus (1831—1898) produces a wooden cart powered by a two-cycle gas engine patterned after Lenoir's. Some claim this to be the first automobile. By 1875, Markus builds a greatly improved version—a four-cycle gasoline engine that drives the rear axle. It has a wheel for steering and goes only one speed since it has no gears.

1864 First significant plan for a subway or underground transit in the United States is proposed by Michigan railroad man Hugh B. Willson. His request for a franchise is rejected by the New York State Legislature.

1864 A.D.

Pullman designs new railroad sleeping car

1864 George M. Pullman (1831—1897) designs his new sleeping car, the forerunner of modern railroad sleepers. It features hinged double berths and is one foot wider and 2.5 feet higher than any other car now in service. He also designs "palace cars" and "hotel cars," equipped with kitchen and dining facilities. Long-distance rail travel becomes almost a pleasure.

1864 In Japan, the Choshu clan operates a miniature locomotive.

1864 American automobile pioneer Ransom E. Olds (1864—1950) is born. Having built a steam three-wheeler in 1893, he turned to gasoline powered-engines, and by 1900 was America's first mass-producer of cars. His easy-to-drive, one-cylinder "curved dash" Oldsmobile became the "merry Oldsmobile" of the popular song. Squabbles led him to leave the Oldsmobile Co. in 1904, and he set up the REO Motor Car Company which never did as well as Oldsmobile.

1864 Longest single span masonry arch in the western hemisphere, the Cabin John Aqueduct and Bridge, is completed across the Cabin John Valley in Montgomery County, Maryland. Designed by Montgomery C. Meigs (1816—1892) and Alfred L. Rives (1830—1903), it has a span of 220 feet and is 20 feet wide. It still supplies water to Washington, D.C. and carries a modern traffic load as well.

1864 Confederate forces build the submarine *Hunley*, to succeed the failed and dangerous *David*. Unlike the steam-powered *David*, this vessel is hand-powered and can thus run completely submerged. Its great length (60 feet) and extreme narrowness make it an inherently unstable vehicle. It goes down with Union ship *Housatonic* after having rammed it. It is sucked into the hole it creates in the *Housatonic*, and is pulled to the bottom with its prey.

1864 Clamp-on device for attaching roller skates to a boot or shoe is designed by Massachusetts inventor Everett H. Barney. Made of metal and adjustable, it can also be used for ice skates.

1864 March 31 German engineer Nikolaus A. Otto (1832—1891) and German industrialist Eugen Langen (1833—1895) sign an agreement forming N. A. Otto & Cie in Cologne, the first and, today, the oldest manufacturing company devoted to making internal combustion engines.

1864 August 28 First permanent railroad post office car for picking up, sorting, and distributing mail en route, begins operations on a run from Chicago, Illinois to Clinton, Iowa.

1865 First proper jet-airplane design is made by French engineer, Jean Charles Louvrie (1821—1894), who takes out a patent on an airplane to be propelled by a jet of gas from burning "a hydro-carbon, or better, vaporized petroleum oil." His plane is never built.

1865 The block signal system of telegraphic communication for railroads is introduced by Ashbel Welch. This system divides a line into sections and allows only one train to be in a section at a time.

1865 Scottish merchant Thomas Glover runs a train at Oura, Nagasaki. The train is later transferred for operation to Kawaguchi, Osaka.

1865 British engineer John Hawkshaw (1811—1891) makes surveys for an English Channel tunnel and finds that the chalk layer of the cliffs on both sides of the Channel is continuous and an excellent medium for tunnelling. (See 1866)

1865 Great Britain, after a long series of restrictive laws pushed by the rail and horse-drawn carriage interests, places another on the statute books requiring that a self-propelled vehicle should not exceed 4 mph and must be preceded by a man carrying a red flag 60 yards in front of it. These regulations are called the "red flag laws." They are not revoked until November 14, 1896.

1865 French writer Achille Eyraud (b. 1821) publishes *Voyage à Venus* (*Voyage to Venus*), which uses the words "reaction motor" to describe how a spaceship is powered. Although what he describes is hydraulic reaction—a kind of water rocket—it correctly forecasts that space propulsion will involve some form of the reaction principle. This book is not as popular as Jules Verne's work.

1865 Jules Verne (1828—1905), French author whose writings influence and inspire space pioneers like Tsiolkovsky, Goddard, and Oberth, publishes *De la terre à la lune (From the Earth to the Moon)*. His space travellers are shot into space by a 900-foot-long cannon while sitting in a padded cylindrical projectile. In the 1870 sequel, *Autour de la lune (Around the Moon)*, the spacecraft orbits but does not land on the moon and eventually splashes down safely in the Pacific Ocean. Verne attempts to incorporate as much actual, scientific information as he can in his novels, accurately describing weightlessness and correctly giving escape velocity at seven miles per second (about 25,000 mph).

1865 ■ Illustration of weightlessness in Jules Verne's *From the Earth to the Moon*.

1865 First boat to be powered by an internal combustion engine is built by French inventor J. J. Etienne Lenoir (1822—1900). As inventor of the internal combustion engine, which uses a mixture of air and gas inside a cylinder, Lenoir applies his new engine to power a boat as well as a horseless carriage. The manager of French newspaper *Le Monde* uses the 40-foot (12-meter) boat with a 6-hp engine to commute on the Seine River from Paris to Charenton.

1865 April 27 Worst maritime disaster in American history occurs as the obsolete and overloaded paddle-wheel steamer, *Sultana*, explodes a few hundred yards from shore, killing over 1,450 people. Normally a freighter able to carry 376 passengers, the ship is packed with some 2,500 Union soldiers who had been prisoners of war and who are returning home. The catastrophe receives little notice, since the Confederacy is defeated and John Wilkes Booth is shot and killed on this same day.

1865 October 2 First railroad in Ceylon (now Sri Lanka) opens between Colombo and Ambepussa.

1865 November 1 First specialty railroad boxcar is built. A railroad tank car specially made for transporting oil takes on its first load at Titusville, Pennsylvania. This is the site of the first U.S. oil well.

1866 French engineer M. de Gamond proposes a tunnel be driven between Folkestone, England and Cap Gris-Nez, France. (See 1867)

1866 German engineer Nikolaus A. Otto (1832—1891) and industrialist Eugen Langen (1833—1895) produce an improved gas engine using the four-cycle sequence. Able to turn consistently between 100 and 180 revolutions per minute, it is also lighter and vibrates less than other similar engines. This engine wins a gold medal at the Paris Exposition of 1867. Both men are interested only in stationary engines, and do not care to put them in horseless carriages. It is this engine that spurs both Gottlieb W. Daimler (1834—1900), who works for Otto, and Karl F. Benz (1844—1929), who does not know Daimler, to independently continue their work.

1866 A.D.

Four-cycle gas engine produced

1866 Automatic railroad block signals are introduced. (See 1865)

1866 French velicopede (early bicycle) makers Michaux et Compagnie introduce a new model made of elegant wrought-iron. Its front wheel is larger than the back one so that each revolution of the pedals will carry the rider farther. They become extremely popular and are called "boneshakers" in England—a word that aptly describes what the rider steadily experiences.

1866 A.D.

Early "boneshaker" bicycle produced

1866 First hotel elevator is installed by the Otis Company in the St. James Hotel in New York City.

1866 ■ "Boneshaker" bicycle with front-wheel crank.

1866 January Percy Sinclair Pilcher (1866—1899), aviation pioneer, born at Leicestershire, England. Inspired directly by Lilienthal whom he had visited, the engineer Pilcher took up the study of flight in 1895 and built his own glider. After four improved glider versions, he was killed when his *Hawk*, a hang-glider with wheeled landing gear, snapped a tail assembly rod and crashed. Pilcher's search for mastery of control was the same correct course followed by the Wrights.

1866 January 12 Aeronautical Society of Great Britain is founded in London (later to become the Royal Aeronautical Society). It soon attracts men of science who take seriously the idea of mechanical flight and who are determined to study it scientifically. This influential society still exists.

1866 June 27 At the first meeting of the newly-founded Aeronautical Society, F. H. Wenham (1824—1908) reads his important and influential paper entitled *Aerial Locomotion*, and communicates the results of his earlier studies. (See 1858)

1866 August 29 First cog railroad opens part of its line for public inspection. Built by Sylvester Marsh (1803—1884) of New Hampshire, the Mt. Washington Cog Railroad remains open today. (See July 3, 1869)

1867 "Velicipedomania" takes over in the larger cities of the United States, as the craze for these pedal-wheel vehicles reaches it height. In New York, any available large hall becomes a rink or riding school in the winter.

1867 One of the first known motorized cycles is built by Frenchmen Ernest Michaux (b. 1841) and L. G. Perreaux. Michaux earlier worked with his brother, Pierre, building the first commercially successful velicopede (early bicycle). This design of a light, single-cylinder steam powered cycle is patented in December 1868.

1867 Proposal for an English Channel tunnel is submitted to Napoleon III (1808—1873) by English and French interests. The Franco-Prussian War of 1870 interrupts consideration. (See 1871)

c. 1867 Steam-powered bicycle is ridden at a number of fairs and circuses in the eastern United States by W. W. Austin. A coal-fired boiler is carried beneath the chassis beam between the wheels. It is believed to be built by Sylvester H. Roper of Roxbury, Massachusetts and is considered, along with Ernest Michaux's (b. 1841) vehicle, one of the first known motorized cycles. (See 1867)

1867 First elevated railroad in the United States begins operation in New York City. Built by the West Side Elevated Railroad Co., this method of actually raising the tracks above street level is the cheapest way of providing a right-of-way for inner suburban trains in large city centers.

1867 First scheduled sleeping and dining car service in North America is begun by Great Western Railway of Canada.

1867 Era of hydraulic elevators begins in France with the invention of Leon Edoux. Power is provided from either a pump worked by a steam engine or, later, directly from high pressure water mains.

1867 Prototype for the Brooklyn Bridge, the Covington-Cincinnati Suspension Bridge, opens to traffic. Built by John A. Roebling (1806—1869) and eventually named the John A. Roebling Bridge, this masonry tower/iron cable suspension bridge is the direct predecessor of his later masterwork. It spans the Ohio River and has a total length of 2,252 feet.

1867 First U.S. ski club is founded in La Porte, California.

1867 Frenchman Joseph Monier (1823—1906) first patents the idea of reinforced concrete. This new material, which is admirably suited to bridge construction, will be heavily used in the 20th century. Embedding metal rods in wet concrete is found to produce a material that has both the compression-withstanding qualities of concrete and the tension-resistance of steel.

1867 April 16 Wilbur Wright (1867—1912) is born in Dayton, Ohio. Co-inventor, with his brother Orville, of the first airplane to achieve powered, sustained, and controlled flight (1903) and the first fully practical powered airplane (1905). Wilbur makes aviation popular world-wide with his flights in France, Italy, and Germany (1908—1909). He died of typhoid fever after a four-week illness.

1867 July 19 First delta-wing airplane designs are suggested by Englishmen J. W. Butler and E. Edwards, who take out patents for delta-wing monoplanes and biplanes to be propelled by jets of steam, compressed air, or gas. Delta wings resemble an isoceles triangle.

1867 November Firm of Otis Brothers & Company is incorporated. When Elisha G. Otis (1811—1861) dies in 1861, his sons, Charles and Norton, carry on the elevator business and build their first factory in 1868 on the site of the present plant in Yonkers, New York.

1867 December 19 Eastbound train from Cleveland to Buffalo derails on the Three Sisters Bridge over Lake Erie, New York. The last car then falls off the bridge into the creek bed and catches fire, killing all 42 passengers inside. This gruesome tragedy seems to catch the attention and imagination of the American public, and it becomes widely known and memorialized.

1868 First proposal and patent for the aileron (a movable part of an airplane wing that gives better side-to-side control) is made by M. P. W. Boulton in England.

1868 Joseph Ravel, a Swiss engineer in Paris, produces an oil-fired, steam tricycle with direct drive. At least one person is killed when the vehicle goes out of control and overturns. Ravel is the father of composer Maurice Ravel (1875—1937).

1868 Use of jinrikisha first begins in Shizuoka, Japan. This is a small, covered, two-wheeled vehicle usually for one passenger and pulled by one man.

Supposedly introduced into Japan by missionaries, they are said to be patterned after the 18th-century French "brouette"——a man-drawn chair on wheels. (See 1896)

1868 First office building in the United States to contain an elevator is the Equitable Life Assurance Society in New York.

1868 January 16 Patent is granted for a railroad refrigerator car to William Davis (1812—1868), a fish market owner in Detroit, Michigan. He designs his first car which he calls an "ice box on wheels." (See 1870)

1868 April 21 First patent for an automatic railroad car coupler is obtained by American Eli H. Janney (1831—1912). A second patent is issued on April 29, 1873 for the basic car-coupler design generally used today.

1868 June First aeronautical exhibition in history is held at the Crystal Palace, London, by the Aeronautical Society, demonstrating the growing status of ideas about flying. The most influential exhibit is John Stringfellow's (1799—1883) steam-powered, model triplane whose design comes from both Cayley and Henson. Despite its later failure to fly, Stringfellow's superposed design (one wing directly above another) is a major influence on Octave Chanute (1832—1910) and, in turn, the Wright Brothers. (See 1896)

1868 June
First aeronautical exhibition takes place

1869 Horse-drawn omnibus service begins between Tokyo and Yokohama, Japan.

1869 Most famous of all the British "tea clippers," the *Cutty Sark*, makes its maiden voyage from England to Australia. Built to carry the new crop of tea from China to London as quickly as possible, this three-masted tall ship is designed as a strong and durable cargo ship with a racing profile. It makes many memorable, speedy voyages and races, and is remembered as the best of its kind.

1869 A.D.
Cutty Sark makes first voyage

1869—1870 American author Edward Everett Hale (1822—1909) makes a fictional proposal for a manned space station in his story "The Brick Moon," published in *Atlantic Monthly*. Hale writes of a large satellite made of brick that is hurled into a 4,000-mile high orbit by gigantic flywheels. It would serve the earth from there as a kind of communications, reconnaissance, and navigation satellite.

1869 January 23 American engineer George Westinghouse (1846—1914) applies for an air-brake patent. His new power braking system uses compressed air as the operating medium, and far surpasses any other method. It is first used on a passenger train, and its final improvement in 1872 makes Westinghouse a rich man.

1869 April 1 First successful cycling magazine, *Le Velocipede Illustre,* is published in France. It touts the virtues of cycling and is critical of most other mechanical modes of transportation.

1869 April 28

Ten miles of railroad track laid in one day

1869 April 28 Greatest length of railroad track laid in one day is accomplished during the construction of the Central Pacific Railroad in Utah. With Charles Crocker (1822—1888) in charge, 4,000 men, mostly Chinese, lay 10 miles, 56 feet (16.11 kilometers) of track. The track-laying advanced at a rate of almost one mile per hour. At day's end, 25,800 ties, 55,000 pounds (24,948 kilograms) of spikes, and 3,250 rails (each 30 feet or 9.1 meters long) were used.

1869 May 10 First transcontinental U.S. railroad is completed with the Golden Spike ceremony. The two lines of the Union Pacific and the Central Pacific Railroads are joined at Promontory Point, Utah, north of the Great Salt Lake.

1869 June 4 First steam road roller is used in the United States. As reported in the June 19 issue of *Scientific American,* the steam-powered machine, weighing 15 tons with four rollers, did a very good job of compacting a road's surface. The machine is built by the English firm of Aveling and Porter and is purchased by the New York Central Park Commissioners.

1869 June 26 Largest hydrogen balloon ever to make a free (untethered) ascent, makes a short flight from the Champs de Mars in Paris, France. Flown by Wilfrid de Fonvielle (c. 1828—1914) and Gaston Tissandier (1843—1899), this huge balloon of Henri Giffard's (1825—1882) has a capacity of 424,000 cubic feet (c. 130,000 cubic meters).

1869 July 3

First mountain cog railroad opens

1869 July 3 First mountain cog railroad opens to carry passengers to the 6,293-foot (1,918-meter) summit of Mt. Washington in New Hampshire. Cog or rack rail have teeth or indentations with which a gear or cog wheel meshes for pulling and climbing power up steep grades.

1869 ■ First Steam Road Roller in U.S. compacts new roads.

1869 October 19 First railroad in Romania opens between Bucharest and Giurgiu.

1869 November 17 Suez Canal, a sea-level waterway across the Isthmus of Suez in Egypt, opens. Built by French diplomat Ferdinand de Lesseps (1805—1894), it takes five years to organize and plan and ten years to construct. Plans to connect the Red Sea and the Mediterranean have existed since 1504, but were never attempted. The canal extends 105 miles (168 kilometers), using several lakes, and is an open cut without locks. Following improvements and widening, it becomes one of the busiest canals, handling a significant portion of the world's sea traffic.

1870 Gustave Trouvé (1839—1902) successfully flies his model ornithopter in France. This strange flapping model gets its lifting power from the successive force of blank cartridges firing into a Bourdon tube, to which are attached the wing-spars (or length-wise wing support). It flies for some 230 feet (c. 70 meters) after a mid-air launch.

1870 Alphonse Penaud (1850—1880), a Frenchman, introduces twisted (as opposed to stretched)

1869 ■ Port Said entrance to Suez Canal, showing harbor and ships, with canal curving off in the distance.

rubber to power his model helicopters. These models become very popular as toys for children and help make the notion of flight a more realistic idea.

1870 One of the earliest forms of roller skates is the American "Pedespeed." These are single wheels, about 14 inches in diameter, that brave young men and women wear on the outside of their feet. They are kept on by rigid, stirrup-like appendages. This vogue does not last long, mainly because of the high casualty rate.

1870 First vehicular tunnel in the United States, the Washington Street Tunnel in Chicago, Illinois, is opened. It is built under the Chicago River by the cut and cover method using cofferdams (watertight enclosures from which water is pumped to expose the bottom of a body of water and permit construction). During the Great Chicago Fire of 1871, it serves the city as the only cross-river connection, since all the bridges burned down. In 1889, it is lowered and converted for cable car use. In 1910, it is again lowered and converted for streetcar use. It closes in 1954.

1870 First railroad use of track tanks which enable locomotives to take water on the run is made on the Pennsylvania Railroad. Water is forced into the tender (a separate, semi-permanently coupled vehicle) by the speed of the train through a special scoop which is lowered into the trough as the steam locomotive passes over it.

1870 First bicycle is imported into Japan.

1870 American Gustavus Franklin Swift (1839—1903) begins his pioneering work in the development of the refrigerated railroad car. His system forces fresh air over ice and then circulates it through the storage compartments. He ships dressed beef successfully for the first time. The refrigerator car becomes an important factor in the development of many food industries.

1870 Julius Hock of Vienna produces a somewhat practical but very dangerous and low-powered, non-compression engine. His "petroleum dynamic engine" sprayed a highly-volatile, gasoline-like fuel directly into the cylinder and was ignited by an open flame. The safety of the Otto four-stroke cycle engine puts this dangerous engine out of business.

1870 First U.S. coast-to-coast railroad run is made from Boston, Massachusetts to San Francisco, California.

1870 August 2 First "tube" railway, the Tower Subway, opens beneath London's River Thames. It uses cable traction. A "tube" is an underground railroad running inside a tunnel excavated by digging.

1870 September—January 1871 During the Franco-Prussian War (1870—1871), over 100 people are evacuated from the city of Paris by balloon. Altogether, 66 balloons are sent out of the besieged city carrying over 10 tons of mail and 400 carrier pigeons, besides people. The pigeons later return to Paris and are used for communications.

1871 The world's first wind tunnel is built for the Aeronautical Society of Great Britain by F. H. Wenham (1824—1908) and John Browning. This highly useful experimental device simulates a moving aircraft by passing air over a stationary model. It is still used today to study the aerodynamics of cars and other vehicles as well as planes.

1871 American Andrew Smith Hallidie (1836—1900) invents the underground continuous moving cable and mechanical gripper for the underside of streetcars. His electric cable car runs two to three times faster than a horse-drawn rail car and can go up the steepest grades. By 1873, his system is running cable cars in San Francisco, California and other American cities. In 1964, this system, which is still running, becomes the first moving National Historic Landmark.

1870
August 2
First "tube" railway opens

1871 A.D.
First wind tunnel built

1871 A.D.
Electric cable car invented

1871 Dr. J. M. Carhart builds a steam buggy in Racine, Wisconsin. His vehicle typifies the American obsession with simply doing away with the horse so as to retain the carriage style and type that most people were used to. This prevented them from evolving any designs suited to the new power plant.

1871 Companies are organized in England and France and a joint commission is set to make a report on a project to tunnel under the English Channel and link England and France. Its report is completed in 1876. (See 1875)

1871 Chisholm Cattle Trail, first and best of all American cattle paths, has its biggest year for cattle traffic as 600,000 head are delivered from San Antonio, Texas to Abilene, Kansas, the "cowboy capital of the world." This 800-mile long trail is a broad, beaten thoroughfare several hundred yards wide. It eventually sees less and less use as the railroads take over its cattle.

1871 August

Model airplane flies

1871 August While continuing to study the problems of flight by making models, Frenchman Alphonse Penaud (1850—1880) makes the first really stable model airplane which flies successfully for over 130 ft. (c. 40 m). Called a *Planophore,* it is propelled by twisted rubber and a propeller at the rear. Its rear tail contributes to its great stability.

1871 August 16 First narrow-gauge U.S. railroad opens a few miles out of Denver, Colorado. The locomotive used, the *Montezuma,* is the first narrow-gauge passenger engine built or operated in the United States. Narrow gauge is any railroad track of less than standard gauge (4 feet, 8½ inches or 1,435 millimeters).

1871 August 19

Orville Wright born

1871 August 19 Orville Wright (1871—1948) is born in Dayton, Ohio. Co-inventor, with his brother Wilbur, of the first airplane to achieve powered, sustained, controlled flight (1903) and the first fully practical powered airplane (1905). Orville piloted the famous first flight at Kill Devil Hills, North Carolina. He was nearly killed in a 1908 crash which killed his passenger but survived and outlived his brother by 36 years.

1872 First river steamboats begin service in Japan.

1872 First major construction project in the United States on which dynamite is used successfully, the Musconetcong Tunnel, is begun. Located on what becomes the Lehigh Valley Railroad in western New Jersey, it uses as much as 17,000 pounds of dynamite a month.

1872 George B. Brayton (1839—1892), born in East Greenwich, Rhode Island, applies for a patent on a two-cylinder gasoline engine. This is the first commercial gas engine of American origin. He also displays his engine at the Philadelphia Centennial where George B. Selden (1846—1922) sends an agent to study the engine. Selden designs a similar engine and makes his famous patent application. (See May 8, 1879)

1872 A railroad line opens between Tokyo and Yokohama, Japan.

1872 First of the important Swiss tunnels, the St. Gotthard, is begun. New rock drills and dynamite speed up the work which still takes ten years to finish. An average of 2,500 men work three shifts for seven years before it is holed through. It quickly becomes an important commercial train route, since it transforms a full day's ride over the mountain into a quick, 12-minute trip. It opens in 1882.

1872 French minister of war abolishes the French rocket troops called "Fuseens" which had been formed in 1827. They had used rockets to fight in China, Algeria, Indochina, and the Crimea. In the same year, the Germans also dissolve their "Raketenstudienburo" or Rocket Research Branch.

1872 "Great Epizootic," a particularly virulent form of equine influenza, strikes the horsecar stables in most of the major eastern U.S. cities. In New York City alone, over 18,000 horses are too sick to pull their rail cars. Following this epidemic which greatly hinders urban transit, transportation officials give horses better care, but also begin thinking seriously about mechanical replacement (by steam or electricity). Draft horses have a short working life on street railways, and their droppings pose a constant hygiene problem for cities.

1872 February 2 Stanislas Dupuy de Lôme's (1816—1885) dirigible (powered) airship makes its only flight, from Fort Vincennes to Mondecourt, France. It is well-designed but under-powered, since its large, four-bladed propeller is driven by eight men turning a crank. Although it manages about 5 mph (c. 8 km/h), it underscores the great need for a light-weight, powerful engine.

1872 February 6 Innovative Swiss engineer Robert Maillart (1872—1940) is born in Bern, Switzerland. His radical use of reinforced concrete revolutionizes masonry arch bridge design. He uses concrete to design incredibly slim but strong bridges in the Swiss Alps that are both engineering and artistic masterpieces.

1872 June 12 First railroad in Japan opens between Yokohama and Shinagawa. It is completed to Tokyo (then Yedo or Jeddo) on October 14, 1872.

1872 July 1 Louis Blériot (1872—1936) is born in Cambrai, France. Pioneer aviator who made the world's first airplane flight across the English Channel (Calais, France to Dover, England). After experimenting first with gliders, he designed and built his own monoplane with a 25 hp engine which took him across the channel on July 25, 1909. He remained active in aviation both during and after World War I.

1872 December 13-14 Paul Haenlein (1835—1905), an Austrian, tests his tethered airship, in Brunn, Czechoslovakia. Although it never flies free and fails most of its tests, it is the first aircraft to be powered by an internal combustion engine. Haenlein uses a new 5-hp Lenoir gas engine which uses the coal-gas contained in the airship's envelope for fuel.

1873 Etienne-Jules Marey (1830—1904), a French physiologist, publishes his book *La Machine Animale*, which contains for the first time a series of rapid sequence photographs of bird flight. Years later, this book will be closely studied by the Wright brothers in America.

1873 English Professor J. Bell Pettigrew (1834—1908), in his book *Animal Locomotion*, describes the motion of a bird's wing as similar to that of a propeller. He is the first since George Cayley (1773—1857) to note this.

1873 Amedee Bollee, a bell-founder from Le Mans, France, builds his practical 12-seater steam carriage or omnibus called *L'Obeissante*. Although powered by steam and not an internal combustion engine, it contains many features that make it a forerunner of a real automobile. It is one of the first vehicles to have pivoting front wheels (Lankensperger steering) as well as an independent front suspension. It weighs over two tons.

c. 1873 First design of a safety bicycle using chain-drive to the rear wheel is made by Englishman H. J. Lawson. It has two medium-size wheels of equal diameter, with the rear being driven by means of a chain and sprockets. (See 1885)

1873 George B. Selden (1846—1922), an engineering-oriented lawyer from Rochester, New York, begins experiments on fuels for internal combustion engines. (See May 8, 1879)

1873 April 1 Worst sea disaster to date occurs as the White Star Line's *Atlantic* is wrecked off the coast of Halifax and 585 people die.

1873 April 1
Shipwreck
kills 585

1873 July 20 Alberto Santos-Dumont (1873—1932), aviation pioneer, is born in Minas Gerais, Brazil. Having first made Europe more air-minded in 1898 with his odd-shaped airships that flew above Paris, he turned to airplanes and built in 1906 his powered *14-bis* based on the principle of the box kite. Although barely able to fly, this airplane drew more attention to aviation in Europe. After his return to Brazil in 1928, he became depressed over the use of the airplane in war and committed suicide.

1873 October 6 Washington H. Donaldson, an American acrobat balloonist, attempts to fly the Atlantic with two others in a huge balloon of 600,000 cubic feet. After leaving New York, the balloon, which has an enclosed car, lands a few hours later in the Catskill Mountains, never to fly again.

c. 1874 Felix Du Temple (1823—1890), a French naval officer, builds a man-sized, powered airplane which is able to take off after going down an inclined ramp. It does not sustain its flight, however. His craft has swept-forward wings and is powered by a hot-air engine.

1874 Henri Farman (1874—1958), aviation pioneer and aircraft builder, is born in France. Europe's outstanding pilot from 1907 to 1910, he is credited with taking up the first passenger in Europe as well as making the first cross-country flight. Before and after World War I, he was a successful aircraft manufacturer with his brother, Maurice, although each designed his own planes.

1874 D. S. Brown, an Englishman, tests his tandem-wing model gliders (one wing directly behind or aligned with another), and publishes the results with illustrations in the Annual Report of the Aeronautical Society for this year. His work on tandem designs may have influenced Langley. (See 1892 and 1896.)

1874 Third rail for trains is invented by American Stephen Field (1846—1913) of New York. This non-running rail carries an electrical current to an electric locomotive and revolutionizes municipal rail transportation by providing a convenient source of electrical power.

1874 A.D.

Underwater railroad tunnel construction begins

1874 First underwater railroad tunnels in the United States are begun. Known as the Hudson Tubes, they are dug under the Hudson River between New York City and Jersey City, New Jersey. Conceived by DeWitt Clinton Haskins, they are the first large projects built with the help of compressed air. Major mishaps stop the project at least three times, and the first tunnel under the Hudson is not completed until 1904.

1874 Smoking is permitted for the first time on Atlantic liners.

1874 May 24

First steel arch bridge opens

1874 May 24 First steel arch bridge, the St. Louis Bridge, opens to traffic. Designed and built by American engineer James B. Eads (1820—1887) to span the Mississippi River, it is ahead of its time in many ways. It is the first to use pneumatic caissons (enclosures with no bottoms in which compressed air keeps out the water) in the laying of the huge piers, and also the first to build arches by the cantilever method without falsework or staging. A cantilever is supported on one end only. Now called the Eads Bridge, it has three arches, spanning more than 1,500 feet. It is built with two decks, the bottom carrying a railroad line and the top carrying a roadway. This very successful bridge is the world's first major construction of any sort with steel, proving it to be the metal of the future.

1874 July 9 Vincent de Groof, a Belgian shoemaker, is killed in London when his ornithopter (part flapping machine, part parachute) is released from a balloon and crashes.

1875 The State of Wisconsin offers a prize of $10,000 to the inventor of a successful steam carriage.

1875 First Pullman railroad parlor car goes into service.

1875 Austrian automobile designer Ferdinand Porsche (1875—1952) is born. One of the most innovative and versatile designers, he begins as an electrical engineer who turns to automobiles. After racing cars, he joins Austria's Daimler Company in 1905, and later the new German firm of Daimler-Benz for a short time. During World War II, he designs the Volkswagen at Hitler's specific command for a "peoples' car." Finally in 1950, he produces a car with his own name on it—the definitive version of the Porsche 356 sports car.

1875 First Japanese steel passenger and freight cars are produced in Kobe.

1875 Work first begins on the English Channel tunnel as two shafts (vertical holes) and short headings (horizontal) are begun by a French company in Sangatte, France. At the same time, the English sink three shafts between Folkestone and Dover, with headings driven out for more than a mile under the sea. These locations will be where the tunnel eventually is built. (See 1882)

1875 Merchant Shipping Act of 1875 is passed by British Parliament and establishes the Plimsoll Line. This line is a fixed mark placed on the hull of every cargo ship indicating the maximum depth to which the ship can be safely loaded. It is invented by British politician and social reformer Samuel Plimsoll (1824—1898), who dedicates himself to saving the lives of crew members aboard "coffin ships"—unseaworthy, overloaded vessels whose owners care little about crew safety. An International Load Line is adopted by 54 nations in 1930, and in 1968, a new standard line takes effect.

1875 Captain Matthew Webb (1848—1883) swims the English Channel from Dover, England to Calais, France in 21 hours, 45 minutes. He later drowns in an attempt to swim the rapids below Niagara Falls.

1875 Experimental steamship the English *Bessemer* is built with a traditional exterior hull shape but with an interior passenger compartment that can swing and always remain level. Built by British engineer Henry Bessemer (1813—1898) to avoid passenger seasickness, the ship's passenger compartment is mounted on metal guides and is moved by hydraulic machinery so that it will always remain level. Trials in heavy seas prove that its engineer-

c. 1875 ■ Passenger train emerges from a tunnel in Mexico.

controlled machinery cannot react fast enough to compensate, and no more are built. It is, however, the precursor of the modern automatic ship stabilizer.

1875 First completely circular ships, the *Admiral Popov* and the *Novgorod,* are built in Russia. Designed with the idea of providing a steady platform for its big guns, these round, iron ships have a diameter of 101 feet (31 meters). Although they do not roll and pitch, their low decks are always awash, and steering is sometimes a problem.

1875 April 15 European scientists Joseph Croce-Spinelli (1845—1875) and Theodore Sivel (1834—1875) both die of asphyxiation during a balloon ascent from Paris to a height of nearly 30,000 feet. A third occupant, French scientist Gaston Tissandier (1843—1899), survives the flight after blacking out several times. Croce-Spinelli and Sivel die despite bringing oxygen containers on their flight.

1875 June Thomas Moy (d. 1904), an English engineer and patent agent, flies his tethered, steam-driven model airplane indoors at the Crystal Palace, London. His 120-pound, tandem-wing (one wing directly behind or aligned with another) model lifts itself off the ground for a short, low flight.

1876 Alphonse Pénaud (1850—1880) patents in France his prophetic design for an amphibious airplane. Although it is never built, it has many features of a modern airplane: twin tractor propellers (props that have a pulling action and are in front of the wings); elliptical wings, slightly curved and set in a small "V"; rear con-

trols; a glass-domed canopy; a single control column; and retractable undercarriage.

1876 First practical, successful, lightweight, four-cycle internal combustion engine is produced by German engineer Nikolaus A. Otto (1832—1891). This is the direct ancestor of all modern reciprocating engines (an engine in which the to-and-fro motion of a piston is transformed into circular motion of the crankshaft). Because of its smooth-running reliability and relative quietness, it is an immediate success.

1876 Early form of paddle boat is a "river velocipede" exhibited in Paris. It is built of two cigar-shaped floats joined by a wooden platform upon which the operator sits and pedals.

1876 First commercial tricycle is produced in England. This three-wheeler has a single, large driving wheel and two small steering wheels in front, mounted on separate forks. It soon is favored by tradesmen who carry and deliver goods and packages.

1876 First plastic boat is made by George Waters of Troy, New York, who makes laminated paper rowing shells. These very light boats are bonded in layers with shellac and are, in a way, precursors of the modern plastic boat.

1876 China lists 64 navigational lights—of which nine are major lighthouses—which dot its major harbors. Only eight years before, these were virtually nonexistent. They are built with the assistance of the British.

1876 A.D.

First tricycle produced

1876 North Sea Canal in Holland in completed. One of Holland's most important canals, this waterway runs 18 miles westward from Amsterdam and makes that city a major seaport.

1876 Scottish mathematician and physicist William Thomson Kelvin (1824—1907) patents his sounding machine which uses three miles (five kilometers) of piano wire. This device, which enables a ship to determine the depth of the sea below it, becomes universally adopted.

1876 First ship to be fitted with electric lights is the French liner *Amérique* which uses them as navigation lights.

1876 August 29 American engineer Charles F. Kettering (1876—1958) is born in Loudonville, Ohio. A major figure in the development of the automobile, his most important invention was the self-starter which did away with muscle power to start a heavy engine and allowed women to easily start a car from the inside. This one device put women behind the wheel.

1877 Enrico Forlanini (1848—1930), an Italian engineer, flies his small, steam-propelled model helicopter. It has two, paddle-like rotors, only one of which revolves, and goes straight up to a height of 42 feet.

1877 French automobile pioneer Louis Renault (1877—1944) is born. The son of a rich Parisian button maker, he remakes a De Dion tricyle, building a new four-wheeled car of his own with a forward-mounted engine and an ingenious direct-drive gearbox. His car is so successful, he and his brothers, Marcel (1872—1903) and Ferdinand (1865—1910), form Automobile Renault Frères.

1877 A.D.

First long underwater tunnel is begun

1877 First long underwater tunnel and the longest railroad tunnel in England, the Severn Tunnel of the Great Western Railway, is begun. Completed in 1886, it is 4.3 miles long and connects Bristol and Cardiff. Digging this tunnel presents some of the worst water pumping problems ever faced. Once flooded in 1879, it takes 14 months to pump dry.

1877 First practical "four-stroke" or four-cycle engine is patented by Otto and Langen's company of Deutz, Germany. During the development of this engine, much of the design work is carried out by two of Otto's employees, Gottlieb Daimler (1834—1900) and Wilhelm Maybach (1846—1929). When Otto cannot be interested in applying his engine to power a vehicle, Daimler and Maybach leave in 1882 to set up their own company in Cannstatt, near Stuttgart, Germany.

1877 British automobile pioneer Charles Stewart Rolls (1877—1910) is born. The privileged son of Lord Llangattock, he is an enthusiastic motorist and racer who, upon seeing the high-quality work Frederick Henry Royce (1863—1933) could produce, joins with him to form the landmark firm of Rolls-Royce Ltd. Rolls leaves the technical work to Royce and takes up flying with similar enthusiasm. He dies on July 12, 1910, crashing his Wright biplane during Bournemouth Aviation Week.

1877 U.S. Supreme Court decides the last of the Granger cases and concludes that the government has the right to regulate railroads. In upholding the power of states to regulate the rates charged by a public utility, the Court marks the beginning of state and federal intervention in the economy.

1877 Kerosene first comes into use to fuel U.S. lighthouses. Before this, the preferred illuminant was first sperm oil, then colza or rapeseed oil, and later lard oil. By 1885, kerosene (which is distilled from coal) is the main fuel for lighthouses.

1877 British naval architect John Thornycroft (1843—1928) patents the concept of the air-cushioned vehicle. He theorizes that drag on a ship's hull could be reduced if the vessel were given a concave bottom in which the air could be contained between hull and water. Despite tests with models, he does not build such a vessel. (See June 7, 1959)

1877 Norwegian Christiania Ski Club holds its first meet. Christiania is now Oslo.

1877 First successful refrigerated steamship, the *Frigorifique*, takes its cargo of beef from Argentina to Europe.

1877 March 21 Maurice Farman (1877—1964), aviation pioneer and manufacturer, is born in Paris, France. In 1908, he made the first circular flight of more than one mile (1.6 kilometers) with his brother, Henri. Although he joined with Henri to form a successful aircraft manufacturing business, he still designed his own planes.

1878 ■ Gilbert steam-powered elevated railroad in New York City.

1877 April 2 First human cannon ball circus act is performed by Zazel at West's Amphitheatre in London, England. Billed as "the beautiful lady fired from a monstrous cannon," Zazel is successfully propelled by elastic springs and gently lands in her safety net.

1877 April 20 First cantilever bridge in United States, the Kentucky River Bridge, is completed. Built by self-taught American engineer C. Shaler Smith (1836—1886) for the Cincinnati Southern Railway, its trusses are continuous for the entire 1,125-foot length of the bridge. A cantilever bridge is essentially two connected beams, each supported only at one end. This wrought-iron bridge is rebuilt in 1911, but is influential in the spread of the cantilever principle for long-span construction.

1877 May 21 First use of telephone communication for railroad purposes occurs during telephone-rail tests in Altoona, Pennsylvania.

1877 July First national rail strike in the United States is held against the Pennsylvania and Baltimore & Ohio (B&O) lines.

1878 First high speed hydraulic elevator is introduced by the Otis Company in the United States.

This new elevator is also fitted with a governor-operated safety device that brings the elevator to a gradual and not a jarring stop during an emergency.

1878 District of Columbia Department of Highways and Traffic is first organized.

1878 Organized ambulance service for civilians is provided in England by the Ambulance Association of the British National Society for Aid to the Sick and Wounded. Starting with a single-wheeled litter, the Association has a special rubber-tire, one-horse ambulance for transport by 1883.

1878 Forerunner of the modern towed ship's log is patented by Englishman Thomas F. Walker, Jr. It consists of a towed rotator connected to a log-line which is connected to a register or dial mounted on the rail of a ship. Reading the log—which indicates a ship's speed and distance covered—now involves only a walk to the stern (rear) to read a dial. (See 1917)

1878 May 21 Glenn Hammond Curtiss (1878—1930) is born in Hammondsport, New York. Pioneer of first years of powered flight and rival of the Wright Brothers. A talented builder of engines for motor-

1878 A.D.
Organized ambulance service begins

cycles and airplanes, he turned to building and racing airplanes. In 1910, he built the first practical seaplane. During World War I, his trainer the *JN-4* or *Jenny* was widely used.

1878 June 12 Charles F. Ritchel (1860—c. 1920), an American professor, builds a cylindrical, man-powered balloon, 25 feet long, which flies in Hartford, Connecticut. The pilot, whom Ritchel hires since he himself is too large a man to fly his device, manages to return the airship to its starting point by means of foot pedals which move the propellers.

1878 July Father of the modern submarine, American John P. Holland (1840—1914), launches his first underwater vehicle, the *Holland I*. The 14-foot unmanned vessel sinks, but it is only a prototype, and Holland continues to experiment. (See 1881)

1879 A French amateur named Biot makes a few short glides at Clamart, France in his full-size glider. This machine is today on exhibit in the Paris Musée de l'Air, and has the distinction of being the earliest surviving full-scale, heavier-than-air aircraft.

1879 Victor Tatin (1843—1913), a French watchmaker, flies his model airplane which whirls around a central pole to which it is tethered. Its importance lies in its new, compressed-air engine and the monoplane design (single set of wings) and front propellers.

1879 Dicycle is first patented in England by E. C. F. Otto. In this vehicle, the rider sits between two wheels of equal diameter that are mounted to one another on a common spindle. The low-sitting driver pedals but steers with difficulty.

1879 A.D.

First electrical street lighting installed

1879 First public electrical street lighting is installed in Cleveland, Ohio by Charles F. Brush. (See March 31, 1880)

1879 First ski school is opened in Telemark, Norway by brothers Torjus and Mikkel Hemmestveit.

1879 First ship to be fitted with internal electric lighting is the Inman Line's *City of Berlin*. Its dining room and engine/boiler rooms are fitted with six arc-lamps.

1879 First major ski meet is held at Huseby Hill, Oslo, Norway. The king and 10,000 spectators are in attendance, demonstrating the growing popularity of skiing.

1879 May 8 George B. Selden (1846—1922) applies for the first U.S. automobile patent, describing a carriage powered by a gasoline engine. Selden's 1903 suit against Henry Ford will stay in the courts until 1911, when it is decided that although his patent is valid, it is limited to the use of a Bratton-type engine. Since Ford does not use that type, he does not infringe Selden's patent. (See November 5, 1895 and 1911)

1879 May 31 First practical electric railroad begins operations at the Berlin Trades Exhibition in Germany. This passenger line, built by German engineer Werner von Siemens (1816—1892), operates on the exhibition grounds and can pull 30 passengers at 4 mph (6.5 km/h). Powered by a 150-volt center rail which drives a 3-hp motor, it is the first practical electric train that gets its current from a stational generator. (See May 12, 1881)

1879 July 31 First manned balloon ascent in Canada is made by Richard Cowan, Charles Grimley, and Charles Page in a hydrogen balloon.

1879 August 29 First Canadian woman to fly in a balloon, Miss Nellie Thurston, flies in Ontario.

1879 September 29 John Wise (1808—1879), an American who made his first balloon flight forty years earlier, disappears in Lake Michigan when his balloon makes a forced landing. Wise and his passenger, George Burn, a local banker, are presumed to have drowned.

1879 December 29 One of the worst bridge disasters occurs as the Tay Bridge at Dundee, Scotland collapses during a storm. An entire passenger train vanishes in the river below, killing at least 75 people. Composed of a series of wrought-iron trusses supported by tall, cast-iron columns built on brick piers founded in concrete, the suspension bridge falls partly because of wind pressure and partly to faults in the cast iron supports. This is the best-known example of bridge failure from lack of aerostatic stability. This is different from a lack of aerodynamic rigidity. In the latter, the wind starts small sways that increase to the point of rocking, which finally tears the bridge apart. In the former, the bridge does not move at all before collapsing, and as the Tay does, it just lets go all at once.

1880 American inventor Thomas Alva Edison (1847—1931) begins experiments with electric railroads on his estate in Menlo Park, New Jersey. He operates an electric locomotive with insulated rails and a fixed dynamo. Edison has little success but contributes more in the field of electricity generation.

1880 U.S. railroad mileage has reached 93,671 miles and covers nearly all major settled areas.

1880 First permanent railroad in China opens. It now forms part of the Peking-Mukden section of the Chinese People's Republic Railways. Following this line, railroad mileage spreads rapidly in China.

1880 League of American Wheelmen is organized when several local bicycle clubs decide to consolidate. Now organized, they begin to lobby for better quality roads, use of road signs, and good maps. (See 1892)

1880 First electrically-powered elevator is built in Germany by Werner von Siemens. His elevator has a motor that drives gears engaged in a fixed tack, via a worm and gear drive. Although it is exhibited at the Industrial Exposition in Mannheim, Siemens does not consider it to be an especially important invention. Siemens and his brother, Karl Wilhelm, go on to numerous other successes in the field of electrical engineering.

1880 First and only railroad to the top of a volcano is built on Mt. Vesuvius in Italy. It is a funicular railway, or one that is cable-operated with ascending and descending vehicles counterbalancing each other. After Italian composer Luigi Denza (1846—1922) writes a song, "Funiculi-Funicular," to commemorate it, German composer Richard Strauss (1864—1949) mistakes the tune for an Italian folksong and incorporates it in the end of his symphony, "Aus Italien." The railway is destroyed when Vesuvius erupts on March 20, 1944.

1880 First humane cattle car is designed by Alonzo C. Mather.

1880 Percy Greg (1836—1889) publishes his novel *Across the Zodiac* which tells of a spaceship travelling to Mars while using a gravity-negating device called "apergy." He describes the "canals" of Mars, obviously reflecting the recent discovery by Italian astronomer Giovanni V. Schiaparelli (1835—1910), whose 1877 description of Mars' "canali" (channels) is interpreted as meaning canals built by intelligent beings.

1880 First steel-hulled ship to enter Atlantic service is the *Buenos Ayrean*. Steel is beginning to be recognized as a metal with properties superior to iron, now that it can be made by a cheaper process.

1880 March 31 First city to have its streets completely lighted by electricity is Wabush, Indiana.

1880 August 3 American Canoe Association is formed by 25 canoe enthusiasts at Crosbyside Park, Lake George, New York.

1881 Louis Pierre Mouillard (1834—1897), a Frenchman living in Cairo, Egypt, publishes in Paris his *L'Empire de l'Air*, which becomes an early bible of gliding. The book recounts his own experiments with soaring and gliding and argues that men can imitate the flight of birds in this way. The book is read eagerly by the Wright brothers, who later acknowledge their debt to him.

1881 A.D.

Pioneer book on gliding published

1881 First practical unicycle or monocycle is produced in England by Pearce. The rider's feet are placed on short stilts connected with the cranks, one on either side of the rim. The rider sits on a spring-seat over the center of the wheel. They are not for the meek.

1881 A.D.

First unicycle produced

1881 All the major elevated railroads in Manhattan, New York are completed. Starting in 1878, Cyrus W. Field (1819—1892) maps out the Island of Manhattan, and the "els" are built even in outlying areas where no neighborhoods exist. It is this planning and foresight that makes New York able to handle the transportation demands that come with its explosive population growth. They are very noisy and disruptive, however.

1881 First steam-heating is installed in passenger trains, replacing older stoves and hot-water heaters.

1881 Russian Nikolai I. Kibalchich (b. 1853), former head of a research laboratory, awaits his execution in prison for attempting to kill Tsar Alexander II and writes of how a rocket's flight can be controlled by changing the direction of the exhausting gases. This valid concept eventually becomes known as vectored thrust—the best way to keep a rocket on course or change its trajectory. This steering principle is eventually used in modern rockets. His work is not published until 1918.

1881 A.D.

Submarine first uses torpedo

1881 First submarine to employ the newly-invented Whitehead torpedo—first built by Englishman Robert Whitehead (1823—1905) in 1872—is the *Nordenfelt I,* begun this year by Swedish engineer Torsten V. Nordenfelt (1842—1920). Since it is powered by steam and subject to all its underwater limitations, it is not a true modern submarine, and has little real naval value.

1881 American inventor John P. Holland (1840—1914) builds his second-generation submarine, the *Holland II* or *Fenian Ram.* This 31-foot-long vessel is much-improved, using one of the earliest internal combustion engines, an American-built Brayton engine for surface propulsion. It uses batteries underwater. He designs his vessel to submerge not by sinking, but by diving under power via its horizontal rudders. **(See 1898)**

1881 First lighted buoy in the United States, an oil gas buoy, is placed near the Scotland Lightship at the entrance to New York Bay.

1881—1882 Tricycle powered by a lead-acid battery is driven in France where battery-powered electric trolley cars also go into service.

1881 March 8 First railroad route to Southern California is completed, via New Mexico and Arizona.

1881 May 11 Air and space pioneer Theodore von Karman (1881—1963) is born in Budapest, Hungary. Educated at the Royal Polytechnic University in Budapest, he became interested in aeronautics in 1908 and was soon doing pioneering work in aerodynamics. In 1930, he was invited to assume direction of the Guggenheim Aeronautical Laboratory at the California Institute of Technology and in 1941, participated in the founding of a corporation to manufacture liquid and solid-propellant rocket engines. He became co-founder of the present Jet Propulsion Laboratory in 1944 and helped found the International Council of the Aeronautical Sciences in 1956 and the International Academy of Astronautics in 1960.

1881 May 12 First public electric railroad to provide regular service to a fare-paying public opens in Germany at Lichterfelde, near Berlin. This line is 1.5 miles (2.5 kilometers) long. The tram-car has an electric motor that gives a 100-volt supply and can carry 26 passengers at 30 mph (48 km/h).

1881 May 26 First successful propeller-driven electric boat is launched on the Seine River in Paris, France. Designed and built by Frenchman Gustave Trouve (1839—1902), the 18-foot- (5.5-meter-) long boat carries three people. Its electric motor is activated by two banks of bichromate-potash batteries and drives a three-bladed propeller. Since the motor can be easily put on and taken off the boat, it is also the first successfully detachable, or outboard, motor.

1881 November 8 Robert-Albert-Charles Esnault-Pelterie (1881—1957) is born in Paris, France. Early aviation pioneer whose own version of the Wright Brothers 1902 glider led him to disagree with their principle of control. This actually set back European aviation for some time. He did invent ailerons (movable wing parts) and built in 1907 one of the first monoplanes. He later turned to theoretical studies of rocketry and coined the word astronautics.

1882 Geoffrey de Havilland (1882—1965), aircraft designer and manufacturer, born in England. Having built and flown an aircraft with a 50 hp engine in 1910, he later originated the British Engineering (B.E.) series of propeller-driven biplanes, and in 1912, built the first single-seat scout and fighter plane in history. He formed the De Havilland Aircraft Company in 1920 which produced the World War II "Mosquito" and pioneered jet-propelled aircraft.

1882 Gottlieb Daimler (1834—1900) and Wilhelm Maybach (1846—1929), on their own at Cannstatt, Germany, begin building several different high-speed gas engines designed specifically to power various vehicles.

1882 High bicycles, later known as penny-farthings, replace the "boneshaker" bicycle. These have a small rear wheel and a large front wheel made as big as the rider's leg length would allow. They give more distance per revolution and a more comfortable ride on rough roads, but are very unsafe. The rider sits almost directly above the straight front forks and is always in danger of being pitched forward.

1882 Only natural tunnel to be used by a railroad opens. Called the Natural Tunnel, it is in Virginia on the Southern Railway. Very little work is needed to transform this natural amphitheater into a railroad tunnel, since it is already 90 feet high and 120 feet wide. It goes through 788 feet of rock that was eroded by water.

1882 French drive a gallery over a mile long under the English Channel in Sangatte, France. This and the earlier French and British digging of 1875 is the only practical work carried out on the Channel Tunnel in the 19th century. Political and military considerations put a stop to any more work for nearly a century. (See 1963)

1882 Fourth Eddystone Lighthouse is completed. Built by Englishman James N. Douglass who generally follows Smeaton's design, it is taller than Smeaton's (140 feet) and is built using more modern equipment and techniques. Douglass uses a cofferdam which allows his crews to work on the sea's bottom and build a solid foundation. His tower sits on a solid, round platform with vertical sides which break up waves before they reach the tower. It still stands today, powered now by electricity instead of oil.

1882 August 20 Wrought iron Kinzua Railway Viaduct, built across the valley of the Kinzua Creek in McKean County, Pennsylvania, is completed. Among the tallest structures of its time, this 2,053-foot-long, 302-foot-high viaduct is composed of 20 linked ironwork towers. Still standing, the original structure is replaced with a similar but stronger structure in 1900.

1882 October 5 Robert H. Goddard (1882—1945), called the "father of American rocketry," is born in Worcester, Massachusetts. Fascinated at an early age by the notion of space travel and inspired by the classic literature of Verne and Wells, he spent his adult life trying to realize his dreams. After receiving a Ph.D. in physics from Clark University in Worcester, he taught there for nearly 30 years, always experimenting with rockets. In 1919 he published a small work, *A Method of Reaching Extreme Altitudes,* which reported on the state of rocketry and spoke of its future potential. By 1923, he had tested his first liquid-fuel rocket (using gasoline and liq-

uid oxygen) and in 1926, he launched successfully the world's first liquid-fuel rocket. He continued to experiment and left Massachusetts for New Mexico where his loud and dramatic launches would not bother anyone. From 1930 to 1935 he launched rockets that went as fast as 550 mph and flew as high as one-and-one-half miles. The U.S. government never took his work seriously, and only realized his worth after World War II when the captured German rocket experts told of how they learned all they knew of liquid-fuel rockets from Goddard's writings. By then he had died.

1883 M. A. Goupil (1843—1909), a Frenchman, designs and builds an unpowered but fairly advanced monoplane (single set of wings) which lifts itself and two men while tethered in a 13 mph wind. During the next year, he publishes his designs in an influential book called *La Locomotion Aerienne.*

1883 A.D.
Unpowered monoplane built

1883 John J. Montgomery (1858—1911), a teacher at Santa Clara College in California, builds and tests unsuccessfully the first of his three full-size gliders. His later efforts (1885 and 1886) do not succeed either.

1883 Edward Butler of England invents a motorized tricycle called the "Petrocycle" whose engine uses benzine or benzoline vapors. (See 1888)

1883 Pedal-principle of the new bicycle is applied to a "velocipede sleigh" patented by James B. Bray of New York. It resembles a bicycle with runners instead of wheels, although it has a toothed center wheel that gives it traction.

1883 Edouard Delamare-Deboutteville (1856—1901) of France begins making a four-cycle gas engine and experiments with a powered tricycle.

1883 Albert de Dion and partners Bouton and Trepardoux begin the manufacture of steam cars. They use two double-acting cylinders separately mounted to drive the front wheels individually. The car also has rear-wheel steering and the wheels are solid rubber. By 1889, one of their steam cars hauls heavy loads at 24 mph.

1883 A.D.
Steam cars manufactured

1883 Stone Arch Bridge in Minneapolis, Minnesota, one of the finest stone viaducts in the world, is completed. Spanning the Mississippi River with 23 semicircular stone arches, it carries the railroad's main transcontinental passenger line across the river, playing an important role in the development of the northwest portion of the United States. Still in use today, it is a double-track structure, 2,100 feet long and 76 feet high. Every stone in the bridge is laid by hand.

1883 March 28 Russian Konstantin E. Tsiolkovsky (1859—1935) writes in his diary a description of what are the essentials of a reaction rocket. He also argues that a rocket will work in the vacuum of space.

1883 May 24

Brooklyn Bridge opens

1883 May 24 Brooklyn Bridge officially opens amid ceremonies attended by U.S. President Chester A. Arthur (1829—1886). Designed by John A. Roebling (1806—1869) and built by his son, Washington A. Roebling (1837—1926), it is hailed as the "eighth wonder of the world." The older Roebling dies of tetanus before work begins, and his engineer son takes over and starts construction in 1870. The longest suspension bridge of its time, its steel cables are strung from two, huge masonry towers and hold a central span of 1,595.5 feet. Including the approaches, the bridge is 5,989 feet long, spanning the East River from Manhattan to Brooklyn, New York.

1883 August 4 First electric railroad in England is Magnus Volk's (1851—1937) Electric Railway running at Brighton. This narrow-gauge line still operates each summer.

1883 September 8 First rail route from the Great Lakes into Washington Territory is commemorated with a spike-driving ceremony. The line is later extended to Puget Sound via the Cascade Mountains on July 1, 1887. Accessibility to these more remote regions means that more people and, eventually, statehood will follow.

1883 October 1 Firm of Benz and Co., gas-engine manufacturers, is formed by Karl F. Benz (1844—1929) in partnership with Max Rose and Wilhelm Esslinger. Their plans include the construction of automobiles.

1883 October 8

Electric-powered airship flies

1883 October 8 French brothers Albert (1839—1906) and Gaston (1843—1899) Tissandier fly their airship from the outskirts of Paris, France. It is 92 feet long and is the first to be powered by electricity (1.5 hp Siemens electric motor). It flies for about one hour but the low power is too weak to steadily move it.

1883 November 18 Standard time, sponsored by the railroads, is adopted throughout the United States. Nearly 100 "local times" observed by railroads are abolished and all railroad clocks and watches are set nationwide on standard time (really four standards, Eastern, Central, Mountain, and Pacific, one hour apart). The necessary time change is sponsored and put into effect by the General Time Convention of Railway Managers, predecessor of the Association of American Railroads.

1884 Hermann Ganswindt (1856—1934), an eccentric German inventor, publishes his book, *Die Lenkbarkeit des aerostatischen Luftschiffes*, in which he proposes a giant rigid airship with what seems like absurd dimensions (500 feet long and a diameter of 50 feet). Although it is never built, the idea seems to have influenced Ferdinand von Zeppelin (1838—1917) in his thinking.

1884 Horatio F. Phillips (1845—1926) patents and publishes in England his design for what will become the true foundation of the modern airfoil (wing shape). After exhaustive wind tunnel research on all shapes, he demonstrates in his patent how and why a curved wing provides lift (the pressure is lower or reduced on the wing top because of the curve than it is on the bottom, and a kind of suction effect is created). This is a major breakthrough in understanding mechanical flight, and will influence future pioneers.

1884 Simplex engine, a four-cycle gas engine, is designed by Edouard Delamare-Deboutteville (1856—1901) and Leon Malandin in Paris. This engine will eventually help break the Otto patent in France in 1886.

1884 John Clegg and his son, Thomas, build the first self-propelled vehicle in Michigan. Their four-wheeled steamer is driven by a single cylinder, with the boiler in the rear, and uses leather belts to transmit power. It seats four and makes its longest drive of 14 miles.

1884 First commercial producer of motorcycles is American Lucius D. Copeland who fits a small steam engine to an American Star "ordinary" or high-wheeler bicycle. Unlike most high-wheelers, the Star has the large driving wheel at the back and the small steering wheel in the front. It is a very stable unpowered bicycle and once was ridden down the steps of the U.S. Capitol for a publicity stunt. Copeland builds about 200 steam-bicycles but soon goes out of business.

1884 Two-wheeled velocipede that converts into a boat is invented by an Englishman named Terry. He crosses the English Channel, changes it back into a cycle, and tours France.

1884 Lenticular truss is first used in America on the Smithfield Street Bridge which opens to traffic. Connecting downtown Pittsburgh, Pennsylvania with that city's south side across the Monongahela River, the bridge's steel frame is in the shape of an elongated lens. It has all the strength of a traditional truss structure, relying as it does on the conventional triangle shape for stability and strength. In 1933 it is given an aluminum deck, lessening its own weight and allowing it to carry more traffic.

1884 English engineer Charles A. Parsons (1854—1931) invents the steam turbine engine. His new engine can dispense with pistons since it has a jet of steam that turns a multibladed shaft which is then connected directly to the propeller. Once perfected and applied to ships, it will revolutionize marine propulsion. (See June 1897)

1884 Steel ball bearings are used for roller skates for the first time by American Levant M. Richardson. His invention allows the skate wheels to turn more freely which makes roller skating a less strenuous activity. It becomes even easier and more popular.

1884 First aids to navigation of any kind in Alaskan waters, 14 iron buoys are placed by the United States.

1884 April 22 British-born American Thomas Stevens (b. 1855) leaves San Francisco, California to bicycle around the world. Stevens perseveres on his uncomfortable and difficult-to-ride two-wheel "penny farthing" bicycle and encounters all manner of difficulty and adversity. He finally arrives in Yokohama, Japan on December 17, 1886, needing only a boat ride across the Atlantic to secure his accomplishment. He later writes a book about his epic, two-wheel journey, and his two volume *Around the World on a Bicycle* is published in New York in 1887—1888.

1884 July Alexander F. Mozhaiski (1825—1890), a Russian naval captain, is able to get his steam-powered monoplane into the air by launching it down a "ski-jump" ramp. It does not sustain itself in the air.

1884 July First commercial electric street railway in the United States begins operations in Cleveland, Ohio. Built by Edward Bentley and Walter Knight, the rail car draws current from an underground wooden pipe carrying two copper-wire conductors placed in a trench between the rails.

1884 August 9 First nearly practical airship flies. Built by Frenchmen Charles Renard (1847—1905) and Arthur C. Krebs (b. 1850), the *La France* is powered by an 9 hp Gramme electric motor driving one large propeller. It flies from Chalais-Meudon and returns, making a fully-controlled circular flight while travelling about five miles at 14½ mph (about 8 kilometers at 23 km/h).

1884 September 15 First railroad in Serbia opens between Belgrade and Nish.

1885 True ancestor of the modern bicycle is the Starley "Rover" Safety Bicycle. Because it has similarly-sized wheels and is much lower and more stable than its predecessor, the high "penny-farthing" or "ordinary" bicycle, it lives up to its "safety" name. This rear-wheel driven bicycle sets the new bicycle style internationally, and sends the high-wheelers and tricycles into irreversible decline. It is designed by Englishman John Kemp Starley (1854—1901), who forms The Rover Company Limited which goes on to produce many successful bicycles, motorcycles, and automobiles.

1885 A.D.

Modern-day bicycle designed

1885 ■ Redesigned "safety" bicycle shifts the drive to the rear wheel and lowers the front wheel, avoiding headers seen here by high "ordinary" bicycles.

1885 Architectural breakthrough is made by American W. L. Jenny (1832—1907) who designs the ten-story-tall Home Insurance Building in Chicago, Illinois. Jenny uses a completely iron frame and begins the age of the "skyscraper" and its elevators. Up to this time, the height of a building was limited by the constructional limit of load-bearing walls, and the higher a traditional building was, the more massive its masonry foundation had to be to support it. With the new steel-frame building technique and the availability of Otis elevators, buildings can now go straight up.

1885 French automobile manufacturing company Peugeot has its origins when Armand Peugeot directs part of his company's iron-making facilities to the construction of bicycles. In 1889 he builds a steam car, and in 1891 a gas-driven model using a Daimler engine. For decades thereafter, Peugeots are at the forefront of automotive technology. Peugeot cars have appeared for over a century and today are well-built, high-quality cars.

1885 Gottlieb Daimler (1834—1900) and Wilhelm Maybach (1846—1929) build a much-improved high-speed, internal combustion engine and install a one-cylinder, four-cycle gas version on a bicycle frame, creating the first motorcycle.

1885 November 7 First transcontinental Canadian railroad, the Canadian Pacific, is completed in British Columbia. It is extended to Vancouver on May 23, 1887, completing a line of 2,879 miles (4,635 kilometers).

1886 Nikolaus A. Otto's (1832—1891) patent for the principle of the four-stroke engine is broken in a

1885 ■ New York Central & Hudson River wreck in Batavia, New York.

court in Leipzig, Germany. This allows such designers as Karl Benz (1844—1929) and Gottlieb Daimler (1834—1900) to develop similar four-stroke engines without first paying expensive license fees to the Benz's Deutz works.

1885 A.D.

Four-cycle gas engine-powered tricycle built

1885 Karl F. Benz (1844—1929) of Mannheim, Germany builds a two-seater tricycle powered by a four-cycle gas engine which drives well in tests on the private grounds adjoining his workshop. This is the first vehicle in which the engine and chassis form a single unit and can be considered the first true automobile. From the beginning, Benz did not attempt to convert a carriage, but rather made designs for an entirely new kind of self-propelled vehicle. He is unaware that Daimler and Maybach are trying to do the same thing only 60 miles away. It is this design he patents in 1886. (See January 26, 1886)

1885 Fernand Forest of France builds a four-cylinder motor and installs improved carburetion. He builds the first water jacket (using hot water) to warm the carburetor.

1886 Danish engineer Albert Hammel and his employee, Hans Urban Johanson, build a vehicle with a two-cylinder, four-stroke engine. It has only one forward speed and can go about 6 mph. They use it to go back and forth to work and do not attempt to market it.

1886 Standardization of the gauge of railroad tracks (4 feet, 8.5 inches) in the U.S. South is completed, making possible the interchange of rail cars throughout the United States for the first time.

1886 First practical tandem bicycle (two or more persons sitting one behind the other) is designed and built by Englishmen D. Albone and A. J. Wilson. It becomes immediately successful. The front driver steers and is usually a man. The person behind is most often a woman, as the rear seat does not have a cross bar but rather a curved tube design. As the first "bicycle built for two," it spawns versions that can transport up to six people.

1885 A.D.

First oil tanker built

1885 First real oil tanker with the characteristic low-slung profile is built. Called the *Gluckauf*, the British-built vessel has separate tanks built into its hull to carry a cargo of oil.

1885 English crew "Oxford eight" rows across the English Channel from Dover, England to Calais, France, in four hours, 20 minutes.

1886 First underwater tunnel to run from one country to another, the St. Clair Tunnel, is begun. Going under the St. Clair River (one of the water links between two Great Lakes—Huron and Erie), it joins Sarnia, Ontario in Canada and Port Huron, Michigan in the United States. Finished in 1890, it is one of the earliest examples of the efficient combined use of compressed air and a mechanized shield. It is over one mile long.

1886 First four-wheeled gas-driven car with a four-stroke engine is built by Gottlieb Daimler (1834—1900) and Wilhelm Maybach (1846—1929) in Cannstatt, Germany. Their landmark vehicle is known today as the "Cannstatt-Daimler." Its one-cylinder engine has only 1.5 hp, but it can do 18 mph.

1886 First U.S. use of electricity for lighthouse purposes occurs as an arc light is placed experimentally in the Statue of Liberty in New York Harbor. (See 1889)

1886 January 26 Karl F. Benz (1844—1929) patents his new, three-wheel car driven by a gas-powered, four-stroke engine.

1886 August German engineer Gottlieb Daimler (1834—1900) tests his 1-hp gas engine on a boat along the River Neckar in Cannstadt, Germany. Within two months, he has redesigned his motorboat, patenting a new position for its prop-shaft, and reaches 6 mph (9.6 km/h).

1886 November True forerunner of the modern motorcycle is successfully driven by Wilhelm Maybach (1846—1929), Gottlieb Daimler's (1834—1900) partner. Having recently left Nikolaus A. Otto (1832—1891), the two men improved his original engine, always with the thought of applying it to a vehicle. Since their new gas-powered engine is not powerful enough to move a full-size horseless carriage, they build it onto their version of one of the new "safety" bicycles. Once their test-runs prove successful, they abandon any further development of the motorcycle and direct their attention to motor-cars.

1886 November 15 German engineer Robert A. Bosch (1861—1942) founds a manufacturing company in Stuttgart for instrument and tool making and electrical engineering. The next year he begins making magneto-ignition systems (a magnet that generates current and provide ignition voltage) for auto engines and later invents the modern spark plug.

1886 ■ Gottfried Daimler on his first motorcycle.

1887 First rotary engine to be applied to aeronautics is built and tested by Lawrence Hargrave (1850—1915) in Australia. It is driven by compressed air, and since its cylinders revolve around a stationary crankshaft, it is a rotary engine. Because of slow communications from Australia, few learn of his rotary-powered models and he does not influence engine history.

1887 Electric cab appears in England, built by Radcliffe Ward. It is followed shortly by his electric omnibus. In 1890, Ward adds another electric bus to his operation, becoming the first fleet operator to use electric propulsion. His second bus is designed by Walter Bersey and travels from Charing Cross to Victoria Station.

1887 Karl Benz (1844—1929) sells an improved version of his 1885 three-wheel auto to Parisian engineer Emile Roger. Roger is also granted sole agency rights for France and assembles and sells Benz's cars there in 1888. This could be considered the beginning of the automobile industry.

1886 ■ Karl Benz (lower left) and his first automobile (lower right) and Ggottfried Daimler (upper right) and his first car (upper left).

1887 American inventor Ransom E. Olds (1864—1950) drives his first steamer on the streets of Lansing, Michigan. The steam for his three-wheeler is generated by gasoline.

1887 A.D.

First electric elevator built

1887 First electric elevator in the United States is built by William Baxter, Jr. who installs it in Baltimore, Maryland.

1887 After extensive tests on 50 freight trains in Burlington, Iowa, automatic, quick-action, triple-valve brakes are adopted for freight service.

1887 First successful electric trolley line is built by Frank J. Sprague (1857—1934) in Richmond, Virginia. (See 1897)

1887 A.D.

U.S. trains use electric lights

1887 U.S. trains fully equipped with electric lights make runs on four different east coast lines. The *Pennsylvania Limited* is the first train so equipped.

1887 Early Soviet rocket pioneer Fridrikh A. Tsander (1887—1933) is born. As a physicist, he was always passionate about interplanetary space flight, and began to work on liquid-propelled rockets during the 1920s. During the 1930s, he worked with Valentin P.

Glushko (b. 1908) at the Soviet Gas Dynamics Laboratory (GDL). He also pioneered the idea of a manned space station.

1887 U.S. Interstate Commerce Commission originates with the passage of the Interstate Commerce Act of 1887. Formed to regulate railroads, it comes to oversee other transportation modes over the years. There are 11 original members, but the number is later reduced to 5, each serving 7 years. Laws passed in 1976, 1980, and 1982 sharply reduce its regulation over railroads, trucking companies, and bus lines. Its creation marks the recognition that national transportation policy has become too large and too important not to be made by the federal government.

1887 February 4 Interstate Commerce Act, creating the Interstate Commerce Commission, is signed by President Grover Cleveland (1837—1908). Among other things, it provides for the first federal regulation of railroads.

1887 April 14 First standard code of train rules in the United States is adopted by the General Time Convention, the predecessor of the Association of American Railroads.

1887 June 17—18 Successful test runs are made of a passenger train pulled by an oil-burning locomotive. It runs from Altoona to Pittsburgh, Pennsylvania and back.

1887 September 20 Patent is issued to American John Charter for what becomes the first practical farm tractor. He then forms the Charter Gas Engine Company in Chicago, Illinois and produces in 1889 the first successful gasoline-powered farm tractor.

1887 December Direct railroad route linking Seattle, Washington and Portland, Oregon with the California cities of San Francisco, Los Angeles, and San Diego is completed.

1888 Michelin brothers Andre (1853—1931) and Edouard (1859—1940) establish the Michelin Tire Company in France to manufacture bicycle tires. (See 1895)

1888 Englishman Edward Butler (1863—1940) builds a gas-powered tricycle he calls a "Petrol-Cycle." Since he patented his designs as early as 1884, many consider his vehicle and not that of Wilhelm Maybach (1846—1929) and Gottlieb Daimler (1834—1900) to be the real ancestor of the modern motorcycle, despite the fact that it has three and not two wheels. (See November 1886)

1888 Englishman Edward Butler's powered tricycle is the first vehicle to have a float-feed carburetor. This is basically a spray carburetor in which the fuel is sprayed from an opening into the center of an air stream. It precedes Wilhelm Maybach's (1834—1900) spray carburetor and has all the basic elements of a modern carburetor. (See 1894)

1888 First American to build and operate a rechargeable electric car is Fred M. Kimball of Boston, Massachusetts.

1888 Scottish veterinarian John B. Dunlop (1840—1921) conceives the idea of pneumatic (air-filled) tires and applies it to his son's bicycle. He first fills a garden hose with air and finds it reduces bumps and makes the ride much smoother. Although invented for the bicycle, whose ride they transform, pneumatic tires come along just in time for the emerging automobile. Dunlop was preceded by Robert W. Thomson (1822—1873) who

patented the idea in 1846, but it is Dunlop who creates an entirely new industry out of it.

1888 Englishman J. K. Starley builds a small, light electric car using bicycle parts.

1888—1889 Leon Serpollet (d. 1907) places his "flash" or instantaneous generation boiler in a tricycle, then in a carriage. This boiler gives steam cars a new lease on life, since he has temporarily solved the problem of no existing boiler being light enough to be carried by anything but a very heavy vehicle. His "flash" system saves weight using a system of coiled tubing which is heated. Serpollet remains an advocate of steam over internal-combustion until he dies.

1888 August 12 First gas-powered aircraft flies. Built by the German experimenter, Wolfert, a powered airship (dirigible) fitted with a 2 hp Daimler benzene engine running two propellers, flies for 2½ miles (c. 4 kilometers) from Seelberg to Kornwestheim, Germany.

1888 September 4 First parachute descents in Canada are made from a hot-air balloon by Edward D. Hogan in Quebec.

1888 September 26 First aeronautical fatality in Canada occurs as Tom Wensley is carried in the air clinging to a balloon rope and falls.

1889 Otto Lilienthal (1848—1896), publishes his *Der Vogelflug als Grundlage der Fliegekunst* (*Bird Flight as the Basis of Aviation*), one of the classics of aviation. His book discusses and analyzes the flight of birds and includes tables of air pressure on curved surfaces at different angles of flight. The Wright Brothers will use this book as their scientific bible and inspiration.

1889 Prolific American inventor Thomas Alva Edison (1847—1931) builds the Edison Experimental Electric car. He is attracted to it as a quiet power source that is free from exhaust fumes. His three-wheel, battery-powered car has only limited range due to the short life of the 5-hp nickel-alkaline storage battery.

1889 A.D.

Edison invents electric car

1889 First "stair climbing elevator" is invented by Frenchman Amiot. Driven by a water-powered engine, it is the forerunner of the modern residence stair elevator.

1889 ■ Typical American stagecoach at Great Hot Springs, Dakota.

1889 Most toll roads in England are by now free and the toll system is abandoned.

1889 First American electric car is built by William Morrison of Des Moines, Iowa. He completes his electric coupe in 1892 and shows it in Chicago.

1889 Sand-clay roads become a cheap, practical method of providing stable road surfaces in many states in the American south. Mixed in proper proportions, the clay acts as a binder and makes for an adequate light-traffic road. It is limited to those areas where the ground does not freeze.

1889 First meeting of the International Maritime Conference is held in Washington, D.C. This broadly-represented and attended conference begins the long process of moving toward international uniformity of all forms of maritime signals. The explosive growth of sea traffic and the rapid technical progress in both ship propulsion and sea lighting make such a conference imperative.

1889 First gas-jet propelled boat, the *Eureka*, is launched in Brooklyn, New York. It is fitted with a series of tubes that open under the water. When a gas/air mixture explodes in rapid succession, the expanding gases push against the surrounding water and move the boat.

1889 First significant reinforced-concrete bridge in the United States, the Alvord Lake Bridge in San Francisco's Golden Gate Park, is completed. Still in use today, it is built to carry one park road above another, and has an arch span of 20 feet and a width of 64 feet. It is designed by Ernest L. Ransome, and contains his pioneering method of twisted-bar reinforcing.

1889 First steam-powered lifeboat, the *Duke of Northumberland*, is built in England. It is a 50-foot (15.2-meter) boat which uses the principle of water-jet propulsion. Since the propeller is not yet perfected, and the paddle-wheel is impractical for smaller boats, this system is preferred.

1889 As a result of experiments with electric lights in the Statue of Liberty, the Sandy Hook Beacon in New York Harbor is electrified with an incandescent electric lamp.

1889 June 1 Longest tunnel in Scotland, the Greenock Tunnel, opens. Located on the former

Caledonian Railway from Glasgow to Gourock, it is over one mile (1,920 meters) long.

1889 June 1 First through train of the *Orient Express* leaves Paris, France and travels to Constantinople (Istanbul), Turkey in 67 hours, 35 minutes. This is the first time passengers do not have to change trains.

1889 June 4 Steepest rack railway in the world, Mt. Pilatus Railway in Switzerland, opens. With a gradient of 50% (100% being vertical), it uses a special rack with horizontal teeth on each side. (See July 3, 1869)

1889 July 22 Longest tunnel in Wales, the Ffestiniog, opens. This railroad tunnel is over two miles (3,407 meters) long.

1889 July 27 Electric tricycle powered by storage batteries is demonstrated in Boston, Massachusetts. It is designed by Philip W. Pratt and built by the Fred W. Kimball Company of Boston.

1889 August 30 British Railways Act goes into effect. The government steps in to impose reliable brakes on all passenger trains and to compel the use of interlocking of signals on main lines, so that one signal cannot conflict with another or with a point (switch).

1889 December 21 First elevator powered by alternating current is installed by the Otis Company in the Desmarest Building in New York. Up to this time, all previous electric elevators had been powered by direct current.

c. 1890 As bicycles are improved and automobiles appear more frequently, interest in the quality of roads is further revived.

1890 Clincher rim is patented by American William E. Bartlett (1830—1900). It allows rubber or pneumatic (air-filled) tires to be firmly attached to the metal wheel rim which has a channel or groove into which the tire's edge fits.

1890 First modern form of the diamond frame bicycle is produced in England. Made by the Humber firm, this machine has all the essential features of a modern bicycle: chain-drive to the rear wheel; a moveable rear wheel set in slotted fork ends to permit chain-tension adjustment; ball bearing raked and set steering head and fork; wheels of the same diameter; and a spring-seat on an adjustable seat tube.

1890 Electric tram runs for the first time in Japan at the Naikoku Industrial Exhibition in Ueno.

1890 First steel cantilever bridge, Forth Bridge, over the Firth of Forth, Scotland, is completed. Designed by English engineers Benjamin Baker (1840—1907) and John Fowler (1817—1898), it spans the firth or estuary at Queensferry. A true cantilever with self-supporting arms reaching out from each of three piers, it carries a railroad track 45 meters above the water and has a main span of 1,710 feet. Overall, it spans 5,330 feet. Called the ugliest bridge by some, it is visually a very powerful and dramatic structure.

1890 April 6 Anthony Herman Gerard Fokker (1890—1939), Dutch pioneer airman and aircraft manufacturer, is born in Kediri, Java. He introduced in Berlin in 1912 the gear system that made it possible for World War I pilots to fire a machine gun through the propeller arc without hitting the blades. His Fokker *D.VIII* was one of the finest all-around fighters of that war. He became a naturalized U. S. citizen and his Fokker *T-2* made the first non-stop flight across the United States. In 1926, the North Pole was overflown in a Fokker trimotor airplane.

1890 October 9 First full-sized manned airplane to leave the ground under its own power (for about 150 feet) is Frenchman Clément Ader's (1841—1925) steam-powered, propeller-driven aircraft at Armainvilliers, France. It has bat-like, canopied wings with a 46-foot span, a 20-hp engine, and a tricycle undercarriage. Although the craft raised itself on its own, Ader's flight was not controlled or sustained. He abandons this plane and begins to rebuild.

1890 December 18 First underground electric rail line or subway, the City & South London Railway, opens in England. Begun in 1866 and built using a shield developed by J. H. Greathead (1844—1896), the tunnel is originally intended for cable operation, but switches to the new electrical method of pulling the cars.

1891 Otto Lilienthal (1848—1896), German engineer, begins a series of experiments with his hang-gliders at Dervitz, Germany. Fully convinced that he must first learn to fly a fixed-wing glider before attempting powered flight, Lilienthal not only launches himself

1890 ■ Forth Bridge, Scotland during construction.

into the air on his gliders, but is able to control his flight. He becomes the first man to be photographed flying in the air, and these pictures receive worldwide publicity. The Wright brothers probably saw them first in *McClure's Magazine* of 1894 and later in Means' *Aeronautical Annuals* for 1896 and 1897.

1891 First American self-propelled vehicle sold for export is a steamer built by Ransom E. Olds (1864—1950). After an article about his steam carriage appears in the *Scientific American*, the Francis Times Company of Bombay, India orders one.

1891 Escalator is invented by American Jesse W. Reno, whose moving, inclined belt provides transportation to passengers riding on cleats attached to the belt. At first the handrail is stationary, but he builds an improved version with a moving handrail in this same year. Modern escalators are inclined at about 30 degrees and are electrically powered, being driven by a chain and sprocket and held in the proper plane by two tracks. Moving ramps have become specialized forms of escalators that carry people and material horizontally.

1891 Shortest railroad tunnel in the United States, the Bee Rock Tunnel, is begun. Built near Ap-

palachia, Virginia on the Louisville and Nashville Railroad, it is only 30 feet (9 meters) long and cuts through a single, huge rock.

1891 First real attempt at theoretical space propulsion is made by a German, Hermann Ganswindt (1856—1934). Lacking any mathematical training, Ganswindt works on a design that marks the beginnings of the "step-rocket" principle. In his plan, steel cartridges fire one after another and continually accelerate until the rocket reaches orbital speed and stays in space. Although he builds nothing workable, his lectures inspire many.

1891 First aluminum boat is built by Escher, Wyss & Co. of Zurich, Switzerland. Powered by a 2-hp naptha engine, it weighs 1,000 pounds and carries eight passengers. The problem with early aluminum for boats is that despite its lightness, it is fairly soft and suffers from "metal fatigue."

1891 Interest in alpine skiing gets a major boost with the English, French, and German translation of arctic explorer Fridtjof Nansen's (1861—1930) book, *Paa Ski Over Grunland.* Among those inspired by the book is Austrian Mathias Zdarsky who develops new methods and better equipment. (See 1897)

1891 A.D.

Escalator invented

1891 First U.S. use of a flashing light as a ship-warning signal is made when a mechanism for revolving lamps around the mast is placed on a lightship. The system does not work well and is discontinued.

1891 July 13 First concrete street pavement in North America is a 220-foot-long, ten-foot-wide strip on the west side of Main Street in Bellefontaine, Ohio. The earliest pavement made of Portland cement is attributed to Inverness, Scotland in 1865. (See July 4, 1909)

1891 September 2 First parachute descent by a Canadian woman is made when Miss Nellie Lamount jumps from a hot-air balloon during a fair in Quebec.

1892 Samuel Pierpont Langley (1834—1906), American physicist and head of the Smithsonian Institution, builds the first of his steam-driven airplane models. He will experiment with several different models, none of which will fly successfully.

1892 New magazine is founded as a result of the Good Roads Movement in the United States. Called *Good Roads,* it is based in New York City and circulates well beyond the bicyclists who started it. It becomes very influential in preparing the public to accept the inevitable taxes that would be required to pay for better roads.

1892 Highest altitude by a main-line railroad is attained as the Central Railway of Peru is completed. The track begins at the coast and reaches 15,806 feet in the Andes Mountains.

1892 First gas-driven outboard motor is tested by its French inventor, Alfred Seguin, in a garage in Geneva, Switzerland. By the spring of 1893, Seguin imports two powered boats to London.

1892 February 27 German inventor Rudolph C. K. Diesel (1858—1913) files a patent application for a new heat engine he has not yet built. He then begins to develop his new type of internal combustion engine that will be more efficient than Otto's four-cycle engine (which loses heat or energy because of temperature changes). (See 1897)

1892 March 29 First state-aid road law becomes operative in New Jersey. It provides that the roads be annually inspected and a systematic plan for improvement be made. The State would pay one-third of the

1892 ■ First State-Aid road in New Jersey pioneers governmental commitment to road improvement.

expense, the adjoining property owners one-tenth, and the local county the remainder.

1892 October 22 Single locomotive disappears completely in England when the ground below its tracks begins to slowly give way. The crew of two jump clear and the train eventually descends to a depth of 200 feet (61 meters). The track had been built in an area of extensive mining, accounting for the great underground spaces. Recovery of the engine is not attempted and the hole is simply filled in.

1892 October 22 Locomotive disappears into ground

1893 The box-kite is invented in Australia by Lawrence Hargrave (1850—1915). This device, which is composed of two four-sided "cells" joined by booms, will be illustrated in Mean's *Aeronautical Annual* for 1896, and will play an important role in Europen aviation by influencing Voisin and Archdeacon. They will use its design to build what will become the classic European biplane. (See 1905).

1893 A.D. Box-kite invented

1893 Forerunner of the U.S. Department of Transportation, the U.S. Office of Road Inquiry, is formed in the Department of Agriculture.

1893 First successful gas-powered car in the United States is demonstrated in Springfield, Massachusetts by Charles E. Duryea (1862—1938) and his brother, J. Frank (b. 1870). Weighing 700 pounds, it is propelled by a 4-hp, two-stroke motor and looks exactly like a buggy without the horse. The Duryea brothers set up the first U.S. company to manufacture cars for sale in 1894. Thirteen are completed in 1896. (See 1894)

1893 A.D. Gas-powered car demonstrated

1893 ■ Charles E. Duryea sits in his third automobile.

1893 First Japanese-made locomotive, Model 860, is produced in Kobe.

1893 First imported automobile into the United States is a Benz version shown at the World's Fair, in Chicago, Illinois.

1893 Pontiac Buggy Company is incorporated in Pontiac, Michigan. This large company eventually makes a successful change from carriage-building to automobile production.

1893 A.D.

Highest railway tunnel opens

1893 Highest railway tunnel in the world, the Galera Tunnel in Peru, opens to traffic. Part of the Central Railway of Peru on the line running from Callao, the port of Lima, up over the Andes Mountains, it is located at 15,655 feet. Trains on this route carry oxygen for passengers suffering the effects of the extremely high altitude.

1893 A.D.

First brick road opens

1893 First rural U.S. road made entirely of brick opens on the Wooster Pike near Cleveland, in Cuyahoga County, Ohio. Four miles of brick pavement are laid atop a heavy, white-clay soil that served as an old stage route.

1893 Air brakes and automatic couplers are now required by law on trains in the United States.

1893 Massachusetts Department of Public Works, Division of Highways, is first organized.

1893 American industrialist Henry Ford (1863—1947) builds and runs his first car in Detroit, Michigan. It has a two-cylinder, 4-hp engine, looks like a buggy, and is the first of several experimental versions. At this time, Ford is ignorant of most of the innovations taking place in Europe.

1893 Corinth Canal, connecting the Aegean and Ionian seas, is built. Conceived initially during the first century A.D. by the Roman Emperor Nero who actually started work on it, this 4.8-mile-(6.3-kilometer-) long canal runs through the mountainous Isthmus of Corinth. As it runs 280 feet (86 meters) below almost vertical rock cliffs, it is probably the most spectacular canal ever built.

1893 March 3 U.S. Office of Road Inquiry (ORI) is approved by Congress and President Benjamin Harrison (1833—1901). This new office is intended to become the research arm of the government concerning the technology of making roads. It forms a testing laboratory in 1900, and in 1905 is merged with other agencies to become the Office of Public Roads.

1893 March 6 First elevated electric city rail line, the Liverpool Overhead Railway, opens in England.

1893 March 21 French scientist Gustave Hermitte (b. 1863) and French balloon pilot Georges Besançon (1866—1934) pioneer the use of unmanned, instrument-carrying balloons for meteorological recording with their *Aerophile* balloon launched at Vaugirard in France. They see no need to risk lives to conduct high-altitude weather research. This is the forerunner of the modern weather balloon.

1893 May Horatio F. Phillips (1845—1926) builds his curious-looking "Venetian blind" airplane which he tests while tethered on a circular ground track at Harrow, England. Powered by a steam engine driving a single propeller, the machine allows Phillips to test his correct airfoil (wing shape) theories.

1893 May 10 First locomotive to exceed 100 mph makes a run in Batavia, New York. A New York Central steam locomotive reaches 112.5 mph.

1893 August 14 Driver's licenses are required of French motorists who must first pass a driver's test. Britain is one of the last countries to require a test. (See 1935)

1893 August 14 Parking restrictions on motor traffic are imposed by a Paris Police Ordinance.

1894 Otto Lilienthal (1848—1896) builds and perfects his most trusty glider, a standard monoplane hang-glider he calls his "Normal-Segelapparat" or "Standard sailing machine." It is with this machine that he makes glides over 1,000 feet.

1894 Octave Chanute (1832—1910), a French-born American civil engineer, publishes his *Progress in Flying Machines*. One of the classics in aviation, this work is the first authoritative account of aviation history. Widely influential, it summarizes the entire course of aeronautical accomplishments to date, and along with Lilienthal's book, is a guiding work for the Wright brothers.

1894 Ransom E. Olds (1864—1950) begins work on his first gasoline car in Lansing, Michigan, and Elwood Haynes (1857—1925) does the same in Kokomo, Indiana. American auto builders begin to see the internal combustion engine as the wave of the future.

1894 First motorcycle to have pneumatic tires and the first with an internal combustion engine to be produced and sold commercially is built in Germany. The Hildebrand & Wolfmuller motorcycle has an open frame formed by four horizontal tubes, between which the engine is mounted. It weighs 115 pounds and can go up to 24 mph. The company goes out of business in 1897.

1894 "Electrobat" cab is built by Henry G. Morris and Pedro G. Salom. The next year they begin operating electric cabs and, by 1897, have a fleet of 12 electric public taxis.

1894 The Benz "Velo" becomes the world's first production car and accounts for most of the 67 Benz vehicles produced this year. Originally fitted with a 1.5-hp engine, it is soon equipped with a 2.75-hp one, and in 1895 is given a third gear.

1894 Emile Levassor (1844—1897) and René Panhard (1841—1908) of France design the Panhard auto which is the forerunner of the modern car. With a front-mounted engine driving the rear wheels via a clutch and gearbox, this vehicle is the archetype of nearly every auto for the next 50 years. Its pioneering chain drive is a vast improvement over the flimsy belt-driven cars.

1894 New Jersey State Highway Department is first organized.

1894 First national road conference in the United States is held with representatives from 11 states. Resolutions passed urge state legislatures to create highway commissions.

1894 First American company formed to produce gasoline autos is the Duryea Motor Wagon Company of Springfield, Massachusetts.

1894 Wilhelm Maybach (1846—1929) invents the atomizing carburetor which directs the fuel spray into the center of an air stream. His version is an improvement of the one invented by Edward Butler in England in 1888.

1894 First toe-irons for snow skis are introduced by Norwegian Fritz Huitfeld. This new binding technique is a major advance which gives the skier real control over the skis and makes skiing on the more difficult Alpine slopes more achievable.

1894 First American aluminum boats are built for the Walter Wellman and the Jackson Arctic Expeditions.

1894 Manchester Ship Canal in England is opened. Built long after the height of the canal era has passed, this important canal makes the industrial city of Manchester a seaport, despite it being 35 miles from the sea. It allows ocean-going vessels access from the Mersey estuary to the city of Manchester.

1894 May 11 Great railroad strike begins in Chicago, Illinois with the Pullman workers. Following the money panics of 1893 and 1894, the Pullman Palace Car Company reduces wages. The workers' strike soon escalates to violence and mobs destroy railroad property. (See June 12, 1894)

1894 A.D.

First gasoline auto company formed

1894 May 11

Great railroad strike begins

1894 June 10 First motor-barge, the 98-foot (30-meter) steel-hulled *l'Idée*, makes a successful trial run on the Tancarville Canal in France. It moves at 6 mph (10 km/h) with 80 tons of ballast on board.

1894 June 12 First national convention of the American Railway Union is held. Under the leadership of Eugene V. Debs (1855—1926), the Union later boycotts the servicing of Pullman cars out of sympathy with the striking Pullman workers. This causes a general strike which paralyzes 50,000 miles of western railroads. (See July 17, 1894)

1894 June 19 Frederick W. Lanchester (1868—1946), British aeronautical and automobile pioneer, announces his theory of circulatory air-flow to the Birmingham Natural History and Philosophical Society in England. This theory is later to become of pivotal importance in aerodynamics. (See 1907)

**1894
June 22**

**First auto
race takes
place**

1894 June 22 First organized automobile race is the Paris-Rouen Reliability Trial. Of the 102 original entries, most are powered by gas or steam, although five cars are driven by springs, five by compressed air, and five by electricity. After elimination runs, 21 cars are left to compete. All finish the 78-mile course, with the De Dion steam tractor (which pulled a carriage) the winner with an average speed of 12 mph. This race gets international publicity and spurs the development of the automobile.

1894 June 25 Hermann J. Oberth (1894—1989), one of rocketry's pioneers along with Tsiolkovsky and Goddard, is born in Hermanstadt, Transylvania (now part of Romania). When his 1922 Ph.D. dissertation on rocket design was rejected, he later published it partly at his own expense and it soon became a classic. His later work on liquid-fueled rockets led him to Peenemünde during World War II where he worked on military rocket development (V-2) for his former assistant, Wernher von Braun (1912—1977). After the war, he worked in Europe and for the United States until he retired in 1958.

1894 July 17

**Federal
intervention
ends railroad
strike**

1894 July 17 Eugene V. Debs (1855—1926), U.S. labor organizer and later Socialist Party presidential candidate, is imprisoned for defying a U.S. Court injunction to stop the railroad strike. Great strike ends two days later, having resulted in some deaths, the involvement of the President, and the invocation of the Constitution. Like the major air traffic controllers' strike nearly a century later, a labor union finds itself no match with the power of the federal government. (See August 3, 1981)

1894 July 31 Hiram Stevens Maxim (1840—1916), an American by birth who later became an English citizen, and famous inventor of the Maxim machine-gun, tests his huge steam-powered airplane at Kent, England. This strange, almost monster-like machine which runs on rails, with additional guard rails above, succeeds in lifting its own weight by the force of its two 180 hp engines, but is brought to a stop after tangling with the guard rails. Maxim's eccentric design is incapable of free flight and proves a dead end.

1895 Otto Lilienthal (1848—1896) builds and flies successfully the first of his three biplane hang-gliders (with two sets of wings). This design gives him better control and more stability, and he can fly in winds up to 24 mph.

1895 James Means (1853—1920), wealthy American industrialist, publishes the first of three successive volumes (1895—1897) of his *Aeronautical Annual*. This three-part work is intended, like Chanute's, to collect the most significant papers in the field and to disseminate them as widely as possible with the deliberate intent of stimulating interest and fostering progress in mechanical flight. It is one of the works which inspired and guided the Wright brothers.

1895 Percy Sinclair Pilcher (1866—1899), English engineer, designs and builds his glider, called the *Bat*, and conducts a series of successful glides—the first ever in England. He thus becomes the first true British aviator.

1895 Connecticut State Highway Department is first organized.

1895 First all-British four-wheeled gas car is designed and built by Frederick W. Lanchester (1868—1946) and his brother, George H. Lanchester (1874—1970), in Birmingham. It is a one-cylinder, 5-hp, air-cooled car. An improved version, their first production car, goes on the market in 1900.

1895 First four-cylinder motorcycle is produced by English civil engineer H. C. Holden. Like all of its predecessors, it runs with a pronounced jerk and has control problems at low speeds.

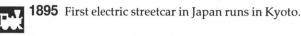

1895 First automotive magazines in the United States appear. They include *The Horseless Age*, *The Motorcycle*, and *Autocar*.

1895 Leland & Faulconer Manufacturing Company, forerunner of the Cadillac Company, is formed in Detroit, Michigan by Henry M. Leland (1843—1932). As a builder of automobile engines and later of complete autos, Leland establishes a record for rigorous and impeccable standards of accuracy and workmanship. (See 1902)

1895 Ransom E. Olds (1864—1950) of Lansing, Michigan brings out his first car powered with an internal combustion engine. One of four built in 1895 by the new Olds Motor Vehicle Company, it has a gas-driven, one-cylinder, 6-hp, water-cooled engine.

1895 First practical subway line in the United States is begun in Boston, Massachusetts. Completed in 1897, it is 1.5 miles (2.4 kilometers) long and uses trolley streetcars or tramcars. It later switches to conventional subway trains.

1895 One of the most important developments for the motorcycle is the introduction of the light, high-speed gas engine by the French firm of De Dion Bouton. This much improved engine, built by Albert de Dion (1856—1946) and Georges Bouton (1847—1938), is small enough to be easily mounted on a bicycle and yet powerful enough to move it about. The De Dion Bouton Company however, chooses the more stable tricycle for its new engine.

1895 Michelin brothers Andre (1853—1931) and Edouard (1859—1940) demonstrate their new, demountable pneumatic tires (air-filled tires held on to the rim by bolts) on a Peugeot racing car which they enter in the Paris-Bordeaux race this year. In the 730-mile race (1,174 kilometers), they use 22 spare tubes and the crew loses count of the number of punctures they repair. They also do not finish the race, which is won by Emile Levassor (1844—1897) in his Panhard. Their performance generates great interest in pneumatic tires.

1895 First steam railroad conversion to electric in the United States is completed on three railroads in Massachusetts, New Jersey, and Maryland.

1895 First electric streetcar in Japan runs in Kyoto.

1895 Russian Konstantin E. Tsiolkovsky (1859—1935) writes a science fiction story about space travel. His "Dreams of the Earth and Sky" is published in *Nature and Men*.

1895 Kiel Canal, best-known canal in Germany, is completed. Providing a short cut between the Baltic Sea and the North Sea, this wide, deep, and fairly straight 61-mile-long canal becomes an immensely busy and important waterway. It has a unique engineering feature at Rendsburg where, to give clearance to the canal's largest ships, the railroad is made to spiral over the city on an ascending viaduct that crosses over itself before returning to the main span above the water.

1895 American inventor Simon Lake (1866—1945) builds a simple, 14-foot-long submersible with no intention of using it for belligerent purposes. Called *Argonaut Junior*, it is built of wood and moves by a hand-crank. (See 1897)

1895 April 24 First man to sail solo around the world, American sea captain Joshua Slocum (b. 1844) leaves Boston, Massachusetts. Three years later he returns, having gone around the world alone, despite being unable to swim. He sails solo again in November 1909 at the age of 65 on a West Indies trip and is never seen again.

1895 April 24
Man first sails around the world

1895 May First aeronautical society in America, the Boston Aeronautical Society, is founded.

1895 November First race for motorcycles in the United States is held in Illinois. At this time, the word "motorcycle" describes almost any mechanically-powered vehicle, regardless of how many wheels it has. The race runs from Chicago to Waukegan.

1895 November
First motorcycle race held

1895 November First club or association of automobile enthusiasts, the American Motor League, is organized in Chicago, Illinois. In its first meeting, it opens its membership to "any man or woman, eighteen years of age or over, of good moral character and respectable standing, friendly to the motor vehicle and its interests." The initiation fee is two dollars.

1895 November 5 U.S. Patent No. 549,160 is issued to George B. Selden (1846—1922) for his gasoline-powered automobile. Selden filed this patent in 1879, and his alleged infringement claims against the Ford Company and a few others brings about the most famous lawsuit in the history of the auto industry. (See 1911)

1895 November 28 First American automobile race, organized by the *Times-Herald* newspaper of Chicago, is held on icy, snow-drifted streets. The $2000 prize is won by a Duryea vehicle which features three forward speeds and a water-cooled, four-stroke engine that gives 18 mph. A Benz car finishes second. This race captures headlines and imaginations throughout the United States, and once again a race spurs renewed interest in the automobile.

1895 December First motorized ambulance is exhibited in Paris at the Salon du Cycle held at the Palais de l'Industrie. It is a Panhard et Levassor vehicle powered by a Daimler engine.

1896 A.D.

Inventor of gyroplane born

1896 Juan de la Cierva (1896—1965), Spanish-born inventor of the gyroplane, is born. Called the autogiro, his aircraft gets its vertical lift from its freely rotating airfoils or what are essentially rotating wings. Having solved the problem of unequal lift—which gave his craft a tendency to roll over—by using flapping hinges on each blade, he made his first successful flight in 1923. By 1933, his rotors were geared to the engine and his autogiro had evolved half-way toward becoming a helicopter. He died in an airplane (not autogiro) crash in England.

1896 Octave Chanute (1832—1910), American civil engineer, designs and builds his own full-size, biplane gliders (two sets of wings). His assistant, Augustus Moore Herring (1867—1926), helps with the design and does the gliding. Chanute's classsic design gives the Wright brothers their general biplane structure, but offers no control help, since Chanute's design has no movable control surfaces.

1896 Percy S. Pilcher (1866—1899) builds and tests his fourth and most successful glider, called the *Hawk*, in Kent, England. It has an undercarriage with wheels, and is often launched by being towed by men or horses.

1896 Automobile Club de France is founded by French Count Albert de Dion (1856—1946). It remains in existence and is a leading authority on international motor sport.

1896 Number of jinrikisha in use in Japan peaks at 210,688. After World War II, their number dwindles to 426 by 1946.

1896 First subway on the European continent opens in Budapest, Hungary. This 2.5-mile (4-kilometer) electric subway uses single cars with trolley poles.

1896 First sale of an American-built, gasoline-powered car is made by the Duryea Motor Wagon Company.

1896 John Henry Knight publishes *Notes on Motor Carriages.*

1896 First front-mounted, four-cylinder engine is built by the firm of Panhard et Levassor of France for competetive racing. It is in one of these powerful new cars that Emile Levassor (1844—1897) is killed in 1897.

1896 First use of the word "automobile" is made by the French who use it to describe the cars beginning to appear in the United States.

1896 First recorded automobile accident in the United States occurs in New York as Henry Wells strikes bicyclist Evelyn Thomas with his Duryea electric.

1896 First automobile track race in the United States is held on a one-mile course at Narragansett Park in Cranston, Rhode Island.

1896 One of the earliest American advertisements showing a photograph of an actual car is published in Kokomo, Indiana. A large ad showing six people sitting in a large Haynes-Apperson, gas-powered, "double cylinder carriage motor" tells how it is a practical machine, available at a modest price, and is promptly delivered. In the same year, the American Electric Vehicle Company of Chicago, Illinois shows a drawing of its electric vehicle, stating its operating costs are one cent per mile.

1896 Frederick W. Lanchester (1868—1946) completes his first horizontally-opposed ("flat") four-cylinder engine and will place it in the center of his 1897 automobile. This car will have many new technical features, one of which reduces vibration to a minimum. It also will have a system of epicyclic gears that can be pres-elected. This design is a forerunner of the modern automatic transmission.

1896 Daimler Company of Stuttgart, Germany is formed in Great Britain at Coventry to manufacture French and German patented cars under license. Until 1900, the English Daimlers are essentially imported German models, but soon after production begins in Coventry, King Edward VII purchases one of the first English-built models.

1896 Rhode Island Department of Public Works, Division of Roads and Bridges, is first organized.

1896 World's first escalator is installed in Coney Island, New York.

1896 Russian Konstantin E. Tsiolkovsky (1859—1935) begins his groundbreaking scientific work on the theoretical aspects of liquid-propellant space rockets. Within two years he designs several rockets and solves the theoretical problem of how reaction (rocket) engines could escape from and reenter the earth's atmosphere. He publishes the results of his work a few years later. **(See 1903)**

1896 Russian Konstantin E. Tsiolkovsky (1859—1935) drafts the first ten chapters of his novel *Outside the Earth*. After making his scientific breakthroughs on rockets, he puts this detailed space novel aside and it is not published until 1918.

1896 First U.S. gas-powered outboard motor is introduced by the American Motors Company of New York. Called the "Portable Boat N Motor with Reversible Propeller," it comes in a single or twin cylinder version.

1896 May 6 Samuel P. Langley (1834—1906) succeeds, after four years of work and failed flights, in obtaining good results with his steam-powered, model-size, tandem-wing (one set behind the other) airplane. His model No. 5 makes a flight of 3,300 feet (c. 1 kilometers).

1896 June First reported automobile theft occurs in Paris, France when a Peugeot owned by Baron de Zuylen is stolen while undergoing repairs.

1896 August 9 Otto Lilienthal (1848—1896) crashes from a height of 50 feet when gliding in one of his monoplane hang-gliders, on the Gollenberg in Germany. He dies of a broken spine the next day in a Berlin clinic. Not only was he the first true aviator, but his work and life directly inspired all those experimenters who followed him.

1896 September 15 In a bizarre public event, William George Crush stages a train wreck as a deliberate disaster. For months before, the aptly-named Crush advertises the great spectacle he has planned to stage in Texas—two trains meeting head-on at top speed. Some 40,000 spectators do come and watch as two locomotives, each pulling six cars loaded with ties, touch cowcatchers and then back away about a mile from each other. With throttles tied down wide open, the two driverless trains careen toward each other at 60 mph. They meet head-on, rear upward together, and both boilers explode. The landscape and the distant crowd are littered with flying metal and wood, but only two spectators are killed and a few others injured. The famous photograph of the two trains, nose-to-nose, seen just before impact was taken by Joe "One-Eye" Deane, who snapped the picture as he was hit by a flying bolt.

1896 October 1 First experimental routes for the free rural delivery of U.S. mail are established in West Virginia, the home state of Postmaster General William L. Wilson (1843—1900). Rural mail delivery soon proves so popular that it gives great impetus to the call for gravel or macadam roads to be built in rural areas.

1896 ■ Free mail delivery to rural areas of the U.S. spurs improvement and construction of roads.

1896 ■ Series of Lilienthal glides prior to his death.

1897 American electrical engineer Frank J. Sprague (1857—1934) invents the multiple-unit electric train in which a single driver can control a number of motor coaches from either end of the train. It is first used on the Chicago South Side Elevated Railway. This invention becomes the key component of all modern, short-haul passenger railways.

1897 Pope Manufacturing Company of Hartford, Connecticut begins marketing its Columbia Mark III Electric Phaetons. By 1899, they have built 500 electric carriages, and after a series of mergers, build some 2,000 electric taxi cabs and buses for New York City.

1897 Blackwell Tunnel in London, England is completed. This is the first of several tunnels dug under the Thames River built specifically for horse-drawn vehicles and pedestrians. It is 3,116 feet long.

1897 First front-wheel drive automobile is the Austrian-built voiturette, Graf & Stift, which is powered by a single-cylinder de Dion engine.

1897 Werner brothers Eugene and Michel, Russian emigres living in Paris, produce the first, practi-cal belt-driven motorcycles. They continue to improve the design, and in 1901 create what becomes the standard design of all motorcycles. (See 1901).

1897 Electric front-wheel drive is introduced by French firm Krieger. In this early electric version, a 770-pound (350-kilogram) battery pack is placed at the front of a carriage. It has a range of about 37 miles (60 kilometers) and can go as fast as 15 mph (24 km/h).

1897 First car insurance policy is purchased by Gilbert Loomis in Westfield, Massachusetts who takes out $1,000 liability coverage on his one-cylinder car. The premium is $7.50.

1897 First automobiles in Japan are steam autos imported from the United States.

1897 First Stanley Steamer takes to the road. Built by two enterprising American twins, Francis E. Stanley (1849—1918) and Freeling O. Stanley (1849—1940), this simple, carriage-looking car with a tiller for steering sells very well, not only because of its reliability but because the identical twins are expert showmen. Dressing alike down to the shape of their long beards, the brothers match their car against gasoline-powered cars at

1896 ■ San Francisco electric streetcar.

every opportunity. When their Steamer climbs Mt. Washington in New Hampshire, it becomes instantly recognized as a good vehicle.

1897 Application is made to the British Patent Office for an electric self-starter by E. J. Clubbe and Alfred W. Southey. It will not be until 1911, however, that American Charles F. Kettering (1876—1958) is able to perfect and sell such a system. It does away with the nuisance of hand-cranking by using the same power to start the engine that turns on its lights and ignites its gasoline.

1897 English novelist and popular historian H. G. Wells (1866—1946) publishes in serial form his story *War of the Worlds*. This story of Martian invaders exerts a powerful influence and stirs a deep awareness concerning outer space. His 1901 novel, *The First Men in the Moon,* uses an anti-gravity device to get his travellers into space. After Wells, turn-of-the-century fiction about spaceflight gets increasingly realistic and believable, based more on facts.

1897 German writer Kurd Lasswitz (1848—1910) publishes his novel *Auf zwei Planeten (On Two Planets)* that describes a trip to earth made by intelligent Mar-

tians. They use a gravity-nullifying device for space propulsion.

1897 Austrian skiing enthusiast Mathias Zdarsky (b. 1856) publishes his book, *Die Lilienfelder Skilauf-Technik,* and pioneers the use of a new crouching method of skiing as well as a new type of metal binding.

1897 American inventor Simon Lake (1866—1945) builds his second non-belligerent submarine, the *Argonaut*. This 36-foot-long submersible is powered on the surface by a gasoline engine and under water by batteries, and makes a 2,000-mile underwater tour of the Chesapeake Bay. This is probably the first extended oceanographic observation of the sea bottom. (See 1902)

1897 First motorized caravan or mobile-home is built in Paris, France by Jeantaud for Prince Oldenburg, the uncle of the Russian Tsar. It is a two-wheel trailer pulled by a 30-hp De Dion steam tractor. The entire rig is nearly 30 feet long and has a kitchen, bathroom, and is panelled in mahogany.

1897 February 27 First reported wedding in which the bridal party leaves in a car is written about in the French magazine *Autocar.* The Parisian corre-

1897 A.D.

First mobile-home built

spondent says, "It was my privilege on Saturday to see the first instance of an autocar ever being used at a wedding."

1897 June First ship to be powered by a Parsons turbine engine, the British *Turbinia,* puts on a spectacular performance as it dashes through lines of assembled warships at a speed of 34.5 knots. Steam turbines for ships prove to be lighter than other engines, and provide more power, higher speeds, and take up less space.

**1897
June 12**

*Two die in
first dirigible
accident*

1897 June 12 German experimenter Wolfert and his mechanic, Robert Knave, are killed in the first flight of Wolfert's new airship, the *Deutschland,* powered by a 6 hp Daimler engine. After leaving Tempelhof, Berlin, flames from the engine ignite gas from the envelope, and the airship explodes and crashes in flames. They are the first to be killed in a dirigible accident.

1897 July 11 Salomon August Andrée (1854—1897), Swedish explorer, sets off with two companions in a balloon from Danes Island, Spitzbergen, Norway in an attempt to fly over the North Pole. They are never seen alive again, but their remains and equipment are found in 1930 preserved underneath the ice. Andree's log tells of the balloon being forced down by the weight of freezing mist and of the men's 200–mile trek before they died of exhaustion and exposure. Andree's preserved and undeveloped photographs were also retrieved from the ice and developed.

1897 October 12—14 Clément Ader (1841—1925) tests his steam-powered, twin-propeller *Avion III* twice on a circular track near Versailles, France. Its design retains the huge, canopied, bat-wings. Neither attempt results in the craft being able to get off the ground, although Ader will later claim he was able to fly.

1897 November 3 First all-metal rigid airship is tested. Built by German designer David Schwarz, its envelope is made of wafer-thin aluminum, an important innovation, and it is powered by a 12–hp Daimler engine driving three propellers. After rising over Berlin, Germany, it crashes soon afterwards.

1898 The Aéro-Club de France is founded in Paris.

1898 Longest railway tunnel in Europe, the Simplon Tunnel passing under Mt. Leone, is begun. Completed in 1906, it is a one-track tunnel 12¼ miles long

1897 ■ First "horseless carriage" built by Olds Motor Vehicle Co.

that facilitates a trip from France, via Switzerland, to Italy. Between 1912 and 1921 it is enlarged to make twin tunnels.

1898 New York Department of Public Works is first organized.

1898 French automobile manufacturing company Renault is founded as Louis Renault (1877-1944) brings out his first automobile and forms Renault Frères with his brothers. Renault disposes of the old chain drive then in use and invents instead shaft drive (directly connecting the engine and the power axle), which revolutionizes the industry. Over the years, Renault cars prove reliable, sturdy, and economical.

1898 First U.S. independent car dealership is opened by William E. Metzger in Detroit, Michigan.

1898 In the United States, the great amounts of dust raised by automobiles becomes first a nuisance and then an indicator of just how much damage automobile tires can do to even a macadam road. The Office of Public Roads Inquiries begins research into better surfaces.

1898 Construction of subway system for Paris, France is begun. Called the Metro (Chemin de Fer Metropolitan), it opens its first—6.25 miles (10 kilometers) long—in 1900. It uses newer cut-and-cover methods that speed its completion.

1898 Vermont Department of Highways is first organized.

1898 Aluminum alloy is introduced into automobile construction by American metallurgical engineer and car-builder Elwood Haynes (1857—1925). Haynes is the first to use aluminum in some parts of his engine.

1898 First female race car driver is a Frenchwoman named Madame Laumaille. She drives a de Dion three-wheeler in the 1898 Marseilles-Nice two-day event in France. She is the fastest in her class the first day and finishes fourth overall, ahead of her sixth-place husband.

1898 Wilhelm Maybach (1846—1929) successfully develops the honeycomb radiator. This new design is composed of a honeycomb of thin, metal fins that radiate heat rapidly and thus cools the hot water it receives from the engine.

1898 First diesel engine is demonstrated by Rudolf Diesel (1858—1913). Although it is some time before the diesel is perfected as a locomotive engine, it will prove more suitable for pulling trains than as an engine for cars or planes. While they are cheaper and safer than gasoline engines, they also are large, very heavy mechanisms.

1898 As horse-drawn traffic comes to a standstill during a New York City blizzard, electric cabs continue to operate.

1898 U.S. battleship *Oregon*, needed in the Gulf of Mexico by the United States during the Spanish-American War, takes 67 days (March 19 to May 24) to sail from San Francisco, California to Key West, Florida. This trip is considered by many to be the most important factor in making Americans feel that a canal across the Isthmus of Panama is necessary.

1898 First truly practical submarine and the first underwater vessel accepted by the U.S. Navy, the *Holland,* is built by American John P. Holland (1840—1914). After obtaining a Navy contract, Holland ignores all its specifications (which he knows will produce a failed ship), and builds the *Holland* to his own designs. His 50-foot-long, five-man submarine is powered by a 45-hp gasoline engine and achieves the first unqualified success in submarine history. It runs easily on the surface, can dive and surface quickly, and fires torpedoes while submerged. The United States orders six, and orders come from England, Japan, and Russia as well.

1898 First electric arc lamp installed in a U.S. lighthouse is placed in the south tower of the Navesink (New Jersey) lighthouse. It is also the first lighthouse to have its own plant for generating electricity.

1898 July 4 French liner *La Bourgogne* collides with steel sailing vessel *Cromartyshire* in dense fog off Nova Scotia. While the latter is virtually undamaged, *La Bourgogne* suffers a rupture in its bow and sinks in 40 minutes, drowning 560 people. Among the 165 who save themselves on lifeboats are the crew of *La Bourgogne.*

1898 July 24 Amelia Earhart (1898—1937), first woman to fly alone across the Atlantic Ocean and one of the world's most famous aviators, is born in Atchison, Kansas. Following her solo Atlantic flight (May 20—21, 1932), she made a similar flight alone from Hawaii to California in 1935. On June 1, 1937, she and copilot Fred Noonan (d. 1937) left Miami in a twin-emgine Lockheed *Electra* in an attempt to fly around the world at the equator. After completing more than two-thirds of the journey, her plane vanished in the South Pacific on July 2, 1937 while heading for Howland Island. In 1992, the International Group for Historic Aircraft Recovery (TIGHAR) announced it had found metal aircraft pieces, an aluminum map box, and a grave on a 3½-mile-long, jungle-covered atoll called Nikumaroro in the island nation of Kiribati, just below Howland Island. The group theorizes that Earhart's plane landed at low tide and that she and Noonan may have survived using the plane's survival gear until 1938 when a severe drought struck.

1898 July 24

Amelia Earhart born

1898 September Alberto Santos-Dumont (1873—1932), a wealthy Brazilian living in Paris, makes the first of several trial flights in his small, one-man, gas-powered airship, from Neuilly, near Paris, France. He will build 14 of these small airships and will make Europe more air-minded by his flights over Parisian roof tops and around the Eiffel Tower. (See also 1901, 1906)

1898 October First self-propelled fire engine is built by Cambier et Cie of Lille, France. This gas-powered vehicle is demonstrated at the French Heavy Autocar Trials held in Versailles, France.

1898 October 10 First American automobile show is held in Boston, Massachusetts. Called the Motor Carriage Exposition of the Massachusetts Charitable Mechanics' Association, it has four exhibitors and holds a motor vehicle race and parade. (See February 1900).

1899 Flag signals are first used by automobile race marshalls. A red flag means stop and a yellow flag means caution.

1899 First official U.S. automobile fatality occurs in New York City when Henry H. Bliss dies after being struck "by a horseless carriage" while stepping off a trolley.

1899 A.D.

First auto salesroom opens

1899 First automobile salesroom is opened in New York City by Percy Owen who sells Winton cars.

1899 Word "petrol" is first used in England to describe the "petroleum spirit" or gasoline that gas-powered car engines now use. The firm of Capel, Carless, and Leonard had registered the word "petrol" as a trade-name in 1896. Terminology in England was quite confusing at first, since gasoline was originally called petroleum spirit and kerosene was petroleum oil. And since the gas or petrol engine was often called an "oil engine," many new car owners did not know what to buy for their engines.

1899 U.S. Post Office conducts mail collection experiments made by motor vehicle in Washington, D.C., Buffalo, New York, and Cleveland, Ohio. In Cleveland, a Winton truck makes 126 stops along 22 miles of streets in less than half the time it takes a horse-drawn wagon.

1899 A.D.

First woman receives driver's license

1899 First driver's license issued to an American woman is received by Mrs. John Phillips of Chicago, Illinois.

1899 By this year, speed gears have become recognized as an essential part of an efficient bicycle. As the means by which the drive ratio can be conveniently changed for varying conditions and for better performance, two and three speed gears are patented during the 1880s. The four-speed gear is patented in 1894. Early gear changing is accomplished by first turning the pedals backwards, causing a flexible metal strip to rotate two segmental pieces around the rear hub, which engages with the edge of the chain and lifts it clear of one rear-wheel sprocket and transfers it to another of a different diameter.

1899 First automobile to exceed one-mile-per-minute (60 mph) is the electric race car called *La Jamais Contente* (The Never Satisfied). This missile or bullet-shaped car weighs 2,200 pounds and is powered by large, expensive batteries. It is driven by dashing, red-bearded Belgian Camille B. Jenatzy (1868—1913) in Acheres, France. Electric cars will never hold another land speed record.

1899 First car with independent front suspension is the French Decauville 3½-hp Voiturelle. Prior to this, front wheels were joined by a rigid axle which sent the effects of a bump throughout the car. Now, with each wheel separately attached by a transverse leaf spring (a kind of layering of metal bands), the shock of a bump remains mostly in that wheel.

1899 First floating factory ship, the *Michail*, is built. The steam-propelled whaling ship is designed to process the entire whale on board after it is caught.

1899 French engineer François Hennebique (1842—1921) builds one of the earliest and most significant reinforced-concrete bridges. The Pont de Chatellerault over the River Vienne in France has three arch spans of 131 feet (40 meters), 164 feet (49 meters), and 131 feet (40 meters). Robert Maillart (1872—1940) is his pupil. (See 1930)

1899 Prototype for all modern car garages is built in England by W. W. Barrett who builds a structure specifically to keep his two cars in and connects it to his house with a convenient passageway. His two-car garage also has two pits below to service his cars. (See December 1901)

1899 March U.S. Congress creates an Isthmian Canal Commission to study plans for building an inter-ocean canal in Central America.

1899 March 17 First radio distress signal from a ship to shore is transmitted by the British lightship at East Goodwin when it sends word that the merchant vessel *Elbe* has run aground. The lightship sends word by radio of its own distress the following month (April 28), when it is rammed by the *R. F. Matthews*.

1899 May 26 Lawrence Hargrave (1850—1915) visits England from Australia, and presents his paper on box-kites to the Aeronautical Society in London.

He also demonstrates how they work and lends the kites to Percy S. Pilcher (1866—1899) for testing.

1899 June 3 First mobile church in the United States is consecrated on Conanicut Island, Rhode Island. This horse-drawn Episcopal chapel is 27 feet long and 18 feet wide and is built on a four-wheel, wooden chassis. Inside the chapel are pews and an altar.

1899 June 7 Automobile Club of America is founded in New York by nine prominent New Yorkers. It soon becomes the most powerful and most successfully organized local automobile club in the United States. Its elite membership makes it more of a national organization that soon becomes recognized by other national auto clubs.

1899 July First woman to make a submarine descent is Clara Barton (1821-1912), founder of the American Red Cross. She makes an underwater trip off Sag Harbor, Long Island, New York in John P. Holland's (1840-1914) vessel, the *Holland VI*.

1899 July 11 Italian automobile manufacturing company Fiat, is founded by Giovanni Agnelli (1866—1945). Its name stands for Fabbrica Italiana Auto-mobili Torino. From its first two-cylinder car steered by a tiller, this company has grown into an industrial giant. It produces mostly well-built, efficient smaller cars that sell very well.

1899 August Wilbur (1867—1912) and Orville (1871—1948) Wright build their first aircraft—a biplane kite—and test its warping ability (the ability to twist and change its curvature, which makes for better control). Without this invention, the Wrights would not have been able to fly successfully.

1899 August
Wright Bros.
build their
first aircraft

1899 September 30 Percy S. Pilcher (1866—1899) crashes in his glider, the *Hawk*, in Leicestershire, England. After being towed into the air by two horses, his rain-soaked glider snaps a tail-assembly rod, and Pilcher crashes from about 30 feet off the ground. He dies from his injuries on October 2 without regaining consciousness.

1899 October 14 *Literary Digest* comments on the new automobiles, saying, "The ordinary horseless carriage is at present a luxury for the wealthy; and although its price will probably fall in the future, it will never, of course, come into as common use as the bicycle."

1900 First U.S. president to ride in a car is William McKinley (1843—1901).

1900 An automobile is first used as a hearse in Buffalo, New York.

1900 First four-wheel-drive car in the United States is built by Charles Cotta of Illinois. It is steam-powered and its drive is achieved by a compensating chain gear.

1900 U.S. car production statistics for the year total 4,192. They break down to steam cars (1,681), electric cars (1,575), and gasoline cars (936). Of the 8,000 powered vehicles on U.S. roads, some 38% are powered by batteries.

1900 Puerto Rico Department of Public Works is first organized.

1900 One of the earliest and most successful modern American motorcycles, the Indian, is made in Springfield, Massachusetts by the Hendee Manufacturing Co. It goes on to be a superior racing machine.

1900 National Good Roads Association (NGRA) is formed during the Chicago Good Roads Convention. It becomes the most active and aggressive of all the U.S. organizations, and mounts a high-powered publicity campaign to rally national support for better roads.

c. 1900 Navies of the world are rapidly becoming mechanized and modernized, adopting turbine engines, propellers, heavy guns, torpedoes, mines, and armor plating.

1900 Iceboating has become popular enough in the United States for the Hudson River Ice Yacht Club to have over 50 iceboats, six of which are very large with over 600 square feet of sail.

1900 First motorized ambulance service for civilians goes into service in Alençon, France.

c. 1900 "Aqua-planing," an early type of water skiing, is invented by Californian J. L. LeRoy, who attaches a rope to a heavy fish box cover and tows a young man from his motor boat. LeRoy offers aquaplaning as a regular attraction at the Coronado Hotel where he works. (See 1914)

c. 1900 A.D.

Early form of water skiing invented

1900 January 2 First "autostage" appears on Fifth Avenue in New York. This electric bus seats eight people inside, four outside, and costs five cents to ride.

1900 February First large, major American automobile show is held in Madison Square Garden, New York. Gas, electric, and steam vehicles fill the Garden's center, around which a track is built for the cars to perform and be test driven. The silent steam cars and the elegant electrics dominate the show, making the gasoline cars seem noisy, smelly, and jerky-moving.

1900 February

First major U.S. auto show held

1900 March First commercial ship to be equipped with wireless telegraphy for the purpose of sending and receiving paid messages is German liner *Kaiser Wilhelm der Grosse*.

1900 May First motorized hearse is an electric-powered vehicle used during a funeral in Buffalo,

New York. Fourteen other electric cars make up the powered funeral procession. (See 1905)

1900 June
Driving lessons offered

1900 June Driving lessons in England are offered for a fee by the Motor Carriage Supply Company of London. It is a sideline to the company's main business concern which is car repair.

1900 June 30 Fire engulfs four German ships all in port at Hoboken Docks, New Jersey. After a blaze breaks out on the cargo ship *Main,* fire spreads from ship to ship and the docks catch as well. As the burning ships are towed into the river, adjoining docks are dynamited to prevent the flames from spreading further. Many crews on the lower decks of the burning ships are trapped, and altogether, three ships are totally burned and 326 people are killed.

1900 July 2 First trial of the first Zeppelin airship, the *LZ-1* (*Luftschiff Zeppelin 1*), takes place over Lake Constance, Germany. The first of the rigid, monster airships, it is 420 feet long and contains 16 separate gas-bags with a total capacity of 338,410 cubic feet. It is tentatively successful, and attains a speed of 8½ mph (c. 14 km/h). It is housed in a floating hangar, the first in history.

1900 July 10
Paris Métro opens

1900 July 10 First section of the Paris Underground, the Métro (Chemin de Fer Métropolitan), opens from Port Vincennes to Porte Maillot.

1900 October Wilbur (1867—1912) and Orville (1871—1948) Wright begin testing their *No. 1* glider at Kitty Hawk, North Carolina. It has wing-warping for better control and is flown both as a kite and with a pilot who lies prone. Wing warping was developed by the Wrights and controls an aircraft's banking and rolling movements by means of twisting the wings with wires to change their angle. By World War I, it was replaced by ailerons which are hinged surfaces on the outboard trailing edges of an airplane's wings which can be raised or lowered to help raise or slow it down.

1901 Samuel Franklin Cody (1861—1913), an American who became a British citizen, patents his man-lifting kite system. This consists of a train of Hargrave box-kites supporting a cable, up which runs another kite with a seat hanging beneath for a passenger.

1901 Mechanical coal stokers for locomotives are introduced in the United States.

1901 First American car to be manufactured in quantity is the "curved dash" Oldsmobile, designed by Ransom E. Olds (1864—1950). In production from 1901 to 1907, this popular "merry Oldsmobile" of the song has a single-cylinder, 7-hp gas engine that gives a top speed of 18 mph (30 km/h). It has a two-speed gearbox with reverse, and sells for about $650. Steered by a hand tiller, it is well suited to heavy going over dirt roads, is easy to drive, and fairly reliable. In 1905, 35 cars a day will be produced. This marks the real beginning of the auto industry.

1901 First automobile traffic laws in the United States are enacted by the State of Connecticut which passes speed limit and registration laws. New York State follows and begins to license cars.

1901 First automobile depicted on a U.S. postage stamp is a Baker Brougham, an electric taxi.

1901 Italian cavalry instructor Federico Caprilli (1868—1907), after a thorough study of the psychology and mechanics of locomotion of the horse, publishes his book *Principi di Equitazione di Campagna*. His ideas completely revolutionize the way of sitting on a horse and establish the forward seat as the best method. This position, in which the rider's weight is centered forward in the saddle over the horse's withers (between his front shoulder bones), is now one of the most frequently used.

1901 First car to use the "Mercedes" name also combines the "modern" features of a pressed-steel chassis frame, honeycomb radiator, and a four-speed gearbox. This dashing car has 35 hp which gives a top speed of 45 mph (72 km/h). It is built by the Daimler company, and not the Benz concern, which have not yet merged. The Mercedes name is that of the oldest daughter of Austrian consul Emil Jellinek, who is one of Daimler's main agents commissioned to sell cars for him. Jellinek buys the new 35-hp cars "on trust" from Daimler and sells them as "Mercedes." The popular car's name has remained the same ever since. (See July 28, 1926)

1901 Werner brothers integrate the motorcycle engine and its frame. In their design, the single-cylinder, 262-cc engine vertically takes the place of the normal bottom bracket where the pedals usually are located. Special lugs hold the engine in place and it becomes an integral part of the entire machine. This improves tremendously its handling and controllability.

The low, centered engine keeps the center of gravity low and the weight evenly distributed. This design is rapidly accepted, and modern motorcycles still have their engines where the Werners put them.

1901 The steering wheel rather than the old-fashioned tiller becomes the accepted and preferred method of driving a car.

1901 Oil is discovered near Beaumont, Texas. These gushers cause the price of crude petroleum to drop below five cents a barrel. Oil discoveries in Texas usher in the era of cheap gasoline, giving the internal combustion engine the economic edge over steam and electric cars.

1901 The beginnings of the American gas station as a place for dispensing fuel and repairing cars takes shape as one is set up in New York City.

1901 First motorized inflatable boat is built by French engineer Clement Ader (1841—1926). Ader's boat has a submerged propeller and works well but is unwieldy and impractical.

1901 First wireless telegraphy exchange between two ships takes place between British ship *Lake Champlain* and Cunard liner *Lucania*.

1901 First ship to exceed 20,000 gross tons is the White Star Line's *Celtic*. Built for comfort rather than speed, this ship represents a wholly new idea in transatlantic travel by combining spacious comfort with economy of operation. Even its third class passengers are fairly comfortable.

1901 February First race to bear the title Grand Prix is run in Pau, France. It is won by Maurice Farman (1877-1964) whose Panhard averages 46.1 mph.

1901 May First driving school in England, the Liver Motor Car Depot and School of Automobilism, opens in Birkenhead. Established by William Lea, it later becomes the Lea School of Motoring.

1901 May First multilevel parking garage opens just off Piccadilly Circus, London, England. Operated by the City & Suburban Electric Carriage Company, it has seven floors and is equipped with an electric elevator to raise cars to the upper levels.

1901 June First gas-driven airplane flies tentatively. American Samuel P. Langley's (1834—1906) one fourth-scale model *Aerodrome* flies with some success but cannot sustain itself horizontally.

1901 July 27 Wilbur (1867—1912) and Orville (1871—1948) Wright make their first of a series of test glides at Kill Devil Hills near Kitty Hawk, North Carolina which will continue through the first half of August. Their redesigned biplane glider *No.* 2 has a larger wing area and wing control worked by a pilot's hip-cradle device. These glides lead to further design changes which improve performance.

1901 August 14 One of the more controversial figures in aviation history, German-born American Gustave Whitehead (1874—1927), is said to have flown a powered airplane for over one mile in Bridgeport, Connecticut. He also supposedly makes a seven-mile (11 kilometers) flight the next year. Despite the lack of any evidence that he did fly first, his claims and supporters still persist.

1901 September First long-distance, American endurance auto race is organized by the Automobile Club of America. It is planned to run the 500 miles from New York City to Buffalo. Of 80 cars that start, 42 reach Rochester, where the race is abandoned when news of President William McKinley's (1843—1901) assassination is received.

1901 October First full-size gas-powered airplane to be built is Wilhelm Kress's seaplane. Kress (1836—1913) is a Russian of German origin who became an Austrian citizen. His tandem-wing flying-boat, driven by a 30-hp Daimler engine, capsizes while being ferried on the Tullnerbach Reservoir, in Austria. Kress abandons his experiments.

1901 October 19 Alberto Santos-Dumont (1873—1932) flies his powered airship, the dirigible *No.* 6, from St. Cloud around the Eiffel Tower and back again in 29½ minutes. His cigar-shaped airship is 110 feet long and has a 12-hp motor that gives a speed of 15 mph. This flight wins the Deutsche prize of 100,000 francs.

1901 October 29 The Aero Club of Great Britain, later to become the Royal Aero Club, is founded.

1901 July 27
Wrights make first series of test glides

1901 November 3 World's longest railroad, the Trans-Siberian Railway, opens to Vladivostock, Russia and uses a ferry to cross Lake Baikal. The Circum-Baikal line is completed on September 25, 1904, the distance from Moscow to Vladivostock being 5,801 miles (9,336 kilometers).

1901 November 5–6 Samuel F. Cody (1861—1913), U.S.-born British citizen, is pulled across the English Channel from Calais, France to Dover, England in a canoe by one of his kites. Cody's 14-foot canvas, folding-type canoe has two masts. After a brisk start, it drifts overnight when the wind falls. With the wind blowing again, Cody hoists his kite and completes the trip in 13 hours.

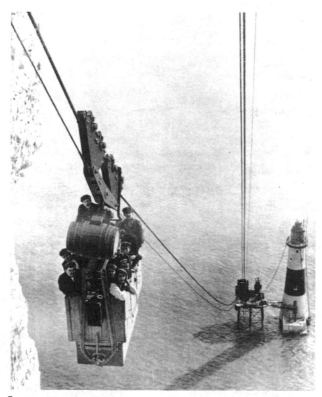

1900 ■ Funicular railway takes workers to and from Beachy Head Lighthouse in the English Channel.

1901 December

Garages built

1901 December Popularity of garages attached to houses becomes apparent as British magazine *The Autocar* reports that, "In Hampstead a number of new houses have recently been erected, the appointments of which include a motor stable."

1902 Philadelphia Electric Company purchases a Mark III electric runabout from the Pennsylvania Electric Company, the first of 56 electric cars and trucks it will buy over the next 15 years.

1902 Running boards—a long step mounted on a car's body under the doors to help passengers get in and out—are first used on a Silent Northern car built by Jonathan D. Maxwell and Charles B. King of Detroit, Michigan. They will become a standard feature on most cars but will disappear in the 1940s.

1902 French automotive pioneer Louis Renault (1877—1944) invents the drum brake. Designed to operate by pressing two semi-circular brake shoes against a circular brake drum, they are soon adopted by nearly all vehicles.

1902 First V-twin, two stroke motorcycle engine is made by the French firm Bichrone. It provides greater power and smoother running.

1902 First "in-line" or straight-eight cylinder engine is the 40-hp model built by CGV (Charron, Girardot and Voight) of Paris. Designed as a racing car, it does not become popular, partly because of its long, unwieldy design necessitated by its coupling of two four-cylinders "in-line."

1902 Cadillac Automobile Company is organized when Henry M. Leland's (1843—1932) company, Leland & Faulconer Manufacturing Co., merges with the Detroit Automobile Company. Known as the "master of precision," Leland will make the Cadillac car synonymous with luxury appointments and precision-made components.

1902 One of the earliest U.S. speeding violations is recorded as a man is arrested and fined $10 for driving in excess of 10 mph in Minneapolis, Minnesota.

1902 Chrome-nickel and tungsten steels are introduced into the manufacture of automobile parts. The use of these alloy steels to make crankshafts, gears, and springs is preferred because of their special properties, like toughness or resistance to wear or corrosion. This is different from the later chrome-plating.

1902 First gas-fueled, four-wheel-drive vehicle is the huge 8.7 litre Dutch Spyker which is built as a racing car. It is powered by the first six-cylinder automotive engine and is also the first car to have four-wheel braking. The Spyker brothers come from Trompenburg near Amsterdam and their car is the most advanced vehicle of its time. It does not go into production, however.

1902 United States establishes the Board for Rivers and Harbors which will review all projects from an engineering and economic viewpoint. This is the beginning of a national policy and structure for its waterways and ocean shipping.

1902 German named Grossman walks on the Danube River wearing water-shoes that are basically aluminum cylinders, 13 feet (4 meters) long. He is able to propel himself "by a treading movement which causes four oar-shaped wings to revolve."

1902 First Trade Exhibition to include a section for motorboats is the 1902 Paris Automobile Salon which has a Marine Motor Section.

1902 First manual published on motorboats is W. J. Woodman's *Launch Motors Today*, published in England.

1902 First British motorboating club, the Marine Motoring Association, is founded.

1902 First working periscope to be fitted on a submarine is constructed by American inventor Simon Lake, who perfects what he calls an "omniscope." It is the forerunner of both the fixed and rotating periscope and provides the heretofore "blind" submarine with an ability to see in all directions.

1902 First wind tunnel in Canada is built in New Brunswick by Wallace R. Turnbull. This experimental device will become an extremely important tool for the emerging science of aeronautics. It enables an engineer to study in the laboratory the effects of air resistance on a particular aeronautical design by passing air over a model.

1902 First "trunnion-bascule" bridge in the United States, the Cortland Street Drawbridge, opens to traffic. This movable bridge over the Chicago River in Chicago, Illinois opens for water traffic by raising the roadway to a nearly vertical position. It is raised or lowered by the operation of a rack and pinion system powered by an electric motor. "Bascule" is the French word for "seesaw," and a trunnion is the axle around which something pivots. This bridge becomes the model for such movable structures.

1902 January The Manly-Balzer radial engine for Samuel P. Langley's full-size *Aerodrome* is first tested in the United States. Built on commission for Langley by Stephen M. Balzer of New York, the engine is improved by Langley's assistant Charles Manly and provides a very high power/weight ratio.

1902 February 4 Charles Augustus Lindbergh (1902—1974), one of the most famous aviators in history, is born in Detroit, Michigan. He made the first nonstop solo flight across the Atlantic Ocean, May 20—21, 1927, and collected a $25,000 prize. His *Spirit of St. Louis* monoplane covered 3,600 miles from New York to Paris in 33 hours, 29 minutes. His flight not only catapulted him to permanent fame, but also molded the public's awareness of the airplane as a serious means of transportation.

1902 February 4 Charles Lindbergh born

1902 March 4 American Automobile Association (AAA) is founded in Chicago, Illinois. Formed by nine auto clubs meeting in that city, the organization will offer members emergency road service and help in planning trips. It is still in existence.

1902 March 4 AAA founded

1902 May 12 Augusto Severo, Brazilian, and his mechanic named Sachet are killed on the first flight of Severo's airship *Pax*. After taking off from Vaugirard in Paris, the airship catches fire, and explodes. It has two propellers, one at each end.

1902 June Ferdinand Ferber (1862—1909), captain in the French artillery, tests in Beuil, France what is Europe's first Wright-type glider. Ferber abandons his Lilienthal-type hang-glider and adopts the Wright style after receiving from Octave Chanute descriptions and illustrations of the first two Wright gliders. Ferber will have a strong influence on European aviation.

1902 July 9 First motorboat to cross the Atlantic, the *Abiel Abbot Low*, leaves New York for Falmouth, England. The 38-foot (11.6-meter) boat, which also has a sail, is operated by William C. Chapman and his 16-year-old son, Edward. It arrives in England on August 14 with both Chapmans feeling the effects of fatigue and nauseating kerosene fumes.

1902 July 9 First motorboat crosses Atlantic

1902 August 13 German engineer Felix Wankel (b. 1902) is born in Lahr, Germany. In 1954, Wankel completed his first design of a rotary-piston engine. Called the "Wankel," this new automobile engine has a pair of three-cornered rotors instead of pistons and cylinders. These rotate inside a chamber, drawing in fuel, compressing it until ignited, and then expelling the burned gases, in one continuous movement. Although his engines are smooth-running and very light, they are not yet economical or fully reliable to warrant a changeover from conventional engines.

1902 September 20

Key Wright glides begin

1902 September 20 The Wrights make the first of nearly 1,000 glides (through the end of October) on their modified *No. 3* glider in Kill Devil Hills, North Carolina. It is this glider, made of spruce wood and cloth, that incorporates for the first time the flight controls of the modern airplane, that is, control in pitch (up and down), in roll (about its horizontal axis) and in yaw (about its vertical axis). After the experience gained and changes made following these controlled glides—the longest of which went 622½ feet—the Wrights have a responsive machine that is ready to be powered.

1902 September 22 Stanley Spencer (d. 1906) becomes the first Englishman to fly in a powered airship over England. His 75-foot-long dirigible is powered by a 3½-hp water-cooled engine. It takes off from the Crystal Palace, near London, and makes a flight of some 30 miles (c. 48 kilometers).

1902 October 13 Ottokar von Bradsky and his mechanic named Morin are killed on the first flight of von Bradsky's sausage-shaped airship from Vaugirard, France when the gondola (suspended car attached to the underside) breaks away in mid-air and crashes in Stains, outside Paris.

1903 A.D.

Buick Co. formed

1903 Buick Motor Car Company is organized by David D. Buick (1854–1929) in Detroit, Michigan with $75,000 capital. Next year its first car called the Flint, with a twin-cylinder, 22-hp engine, comes out in July.

1903 Automobile innovations this year are all steel car bodies and pressed steel frames, shock absorbers, and glass windshields.

1903 American aviation pioneer Glenn Curtiss (1878–1930) becomes interested in motorcycles and begins building his own. Beginning with single-cylinder engines and progressing to V-twins, he eventu-

ally builds the first motorcycle to have eight cylinders. His V8 is timed at 136.36 mph (219.45 km/h) on Ormond Beach, Florida. No single engine for a motorcycle has ever had more cylinders.

1903 Sidecars are introduced as an ideal means for transforming a motorcycle into a passenger-carrying vehicle. They are continuously improved, and by the outbreak of war in 1914, are adapted for various military purposes, primarily as a machine-gun carrier.

1903 First Australian motoring organization, the Australian Automobile Club, is formed in Sydney. The national Australian Automobile Association comes into being in 1924.

1903 The Motor Car Act in Great Britain raises the speed limit to 20 mph (32 km/h). This Act also requires that driver's licenses and car registration numbers be obtained. Some resistance to being "numbered like convicts and labelled like hackney carriages" is voiced. The 20-mph limit stays in force until 1930.

1903 First gearless traction elevators are installed by the Otis Company in the 182-foot Beaver Building in New York. This electrically-powered system is the forerunner of what we have today. Its operating principle is similar to the way a locomotive pulls a train because of the traction between the steel wheels and the rails. Here, the elevator cables are wrapped around the drive sheave in special grooves. When the motor turns the sheave, it presses the cables down on the grooves which hoist with almost no slippage.

1903 Ford Motor Company of the United States moves into the Japanese market.

1903 First automobile used as a police car in the United States is a Stanley Steamer in Boston, Massachusetts. It has a top speed of 10 mph.

1903 Harley-Davidson Company of Milwaukee, Wisconsin produces its first motorcycle. William S. Harley and Arthur Davidson are joined within a year by Davidson's brothers, William and Walter. Their first motorcycle is a single-cylinder machine with 2 hp. The firm will become internationally famous after World War I, and remains in business today.

1903 Pennsylvania Department of Highways is first organized.

1903 A groundbreaking scientific work on space flight is written. Konstantin E. Tsiolkovsky's (1859—1935) article, "A Rocket into Cosmic Space" is published by the Russian journal *Nauchnoye Obozreniye (Scientific Review)*. This contains not only the theoretical solutions and basic principles of flight in space, but designs of several rockets powered by liquid oxygen and liquid hydrogen—fuels that are used even today. Most of these discoveries are ignored by his contemporaries.

1903 First coastal lighthouse in Alaska, the Scotch Cap Lighthouse, begins operations. It is located near the west end of Unimak Island on the Pacific side of Unimak Pass, the main passage through the Aleutian Islands into the Bering Sea.

1903 January Parsons non-skid chains are introduced for better automobile traction. They fit over tires much as snow chains do today.

1903 February 1 International distress call at sea is decided by Marconi Wireless Telegraph Company to be the Morse Code for "CQD" which stands for "Come Quick Danger." At a 1906 international conference, Germany suggests that "SOE" should be adopted, since it is quicker to send. Finally, the "E" is replaced by an "S," since the former is only a single dot in Morse Code, and might be easily missed. "SOS" (··· - - ···) is ratified internationally in 1908 as the international call for help.

1903 April 2 Octave Chanute (1832—1910) lectures at the Aéro-Club de France in Paris, and describes in detail, with sketches and photographs, the sophisticated No. 3 Wright glider of 1902. This speech will, in the long run, give the main impetus to the rebirth of European aviation, but at the time it has little real effect. Chanute's lecture gives the Europeans many of the necessary essentials that the Wrights had learned about flight, but few realize it.

1903 May 3 First steam railroad in England to be converted to electric is the Mersey railway.

1903 June 16 American automobile manufacturer Ford Motor Company is organized in Detroit, Michigan by Henry Ford (1863—1947). The entire property of the newly opened factory consists of $28,000 capital put up by 12 shareholders and a number of patents. Ford builds the Model T in 1908, a car that many regard as the first really practical American automobile, and changes the course of the history of the American car. He also establishes the moving assembly line to produce cars in volume, and makes them affordable to greater numbers of people. With its lines of Ford, Lincoln, and Mercury, it has today developed into a large, multinational enterprise.

1903 July 26 First coast-to-coast crossing of the United States by car is made by a Winton Touring Car. Begun on May 23, the trip takes 65 days, 20 of which are spent making repairs due mainly to bad road conditions.

1903 August 10 Subway disaster aboard Paris Métro (Chemin de Fer Metropolitan) kills 84 people and reinforces passengers' anxiety about traveling underground. An intense electrical fire at the Couronnes Street Station devours the cars made of resinous varnished wood, creating a smoky inferno that consumes all the oxygen below ground and suffocates its victims.

1903 August 18 Karl Jatho (1873—1933), a German civil servant, tests what can be described as a powered kite. His "running jump" and a 9-hp gas engine, propel him 18 meters. This test near Hanover, coupled with another, longer one (60 meters) in November, gives him claim to the title of first German to leave the ground in a powered aircraft.

1903 September 7 First U.S. motorcycle association, the Federation of American Motorcyclists, is formed in Manhattan Beach, New York. About 200 delegates attend this first meeting. Today, motorcyclists gather in less formal groupings.

1903 October First boat to be powered by a diesel engine, French canal barge *Petit-Pierre*, is driven by Rudolf Diesel (1858—1913) along the Rhine-Marne Canal. The engine for this large barge produces 25 hp at 360 rpm.

1903 October 7 Samuel P. Langley's (1834—1906) full-size *Aerodrome A*, piloted by Charles M. Manly (1876—1927), crashes into the Potomac River on its first attempt to fly. After being catapulted from a houseboat, the tandem-wing monoplane becomes tangled with the catapult gear. Manly is unhurt. Langley's control sys-

1903
August 10

Subway accident kills 84

1903
August 18

Powered kite tested

1903
October

First diesel-powered boat sails

c. 1900 ■ U.S. Life Saving crew at Salisbury Beach.

tem is primitive and the craft has probable structural weaknesses that make its ability to fly suspect.

1903 November 12　First fully practical airship, the *Lebaudy*, makes a successful flight from Moison to Paris, France. Commissioned by brothers Paul (1858—1937) and Pierre Lebaudy (1880—c. 1940), who are French sugar refiners, and designed by Henry Juillot and Don Simoni, the semi-rigid, 190-foot-long airship makes a flight of 38½ miles. It is powered by a 35-hp Daimler engine and achieves a speed of over 25 mph.

1903 December 8　Samuel P. Langley (1834—1906) makes a second attempt to fly his *Aerodrome A*, with Charles M. Manly (1876—1927) as pilot. Choosing a different spot on the Potomac River but using the same houseboat catapult launch methods, Langley sees his craft fall again into the water directly after launch. Manly is rescued but Langley's reputation is not, and the press makes great fun of his failures.

1903 December 14　Wilbur Wright (1867—1912) makes the first and unsuccessful attempt at powered flight at Kill Devil Hills, North Carolina. The aircraft stalls after 3½ seconds in the air and crash lands 105 feet away. Five men from the Kill Devil Hills Life Saving Station are present.

1903 December 17　First sustained, controlled, powered flight is made by Orville Wright (1871—1948) in the *Flyer* at Kill Devil Hills near Kitty Hawk, North Carolina. He and Wilbur (1867—1912) make four flights this day, all from level ground and without any take-off assistance. The historic first flight lasts 12 seconds and covers 120 feet. The second (Wilbur) covers about 175 feet; the third (Orville) goes some 200 feet; and the fourth (Wilbur) and longest, lasts 59 seconds and covers 852 feet (c. 260 meters).

1904　First large dirigible (powered airship) in America is built. Called the *California Arrow*, it is 52 feet long and 17 feet in diameter. Built by Thomas Baldwin (1854—1923) and powered by a Curtiss engine, it makes a promising first flight during August of 1904.

1904　First woman to fly in an airship is Madame Paul Lebaudy. She is a passenger in a Paul and Pierre Lebaudy-built airship called *Jaune* which flies in Moisson, France. This airship also becomes the first to accommodate photographers and to make a night flight.

1904 First British six-cylinder car is the 30-hp Napier which has its cylinders cast in pairs rather than cast in a single block of aluminum. Napier cars become a very high calibre car synonymous with perfection. They disappear during the lean years of the late 1920s.

1904 First national inventory of roads is conducted by the U.S. Office of Public Road Inquiries (OPRI). The study shows that there are 2,151,570 miles of rural public roads in the United States, plus 1,598 miles of stone-surfaced toll roads. Of the over two million miles of public roads, only 153,662 miles have any kind of surfacing.

1904 All-steel railroad passenger cars are placed in steam service in the United States. (See August 13, 1906)

1904 The four-speed gearbox for motorcycles becomes more common, with such British companies as Roc and Zenith leading the trend.

1904 First exhibition in America of a Diesel engine is made at the St. Louis Exposition.

1904 Iowa State Highway Commission is first organized.

1904 One-third of all the powered vehicles on the streets of Boston, New York, and Chicago are electric. Horses still predominate, however.

1904 First person to exceed 100 mph in an automobile is Frenchman Louis E. Rigolly whose large Gobron-Brille is timed at 103.56 mph in Ostend, Belgium.

1904 First U.S. automobile speed law is passed in New York State. A speed limit of 10 mph is set for closely built-up districts; 15 mph in villages; and 20 mph in open country.

1904 Ohio Department of Highways is first organized.

1904 The left-hand rule of the road for horse-drawn vehicles is carried over into the British Motor Car Order of 1904 which orders that automobiles must keep to the left of oncoming traffic and pass traffic going in the same direction on the right. For this reason, English-made cars have the steering wheel on the right side of the car, so the driver can better judge the clearance of on-coming vehicles to his right. (See 1756)

1904 First true automatic transmission is introduced by Sturtevant of Boston, Massachusetts. His company is short-lived.

1904 First motor vehicle known to have been made in Japan is a steam car built by Yamaha Torao in Okayama.

1904 Governor-type speedometer for automobiles is invented by Englishman L. E. Cowley. This device is used primarily to regulate a vehicle's speed. (See 1911)

1904 A.D.

Speedometers invented

1904 First successful caterpillar-type tractor (endless chain) is patented by American Benjamin Holt (1849—1920). In 1906, the Holt Tractor Company begins producing them commercially.

1904 First patent for a radar-like system is granted to German engineer Christian Hulsmeyer (1881—1957). Although his system works in a demonstration, it is ineffective beyond one mile. The principles involved have been known theoretically due to Michael Faraday (1791—1867) and James Clerk Maxwell's (1831—1879) work. In 1886, Heinrich R. Hertz (1857-1894) demonstrated not only the existence of radio waves but the fact that they could be reflected from solid objects. This is the principle of radar. (See 1935)

1904 A.D.

First radar-like system patented

1904 First American and first British motor lifeboats are launched this year. The British *J. McConnell Hussy* has a 9-hp gas motor, and the American *Dreadnought* has a 27-hp engine.

1904 First U.S. lightship to be permanently equipped for radio communications is the *Nantucket Lightship,* about 50 miles southeast of Nantucket Island in the Atlantic Ocean.

1904 Scooter-boards become a popular youngster's toy in the United States. These forerunners of the modern skateboard are put together by nailing over-the-shoe roller skates onto a 2 x 4 board and attaching this to a vertical crate or box, and adding handle bar slats. (See 1958)

1904 National Association of Engine & Boat Manufacturers is founded in the United States. It now has over 350 companies as members.

1904 February 8 Russo-Japanese War (1904—1905) begins as Japan launches a surprise attack on Russian forces at Port Arthur, China. Japan eventually destroys the Russian fleet, becoming the first modern Asian power to defeat a European nation. Both navies use torpedoes and mines to devastating effect.

1904 April Ernest Archdeacon (1863—1957), a wealthy Paris lawyer and one of the founders of the Aéro-Club de France, has a Wright-type glider built, which Ferdinand Ferber (1862—1909) and Gabriel Voisin (1880—1973) fly briefly for him.

1904 April 1 Self-taught British engineer Frederick Henry Royce (1863—1933) puts his first twin-cylinder experimental car on the road. Soon after, a meeting is arranged between him and aristocratic motoring enthusiast Charles Stewart Rolls (1877—1910). The perfectionist Rolls is so impressed by Royce's hand-tooled car, that he forms Rolls-Royce Ltd., to build cars of the highest standards for quality, reliability, refinement, and silence. (See May 1904)

1904 May Robert Esnault-Pelterie (1881—1957), French engineer and inventor, builds and tests his own version of the Wright glider, but without success. He does not see the value of wing-warping for control. (See October 1904).

1904 May Wilbur (1867—1912) and Orville (1871—1948) Wright begin flying their redesigned, powered *Flyer II* at the Huffman Prairie, near Dayton, Ohio. Their new version also has a more efficient engine. Until they stop for the winter, they will make some 80 brief flights.

1904 May

Rolls-Royce founded

1904 May British automobile manufacturing company Rolls-Royce Ltd. originates in an arranged meeting between engineer Frederick Henry Royce (1863—1933) and the rich Charles Stewart Rolls (1877—1910). Rolls is so impressed by the high quality of Royce's work, he becomes partners with him to build "the best car in the world." Royce turns out the remarkable and revolutionary "Silver Ghost" in 1906. The firm has maintained its standards over the years to the degree that it has become a legend, building cars of the highest quality and the highest price.

1904 June 15 Large pleasure boat, the *General Slocum*, catches fire on the Hudson River while carrying 1,400 German-Americans from the Lower East Side of New York to Long Island Sound for a church picnic. More than 1,030 are killed in this terrible catastrophe that nearly wipes out an entire community. The captain is convicted of negligence and goes to prison.

1904 September 7 Wilbur (1867—1912) and Orville (1871—1948) Wright first use their weight-and-derrick-assisted take-off device in order to make themselves independent of the wind and weather. When the heavy weight is released, the rope pulls the aircraft, which sits on a flatbed truck, over the launching track, thus assisting its take-off.

1904 September 20 First circular flight is made by Wilbur Wright (1867—1912) on the *Flyer III* in Huffman Prairie, Ohio. Increasingly, more people see these flights, and this one is witnessed by Amos Root who writes a vivid description for his magazine *Gleanings in Bee Culture*. It is published January, 1905.

1904 October Robert Esnault-Pelterie (1881—1957) tests unsuccessfully his modified Wright glider near Boulogne, France. His machine is important, however, because he adds ailerons (movable surfaces to control the rolling motion of an airplane) to the front of the wings. These are the first real ailerons, and will lead to the modern aileron system.

1904 October Ferdinand Ferber (1862—1909) completely rebuilds his version of the Wright-type glider and, most importantly, adds a tailplane to give longitudinal stability. His new machine marks the beginnings of the stable, full-size airplane in Europe.

1904 October 27 New York City opens the first section of what becomes the largest subway system in the world. This system now moves one billion people a year over 710 miles of track.

1904 November 9 Wilbur Wright (1867—1912) flies for five minutes, four seconds over Huffman Prairie, Ohio. He covers 2¾ miles (c. 4.4 kilometers), making almost four circles of the field. This best and longest

1904 ■ Brooklyn Bridge, New York.

flight of the year will not be exceeded in duration by any European pilot until May 1908.

1905 Society of Automotive Engineers is formed in the United States. It is created to set standards for the automotive industry. It also publishes research papers.

1905 American Motor Car Manufacturers Association (AMCMA) is formed in Chicago by a group of independent car-makers led by Henry Ford (1863—1947) who organize to fight the restrictive patent claims of Henry Selden (1846—1922). It serves as a rival organization to the Association of Licensed Automobile Manufacturers (ALAM), a trade association of companies who have obtained the right to make gasoline cars under the Selden patent. Once the suit is resolved, both organizations break up and are replaced by the National Automobile Chamber of Commerce in 1914 and, in 1932, the Automobile Manufacturers Association.

1905 Automobile innovations during the year include ignition locks, tire chains, spare tires, and folding car tops.

1905 English-born American Charles Knight invents the sleeve-valve engine. Unlike an ordinary gas engine that has poppet (disc or mushroom-shaped) valves, this sleeve or sliding-valve engine has only a tubular sleeve or liner with holes. Despite its high oil consumption, it becomes the vogue for some time. It is rarely used now.

1905 First motorcycle to have a horizontally opposed twin-cylinder engine is the Fee, designed by J. F. Barter. This solves the problem of balance and equal firing impulses. It is later developed in England by the Douglas motorcycle and in Germany by BMW.

1905 Between 1905 and 1916, practically every modern motorcycle design feature makes its first appearance.

1905 Illinois Department of Public Works and Buildings, Division of Highways, is first organized.

1905 Michigan State Highway Department is first organized.

1905 Washington State Highway Commission, Department of Highways, is first organized.

1905 ■ Steamer *Keystone State* in Wheeling, West Virginia.

1905 Minnesota Department of Highways is first organized.

1905 New Hampshire Department of Public Works and Highways is first organized.

1905 Experiments begin in several U.S. states using coal tar and crude oil to resurface older macadam roads now in need of repair. The State Board of Public Roads of Rhode Island becomes a pioneering state in carrying out experiments on these new types of roads.

1905 A.D.

Removable tire rims introduced

1905 First removable automobile tire rims are introduced by the Michelin Company of France. Before these, punctured or damaged tires had to fixed on the spot with the wheels remaining attached to the car.

1905 First turbine steamer to cross the Atlantic is a British ship, the *Victorian*. It is also the first liner to have triple propellers.

1905 First vehicle built specifically as a hearse is a 24-hp De Dion made in Paris, France.

1905 First true hydrofoil is operated by its Italian inventor, Enrico Forlanini (1848—1930). The hydrofoil principle eliminates drag on the hull of a boat by going fast enough so that its foils (fins or skis attached to the hull) come to the surface and the vessel skids along the top of the water. This vehicle is powered by an airplane propeller.

1905 First U.S. National Boat Show is held in New York City.

1905 March First use of an aerodrome (an old-fashioned word for airfield or airport) in Europe. The French military ground, "Champ de Manoeuvres," at Issy-les-Moulineaux, Paris is used by Ernest Archdeacon (1863—1957) to test his second glider. This aerodrome becomes the site of many famous aeronautical events, and much later, the Paris heliport.

1905 March 16 First glider descent from a balloon. S. M. Maloney, a professional balloon-parachute jumper, makes a successful glide to earth in a tandem-wing glider built by John J. Montgomery (1858-1911), a professor at Santa Clara College in California. Maloney will be killed in the same glider in July of this year, and Montgomery will also die during a glider flight in October 1911. (See July 1905)

1905 June Lawrence Hargrave's (1850—1915) box-kite configuration is first incorporated in two unpowered airplanes, the *Voisin-Archdeacon* and *Voisin-Blériot* float-gliders in France. They are to be mounted on floats and towed into the air by a motorboat. This is the beginning of the classic European biplane design.

1905 June 11 Pennsylvania Railroad begins an 18-hour train between New York and Chicago, Illinois, calling it "the fastest train in the world." One week later, New York Central Railroad begins its same 18-hour service, calling it the "Twentieth Century Ltd." Within a week, both trains suffer wrecks and 19 people are killed. (See June 12, 1905)

1905 June 12 Fastest train speed officially recorded on an American railroad—the "Pennsyl-

c. 1900 ■ Alpine rack or cog railway in Balzano, Italy.

vania Special" reaches 127 mph—is made on a three-mile run near Ada, Ohio.

1905 June 23 Wilbur (1867—1912) and Orville (1871—1948) make their first flight of 1905 in Huffman Prairie, Ohio in their new *Flyer III*, the first real practical airplane in history. In a series of 50 flights between now and October, the new *Flyer* proves that it can bank, turn, circle, and easily fly over half an hour at a time.

1905 July 18 Third airplane fatality in history occurs when S. M. Maloney is killed in Santa Clara, California while flying a Montgomery tandem-wing balloon-launched glider. Montgomery's aircraft has tandem wings or one behind the other which he calls "following surfaces." The glider is damaged at take-off and crashes.

1905 October 5 Longest flight of the year is made by Wilbur Wright (1867—1912) in Huffman Prairie, Ohio. Flying 24 1/5 miles in 39 minutes, 23 seconds, the *Flyer III* averages 38 mph. This one flight is longer than all of their 1904 flights (105) combined.

1905 October 14 The Fédération Aéronautique Internationale (F.A.I.) is founded in Paris by Comte Henri de la Vaulx (1870—1930). Its aim is "to regulate the various aviation meetings, and advance the science and sport of aeronautics."

1905 November Aero Club of America is founded with headquarters in New York City by 300 members interested in ballooning.

1905 November 8 Electric lights are used inside a railroad train for the first time on a train from Chicago to California.

1906 Third longest railway tunnel in the Alps, the Lotschberg Tunnel, is begun. Over nine miles long, it is a double-track tunnel. Intended to be shorter, a detour is made adding a half mile, when a severe water problem cannot be solved. Completed in 1913, it is important commercially as it provides a link between Europe north of Switzerland and the Simplon line into Italy.

1906 One of the earliest tunnels to be built by the trench method is begun. This underwater tunnel between Canada and the United States connects Windsor and Detroit on the Michigan Central Railroad. With this method, a trench is first dug in the river bottom. Long steel tubes are then built on land, made watertight, floated to the trench site, and then sunk. Divers join the

1906 A.D.

Detroit-Windsor tunnel built

sections which are covered with earth and rock. To make this one-and-one-half-mile tunnel, 11 sections are sunk in a trench dredged 30 to 50 feet.

1906 A.D.

Motorized roller skates invented

1906 Motorized roller skates are invented by Parisian inventor M. Constantini. Each gas-driven, four-wheel skate weighs over 13 pounds. The Shah of Persia orders three pairs after they are exhibited at the Paris Automobile Show.

1906 British automobile manufacturing company Austin is founded by Herbert Austin (1866-1941). It is best known for its Austin Seven in the 1920s which brings automobiles within the reach of ordinary people. Known today as Austin Rover, it is really a group of companies, called BL Public Limited Company, that is composed of Austin, Morris, Rover, MG, and Triumph.

1906 Automobile innovations during the year are front bumpers, asbestos brake linings, high voltage magnetos, and air brakes. Brake linings made of asbestos are highly resistant to burning and do not conduct heat or electricity; the new magnetos generate sufficiently high voltage to jump a spark plug gap without an ignition coil; and the use of air pressure instead of fluid pressure to operate brake shoes or pads is found to be very effective for heavy duty truck braking.

1906 Buick produces its first four-cylinder engine and first sliding gear transmission. Called the Model D, it costs $2500 and has individually cast cylinders of a T-head design. This has intake valves located in pockets on one side of the engine and exhaust valves in pockets on the other. It has between 24 and 35 hp.

1906 Virginia Department of Highways is first organized.

1906 The term "outboard motor" is coined by American Cameron B. Waterman, whose company, Waterman Porto Outboard Motor, makes its first one in Detroit this year.

1906 A.D.

First Mack trucks built

1906 First Mack trucks are built in Allentown, Pennsylvania by the Mack Brothers, John, William, and Augustus. Their 10-ton trucks have great hauling power and strength.

1906 Woodrow Wilson (1856—1924), president of Princeton University and later president of the United States, states his anti-automobile beliefs saying, "Nothing has spread socialistic feeling in this country more than the use of the automobile. To the countryman, they are a picture of the arrogance of wealth, with all its independence and carelessness."

1906 First U-boat is delivered to the German Navy by the Krupp Shipbuilding Company of Kiel, Germany. Designated the *Untersee Bote U1*, this 128-foot-long submarine has a range of about 2,000 miles. This new vessel is perceived as an offensive weapon that is truly seaworthy and not just useful for coastal defense purposes.

1906 January First Aero Exhibition in America held in New York in connection with the Automobile Show, under the auspices of the Aero Club of America.

1906 January Wilbur (1867—1912) and Orville (1871—1948) Wright publish their patent in the French journal, *L'Aérophile*, the official organ of the Aéro Club de France. It contains descriptions and drawings showing how they control their airplane.

1906 January 17 Second Zeppelin (*LZ-2*) built makes its first successful flight over Lake Constance, Germany, achieving a speed of 25 mph (c. 40 km/h). It will later be destroyed on the ground in a storm.

1906 March 18 A monoplane is first tested in France by Trajan Vuia, a Rumanian. Although it only hops and does not fly, Louis Blériot (1872—1936) decides that its monoplane design is superior to his biplane.

1906 May 22 U.S. Patent Office grants the basic Wright patent, No. 821,393, for a flying machine.

1906 July 13 First dirigible (powered blimp) flight in Canada is made by American Charles K. Hamilton.

1906 August 13 Pennsylvania Railroad announces that from now on, all its coaches will be made of steel, and wooden coaches will be abandoned.

1906 September First Gordon Bennett Balloon Race is won by American Frank P. Lahm (1877—1963) in his balloon, *United States*. Lahm flies 420 miles (647 kilometers) to Flyingdales, in Yorkshire, England.

1906 September 12 J. C. H. Ellehammer (1871—1946), Danish engineer, makes a hop-flight of some 140 feet (42 meters). His biplane is tethered to a central post and does not fly freely.

1906 October 3 Britain's new battleship, the *Dreadnought*, begins sea trials. As the first major battleship to have turbine engines and all "big guns," it makes every other battleship obsolete and starts a battleship arms race.

1906 October 23 Alberto Santos-Dumont (1873—1932), a Brazilian, makes the first successful powered flight in Europe, in Bagatelle, France. His airplane flies some 200 feet (60 meters).

1906 ■ *Santos Dumont* airship flies over Paris.

1906 November 12 Alberto Santos-Dumont (1873—1932) flies some 720 feet (220 meters) and wins the Aéro-Club de France prize for exceeding 100 meters.

1906 December 30 Soviet rocket and spacecraft designer Sergei P. Korolev (1906—1966) is born in Zhitomir, now in the Ukraine. Interested in aviation as a teenager, he studied under the likes of Andrey Tupolev (1888—1972) and in 1931 formed with F. A. Tsander (1887—1933), the Moscow Group for the Study of Reactive Motion. Following World War II, he modified the captured German V-2 rockets and later produced the Soviet Union's first intercontinental ballistic missile. He also ran the Soviet space program, designed its spacecraft, and was directly responsible for all of its early manned and unmanned successes.

1907 ■ Six-cylinder, 48-hp Rolls-Royce "Silver Ghost."

1907 First tentative hop-flight in Britain is made in the spring of this year by 62-year-old Horatio F. Phillips (1845—1926) in his multi-slat (Venetian blind-like) machine. It hop-flies about 500 feet (c. 150 meters) in Streatham near London.

1907 In England, Frederick W. Lanchester (1868—1946) publishes his book *Aerodynamics* which, although it is the first account of an important aeronautical theory, is so difficult that it is understood by very few and has no impact.

1906 November Rolls-Royce introduces its 40—50 hp six-cylinder "Silver Ghost." This incomparable luxury car becomes a milestone in the history of automobile design. The exquisite engineering and high craftsmanship that go into careful manufacture of this car make for a silent, smooth-running, absolutely reliable and durable vehicle.

1907 First supercharged engine is built by the Chadwick Company of the United States for racing purposes. It is not used in their production models. An engine gets considerably more power when a mechanical pump or compressor increases the pressure of incoming air or gases in the engine.

1907 Oldest vehicular and pedestrian tunnel on the European continent, the Elbe Tunnel, is begun. Running under the Elbe River in Hamburg, Germany, it is 1,312-feet long and mainly transports workers back and forth from the shipyards. It opens in 1911.

1907 Large, metal wheel skates are invented by M. Koller of Winterthur, Switzerland. The skater's foot fits on the inside of a 12-inch diameter metal wheel and he basically pedals instead of walking. The poor, uneven quality of most road surfaces made small roller wheels almost impossible to use. Thus the design of very large wheels.

1907 Wisconsin State Highway Commission is first organized.

1907 A.D.

Speed bumps installed

1907 Speed bumps are installed on the streets of Glencoe, Illinois to discourage automobile speeders. They are still in use today in America's suburbs and parking lots.

1907 A.D.

Taxis appear in NYC

1907 Automobile taxicabs appear in New York City. The standard fare for a short ride is a "jitney"—a common term for a nickel. The term soon becomes synonymous with the service itself.

1907 Motorcycle advances made this year are: a foot operated gear lever; pneumatic front and rear suspension; and the high tension magneto spark for ignition.

1907 Philadelphia, Pennsylvania subway system opens for business.

1907 Maine State Highway Commission is first organized.

1907 First modern amphibious car is demonstrated in Paris by French builder Ravailler. It is later taken to the United States where it is named "Water-Land I." (See 1804)

1907 Association of Licensed Automobile Manufacturers (ALAM) devises a formula for figuring horsepower which is adopted by several states as a means of calculating taxes to be owed.

1907 Hawaiian George Freeth (b. 1883) teaches himself to ride a surfboard standing up and designs a shorter, chopped-down version of the ancient Hawaiian board. He introduces the art of surfing to the United States this year, becoming nationally famous as a lifeguard who uses a surfboard in his rescues.

1907 International Peace Convention in The Hague, Netherlands first lays down the conditions under which hospital ships are given immunity during wartime. Basically, they must be painted white with a horizontal band of green around the hull and should have red crosses painted on their sides. Less than ten years later, the first hospital ship is sunk.

1907 Union Station in Washington, D.C. is completed. Designed by Chicago architect Daniel H. Burnham (1846—1912) and patterned after the Baths of Diocletian and the Arch of Constantine in Rome, the railroad station will reach a sad state of disrepair by the 1970s. However, by 1990 it is totally renovated and restored and becomes a pleasure to use once again.

1907 First international motorboating club, the International Association of Automobile Yachting, is founded.

1907 First U.S. hydrofoil is built by Peter C. Hewitt. Weighing 2,500 pounds, it attains a speed of 30 mph (48 km/ph).

1907 March The Voisin Brothers build what becomes the classic European biplane, incorporating some Wright features. Built for Leon Delagrange (1873—1910) and called the *Voisin-Delagrange I*, it makes six test hop-flights in France.

1907 March First Canadian technical paper on aeronautics is Wallace R. Turnbull's "Research on the Forms and Stability of Aeroplanes," published in *Physical Review*.

1907 April Louis Blériot (1872—1936) builds and tests his *No. V*, the first cantilever monoplane, (a design that has a wing or some other part supported at one end only). This "tail-first" airplane manages a takeoff but crashes in Bagatelle, France.

1907 July Aeronautical Division is established in the Office of Chief Signal Officer, U.S. Army, thereby marking the beginning of an Army air force.

1907 August First Canadian glider flight is made at Montreal by Lawrence J. Lash.

1907 August 29 One of the worst disasters in bridge construction history occurs as the Quebec Bridge collapses while being built. This steel cantilever bridge is planned to be longer than the Forth Railway Bridge, but it succumbs to bad engineering and cheap materials, killing approximately 80 men. It takes two years to remove the 9,000 tons of twisted steel on the Canadian side of the St. Lawrence River. Another steel cantilever bridge is built on the same spot and is completed in August 1918.

1907 September The Voisin Brothers build their improved version for Henri Farman (1874—1958). Called the *Voisin-Farman I*, their airplane has a 50-hp Antoinette engine and is flown by Farman himself at Issy-les-Moulineaux, France. He soon becomes the outstanding pilot in Europe.

1907 September First liner to exceed 30,000 gross tons, the Cunard Line's *Lusitania*, is completed. It is also the first quadruple-propeller steamer, and sets records with its speedy Atlantic crossings. It is best remembered for its tragic end. On May 7, 1915, it is torpedoed by a German submarine and sinks in 22 minutes, killing 1,198 people. The deaths of 124 Americans on board influences public opinion in the United States about involving itself in the First World War.

1907 September 2 Walter Wellman (1858—1934), American explorer, readies his first attempt at Spitzbergen, Norway, to fly over the North Pole in an airship. Storms force the attempt to be postponed. (See October 15, 1909).

1907 September 19 First piloted helicopter rises at Douai in France. Built by Louis (1880—1955) and Jacques Breguet and Charles Richet (1850—1935), and piloted by Volumard, it rises only about two feet (60 centimeters) and is steadied by the men on the ground. This does not constitute free, vertical flight.

1907 September 29 The Breguet-Richet helicopter manages to rise about five feet (1.5 meters) but is still supported from the ground.

1907 October The Aerial Experiment Association (A.E.A.) is formed by Alexander Graham Bell (1847—1922), Glenn Curtiss (1878—1930), J. A. D. McCurdy (b. 1886) and others. Based first at Baddeck Bay, Nova Scotia, and then at Hammondsport on Lake Keuka, New York, the Association will sponsor the building of a series of biplanes.

1907 October 5 First British Government airship, the *Nulli Secundus*, flies from Farnborough to the Crystal Palace, near London, piloted by J. E. Capper and S. F. Cody.

1907 November Curtiss Motor Vehicle Company is formed in Hammondsport, New York to manufacture engines, motorcycles, airships, airplanes, and low-priced automobiles.

1907 November 10 Louis Blériot (1872—1936) introduces in France what will become the modern-configuration of the airplane. His *No. VII* has an enclosed or covered fuselage (body), a single set of wings (monoplane), a tail unit, and a propeller in front of the engine. Despite this prophetic design, Blériot's airplane can hardly fly.

1907 November 10 First flight in Europe of over one minute is made by Henri Farman (1874—1958) in his *Voisin-Farman I* biplane, in Issy-les-Moulineaux, France.

1907 November 13 First piloted helicopter rises vertically in free flight, in Lisieux, France. Built by Paul Cornu (1881—1914), it is powered by a 24-hp Antoinette engine driving two rotors. Although a major achievement, the practical helicopter will not appear until the 1930s.

1907 November 30 In France, the Lebaudy airship *Patrie* built for the French Army breaks loose from its ground crew in a high wind, and flies off by itself. It disappears in the direction of the Atlantic Ocean and is never seen again.

1907 December U.S. Army Signal Corps advertises for bids on an airplane. The Wright brothers, J. F. Scott, and A. M. Herring (1867—1926) all submit proposals and make the 10% deposit required. The Wrights' bid is $25,000.

1908 Automobile innovations during the year are motor-driven horns, silent timing gear chains (the drive axle was powered by a chain running from the transmission), left-handed steering, and baked enamel finish. In the latter, the enamel-painted car body is placed in a drying room at an elevated temperature to cure and harden the paint. This results in a hard, durable finish much superior to air dry finishes.

1908 Alfred Scott of England pioneers the water-cooled, two-stroke twin motorcycle engine and the triangulated bicycle frame. His motorcycles soon become legendary for their acceleration, speed, and handling qualities.

1908 Self-closing doors on elevators are first exhibited at the Manchester Electrical Exhibition in England. These doors cannot be opened unless the elevator is at the proper position in relation to the landing.

1908 A.D.

Standard auto parts introduced

1908 First use of interchangeable or standard automobile parts is introduced by the Cadillac Company.

1908 Maryland State Roads Commission is first organized.

1908 The word "pit" first enters motor-racing terminology at a Grand Prix race in Dieppe, France when a divided trench with a counter just above ground-level is provided for crews. Although today's auto race team crews no longer work below ground, the name remains.

1908 A.D.

Tire treads invented

1908 Tire treads are invented by Frank Seiberling who perfects a machine that cuts grooves in the tire surfaces. Up to now, tires have smooth surfaces and can give little traction when roads are bad.

c. 1908 The name *Sex-Auto* is given, supposedly in all innocence, to a six-wheeled car built by the Reeves Manufacturing Company of America. It is an otherwise normal four-cylinder car with an extra axle and a pair of wheels near its center. The company goes out of business soon after it builds an *Octo-Auto*.

1908 Coil and distributor ignition is first introduced by Delco in the United States. This system increases the very low battery volts to a voltage high enough so a spark of electricity can jump a spark plug's gap and ignite a mixture of fuel and air.

1908 Denver electric car maker Oliver P. Ritchie drives his electric car to New York City in five weeks. Much of this 2,000-mile trip is spent recharging his car's batteries.

c. 1908 First motorized vehicle to be used in Antarctica is the Arrol-Johnson motor car used by British explorer Ernest H. Shackleton (1874—1922) during the British Antarctic Expedition of 1908—1909. Although it has special steel-ribbed snow tires for extra traction, it proves useless in soft snow. Its air-cooled engine has 15 hp.

1908 England pioneers the use of diesel engines in submarines. These engines are fired by compression rather than an electric spark, and are less toxic, less volatile, and cheaper to operate than gasoline-powered engines. Diesel engines are considered nearly ideal for submarines.

1908 First workable gyrocompass is installed and used on the German battleship *Deutschland*. Produced by German engineer Hermann Anschutz-Kampfe, it is in no way related to the traditional magnetic compass. Rather, it employs the principle of the gyroscope—a device whose spinning wheel, if mounted correctly, maintains its orientation despite any movements about it. Once set or oriented in a certain direction (north), it resists being turned out of that plane. Since it is not influenced by any iron or steel around it, as a magnetic compass is, it is the first major improvement on the compass in a thousand years. (See Sperry, 1911)

1908 January 13 First European to fly one kilometer in a circle is Henri Farman (1874—1958) in his Voisin-Farman. Farman flies for 1 minute, 28 seconds at Issy-les-Moulinoux, France and wins the 50,000-franc Grand Prix d'Aviation Deutsche-Archdeacon.

1908 February 10 First formal Army airplane contract is signed by the U.S. Signal Corps with the Wright brothers who agree to deliver, for $25,000, a heavier-than-air flying machine meeting set specifications by August 28, 1908.

1908 March 12 First powered airplane flight by a Canadian is made by F. W. Baldwin who flies a Curtiss biplane in Hammondsport, New York for the Aerial Experiment Association. American inventor Alexander Graham Bell (1847—1922) is its founding member.

 **1908 May 6** Wilbur (1867—1912) and Orville (1871—1948) Wright fly for the first time since 1905, covering a distance of 1,008 feet at an average speed of 41 mph at Kill Devil Hills, North Carolina. They use the 1905 *Flyer III*, modified for the pilot and a passenger to sit upright. They make a series of 22 flights until May 14.

1908 ∎ Wilbur Wright flies in France.

 **1908 May 14** First passenger flies in an airplane. Wilbur Wright (1867—1912) takes Charles W. Furnas of Dayton, Ohio on a 28 3/5 second flight that covers 600 meters at Kill Devil Hills, North Carolina.

 **1908 May 23** First airplane flight in Italy is made by Leon Delagrange (1873—1910) in Rome.

 **1908 May 29** First passenger flight in Europe occurs as Henri Farman (1874—1958) takes up Ernest Archdeacon (1863—1957) for a brief flight at Issy-les-Moulineaux, France.

 **1908 May 30** First European flight of over 15 minutes. Léon Delagrange (1873—1910) flies his Voisin-Delagrange in France.

 **1908 June** Glenn Curtiss (1878—1930) flies the *June Bug* of his own design and wins the *Scientific American* magazine's prize for the first public U.S. flight of more than a mile. Curtiss is the first American after the Wrights to fly with any ability.

 **1908 June** A. V. Roe (1877—1958) tests his Wright-based biplane in England. He succeeds in making hop-flights of up to 150 feet (c. 46 meters), probably with a downhill assisted take-off.

 **1908 June 28** J. C. H. Ellehammer (1871—1946) of Denmark makes the first hop-flights in Germany at Kiel in his biplane. His best lasts 11 seconds.

 **1908 July 4** Zeppelin *LZ-4* makes a 12-hour flight crossing the Alps. It covers the 235 miles (c. 378 kilometers) from Friedrichshafen to Lucerne and Zürich, and reaches speeds of 32 mph (c. 52 km/h).

 **1908 July 8** First woman flies as an airplane passenger. Madame Therese Peltier flies with Leon Delagrange (1873—1910) at Turin, Italy. They make a flight of 500 feet (150 meters) in his Voisin biplane.

 **1908 July 17** First city ordinance in the United States pertaining to aircraft is passed by the town of Kissimmee, Florida. It prescribes flight limits and an annual license and covers such details as brakes, lights, and signal systems.

 **1908 July 22** Fisher Closed Body Company is organized by the Fisher brothers. The Fishers are coachbuilders who consider it unreasonable (as well as uncomfortable) to ride in an open car and be subject to the dust and rain of the road. They therefore design and build completely closed bodies for cars. Cadillac orders 150 bodies in 1910, and eventually all cars become enclosed.

 **1908 August 4** Zeppelin *LZ-4*, which had just crossed the Alps, begins its government acceptance trials in Germany and is completely destroyed on the ground by a storm after landing for engine repairs.

 **1908 August 4** Wilbur Wright (1867—1912) flies at Hunaudières, near Le Mans, France, for 1 minute,

1908 July 8

First woman airplane passenger flies

45 seconds using stick control for the first time. This is the first of 123 August to December flights in France, first at Hunaudières, then at Auvours, also near Le Mans. During these flights, he is airborne over 25 hours, making one flight last over two hours. He also takes up passengers on more than 60 occasions. Europeans finally realize that flight is here to stay.

1908 August 20 Soviet rocket pioneer Valentin P. Glushko (b. 1908) is born. Interested in the notion of reactive rocket power for spaceflight as a pre-teenager, he wrote to the great Tsiolkovsky in 1923 about his ideas. When only 23, he proposed making liquid-fuel rockets for the Soviet government, and it responded by making him a department head of its Gas Dynamics Laboratory (GDL). There he built and launched the first Soviet liquid-fueled rocket and experimented with various other fuel possibilities. After World War II, he helped develop the boosters for the Soviet space program.

1908 September 1 Réné Lorin (1877—1933), French artillery officer, publishes in *L'Aérophile* the first of his articles concerning a new method of jet propulsion of airplanes. He suggests that the exhaust from two gas engines would push a plane forward and that tilted downward, they could assist in taking off vertically. French military authorities are not interested at the time, and his ideas will have to wait for Frank Whittle (b. 1907) a generation later. (See 1937)

1908 September 3 Orville Wright (1871—1948), in preparation for forthcoming trials in fulfilling the Army contract, makes his first flight at Fort Meyer, Virginia near Washington, D.C., circling the field one-and-one-half times. During the next two weeks, he conducts a series of 14 long, high, and impressive flights, many of which set new records and are witnessed by many government officials.

**1908
September 5

Full-size tri-
plane flies**

1908 September 5 First flight of a full-size triplane aircraft, the French *Goupy*, is made. Built by Ambroise Goupy, it has three sets of wings, each stacked above the other. It is powered by a 50-hp Renault engine.

1908 September 17 First fatality in a powered airplane occurs when Lt. Thomas E. Selfridge is killed when flying with Orville Wright (1871—1948) at Fort Meyer, Virginia. After a propeller blade breaks and severs control wires, the airplane crashes from a height of about 75 feet. Orville is severely injured and lives with back pain the rest of his life, but he will fly again.

1908 September 26 American automobile manufacturing company General Motors Corporation is founded by William C. Durant (1861—1947). Later that year, he takes over the Buick Motor Company and adds Cadillac, Oakland, and Oldsmobile in 1909. Later, Chevrolet Motor Car Co. comes into the fold. The company decides in the 1920s to offer a wide range of cars, from the prestigious Cadillac to the affordable Chevrolet. Today it is the largest car producer in the world.

1908 October Hans Grade (1879—1946) becomes the first native German to fly a plane in Germany. He makes tentative flights in Magdeburg in a triplane of his own construction but derived from Ellehammer.

1908 October First practical use of ailerons (movable surfaces to control the rolling movements of an airplane) on a monoplane is by Frenchman Leon Levavasseur (1863—1922) on his *Antoinette IV*.

1908 October First practical use of ailerons (movable surfaces to control the rolling movements of an airplane) on a biplane is by Henri Farman (1874—1958) who fits four large, flap-type ailerons on his Voisin-Farman biplane for a flight in France.

1908 October Legendary Model T Ford Tin Lizzie, the first of the "People's Cars," is introduced. It is the first Ford with left-hand steering and has a four-cylinder engine that gives 20 hp. Easy to drive and easy to fix, its production will continue until 1927, when total production reaches 16,536,075 vehicles—a record which stands until 1972. At the end of its run, it sells for an all-time low $260.

1908 October 6 First passenger flight of over one hour occurs as Wilbur Wright (1867—1912) takes French writer Arnold Fordyce up at Auvours, France for 1 hour, 4 minutes, 26 seconds.

1908 October 16 First powered flight in Britain is made by Samuel F. Cody (1861—1913), an American who becomes a British citizen in 1909. Cody flies 1,390 feet (c. 424 meters) in 27 seconds before crashing at Farnborough.

1909 ■ "Touring" version of Model T.

1909 ■ Louis Bleriot flies across the English Channel.

1908 October 30 First cross-country flight is made by Henri Farman (1874—1958) who flies from Bouy to Reims, France, about 16½ miles (27 kilometers) in 20 minutes. His modified Voisin-Farman biplane is fitted with four large, flap-type ailerons (movable surfaces to control the rolling movements of an airplane).

1908 October 31 Louis Blériot (1872—1936) flies cross-country in France from Toury, around Artenay, and back, making two landings and flying some 17 miles (28 kilometers) in 22 minutes.

1908 November 30 La Compagnie Generale de Navigation Aérienne, the French Wright company, is organized.

1908 December The Aerial Experiment Association's airplane, the *Silver Dart*, is first test flown by J. A. D. McCurdy (b. 1886), its Canadian designer.

1908 December 31 First flight over two hours is made by Wilbur Wright (1867—1912) at Auvours, France. He flies for two hours, 20 minutes, and 23 seconds, covers some 77 miles (124 kilometers), and wins the Michelin Cup for 1908 and 20,000 francs.

1909 Glenn L. Martin Company is formed, as Glenn Martin (1886—1955) organizes his new business around his modest airplane construction shop located in an abandoned church in Santa Ana, California. Chiefly noted for its bomber designs, the company takes part in "Billy" Mitchell's successful 1921 bombing trials and builds one of World War II's best tactical bombers,

Marauder. Today, it is primarily associated with missile and space systems.

1909 Selden patent is upheld by Judge Hough in the U.S. District Court. (See 1911)

1909 The Knight sleeve-valve engine is adopted for the Daimler 38 and 48 hp models. (See 1905)

1909 German automobile manufacturing company Audi is founded by August Horsch—Audi being a Latin version of the name Horsch. The current company is an amalgam of several different, older companies and has begun to produce prestige models as it did in its early years.

1909 A.D.
Audi is founded

1909 Utah State Road Commission is first organized.

1909 First U.S. president to order an official White House car is William Howard Taft (1857—1930) who gets a steam-powered White Steam Car. It is a small, buggy-like vehicle with a tiller and not a steering wheel.

1909 A.D.
Pres. Taft orders car

1909 Indianapolis Speedway in Indiana opens. Designed by P. T. Andrews, this famed automobile race track provides a rigorous competitive testing ground for new components, systems, and designs. It is a two-and-one-half-mile (four-kilometer) oval track with four slightly banked turns. After its surface is torn up during this first meet, it is resurfaced with 3,200,000 bricks—resulting in its being called "The Brickyard." (See 1911)

1909   Automobile innovations made during the year are electric head-lights, the electric generator, four-door bodies, and oil gauges on the dashboard.

1909 A.D.

Derailleur gears invented

1909   Derailleur type gear for bicycles is first made in France. This still-popular system consists of two or more rear wheel sprockets of different diameters, a chain looped over a mechanism which both lifts and transfers it from one sprocket to another to provide a change of gear ratios, and also a chain-tensioning device to take up the slack that is necessary to permit the chain transfer to take place. This extremely simple system also allows for direct drive on all ratios.

1909   Motor Cycle Racing Club is formed in England.

1909   Arizona State Highway Department is first organized.

1909 A.D.

Alfa Romeo founded

1909   Italian automobile manufacturing company Alfa Romeo is founded as the Anonima Lombardo Fabbrica Automobili. Nicola Romeo takes over the company in 1915 and after World War I markets his cars as Alfa Romeos. The company is nationalized by the Italian government from 1933 to 1986. Still in existence, Alfa Romeo produces sporty, high-performance, well-built cars.

1909   Colorado Department of Highways is first organized.

1909   American physics professor Robert H. Goddard (1882—1945) begins his studies of liquid-propellant rockets and concludes that liquid oxygen and liquid hydrogen would be excellent rocket fuels.

1909   *Colliers* magazine calls the automobile the greatest social force in America—greater than rural free mail delivery or the telephone. While this article is correct that the automobile has changed life in America, that influence is still only slight compared to the later role of the car in American life.

1909   Self-contained diving system is design by Draeger who equips a diver with a backpack of compressed oxygen. (See 1917)

1909 January   First flying school is opened by the Wright brothers in Pau, France, a French resort town at the edge of the Pyrenées, selected because of its warm climate.

1909 January 18   First book to treat the work and accomplishments of the Wright brothers, *Les Premiers Hommes-Oiseaux: Wilbur et Orville Wright*, is written by François Peyrey (1873—1934) and published in France.

1909 January 23   First flight of French *Blériot XI*, one of the most successful monoplanes designed and built before World War I, is made. It becomes the airplane of choice, purchased by both individuals and countries. Louis Blériot (1872—1936) uses this aircraft to fly the Channel. (See July 25, 1909)

1909 January 23   First instance of wireless telegraphy being used at sea to call for help occurs when the *Republic* and the *Florida* collide in a fog off Nantucket, Massachusetts. Five liners come to aid of the sinking *Republic*, saving its passengers and crew.

1909 February 23   First flight in Canada by a powered aircraft is made in Nova Scotia by J. A. D. McCurdy of the Aerial Experiment Association. American inventor Alexander Graham Bell (1847—1922) is its founding member.

1909 March 30   Queensboro Bridge opens to traffic in New York City. Spanning the East River, this huge cantilever bridge is criticized from the start, and is a good example of an over-designed, over-built, and over-decorated bridge. Its heavy, clumsy appearance prompts its consulting architect to exclaim upon first seeing it completed, "My God—it's a blacksmith's shop!"

1909 April   Henri Farman (1874—1958) first flies *Henri Farman III*, the first machine wholly designed by him. This classic biplane with four-wheeled landing gear plus skids becomes popular as a safe sporting machine and is also the first practical aileroned biplane.

1909 April   First Canadian aviation company, the Canadian Aerodrome Company, is formed in Nova Scotia.

1909 April 15 Wilbur Wright (1867—1912) makes his first flight in Italy at Centocelle Field near Rome. He flies for 10 minutes and reaches an altitude of 30 meters and is watched by a large, enthusiastic crowd. Between now and April 26, he makes 50 flights, many with passengers.

1909 April 24 Wilbur Wright (1867—1912) makes five flights in Centocelle, Italy with King Victor Emmanuel III (1869—1947) of Italy present. He also takes up U.S. Ambassador to Italy Lloyd C. Grissom as a passenger on his last flight. During one flight, a Universal News Agency cameraman accompanies him and takes the first motion pictures from an airplane in flight.

1909 June First airship built by one nation for another is the French Lebaudy airship *Russie,* commissioned by Russia. It passes its trials and is shipped from France to Russia.

1909 The Gnome rotary engine, made by French brothers Louis and Laurent Seguin, first goes into service, powering Louis Paulhan's (1883—1963) Voisin aircraft. The brothers' rotary is a seven-cylinder, 50-hp engine whose improving power makes it very popular with pilots between 1909 and 1914.

1909 June 5 First monoplane flight of over one hour is made by Englishman Hubert Latham (1883—1912) on the *Antoinette IV* for one hour, seven minutes, 37 seconds.

1909 June 22 Airplane sales agency is established by Wyckoff, Church & Partridge, an automobile dealer in New York, to handle sales of Curtiss airplanes.

1909 June 26 First commercial sale of an airplane in the United States is made as Glenn H. Curtiss (1878—1930) sells one of his planes to the Aeronautic Society of New York for $7,500. This action spurs the Wright brothers to begin a patent suit to prevent him from selling airplanes without a license.

1909 July 4 First U.S. rural public road surfaced with Portland cement opens in Wayne County, Michigan. A one-mile strip on Woodward Avenue leading from Detroit, Michigan to the State Fair Grounds is resurfaced with two courses of cement. In 1907, Windsor, in the province of Ontario, Canada, was the first municipality in North America to pave streets extensively with Portland cement concrete. (See July 13, 1891)

1909 July 19 First attempt to fly the English Channel is made by Englishman Hubert Latham (1883—1912) on his *Antoinette IV* monoplane. Attempting to fly from Sangette, near Calais, France, he has engine failure at seven or eight miles out and crashes into the sea. He is rescued unhurt by an escorting French destroyer.

1909 July 25 First flight in Russia is made by Van den Schkrouff on a Voisin biplane at Odessa.

1909 July 25 First airplane crossing of the English Channel is made by Louis Blériot (1872—1936) of France who flies his Blériot *No. XI* monoplane from Les Baraques near Calais to Dover, England in 37 minutes. This event increases public and governmental awareness of the possible military aspects of the airplane.

1909 July 25
Airplane first crosses English Channel

1909 July 27 Orville Wright (1871—1948), with Lt. Frank P. Lahm (1877—1963) as passenger, makes the first official test flight of the U.S. Army's first airplane in Fort Myer, Virginia. He flies for one hour, 12½ minutes and fulfills the Army's requirements. The flight is witnessed by President William Howard Taft, his cabinet, and an estimated crowd of 10,000 enthusiastic spectators.

1909 July 27 General Motors acquires the Cadillac Automobile Company. William C. Durant (1861—1947) adds this maker of high quality, limited number, prestige automobiles to his growing line of car types. GM will eventually attempt to offer "a car for every wish and every pocket."

1909 July 27
GM acquires Cadillac

1909 July 29 First airplane flight in Sweden is made by Georges Legagneux in his Voisin biplane in Stockholm.

1909 August 2 First flying machine purchased and put into service by a government is the Wright *Flyer.* The U.S. Army accepts its first airplane and pays the Wrights $25,000, plus a $5,000 bonus, because the machine exceeded the speed requirement of 40 mph.

1909 August 22—29 The first great aviation meeting, in Bétheny, France, north of Reims, opens as 23 European airplanes make 87 flights during this one week. This meeting will have a strong influence on the technical and military aspects of flight.

1909 September 7 U.S. Army's first "aerodrome," an airfield or airport, is established in College Park, Maryland.

1909 October 15 Walter Wellman (1858—1934) departs Spitzbergen, Norway in an airship with three companions and attempts to fly over the North Pole. Mechanical problems force the flight to be abandoned after 12 miles (c. 19 kilometers), and Wellmann later abandons the project altogether after Robert E. Peary (1856—1920) reaches the North Pole.

**1909
October 16

World's first
commercial
airline
formed**

1909 October 16 World's first commercial airline is formed by German Count Ferdinand von Zeppelin (1838—1917). Between 1910 and 1913, Delag airships (Die Deutsche Luftschiffahrt Aktiengesellschaft) carry more than 34,000 passengers between major cities in Germany.

1909 October 18 Charles Comte de Lambert (b. 1865), Wilbur Wright's (1867—1912) first aviation pupil, flies around the Eiffel Tower in Paris.

**1909
November 22

Wright Co.
incorporated**

1909 November 22 Wright Company is incorporated with a capital stock of $1,000,000. Formed to manufacture airplanes, the company's president is Wilbur Wright (1867—1912), and Orville (1871—1948) is one of the vice-presidents. Cornelius Vanderbilt III (1873—1942) is a member of its executive committee.

1910 Although the majority of the more than 500 delivery vans in the United States are electrics with increased range, they are still expensive vehicles to maintain.

**1910 A.D.

Bolt-on
wheels
introduced**

1910 First modern bolt-on wheels are introduced by the Sankey Company of England. These did much to replace the old, wooden-rim/cast iron car wheel. The Sankey wheel has five bolts and is a godsend for drivers. It can be unbolted and replaced with a spare in minutes. It is made of pressed steel and is strong and light.

1910 Electrical lighting for bicycles becomes a practical system with the introduction of the Bowden cycle dynamo. Driven by means of a small friction wheel pressing against the side of the front tire, it replaces the heavy and inefficient early batteries.

1910 First U.S. car manufacturer to offer enclosed, weatherproof bodies as standard equipment is

Cadillac. The bodies are made by Fisher. (See July 22, 1908)

1910 First production car to be successfully fitted with four-wheel brakes is the Scottish car Argyll. Built by Arrol-Johnson, it uses a diagonal control system invented by French engineer Henri Perrot. Brakes on all four wheels do not come into regular use until the mid-1920s.

1910 American Association for Highway Improvement is formed as a large, umbrella-type organization to coordinate the scores of Good Roads organizations. In 1912 it shortens its name to American Highway Association and joins with the American Automobile Association to sponsor American Road Congresses. In December 1914, the American Association of State Highway Officials is organized to coordinate state activity and work with the federal government.

c. 1910 ■ Electric streetcar advertising in Providence, Rhode Island.

1910 First driverless underground railroad opens in Munich, Germany. It runs from the post office in Hofenstrasse to the Starnberger railway station.

1910 Louisiana Department of Highways is first organized.

1910 First Japanese motorboat is a 24-foot (7-meter) boat with a 10—12-hp Waterman engine built by Ishikawazima Ship Building Company.

1910 First clear analysis of the physics and dynamics of skiing is written by English artist

Vivian Caulfield. His book, *How To Ski and How Not To*, becomes one of the most influential early books on skiing.

1910 Federation Internationale de Ski (FIS), the worldwide ruling body for this sport, is formed. The First International Ski Congress also meets for the first time this year in Christiania (Oslo), Norway.

1910 January 26 First practical seaplane flies. Built and flown by American Glenn H. Curtiss (1878—1930), it lands and takes off in the waters off San Diego, California.

1910 January 10—20 The first aviation meet in the United States is held in Los Angeles, California. Enthusiastic audiences range each day between 20,000 and 50,000.

1910 February A patent is granted to German engineer Hugo Junkers (1859—1935) for "an aeroplane consisting of one wing, which would house all components, engines, crew, passengers, fuel and framework." This marks the beginning of his "flying wing" concept. Junkers later founds the famous German aircraft company of the same name.

1910 March 8 First woman to become a qualified pilot is the Baroness de Laroche who receives her "brevet de pilote d'aéroplane" (pilot's license) in France. She dies in 1919 in an airplane accident.

1910 March 10 First flight at night is made by Frenchman Emile Aubrun in Argentina on a Blériot airplane. Aubrun makes two flights in the dark, each about 20 kilometers from Buenos Aires and back again.

1910 March 13 First airplane flight in Switzerland is made by German Capt. P. Englehardt who takes off in a Wright *Flyer* from a frozen lake in St. Moritz.

1910 March 28 First takeoff from water by an aircraft is made by Henri Fabre (b. 1882) in his tail-first float-plane, powered by a Gnome engine, in Martigues, near Marseilles, France.

1910 April 5 Trans-Andine Railway opens between Los Andes, Chile and Mendosa, Argentina.

1910 May 25 Orville Wright (1871—1948) takes his 82-year-old father for his first airplane ride.

Also on this day, Wilbur and Orville fly together for the only time in a six-and-one-half minute flight at Simms Station, near Dayton, Ohio.

1910 June 22 First regular passenger-carrying airship service is inaugurated by the German firm "Delag" (Deutsche Luftschiffahrt Aktiengesellschaft). Between 1910 and 1914, its five Zeppelin airships carry nearly 35,000 passengers without a fatality over inland German routes.

1910 June 25 First Canadian aviation meet is held in Lakeside (now Pointe Claire), Quebec. Sponsored by the Automobile & Aero Club of Canada, the meet sees Wright biplanes and Bleriot monoplanes fly, as well as balloons.

1910 June 30 First airplane bombing tests are made as Glenn H. Curtiss (1878—1930) drops dummy bombs from his own Curtiss biplane on the shape of a battleship marked by flagged buoys on Lake Keuka, New York.

1910 June 30

First airplane bombing tests made

1910 August 17 First English Channel crossing by an airplane with a passenger is made by John B. Moisant (1868—1910) who takes his mechanic in his two-seater Blériot on the flight from Calais, France to Dover, England.

1910 August 27 Radio is first used to send messages between the ground and an airplane when James A. D. McCurdy (b. 1886) both sends and receives messages from a Curtiss biplane at Sheepshead Bay, New York, using an H. M. Horton wireless set.

1910 August 28 Armand Dufaux, the first native Swiss pilot, flies across Lake Geneva, Switzerland in his Dufaux biplane.

1910 September 2 First American woman to fly an aircraft solo is Blanche Scott.

1910 September 8 First mid-air collision occurs in Austria as two airplanes piloted by brothers named Warchalovski collide. No deaths are recorded.

1910 September 8

First mid-air crash occurs

1910 September 8 New railroad terminal, Pennsylvania Station, opens in New York City. Built in a deliberately monumental style, it covers two square blocks of the city and has 35-feet-high columns and a 150-foot ceiling.

1910 September 23   First airplane flight over the Alps is made by Peruvian Georges Chavez (1887—1910), who flies over the Simplon Pass (Lepontine Alps between Italy and Switzerland). This spectacular flight ends in tragedy as Chavez is killed in a crash-landing at Domodossola, Italy.

1910 October 2   First mid-air collision at an aviation meet takes place in Milan, Italy between M. Thomas on an Antoinette monoplane and Capt. Bertram Dickson on a Henri Farman biplane. Thomas's plane dives onto the top of Dickson's plane. Both pilots survive, although Dickson is seriously injured.

1910 October 15   Walter Wellman (1858—1934) and a crew of five attempt to fly the Atlantic by airship. After leaving from Atlantic City, New Jersey, Wellman develops engine trouble and is forced to radio for help. This is the first airship-to-land use of radio. The entire crew and a cat are rescued in their lifeboat 400 miles (c. 644 kilometers) off the coast by a steamer.

1910 October 17—24   Alan R. Hawly (1869—1938) and Augustus Post (1873—1952) fly 1,173 miles (1,890 kilometers) in a balloon from St. Louis, Missouri to North Lake Chilogoma, Canada. This is one of the longest balloon voyages in America.

1910 October 22—31   Belmont Park International Aviation Meeting is held at Long Island, New York. This international meet helps to popularize aviation in America and gets the attention of its financial and military groups as well. About forty planes compete and are shown, and a race to the Statue of Liberty is held.

1910 October 23   First Canadian to receive a pilot's license is J. A. D. McCurdy who earns an American license.

1910 November 4   First dirigible to fly from England to France is the British non-rigid airship *City of Cardiff*, built by E. T. Willows (d. 1926). A dirigible is an alternative name for a steerable lighter-than-air aircraft with its own engine. It means literally "able to steer."

1910 November 7   First use of an airplane to carry commercial freight is the Wright Company's

airplane which flies from Dayton to Columbus, Ohio carrying 10 bolts of silk to the Morehouse-Martens Co. The pilot is Phillip O. Parmalee.

1910 November 14   Birth of the aircraft-carrier occurs when Eugene B. Ely (1886—1911) takes off from the cruiser *USS Birmingham* in Hampton Roads, Virginia, on a Curtiss biplane. This warship has an 83-foot platform built over the fore-deck for the take-off. (See January 18, 1911)

1910 ■ Ely flies his Curtiss biplane off deck of cruiser *Birmingham*.

1911   First oleo-undercarriage is produced by Frenchman Robert Esnault-Pelterie (1881—1957). This new landing-gear device is essentially a cylindrical strut with a built-in telescopic shock absorber that lessens the wheel's impact as it touches down.

1911   Earliest known airplane to be equipped with a machine-gun is a Blériot two-seat monoplane modified by Edouard Nieuport (1875—1911) in France.

1911   First use of a rearview mirror in the United States occurs at the Indianapolis 500 race when driver Ray Harroun puts one in his Marmon Wasp racing car. Harroun wins the race averaging 74.59 mph.

1911 Largest canal tunnel of its time, the Rove Tunnel in France, is begun. Part of the Rhone-Marseilles Canal, it is delayed by World War I and not finished until 1927. It is four-and-one-half miles long and can handle boats that are as long as 197 feet. Cut through limestone, it is as wide as a six-lane highway, 51 feet high and 72 feet wide, with a six-foot towpath on each side.

1911 Alabama State Highway Department is first organized.

1911 Original predecessor of Japanese Nissan Motor Company is formed as the Kwaishinsha Motor Car Works. The company produces the DAT car and in 1931 becomes Datson, then Datsun in 1932. In 1934 they settle finally on Nissan for the company's name.

1911 Automobile innovations during the year are detachable wheel rims, worm gear drive for trucks, and improved electric horns. The rim is the part of the wheel on which the tire is mounted, and changing tires becomes easier and quicker with detachable rims. The worm gear is the end of the steering column which is cut with a spiral thread. As it turns, the thread moves a sleeve-like nut back and forth and turns the wheels.

1911 California Department of Public Works, Division of Highways, is first organized.

1911 Oklahoma State Highway Department is first organized.

1911 First electric starter, invented by Charles F. Kettering (1876—1958), is installed on a Cadillac. Kettering works for General Motors' Delco (Dayton Engineering Laboratories Company). This finally does away with the difficult and sometimes dangerous business of hand-cranking and makes it much easier for a woman to start a car by herself from inside the car with the touch of her toe. It also makes gasoline the fuel of choice over steam, since electric starters make gas-powered automobiles start up at once. Owners of steam vehicles must wait for them to heat to the required pressure.

1911 Selden patent is declared valid but of limited applicability by the U.S. Court of Appeals. In this final ruling, the court says that Selden's patent is limited to a certain type of engine (Bratton), and that Ford and other cars are not an infringement.

1911 Russian Konstantin E. Tsiolkovsky (1859—1935) publishes his article "Investigation of Universal Space by Means of Reactive Devices." Here he further refines and elaborates on his 1903 theories and designs, offering such correct particulars as the necessary speed for escape velocity (25,050 mph). He computes the time for a moon mission (4.8 days, which is what it takes the U.S. Apollo moon mission 58 years later), and suggests methods for steering a rocket into earth orbit. He updates and improves this work in 1912 and again in 1914.

1911 Mechanical speedometer that not only measures but indicates an automobile's speed is built by German W. H. Grossman. Speedometers work by measuring the rotation speed of the car's transmission, and use a flexible cable that is attached to a pointer on an indicator display. The odometer, which measures distance travelled, is connected by gears to the speedometer spindle, and works off it.

1911 First unofficial outboard motor boat race in the United States takes place on Lake Pewaukee, Wisconsin.

1911 English cleric Sidney Swann rows a racing skiff across the English Channel in 3 hours, 50 minutes.

1911 Gyrocompass is marketed by American inventor Elmer A. Sperry (1860—1930). Sperry, working on applying the principle of a gyroscope to navigation since 1896, finally perfects his electrically-driven gyrocompass which always points north. During this year, his device is installed on the American battleship *Delaware*. In 1909, Sperry invents the first automatic pilot for aircraft. (See 1908)

1911 First SAE handbook on standardization is published by the six-year-old U.S. Society of Automotive Engineers. Issuing standards and specifications for spark plugs and carburetor parts, it eventually will standardize all automobile components. Standards are essential for interchangeability, reliability, and quality control.

1911 First escalator in England is installed in a London subway station which hires a one-legged man to ride up and down. Management has to convince the public they have nothing to fear from a moving staircase.

1911 A.D.
Speed-
ometer and
odometer
invented

1911 Last horse-drawn bus of the London General Omnibus Company is retired. Automobiles, trucks, and motorized buses are fast replacing the horse on London's roads.

1911 First white center line dividing a road surface is made by Edward N. Hines, road commissioner for Wayne County, Michigan. His "center line safety stripe" is painted on River Road near Trenton, Michigan.

1911 Principles of echo-sounding at sea are discovered as Alexander Behm of Germany experiments in an aquarium to show that it is possible to measure the sea's depth by timing the echo of an underwater explosion.

1911 First bomb-sight is made in the United States by Lt. Riley Scott.

1911 January 18 Eugene B. Ely (1886—1911) lands his Curtiss biplane on the cruiser *USS Pennsylvania* after taking off from San Francisco, California. He then takes off again and returns to the city.

1911 January 18 U.S. House of Representatives passes an appropriation of $125,000 for Army aeronautics.

1911 February First amphibian airplane (able to take off and land on both water and land) is built by American Glenn Curtiss (1878—1930) who fits wheels to his seaplane. Curtiss will become the world's leading pioneer and promoter of seaplanes.

1911 February 18 First official government air mail flight is made in India as French pilot Henri Pequet flies some 6,500 letters a distance of about five miles (8 kilometers).

1911 April 21 Aeronautical Manufacturers Association is incorporated under the laws of Connecticut as a membership corporation.

1911 May 30 First Indianapolis 500 auto race is run. This traditional Memorial Day race has become the largest single-day sporting event in the world in terms of spectator attendance. This race is won with an average speed of 74.59 mph (120 km/h). Eighty years later, the winner's average speed is 176.5 mph (284 km/h).

1911 June 28 First airplane charter flight is made by English aviator Thomas Sopwith (1888—1989) who is hired by Wannamaker's New York store to deliver repaired glasses to Philadelphia merchant W. A. Burpee (1858—1915). Burpee is on the liner *Olympic*, bound for London, and Sopwith catches up with the ship at sea and drops the carefully wrapped package onto its deck.

1911 July 31 First automobile securities listed on New York Stock Exchange is General Motors.

1911 August First air-sea rescue is successfully carried out by Hugh Robinson (b. 1881) in a Curtiss seaplane, when he lands on Lake Michigan and rescues another pilot who had crashed there.

1911 August 2 First woman in the United States licensed as a qualified pilot is Harriet Quimby (1884—1912), a drama critic. (See April 16, 1912)

1911 August 15 First Canadian pilot to die in an aircraft, St. Croix Johnstone, is killed as his Moisant monoplane crashes in the United States.

1911 September 17—November 5 Calbraith P. Rodgers (1879—1912) flies across the United States in a Wright EX biplane. He flies from Long Island, New York to Long Beach, California, via Chicago, Illinois and San Antonio, Texas, covering 4,000 miles (c. 6400 kilometers) in 82 flying hours over 49 days. His airplane crashes 19 times and is virtually rebuilt, using spare parts carried in a following train, by the time it reaches California.

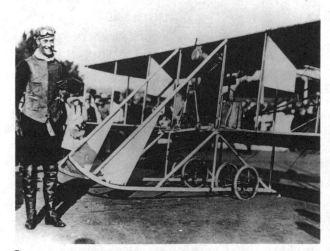

1911 ■ Cal Rodgers and *Vin Fiz* in Binghampton, New York during his transcontinental flight.

1911 ■ Typical American buggy at the turn-of-the century.

 **1911 September 23** First air mail in the United States is carried by Earl L. Ovington (b. 1879) in a Blériot monoplane from Nassau Boulevard Aerodrome, Long Island to Mineola, Long Island.

1911 October 22 First use of an airplane in war is made by Italian Captain Piazza in a Blériot monoplane which makes a reconnaissance flight of about an hour from Tripoli to Azizia, to observe positions of Turkish soldiers.

1911 October—November First "Concours Militaire," a display of aircraft that could be used in war, is held at Reims, France and arouses widespread official interest.

1912 First successful and practical seaplanes or flying-boats make their appearance. Built first by Glenn Curtiss (1878—1930) in the United States and then by Denhaut in France, the design by Denhaut sets the basic style for future seaplanes.

1912 First use of the monocoque fuselage at La Vidamée in France. Taken from the French word meaning "egg-shell," this new design is a hollow, shell-like structure in which the shell itself carries most of the load and stress. Designed by Swiss designer Ruchonnet, and applied by L. Béchereau for the Deperdussin monoplane called *Monocoque Deperdussin*, this invention is one of the milestones in aviation, since it is the fuselage (body or hull) design of the future.

1912 Sopwith Aviation Company, famous for its World War I fighter aircraft, is founded by Thomas O. M. Sopwith (b. 1888). Its best-known fighter, the *F1 Camel*, is highly successful during the war and becomes the standard fighter of the RAF after the war. In 1920, the company is absorbed by the Hawker Aircraft Company.

1912 German professor H. Reissner (b. 1874) adopts corrugated aluminum wings, without fabric covering, in his canard-type (tail-first) monoplane. This anticipates the cantilevered (supported on one end only) aluminum wing of Hugo Junkers.

1912 The first single-seat scout airplane, the British Farnborough *B.S. 1* biplane, flies successfully. Designed by Geoffrey de Havilland (1882—1965), this airplane is the direct ancestor of every subsequent scout and fighter plane.

1912 A.D.

First scout plane flies

1912 Newly-invented gyroscopic autopilot invented by American Elmer A. Sperry (1860—1930) is successfully demonstrated on a Curtiss seaplane. Improved and refined over the years, gyroscope-based systems have become an integral part of every aircraft's operating system.

1912 First diesel locomotive is an experimental, direct-drive, 1000-hp Diesel-Klose-Sulzer unit built in Germany. It runs for only a few months.

1912 Japanese automobile manufacturing company Nissan has its origins in the founding of the Kwaishinsha Motor Car Works of Tokyo. Its cars are named DAT, taken from the first initials of the three men involved (Den, Aoyama, Takeuchi). Their 1931 car is named the son of DAT, and Datson becomes the name of the new car and the new company as well. Next they change it to Datsun and then finally to Nissan Motor Company Ltd. in 1934. They become the second largest car maker in Japan, finding an enormously receptive market in the United States.

1912 The Morris Oxford, popularly known as the "bull-nose" Morris, is built by William R. Morris (1877—1963) of Oxford, England. The small two-seater has a four cylinder, water-cooled engine and serves as Britain's answer to the Model T until the more popular Austin Seven comes along. (See 1922)

1912 Electric vehicles reach their high point of production and acceptance in the United States. From now on, they will decline and virtually disappear in favor of the gasoline-powered car.

1912 A.D.

*Japanese
taxi business
begins*

1912 First taxicab business in Japan begins operations with six Ford automobiles.

1912 New Mexico State Highway Commission is first organized.

1912 Kentucky Department of Highways is first organized.

1912 Use of sound waves for underwater detection of objects is investigated by English physicists John W. S. Rayleigh (1842—1919) and Lewis F. Richardson (1881—1953). Richardson seeks a way to locate submerged icebergs, following the *Titanic* disaster. His work leads to the development of sonar, or "sound navigation and ranging." (See 1917)

1912 Brazil opens the Madeira-Mamoro Railway, 255 miles of track built to transport its Amazon rubber to market. It takes six years and 6,000 lives to build it, but will soon become useless as the market for natural rubber falls.

1912 February 22 First large, ocean-going ship to be propelled by an internal combustion engine (four-stroke, single-acting diesel engine), the Danish *Selandia*, makes its maiden voyage.

1912 March The first seaplane meet is held in Monaco. Seven pilots attend, all on biplanes, and first prize is won by Fischer, flying a *Henri Farman*.

1912 March 23 German rocket pioneer Wernher von Braun (1912—1977) is born in Wirsitz, Germany. Inspired while young by the ideas of space travel, he began serious rocket research after receiving his Ph.D. in 1934 from the University of Berlin. He had joined the German Rocket Society in 1930 and eventually began rocket work as a civilian for the German army. By the time war broke out, he was one of Germany's most influential rocket pioneers and was working at Peenemünde under the command of Walter Dornberger (1895—1980). There he developed the V-2 rocket which was used as a terror weapon late in the war. He surrendered to the Americans along with his large staff, and accompanied scores of V-2 rockets to the United States. He and his team were set up in Huntsville, Alabama and he became chief of the U.S. Army ballistic weapon team. It was this team that launched the first U.S. satellite, *Explorer 1*, on January 31, 1958. He went on to become the driving force behind the massive Saturn V launch vehicle used to send Americans to the moon. He died after leaving NASA (National Aeronautics and Space Administration) for private industry.

1912 April 10 Largest ship of its time, the British *Titanic*, leaves Southampton, England for New York on its maiden voyage. Already named "unsinkable" at the time of its launching, this mammoth ship is 882 feet (269 meters) long and has a double bottom subdivided by 15 transverse bulkheads. Carrying 1,316 passengers and a crew of 891, it is 300 miles (483 kilometers) southeast of Newfoundland when its hull hits a 100-foot (30.5-meter) iceberg on April 14. The collision is so gentle that few take note, but five of its six watertight compartments on the starboard (right) side are ripped open, and the ship is doomed. Carrying an insufficient number of lifeboats to save everyone (although it actually has more than it is legally bound to stow), the ship sinks slowly, killing 1,502 still aboard. Only 705 people are saved. Following the tragedy, new lifeboat regulations are passed and an International Ice Patrol is established.

1914 ■ Transverse (amidship) section of the *Titanic*.

1912 April 16 First woman to fly across the English Channel is Harriet Quimby (1884—1912). She flies from Deal, England to Cape Gris-Nez in a Blériot monoplane. (See July 1, 1912)

1912 May 1 As a result of *Titanic* disaster, U.S. federal inspectors mandate that all steamships must carry enough lifeboats to hold all passengers.

1912 July 1 First woman pilot to be killed is Harriet Quimby (1884—1912) in Boston, Massachusetts.

1912 August First enclosed cabin airplanes fly at the Military Trials in England. Built by the Avro Company, the Avro cabin monoplane and Avro cabin

biplane have the pilot sitting inside. The company's founder is Englishman Alliot Verdon Roe (1877—1958).

1912 September 6 Proposal for a transcontinental U.S. highway, called the Lincoln Highway, is made by Carl G. Fisher (1874—1939) to a group of automobile manufacturers. They form the Lincoln Highway Association in 1913 and become an effective lobbying group to focus attention on this growing national transportation need.

1912 September 28 Japanese steamer *Kiche Maru* sinks off the Japan coast with a loss of approximately 1,000 lives.

1912 ■ Panama Canal under construction as Culebra cut is dug.

1912 November 12 First successful catapult launch of a seaplane is made at the Washington (D.C.) Navy Yard. Catapulted by a compressed air system from an anchored barge, the float-plane is a Curtiss *A-1* and the pilot is Lt. T. Ellyson (1885—1928).

1913 The improved French monoplane *Monocoque Deperdussin* first flies and breaks the world's speed record three times during this year, the best being 126.67 mph (203.86 km/h). This classic, streamlined-looking aircraft appears very modern.

1913 The Avro 504 two-seater biplane first flies in England, and becomes one of the world's outstanding trainers, over 10,000 being built into the 1930s.

1913 First large multi-engined airplane flies. Russian engineer Igor Sikorsky (1889—1972) builds

*1912
Sept. 6*

Transcontinental U.S. highway proposed

1913 A.D.

French monoplane breaks speed record

and flies a four-engined biplane, *Bolshoi*, in St. Petersburg, Russia. This precursor aircraft has no precedent, and is revolutionary in size (span of 92½ feet or 28 meters), power (four 100-hp Argus engines), and capacity (its cabin holds six passengers who can sit on armchairs or a sofa). This large airplane directly inspires the German Zeppelin to later design airplanes on this large scale.

1913 Idaho Department of Highways is first organized.

1913 First diesel locomotive in regular service is a diesel-electric train that runs in Sweden.

1913 National Automobile Chamber of Commerce is organized in the United States. Later it becomes the Automobile Manufacturers Association.

1913 Buenos Aires, Argentina subway system first opens.

1913 Henry Ford sets up his first assembly line production of Model T cars and pays his workers an unheard of $5 day. Using a system adapted from the meat packer's conveyer belt system, Ford revolutionizes the manufacture of automobiles and soon turns out 1,000 cars a day.

1913 A.D.

Model T assembly line begins

1913 South Dakota Department of Highways is first organized.

1913 Missouri State Highway Commission is first organized.

1913 A.D.

Installment payment plan used for cars

1913 Installment plan is first used in San Francisco, California to sell automobiles. This is a loan payment plan that allows the buyer to purchase a car "on time" by making specified payment amounts over a certain period of time. It has become the standard method of car-buying in the United States today.

1913 West Virginia State Road Commission is first organized.

1913 Orgeon State Highway Commission is first organized.

1913 Wire wheels are introduced as standard equipment on several cars. Their hub and rim are linked by radiating wire spokes that help support the outer wheel surface.

1913 Longest railroad tunnel in India is begun. Called the Parsik Tunnel, it is 4,322 feet long and has double track. It is on the Bombay-Kalyan line.

1913 First free U.S. road maps are distributed by the Gulf Oil Company. This smart policy encourages Americans to take to the road in their cars. Now that everyone is on the road, the maps are no longer free.

1913 North Dakota State Highway commission is first organized.

1913 Nebraska Department of Roads, Bureau of Highways, is first organized.

1913 Montana State Highway Commission is first organized.

1913 Arkansas State Highway Department is first organized.

1913 Grand Central Station opens at 42nd Street in New York City. This major facility will serve as the terminal for New York Central and New York, New Haven, and Hartford passenger trains.

1913 June Grover C. Loening (1888—1976), the first person in the United States to write a thesis on aeronautics for a university degree, is hired by the Wright Company as an engineer.

1913 June Jerome C. Hunsaker (1886—1984) is detailed to Massachusetts Institute of Technology by Secretary of the Navy Daniels, to develop courses in aerodynamics. He becomes an innovative aeronautical engineer and later chairman of the U.S. National Advisory Committee for Aeronautics from 1941 to 1957.

1913 June 18 First liner to exceed 50,000 gross tons, the German *Imperator*, goes into service. The largest ship in the world at this time, it becomes a Cunard liner named *Berengaria* after World War I.

1913 June 21 First woman to make a parachute jump from an airplane is Georgia "Tiny" Broadwick. The 18-year-old American descends 1,000 feet over Los Angeles, California.

1913 July 19 Skywriting by airplane, a new form of advertising, is introduced over the skies of Seattle, Washington by Milton J. Bryant.

1913 August 6 First fatal air crash in Canada occurs as John B. Bryant crashes his Curtiss aircraft in British Columbia.

1913 August 19 First parachute jump from an airplane in Europe is made by Frenchman Adolphe Pégoud (1889—1915) from a Blériot monoplane.

1913 August 23 First U.S. post-road project begins construction in Alabama. This and other new roads are made possible by the Post Office Appropriation Bill of 1912 which revives the intensive construction of roads on a nationwide scale using U.S. Treasury funds.

1913 August 27 First loop-the-loop is performed by Lt. Petr Nikolaevich Nesterov of the Imperial Russian Army on a Nieuport Type IV monoplane in Kiev, Russia. This complete circle and other intentional acrobatic stunts prove to be valuable experience for the wartime maneuvers needed during aerial battles.

1913 October 9 Franklin D. Roosevelt (1882—1945), acting secretary of the Navy, appoints Capt. Charles W. I. Chambers to draw plans for the organization of a Naval Aeronautic Service.

1913 November K. M. Turner (b. 1859) develops the "aviaphone" or "airophone," making communication possible between pilot and passengers during flight.

1913 November 29—29 December Jules Védrines (1881—1919) flies long-distance from Nancy, France to Cairo, Egypt (via Prague, Vienna, Belgrade, Sofia, Constantinople, and Tripoli). He stops many times in his Blériot monoplane and covers 2,500 miles (c. 4000 kilometers).

1914 First use of flaps are made by the Royal Aircraft Factory's Farnborough *S.E.4* biplane in England. The flaps are movable, often hinged, surfaces that can be changed to provide more lift or more drag.

1914 The U.S. firm Indian offers a motorcycle with an advanced electrical system that powers all the lighting and ignition and turns the engine over for starting as well.

1914 First use of a radio in railroad communication is made.

1914 Gasoline pumps are barred from their curbside locations in Detroit, Michigan.

1914 First American high-speed V-8 automobile engine is the water-cooled powerplant offered by the Cadillac Company. It is rated at 60 hp and is considered by many of its time to be the ultimate engine.

1914 A.D.
V-8 engine first used in cars

1914 First use of a STOP sign is made in Detroit, Michigan.

1914 First electric automobile traffic light is introduced in Cleveland, Ohio.

1914 A.D.
Electric traffic light first used

1914 Houston Ship canal opens to traffic. This 50-mile-long canal gives the city of Houston, Texas an outlet to Galveston Bay on the Gulf of Mexico and makes it a major U.S. deep-water port.

1914 Europe adopts "aquaplaning" or being towed on a board behind a motorboat. It is called planking or plank-gliding in England, where regular contests are held.

1914 January Igor Sikorsky's (1889—1972) four-engine, cabined biplane, *Ilya Mouriametz*, an improved version of his *Bolshoi*, first flies in Russia. Able to carry 16 people, it will make about 400 bombing sorties during World War I.

1914 January Permanent U.S. Naval Aeronautical Center, with Lt. John H. Towers (1885—1955) in command, is established in Pensacola, Florida. Nine airplanes are assigned to the base.

1914 January 1 U.S. Weather Bureau begins daily publication of a weather map of the Northern Hemisphere designed specifically as an aid to aviation.

1914 January 13 Legal suit by Wright brothers begun in 1909 against Glenn H. Curtiss (1878—1930) is decided in their favor by U.S. Circuit Court of Appeals of New York. The decision recognizes the

1914 ■ Glenn Curtiss' flying boat *America* takes off from Lake Keuka, New York.

Wright patent as a pioneer patent entitled to very broad interpretation.

**1914
January 15

*Passenger
airline
service
begins***

1914 January 15 First regularly scheduled passenger airline in the United States begins service. The Benoist Company, flying its Benoist flying boat, runs a line between St. Petersburg and Tampa, Florida (22 miles or 35 kilometers). The business lasts four months.

1914 February 11—13 Distance record for balloons over land is set by H. Berliner, who flies 1,890 miles (c. 3,040 kilometers) from Bitterfeldt, Germany to Kirgischano, Russia.

**1914 July 7

*Goddard
receives
rocket patent***

1914 July 7 American physics professor Robert H. Goddard (1882—1945) receives a patent for his two-stage solid fuel rocket. (*See 1917*)

1914 July 28 World War I (1914—1918) begins with Austria-Hungary, Germany, and Turkey opposed by Russia, France, Great Britain and later the United States. Although Germany and Great Britain have two of the greatest battle fleets in the world, surface warships prove less significant than submarines. With the defeat of Germany on November 11, 1918, the bulk of its ships are sold to pay for reparations under the terms of the Versailles Treaty.

1914 July 29 Cape Cod Canal, cut through the Cape Cod, Massachusetts peninsula, officially opens. This short-cut which was considered by the 17th century colonists, reduces the distance between New York and Boston by 70 miles.

1914 August 15 Panama Canal, linking the Atlantic and Pacific Oceans, officially opens. Built across the Isthmus of Panama by American engineer George Washington Goethals (1858—1928), it is really three major engineering projects in one. First an enormous dam is built to control the Chagras River and create a lake; next a deep cut is made through the hill whose top is the Continental Divide; and then giant locks are built at each end of the canal to move ships up and down the 85 feet. It takes about eight years of work to complete this massive, 51.2-mile (85-kilometer) canal. The minimum channel depth is 37 feet (11.3 meters) and the width is 300 feet (91 meters). There are six sets of double locks, three at each end, and each lock is 1,000 feet long. Ships run under their own power except in the locks, where they are towed by electric locomotives. Like the Suez Canal, the Panama Canal saves tremendous distances for ships— nearly 6,000 miles are cut off a journey from England to California; nearly 8,000 miles from a trip from New York to San Francisco; and over 10,000 from San Francisco to the Strait of Gibraltar.

1914 August 26 First aerial ramming in combat occurs as Russian Capt. P. N. Nesterov brings down an attacking Austrian aircraft by ramming it with his unarmed Morane *Type M* monoplane. Both pilots are killed.

1914 August 30 Paris, France becomes the first capital to be bombed by an airplane. German Lt. Ferdinand von Hidessen flies a Rumpler *Taube*, a monoplane with swept-back bird-like wings, over the city.

1914 September First U.S. tactical air unit, the First Aero Squadron, is organized because of the August outbreak of war in Europe. Based in San Diego, California, the unit has 16 officers, 77 enlisted men, and eight airplanes.

1914 September 16 Canadian Aviation Corps is authorized to be formed by the Minister of Militia and Defence. This is the beginning of Canada's military air force.

1914 October 5 First aircraft to be shot down by another is the German two-seater *Aviatik* over Jonchery, Reims in France by Sgt. Joseph Frantz and Cpl. Quénault in a Voisin *Escadrille VB 24*. They use a Hotchkiss machine-gun.

1915 Thermostatic control of the cooling system is introduced by Cadillac. This system uses a temperature-activated valve to control coolant flow according to its temperature.

1915 Tennessee Department of Highways is first organized.

1915 Florida State Road Department is first organized.

1915 Placement of the spare tire in a car's trunk is introduced by the American Franklin car.

1915 Tilt-beam headlights are first offered by Cadillac.

1915 Otis Elevator Company in the United States develops the Micro-drive, a self-levelling device for elevators. This new feature greatly reduces the tripping hazard for passengers as they step off.

1915 North Carolina State Highway Commission is first organized.

1915 Automobile innovations include aluminum pistons and torsional vibration dampers. Pistons made of aluminum are lightweight, easily machined, and resistant to corrosion. The damper minimizes the twisting and untwisting action developed in a shaft when loads are applied.

1915 First American 12-cylinder automobile engine and the first to have aluminum pistons is the Packard Twin Six (V12) model. Built by the innovative Jesse G. Vincent, it becomes the car of choice for such prominent personalities as Russian Czar Nicholas II (1868—1918) and the Maharajah of India. Packard showrooms are forced to remain open 24 hours a day to accommodate crowds wanting to see this grand car.

1915 American physics professor Robert H. Goddard (1882—1945) proves the validity of his rocket propulsion principles in a vacuum test at Clark University, Worcester, Massachusetts.

1915 Oil fuel begins to replace coal for boilers in the ships of England's battle fleet.

1915 Hawaiian Olympic Games swimming champion Duke Paoa Kahanamoku (1890—1968) introduces surfboard riding to Australia. His international reputation and association with surfing inspires many to take up the sport.

1915 January 15 Joint U.S. Congressional Committee reports that Federal aid for road improvement would accomplish several Constitutional objectives: establish post roads, regulate commerce, provide for the common defense, and promote the general welfare. This leads to the Federal Aid Road Act of 1916. (See July 11, 1916)

1915 January 19 First Zeppelin raid on Britain occurs as three German Navy rigid airship Zeppelins drop bombs on four cities. During the war, Zeppelins make 53 bombing raids on Britain, in which 556 people are killed, but with no real strategic effect. England responds with blackouts of cities, anti-aircraft guns, and aircraft attacks.

1915 February 4 Germany declares the waters around Great Britain and Ireland, including the English Channel, to be a war zone. It states that all British shipping would be sunk by U-boats on sight, and that the safety of neutrals could not be guaranteed because of the difficulty of identifying flags at a distance as well as the British practice of running up neutral flags when necessary. Both Germany and England argue that they have international law on their side. (See May 7, 1915)

1915 March 3 The National Advisory Committee for Aeronautics (NACA) is established by an Act of Congress, "to supervise and direct the scientific

1915 A.D.
Surfboarding introduced in Australia

1915 January 19
Zeppelins drop bombs

1915 ■ *Lusitania* prior to sinking.

study of the problems of flight, with a view of their practical solution." Until its functions are transferred to the National Aeronautics and Space Administration (NASA) in 1958, this body functions as the major government aeronautical research body in the United States.

1915 March 31 Work begins in Oregon on the first major highway tunnel in the United States. Called Mitchell's Point Tunnel or Storm Cliff Tunnel, it is excavated from solid rock and resembles an elongated cave opening. It has a domed or rounded ceiling and five side openings or windows, each 16 feet wide, making a magnificent scenic drive. Its only man-made elements are the masonry railings across the windows.

1915 April 1 Era of the true fighter airplane begins as French pilot Roland Garros (1888—1918) shoots down a German Albatros by firing through the propeller of his Moranie-Saulnier monoplane. This is accomplished by using metal deflector plates, invented by Raymond Saulnier, on the blades. The Germans discover this secret when they later capture Garros's downed plane, and it is Anthony H. G. Fokker (1890—1939) who improves on it with his interrupter gear or synchronized firing device.

1915 May 7

Germans sink Lusitania

1915 May 7 Cunard liner *Lusitania* is sunk off the coast of Ireland by a single torpedo from the German *U20* submarine. After being struck squarely amidships, the liner sinks within 20 minutes of a huge second explosion. Nearly 1,200 people are killed and world opinion turns solidly against this mistaken German policy of attacking civilian vessels. Despite this, submarines will prove a major weapon for both sides in this war and the next.

1915 May 22 Worst rail disaster in Britain occurs near Carlisle, Scotland. A signalling error allows a military train to collide with a standing train, and less than one minute later, an express train coming from the other direction plows into the wreckage, totalling 227 people killed.

1915 May 31 First Zeppelin airship is destroyed in the air. Zeppelin *LZ-37* is bombed by a British aircraft over Ghent, Belgium.

1915 June 24 One of the worst maritime disasters in U.S. history occurs without the ship ever leaving shore. As the Great Lakes excursion ship *Eastland* takes on 1,000 passengers for a pleasure trip on Lake Michigan and prepares to leave the dock, it starts to lean badly to one side. When the ship rolls completely on its side, it kills 812 people, among which are 22 entire families.

1915 July 10 U.S. Naval Aeronautic Section, Pensacola, Florida, tests a sextant (an instrument used to navigate by the stars) equipped with a pendulum-type artificial horizon and reports that this type is unsatisfactory for aircraft use, but that a sextant with a gyroscopically stabilized artificial horizon might be acceptable.

1915 July 16 First warships to pass through Panama Canal are American vessels *Missouri, Ohio,* and *Wisconsin.* All three make a successful canal passage during U.S. fleet maneuvers.

1915 August 1 First Allied aircraft is shot down over Douai in France by a German Fokker *Eindecker*

1 using a synchronized gun and propeller invented by Fokker.

1915 October William Edward Boeing (1881—1956) becomes interested in aeronautics and enters Glenn L. Martin's school in California for flying lessons. Boeing later founds the Boeing Airplane Company, a firm specializing in large commercial and military aircraft.

1915 November 6 First catapult launching of an airplane from a moving ship is made from the *USS North Carolina* in Pensacola, Florida.

1915 November 6 Largest reinforced-concrete bridge, the Tunkhannock Viaduct, opens to traffic. This railroad bridge in Nicholson, Pennsylvania consists of ten 180-foot-high arches. Over 162,000 cubic yards of concrete are used as well as 2,275,000 pounds of reinforcing steel. The 245-foot-high, 2,375-foot-long viaduct is still in use today.

1915 December First successful all-metal, fully cantilever-wing airplane, the *J-1* monoplane, flies in Dessau, Germany. Built by German designer Hugo Junkers (1859—1935), the cantilever wings of this revolutionary, iron-and-steel airplane are supported at the base only, and have no external bracing.

1915 December 9 First technical report issued by NACA is Report No. 1, a two-part *Report on Behavior of Aeroplanes in Gusts* by Jerome Hunsaker (b. 1886) and E. B. Wilson of the Massachusetts Institute of Technology.

1916 Loughead Aircraft Manufacturing Company is formed by the British Loughead brothers who change the company's name to Lockheed after World War I. Following business difficulties, it is reformed in 1926 and builds the pre-war Model-14, the fastest airliner of its day. During World War II, its *P-38 Lightning* fighter is one of the most important planes, serving successfully in every major combat theater for the British. In 1943, its *Constellation* becomes a popular airplane with passenger airlines, but its contemporary wide-bodied *Tristar* does not fare as well.

1916 Radio-controlled pilotless monoplane called the *Aerial Target* flies at the British Royal Aircraft Establishment in Farnborough. H. P. Folland designs the plane and A. M. Low is responsible for the radio gear.

1916 The supercharger is successfully adapted to airplane engines at the Royal Aircraft Factory in Farnborough, England. This is a pump or compressor that forces more air or fuel-air mixture into an engine. It allows an aircraft engine to maintain its power at high altitudes where the air is thinner.

1916 First mechanical (hand-operated) windshield wipers are introduced in America. One of the earliest is on the enclosed Willys-Knight. This two-seater has a high body design and large windows for unusually good visibility.

1916 A.D.
Mechanical windshield wipers introduced

1916 German automobile manufacturing company BMW is founded originally as the Bayerische Flugzeug Werke to make aircraft engines. In 1922, the name is changed to Bayerische Motoren Werke, and the first BMW motorcycle is built in 1923. Production of the first true BMW car starts in 1932. Today, it produces precision-built cars with sporty lines.

1916 Motorized scooter called an "autoped" appears on some American streets. This is a two-wheel vehicle that resembles a child's scooter which the user pushes with one foot and then stands upon with two while holding the handle bars.

1916 A.D.
Motorized scooter appears

1916 Mississippi State Highway Commission is first organized.

1916 Renault taxicabs from Paris are commandeered to rush French troops to the Marne River to stop the German advance during World War I. These four-cylinder, 30-hp cars have ever since been called "Taxis de la Marne."

1916 Georgia State Highway Department is first organized.

1916 U.S. Federal Maritime Commission originates with the passage of the Shipping Act of 1916 which creates the U.S. Shipping Board. This body is given jurisdiction over U.S.-flag shipping companies in interstate or foreign commerce and on the Great Lakes. The original Act provides a way to regulate against "cut-throat" competition. The Shipping Act of 1984 modernizes its regulations in an attempt to revitalize the liner segment of the U.S. maritime industry and to permit it to compete more effectively with foreign carriers.

1916 Italian G. Galansimo demonstrates his Hydro-Ski Risso on a lake in France. By swinging his feet while standing atop two torpedo-like cylinders, he turns the blades of a water-vane or paddle and moves himself forward.

1916 Heaviest bridge, the Hell Gate Bridge crossing the East River in New York, is completed. Designed by Gustav Lindenthal (1850—1935), the arch for this enormous bridge has to be cantilevered out from both sides until joined. Besides being the heaviest bridge, it also has the strongest steel arch ever built (capable of carrying a live load on its railroad tracks of 22,000 pounds per foot (32,400 kilograms per meter) of its length.

1916 February 12 U.S. Post Office Department issues its first air mail advertisement, inviting bids for carrying the mail by airplane in Massachusetts and Alaska.

1916 February 14 Longest tunnel in Argentina opens. This single-line freight-only railroad goes under the city of Buenos Aires and is about three miles (4.8 kilometers) long.

1916 April First air-to-air combat rockets are used by French aviators against German Zeppelins. Four Le Prieur rockets are attached to each strut of the French Nieuport fighters which down a German hydrogen-filled Zeppelin *LC-77*.

1916 July 11

Federal Aid Road Act signed

1916 July 11 Federal Aid Road Act is signed by President Woodrow Wilson (1856—1924). Intended to coordinate the main interstate roads of the nation, this law is the first comprehensive act of the federal government aimed at the establishment of a nationwide system of interstate highways. The commonly-experienced difficulties of driving from one state with good roads into another with unimproved roads forces a national solution to the problem.

1916 September 12 First pilotless radio-controlled aerial bomb is tested in the United States. Designed by Lawrence B. Sperry (1893—1923) and built by Glenn H. Curtiss (1878—1912), it is actually a small biplane that can fly radio-guided for 50 miles (c. 80 kilometers) with 308 pounds (c. 140 kilograms) of bombs. It is the ancestor of the World War II German *V-1 Flying Bomb* and the contemporary U.S. cruise missile.

1916 October 5 National Advisory Committee for Aeronautics (NACA) first recommends the inauguration of air mail service.

1916 December 6 Longest tunnel in Canada, the Connaught Tunnel in the Selkirk Mountains on the Canadian Pacific Railway, opens. This double-track tunnel is over five miles (8,083 meters) long. (See 1984)

1917 Kansas State Highway Commission is first organized.

1917 Push-button electric gear selector, known as the Cutler-Hammer Magnetic Gear Shift, is introduced on Premier touring car models. It is a solenoid-operated, semi-automatic system. A solenoid is a heavy duty electromagnetic switch which remains closed only as long as the current passes through its coil.

1917 Nevada Department of Highways is first organized.

1917 Delaware State Highway Department is first organized.

1917 Texas State Highway Department is first organized.

1917 South Carolina State Highway Department is first organized.

1917 Steel disc wheels for automobiles first appear. Built in the shape of a disc, their drop center rim design allows lower pressure tires to be used. Today's auto wheels still use this rim concept for keeping the tires on the wheel.

1917 Wyoming State Highway Department is first organized.

1917 Japanese automobile manufacturing company Mitsubishi is founded. It builds trucks and aircraft for some time, and in 1959 begins a line of small economy cars. It greatly expands in 1965, and today is a major Japanese automaker.

1917 American rocket engineering pioneer Robert H. Goddard (1882—1945) receives a $5,000 research grant from the Smithsonian Institution to continue his research on the problems of rocket propulsion.

1917 French physicist Paul Langevin (1872—1946) succeeds in using sound waves or an acoustical echo as an underwater detector. His system uses piezo-electricity to create ultrasonic waves. This employs the principle that certain sound vibrations can cause an electrical effect. By World War II, the system called "sonar" (sound navigation and ranging) is perfected. Modern sonar, which employs a transducer (a device that converts energy from one form to another), is used for mapping ocean bottoms and fish or wreck location as well as submarine detection.

1917 New railroad warning sign, "Stop-Look-Listen," is first used in Seattle, Washington to replace the less insistent, "Watch for Engines" in common use.

1917 Draeger designs a self-contained diving system consisting of a backpack containing a mixture of compressed air and oxygen which is recirculated over a carbon dioxide scrubber and connected to a diving helmet. Called the DM-40 system, it allows a diver to descend to 125 feet (40 meters) for extended periods entirely free from a surface air supply.

1917 Trolley car ridership in the United States reaches 11 billion passengers riding on some 80,000 electric streetcars. Connecting lines make it possible to ride from New York to Boston, Massachusetts.

1917 Electrically-operated ship's log—device by which a ship's speed and distance covered can be calculated—is developed by B. Chernikoff of the Russian Navy. A small rotator attached to the ship's bottom drives an electrical transmitter connected to recording apparatus carried onboard.

c. 1917 Earliest diver propulsion vehicle is designed and built by Italians Raffaele Rossetti and Raffaele Paolucci, who use an underwater "chariot" to attach a bomb and sink the Austrian battleship *Viribus Unitis* at Pula Harbor in Yugoslavia during World War I. The vehicle that propels them underwater is powered by compressed air. After planting the bomb, the men discover that the ship has already been captured by the Allies. Although they board the ship, warning of the bomb, it explodes. They escape, but several men, including the captain, are killed.

1917 February 13 Aircraft Manufacturers Association is formed with Frank H. Russell as its first president.

1917 March American Short Line Railroad Association is organized.

1917 April 6 United States declares war on Germany. There are 35 American pilots in the Signal Corps, 38 in the Navy, and 10 in the Marines.

1917 April 30 Pacific Aero Products Company changes its name to Boeing Airplane Company, with William E. Boeing (1881—1956) as its president.

1917 May 20 First sinking of a submarine by an aircraft occurs when the German *U-36* is sunk in the North Sea by a British flying boat.

1917 June 5 First organized unit of U.S. naval aviators lands in Bordeaux, France. It is comprised of six officers and 63 enlisted men.

1917 June 13 First heavy daylight raid on London is made by 14 German *Gotha* two-engine airplanes, none of which are shot down.

1917 June 13

Two-engine planes raid London

1917 July Between this month and the time the armistice is signed (November 11, 1918) ending the war, 13,943 airplanes are manufactured in the United States under the cross-licensing agreement of the recently-formed Aircraft Manufacturers Association.

1917 July 1 School of Aeronautics is formed at the University of Toronto in Canada.

1917 August National Advisory Committee for Aeronautics (NACA) recommends that funds be given to the U.S. Weather Bureau in order to promote safety in aerial navigation.

1917 October 22　Trans-Australian Railway opens between Kalgoorlie and Port Augusta. The entire line is 1,052 miles (1,693 kilometers), and during one stretch on the Nullarbor Plain, it includes the longest run of dead-straight tracks (over 300 miles) in the world.

1917 December 6

Munitions ship explodes in Halifax

1917 December 6　Munitions ship carrying TNT, the *Mont Blanc*, explodes in Halifax, Nova Scotia harbor after colliding with Belgian relief ship *Imo*. Twenty minutes after the collision and fire, an explosion levels half of Halifax (an area of about 2.5 square miles), killing 1,266, injuring twice as many, and leaving 400 people blinded. The force of the explosion creates a small tidal wave and is heard 60 miles away. Things worsen as the next day brings a severe blizzard which prevents any help from reaching the city for days.

1917 December 12　Worst railroad disaster in terms of casualties is believed to have occurred on the Mount Cenis Tunnel route in the Alpine region of southeastern France. A train heavily overloaded with soldiers returning home for Christmas runs out of control on a steep grade and derails at a wooden bridge on a sharp curve. The cars pile up and catch fire. Although the deaths are officially announced at 543, most estimates place the grim total much higher.

1918 A.D.

GM develops ethyl gas

1918　Ethyl gasoline is developed by General Motors Laboratories. This is a fluid additive put into gasoline that reduces engine knocking by slowing down the air/fuel burn rate. As a lead compound however, it is found to be a harmful and toxic contaminant and is no longer allowed in gasoline.

1918　First practical Anti-Submarine Detection Indicator Chart (ASDIC) is developed by French physicist Paul Langevin (1872—1944). This is essentially an echo-sounding device.

1918　First boat powered by an airplane engine that drives an immersed propeller is the American-made *Miss Detroit III*. Soon, all power racing boats will have similar engines.

1918　Fruehoff Trailer Company is founded by blacksmith-wagonmaker August Fruehoff of Detroit, Michigan. It will become the largest maker of tractor trailer trucks in the world.

1918　First armored car for commercial use is employed by Brink's, Inc., of Chicago, Illinois. Used to transport cash, it is a standard vehicle covered with armor-plate steel.

1918　First use of a parachute from an airplane in warfare is made by Capt. Sarrat of the French Air Force.

1918 January　National Advisory Committee for Aeronautics establishes the Office of Aeronautical Intelligence to collect and distribute scientific and technical data on aeronautics.

1918 February 28　Regulation of the airways begins as U.S. President Woodrow Wilson (1856—1924) issues an order requiring licenses for civilian airplane pilots or owners. Over 800 licenses are issued.

1918 March　First Canadian magazine devoted to aeronautics, *Aviation News*, is published in Toronto. It soon becomes *Aviation & Wireless News*.

1918 March 19　First operational flights are made by U.S. airplanes in France.

1918 April 21　The Red Baron, German Rittmeister Manfred von Richthofen (1892—1918), also called the Ace of Aces, is shot down in action over France by Canadian Capt. A. Roy Brown (b. 1893). Richthofen was credited with 80 aerial victories.

1918 May 2　General Motors Corporation buys the Chevrolet Motor Company.

1918 May 15　First regular air mail service begins with regular flights between Washington, D.C. and New York City. It is operated by the U.S. Army Signal Corps.

1918 May 28　American Railroad Express Company is organized under federal supervision by an enforced merger of the Adams, American, Southern Express, and Wells-Fargo Companies. The government justifies this as a necessary wartime move to improve the shipment of war goods and supplies.

1918 June 24 First air mail in Canada is flown from Montreal to Toronto.

1918 July 9 Two trains collide head-on in Nashville, Tennessee, killing 101 and injuring 171. The accident is caused by an inbound local train running a stop signal and entering the same track as an outbound express traveling 60 mph.

1918 July 28—August 8 First flight from England to Egypt is made by Major A. S. MacLaren and Brig. Gen. A. E. Borton flying a *Handley Page O/400.*

1918 September 10 First time the mail is delivered from Chicago, Illinois to New York in one day. Actual flying time is 10 hours, five minutes.

1918 November 2 New York subway accident kills 97 and injures 100 as a train jumps a track at 30 mph. It is driven by a supervisor because the motormen are on strike. The train is speeding when it crashes.

1918 November 27 U.S. Navy's giant new seaplane, *NC-1,* carries an unheard-of number of passengers when it flies from Rockaway, New York with 50 men on board. This new class of plane flies across the Atlantic, with stops, in 1919. **(See May 16, 1919)**

1918 December By the end of the war, Germany drops a total of 275 tons of bombs on Britain by Zeppelin and airplane. Britain drops 5,000 tons of bombs on Germany during 1918.

1918 December 8 With the end of World War I, the United States removes an anti-submarine device from New York Harbor. A huge steel net had been stretched underwater across the harbor narrows.

1918 December 13—January 16, 1919 First flight from England to India is made by A. S. MacLaren, Halley, and McEwen in a Handley Page *V-1500* four-engined bomber.

1919 German Hugo Junkers (1859—1935) invents auxiliary aerofoil wing-flaps, making for improved control. Slotted flaps, which reduce turbulence, are developed by Englishman Frederick Handley Page (b. 1885) in 1919, and both types come into regular use in the late 1930s.

1919 Motorcycling industry in the United States barely exists as mass-produced American automobiles dominate the market. Only the firms of Indian and Harley-Davidson remain as substantial manufacturers. In England however, the motorcycle industry flourishes, with over 100 firms offering more than 200 different types of motorcycles.

1919 Indiana State Highway Commission is first organized.

1919 German firm Krupp builds a motorized scooter with front-wheel drive.

1919 World's first traffic light is installed in Detroit, Michigan.

1919 Studebaker Company is still making horse-drawn wagons alongside their cars and trucks.

1919 French automobile manufacturing company Citroen is founded by André Citroen (1878—1935). He and his company are at the forefront of popularizing the automobile. Although always at the forefront of auto technology, it also provided cheap, basic transportation with its classic 2 CV. One of the oldest car companies, it is still producing unconventional but excellent cars.

1919 The 3-liter Bentley debuts at the London Car Show and creates a sensation. Designed by British engineer Walter O. Bentley, it combines brute power and strength with elegance, and becomes identified with all that is smart and sporting. Called the "Red Label" model for its signature radiator color, it has four cylinders and can go 80 mph.

1919 First servo-assisted front-wheel braking is on the Type H6 Hispano-Suiza designed by Spanish-backed Swiss Marc Birkigt. A servo is a mechanism that supplements a person's efforts. In this case, it boosts the force they apply to the brakes.

1919 Mobile home trailer is invented by American aviation pioneer Glenn H. Curtiss (1878—1930). Curtiss designs and builds his own custom trailer, called the Aerocar, which is twice as long as his car and has four Pullman berths, a galley, closets, running water, and a telephone to the car pulling it. **(See 1929)**

1919 January 18 Following the end of World War I, the Paris Peace Conference opens. Among the terms presented to Germany in the Treaty of Versailles are very strict limitations on the building and use of powered aircraft. These limitations stimulate a renaissance of gliding and soaring activity in Germany, since it is unpowered and therefore legal. It gives Germany advantageous experience in aerodynamics and the efficient use of light materials. It also offers flight training experience to future German pilots.

1919 February 5 First civil airline for passengers with sustained, scheduled daily air service begins as German company Deutsche Luftreederei offers service between Berlin, Leipzig, and Weimar.

1919 February 8 First international passenger flight is made by French company Lignes Aériennes Farman, which flies 11 passengers from Paris to London in a Farman Goliath.

1919 February 25

First gas tax levied

1919 February 25 First gasoline tax levied by a U.S. state occurs in Oregon. It places a one-cent-a-gallon tax on all motor fuel and uses the funds for road maintenance and construction. (See June 21, 1932)

1919 February 26 President Woodrow Wilson (1856—1924) approves and submits to the House of Representatives recommendations of the National Advisory Committee for Aeronautics for legislation placing licensing and regulation of aviation in charge of the Department of Commerce.

1919 March 1 The RAF (Royal Air Force, formerly Royal Aircraft Factory) starts an air mail service from Folkestone, England to Cologne, Germany for its post-war occupation forces in the Rhineland.

1919 March 3 First international mail from Canada flies from Vancouver to Seattle, Washington.

1919 April 28 American Leslie Irvin (b. 1895) makes the first jump from an airplane using a free-type (to be opened at will by a rip chord) back-pack parachute and lands at McCook Field in Dayton, Ohio. The parachute is designed by Floyd Smith.

1919 May 6 First commercial flight, Canada to the United States, occurs as a Canadian Curtiss aircraft flies 150 pounds of raw furs from Toronto to Elizabeth, New Jersey. It is not a non-stop flight.

1919 May 15 U.S. Post Office Department begins its first air mail service operations between Chicago and Cleveland, later extended to New York and San Francisco. Carrying the mail is a De Havilland *D.H. 4-A.*

1919 May 16—27 First transatlantic flight is made in stages by the U.S. Navy's Curtiss *NC-4* seaplane flown by Lt. Cdr. A. C. Read (1887—1967) and his crew. Leaving from Trepassey Bay, Newfoundland, it flies to Plymouth, England, via two stops in the Azores and Lisbon, Spain. Three Navy seaplanes originally attempt the crossing, but one is damaged on landing in the Azores and another crashes at sea. The crew is rescued by a Greek steamer.

1919 May 26 American Robert H. Goddard (1882—1945) submits to the Smithsonian Institution his report, "A Method of Reaching Extreme Altitudes" (published in January 1920). This classic work in the literature of astronautical science demonstrates conclusively that rockets can be used to reach outer space. It also suggests that for dramatic effect and proof, a rocket carrying magnesium powder could be crashed on the moon, producing a flash visible from earth with a telescope.

1919 June 14—15 First direct non-stop crossing of the Atlantic by airplane is made by a British two-man team. Capt. John Alcock (1882—1919) and Lt. Arthur Whitten-Brown (1886—1948) fly a Vickers *Vimy* bomber from St. Johns, Newfoundland to Clifden, Ireland. They crash-land safely in a bog after flying some 1,950 miles in 16 hours, 27 minutes. This flight increases in the public's mind the importance of flying.

1919 July 2—13 First crossing of the Atlantic by airship, as well as the first double crossing (return flight), is made by the British rigid airship, *R-34.* This giant dirigible, which flies nonstop from Scotland to Long Island, New York, has a 30-man crew and is piloted by Maj. G. H. Scott. A dirigible is an alternative name for a steerable lighter-than-air aircraft with its own engine. It means literally "able to steer."

1919 July 21 Thirteen people are killed as a 158-foot-long dirigible crashes through the roof of a bank in Chicago, Illinois.

1919 August 20 First flight is made by Zeppelin *LX 120 Bodensee*, a small rigid airship built by the Germans after World War I for commercial use. It begins the first regularly scheduled passenger service by airship with its run between Friedrichshafen and Berlin from August to November 1919.

1919 August 25 First daily commercial scheduled international air passenger service starts between London and Paris. An Airco De Havilland *D.H. 4-A* flies from Hounslow to LeBourget in two-and-one-half hours. Single fare to Paris is 21 pounds.

1919 August 28 International Air Traffic Association (IATA) is formed at The Hague, Holland. It is the predecessor of the International Air Transport Association (IATA), the airlines association formed in 1945 for the economic control of international air transportation.

1919 September U.S. Navy Department announces that all U.S. battleships of first and second class are to be equipped with a seaplane which is to be launched by catapult.

1919 October 7 Dutch airline K. L. M. (Konninklijke Luftvarrt Maatschappij) is formed by Albert Plesman.

1919 October 13 International Convention for the Regulation of Air Navigation (ICAN) is signed in Paris. This reaffirms the principle of national sovereignty of airspace and establishes a Commission for Aerial Navigation under the League of Nations to regulate international air commerce.

1919 November 12—December 10 First flight from England to Australia is made by Ross (1892—1922), Keith Smith (1890—1955), and their crew in a Vickers *Vimy* bomber. They fly over 11,000 miles in 27 days, 20 hours.

1919 November 20 First municipal airport in the United States opens in Tucson, Arizona. It is still in use.

1920 Split wing-flaps are invented by Orville Wright (1871—1948) and J. M. Jacobs in the United States. These flaps, which come into widespread use in the mid-1930s, allow for slower and safer landing speeds since they preserve maximum lift at minimum speeds.

1920 First airplane with modern, fully-retractable under-carriage flies. The wheels of the American Dayton-Wright R.B. high-wing racing monoplane retract directly into the fuselage. This aids streamlining and cuts down on drag.

1920 Hawker Aircraft Company is formed as a successor to the Sopwith Aviation Company. It becomes a maker of fighter aircraft and its *Hurricane* fighters destroy more enemy aircraft in the Battle of Britain (1940) than all other RAF fighters. After World War II, it develops jet fighters and in 1963, becomes part of Hawker Siddeley Aviation.

1920 United States creates a national program of highway research to solve the deteriorating road problem created by heavy automobile use. Following a conference, the Highway Research Board of the National Research Council is organized to provide a clearinghouse and a forum for all branches of highway engineering.

1920 First long underwater tunnel in the United States designed specifically for automobiles, the Holland Tunnel, is begun. Consisting of twin tubes, each of which carries two lanes of traffic one way, it is finished in 1927 after solving new and serious ventilation problems concerning carbon monoxide. One tube is 8,557 feet and the other is 8,371 feet. It connects Manhattan, New York with Jersey City, New Jersey.

1920 U.S. Congress passes the Transportation Act of 1920 whose stated purpose is to promote an adequate national transportation system. It also relaxes some of the more stringent regulations against railroad competition.

1920 First rigid six-wheeler truck is made by American Goodyear Tire Company. This one-piece truck increases its load area by using three axles on a rigid chassis. Goodyear builds this vehicle to demonstrate their new, large pneumatic tires.

1920 A.D.

First six-wheeler truck made

1920—1922 American Robert H. Goddard (1882—1945) experiments with liquid oxygen and other liquid hydrocarbons, including gasoline, liquid propane, and ether for use as rocket fuels. He concludes that "the most practical combination appears to be liquid oxygen and gasoline."

1920 January Raymond Orteig (d. 1939), of Paris, France offers $25,000 through the Aero Club of America to the first pilot to make a nonstop flight from New York to Paris. It is this prize that helps Charles A. Lindbergh (1902—1974) persuade a group of St. Louis businessmen to give him financial backing for his attempt. Lindbergh collects the prize after making his historic flight in the *Spirit of St. Louis* on May 20—21, 1927.

1920 February 14—May 31 First flight from Rome, Italy, to Tokyo, Japan is made by two Italian airmen, Ferrarin and Masiero, who fly 12,000 miles (c. 19,300 kilometers) in two airplanes.

1920 April 27 First warrant in the United States for reckless aerial diving is issued against Omer Locklear (d. 1920) in Los Angeles, California.

1920 July 19 First flight of British rigid airship *Vickers R-80*, the first truly streamlined airship. Its design reflected important advances in aerodynamics. Lack of both military and civilian interest and confusion about the exact role of airships make the very fast *R-80* a little-used craft.

1920 August 2 Omer Locklear (d. 1920), aerial stuntman, is killed in a night flight in Los Angeles, California.

1920 August 15 First sustained soaring flight is made over a closed circuit in a slope lift (using ascending air currents that come up the lee or sheltered side of a hill). This sailplane is a *Weltensegler* built by German Frederic Wenk and flown over the Feldberg near Fribourg, Germany. The pilot is named Peschke.

1920 September 8 First transcontinental U.S. air mail service begins from New York to San Francisco.

1920 September 30 Forerunner of the modern, large, all-metal airliner, the *Zeppelin-Staaken E-4/20*, is completed in Germany. This four-engined, 18-passenger transport monoplane is designed by Adolf Rohrbach (1889—1939) and flies soon afterward. Despite all its advances, the Allies decree after the war that every E-4/20 must be destroyed.

1920 October Donald W. Douglas (1892—1981), formerly chief engineer at the Glenn L. Martin Company, organizes the Davis-Douglas Company. Douglas becomes, with Boeing, one of aviation's pioneers, building the "modern type" passenger airliners in 1933.

1920 October 31 The city of Toledo, Ohio is the recipient of leaflets dropped from airplanes on behalf of Socialist presidential candidate Eugene V. Debs (1855—1926).

1921 The first left-hand drive option by a British auto manufacturer is offered by the Lanchester Company on cars sold in the United States. American cars have the steering wheel and driver's seat on the left (the side that is closest to the middle of the road).

1921 Second longest double-track railroad tunnel, the Apennine Tunnel, is begun. This enormous, double-track tunnel is dug despite major flooding and eruptions of gas. It is finished in 1934 and its 11½ miles bore through the heart of the Apennine Mountains on the railroad line between Bologna and Florence, Italy.

c. 1920 ■ Work on street rails near the White House, Washington, D.C.

1921 Federal Highway Act of 1921 resolves the U.S. debate as to whether the federal government should construct a national system of highways directly or continue under a cooperative plan with the states, in favor of a federal-state cooperative system in which the states would construct and maintain the highways with federal aid.

1921 English-built Brough Superior motorcycle becomes known as the "Rolls-Royce of Motorcycles." Built to exacting standards, this high-performance motorcycle wins races, rides smoothly and quietly, and is very expensive. It is on his beloved Brough Superior that British soldier, scholar, and author T. E. Lawrence (1888—1935), known as Lawrence of Arabia, dies in a road accident.

1921 First hydraulic four-wheel brakes are fitted to the Dusenberg Model A straight-8 automobile. Developed by Malcolm Loughhead (later to change his name to Lockheed and become famous in aeronautics), hydraulic brakes will become very popular and standard on all cars. They operate by the resistance offered or pressure transmitted when a fluid is forced through a small tube.

1921 Tri-Continental Corporation of Buffalo, New York introduces its vacuum-operated windshield wiper motor. The motor uses gearing, cams, and other components to translate circular motion into the needed back-and-forth motion. This gradually replaces the hand-operated "Crescent Cleaner" and becomes standard equipment on all U.S. passenger cars. Its vacuum motor is later replaced by today's electric motor.

1921 First series production car with swing-axle rear suspension is the rear-engine sedan car from Germany designed by Edmund Rumpler. A swing-axle allows each wheel to move up and down independently. This odd-shaped car has a "teardrop" shape with fins if viewed from above, and its drag coefficient (resistance of an object moving through air) of 0.28 is not matched on production road cars until the 1960s.

1921 Douglas Sea and Swell Scale is devised by British Navy Captain H. P. Douglas. Designed to provide a standardized method of measuring the degree of roughness of the ocean, it becomes a recognized code that is recommended for general use by the 1929 International Meteorological Conference. It is closely related to the strength of the wind and therefore to the Beaufort Scale. (See 1806)

1921 Prototype for the modern bus is the Safety Coach, introduced by brothers Frank and William Fageol of Oakland, California. This 22-passenger, single-deck bus has a fully enclosed body and a low-slung chassis allowing only 19 in between the floor and the ground. This new design, along with a much wider body, gives it

1921 ■ Jinricksha at the Grand Hotel, Yokohama, Japan.

a totally new appearance. It becomes very popular. (See 1927)

1921 January 25 Committee on Law of Aviation of the American Bar Association files an initial report on the necessity of aerial legislation.

1921 February 21—24 First solo coast-to-coast flight across the United States is made by Lt. William D. Coney. He flies from San Diego, California to Jacksonville, Florida in 22 hours, 27 minutes.

1921 February 22—23 First coast-to-coast airmail flight in the United States (from San Francisco, California to Mineola, Long Island, New York) is made in 33 hours, 20 minutes by Jack Knight (b. 1893) and others in a De Havilland *D.H. 4* with stops in Nebraska and Illinois.

1921 March 1 New Soviet government establishes a state-supported laboratory for solid-propellant rocket research. This is the result of N. I. Tikhomirov's (1860—1930) appealing directly to Lenin for research support.

1921 April 30 Transportation in and out of New York and New Jersey becomes so large and complicated that the two states create the Port of New York Authority. This organization will administer marine terminals, tunnels, bridges, airports, rail and bus terminals, helicopter pads, and office buildings.

1921 April 30

Port of New York Authority created

 1921 June 8 First flight of a U.S. Army Air Service pressurized cabin airplane is made with a *D-9-*

A aircraft. This allows flying beyond the "comfortable" breathing altitude of about 8,000 feet.

1921 ■ Nyach-Tarrytown ferry boat.

**1921
July 13—21

Bombing
tests con-
ducted**

 **1921 July 13—21** Brig. Gen. William (Billy) Mitchell's (1879—1936) attempts to focus government attention on the bomber as a powerful weapon of war spur the Army and Navy to conduct bombing tests on captured German vessels. As a result, a German submarine, destroyer, light cruiser, and a supposedly unsinkable battleship are all bombed by Mitchell from the air and sunk, demonstrating the vulnerability of naval vessels to air attack.

1921 July 18 John H. Glenn, Jr., the first American to orbit the earth, is born in Cambridge, Ohio. After flying combat missions in the Korean War as a Marine, he became a test pilot and set a record by flying an *F8U* from Los Angeles, California to New York in three hours, 23 minutes. After being selected by NASA (National Aeronautics and Space Administration) with the first group of astronauts in 1959, he made his historic orbital flight on February 20, 1962. He is currently a U.S. senator from Ohio.

1921 August First recorded instance of a radio receiver in a private car occurs when the Cardiff and South Wales Wireless Society installs a set. American car manufacturers begin to offer car radios in 1928.

1921 August 4 Five thousand catalpa trees near Troy, Ohio are successfully sprayed from an airplane in 15 minutes, demonstrating the efficiency of aerial crop spraying and dusting.

1921 August 14 First soaring flight in which a transfer from slope lift (gentle up-currents on the side of a hill) to thermal lift (strong, vertical up-currents caused by convection or temperature differences) is made in Germany by a Wenk *Weltensegler* sailplane over the Wasserkuppe mountain peak in the Rhön. The pilot, Wilhelm Leusch, is killed when his plane's wings collapse.

1921 September 1 President Warren G. Harding (1865—1923) authorizes the creation of the Navy Bureau of Aeronautics, with Rear Adm. W. A. Moffet (1869—1933) as its chief.

1921 September 13 Frederic Harth, on a sailplane of his own design, effectively exploits the up-currents and breaks the soaring endurance record established by Orville Wright (1871—1948) in 1911 with a sustained flight of 21 minutes, 30 seconds near Hidenstein, Germany.

1921 October Appalachian Trail idea is first articulated by American forester and philosopher Benton MacKaye, in his plan titled, "The Appalachian Trail, an Experiment in Regional Planning," published in the *Journal of the American Institute of Architects*. It becomes a reality under the leadership of Connecticut lawyer Arthur Perkins. This mountain footpath for hikers presently extends southward for 2,000 miles (3,000 kilometers) from Mt. Katahdin, Maine to Springer Mountain, Georgia. Following the crest of the Appalachian Mountains, it passes through 14 states, 8 national forests, and 2 national parks. Each hiker is responsible for the upkeep of the rough shelters and trail-side campsites located every seven or eight miles. The first hiker to cover its full length is Earl V. Shaffer of York, Pennsylvania. Leaving Mt. Ogelthorpe, Georgia on April 14, 1948, he reaches Mt. Katahdin, Maine on August 5 after spending 123 nights on the trail.

1921 November 12 First air-to-air refueling is made when American Wesley May steps from the wing of one aircraft to that of another carrying a five-gallon can of gasoline strapped to his back.

1921 November 28 Major contribution to theoretical basis of applied aerodynamics is made by Ludwig Prandtl (1875—1953) of Gottingen University in Germany, and is published as NACA Report No. 116 titled *Applications of Modern Hydrodynamics to Aeronautics*.

1922 ■ Mobile home (front) pulls a detachable candy store in Austria.

1921 December 4 First regular air service in Australia begins as West Australian Airways opens a line between Derby and Geraldton using Bristol Tourer Coupé aiplanes.

1922 First airship to be filled with helium gas is U.S. Army's *C-7* non-rigid dirigible. Helium is a rare, inert gas that weighs twice as much as hydrogen and has slightly less lifting capacity. It is also expensive. Unlike hydrogen, it is nonflammable and promises to make airships much safer from the risk of fire.

1922 Regulations for elevators are established with the American Standard safety code. Most of these newly-codified laws apply to passenger safety, and they are updated continually. Most U.S. elevators conform to these standards.

1922 Balloon tires are introduced by American manufacturer Firestone. They are low pressure, pneumatic (air-filled) tires that cushion by their flexible, large cross-sections. They are outdated in a decade.

1922 Longest railroad tunnel in the world, the second of two Simplon tunnels in Switzerland, opens a passage through the Alps between Switzerland and Italy. It is 12 miles, 559 yards long (19,823 kilometers).

1922 The automatic choke is introduced by Cadillac. A choke increases the gas flow in the carburetor by decreasing the airflow. This choke is designed to open a butterfly plate automatically as the engine warms up.

1922 Motoring at its most basic and cheapest is probably the Smith Flyer offered by a Wisconsin company. Consisting of four cycle wheels linked by boards serving as both floor and suspension, the vehicle has no body except two bucket seats. It is powered by a 12-volt electric battery and is later sold by Briggs & Stratton Company of Milwaukee, Wisconsin. Called the "Red Bug Buckboard," it costs between $125 and $150.

1922 First British "peoples' car," the Austin Seven, is introduced. Nicknamed the "Chummy," it plays a major role in the emerging British car industry. A small, four-seater with a four-cylinder engine, it meets the growing demand for affordable cars by rationalizing production methods, like Ford.

1922 First chrome-plated automobile bumpers and grills are on the Cadillac Sport Touring car.

1922 A.D.

*Automatic
choke
introduced*

This hard, shiny coating plated onto a metal surface is a mixture of chromium and other chemical elements such as nickel and copper.

1922 First "million year" ever attained by any automobile manufacturer is achieved by Ford Motor Company which delivers 1,216,792 units of its Model T. (See 1962)

1922 British automobile manufacturing company Aston Martin is founded by Lionel Martin. He adds the name Aston to his because it is the name of a 1913 race he won. Under a series of different owners over the years, the company produces a consistently high-performance sports-racing car that ranks among the leaders in high quality and prestige value.

1922 Barker headlamps which move mechanically are offered on such British cars as Alvis and Morris.

1922 Motorized perambulators or baby carriages are offered for sale in England. They are powered by a small two-stroke engine and contain a platform at the rear for the nursemaid. Unfortunately, British law does not allow such vehicles on the sidewalk.

1922 Hermann Oberth (b. 1894) submits his Ph.D thesis which sets forth in considerable detail his theoretical proposals for achieving space flight with liquid fuel rockets. Heidelberg University rejects his thesis and he publishes it in 1923 in Germany at his own expense under the title, *Die Rakete zu den Planetenraumen (The Rocket into Interplanetary Space)*.

1922 American Ralph Samuelson (b. 1904) builds a specially made pair of skis for water and is successfully towed behind a motorboat. He is believed to be the first to use what are essentially modern water skis. He puts on water skiing exhibitions, being towed by a seaplane as well as a boat, and going over greased ski jumps.

1922 Checker Cab Manufacturing Corporation is founded in Kalamazoo, Michigan by Russian-born American Morris Markin.

1922 First major outboard motorboat race takes place in Stockholm, Sweden. There are 75 boats involved.

1922 A.D.

Checker Cab founded

1922 International Railway Union is created. This international body reestablishes channels of communication following World War I and begins the long process of promoting technical unity and standardization among Europe's national railroad systems.

1922 January 1 Underwriter's Laboratories in Chicago, Illinois begins registration of U.S. aircraft for the benefit of insurance companies.

1922 March American Robert H. Goddard (1882—1945) conducts unsuccessful tests on his first liquid-fueled rocket engine. He soon devises small, high-pressure pumps to force fuel into the combustion chamber.

1922 March 13 First flight across the South Atlantic is made in stages by Portuguese pilots Capt. Sacadura Cabral and Capt. Gago Coutinho. Leaving Lisbon in a Fairey *IIIC* seaplane, they arrive in Brazil on June 16 in a Fairey *IIID*, having crashed their original plane.

1922 April 7 First mid-air collision between passenger-carrying aircraft on scheduled flights occurs over France when a De Havilland and a Farman collide. Both pilots were visually following the same road below. Seven people are killed.

1922 June 16 A hybrid aircraft—part airplane (three fixed wings) and part helicopter (twin rotor blades)—makes a short vertical flight. Designed by American inventor Emile Berliner (1851—1929) and flown by his son, Henry, it flies again on July 16 and rises and hovers successfully as Army officials watch.

1922 August 18 First soaring flight of one hour in slope lift (using hill currents) is made by Arthur Martens (1897—1937) in a *Vampyr* sailplane designed by Wolfgang Klemmperer at the Wasserkuppe, Rhön, Germany.

1922 August 19 First true thermal soaring flight (using strong, vertical, temperature-driven up-currents) in which height was gained only by circling in lift is made by a Henri Farman sailplane flown by French pilot Bossoutrot in Combegrasse, France.

1922 September 4 First coast-to-coast crossing of the United States in one day is made by Lt. James

1923 ■ De Bothezat helicopter in flight.

H. Doolittle (b. 1896), U.S. Army Air Service in a De Havilland *D.H. 4-b.* He flies 2,163 miles (c. 3480 kilometers) from Pablo Beach, Florida to San Diego, California in 21 hours, 20 minutes.

1922 October Soviet rocket pioneer Fridrich A. Tsander (1887—1933) completes his study, "An Airplane for a Flight Beyond the Earth's Atmosphere for Flights to Other Planets." Here he suggests a vehicle that first takes off using propellers like an airplane which then uses liquid-fuel rocket engines to reach space.

1922 October 1 The RAF takes over military control of Iraq, becoming the first Air Force to assume complete control of a military command. After seizing many Arab provinces from the Ottoman Turks in World War I, the British rule Iraq until 1932. Following the Cairo Conference of 1921 and the Anglo-Iraqi Treaty of 1922, the British face increasing nationalist sentiment and feel forced to assert military control.

1922 October 3 In a reply to American Robert H. Goddard's (1882—1945) report on his recent accomplishments with a multiple-charge rocket, Charles G. Abbott of the Smithsonian Institution replies: "I regret that the Institution does not see its way to obtain funds to further promote your experiments. We find these very tight times..."

1922 December 18 A four-rotor helicopter powered by a 180-hp LeRhone engine and designed by Russian emigre George DeBothezat flies for about one-and-one-half minutes at McCook Field (now Wright Field), Ohio, rising about six feet in the air.

1923 Work begins on the Moffat Tunnel which pierces the Rocky Mountains. Designed to speed up travel to the West Coast, it is on the Denver and Rio Grande Western Railroad in Colorado. Completed in 1928, it is over six miles long, 24 feet high, 16 feet wide, and 9,000 feet above sea level.

1923 First motorcycle with disc brakes to win a race is the Douglas. The new brakes are made by the Research Association in England.

1923 First complete BMW motorcycle to carry that name is introduced. Its transverse-cylindered, flat-twin engine proves very popular. Its innovative design, in which the engine drives the rear wheel through a car-type clutch and gearbox and shaft, is a sophisticated way of doing away with a motorcycle's transmission chains. BMW stands for the Bayerische Motoren Werke (Bavarian Motor Works).

1923 Pan-American Highway idea is originally conceived at the Fifth International Conference of American States held in Santiago, Chile. First thought of as a single route connecting North and South America, the concept grows to include a number of designated highways in participating countries. The United States begins assisting Central American countries in building their own highways in 1930, and today, it is an international highway system extending nearly 17,000 miles (27,000 kilometers) south from Alaska across Canada and the United States, through Mexico and Central America, into Chile. Connecting routes extend the system through Paraguay, Argentina, and Brazil. It is continuous except for a 52-mile (84-kilometer) gap after Panama where northwest Colombia begins.

1923 First U.S. diesel-electric to turn a profit is built by American Locomotive Company (ALCO) and operates on 13 different lines.

1923 The last National Automobile Show at which an electric vehicle appears is held.

1923 A.D.

First MG introduced

1923 First MG is introduced in England. A sporty car with no windshield, wire wheels, and a hand brake outside the body, it can reach 80 mph. MG stands for "Morris Garages," the name of William R. Morris's (1877—1963) original retail and repair business in Oxford.

1923 First use of a power-operated railroad car retarder system is made by the Indiana Harbor Belt Line Railway. Another name for a rail brake, this system regulates the speed of freight vehicles being moved about in mechanized marshalling yards. Marshalling yards are areas where railroad cars are sorted, assembled, and marshalled into trains.

1923 First Le Mans Grand Prix d'Endurance is run in France and won by Lagache and Leonard who average 57.21 mph in a Chenard et Walcker. This famous 24-hour automobile race is conceived as a test of a touring car's endurance rather than speed, and it is still run today.

1923 Hertz Drive-Ur-Self System is founded by John D. Hertz, president of the Yellow Cab Company in Chicago, Illinois. (See 1925)

1923 January 3 First soaring flight of more than five hours is made by French Lt. Thoret in a Hanriot *HD-14* biplane as he flies with his engine stopped in a slope lift (using hill-side air currents) in Biskra, France.

1923 January 9 First flight of a practical gyroplane or rotorcraft is made by Juan de la Cierva's (1886—1936) *C-3 Autogiro* which is flown by Spenser Gomes at Cuatro Vientos, Madrid, Spain. Unlike an airplane, a gyroplane derives its lift and/or thrust from rotating airfoils or wings. Although this version is not a true helicopter since it has wings, it does help develop the first practical helicopter which appears in the 1930s.

1923 March 21 American Robert H. Goddard (1882—1945) describes his rocket accomplishments

to the president and trustees of Clark University, Worcester, Massachusetts and requests $1000 to complete his tests on liquid fuel mixes and combustion.

1923 May 2—3 First nonstop flight across continental United States is made by Lt. J. A. Macready (b. 1897) and Lt. Oakley Kelly, U.S. Air Service. The two men fly 2,520 miles (4055 kilometers) from New Tork to San Diego, California in 26 hours, 50 minutes in an Army *T-2 Fokker Transport*.

1923 June 27 First refuelling in mid-air (with hose) of one airplane by another is made by a De Havilland *D.H. 4-b* from another one over San Diego, California. The planes are flown by Capt. L. H. Smith (b. 1892) and Lt. J. P. Richter.

1923 July 19 American Robert H. Goddard (1882—1945) receives from Hermann Oberth (b. 1894) a copy of Oberth's book, *The Rocket into Interplanetary Space.* Oberth asks for Goddard's paper, "A Method of Reaching Extreme Altitudes," in return.

1923 August 21 First use of electric beacons mounted on the ground to provide sight direction for night flying is made in the United States.

1923 September Boston, Massachusetts Municipal Airport opens officially. It forms the core of what becomes Logan International Airport, named in 1939 after Boston's local war hero and judge, Edward L. Logan (1875—1939).

1923 September 1 The Royal Australian Air Force is formed.

1923 October 1 Goodyear Tire & Rubber acquires Zeppelin rights for the manufacture of rigid airships.

1923 November 1 American Robert H. Goddard (1882—1945) successfully operates a liquid oxygen and gasoline rocket motor on a testing frame. Both fuels are supplied by his pumps installed in the rocket. In two tests runs, his motor achieves 25 pounds of thrust for 12 seconds and 50 pounds of thrust for 15 seconds.

1923 November 5 United States conducts a series of tests demonstrating the feasibility of storing, assembling, and launching a seaplane from a subma-

1923 ■ Raul P. Pescara lands his 16-bladed helicopter.

rine. A Martin *MS-1* is assembled and successfully "launched" when the submarine submerges.

1923 November 18 Alan B. Shepard, the first American to fly in space, is born in East Derry, New Hampshire. A graduate of the U.S. Naval Academy, he was chosen with the first group of astronauts in 1959 and made his historic sub-orbital Mercury flight on May 5, 1961. He was grounded by an inner ear ailment until 1969 when he was able to walk on the moon during *Apollo 14*. He is currently president of Seven-Fourteen Enterprises in Houston, Texas.

1924 First flight of the Junkers *G-23*, an all-metal, three-engine, monoplane airliner. This aircraft starts the trimotor era in 1925 when it becomes the first all-metal trimotor to enter commercial airline service. (See May 1925)

1924 Trial run for transcontinental air mail from New York to San Francisco, California is made in 27 hours. The best previous time was seven-and-one-half days by train in 1869.

1924 Fowler flaps are invented in the United States. These new flaps increase a wing's area by projecting out and forming an extension of the trailing edge. This makes for faster, longer range airplanes.

1924 The variable-pitch, constant-speed propeller is demonstrated and patented in England. Designed by H. S. Hele-Shaw and T. E. Beacham, this important invention allows an aircraft's propeller to maintain optimum thrust under all conditions. It does this by varying its pitch or changing its blade angle.

1924 First step toward automatic elevator controls is taken by the Otis Company which develops the Signal Command System for the new Standard Oil Company building in New York. The operator only presses the floor button and closes the doors, and the Control System selects which floor to respond to, when to accelerate, slow down, and stop.

1924 Four-wheel brakes are perfected by Buick in 1923 and appear in 1924. (See 1921)

1924 Price of a Ford automobile hits its lowest point ever at $290 (without a self-starter). The price for a Model T in 1909 was $950.

1924 Double-filament headlamp bulbs are introduced in the United States. This more powerful lamp increases a driver's visibility at night.

1924 Ethyl Gasoline Corporation is formed in Delaware by General Motors and Standard Oil Company of New Jersey to market "knockless" automobile motor fuel. The new corporation attains a wide market for its product in a very short time.

1924 A.D.

Oil filters introduced

1924 Oil filters are first introduced for automobile engines. As filtering devices that strain and remove foreign particles from an engine's circulating oil, they must also be designed so as to retain oil after an engine stops and minimize the removal of oil additives.

1924 American Tom Blake (b. 1902) introduces the hollow surfboard. His 15-foot board is shaped in the ancient Hawaiian tradition, but he hollows it out to lighten it and make it more maneuverable. (See 1946)

1924 January 21 American Robert H. Goddard (1882—1945) receives a $500 grant from the Smithsonian Institution despite its earlier refusal. The new fund source is the Cottrell Fund, established by the Research Corporation of New York to honor its founder, Frederick G. Cottrell. From now until 1928, Goddard will receive a total of $5000 from this fund to support his work on liquid fuel rockets.

1924
March 4

Bombs clear ice jam

1924 March 4 Two Martin bombers and two *DH-4B*'s from the Army Air Service prevent a flood on the Platte River in North Bend, Nebraska, by dropping bombs to clear an ice jam.

1924 April Fridrich A. Tsander (1887—1933), Konstantin E. Tsiolkovsky (1859—1935), and Felix E. Dzherzhinsky (1877—1926) form, in the Soviet Union, the Society for the Study of Interplanetary Travel with a membership near 200. Also in the Soviet Union during this month, the Central Committee for the Study of Rocket Propulsion is established. The new, post-revolution Soviet Union treats the notion of space flight with a great deal more respect and seriousness than does Europe or the United States.

1924 April 1 The Royal Canadian Air Force is formed.

1924 April 1 The British national "chosen-instrument" airline, Imperial Airways, is formed by the merger of Handley Page Transport, Aircraft Transport and Travel, the Instone Airline, and the British Marine Air Navigation Co.

1924 April 6 First successful flight around the world starts as four Douglas *World Cruisers* leave from Seattle, Washington. Of the four, only two complete the circumnavigation as they each fly 27,553 miles (44,340 kilometers) in 175 days, and return to Seattle on September 28. The actual flying time is 371 hours, 11 minutes, and the successful pilots are Lt. Lowell H. Smith (b. 1892) and Lt. Erik Nelson.

1924 April 19 The Argentinian Marquis de I. Pescara's helicopter establishes in France a flying record of 2550 feet (c. 777 meters) in four minutes, 11 seconds. His helicopter provides for auto-rotation (free blade rotation) in case of engine failure. This invention is a life-saving device, as it allows for a measure of control and lift.

1924 May 4 First helicopter flight in a closed circle is made in France by Etienne Oehmichen's helicopter No. 2. The previous month, it established a world record by flying 1,182 feet (360 meters).

1924 May 23 First scheduled air service in Canada begins. Laurentide Air Service Ltd. offers flights between Angliers, Lake Fortune and Rouyn, Quebec.

1924 August 22 American Fred Waller patents a twin "aquaplane" system, an early form of water skis. Called "Akwa-Skees," it is a complicated system in which each ski is attached to a boat tow rope, and a hand rope is attached to the back end of each ski which, in turn, are connected. (See 1922)

1924 August 24 First flight of the Zeppelin *LZ-126* rigid airship is made in Germany. Later in the year it flies the Atlantic and is supplied to the U.S. Navy as war reparations and becomes the *Los Angeles*. This very successful airship flies for seven years, making 331 flights and logging more than 5,000 hours.

1924 September First modern highway opens in Italy between Milan and Varese. Called the "autostrada" or automobile road, it is built by the Italian government and operates as a toll road. It has three undivided lanes on a 33-foot (10-meter) roadway with three-foot shoulders. Access is limited, with restrictions on commercial vehicles. It is a forerunner of the modern, high-volume, high-speed highway.

1924 September 3 Regular air mail service in Canada begins with flights between Ontario and Quebec.

1924 October 15 Lido A. Iacocca, automotive manufacturing executive, is born in Allentown, Pennsylvania. Known as Lee, he joins Ford Motor Company after leaving Princeton University with a post-graduate engineering degree, and successively climbs from the sales staff to become its president in 1970. During that time, he is responsible for one of the industry's major success stories, as his new sporty and glamorous small car, the Mustang, is introduced in 1964 and makes Ford a profitable company again. He leaves Ford in 1978 and becomes president and chief operating officer of Chrysler Corporation in 1979. He again performs miracles and resurrects a dying company, via a $1.5 billion federal loan guarantee and by selling his new fuel-efficient, front-wheel drive "K" cars beginning in 1980.

1924 December 9 The Civil Aeronautics Act, proposing the establishment of a Bureau of Civil Aeronautics in the Department of Commerce, is reintroduced in the U.S. Congress.

1925 In Germany, H. A. Wagner develops his "Tension Field Beam Theory" which is to make an important contribution to A. Rohrbach's design of all-metal stressed-skin aircraft. The modern concept of stressed skin construction involves the idea that the skin or outer covering of an airplane can support part of its load and stresses.

1925 First flight of the first Daimler Klemm *L-20* wooden, low-wing light monoplane. This two-seater German design marks an important step in light airplane development.

1925 Longest railroad tunnel in the Western Hemisphere, the 7.8-mile-long Cascade Tunnel of the Great Northern Railroad in the state of Washington, is begun. It opens to great fanfare on January 29, 1929. A single-track tunnel, it is 21 feet, 5 inches high and 16 feet wide.

1925 Of the over 1,000 automobile manufacturers that started in business before 1905, 15 are still in existence. They are: Haynes (1896), Olds (1897), Studebaker (1898), Locomobile (1899), Franklin (1900), Peerless (1900), Stearns (1900), Apperson (1901), Pierce-Arrow (1901), Cadillac (1902), Overland (1902), Packard (1902), Buick (1903), Ford (1903), and Maxwell (1904).

1925 First known use of an oil-warning light is on the Italian Fiat 509 model. This light goes on inside the car when engine oil pressure drops to 5—7 psi (pounds per square inch). At this point, the engine should be stopped immediately.

1925 American automobile manufacturing company Chrysler Corporation is founded by Walter P. Chrysler (1875—1940) who takes over Maxwell cars. In 1928, Dodge is taken over and two new lines, DeSoto and Plymouth, are created. In 1954, Imperial becomes a separate model, having been a Chrysler model. A government bail-out helps it avert financial disaster in the 1970s, and it is competitive again with its models reduced.

1925 A.D.

Chrysler founded

1925 ■ Termini Station after inaugural run of Rome's first subway.

1925 Walter Hohmann (b. 1880) defines the principles of a rocket moving through space in his book, *Die Erreichbarkeit der Himmelskorper (The Attainability of Celestial Bodies)*.

1925 Ford car dealers now receive their Model T's from the factory "knocked down" and assemble them themselves. Since seven "knocked down" cars can be shipped in the same railroad car that would hold only two assembled cars, and a good mechanic can put one together in half a day, economics dictates the new way of doing things.

1925 Chicago taxi fleet operator John D. Hertz sells his Hertz Drive-Ur-Self System to General Motors. He also sells his Yellow Truck and Coach Manufacturing Company to General Motors. Hertz will become the world's largest rental car company.

1925 February 15 First "hook-on" of an airplane to an airship in flight is made when the biplane *Sperry Messenger* is captured by the "hook on" trapeze structure of a U.S. Army non-rigid dirigible over Scott Field, Illinois.

1925 February 22 First flight of the De Havilland *D.H. 60 Moth*. It becomes the most popular and widely used light airplane of this time, preferred by private and sport fliers alike. It is light, strong, and easy to fly, and remains in use for thirty years.

1925
March 2

Uniform
road signs
adopted

1925 March 2 Uniform road signs are the aim of the newly-formed U.S. Joint Board of State and Federal Highway Officials. Besides route names and numbers, the Board agrees on standard shapes and color schemes for certain categories of road signs. Thus "Stop" signs become octagonal and caution signs have black letters on a yellow background.

1925 April U.S. Navy tests Oleo landing gear and determines it to be superior to old landing gear systems. The Oleo method has a cylindrical strut with a built-in telescopic shock absorber that allows a degree of give when the airplane wheels touch down.

1925 April 21—November 9 An Italian Savoia seaplane flies from Rome to Japan and Australia and makes a return flight to Italy, totalling 34,000 miles (c. 54,720 kilometers).

1925 April 13 The first regular U.S. air-freight service is initiated by Henry Ford, linking Detroit, Michigan and Chicago, Illinois.

1925 May 15 Four Junkers *G-23s*, the first all-metal, trimotor monoplane airliners, go into commercial service between Malmö, Sweden, Hamburg, Germany, and Amsterdam, Holland.

1925 May 21—June 17 First attempt to reach the North Pole by airplane fails as Roald Amundsen (1872—1928) of Norway and Lincoln Ellsworth (1880—1951) of the United States and their crews land 140 miles (225 kilometers) short of the Pole in their Dornier seaplanes.

1925 June 12 Wealthy American industrialist Daniel Guggenheim (1856—1930) donates $500,000 toward the establishment of a School of Aeronautics at New York University.

1925 July In an experiment at Wright Air Field, Dayton, Ohio, the U.S. Air Service controls and moves a small car on the ground by radio from an airplane 2,000 feet above.

1925 July 15 First to use airplanes for exploration is A. Hamilton Rice (b. 1875) whose Rice Expedition returns from exploring the headwaters of the Amazon River.

1925 July 26 First soaring flight of 10 hours is made near Cherbourg, France by Belgian Massaux in a Poncelet sailplane.

1925 September 3 Airship *Shenandoah*, pride of the U.S. Navy, is ripped apart in the air near Marietta, Ohio by violent weather. After being driven upward and suddenly downward several times, the structurally-weak airship comes apart, killing 14.

1925 September 4 First flight of the Fokker *F-VII/3m* trimotor airliner is made. It becomes widely used throughout Europe and North America and wins the Ford Reliability Trial in the United States.

1925 November 16—March 13 1926 First round trip flight from London, England to Cape Town, South Africa, is made by Alan Cobham (1894—1973) and crew in a De Havilland *D.H. 50*.

1925 December 6 American Robert H. Goddard (1882—1945) conducts a static test of his liquid fuel rocket engine at Clark University, Worcester, Massachusetts, and reports that "this was the first test in which a liquid-propelled rocket operated satisfactorily and lifted its own weight."

1925 December 17 General William E. Mitchell (1879—1936) of the U.S. Army is found guilty by a court-martial of "insubordination and conduct unbecoming to an officer." His public accusations of the U.S. War and Navy departments' incompetency following the airship *Shenandoah*'s fatal crash makes his conviction inevitable.

1925 December 27 Wealthy American industrialist Daniel Guggenheim (1856—1930) creates a $2,500,000 foundation for the promotion of civil aviation in the United States.

1926 First practical proposal for gas turbine propeller propulsion is made in England in a report by A. A. Griffith to the Royal Aircraft Establishment (RAE). Unlike piston engines, gas turbines have a rotary shaft and operate continuously. Griffith's plans are not however for a pure jet engine, but for a turbo-prop.

1926 ■ U.S. Coast Guard cutter *Tampa*.

1926 Raleigh bicycles (in England) pioneers the evolution of tube steels of considerable strength, making possible the production of the lightweight bicycle frame. Using new metal blends, they make bicycles both lighter and stronger.

1926 Turn signal indicators are available on British 14/40 Talbot automobiles. They are directional arrows located on either side of the number plates.

1926 First private car in the U.S.S.R. is the NAMI-1, a small twin-cylinder automobile.

1926 Car heaters that use the heat obtained from the engine's cooling system first appear in the United States. Foot-warmers similarly operated were found on pre-1900 Cannstatt-Daimlers in Germany.

1926 First car with safety glass windows as standard equipment is offered by Cadillac. This new ceramic glazing material prevents a car's windows from shattering or falling apart when broken.

1926 The first British V-12 engine drives the English Daimler "Double Six." This very large car has an engine cast in four blocks of three cylinders each and a wheelbase of 12 feet, 11½ inches (3.9 meters). An extremely quiet luxury car, it is purchased by the king of England.

1926 Plans are announced for the construction of a bridge across the Hudson River to Manhattan. Terminal sites decided upon are Fort Lee in New Jersey, and Fort Washington on Manhattan. The bridge is later called the George Washington Bridge. (See October 1931)

1926 First frameless tractor/trailer truck in which a large cylindrical tank provides its own frame is made by Scammel in England. These rear-wheel only cylinders are still used today to transport milk, chemicals, and other liquids and gases.

1926 First antifreeze for automobiles is introduced by Union Carbide and Carbo Company. Called Prestone, it is ethylene glycol and sells for $5 a gallon.

1926 A.D.
Antifreeze introduced

1926 American Gertrude Ederle (b. c. 1907) swims the English Channel from Cap Gris Nez, France to St. Margaret's Bay, England, in 14 hours, 34 minutes.

1926 Greyhound Corporation is incorporated to compete with intercity passenger rail service. It does well and begins to grow, soon buying up other bus companies.

1926 Standards for engine oil viscosity (lubricating ability) are set in the United States by the Society of Automotive Engineers (SAE), as engineers agree on numbers ranging from 50 (heavy oil) to 10 (light oil).

1926 A.D.
Engine oil viscosity standards set

1926 First designated pedestrian crossing in Britain is marked in Parliament Square, London. The London Traffic Advisory Committee paints two parallel white lines across the road and erects a square white sign high on a post with a cross and an arrow that says, "Please Cross Here."

1926 January 22—February 10 First east-west airplane crossing of the South Atlantic is made by Spaniard Ramon Franco (1896—1938) in a Dornier seaplane. He flies from Spain to Rio de Janiero in stages.

1926
March 16

First free flight of liquid-fueled rocket

1926 March 16 First free flight of a liquid-fueled rocket is made at a farm in Auburn, Massachusetts. Designed and built by Robert H. Goddard (1882—1945), it burns liquid oxygen and gasoline. Successfully launched from a 2-meter-tall A-frame, the small rocket accelerates to a height of 12.5 meters with an average speed of 60 mph (96 km/h) in its two-and-one-half-second flight. It lands 184 feet (56 meters) away in a cabbage patch. This brief flight is to rocketry what the Wright Brothers' 12-second Kitty Hawk flight is to aviation.

1926 ■ Robert H. Goddard and the first liquid-fuel rocket.

1926 April 3 American Robert H. Goddard (1882—1945) conducts the second successful launch of a liquid-fuel rocket. It lands 50 feet from the test stand after being in the air 4.2 seconds.

1926 May 5 American Robert H. Goddard (1882—1945) communicates the results of his successful liquid-fuel rocket flight of March 16 to the Smithsonian Institution. He tells Secretary Charles G. Abbott, "To me, personally, these tests, taken together, proved conclusively the practicality of the liquid-propelled rocket..."

1926 May 8 First Federal legislation regulating civil aeronautics. U.S. Congress passes the Air Commerce Act authorizing the Weather Bureau to provide meteorological service over routes designated by the Secretary of Commerce as suitable for air commerce as well as those over the high seas; to establish and maintain stations in aid of air navigation; and to conduct aeronautical research and study. President Calvin Coolidge (1872—1933) signs the Act, known also as the Bingham-Parker Bill, on May 20.

1926 May 9 First airplane flight over the North Pole is made by Americans Lt. Cdr. Richard E. Byrd (1888—1957) and Floyd Bennett (1890—1928) in a Fokker *F-VII/3m.* Their total distance from Spitzbergen, Norway is 1,600 miles (2,575 kilometers).

1926 May 11—14 First airship flight over the North Pole and the first crossing of the Arctic Ocean is made by Roald Amundsen (1872—1928) of Norway, Umberto Nobile (1885—1978) of Italy, Lincoln Ellsworth (1880—1951) of the United States, and their crew in an Italian-built semi-rigid airship, N-1, *Norge.* They fly from Spitzbergen, Norway to Teller, Alaska. Two years later, Nobile's airship crashes returning from another trip over the Pole, and Amundsen's attempted airship rescue disappears over the waters of the Arctic Circle. Amundsen is never seen again, but Nobile is rescued by a Russian ice-breaker.

1926 June 11 First flight of the Ford *4-AT* trimotor, an all-metal monoplane which competes with the three-engine Fokker and becomes a pioneer American airliner. It is known affectionately as the "Tin Goose."

1926 June 30—October 1 First flight from England to Australia and back again is made by Britain's Alan Cobham (1894—1973) in a De Havilland *D.H. 50* seaplane. The trip takes five weeks outbound, and three weeks six days homeward. This and other Cobham flights help lay the groundwork for a future British Empire commercial air network.

1926 July 1 The Royal Swedish Air Force is formed.

1926 July 2 The U.S. Army Air Corps is formed out of the former Air Service. Provisions are also made for an assistant secretary of war for air and a five year Air Corps expansion program.

1926 July 28 U.S. submarine *S-1* surfaces and launches a Cox-Klemin *XS-2* seaplane which is later recovered by the sub, stowed, then the submarine submerges. This is the first time such a complete cycle of these feasibility experiments is completed. The system never becomes operational.

1926 July 28 German automobile manufacturing company Mercedes-Benz is founded as the Daimler-Benz AG. It is the result of the merger of the separate Daimler (Mercedes) and Benz companies. Post-war inflation in Germany was devastating to both companies and they had been cooperating increasingly from 1923. Over the years, this company has been able to link innovation with dependable high quality, to produce one of the best cars made today.

1926 October 4 H. H. Culver (b. 1880) is arrested by an air traffic policeman on a charge of reckless flying and is held on $25 bail for a court appearance in Delmonte, California.

1926 November 3 Capt. Charles A. Lindbergh (1902—1974) jumps from his disabled airplane during a night air mail flight, making this the fourth time he has had to use his parachute to save his life.

1927 George A. Townend of the National Physical Laboratory in England invents what comes to be called the "Townend Ring," an engine-cowling device for radial engines. A cowling covers an aircraft's engine, and his design largely solves the problem of engine drag or resistance of the air. A similar design is independently invented in America at about the same time by the National Advisory Committee for Aeronautics (NACA) and is called the "NACA Cowling." (See 1928)

1927 National Advisory Committee for Aeronautics (NACA) builds the first wind tunnel large

enough to test a full-size airplane at its Langley Field, Virginia facilities.

1927 Cessna Aircraft Company is founded in Wichita, Kansas by Clyde V. Cessna. Specializing in light aircraft construction, the company is today synonymous with the privately-owned light plane, although it produced World War II trainers and, now, twin-jet executive transports.

1927 Bicycles for women are built to reflect changes in women's clothing. The heavy, cumbersome cycles built to accommodate the long, voluminous skirts women wore are replaced by simpler, lightweight bicycles now that women are able to wear skirts and slacks.

1927 United States passes the Oldfield Act providing for federal participation in the cost of constructing toll bridges on the federal-aid system, subject to the condition that the bridges would become toll-free when the state's share of the cost is collected.

1927 First subway in Japan opens in Tokyo. Called the Chikatetsu Line, it is only 1¼ miles long but will grow to have eight lines with 102.9 miles of track. It rivals any urban rapid transit system in terms of efficiency.

1927 Revolutionary bus design is offered by the Fageol brothers (Frank and William) of California. Called the Twin Coach, it looks almost identical at the front or the rear, seats 43, and is powered by two 4-cylinder engines mounted on each side of the chassis. Its radical design has a flat front and back and the entrance door is placed ahead of the front axle. It also has driver-controlled pneumatic doors. Most buses today look quite similar to the Twin Coach. (See 1921)

1927 January 7 Regular air service between Cairo, Egypt and Basra, Iraq is started by British company Imperial Airways, using De Havilland Hercules trimotor airliners.

1927 March 29 First man to exceed 200 mph on land is Englishman Henry Seagrave. He drives his twin-engine 1,000-hp Sunbeam at a top speed of 207 mph in a race in Daytona Beach, Florida.

1927 April U.S. Bureau of Aeronautics and the Department of Commerce conduct experiments to

1927 A.D.

Bus designed

1927 March 29

Racer drives 207 mph

find a substitute for imported Japanese silk for parachutes in an effort to make the United States less dependent on foreign raw materials.

1927 April Lt. Cdr. Richard Byrd (1888—1957) and crew of three crash their Fokker monoplane in its trial flight. This plane is planned for a New York to Paris flight.

1927 April 26 Lt. Cdr. Noel Davis and Lt. H. S. Wooster are killed when their biplane, which they plan to fly to Paris within the next few weeks, crashes on a test flight at Messick, Virginia.

1927 May 20–21 Lindbergh flies non-stop across Atlantic

1927 May 20–21 First solo non-stop flight across the Atlantic is made by Charles A. Lindbergh (1902—1974). Lindbergh leaves Roosevelt Field, Long Island, New York at 7:55 A.M., so laden with fuel that his Ryan monoplane, *Spirit of St. Louis,* barely clears the telephone wires. Navigating at times by dead reckoning, he lands at Le Bourget Airfield, Paris on May 21 at 10:24 P.M. He covers 3,600 miles in 33 hours, 29 minutes and wins the Orteig Prize of $25,000. Lindbergh's daring and romantic solo flight has a tremendous impact and serves to make the United States and the world more aware of the true potential of aviation.

1927 ■ Charles A. Lindbergh and his *Spirit of St. Louis.*

1927 June First World Exhibition of Interplanetary Machines and Mechanisms is held in Moscow, U.S.S.R. The exhibit includes models of spaceships, schematics of space suits, and books and photographs reflecting the work of rocket pioneers like Tsiolkovsky, Oberth, Goddard, Esnault-Pelterie, and Tsander. The Soviet Union appears to officially embrace the notion of space flight.

1927 June 4 Daniel Guggenheim School of Aeronautics officially opens at New York University.

1927 June 5 Verein für Raumschiffahrt, known as the VfR (Society for Space Travel), is founded in Germany and soon grows to several hundred interested and enthusiastic members. Among its founding members are Johannes Winkler, Max Valier, and Rudolf Nebel. It begins publishing a journal as well as books, and later includes sponsorship of practical experiments and demonstrations. It disbands in 1933.

1927 June 8 The Astronautics Committee of the Société Astronomique Française (Astronomy Society of France) is established in France. French aviation and rocket pioneer Robert Esnault-Pelterie (1881—1957) lectures to the Society on the possibility of probing the upper atmosphere and exploring space. In this speech he first uses the word "astronautics," invented by Belgian writer J. J. Rosny (1856—1940) (who writes under the name Joseph-Henri-Honoré Boex), and which he and banker André Hirsch coin and popularize to mean the range of activities covering space propulsion and navigation.

1927 June 4—5 First nonstop flight from New York to Eisleben, Germany is made by Americans Clarence D. Chamberlain (b. 1893) and Charles A. Levine in a Bellanca monoplane. They fly 3,905 miles in 42 hours, 15 minutes.

1927 June 28—29 First non-stop flight between the United States and Hawaii is made by U.S. Lts. Albert F. Hegenberger (1895—1983) and Lester J. Maitland (b. 1899). They fly 2,407 miles (3,874 kilometers) from Oakland to Honolulu in 25 hours, 30 minutes.

1927 July 4 First flight of the Lockheed *Vega,* a single-engine, high-wing, monoplane which can carry eight passengers. This small transport marks an important step towards the low-drag monoplanes which would set the fashion and pace for general purpose aircraft. It also influences the design of larger transport of the 1930s.

1927 July 25 Coordinated system of centralized rail traffic control is installed on a 40-mile route in Berwick, Ohio. CTC has since been installed on more than 40,000 miles of U.S. track.

1927 September 1 American Railway Express Company begins large-scale air express operations in the United States by negotiating with all the major airlines.

1927 October 14—15 First non-stop airplane crossing of the South Atlantic is made by Capt. Dieudonné Costes and Lt. Cdr. Joseph Le Brix in a Breguet *XIX* from Saint-Louis, Senegal to Port Natal, Brazil. They fly 2,125 miles (3,420 kilometers) in 19 hours, 50 minutes.

1927 October 19 Pan American Airways begins its first regular service between Key West, Florida and Havana, Cuba.

1927 November 22 First U.S. snowmobile patent is obtained by Carl J. E. Eliason of Sayner, Wisconsin. His "vehicle for snow travel" is given U.S. Patent No. 1,650,334.

1928 First refrigerated wind tunnel for research on the prevention of icing of wings and propellers begins operations at Langley Laboratory, Virginia.

1928 American C. S. Caldwell demonstrates his variable-pitch propeller. This design is later developed and put into service by Hamilton Standard and becomes the most popular of the first variable-pitch propellers. This system allows an aircraft's propeller to maintain optimum thrust under all conditions by varying its pitch or changing its blade angle. (See August 1933)

1928 Fred Weick of the U.S. National Advisory Committee for Aeronautics (NACA) invents the long-chord cowling for radial engines. Called the "NACA cowling," it is an engine-covering design that reduces engine drag or its resistance to the air.

1928 German automobile industrialist Fritz von Opel (1899—1971) produces a rocket-propelled motorcycle as an extension of earlier tests on a rocket-car.

He obtains high speeds but finds nothing to recommend them commercially.

1928 Last private car fitted with solid rubber tires is the British Trojan Type XL built by Leyland Motors. It is small, very affordable, and has a two-cycle, four-cylinder engine that drives the solid rear axle by a chain. It is durable and gives a surprisingly smooth ride because of its springs.

1928 Mechanical fuel pump for automobiles is brought out by AC Spark Plug Co. It is mounted on the engine block and powered by the engine's camshaft. It moves the fuel from the car's tank to the engine's carburetor.

1928 First three-color traffic light in England is used in Wolverhampton.

1928 First synchromesh transmissions are built in LaSalle and Cadillac cars. This is a manual transmission with two or more gear ratios (the speed at which the gears rotate) in constant contact with one another. Manual gear shifting is made easier and smoother.

1928 First front-wheel drive car with all-independent suspension is the Alvis Compressor built by the British firm of T. G. John, Ltd. of Great Britain. This dashing sports car has a 75-hp, four-cylinder, supercharged engine and runs in many races.

1928 In Moscow and Leningrad, U.S.S.R., the GIRD or Gruppa Isutcheniya Reaktivnovo Dvisheniya (Group for the Study of Reactive Motion) is formed to promote space flight, support local activities, and develop active test programs leading toward the successful flight of a Soviet rocket.

1928 In Austria, Franz von Hoefft of Vienna's Gesellschaft für Hohenforschung (Society for Altitude Research) proposes plans for a 30-ton rocket-powered lifting body capable of taking off from water like a hydroplane. It has an upper stage with orbiting capability. It is never built.

1928 First of nine volumes of the first encyclopedia of rocketry and space flight, *Mezhplanetyne Soobshcheniya (Interplanetary Communications)*, is published by Professor Nikolai A. Rynin in the Soviet Union. It covers everything from myths and legends of space travel and the fiction of Verne and Wells, to the work of Tsiolkovsky, Goddard, and Esnault-Pelterie. The final volume appears in 1932.

1928 The Soviet Union establishes at Leningrad a Gas Dynamics Laboratory for work on liquid rockets. This leads to the testing of the ORM-1 rocket two years later.

1928 Viennese student Joseph Krupka builds a light, portable water ski he uses to glide over water. He propels himself forward on two skis by using double-bladed paddles like a snow skier's poles. It catches on in Europe and is called "water skijoring." Skijoring is snow skiing while being pulled by a galloping horse.

1928 January 27 U.S. Navy's dirigible *USS Los Angeles* successfully lands on the deck of the aircraft carrier *Saratoga* while at sea.

1928 February 1 Robert Esnault-Pelterie (1881—1957) and French banker André Hirsch establish the REP-Hirsch International Astronautics Prize of 5,000 francs to be awarded annually for the best original scientific work, either theoretical or experimental, that advances space travel. Hermann Oberth (b. 1894) is the first recipient for his book *Wege zur Raumschiffahrt (The Roads to Space Travel)*.

1928 February 7—22 First solo flight from England to Australia is made by Australian Sqn. Ldr. H. J. L. "Bert" Hinkler (1892—1933), in an Avro *581 Avian* light airplane. He flies 11,005 miles (17,711 kilometers) in 15½ days.

1928 March 1—15 Robert Esnault-Pelterie (1881—1957) publishes an article in the French aeronautical journal, *L'Aérophile*. Titled "Intersidereal Navigation or Astronautics," it deals with space travel by liquid-fuel rockets.

1928 March 13 First Canadian woman to obtain a pilot's license, Miss Eileen M. Vollick, passes her flight tests in Hamilton, Ontario on a Curtiss aircraft.

1928 March 15 First manned rocket-propelled automobile is tested in Berlin, Germany. Built by Fritz von Opel (1899—1971), Friedrich W. Sander and

others, it reaches 45 mph but does not perform well, so a specially-built car is made, called Opel-Rak 1. (See April 12, 1928)

1928 April 12 Redesigned rocket-propelled automobile, Opel-Rak 1, achieves speeds of 55 mph in Germany. A more streamlined version, Opel-Rak 2, is later driven by Fritz von Opel (1899—1971) and reaches speed of nearly 125 mph.in the Rhön Mountains of Germany. Stamer's tail-first glider flies about one mile. Its rocket takeoff is assisted by an elastic launching rope and another rocket fires while airborne. German aerodynamicist A. Lippisch (1894—1976) directs the experiment, whose rockets are provided by F. W. Sander.

1928 April 12—13 First east-west crossing of the Atlantic by airplane is made by Germans Hermann Kohl (1888—1938), Gunther von Hunefeld, and Irish Capt. James Fitzmaurice flying a Junkers *W33* monoplane. They fly from Dublin, Ireland and crash-land off Labrador. Eight previous attempts to make an east-west crossing killed seven people.

1928 April 15—21 First west-east airplane crossing of the Arctic Ocean is made by Australians George H. Wilkins (1888—1958) and Carl B. Eielson (1897—1929) in a Lockheed *Vega* from Point Barrow, Alaska to Spitzbergen, Norway. Flight time includes the five days they spend in their airplane cabin when forced by bad weather to land on Dead Man's Island, only one-half hour away from Spitzbergen.

1928 May Aeronautics Branch of the Department of Commerce creates a board to review aircraft accident reports and to determine original causes so far as possible. A board to determine standard measurements of airway distances is also created. The creation of both boards indicates that American aviation is growing, maturing, and in need of coordination, regulation, and organization.

1928 May 31—June 9 First airplane flight across the Pacific is made by British Capt. Charles Kingsford-Smith (1899—1935) and crew in a Fokker *F-VIIB/3m*. They fly from Oakland Field, California to Brisbane, Australia, 7,389 miles (11,890 kilometers), in 83 hours, 38 minutes. On the way, it becomes the first airplane to land in Fiji.

1928 May 1 World's longest non-stop railway run opens between London and Edinburgh. The 393-mile (632.5-kilometer) line is operated by London & North Eastern Railway.

1928 May 12 A 3,000-square-mile aerial map of the Florida Everglades is completed by Air Corps Reserve Lt. Julian S. Dexter. The project takes 65 hours of flying spread over two months. Today, the same results can be achieved by one satellite overflight, and these photographs can be in several spectral bands, providing a wealth of information beyond the simply cartographic.

1928 June 11 First rocket-powered manned airplane flight is made by Frederich Stamer from the Wasserkuppe peak in the Rhön Mountains of Germany. Stamer's tail-first glider flies about one mile. Its rocket takeoff is assisted by an elastic launching rope and another rocket fires while airborne. German aerodynamicist Alexander Lippisch (1894—1976) directs the experiment, whose rockets are provided by F. W. Sander.

1928 June 15 Mail is successfully transferred from an airplane in flight to a train as Lt. Karl S. Axtater flies directly over an Illinois Central train and transfers a mail bag to a railway clerk.

1928 June 17—18 Amelia Earhart (1898—1937) becomes the first woman to fly across the Atlantic as a passenger as she accompanies pilot Wilmer Stiltz and mechanic Louis Gordon on their flight from Newfoundland to Wales in a Fokker C-2. Less than four years later, she flies the Atlantic alone. (See 1932)

1928 July 3—5 Non-stop flight from Rome, Italy to Pont Genipabu, Brazil, is made by Italians Arturo Ferrarin and Carlo Del Prete. Their Savoia *S.64* travels 4,466 miles (c. 7188 kilometers).

1928 July 18 Longest tunnel on the French railroad system, the Somport Tunnel, opens. Actually between France and Spain, it is over four miles (7,874 meters) long.

1928 September First buses equipped with sleeping facilities for U.S. coast-to-coast travel are Pickwick Stages, Inc.'s "nite coaches."

1928 September 18 First rotating-wing aircraft to fly the English Channel is the Cierva *C-8L Autogyro* flown by its designer, Spaniard Juan de la Cierva (1886—1936). He flies with a pasennger from Croydon, England to Le Bourget, France.

1928 September 18 First flight of the Zeppelin LZ-127 *Graf Zeppelin*, the most successful rigid airship ever built. Operated commercially by the Zeppelin Company, especially on a regular service from Europe to South America, it flies over a million miles and carries some 13,100 passengers before its demise in 1940.

1928 September 18 Graf Zeppelin makes first flight

1928 September 19 First diesel engine to power a heavier-than-air aircraft is flight tested in Utica, Michigan. It is made by the Packard Motor Car Company.

1928 September 23 Lt. James H. Doolittle (b. 1896) makes a flight to an altitude of 37,200 feet and obtains an aerial photograph covering 33 square miles.

1928 October U.S. Air Corps develops an 84-foot diameter parachute strong enough to support the weight of an airplane and its passengers. This system does not become operational.

1928 October 11—15 First transatlantic crossing by an airship carrying paying passengers is made by the German airship *Graf Zeppelin* (LZ-127). It travels from Friedrichshafen, Germany to Lakehurst, New Jersey in almost 112 hours carrying a crew of 37 and 20 passengers.

1928 October 31 Robert Esnault-Pelterie (1881—1957) continues to argue the case for space research and gives a free lecture at the Royal Aero Club in London, England. His talk is titled "The Exploration of the Upper Atmosphere by Rockets and the Possibility of Interplanetary Flight."

1928 November Ancestor of the modern container ship, the *Seatrain New Orleans,* begins a new transport service. The major innovation of the New Orleans-Havana, Cuba line is its use of sealed containers which the shipper places on railroad flats. They are not unloaded until they reach their destination. This prepackaging of goods will become an efficient way of transporting cargo.

c. 1929 ■ Opel rocket-powered motorboat.

1928 December 7 Railway Express Agency is formed to handle nationwide U.S. express business. Its name is changed to REA EXpress in 1960.

*1928
December 20

First flight
over
Antarctica*

1928 December 20 First flight over Antarctica is made by Australian George H. Wilkins (1888—1958) and Lt. Carl B. Eielson (1897—1929). They use a Lockheed *Vega* for the 10-hour flight.

1928 December 23—February 25 1929 The Royal Air Force (RAF) conducts the first emergency airlift and evacuates 586 people by air from Kabul, Afghanistan.

1929 British professor Bennett Melvill Jones (b. 1887) publishes his influential paper titled *The Streamline Aeroplane*. It is not until the publication of this paper that airplane designers begin to pay any attention to the theoretical approach to the problem of drag (the force exerted by resistant air upon a body). From this point on, the science of aerodynamics (the field of dynamics concerned with the motion of air) plays a major role.

1929 Electric fuel gauges are developed to determine the amount of fuel left in an automobile's gas tank. It consists of a remote sensing unit in the fuel tank and an indicator gauge in the dashboard.

1929 Hawaii Department of Transportation, Division of Highways, is first organized.

1929 First station wagon offered as a private car and not as a commercial vehicle is a version of the Ford Model A. Once established as a practical vehicle, nearly every American family with children will drive some version of a station wagon.

1929 In Leningrad, U.S.S.R., a group is formed within the Gas Dynamics Laboratory (GDL) under Valentin P. Glushko (b. 1908) to develop electric and liquid-propellant rocket engines.

1929 Yuri V. Kondratyuk publishes his book *Zavoevanie mezhplanetnykh prostranstv (The Conquest of Interplanetary Space)*, which contains the first known statement of an orbital technique for landing on planetary bodies. It is remarkably similar to how the U.S. *Apollo 11* spacecraft will land on the moon 40 years later. He says: "The entire vehicle need not land ... the machine part separates from it ... subsequently rejoining the remainder of the vehicle."

1929 First successful rocket-propelled boat, the *Dixie Torpedo*, runs on Biscayne Bay. Built by American Malcolm Pope, it is powered by 40 electrically-controlled rockets fitted at the stern, and can reach 55 mph (102 km/h).

1929 First mobile home trailers for sale are on display in the Hudson Motor Car Company's showrooms in New York.

1929 January 7 First science-fiction comic strip, "Buck Rogers in the 25th Century," introduces space travel and scores of other futuristic concepts and devices to millions of readers in daily newspapers served

1929 ▪ *Graf Zeppelin* airship.

by the National Newspaper Syndicate of Chicago. Written by Philip Nowlan and drawn by Richard Calkins, it spawns radio programs, toys, and later a TV program, making the phrase "Buck Rogers" synonymous with anything futuristic. It also inspires and excites an entire generation about space the way the writings of Jules Verne and H. G. Wells did earlier.

1929 January 12 First U.S. air mail stamped envelopes are available for sale.

1929 April 10 German inventor Friedrich W. Sander (1896—1934) claims to have launched Europe's first liquid-propelled rocket, but no witnesses can substantiate his claim since Sander tests his rocket in secret. (*See* March 14, 1931)

1929 April 24—26 First non-stop flight from England to India (Lincolnshire to Karachi) is made by R.A.F. crew led by A. G. Jones-Williams and N. H. Jenkins flying a Fairey long range monoplane. Their flight takes 50 hours, 48 minutes.

1929 May 16 At the first Academy Award ceremonies in Los Angeles, California, the Oscar for

Best Picture for 1927—1928 goes to the Paramount movie, *Wings*. This World War I flying epic starring Richard Arlen, Buddy Rogers, and Clara Bow (1905—1965) remains a classic today.

1929 July 1 Airworthiness Requirements for Aircraft, as set down by the U.S. Aeronautics Branch, Department of Commerce, become effective.

1929 July 7 Transcontinental Air Transport, Inc. inaugurates a 48-hour combined rail and air passenger service from coast to coast. Col. Charles A. Lindbergh (1902—1974) flies the first plane over the air route.

1929 July 7

Rail-air passenger service begins

1929 July 17 Robert H. Goddard (1882—1945) launches his fifth liquid-fueled rocket in Auburn, Massachusetts. His instrumented rocket carries a camera, thermometer, and barometer, all of which are recovered intact 171 feet away. This flight is particularly bright and noisy, and attracts public attention, much of it negative or derisive. Goddard is called the "moon professor" by the local papers.

1929 August 8—29 First flight around the world by an airship is made by the Zeppelin LZ-127 *Graf*

Zeppelin. Captained by Hugo Eckener (b. 1868), the airship make its 21,500-mile circumnavigation in 21 days, 7 hours, 34 minutes. Starting from Lakehurst, New Jersey, it stops at Friedrichshafen, Tokyo, and Los Angeles before returning to Lakehurst.

1929 August 20 Austrian rocketry pioneer Max Valier (1895—1930) writes in the newspaper *Recklinghauser Zeitung* that he plans to fly by rocket across the English Channel just as Bleriot did with an airplane 20 years before, proving airplanes were practical. Valier cannot get sufficient financial backing and is killed in 1930 during an experiment with a rocket engine for a rocket-propelled car. (See May 17, 1930)

1929 September 9 First air conditioned Pullman rail car is operated between Chicago, Illinois and Los Angeles, California.

1929 September 24 First public demonstration of a "blind" airplane flight is piloted by Lt. James H. Doolittle (b. 1896) at Mitchell Field, New York. Using Sperry's gyro horizon and directional gyro in a Consolidated *NY-2* biplane, Doolittle is able "to take off, fly a specific course, and land without reference to the earth." Instrument flying eventually becomes routine for all military and commercial planes.

1929 September 30 German industrialist and inventor Fritz von Opel (1899—1971) flies his solid-rocket propelled glider at Rebstock, near Frankfurt, Germany for over one mile and reaches a speed of 100 mph (161 km/h).

1929 October 15 The premier is held of the film *Frau im Mond (The Girl in the Moon).* Made by the German Ufa Film Company and directed by Austrian filmmaker Fritz Lang (1890—1976), this film has Hermann Oberth (b. 1894) as technical adviser. Oberth builds a rocket and motor with friends Rudolf Nebel (1894—1978) and Alexander Scherschevsky, but cannot make a real working model for use in the film. The movie helps boost popular awareness in Germany of the potential of space flight. An English language version is shown in the United States in 1930.

1929 October 21 Giant monoplane seaplane, the German Dornier *DO-X,* carries 169 passengers in an hour-long flight over Lake Constance, Switzerland. With a span of 157½ feet and twelve 525-hp engines, this huge aircraft is called an ambitious freak, since most seaplanes of its time are smaller by far and accommodate about 20 passengers.

1929 November 28—29 First flight over the South Pole is made by Americans Cdr. Richard E. Byrd (1888—1957) and Bernt Balchen (b. 1899) and crew, in a Ford *4-AT* Trimotor monoplane.

1929 December First ski school in the United States is formed at Peckett's Inn on Sugar Hill in Franconia, New Hampshire.

1929 December 22 Austrian rocket pioneer Max Valier (1895—1930) begins a series of experimental runs in Berlin, Germany with his new rocket car, Rak 6, which uses carbon dioxide as fuel. (See May 17, 1930)

1930 National Advisory Committee for Aeronautics (NACA) makes confidential recommendations to U.S. industry and military for the best location of engine nacelles (housings), stating that engines built into the leading edges of the wings are most favorable. This report influences the design of all multiengine aircraft hereon.

1930 In England, Frank Whittle (b. 1907), inventor of the jet engine, takes out his first jet-engine patent. Published in 1932, it is here that Whittle offers the conception for a simple, light-weight engine for propelling aircraft at high speeds by reaction propulsion.

1930 In Japan, Osaka Hatsudoki Company puts a three-wheeled automobile called "Tsubasa-go" on the market.

1930 First U.S. 16-cylinder automobile engine is introduced by Cadillac. First European 16-cylinder is the V16 Bugatti Type 47.

1930 Automobile oil cooling systems are introduced as well as the automotive use of stainless steel. Alloyed with four or more percent chromium to prevent rusting and increase resistance to corrosion, stainless steel is especially useful for car manufacture.

1930 Valentin P. Glushko (b. 1908) designs the Soviet Union's first liquid-fuel rocket engine, called the ORM-1.

1930 French aviation and rocket pioneer Robert Esnault-Pelterie (1881—1957) publishes his major work, *L'Astronautique (Astronautics)*, marking the first time the word "astronautics" appears in the title of a book. This classic is followed by a supplement in 1934 which together cover all known experiments, tests, and philosophies concerning rocketry and space flight.

c. 1930 ■ Typical Coast Guard lightship serves as a floating lighthouse.

1930 Bathysphere is developed by American naturalist Charles W. Beebe (1877-1962) and American engineer Otis Barton. This steel spherical underwater vessel is capable of maintaining an interior environment of ordinary pressure when lowered beneath the sea. It has thick quartz windows or portholes for observation and is suspended by a cable from a boat. In 1934, Beebe and Barton descend to a depth of 3,028 feet. The bathysphere proves difficult to operate and potentially dangerous, and since it is not able to maneuver about, it is eventually replaced by the safer, more maneuverable bathyscaphe. (See 1948)

1930 Courlieu in France develops the rubber foot fin for divers. This simple device greatly extends a diver's swimming range.

1930 Swiss engineer Robert Maillart (1872—1940) builds his longest bridge, the Salginatobel Bridge over the Schrau River in Switzerland. Spanning 246 feet, his reinforced-concrete bridge demonstrates that this new material can be elegant and refined while still very strong. Using concrete in an entirely rational manner and ignoring traditional forms, Maillart innovates a radical bridge design that is far ahead of its time. He uses the formerly passive deck of the bridge as an integral part of the structure. By making it a bearing surface, he does away with all extra material, making for a slim and stylized but very strong bridge. His designs are not adopted in the United States, since they are considered too light for railroad traffic and too expensive for normal highway spans.

1930 Sweden pioneers the construction of offshore, unmanned lighthouses to replace lightships. These are telescoped concrete towers, topped by cast-iron lanterns, that are built on land, towed to the site, and sunk. The unmanned lights are controlled by switches on the mainland.

1930 April 4 American Interplanetary Society, led by G. Edward Pendray (1901—1987) and David Lasser (b. 1902), is formed in New York. Its announced aims are to promote "interest in and the experimentation toward interplanetary expeditions and travel." In 1934, it is renamed the American Rocket Society. (See April 6, 1934)

1930 April 4

American Interplanetary Society formed

1930 May 5—24 First solo flight from England to Australia by a woman is made by Britisher Amy Johnson (1903—1941) in a De Havilland *D.H. 60G Moth*. She flies from Croydon, England to Darwin, Australia in 19 days.

1930 May 15 First airline stewardess is Ellen Church, a nurse who flies on the Boeing Air Transport flight between San Francisco, California and Cheyenne, Wyoming.

1930 May 15

First airline stewardess hired

1930 May 17 Austrian rocket pioneer Max Valier (1895—1930) is killed when his rocket car motor fueled by a kerosene/water mixture and liquid oxygen is being static tested and explodes.

1930 July 23 Hermann Oberth (1894—1989) and associates of VfR (Verein für Raumschiffahrt) successfully test, in Germany, a liquid oxygen and gasoline rocket motor for 90 seconds.

1930 August 5 Neil A. Armstrong, the first person to walk on the moon, is born in Wapakoneta, Ohio. A civilian test pilot in the *X-15* rocket plane program, he was chosen by NASA (National Aeronautics and Space Administration) with the second group of astronauts in 1962. He first flew in space aboard *Gemini 8* in 1966. He was commander of the *Apollo 11* moon mission and first stepped on the moon on July 20, 1969. He was awarded the Congressional Space Medal of Honor in 1978. He is currently chairman of the board of Computing Technologies for Aviation, Inc.

1930
August
18—26

First east-
west
crossing of
Atlantic
made

1930 August 18—26 First east-west seaplane crossing of the Atlantic is made in stages by Capt. Wolfgang von Gronau and crew in a Dornier *Wal* from the German island of Sylt to New York harbor.

1930 September 1—2 First non-stop flight from Paris to New York is made by Capt. Dieudonné Costes (1892—1973) and Maurice Bellonte (b. 1892) in a Breguet *XIX* in 37 hours, 18 minutes.

1930 September 10 First flight of the Taylor E-2 *Cub*, a two-seat, light monoplane with a 37-hp engine, a cruising speed of 74 mph, and a range of 210 miles. This American design develops into the Piper *Cub*, which is to become one of the world's most popular light aircraft.

1930 September 27 Verein für Raumschiffahrt (VfR) or Society for Space Travel opens its "Raketenflugplatze" launching site for rockets in Reinickendorf, a suburb of Berlin. As an unused ammunition storage depot, its protected facilities are ideal for rocket experiments. Among the members are Hermann Oberth (1894—1989), Rudolf Nebel (1894—1978), Klaus Riedel (1907—1944), Willy Ley (1906—1969), and a young student named Wernher von Braun (1912—1977). All gain valuable practical experience building, testing, and launching liquid-fuel rockets.

1930 October 5 Britain ceases development of airships following a British airship crash in Beauvais, France, which kills 48 people, including the British air minister and director of civil aviation.

1930 October 7—13 Robert H. Goddard (1888—1945) establishes his new test site in Roswell, New Mexico and builds a launch tower from which he will launch several record-breaking rockets.

1930 October 8—10 A helicopter designed by Italian Corradino d'Ascanio establishes a new

world record for altitude, time in the air, and distance. It rises to 59 feet, stays aloft for eight minutes, 45 seconds, and covers 3,540 feet (c. 1078 meters). These extremely modest numbers illustrate graphically how far behind helicopters are in their development compared to aircraft.

1930 October 18 First subway in South America opens in Buenos Aires, Argentina. The Lacroze line of the Ferrocarril Terminal Central de Buenos Aires, is built in less than two years.

1930 October 19 Gottlob Espenlaub flies a rocket-propelled glider in Dusseldorf, Germany. Powered by solid-fuel rockets built by Friedrich Sander (1896—1934), his plane reaches a speed of 60 mph (90 km/h).

1930 October 25 First coast-to-coast air service across the United States is started by Transcontinental and Western Air (today's TWA), between New York and Los Angeles.

1930 November World's first "old car" club, the Veteran Car Club of Great Britain, is founded in Brighton.

1930 November 30 Detroit-Windsor Tunnel opens to automobile traffic. Built under the Detroit River, it is made of prefabricated tubes that are floated over a trench dug at the river bottom, sunk, and then connected underwater.

1930 December 17 German Army Ordnance Office reviews work of Goddard, Oberth, and others, and decides that rockets have some military potential. It establishes a rocket program and equips an artillery proving ground at Kummersdorff to develop military rockets. Capt. Walter Dornberger (1895—1980) is placed in charge. From this beginning will spring the V-2 rocket.

1930 December 30 Robert H. Goddard (1882—1945) launches an 11-foot-long, liquid-fueled rocket to an altitude of 2,000 feet, reaching a speed of 500 miles per hour. This is the first launch at his new test site in Roswell, New Mexico. The rocket weighes 33.5 pounds and uses a gas pressure tank to force the liquid oxygen and gasoline propellants into the combustion chamber.

1931 First applied use of the principle of jet-propulsion is made when the Italian airship *Omniadir* uses compressed air for propulsion.

1931 First practical delta-wing aircraft flies in Germany. Built by Alexander Lippisch (1894—1976), the chief pioneer of the delta-wing airplane, this modern design has wings shaped to resemble an isosceles triangle. The true delta and its real flourishing must await the development of the practical jet engine.

1931 First cast-iron road ever built opens on a 100-yard section of Romford Road in London, England. Built by Frank Hough, the road is composed of triangular iron plates resting on asphalt which in turn is atop a concrete foundation. Iron roads are too expensive to build.

1931 Front-wheel drive automobile with transverse engine layout originates on the two-cylinder DKW F1 model from Germany. This car's engine block is mounted perpendicular (at a right angle) to a car's length. It is done now to save space and has become popular on small, front-wheel drive cars.

1931 Japanese automobile manufacturing company Mazda begins making cars as the Toyo Kogyo Company Ltd. When its car factories in Hiroshima are destroyed during World War II by the 1945 atomic bomb that levelled that city, it does not produce another production car until 1960. It grows into one of the leading car-makers in Japan by concentrating on manufacturing smaller cars.

1931 German rocket pioneer, Eugene Sänger (1905—1964) begins a series of rocket motor experiments at the University of Vienna. He obtains high combustion pressure using very advanced fuel injection techniques.

1931 Austrian Society for Rocket Technology (Osterreichische Gesellschaft für Raketentechnik) is founded in Vienna by Baron Guido von Pirquet (b. 1880) and Rudolf Zwerina. It seeks to promote space travel by presenting lectures and programs. It conducts no experiments and soon disbands.

1931 Automobile ferry across the English Channel, the 850-ton Autocarrier, is begun by British

Southern Railway. It carries 35 automobiles and bases its rates according to wheelbase size.

1931 January 1 Turkestan-Turksib (Siberia) Railway opens.

1931 February First mail delivered by rocket occurs as Austrian Friedrich Schmiedel begins air mail service between two Austrian towns. This service, powered by solid-fuel rockets, continues until March 16, 1933.

1931 February Rocket mail service begins

1931 March 13 First successful sounding rocket (used to obtain scientific information on the atmosphere) is launched by German rocket experimenter Karl Poggensee, an engineering student at the Ingenieur Akademie of the University of Oldenburg. His solid propellant rocket flies to 1,500 feet and carries a radio transmitter, an altimeter, a camera, and a velocity meter.

1931 March 14 First liquid-fuel rocket successfully fired in Europe is made by German Johannes Winkler (1897—1947) in Dessau, Germany. His two-foot-long, 12-inch diameter rocket is fueled by liquid oxygen and methane and flies 180 feet high. Winkler conducts his tests alone, and not as part of any group.

1931 April 15 German Reinhold Tiling (d. 1933) demonstrates his solid-propellant rocket made of aluminum. It is six feet (1.82 meters) long and has folding wings which open for landing. One of these launches reaches as high as 6,600 feet and nearly 700 mph.

1931 April 29 Boeing *B-9* bomber flies for the first time and marks the next step in airframe development in the evolution of the Boeing *247*, the first modern-type airliner. (See February 1933)

1931 April 29 First B-9 bomber flies

1931 May 14 German VfR group (Verein für Raumschiffahrt) has its first rocket launch success with a liquid-fueled rocket which rises about 200 feet before falling back to earth. By late summer, VfR rockets had flown more than one kilometer, and the society feels confident enough to ask for support from the German Army.

1931 May 24 First completely air conditioned passenger train is operated by the Baltimore & Ohio (B&O) Railroad and goes into service between Washington, D.C. and New York.

1931 May 27 Balloon height record of 51,775 feet (c. 15,780 meters) is attained by Swiss physics professor Auguste Piccard (1884—1962) and his assistant, Paul Kipfer, in Augsburg, Germany. Balloons are now beginning to enjoy a comeback, mainly due to equipment improvements. Piccard's gondola is hermetically sealed and has an automatic oxygen supply. Upon his safe descent, he is hailed as conquerer of the stratosphere, since no airplane to date can rise as high as he has.

1931 June 11 Handley Page *HP-42* four-engine biplane enters service with the British airline Imperial Airways and sets new standards of passenger service and comfort. It carries 40 passengers.

1931 July 1 First mail delivered by rocket in the United States is claimed by three Struthers, Ohio high school students led by philatelist John Kiktavi. He sends mail from Struthers to Poland, Ohio.

1931 July 28—30 First non-stop flight from New York to Istanbul, Turkey is made by Russell Boardman (b. 1898) and John Polando (b. 1901) in a Bellanca monoplane.

1931 September 25 First flight of the American-built rigid airship *Akron* which, with its sister ship *Macon*, is built to act as the eyes and ears of the U.S. Navy. The *Akron* and 76 men are lost at sea (only three survive) in an April 1933 accident, and the *Macon* is also lost at sea in February 1935 (only two die). Both are unable to withstand severe weather at sea and the Navy abandons for good any further airship development.

1931 October

George Washington Bridge opens

1931 October George Washington Bridge opens to traffic, connecting New York with New Jersey by spanning the Hudson River. Designed by Othmar H. Ammann (1879—1965), this massive suspension bridge is built on the same principle as a skyscraper—-a steel frame. Using steel for its towers instead of the traditional masonry of the Brooklyn Bridge, it is able to bear a span 3,500 feet (1,067 meters). It is higher and far stronger, ranking as the strongest suspension bridge (capable of carrying 5,000 pounds per foot or 7,560 kilograms per meter). Below its roadway is a second deck intended for a tramway. This is converted in 1962 to another roadway, and it becomes a double deck automobile bridge carrying 14 lanes of traffic.

1931 October 9 Frenchman Robert Esnault-Pelterie (1881—1957) loses four fingers on his left hand during an explosion. He is experimenting with liquid tetranitromethane as a rocket fuel, seeking a more powerful mix.

1931 October 3—5 First non-stop flight across the North Pacific is made by Americans Hugh Herndon (b. 1904) and Clyde Pangborn (1893—1958), who fly from Tokyo, Japan to Wenatchee, Washington, 4,558 miles (c. 7330 kilometers) in 41 hours, 13 minutes in a Bellanca *Pacemaker*. This is one leg of their round-the-world flight.

1932 First appearance and production of Junkers *Ju-52*, a highly successful three-engine transport which becomes one of the mainstays of European airlines and is later mass-produced for German freight and troop transport.

1932 First high-speed diesel train is the German streamlined "Flying Hamburger." In regular service between Berlin and Hamburg, it averages 77 mph (124 km/h).

1932 First fully modern highway system, the German autobahn network ("automobile road"), opens to traffic. First conceived in 1926, this high-speed, limited access highway consists of dual roadways separated by a substantial median area. By 1942, it had been extended to a national highway network which would be able to meet the military transportation needs of a nation going to war. After World War II, construction resumes in 1957. Prior to German unification, both East and West Germany had their own autobahn systems.

1932 U.S. Route 66 opens and links Chicago, Illinois with Los Angeles, California. Heading west via St. Louis, Joplin, Oklahoma City, Amarillo, Gallup, Flagstaff, Winona, Kingman, Barstow, and San Bernadino, it becomes popularized in both song and television.

1932 First patent application for a parking meter is made by Carl C. Magee, editor of the *Oklahoma City News*. Soon, 174 of his "Dual Park-O-Meters" will be installed. (See July 1935)

1932 First U.S. state to introduce mandatory car inspections is Maryland.

1932 Bridgestone Tire Company is founded in Japan by Shojiro Ishibashi whose name means "stone bridge."

1932 Last steam-powered private car in the United States is the Doble, built by Abner Doble of California. It is also the best, most expensive, and most complex American steam car. It has a flash boiler at the front and a four-cylinder horizontal engine geared directly to the back axle. It can start cold and be driven away in 30 seconds. Priced at up to $20,000, it simply costs too much.

1932 In Japan, a road built exclusively for automobiles is completed between Atami and Hakone.

1932 German VfR group (Verein für Raumschiffahrt) makes its first rocket demonstration flight for the German Army. It rises to a height of 200 feet.

1932 January 22 During the production of the documentary film on space travel, *"All Aboard for the Moon,"* the producers (Bray Studios of New York) ask Robert H. Goddard (1888—1945) for technical assistance. Goddard declines, explaining that his work is under the supervision of an advisory committee who want to make public "only the scientific results of the work."

1932 March 19 Sydney Harbour Bridge, the longest steel arch bridge constructed without centering (built from each side without support, like the Eads Bridge of 1874), is completed. Designed by English engineer Ralph Freeman (1880—1950), the arch carries suspended below it, four inter-urban railway tracks, a 57-foot-wide road, and two footpaths over the harbor in New South Wales, Australia.

1932 March 28 After a visit to Robert H. Goddard (1888—1945) in Roswell, New Mexico, a U.S. Army Ordnance representative reports to his Chief that "Prof. Goddard does not desire publicity or visits by curious public." Also, he "did not desire to show Ordnance representative experimental equipment or manufacturing shops."

1932 April 19 Robert H. Goddard (1882—1945) launches in Roswell, New Mexico his first rocket with gyroscope-controlled vanes (similar to fins moved by a gyroscope which automatically stabilize its flight).

The rocket is nearly 11 feet long and flies to 135 feet in five seconds.

1932 May 9 First totally blind solo flight (without a check pilot aboard) is made solely on instruments by Capt. A. F. Hegenberger (1895—1983) (Army Air Corps) in Dayton, Ohio.

1932 May 20—21 First solo flight by a woman pilot across the Atlantic is made by American Amelia Earhart (1898—1937). She flies from Harbor Grace, Newfoundland to Londonderry, Northern Ireland in a Lockheed *Vega* monoplane in 13 hours, 30 minutes. Earhart solidifies the fame she reached by her 1928 Atlantic crossing as a passenger.

1932 May 20—21 Amelia Earhart flies across Atlantic

1932 June 21 First federal tax on gasoline levied by the United States goes into effect. The Revenue Act of 1932 places a one-cent-a-gallon tax on all motor fuels. This tax has never been repealed and its revenues are used for more than road maintenance and construction.

1932 July 21—November 9 First flight around the world by a seaplane is made by Wolfgang von Gronau and a three-man crew in a Dornier *Wal.* Their flight takes 111 days.

1932 August The German Army formalizes its rocket development work with the VfR (Verein für Raumschiffahrt) group with Capt. Walter Dornberger (1895—1980) in charge. Wernher von Braun (1912—1977) transfers from VfR's Raketenflugplatz location to the Army's site at Kummersdorf.

1932 August 18 Balloon altitude record of 53,153 feet (c. 16,200 meters) is set by Swiss Auguste Piccard (1884—1962) and Belgian Max Cosyns over Switzerland. Ascending from Dubendorf airport in Zurich, Switzerland, Piccard breaks his own record of 1930. Piccard never again ascends so high, and turns his attention to deep-sea diving and underwater research.

1932 August 18 Balloon altitude record set

1932 August 18 First solo flight east to west across the Atlantic by a light airplane. Britisher J. A. Mollison (b. 1905) flies a De Havilland *Puss Moth* from Portmarnock Strand, Dublin, Ireland, to Pennfield Ridge, New Brunswick, Canada. He later marries Amy Johnson (1903—1941), herself a British long-distance flier.

1932 August 25 First woman to fly nonstop across the United States is Amelia Earhart (1898—1937). Three months after her transatlantic crossing in a Lockheed *Vega,* she uses the same model for a transcontinental flight. The reliable *Vega* was also used by George H. Wilkins (1888—1958) in his trans-Arctic flight and by Wally Post (1899—1935) for his round-the-world speed records.

1932 October 1 Wernher von Braun (1912—1977) officially joins the German Army Ordnance office rocket program in Kummersdorf. He becomes a civilian employee under Walter Dornberger (1895—1980) and is in charge of developing liquid-fuel rockets.

1932 October 15 Institute of the Aeronautical Sciences (United States) is incorporated in the state of New York. Its president is Jerome C. Hunsaker (1886—1984) and Lester D. Gardner is secretary.

1932 November 12 Members of the American Interplanetary Society make their first rocket firing attempt on a farm in Stockton, New Jersey. In the static firing test, the liquid oxygen/gasoline engine produces 60 pounds of thrust for 20—30 seconds and catches fire.

1932 November 28 Responding to an inquiry from the Japanese Navy about his patented turbine aircraft, American Robert H. Goddard (1888—1945) writes that no further work has been done because of the Depression. Goddard's turbine plane patent describes a high-speed turbine blade at the rear of the aircraft that is driven by rocket exhaust.

1932 November 14—18 Amy Johnson (1903—1941) of Britain flies solo from England to Cape Town, South Africa, in four days, 54 minutes.

1932 December 21 Wernher von Braun (1912—1977) and Walter Riedel test their first new rocket for the German Army and Capt. Walter Dornberger (1895—1980). Fueled by liquid-oxygen and ethyl alcohol, it explodes violently but no one is hurt.

1933 "Knee action" for automobiles is first introduced on General Motors cars. As the first individual front wheel suspension system, it gives a car good road handling ability.

1933 In Japan, a subway opens in Osaka.

1933 German rocket propulsion engineer Eugen Sänger (1905—1964) publishes his classic *Raketen-flugtechnik (The Technique of Rocket-Flight).* He reveals his designs for a rocket motor to power a stratospheric aircraft.

1933 First "schnorchel" device—German for snout—is invented by Dutch officer Jan J. Wichers. Called a "snorkel" by Americans, it is a pair of breathing tubes to supply fresh air to a submarine while running submerged and to exhaust engine fumes.

1933 First daylight fluorescent pigments ("Day-Glo") are invented by young American Joseph Switzer. Inspired after learning about "black light," or invisible ultra-violet light, Switzer experiments using chemicals from his father's store and produces a paint that has a brilliance in daytime. These paints are eventually marketed and used on inflatable boats and life jackets, since they are three times more brilliant (and therefore noticeable) than their old, orange World War II counterpart.

1933 White Sea Canal in Russia is opened. This 140-mile-long canal has 19 locks and runs from the White Sea to Lake Onega where it joins Leningrad on the Baltic Sea, thus providing a passage between the two seas. It freezes over from October to May.

1933 February Modern airliner is born in the United States as Boeing *247* flies for the first time. Along with the Douglas *DC-1* and the Lockheed *Electra,* the Boeing aircraft revolutionizes all aspects of air transport and defines the future shape and features of airliners. Its dominating features are: all-metal, low-wing monoplane; two powerful, supercharged, air-cooled engines mounted on the wings; variable-pitch propellers; and retractable undercarriage.

1933 February 25 First U.S. aircraft carrier, *Ranger,* is launched at Newport News, Virginia. As the first U.S. ship designed specifically as a carrier, it is essentially an airfield at sea, equipped with catapults for take-offs and hooks and wires for landings. The ship is named after the famous vessel commanded by American naval hero John Paul Jones (1747—1792).

1933 March 1 U.S. Air Commerce Regulations are amended to increase the flying time required for a pilot's license from 10 hours to 50 hours.

1933 April 1   The Indian Air Force is formed.

1933 May   The Junkers *Ju-52/3m* three-engine airliner enters service with Lufthansa.

1933 May 14   American Interplanetary Society (AIS) launches its first liquid-fueled rocket (No. 2) at Marine Park, Staten Island, New York. During its second flight, it reaches an altitude of 250 feet. Robert H. Goddard (1882—1945), who has already launched his very sophisticated rockets in New Mexico, is not affiliated with the AIS, although he is invited to join.

1933 June   United States passes the National Industrial Recovery Act which, among other measures, assigns $400 million to the states for highway construction, thus providing work for the unemployed during the Great Depression. Much of this money goes to build local secondary or feeder roads and farm-to-market roads, many of which are not surfaced.

1933 July 1   Douglas *DC-1* flies for the first time. One of the first modern airliners and forerunner of the famous *DC-3*.

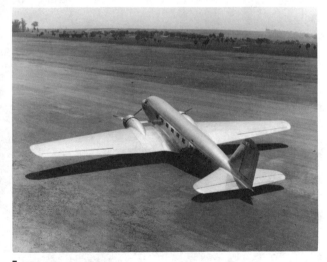

1933 ■ Douglas *DC-1*.

1933 July 5   Daniel and Florence Guggenheim Foundation authorizes a grant of $2,500 to Robert H. Goddard (1888—1945) for rocket research. Goddard had asked for $25,000.

1933 July 15—22   First solo flight around the world is made by one-eyed American pilot Wiley

Post (1899—1935). Flying a Lockheed *Vega* named *Winnie Mae,* he covers 15,596 miles (25,099 kilometers) in seven days, 18 hours, 49 minutes. He flies from New York via Berlin, Moscow, Irkutsk, and Alaska and back to New York. Post pioneers the early development of a pressure suit and proves the value of navigating instruments, especially the automatic pilot. This device, built by the Sperry Gyroscope Company, enabled him to cut nearly one day from his 1931 circumnavigation record flight which was not a solo.

1933 July 22—24   First direct flight from England to the United States is made by newlyweds Jim Mollison (b. 1905) and Amy (Johnson) Mollison (1903—1941) in a De Havilland *Dragon* from Pendine Sands in Wales to Bridgeport, Connecticut.

1933 August   First practical variable-pitch two-position propeller is introduced into airline service by Hamilton Standard in Curtiss *Condor* biplanes. (See 1928)

1933 August   Only Italian liner to hold the transatlantic speed record, the *Rex,* leaves Gibraltar for New York. Its record time is 4 days, 13 hours, 58 minutes for an average speed of 28.92 knots.

1933 August 17   First Soviet liquid-fueled rocket is launched successfully to an estimated 400 meters. It weighs 19 kilograms fueled, is 2.4 meters long and is actually a hybrid of liquid and solid fuel. Sergei P. Korolev (1906—1966) and Mikhail K. Tikhonravov lead the Soviet rocket team.

1933 August 30   Air France, the French "flag" or national airline, is formed.

1933 September 21   Soviet Union establishes the Reaktirnyi Nauchno Issledovatel'kii Institut (RNII) or Reaction Propulsion Research Institute, combining all its best talents in the field.

1933 October 10   German rocket pioneer Reinhold Tiling (d. 1933) and two assistants are killed in an explosion while compressing some 40 pounds (18 kilograms) of black powder into fuel pellets for their rocket.

1933 October 13   British Interplanetary Society (BIS), led by Philip E. Cleator, holds its inaugural meeting in London, England. The society is dedicated to

1933
August 17
First Soviet liquid-fueled rocket launched

1934 ■ Igor Sikorsky's S-40 flying boat.

gaining support for space flight research and to foster experimental research. It begins a publication in 1934, the *BIS Journal,* which continues today. (See January 1934)

1933 December 31 First monoplane fighter aircraft to have an enclosed cockpit and fully retractable landing gear, the Soviet Union's Polikarpov *I-16 Mosca,* makes its first flight. This is the pre-World War II high point of Soviet aviation.

1934 A.D.

Hughes Aircraft Co. forms

1934 Hughes Aircraft Company begins business with a small design team assembled in Culver City, California by Howard R. Hughes (1905—1976). A Hughes *H-1* establishes a new speed record in September 1935 and a new coast-to-coast U.S. record in November 1937. Hughes builds unsuccessful long-range reconnaissance prototypes after the war, and the last aircraft he is personally involved with is the giant, eight-engined, wooden seaplane or flying boat derisively called the *Spruce Goose.* Hughes becomes a reclusive and eccentric millionaire, whose aircraft business later focuses primarily and successfully on helicopters.

1934 Douglas Aircraft begins development of the twin-engined transport, its new *DC-3.* (See December 1935)

1934 Concerted effort begins in the United States to eliminate the most dangerous, as well as the most time-consuming, highway railroad crossings. There are 236,486 such crossings on the 178,597 miles of Class I railways in the United States. Elimination entails changing their grades or levels, allowing trains to pass over highways via bridges. (See 1935)

1934 First mass-produced front-wheel drive passenger car with unitary chassis/body construction is France's four-cylinder Citroen. Called the "Traction Avant," it seats five comfortably because its wheels are placed at the extreme front and rear. This also gives the car a good ride and provides maximum road-holding.

1934 First coil-spring independent front-suspension system is introduced by Cadillac. These heavy spring steel rods are shaped in a spiral and are used to provide support between the front wheels and the car body.

1934 First drive-in movie opens in Camden, New Jersey. Although few now remain, these "passion pits" catered to the American teenagers' love of (and in) the automobile.

1933 ■ Douglas *DC-3.*

1934 ■ Philadelphia street scene.

1934 "Cat's eyes," the rubber-mounted reflectors that "line" traffic lanes at night or in fog, are invented by Englishman Percy Shaw. These reflectors are built into studs that are placed on the surface of the road and reflect light back the way from which it comes. The studs are carefully engineered prisms with a sealed, vacuum-deposited layer of aluminum forming the mirror.

1934 Chessie trademark of a sleeping cat is adopted by the Chesapeake & Ohio Railroad (C&O) to symbolize the smooth ride its trains give because of their well-built roadbeds.

1934 First skiing rope tow is installed in the United States in Woodstock, Vermont. It is a system of pulleys over which a rope travels in a long loop, the lower part of which is used by skiers to travel uphill. The simple rope tow is eventually replaced by the T-bar or J-bar lift which tow skiers uphill.

1934 First all-plywood boat, a 12-foot (3.7-meter) fishing skiff, is built by the Harbor Plywood Corporation of the United States. It uses resin-bonded plywood.

1934 Cunard line director Thomas Royden meets with British King George V, intending to get his permission to name his new transatlantic liner after Queen Victoria. Royden asks the king if he may name the ship "after the greatest queen this country has ever known," and the king replies that his wife, Queen Mary, would be delighted. Naturally, the ship becomes the *Queen Mary*.

1934 January First issue of the *Journal of the British Interplanetary Society* appears.

1934 February Lockheed *Electra* flies for the first time. It was one of the first modern airliners.

1934 March 9 Yuri A. Gagarin (1934—1968), first man to fly in space, is born in the Gzhast district, Smolensk region of the U.S.S.R. A military pilot, he was chosen to be a cosmonaut in 1960. After his famous first flight of April 12, 1961 in which he made a single orbit of the earth, he became a world-famous celebrity but still remained active in the Soviet manned space program. He was planning to fly in space again when he was killed in a crash of his training aircraft on March 27, 1968.

1934 April 6 American Interplanetary Society is renamed the American Rocket Society at its fourth annual meeting. Many members feel the change is necessary because of its unserious "Buck Rogers" connotations. In 1963, it merges with the Institute of Aerospace Sciences to become the American Institute of Aeronautics and Astronautics.

1934 May 19 First flight of the Russian Tupolev *Ant-20 Maxim Gorki*, at this time the largest aircraft in the world. Powered by eight engines, it has a wing span of 207 feet (63 meters). Capable of carrying 80 passengers, it is used mainly as a mobile propaganda office. This strange aircraft contains a cinema, printing press, photo lab, and radio and telephone equipment. It also has loudspeakers and lights under its wings to broadcast messages while in flight.

1934 May 26 First U.S. diesel-powered steamlined train runs the 1,015 miles between Denver and Chicago at an average (nonstop) speed of 77.6 mph. It

1934
March 9

Yuri Gagarin
born

is operated by the Chicago, Burlington & Quincy Railroad.

1934 June 10 American Rocket Society attempts its fourth rocket launch in Staten Island, New York. The 90-inch-tall rocket does not fly but does three months later after modifications. (See September 9, 1934)

1934 July
Mersey
Tunnel
opens

1934 July Mersey Tunnel, one of England's most important automobile tunnels, opens to traffic. Connecting Liverpool and Birkenhead under the estuary (a water passage where the ocean tide meets a river current) of the Mersey River, it has the largest bore (inside width or diameter) of any underwater tunnel. Its 44 feet allow two lanes of traffic in both directions within a single tube. If all its sections are counted together, it is the longest underwater automobile tunnel at nearly three miles long.

1934 July 1 Aeronautics Branch changes its name to the Bureau of Air Commerce as part of the U.S. Department of Commerce.

1934 July 12 British Rocket Syndicate of London is formed to conduct any and all rocket-related business "pertaining to rockets or rocket-like projectiles, aeroplanes, gyroscopes, gliding planes, vehicles, and boats." The company is put out of business by a 300-year-old law which prohibits private rocket experimentation.

1934 July 28 American balloon altitude record of 60,613 feet (c. 18,475 meters) is set by William E. Kepner (b. 1893), Albert W. Stevens (b. 1886), and Orville A. Anderson (b. 1895) in *Explorer I*. In this joint venture between the U.S. Army Air Corps and the National Geographical Society, the balloon's gondola rips off at 6,500 feet during descent, but the crew uses their parachutes and land safely.

1934 September 9 American Rocket Society launches a seven-and-one-half-foot-long rocket (Number 4) that possibly approaches 700 mph, becoming the first to pass the sonic barrier (or surpass the speed of sound). It climbs to nearly 400 feet and travels downrange 1,338 feet.

1934
September 26
Queen Mary
sets sail

1934 September 26 *Queen Mary*, most famous transatlantic liner of all time, leaves Southampton, England on its maiden voyage to New York. It becomes the fastest liner for some years, and carries 2,139 passengers and a crew of 1,101. It is over 80,000 gross tons and is 1,019 feet (310.6 meters) long. During World War II, it serves as a troopship. It is now anchored in Long Beach, California as a floating museum.

1934 October 12 Association of American Railroads is formed by the merger of the American Railway Association and four other organizations. It acts in regard to all research, operations, traffic, accounting, and finance matters.

1934 October 22—November 4 First flight from Australia to North America is made in a Lockheed *Altair* by Englishmen Charles Kingsford-Smith (1899—1935) and Capt. P. G. Taylor. They fly from Brisbane to Oakland, California after stopping in Fiji and Hawaii.

1934 November 11 First lightweight streamlined passenger train to use diesel-electric power and the first to go into regular, daily service, begins operations between Lincoln, Nebraska and Kansas City, Missouri.

1934 November 18 U.S. Navy contracts with Northrop Aviation for the *XBT-1*, a two-seat scout and 1,000-pound bomb dive bomber. This prototype leads to the *SBD Dauntless* series of dive bombers used throughout World War II.

1934 December German Army Kummersdorf rocket development group (Reidel, Von Braun, Dornberger) fires the A-2 rocket straight up for a distance of over one mile. Launched on the North Sea island of Borkum, it begins a series of successful A-2 flights that demonstrate the rocket's military potential. The groundwork for the future V-2 rocket is now laid. (See Oct. 1939)

1934 December 4 First Australian rocket mail experiment is conducted at Brisbane. A solid-fuel (gunpowder) rocket carries 900 letters from the deck of a ship.

1935 Adolf Busemann (b. 1901), German scientist at the Volta Conference in Rome, suggests the use of swept-back wings and tails to delay and reduce the sharp increase in drag and pressure that occurs as the speed of sound is approached and exceeded. (See January 20, 1945)

1935 U.S. road builders and city planners adopt viaducts for cars as a solution to the increasingly hazardous places where trains cross highways. These elevated overpasses or bridges allow cars to pass over the tracks, thus avoiding both delays and train-car accidents.

c. 1935 By this time, motorcycles are developing the all-enclosed engine as a means of giving it a smooth, weatherproof, and easily-cleaned exterior. Twist-grip throttle controls and foot-operated gear change mechanisms are now standard. The old form rear stand is being replaced by the simpler and easier lean-to side stand.

1935 New bicycle gear system, the single epicyclic gear-train, three-speed hub gears are produced in England by Sturmey-Archer. It uses a new trigger-control for gear changing that is mounted on the handlebars and offers a simpler and easier way of changing gears.

1935 First automobile headlight flashers appear on the Fiat 1500 model in Italy.

1935 First car to offer windshield washers is the British Triumph.

1935 Japanese automobile manufacturing company Toyota is founded by Kiichiro Toyoda. Changing the name to the more phonetic Toyota Motor Company in 1937, the firm excels at taking an existing car model and making their copy entirely better than the original. It has become the largest car maker in Japan, selling huge numbers of its quality cars in the United States.

1935 U.S. automobile manufacturers begin serious manipulation of the market by changing their annual New York auto show from January to November (maintaining demand through the usually slack winter months), and by advertising new body style changes made each year as significant and desirable.

1935 Soviet rocket designed by Mikhail K. Tikhonravov successfully reaches an altitude of six miles in a meteorological experiment.

1935 Modern radar system is developed by Scottish physicist Robert A. Watson-Watt (1892—1973). Using the known principle that radio waves travel at the velocity of light and are reflected back to the sender when they strike a solid object, he builds a warning system for enemy aircraft that is secretly adopted by the British and put into operation. By the time of the Battle of Britain in 1940, the British are able to detect all incoming German aircraft in any weather or at night. These ground stations are quickly developed into airborne systems as well. Radar is named by Watson-Watt who originally calls it "radio detection and ranging." Today it is used at all airports for air-traffic control and for landing planes during zero visibility. In the future, radar may be used on automobiles as collision-avoidance systems.

1935 Motor Carriers Act of 1935 becomes U.S. law and requires the licensing and publication of rates by road transport "common carriers." It also gives the Interstate Commerce Commission the power to regulate rates. This act comes about as the previously-unregulated road transport industry undercuts rail rates and threatens to financially wreck the rail system.

1935 January 31 First lightweight streamlined train equipped with distillate-electric power goes into service between Salina, Kansas and Kansas City, Missouri.

1935 March 6 U.S. secretary of commerce signs a special air traffic regulation that prohibits air flights over parts of Washington, D.C.

1935 March 8 American Robert H. Goddard (1888—1945) launches a rocket equipped with a 10-foot recovery parachute. It reaches an altitude of 1,000 feet and lands 11,000 feet from the tower. He later describes this as "the best flight we have ever had during the entire research. The streamlined rocket traveled nearly 700 mph...."

1935 March 9 Hermann Goering (1893—1946), former German World War I air ace, openly announces the formation of the German Air Force (Luftwaffe). This marks Germany's unilateral rejection of the Treaty of Versailles which, after World War I, had prohibited it from forming an air force. Goering eventually is promoted to the unique rank of "Reichs-marshall" for his part in Germany's 1940 air victory over France.

1935 March 28 Robert H. Goddard (1888—1945) launches a rocket with improved gyroscopic controls in Roswell, New Mexico. The nearly 15-foot-long rocket reaches an altitude of 4,800 feet and a range of

*1935
March 9
German Air
Force
formed*

1935 ■ Robert H. Goddard and Charles A. Lindbergh meet in New Mexico.

1935 ■ Rotary Club ambulance in Sea Isle City, New Jersey.

13,000 feet. During its 20-second flight, it goes nearly supersonic and averages 550 mph.

1935 May Only French liner to hold the transatlantic speed record, the *Normandie*, leaves Le Havre, France on its maiden voyage.

1935 May 15

Moscow subway opens

1935 May 15 Moscow subway system opens its 22-station core. This first section is built mostly by hand by the cut-and-cover method. With its extension after World War II, it becomes the world's busiest underground system, moving 6.5 million passengers a day.

1935 May 31 Robert H. Goddard (1888—1945) launches an 84-pound, 15-foot rocket to an altitude of 7,500 feet in Roswell, New Mexico. This is the highest altitude yet reached by Goddard. It lands over one mile away from the tower, digging a 10-foot-deep hole in the ground.

1935 June 26 Louis Breguet (1880—1955) successfully flies his helicopter after a long period of development. Called the Breguet *Dorand 314*, it has twin co-axial rotors. Although it marks an advance, it is neither fully practical nor controllable.

1935 July World's first parking meter is installed in Oklahoma City, Oklahoma. It looks almost exactly like today's meters, except it is shorter. Meters do not appear in Great Britain until 1958.

1935 July 28 Boeing *Model 299*, called the *XB-17*, a four-engine U.S. bomber prototype, makes it first flight. Its successor, the *B-17*, becomes one of the most successful bombers of World War II.

1935 August 15 Record-setting American pilot Wiley Post (1899—1935) and his passenger, American humorist Will Rogers (1879—1935), are killed in an airplane crash near Point Barrow, Alaska. Post is setting out to survey a new air route over Siberia when his Lockheed *Orion* crashes on takeoff.

1935 September First ship to be equipped with radar, the German vessel *Welle*, undergoes sea trials. The ship is able to detect and range coastlines from as far away as 12 miles and can detect other ships at five miles.

1935 October 1 British Airways is formed out of an amalgamation of three smaller private airlines, Hillman's Airways, Spartan Air Lines, and United Airways.

1935 October 30 First *B-17* prototype crashes on takeoff during flight tests. Despite this early failure, the *B-17* comes to be known as the *Flying Fortress* during World War II. It becomes the "classic" American day bomber during the war.

1935 November 6 British prototype of the Hawker *Hurricane* fighter makes its first flight. Later models of this fighter destroy more enemy aircraft in the Battle of Britain (1940) than all other British defenses, air and ground, combined.

1935 November 11 Altitude record for balloons of 72,395 feet (c. 22,656 meters) is established in the United States by Orville A. Anderson (b. 1895) and Albert W. Stevens (b. 1886) in *Explorer II*. After a trip of 125 miles (200 kilometers) from their starting point, they fly for a total of eight hours, 13 minutes. This altitude record for free balloons remains until November 1956.

1935 ■ First prototype Volkswagen "Beetle" (top) and 50th anniversary version (bottom).

1935 November 22 First scheduled air mail flight across the Pacific from San Francisco, California to the Philippines is made by pilot Edwin C. Musick in a Pan American Martin *Clipper*.

1935 December 17 First flight of Douglas *DC-3* is made. One of the most famous and popular airplanes of all time, it is the definitive expression of the new American transport aircraft, with its all-metal structure, low-wing configuration, twin radial engines, and retractable landing gear. It is rugged, handles well, and is

almost as comfortable as a train. All it needs to be a truly modern airliner is cabin pressurization. Altogether, 10,654 are built, and some are still in use today. It is possibly the greatest transport aircraft of all time.

1936 First pop-up headlights are offered on the innovative Cord Model 810 automobile. The lights are raised by manual winding. This interesting car has a V-8 engine giving 125 hp, front-wheel drive, and a four-speed transmission.

1936 First diesel-engine automobile offered for sale to the public is the Mercedes-Benz 260 D from Germany. An extremely sturdy car, it demonstrates that diesel engines can be used on autos as well as trucks. Mercedes still offers a diesel on certain models.

1936 Jaguar automobile's famous "big cat" hood ornament is designed by Frederick Gordon-Crosby. At first an optional extra and later an obligatory ornament, it disappears for good in 1970 because of safety regulations.

1936 Age of the American trailer begins in earnest. It is estimated that 160,000 trailers are on the road this year as Americans take advantage of their new, affordable mobility by hitching camping trailers to the back of their cars and seeing America.

1936 Hungarian-born engineer Theodore von Kármán (1881—1963) co-founds a group which begins experiments in design fundamentals of high altitude sounding rockets. Called Galcit (Guggenheim Aeronautical Laboratory of the California Institute of Technology), this program eventually leads to the creation of the Jet Propulsion Laboratory. Besides von Karman, the group consists of Weld Arnold, Frank J. Malina (1912—1981), Hsue-shen Tsien, Edward S. Farman, John W. Parsons, and A. M. O. Smith (b. 1911). (See November 1, 1944)

1936 U.S. Congress passes the Merchant Marine Act of 1936 which eventually results in a long range shipbuilding program subsidized by the federal government. During this year, the U.S. Maritime Commission is also created.

1936 Second longest steel arch bridge, the Bayonne Bridge, is built over the Kill van Kull, between Newark, New Jersey and Staten Island, New York. Designed by Othmar H. Ammann (1879—1965), this

1,652-foot-long bridge carries two rail tracks and six lanes for automobiles.

1936 First practical hydrofoil is built in Germany by Hanns von Schertel. His newly-developed V-shaped foil system allows him to finally solve the problem of stability in rough water. It works so well in tests on the Rhine River, that the German Navy places orders for military hydrofoils.

1936 February German Army Kummersdorf rocket group (Reidel, Von Braun, Dornberger) test an A-3 rocket with 3,300 pounds of thrust. Specifications for its design are based on military considerations, and it is a precursor to the planned A-4, long-range weapon.

1936
March 4

Hindenburg
makes first
flight

1936 March 4 First flight of the German Zeppelin *LZ-129 Hindenburg* is made in Germany. She and her sister-ship, *LZ-138 Graf Zeppelin II*, are the last rigid airships built. (See May 6, 1937)

1936 March 5 First flight of the prototype of the British Supermarine *Spitfire*, a single-seater, monoplane fighter. It is the only British aircraft to remain in production throughout the war and is perhaps the most famous aircraft of World War II.

1936 March 5 The Russians are reportedly launching liquid-fuel rockets into the stratosphere (about seven miles up and higher) that carry instruments and recovery parachutes.

1936 March 16 The Smithsonian Institution publishes Robert H. Goddard's (1888—1945) report, "Liquid Propellant Rocket Development." This report reviews his liquid-fuel rocket research and flight testing done since his first 1919 report.

1936 May 9 German airship *Hindenburg* lands at Lakehurst, New Jersey after its first scheduled transatlantic flight. Built by German firm Zeppelin Transport Company, it is powered by four 1,050-hp Daimler Benz diesel engines and has a range of 8,000 miles. (See May 6, 1937)

1936 May 13 The Australian National Airways (ANA) is formed by incorporating Holyman's Airways, Adelaide Airways, Airlines of Australia, and West Australian Airways.

1936 May 22 Herrick *Vertaplane*, designed by American Gerald Herrick, undergoes safety tests and speed trials. This is Herrick's second attempt at a combination aircraft/autogyro. It has two wings, the upper serving either as a fixed, second wing (airplane) or as a lifting rotor (gyroplane). During 1937, it converts successfully from biplane to autogyro, but experiences other aerodynamic problems that prevent it from ever becoming operational.

1936 June 26 First flight of the first practical helicopter with two side-by-side rotors is made in Germany. Designed by Heinrich Focke (b. 1890), the Focke-Achgelis *FW-61* makes many flights, the longest being one hour and 20 minutes. It is a stable and controllable aircraft, but its success is not immediately exploited. (See 1937)

1936 July 18 Spanish Civil War begins and gives Germans, Italians, and Russians the opportunity to test their aircraft and air units under battle conditions.

1936 October 13 Robert H. Goddard (1888—1945) is visited by U.S. Lt. John W. Sessums who is to officially evaluate the military potential of Goddard's rocket research. Sessums later reports there is little military value, although rockets may be useful to drive turbines.

1936 October 14 Dover-Dunkirk train ferry service and through trains opens between London and Paris.

1936 October 21 First transpacific passenger service begins as Pan American Airways uses Hawaii, Midway, Wake Island, and Guam as stepping stones to the Phillipines. A graceful Martin four-engine *China Clipper* makes the round trip to Manila.

1936 November 7 American Robert H. Goddard (1888—1945) launches what is probably the first four-chambered liquid-propelled rocket ever. The 13.5-foot rocket reaches about 200 feet using a cluster of four, 5.75 inches diameter combustion chambers.

1936 November 10 President Franklin D. Roosevelt (1882—1945) states a new U.S. policy covering the export of military planes, which stipulates that foreign countries wishing to buy American-made aircraft types used by the United States, must wait two years for delivery.

1936 ■ West bay crossing of San Francisco-Oakland Bay Bridge.

1936 November 12 San Francisco-Oakland Bay Bridge is first opened to automobile traffic. Before this six-lane bridge was built, 35 million ferry boat commuters annually pass over the bay in trips that average one hour. The physical linking of San Francisco and Oakland, California is accomplished by what is actually two suspension bridges joined end to end at a common anchorage point, a 540-foot (165-meter) tunnel through Yerba Buena Island, and a 1,400-foot (426-meter) span cantilever bridge to the mainland. The whole adds up to a four-and-one-half-mile (6.8-kilometer) crossing on two decks, with six lanes of traffic on the upper and three lanes for heavy vehicles on the lower plus two interurban tracks. Over 50 years later, it is damaged by an earthquake. (See October 17, 1989)

1937 First flight of the *Ju-87* single-engine dive-bomber is made. It is the prototype of the *Stuka* which is used effectively by the Germans in the Spanish Civil War and also in support of their armies during World War II.

1937 First flight of over an hour by a helicopter is made in Germany by the Focke-Achgelis *FW-61*.

1937 First drive-in bank opens in Los Angeles, California. In the United States today, drive-in (or drive-through) fast food establishments outnumber drive-in banks.

1937 A.D.

First drive-in bank opens

1937 First American car to offer windshield washers is the Studebaker.

1937 Soviet Union realizes the obvious military potential of rockets and establishes test centers at Kazan, Moscow, and Leningrad.

1937 As electric power is extended even to the more remote parts of the United States, the Lighthouse Service has converted most of its lighthouses to electric lights.

1937 Passenger train ferry service is established between Dover, England and Dunkirk, France.

1937 First turbine propulsion system using oxygen generated by hydrogen peroxide is invented by German engineer Hellmuth Walter (b. 1900). Prior to this system, submarines have to surface and run their diesel engines to recharge the underwater batteries. Walter's new engine uses chemical catalysts to break down hydrogen peroxide into water and oxygen. The freed oxygen is fed into a combustion chamber with diesel fuel to produce steam which runs a turbine. Submarines can now carry their own oxygen for power consumption.

1937 January 1 First laboratory for physiological research is established at Wright Field by the U.S. Air Corps to study all aspects of flight-related stress and discomfort.

1937 January 29 The National Air Show, New York's first in seven years, opens and achieves a one-week record attendance of over 250,000 people and a sales of planes and accessories of over $1 million.

1937 March A two-way train telephone communication system is begun between Albion, Pennsylvania and North Bessemer Yard, Pittsburgh.

1937 March 21 First air transport suicide in the United States occurs as Anatole Maren leaps from a United Airlines plane near Bakersfield, California.

1937 ■ *Hindenburg* is destroyed by fire in Lakehurst, New Jersey.

1937 April First set of U.S. radar equipment is installed on a ship and successfully demonstrated in Chesapeake Bay. This system is developed at the U.S. Naval Research Laboratory.

1937 April 12

Jet engine tested

1937 April 12 First practical jet engine is bench-tested by its inventor, Englishman Frank Whittle (b. 1907), at the laboratories of Cambridge University in England.

1937 April 26 The bombing of Guernica, a Basque fishing village in northern Spain, is conducted by German aircraft supporting General Francisco Franco's (1892—1975) Nationalists. This particluarly terroristic act later motivates Spanish artist Pablo Picasso (1881—1973), who creates a large oil painting named "Guernica." The popular anti-war painting makes the town's name synonymous with the inhumanity of war, especially modern aerial warfare.

1937 April 28 First commercial flight across the Pacific is made as a Pan-American Boeing *314 Clipper* seaplane arrives in Hong Kong.

1937 May The German Army rocket experiment station at Peenemünde is opened. Capt. Walter Dornberger (1895—1980) and the Kummerdorf group need a larger and more secret location to test their more powerful rockets. The Peenemünde site is recommended by civilian Wernher von Braun (1912—1977) who discovers its remoteness during a holiday visit to relatives in 1935.

1937 May Golden Gate Bridge across San Francisco Bay, California, is opened to traffic. Designed by Joseph B. Strauss (1870—1938), this suspension bridge with a 4,200-foot (1,280-meter) span links San Francisco to Marin County in the north across the bay. Securing its steel towers presents unique problems, as the south tower is 1,125 feet (343 meters) from shore, virtually in the open sea. These beautifully designed towers are eventually laid upon solid rock and rise some 746 feet above the water, making for a striking feature.

1937 May 6 German airship *Hindenburg* explodes into flames at Lakehurst, New Jersey while attempting to dock after a transatlantic flight. Thirty-six of the ninety-seven people aboard die, with many survivors suffering burns. The demise of this huge airship, which offered luxury round trip passage at $720, brings to an inglorious end the era of the great airships.

1937 May 7 First successful pressurized airplane cabin is achieved in the Lockheed *XC-35*. As the new generation of aircraft fly higher, passenger comfort becomes a problem, since the higher air is both extremely cold and thin, and difficult to breathe. Once Lockheed solves the problem of making the fuselage or cabin airtight, it begins regular, high-altitude flights.

1937 May 9 Hugh F. Pierce launches his independently-built liquid-fuel rocket to about 250 feet in the Bronx, New York. He later founds, with three others, Reaction Motors, Inc. This is the first U.S. commercial liquid-fuel rocket company. (See 1941)

1937 May 23 U.S. Bureau of Air Commerce begins work on an estimated $5 million airways modernization program covering 23,000 miles of government-controlled airways.

1937 July 2 Amelia Earhart (1898—1937) and navigator Fred Noonan are lost over the South Pacific near Howland Island in a Lockheed *Electra*. This is to be her last long-distance attempt, and she intends to conclude her career with a very long (27,000 mile), round-the-world flight close to the bulge of the equator. It is assumed that she suffers engine failure during a storm, but no one knows for sure.

1937 July 12—14 First non-stop flight from Moscow, U.S.S.R. to California over Arctic regions of 6,750 miles (c. 10,860 kilometers) is made by the Soviet crew of Gromov, Umasheff, and Danilin in an Antonov *ANT 25*.

1937 September Feathering propellers are used on a Lockheed *Model 14* transport aircraft in the United States. These cut the drag of a dead engine on multi-engined aircraft by changing the propeller blade angle.

1937 September 30 Air mail service begins between the United States and Paraguay.

1937 September 30 U.S. Navy's newest aircraft carrier, the *USS Yorktown,* with a capacity for carrying 72 airplanes, is commissioned at Newport News, Virginia.

1937 December U.S. Naval Academy midshipman Robert A. Truax develops, builds, and tests a small liquid propellent rocket engine that delivers an initial thrust of 25 pounds. His work leads to the wartime Navy-sponsored rocket research program in Annapolis, Maryland.

1938 German scientist Heinz von Diringshofen (b. 1900) conducts research on the human ability to tolerate multiple g-loads by exposing test subjects to a few seconds of increased force or pressure on their bodies by having an aircraft make a vertical dive.

1938 In studies of hypoxia (oxygen deficiency), the duration factor is shown to be of vital importance to a pilot's performance. This is demonstrated in animal experiments conducted by H. G. Armstrong (b. 1899) and J. W. Heim.

1938 First year of the longest-ever automobile production run, the Volkswagen "Beetle." Designed by Ferdinand Porsche (1875—1952), a versatile, Austro-Hungarian automotive designer and sponsored by the German government as a "people's car," it is conceived as an economical, not too small, sturdy, low-priced car for a soon-to-be-mobile public. It is enthusiastically received, especially when the government introduces a plan allowing anyone to reserve a new VW by paying a certain amount every month.

1938 First steering column gear shift is introduced in the United States by Cadillac and becomes common on most manual shift cars.

1938 First automobile air conditioning system is offered by Nash. This system filters and heats air from the outside before it enters the car's interior. It will evolve into a total system that regulates the air temperature and humidity of a car's interior and will make driving more comfortable and quiet.

1938 Eugen Sänger (1905—1964) and his fellow worker (and later his wife), Irene Brendt, begin designing an "antipodal rocket bomber" at Germany's Research Institute for the Technique of Rocket Flight. This plan envisions a 92-foot-long rocket launched from a track that would attain 1,000 mph. Its liquid-fuel rockets

1938 ■ Hanna Reitsch flies a Focke helicopter inside a Berlin sports arena.

would send it to 160 miles high where it would skip along the upper edge of the atmosphere like a stone on a pond. When war breaks out, Sänger suggests the plane be used to deliver a bomb to New York City. It is never built.

1938 A.D.

First inflatable life rafts produced

1938 First inflatable canopied life rafts are produced by the RFD Company, named after Englishman Reginald F. Dagnall. They are first adopted by the Royal Canadian Air Force.

1938 First usable, sea-going radar system is installed on the British ship *Rodney*.

1938 February Hanna Reitsch, German aviator and the first woman to pilot a helicopter, demonstrates a Focke-Achgelis Fa-61 twin-rotor helicopter by flying every night for three weeks inside the cavernous Deutschlandhalle arena in Berlin, Germany. Every performance is packed, and the Nazis score a publicity coup.

1938 April 20

First rocket with barograph launched

1938 April 20 American Robert H. Goddard (1888—1945) launches a rocket carrying a National Aeronautics Association barograph to certify its altitude. The 18-foot-tall, liquid-fuel rocket reaches an average height of 4,215 feet.

1938 April 21 Tests in National Advisory Committee for Aeronautics' (NACA) full-scale wind tunnel on the *XF2A-1* show testers how to redesign and increase aircraft speed by 31 mph. These dramatic performance improvements show how valuable wind tunnel tests are and lead to their use by the Army and Navy.

1938 April 22 American World War I ace Eddie Rickenbacker (1890—1973) buys Eastern Air Lines from North American Aviation for $3.5 million. This is roughly the cost of a single engine for a Boeing *757* today.

1938 August 11—14 First round trip flight, Germany to United States (Berlin-New York-Berlin), is made by the four-engine transport, Focke-Wulf *Condor* in 24 hours, 56 minutes outbound, and 19 hours, 55 minutes upon its return.

1938 August 22 The Civil Aeronautics Act becomes effective in the United States, coordinating all nonmilitary aviation under the Civil Aeronautics Authority.

1938 September 12 Advances in wind tunnel research continue as the Massachusetts Institute of Technology dedicates a wind tunnel capable of simulating altitudes of 37,000 feet.

1938 October 17 Trans-Canada Air Lines begins operations. It later becomes Air Canada.

1938 November 5—7 First non-stop flight from Egypt to Australia is made by two British Vickers *Wellesleys*. Covering 7,158 miles (11,520 kilometers) between Ismailia and Darwin, this is the longest non-stop, unrefuelled distance flown by a military aircraft prior to World War II.

1938 November 19 Construction begins on a new airport serving the nation's capital, Washington, D.C. Actually built in nearby Virginia, this becomes what is today National Airport.

1938 ■ Boeing B-314 *Yankee Clipper.*

1938 November 29—30 A record for airplanes weighing less than 700 pounds is set as Johnny Jones flies nonstop from Los Angeles, California to New York in a Piper *Cub* in 30 hours, 37 minutes.

1938 December 10 First static test of American James H. Wyld's regeneratively cooled rocket thrust chambers are made, achieving a thrust of 90 pounds. Circulation of the fuel itself, instead of water or air, is used to cool the combustion chamber.

1938 December 15 Minimum wage for employees in the aircraft industry is fixed by the U.S. Department of Labor at 50 cents an hour, equalling $20 for a 40-hour week.

1938 December 31 First flight of Boeing *307 Stratoliner*, the first passenger plane to have a pressurized cabin, is made. This four-engine aircraft carries 33 passengers over long distances. With the cabin pressurized with warm air for passenger comfort, the new generation of airliners could take advantage of high-altitude operation where maximum speed could be attained for minimum power. (See March 21, 1940)

1939 American aircraft industry now ranks as 44th largest in the United States and reaches the highest level of activity in its 30-year history.

1939 Superchargers that are gear-driven and have multi-speeds are brought into use on airplane engines in England. These help an engine maintain efficiency at high altitudes where the air is thinner, by compressing the air as it is drawn into each cylinder.

1939 U.S. Bureau of Public Roads submits its report, *Toll Roads and Free Roads,* to Congress. It concludes that the construction of six superhighways criss-crossing the country was practical and needed, but was too expensive. This document, along with its 1944 report, *Interregional Highways,* serve as basic studies leading to 1944 legislation providing for a National System of Interstate Highways. (See 1944)

1939 First Pope to use an automobile regularly is Pope Pius XII (1876—1958). Pius X (1835-1914) was presented with an Italian car as early as 1909, but refused to ride in it.

1939 A.D.

Pope Pius XII uses car

1939 As World War II begins in Europe, light folding bicycles are produced in England for military transport purposes, especially for airborne troops.

1939 Longest underwater auto tunnel in Japan and the world's first under-ocean tunnel, the Kanmon Tunnel, is begun. Connecting Honshu and Kyushu Islands, it is under the sea (the Kanmon Straits) rather than a river. Although it is 2.2 miles long, it is also used by many pedestrians upon completion in 1958.

1939 Flashing turn signals for automobiles, developed by the Guide Lamp Division of the General Motors Corporation, are introduced by Buick.

c. 1939 Autocycle is established in Europe as an economical form of personal motor transport. As a sort of ultra-light motorcycle, it has a small two-stroke engine, a hand clutch, and pedalling gear. It becomes even more popular in Europe after World War II.

1939 First proposal for a nuclear-powered submarine is made by American physicist Ross Gunn (1897—1966) of the U.S. Naval Research Laboratory. His work is put off while the United States concentrates on building an atomic bomb during World War II. (See 1946)

1939 Albert Canal, perhaps Belgium's best-known waterway, is completed. Built to connect the Meuse River with the Scheldt River from Liege to Antwerp, it is 81 miles long. At one point, the Geer River passes under the canal via a large pipe.

1939 January

Trans-Iranian Railway completed

1939 January Trans-Iranian Railway is completed after nearly 12 years under construction. It links the Caspian Sea with the Persian Gulf.

1939 April 23 U.S. Civil Aeronautics Authority raises the eligibility age for obtaining a private pilot license to 18 years from previous 16 years of age.

1939 May 20 First North Atlantic air mail service is started by Pan American Airways which carries the mail between Long Island, New York, the Azores, Portugal, and Marseille, France.

1939 June 18 First direct transatlantic seaplane service is begun by Pan American Airways. It flies from New York to Southampton, England, by way of Botwood, Newfoundland, and Foynes, Ireland.

1939 July 1 National Academy of Sciences sponsors the establishment of the Jet Propulsion Research Project at the California Institute of Technology. It gives $10,000 to develop a rocket suitable to boost planes during take-off. It becomes known as the JATO (jet assisted take off) project.

1939 August 5—7 First British transatlantic airmail service from England to Canada is begun by Imperial Airways. A flight-refuelled seaplane flies from Southampton to Montreal by way of Foynes, Ireland and Botwood, Newfoundland.

1939 August 27

First fully jet-propelled plane flies

1939 August 27 First fully jet-propelled aircraft to fly is Germany's *Heinkel 178*. It is powered by an He S3b centrifugal flow turbojet engine designed by Han von Ohain and piloted by Erich Warsitz. Although the Englishman Frank Whittle (b. 1907) was the pioneer of jet engines and produced one in 1937, it is the Germans who produce the first jet plane with an engine design very different from the British. Jet propulsion will revolutionize flying, but at this time, neither the Germans nor the British see its full potential, and operational jet aircraft do not appear until late in World War II. When they do emerge, however, they outclass everything else.

1939 September 1—3 Germany invades Poland using "blitzkrieg" (a fierce surprise offensive by air forces and ground forces in close coordination) techniques of modern war technology. England and France declare war on Germany.

1939 September 3 World War II (1939—1945) breaks out, eventually pitting Germany, Japan, and Italy against Britain, France, the Soviet Union, and the United States. Sea power plays an extremely important role in the war, especially given the vast armada required for the D-Day invasion of Normandy, France (June 6, 1944), but air power proves decisive.

1939 September 14 Igor Sikorsky (1889—1972) makes a tethered flight in his helicopter, the *VS-300*. It is from this basic design that most modern helicopters have descended. Sikorsky's new design has only one rotor for lift and two small tail rotors to counteract torque (the natural tendency of the body to twist with the rotors). Although crude-looking, it is the design of the future. (See May 13, 1940)

1939 ■ Igor Sikorsky flies his *VS-300* helicopter.

1939 October The German Army rocket group at Peenemünde launches the new A-5 rocket to an altitude of 7.5 miles and a range of 11 miles. The 2,000-

pound A-5 is an interim test vehicle between the A-3 and the larger A-4 (V-2). It is needed to test an improved guidance and control system. Several of the A-5's are recovered by parachute and flown again.

1939 October 15 New York Municipal Airport in North Beach, Queens, New York is officially dedicated as LaGuardia Field.

1939 October 24 A new "fighting harness" that anchors the pilot to his seat but can be released easily by pushing a button is developed by the U.S. Army Air Corps.

1939 November 26 British Overseas Airways Corporation (BOAC) is established by the amalgamation of Imperial Airways and British Airways.

1939 December 2 War in Europe spurs the U.S. Army Air Corps to begin development of a four-engine bomber with a 2,000 mile radius of action. This leads to the Boeing *B-29 Superfortress*.

1939 December 29 First flight of the prototype Consolidated *B-24 Liberator*. This four-engine heavy bomber is built in greater numbers than any other U.S. aircraft. More than 18,000 are completed, and it plays a major role in Europe and North Africa during World War II.

1940 In Japan, the project for Shinkansen (bullet train) is first conceived.

1940 First modern-type automatic transmission is offered as an option by General Motors on their Oldsmobile models. Called "Hydra-Matic," it makes gear changes according to varying road and load conditions, without the driver having to do anything, since each gear is controlled through fluid pressure which regulates brake band clamping and engages or disengages a clutch.

1940 Bantam Car Company of Butler, Pennsylvania makes a very functional, four-wheel drive, light military scout car for the U.S. Army. These four-cylinder vehicles can climb a 69% grade fully loaded and, with special canvas sides and a snorkel, even cross streams up to six feet deep. They eventually become known as Jeeps, a variation on the abbreviation for "General Purpose"—G.P. In 1941, the Ford and Willys-Overland companies begin producing them, since Bantam cannot meet the demand.

1940 Pennsylvania Turnpike is completed from Carlisle to Irvin, 11 miles east of Pittsburgh. This 160-mile highway has seven tunnels that divert high speed traffic around towns and through the Alleghany Mountains.

c. 1940 Thin rubber suit is developed by the U.S. Navy for "frogmen." This is a watertight suit under which divers wear an insulating wool suit.

1940 February 1 Bell *P-39 Airacobra* reaches flying speeds of over 600 mph during flight tests. This is the only single-engine, piston-powered airplane with the engine built into the middle of the fuselage that is ever mass produced. Bell places the engine in the middle so as to install a 37-mm cannon in front of the fuselage where it can fire through the hollow hub of the propeller. It also tends to increase the plane's maneuverability. Over 9,000 are built during World War II.

1940 February 28 Soviet rocket-powered glider designed by Sergei P. Korolev (1906—1966) flies under power and attains a top speed of 124 mph (200 km/h).

1940 March 21 Pan American Airways takes delivery of the first of its fleet of new Boeing *307* supercharged, pressure-cabin, passenger *Stratoliners*. It is the arrival of this new aircraft that marks the beginning of the era of truly efficient and comfortable long-haul passenger transport.

1940 March 25 United States releases over 600 aircraft under construction to Allies, giving them access to their latest models of warplanes.

1940 April North American Aircraft builds in 120 days, according to British design specifications, the prototype fighter/escort called the *P-51 Mustang*. It is the first airplane to utilize the new NACA low-drag wing, and proves to be an excellent fighter aircraft with long range.

1940 May 13 First successful free flight of a true helicopter is made by Igor I. Sikorsky's (1881—1972) single-rotor *VS-300*. Built by Vought-Sikorsky in the United States, the helicopter flies but is underpowered.

1940 May 16 U.S. President Franklin D. Roosevelt (1882—1945) asks Congress to pass legislation making it possible to increase the aircraft industry's production capacity to 50,000 airplanes per year. (See September 1, 1943)

1940 May 26 One of the most massive transport operations ever conducted—-the World War II Dunkirk evacuation—-begins as the British Cabinet authorizes the evacuation of Belgian, French, and English troops from this coastal area in northern France where they have been driven by German forces. Using warships, ferries, trawlers, and a wide variety of civilian water craft, they evacuate to England 338,225 men by June 4. This transport dilemma is solved by what is now recognized as a masterpiece of improvised logistics.

1940 May 28 Robert H. Goddard (1888—1945) offers U.S. military authorities (Army Ordnance, Army Air Corps, and Navy Bureau of Aeronautics) all his research data and rocket information, as well as patents and facilities, at a meeting arranged by Harry Guggenheim. Nothing comes from his offer except an interest in the possible use of rockets for jet-assisted takeoffs. U.S. authorities are either unable to see any military potential in rocket research or simply do not think his work has value.

1940 May 29 A new U.S. Navy fighter plane, the *F4U Corsair*, built by Chance Vought, makes its first test flight. This small fighter proves an excellent carrier aircraft, capable of high performance and carrying large offensive loads, and is called by many the best of all the Allied fighter planes.

1940 June 1 U.S. Army Air Corps announces plans for the construction of the world's most powerful wind tunnel at Wright Field, Dayton, Ohio.

1940 June 26 Paul Kollsman (b. 1900) and the Square D Company of Detroit make a gift of $50,000 to the Institute of the Aeronautical Sciences for the establishment of a nationwide aeronautical lending library.

1940 July 1 U.S. Civil Aeronautics Authority (CAA) becomes the Civil Aeronautics Board and part of the Commerce Department, directly under the secretary, Harry L. Hopkins.

1940 July 2 Lake Washington Floating Bridge opens to traffic in Seattle, Washington. The main portion of the bridge floats on huge concrete pontoons. It

is the largest floating structure built, until it is replaced in 1963 by the second Lake Washington Bridge. This new structure is 7,998 feet (2437.8 meters) long and has movable sections that can be temporarily moved to let ships pass.

1940 August Sir Henry Tizard (1885—1959), science advisor to the British Ministry of Aircraft Production, visits the United States and briefs Americans on advanced devices under active development by the British for use in the war. This begins a period of U.S.-U.K. cooperation, enabling the United States (which was not yet in the war) to catch up with Britain's war-accelerated progress in both aeronautics and rocketry.

1940 August 8—October 31 The Battle of Britain, one of the greatest air battles ever, is fought over Southeast England between the German Luftwaffe and England's RAF Fighter Command. The Germans fail to gain mastery of the air despite a much larger force, mainly due to British radar (which the Germans do not have) and flexible tactics. As a consequence, England is not invaded.

1940 August 19 First flight of the prototype North American *B-25 Mitchell*, named after American airpower advocate "Billy" Mitchell (1879—1936). It becomes one of the most successful Allied medium bombers of World War II.

1940 August 27 First flight of the experimental Caproni-Campini *N-1* piston-engine-driven compressor jet airplane is made at Tatiedo near Milan, Italy. (See November 30, 1941)

1940 September 28 U.S. Defense Commission informs all airplane manufacturers that they cannot accept orders for commercial transport planes without obtaining permission from the Commission.

1940 November 7 Tacoma Narrows Bridge over the Puget Sound, connecting the Olympic Peninsula with the mainland of the state of Washington, collapses due to wind vibration. As the third longest suspension bridge when built, it fails only four months after its completion. An extremely flexible bridge that gives signs of movement almost from the beginning, it starts to oscillate slowly during a wind between 42 and 44 mph, and then its undulations increase in severity until a 600-foot length falls into the Sound. Investigators learn an

1940 ■ Tacoma (Washington) bridge collapses.

important lesson about "aerodynamic instability," and ever since have tested scale models of bridges in wind tunnels. No one is killed in the collapse since the vibrating bridge is closed.

1940 November 25 British De Havilland *Mosquito* makes its first flight. One of the most versatile and fascinating aircraft of the war, this all-wood bomber has two Rolls-Royce Merlin engines that allow it to fly so fast that it does not need armament. During most of the war, it roams unmolested, performimg any task needed, whether high-speed bombing, fighting, or reconnaissance.

1940 November 26 U.S. Automotive Committee for Air Defense is organized in Detroit, Michigan to make automotive resources available for the production of parts and subassemblies for the aircraft manufacturing industry.

1940 December First Los Angeles freeway, the Arroyo Seco Parkway, is dedicated in California. This is the first step of what will become the ultimate example of a modern urban environment being defined by the automobile. By 1970 alone, some 60 percent of downtown Los Angeles will be dedicated to highway or parking needs.

1941 First four-wheel drive private car in series production is the six-cylinder GAZ-61 from the U.S.S.R. GAZ stands for the state-owned Gorkovski Auto Zavod in Gorki.

1941 First diesel-electric freight locomotives are placed into regular service in the United States on the "Santa Fe."

1941 First American company formed solely to build rockets is Reaction Motors, Inc. of Pompton Plains, New Jersey. It is founded late in this year by members of the American Rocket Society. One of its members, James H. Wyld, conducts successful tests of a liquid fuel rocket motor with an average thrust of 125 pounds, and the company is formed to continue work on this design.

1941 A.D.

First U.S. rocket company formed

1941 Largest, heaviest, and most powerful steam locomotive, the *Big Boy* of the Union Pacific Railroad, makes its first run. Capable of pulling up to 4,200 tons up a 60-mile mountain climb, the locomotive is 132 feet long and must be articulated or hinged to get around curves. These American locomotives prove highly successful, with the last being retired in 1962.

1941 January 9 First flight of the prototype Avro *Lancaster*, a four-engine, heavy bomber, which becomes the most successful British bomber of World War II. Nearly 7,400 *Lancasters* are built.

1941 April 1 British Royal Air Force equips all its fighter pilots's parachute packs with a one-man, yellow inflatable dinghy. It is developed by Reginald F. Dinhall's RFD Company. After World War II, it is estimated that 17,000 Allied airmen are saved after ditching because of these rafts.

1941 April 16 Igor I. Sikorsky (1889—1972) impressively demonstrates the capabilities of his *VS-300* helicopter by hovering virtually motionless over Stratford (Connecticut) Airport for one hour, five minutes. Powered by a larger, 90-hp engine, it sets a new helicopter record.

1941 May 6 First flight of the prototype Republic's *P-47 Thunderbolt*, one of the most successful American fighters of World War II.

1941 May 15 First British jet-propelled aircraft to fly is the turbojet, Gloster *E28/39*, which flies for 17 minutes powered by a Whittle W1 engine.

1941 June Record-setting pilot Jacqueline Cochrane becomes the first woman to ferry a bomber across the Atlantic from Canada to the British Isles to help out in the war effort.

1941

June 22

U.S. Army Air Forces formed

1941 June 22 U.S. War Department announces the reorganization of the U.S. Army Air Corps, unifying its air activities in a new unit to be known as the Army Air Forces, with Major Gen. H. H. Arnold (1886—1950) as chief.

1941 July—August First JATO (jet assisted take off) flights in the United States are made by Lt. Homer A. Boushey, U.S. Army Air Force, who flies a solid rocket-propelled Ercoupe monoplane on several occasions. Using the rockets developed by Cal Tech, the plane takes off in 7.5 seconds using 300 feet of runway compared to its normal, 13.1-second, 580-foot takeoff.

1941 September The Whittle jet-engine is flown from Britain to the United States and provides the model for the first practical American jet-engines built by General Electric.

1943 ∎ *Liberty* ship launch.

1941 September Robert H. Goddard (1888—1945) begins work on liquid-fuel JATO (jet assisted take off) for the Navy's Bureau of Aeronautics.

1941 September 27 First U.S. Liberty ship, the *Patrick Henry*, is launched. This is the first of 2,710 such ships produced by the United States during World War II. All share the same standard cargo ship design, and as American shipyard efficiency improves, they are built with increasing speed. In September 1942, three new ships are delivered every day, totalling 93 for that month alone. They prove to be excellent ships for cargo and troop transport, with turbine engines that give speeds up to 17 knots. Today, the only remaining preserved Liberty ship, the *Jeremiah O'Brien*, can be seen near Fisherman's Wharf in San Francisco, California.

1941 October 11 U.S. Civil Aeronautics Board amends Civil Air Regulations to require certification of every pilot and aircraft in the United States regardless of whether or not they are engaged in commercial activities.

1941 October 24 Record parachute descent is made by Arthur Starns who jumps from 30,500 feet and falls five miles in one minute, 55 seconds before pulling the rip cord.

1941 October 24 First true "flying wing" tailless bomber is announced by the U.S. Army Air Forces to be developed by Northrop Aircraft, Inc. In November, Northrop is given the contract to develop prototypes for what is to be called the *XB-35*. A flying wing is an aircraft consisting entirely of a single large, V-shaped wing within which is contained the engine, crew, and all its other systems.

1941 November 30 First Italian jet aircraft, the Caproni-Campini *CC2*, flies 475 kilometers from Turin to Rome in two hours, 11 minutes. Although called a "jet" plane, it is really a ducted propeller and afterburning jet. This is an extra burner attached to the tail pipe of a turbojet engine used for injecting fuel into the hot exhaust gases and burning that fuel to provide extra thrust.

1941 December 7 At 7:55 A.M. the U.S. Fleet at Pearl Harbor, Hawaii is attacked by a first wave of 183 Japanese planes. This surprise attack allows them to bomb and torpedo almost without interference. After a second wave of 170 Japanese planes wreak similar destruction, more than 2,000 Americans are killed and American power in the Pacific is virtually destroyed.

1941 December 18 Office of Defense Transportation is created by order of President Franklin D. Roosevelt (1882—1945). This decision comes less than two weeks after the Japanese bombing of Pearl Harbor. Roosevelt must see war as inevitable and realizes the crucial importance of all aspects of transportation to the coming effort.

1942 First affordable American car built with full unitary construction is the Nash 600 sedan. It has a box section frame that is fully welded directly to the body. Such a unitary frame, in which all its parts or members are interrelated and carry loads, is both better built and safer.

1942 Only trench-type tunnel in Europe opens to traffic. Built under the Maas River at Rotterdam, Holland, it is a twin-tube tunnel, 3,512 feet long with four separate lanes for autos, bicyclists, and pedestrians. (See 1906)

1942 January 13 First fully-practical, single rotor helicopter makes a successful flight as Igor I.

Sikorsky's (1889—1972) *XR-4* clearly demonstrates he has solved the problems of control and stability inherent in rotating (advancing and retreating) blades or rotors. This is the first classic helicopter to use a single powered rotor to accomplish all the things that a helicopter should do: vertical take-off and landing; hovering stationary in the air; progressing through the air; flying backwards, sideways, and forward.

1942 February 10 Last new U.S. automobile produced until 1945 rolls off the Ford assembly line. Automakers will now switch to producing tanks, jeeps, aircraft, and other transportation-related material.

1942 February 14 First flight of a four-engined airliner, the Douglas *DC-4*, is made in the United States. This is the first modern-type, long-range airliner and sets the trend for many post-war piston-engined transports.

1942 February 17 U.S. War Production Board restricts sales of light planes to government agencies only, or to individuals they approve.

1942 March 10 Largest single highway construction project to date begins as the United States, citing strategic importance of Alaska during World War II, decides to build the Alaska Highway as quickly as possible. Ten thousand troops cut through forests and frozen ground, followed by 14,000 civilian workmen with heavy road-building machinery. In about 20 months, a 1,480-mile road opens to vehicular traffic, extending from Dawson Creek to Fairbanks.

1942 March 10 Construction of Alaska Highway begins

1942 March 19 Pioneer U.S. rocket-building company Aerojet Engineering Corporation is organized in Azusa, California by a group associated with the California Institute of Technology. It builds JATO (jet assisted take off) units during the war. It is eventually absorbed by the General Tire and Rubber Company in 1944.

1942 April 19 Two feasibility tests using drone (pilotless) aircraft are conducted by the U.S. Navy in Chesapeake Bay. The most successful is Project Fox *BG-2*, a drone equipped with a target-viewing television camera, which dives onto a moving raft while being guided by an airborne control pilot 11 miles away. This successful, remote-control craft can be viewed as a precursor to the "smart" bombs used today.

1942 June 13 First long-range strategic weapon system propelled by a rocket motor, the German A-4 (V-2) rocket, is launched at Peenemünde for the first time. It rises above the cloud cover, and then falls back and explodes, after a climb to 0.8 miles. The V-2 missile stands 46 feet, 11 inches tall, and is five feet, five inches in diameter, weighing 14 tons at takeoff. It would carry a warhead variously listed as 1,650 and 2,150 pounds. Its maximum range would be about 200 miles, with a combat trajectory height of 60 miles. Its speed is approximately 3,300 mph at burnout.

1942 June 17 U.S. Army Air Forces conduct test at Wright Field in Dayton, Ohio, successfully picking up gliders from the ground by an airplane flying at more than 100 mph.

1942 June 27 U.S. Naval Aircraft Factory is directed to join the Army's efforts to develop a high-altitude pressure flying suit for pilots and crew.

1942 July 18 First flight with two turbojet engines is made by German Messerschmitt *Me-262* turbojet fighter. This concludes a series of spectacular flight tests, using Junkers turbojet engines, that began during May 1942.

1942 July 27

Flight jacket parachute patented

1942 July 27 A new patent is granted to U.S. Navy Lt. Cmdr. A. B. Vosseller (b. 1903) covering a new parachute that is built directly into the back of an aviator's flight jacket.

1942 September Robert H. Goddard (1888—1945) delivers a JATO (jet assisted take off) device to the U.S. Navy. Until his death in 1945, he works on variable thrust engines as director of research in jet propulsion at the Naval Engineering Experiment Station in Annapolis, Maryland.

1942 September

Wartime gas rationing begins

1942 September Wartime conservation measures force the United States to order nationwide gasoline rationing, mainly to conserve dwindling rubber supplies. All motorists are assigned a gas ration sticker according to their needs, and pleasure driving is banned. A 35 mph speed limit is established on all U.S. highways.

1942 September 21 First flight is made by the Boeing *XB-29* bomber, which comes to be known as the *Superfortress*. It becomes an indispensable aircraft in the Pacific, and leads the first major air attack on Tokyo, Japan in November 1944.

1942 October 1 First U.S.-built jet-propelled aircraft, Bell's *XP-59*, flies at Muroc Dry Lake, California. Powered by two General Electric I-16 engines and piloted by Robert Stanley (b. 1903), it becomes known as Bell Aircraft's *Airacomet*. It is not a very successful fighter, however, and sees no action in the war.

1942 October 3 First successful launch of A-4 (V-2) rocket is made at Peenemünde. It climbs over 50 miles high and travels to a point 118 miles away, veering off course by only 4 kilometers. Called "Vergeltungswafen" or weapons of retaliation, the V-2 is 46.1 feet long and weighs 27,000 pounds with a pointed nose and finned bottom.

1942 November 30 Alcan International Highway officially opens. It is a cooperative venture between the United States and Canada to link Alaska with the Canadian province of Alberta.

1943 First jet-propelled rotor helicopter, the Doblhoff *V1*, flies successfully. Built in Austria by the Wiener Neustadter Flugzeugwerke (WNF), it has an afterburner rather than a pure jet engine. It is damaged during air raids in Vienna.

1943 The only U.S. aircraft built with both a piston/propeller engine and a jet engine is begun by Ryan Aircraft. Called the *FR Fireball* fighter, this long-range, high-performance plane sees service after the war, using its economical piston engine in its nose for long-range cruising and its jet engine in the tail for high performance in combat.

1943 Chicago, Illinois subway system first opens.

1943 Aqualung or scuba gear (self-contained underwater breathing apparatus) is developed by Frenchmen Jacques-Yves Cousteau (b. 1910) and Emile Gagnan. This system allows a diver to swim freely down to about 180 feet (55 meters). It consists of three small bottles of highly compressed air that the diver wears on his back, and which is connected to a demand regulator which automatically supplies air at the correct pressure according to the diver's depth. Later, this system will be improved and divers will use a mixture of oxygen and helium rather than normal air (oxygen and nitrogen), since this will allow them to operate as deep as 1,640 feet (500 meters).

1943 January 8 First U.S. aircraft with a permanently installed JATO (jet assisted take off) rocket powerplant takes off at Muroc, California. It is an *A-20A* medium bomber.

1943 March First wholly American-designed turbojet engine, the X-19A, is completed by Westinghouse Electric. It is the precursor of the J series engines (J30, J34, J40, J46, and J54).

1943 March 5 First flight of the British jet-propelled prototype Gloster *Meteor*, the first Allied jet-fighter to see combat action during World War II. It is a single-seat twin-jet fighter with a maximum speed of 480 mph and a ceiling of 40,000 feet.

1943 April 15 British Prime Minister Winston Churchill (1874—1965) first learns of German experiments at Peenemünde with long-range rockets.

1943 May 22 Germans conduct test flights of Messerschmitt *Me-262* turbojet prototype fighter. Production does not begin until 1944.

1943 June 15 The Greyhound Corporation files an application with the Civil Aeronautics Board for an extensive network of 78 helicopter routes covering 43,103 miles and serving 1,043 terminals and intermediate points. Making some brave corporate advanced planning, Greyhound feels that if helicopters replace buses for inter-city travel in postwar America, it will have a decided competitive edge.

1943 June 15 First flight of the first operational jet-bomber is made. The German-built Arado *Ar-234 Blitz* is very advanced, but enters the war too late to be a factor.

1943 July 7 Adolf Hitler (1889—1945) meets with Dornberger, von Braun and others and is briefed with launch films and A-4 (V-2) models. Hitler is desperate as well as impressed, and assigns the highest military authority and priority to the V-2 program. He also demands an impossible production rate of 2,000 rockets a month.

1943 July 22 Regular Canadian transatlantic air service is begun by Trans-Canada Air Lines.

1943 August 17 The British carry out a saturation bombing air raid on the Peenemünde rocket development center in Germany and wreck much of the facility. German planners intend to rebuild Peenemünde as a research station and to move launch facilities 600 kilometers away to Poland.

1943 September 1 United States has produced 123,000 airplanes and 349,000 airplane engines from May 1940 until this day. This is slightly under President Franklin Roosevelt's stated production goal of 50,000 aircraft a year.

1943 November 6 U.S. airplane using aviation fuel processed from coal makes its first flight from Morgantown, West Virginia to Washington, D.C. A plentiful and cheap oil supply as well as expensive and difficult processing will keep alternative fuels such as this off the market.

1943 December A rocket research program is conceived by National Advisory Committee for Aeronautics' (NACA) John Stack (b. 1906) which will investigate the flight characteristics of an airplane flying beyond Mach 1 (the speed of sound). This marks the very early beginnings of a postwar U.S. effort to break what is considered a serious technological obstacle to aviation progress—the sound barrier. This program leads eventually to the *X-1* research airplane project.

1944 First rocket-powered airplane enters service with the German Luftwaffe. The Messerschmitt *Me-163* has swept-back wings, a liquid-fuel rocket motor, and can climb to 30,000 feet in two-and-one-half minutes. Because it is rocket- and not jet-powered, it can only fly at maximum speed (590 mph) for 8 to 10 minutes. It enters the war too late to have any effect.

1944 First full-scale supersonic wind tunnel is begun at National Advisory Committee for Aeronautics (NACA) Lewis Laboratory in Cleveland, Ohio. Conceived and designed by Abe Silverstein, it can accommodate a full-size supersonic engine and can test speed variations between Mach 1.4 and Mach 2 (Mach 1 being the speed of sound).

1944 ■ German World War II "Buzz Bomb."

1944 Volvo of Sweden first introduces its PV444 model, although it is not available until 1947. This two-door fastback seats four and has a four-cylinder, water-cooled engine that gives 44 hp. It is the first to sell in any numbers outside of Scandinavia and is produced with little outward changes until 1965.

1944 United States enacts Federal-Aid Highway Act of 1944. This landmark law not only expands the existing federal-aid program, but establishes two new continuing programs by authorizing funds specifically for a system of secondary highways and of arterial routes in urban areas. It calls for a National System of Interstate Highways which would connect the principle metropolitan areas, cities, and industrial centers. It also calls for uniform signs, traffic signals, and markings. No funds are provided however until 1952. **(See 1956)**

1944 Germans conduct several piloted V-1 "buzz bomb" test flights for possible suicide missions. The 27-foot-long V-1, now called V-1e, is outfitted with a cockpit and instruments and air-launched from an *He-111* aircraft. Code named Project Reichenberg after the experimental station in Reichen, Germany, the V-1e is flown several times by a woman test pilot, Hanna Reitsch (1912—1979).

1944 Germans convert an unused underground oil depot into an underground rocket assembly plant called Mittelwerke. Using slave labor, it produces 300 V-2 rockets a month.

1944 January 8 U.S. Army's new *P-61 Black Widow* is publicly unveiled at the Army-Navy Los Angeles Air Show. Built by Northrop Aircraft, Inc., this is the first American aircraft designed specifically as a night fighter since it is equipped with radar. It becomes operational during the summer of 1944.

1944 January 8 First flight of Lockheed *XP-80* is made at Muroc Dry Lake, California. Powered by a British Halford turbojet engine, it is the first American plane to be designed from the beginning as a jet-propelled aircraft and the first American fighter to exceed 500 mph in level flight. Called the *Shooting Star,* it is rushed through development in 143 days, but sees no World War II service. It does see action in the Korean War.

1944 March 16 U.S. National Advisory Committee for Aeronautics (NACA) proposes, after considerable study, that a jet-propelled transonic research aircraft be developed. Transonic speed is the complex area just above and below Mach 1 or the speed of sound. This is expressed as Mach 0.85—1.15. At these speeds, there are great changes in flow characteristics, and various parts of an aircraft may be simultaneously experiencing subsonic, sonic, and supersonic airflows. This eventually leads to the Bell *X-1.*

1944 June 6 A huge airborne armada, nine planes wide and 200 miles long, carries American and British troops across the English Channel for the D-Day invasion of Europe.

1944 June 6 Largest amphibious operation ever, the D-Day invasion of Europe by the Allied forces, occurs on the beaches of Normandy, France. Troops of all kinds from several different nations participate in this massive, directed movement of soldiers. Altogether, 1,213 warships and 4,126 landing ships and small craft carry 176,000 troops and their equipment. Allied airplanes fly 14,000 sorties in one day. No transporting venture before or since has matched this magnitude of scale.

1944 June 13 First German V-1 "buzz bomb" explodes in the center of London. This fairly conventional weapon is a subsonic rocket with wings with a pulsejet engine that operates on gasoline. Although more than 8,000 rain down on London during the war, they are inefficient and unreliable, and have no real strategic effect. The V-1 missile has a speed of less than 400 mph and a range of 190 miles while carrying a warhead of 1,988 pounds.

1944 July 5 First U.S. rocket-powered military aircraft, the *MX-324*, flies at Harper Dry Lake, California. Built by Northrop and piloted by Harry Crosby (b. 1907), it is powered by an Aerojet XCAL-200 rocket motor. A rocket aircraft differs from a jet plane in that a jet-propelled aircraft has an oxygen-burning engine and can do what engines normally do—alter speed, go on and off, etc. A rocket is self-contained, burns no oxygen from the atmosphere, and burns itself out relatively quickly. Both, however, move an aircraft by propulsive, rearward thrust.

1944 July 5 First U.S. rocket plane, the Northrop *MX-324*, is flown at Harper Dry Lake, California by Harry Crosby. Three of these very advanced "flying wing" type aircraft, powered by a 2,000-pound thrust rocket engine, are built. None performs well or safely, and the project is discontinued.

1944 August 2 Beginning its postwar planning, the U.S. Defense Plant Corporation completes its arrangements for the sale of war surplus airplanes at 30 sales centers throughout the country.

1944 August 4 First piston engine aircraft to exceed 500 mph is Republic's *XP-47J Thunderbolt*. This speedy aircraft proves to be one of the outstanding American fighter planes of World War II.

1944 August 4 German V-1 "buzz bomb" is destroyed for the first time by a British aircraft. The pilot manuevers his Meteor *EE 216* aircraft close enough to the slow-flying V-1 to be able to flip it with his wingtip.

1944 September 6 First V-2 launch against a European city occurs as two missiles are launched against Paris. They are not successful launches. (See September 8, 1944)

1944 September 8 German V-2 missile offensive against England begins with mobile launches made from the Netherlands at the rate of two a day. During the war, more than 1,500 V-2s land in southern England or just off its shores, killing more than 2,500 people. Paris, France is also hit by a V-2 the same day.

1944 September 14 First successful flight into the eye of a hurricane is made by a three-man American crew flying a Douglas *A-20 Havoc*. They demonstrate that valuable scientific information can be obtained in this manner. This is still done today.

1944 November 1 International Civil Aviation Conference opens in Chicago. It is attended by representatives from all the major nations, except the Soviet Union.

1944 November 1 First U.S. center devoted to the research and development of rocket propulsion systems, Galcit, founded in 1936, is reorganized and changes its name to the Jet Propulsion Laboratory.

1944 December U.S. Army Ordnance makes plans to study any German V-2 rockets the United States can acquire once the war ends. Army Ordnance contracts with the General Electric Company in what becomes known as the Hermes program.

1945 A comparison between the speeds of WWI and WWII (non-jet) aircraft shows an increase of 300—400 mph. Three-fourths of this gain is attributed to more horsepower and one-fourth results from aerodynamic improvements.

1945 Motorcycle improvements for the year include: torsion bar suspension; frameless stressed-engine construction; four brakes; and a servo-aided clutch.

1945 U.S. Federal Communication Commission (FCC) allocates radio channels for exclusive railroad use.

1944
Sept. 14

Plane flies into eye of hurricane

1945 January Commercial air transport service across the Atlantic resumes.

1945 January Wernher von Braun (1912—1977) meets secretly with his top Peenemünde staff members in view of Germany's imminent collapse, and all agree to head south to attempt to contact the American forces and avoid the Soviet troops.

1945 January 20 The swept-back wing concept is formulated by American aeronautical scientist Robert T. Jones (b. 1910). Unaware of German Adolf Busemann's (b. 1901) prior work, he argues correctly that at high speeds, angled-back wings delay the onset of compressibility (the steep pressures or shock waves that build up on an aircraft's wings and body surfaces). This is demonstrated experimentally in a wind tunnel test in March 1945.

1945 January 24 Peak of German wartime rocket research is reached with the successful launch of a winged version of the V-2, called the A-9 (also A-4b). The von Braun team produces several other theoretical designs, but is only able to build and test this advanced idea. The winged A-9 would later sit atop a new, larger A-10 and be the upper stage of a two-stage rocket. This winged, A-9 second stage could become a transcontinental transporter if manned and equipped with landing gear, or an ICBM (intercontinental ballistic missile) for ultimate attack on North America. In this one and only launch, it reaches an altitude of 50 miles, and a speed of 2,700 mph.

1945 February First vertically-launched rocket airplane is tested by the Bachem-Werke firm for the German Luftwaffe. Called the *BA-349* or more commonly, the Natter, its cockpit cover flies off at 492 feet (150 meters), killing the pilot, and the plane flips and crashes.

1945 February 20 The U.S. secretary of war approves Army Ordnance plans to establish the White Sands Proving Ground in New Mexico.

*1945
March 13

Aviation
courses
increase in
popularity*

1945 March 13 U.S. interest in flight is so popular that courses in aviation are being taught at this point in 14,000 of America's 25,686 high schools.

1945 April 10–11 U.S. troops enter Peenemünde rocket center and discover completely intact assembly lines of V-1 and V-2 rockets. Under orders from Col. Holger N. Toftoy, "Special Mission V-2" is hastily created to ship all of the rockets from Nordhausen to Antwerp. From May 22 to May 31, 341 railroad cars are loaded with about 100 V-2 rockets on their way to Antwerp, then to New Orleans via Liberty ships, and then to the New Mexico desert. The Soviets are expected to occupy the Peenemünde area on June 1 by agreement at the recent Yalta Conference.

1945 April 12 Franklin Delano Roosevelt (1882—1945), the first president of the United States to fly in an airplane, dies in Warm Springs, Georgia.

1945 April 19 International Air Transport Association (IATA) is inaugurated at Havana, Cuba as a non-governmental organization of airlines to perform technical and economic regulation of the airline industry. It succeeds the International Air Traffic Association formed in 1919 at The Hague, Holland.

 1945 ■ British test-firing of the first captured V-2 rocket in Peenemünde.

1945 April 25 U.S. Aeronautical Chamber of Commerce changes its name to Aircraft Industries Association of America (A.I.A.).

1945 May Wernher von Braun (1912—1977), Walter Dornberger (1895—1980), and others leave their mountain retreat and turn themselves over to the Americans, after learning of Adolf Hitler's suicide on April 30.

1945 May 8 World War II in Europe ends as German resistance collapses.

1945 July 13 The White Sands Proving Ground, New Mexico, is formally activated.

1945 July 19 U.S. intelligence project conducted before war's end, with the goal of compiling a list of key German rocket personnel to be found and interrogated, is christened "Overcast." Nine months later the project has the key scientists in hand and is renamed "Operation Paperclip."

1945 July 23 First modern, vista-domed passenger observation rail car is introduced on the Burlington route between Chicago, Illinois and Minneapolis, Minnesota.

1945 July 23 *Life* magazine publishes detailed drawings of a large manned space station, including a large space mirror, as envisioned by the German scientists of Peenemünde.

1945 July 28 B-25 light bomber crashes into the Empire State Building in New York City. It rips a hole between the 78th and 79th floors, killing the crew of three as well as ten others on the ground. Some of the victims are killed when one of the building's elevators has its cables and safety gear destroyed in the crash.

1945 August Components for approximately 100 V-2 rockets are shipped from Europe to White Sands Proving Ground, New Mexico.

1945 August 6 U.S. Boeing *B-29* bomber, the *Enola Gay*, drops the first atomic fission bomb on Hiroshima, Japan, destroying that city. Simultaneously, 580 more *B-29* bombers drop 3,850 tons of incendiary bombs on five other Japanese industrial cities.

1945 August 14 World War II ends as Japan surrenders. During four years of war, U.S. Army Air Forces aircraft flew over 108 million hours and dropped over two million tons of bombs.

1945 August 17 U.S. War Department sends 4,500 telegrams to aircraft manufacturers in 11 northeastern states canceling aircraft contracts.

1945 September 2 As VJ day (Victory in Japan) ends World War II, American railroads had moved 90% of all Army and Navy freight and more than 97% of all military personnel in organized groups within the United States.

1945 September 2 VJ Day ends WWII

1945 September 20 First flight of an aircraft powered completely by turboprop engines (Rolls Royce Trent) is made by a British Gloster *Meteor F.1*. A turboprop or prop-jet is an aircraft with a propeller that is driven by a gas turbine engine.

1945 September 26 First development flight of a U.S. Army WAC Corporal rocket is made and reaches an altitude of 43.5 miles at the newly opened White Sands Proving Ground in New Mexico. This is the first liquid-fueled rocket developed with government funds.

1945 September 29 The *New York Times* reports that building an interplanetary rocket is no longer viewed as an insurmountable task.

1945 October U.S. Secretary of War Patterson approves a plan to bring top German scientists to the United States to work on military research and development. This includes the small group of German rocket specialists who compose Operation Paperclip. They are to work on missile development at Fort Bliss, Texas and White Sands Proving Ground, New Mexico.

1945 October U.S. Army Air Force invites selected aircraft companies to submit proposals for participation in a long-range guided missile development program.

1945 October 3 U.S. Navy Committee for Evaluating the Feasibility of Space Rocketry (CEFSR) is established by the Bureau of Aeronautics. In November, the committee recommends a high priority be given to the development of a satellite program.

1945 October 5 First department store to sell aircraft as merchandise is Wannamaker's of New York City. Three different models from the Piper Aircraft Corporation are displayed on the floor.

1945 October 23 American Overseas Airlines inaugurates a scheduled passenger service across the North Atlantic with Douglas *DC-4*'s. A successor to American Export Airlines, it is later absorbed by Pan American Airways.

1945
November 6
Plane lands
on aircraft
carrier

1945 November 6 First jet plane to land on an aircraft carrier is a Ryan *FR-1* piloted by U.S. Navy Ens. Jake C. West.

1945 November 7 First speed record of over 600 mph is established by British pilot Hugh J. Wilson in a Gloster *Meteor* jet-fighter at 606 mph (c. 975 km/h).

1945 November 29 First air-sea rescue is made by a U.S. Army Sikorsky R-5 helicopter off the coast of Long Island, New York.

1945 December One hundred twenty seven German rocket scientists and engineers who agreed to come to the United States as part of Operation Paperclip, arrive at Fort Bliss, Texas.

1946 A.D.
India builds
car

1946 First Indian-built private car is the Hindustan Ten. Identical to the 10-hp English Morris Series M, this British car is assembled or manufactured in India under a licensing agreement. The Hindustan Company begins building cars of its own in the 1950s.

1946 First British car to have steering column-mounted gear shift is the Triumph 1800 model.

1946 Bermuda finally permits automobiles to operate on the island. This ends a half-century ban on vehicles other than bicycles and horse-drawn carriages and wagons. Trucks had been permitted for special reasons.

1946 Italian-made Vespa motor scooters are introduced in Italy. Built by Italian aircraft manufacturer Enrico Piaggio as an excuse to get his wartime-destroyed factory back into production, the scooters prove successful both in Europe and the United States.

1946 First fiberglass surfboard is made. This new light, durable synthetic will transform surfboards, making this the first modern board. (See 1970)

1946 Last major bid to challenge the big three U.S. automakers (Ford, General Motors, and Chrysler) is made as Kaiser-Frazer automobiles are introduced. The new company sees Henry J. Kaiser (1882—1967) of Kaiser Aluminum and Willys-Overland president Joseph W. Frazer merge their interests. It never manages to sell many cars and eventually goes under.

1946 Work on a nuclear-powered submarine is resumed after the war by American physicist Ross Gunn (1897—1966) and American physical chemist Philip H. Abelson (b. 1913) who present their plans to the U.S. Navy. (See January 17, 1955)

1946 January 16 United States forms a panel of various government agencies and plans a program of upper atmosphere research using V-2 rockets.

1946 January 26 U.S. Army Air Force creates the First Experimental Guided Missiles Group formed to develop and test rockets at Eglin Field, Florida.

1946 January 31 Only 23 aircraft engines for military planes are produced this month in the United States as compared to a single wartime month's production total of 24,102.

1946 March U.S. Army Air Force begins a program to study ballistic missile defense, feeling it needs to develop an interceptor missile to cope with the likes of V-2 type missiles.

1946 March Project RAND is established by the U.S. Army Air Force as an advisory and consultative board on military weapons development. It is formed principally by the Douglas Aircraft Co., with the participation of North American Aviation and Northrop.

1946 March 12 First commercial helicopter license issued by the U.S. Civil Aeronautics Administration is granted to Bell Aircraft Corporation for its Bell 47. This classic model provides the basic design for several decades of Bell helicopters. The implications of a helicopter's independence from airports for landings as well as its special ability to hover or fly slowly, soon make police departments begin to adopt them as excellent surveillance and pursuit vehicles.

1946 March 14 First static firing in the United States of an American-assembled German V-2 rocket is made at White Sands Proving Ground, New Mexico. This is a necessary, preliminary step to later test flights.

1946 March 22 First U.S.-built rocket to escape the earth's atmosphere is the Jet Propulsion Laboratory WAC Corporal. It climbs to 50 miles after launch from White Sands Proving Ground, New Mexico.

1946 April 4 Sears, Roebuck & Company begins a new, regular weekly overnight shipment of women's clothing from New York to the West Coast by airplane.

1946 April 16 First launch of an American-adapted German V-2 rocket is made at White Sands Proving Ground, New Mexico. It climbs five miles.

1946 April 19 Project MX-774 is begun by the U.S. Army Air Force with Consolidated-Vultee to study rocket capabilities leading to an ICBM (ntercontinental ballistic missile).

1946 April 22 North American Aviation obtains a contract to develop the Navaho rocket, a winged cruise missile with a range up to 500 miles. Although it never reaches operational status, it contributes valuable systems and components used later, such as its large liquid fuel motor which is used in the Thor, Jupiter, Atlas, and Saturn launch vehicles.

1946 April 24 First flights of the first Soviet designed and built jet aircrafts, *MiG-9* and *Yak-15*, are made. A member of the company test team for the *Yak-15*, Olga Yamschikova, is probably the first woman to fly a turbojet powered aircraft when she flies in 1947.

1946 May 9 First major league baseball team to use air transportation for its full schedule is the New York Yankees of the American League. The Yankees sign with United Air Lines to travel by air throughout this season.

1946 May 12 Project RAND presents its report to the Army Air Force entitled "Preliminary Design of an Experimental World-Circling Space Ship." This report (SM-11827) indicates the technical feasibility of building and launching an artificial satellite launched using technology similar to the German V-2 rocket.

1946 May 13 President Harry S. Truman (1884—1972) signs the Federal Airport Bill authorizing a federal expenditure on a state-matching basis of $500 million for an airport construction and development program over the next seven years.

1946 May 13
Airport bill signed

1946 June 26 U.S. Army Air Forces and Navy adopt the "knot" and "nautical mile" as standard aeronautical units of speed and distance. A nautical mile is about 6,080 feet (1,853 meters), and a knot is the equivalent of one nautical mile per hour.

1946 June 28 First V-2 fully instrumented for upper atmosphere research is launched by the Naval Research Laboratory at White Sands Proving Ground, New Mexico. It attains an altitude of 67 miles.

1946 July In a series of launches, V-2 Nos. 5 and 9 set new altitude records of over 100 miles, and No. 17 sets a velocity record of 3,600 mph.

1946 July
New altitude records set

1946 July Soviet rocket engineer Sergei P. Korolev (1906—1966) uses captured German V-2 and designs a "stretched" version by lengthening its propellant tanks and increasing engine thrust.

1946 July 9 A subcommittee of the Guided Missile Committee of the U.S. Joint Chiefs of Staff recommends that a search be made for a missile range to test ballistic missiles with a range of up to 2,000 miles.

1946 August 1 British European Airways (BEA) and British South American Airways are established under the Civil Aviation Act of 1946. The entire British air transport industry is now nationalized.

1946 August 6 Two Boeing *B-17* bombers are flown nonstop from Hilo, Hawaii to Muroc Lake, California without pilots or crews and controlled entirely by radio.

1946 August 8 First flight of the Convair *B-36* heavy bomber is made. The requirements for this huge bomber were drawn up early in the war when it seemed likely that all of Europe would be overrun, and that strategic missions would have to be flown directly from the United States. After the war, it is used to conduct strategic reconnaissance.

1946 August 12 President Harry S. Truman (1884—1972) signs a bill authorizing an appropriation of $50,000 to establish a National Air Museum in the Smithsonian Institution in Washington, D.C. This small museum eventually grows into the National Air and Space Museum of today—the most visited museum in the world.

1946 August 13 Agreement is reached to form the consortium airline Scandinavian Airlines System (SAS) as the joint Swedish, Norwegian and Danish flag airline.

1946
August 17

First airplane
ejection
takes place

1946 August 17 First person in the United States to be ejected from an airplane by means of its emergency escape equipment is Sgt. Lambert of Wright Field, Ohio. He is ejected from a *P-61* traveling 302 mph at an altitude of 7,800 feet.

1946 August 27 A new pilot ejector seat, designed to catapult a pilot from the cockpit of his high-speed plane, is successfully tested by the Army at Wright Field. This system has proven itself over time and is still used to save lives in certain critical situations.

1946 September 24 U.S. Civil Aeronautics Board (CAB) issues new safety regulations to minimize fire hazards in transport aircraft, requiring all existing commercial transports, and new ones, to incorporate certain specified design changes. As a government agency that surpervises airline activity, the CAB is terminated once deregulation goes into full effect in 1984.

1946 September 28 U.S. rocket pioneer Frank J. Malina (1912—1981) publishes with colleague Summerfield an article, "The Problem of Escape from Earth by Rocket," which sets out the requirements for multistage rockets capable of achieving escape velocity.

1946 October U.S. Army Ordnance initiates Project Bumper that leads to the development of a two-stage missile. It plans to put an American WAC Corporal rocket on top of a V-2, to create a two-stage missile. This would reach higher altitudes and provide needed experience with staged vehicles. (See May 13, 1948)

1946 October 6 First non-stop flight between Hawaii and Egypt by way of the North Pole is made by a Boeing *B-29 Superfortress*. It covers 10,873 miles (17,498 kilometers).

1946 October 11 First glide flight of the Bell *X-1* is made by pilot Chalmers Goodlin in Muroc, California.

1946 October 24 V-2 rocket No. 13 is launched at White Sands Proving Ground, New Mexico carrying a camera that takes motion pictures of the earth. Taken from an altitude of about 65 miles, the film covers 40,000 square miles.

1946 December 8 Bell *X-1* rocket-powered test plane makes its first successful flight and reaches a speed of 550 mph. This is the first U.S. aircraft designed for supersonic speeds.

1946 December 17 A program of space biological research is initiated by the U.S. National Institutes of Health at Holloman Air Force Base, New Mexico. Much is needed to be learned about the factors affecting a biological organism sent into space.

1946 December 23 In a work that basically describes the early flights of the U.S. Mercury program 15 years later, a British study group (led by R. A. Smith and H. E. Ross) designs a German V-2 rocket that can carry a man in a pressurized cabin into space. The appropriate British Ministry does not adopt the study.

1947 First new post-war British car design is the Vanguard. Made by the Standard Motor Company, this round-featured "fastback" car has a four cylinder engine, shift on the column, and seats six.

1947 First motorboat to be powered by a turbo-jet engine, a *Bluebird* version called *Slipper*, is run in unsuccessful trials by Englishman Malcolm Campbell (1885—1948). It is powered by a De Havilland Goblin II jet engine giving 5,000 pounds of thrust. Campbell later sets world speed records with the *Bluebird*.

1947 The replacement of many passenger ships lost or damaged during the war is begun by many countries.

1947 January 23 V-2 rocket carrying telemetry for the first time is launched at White Sands Proving Ground, New Mexico and climbs to 31 miles.

1947 February 20 In the first of a series of tests called Blossom Project, a V-2 rocket (No. 20) ejects a canister which is recovered by parachute. The canister contains fruit flies and various seeds exposed to cosmic rays after a climb to 68 miles.

1947 February 25 U.S. Civil Aviation Administration (CAA) demonstrates a new stall-warning instrument it has developed. Such devices, which give advance warning to a pilot that his plane is beginning to lose lift or "stalling," are standard equipment in today's planes. The CAA is the forerunner of the Federal Aviation Administration (FAA).

1947 March 6 First four-engine jet bomber to fly in the United States makes its first test flight in Muroc, California. Built by North American, the *XB-45* also becomes the first operational jet bomber during the next year.

1947 March 7 First photograph taken from an altitude of 100 miles is made during a V-2 launch at White Sands Proving Ground, New Mexico. The photograph is not released by the U.S. Navy until March 20, since it takes search parties several days to locate the returned cameras.

1947 March 14 A poll of 1,000 passengers taken by the U.S. Air Transport Command reveals that 96 percent prefer riding in seats that face the rear of the airplane. Contemporary planes no longer offer the passenger an option of which way to face while flying, so it is difficult to know whether people have changed their attitudes and preferences over the years.

1947 April U.S. Army Air Force awards a contract to Aerojet Engineering Corporation to build an experimental rocket engine test station in Muroc, California. This later becomes Edwards Air Force Base.

1947 April 4 The International Civil Aviation Organization (ICAO) comes into being after ratification at the Chicago Convention of 1944. As a specialized agency of the United Nations, its objectives are to develop air technologies, to foster the planning and development of international air transport, and to insure its safe and orderly growth.

1947 April 14 Bell Aircraft begins to build a second rocket-powered supersonic airplane, the *XS-2*, for the U.S. Army.

1947 April 24 The French government opens a new rocket test range at Colomb Bechar, Algeria in the Sahara Desert.

1947 May 29 New safety measures and procedures are instituted at White Sands Proving Ground, New Mexico as a V-2 rocket launched from there veers off course and impacts only one-and-one-half miles south of Juarez, New Mexico.

1947 May 31 Eastern Airlines *DC-4* flying to Florida crashes near Perryville, Maryland, killing all 53 people aboard. A tail assembly defect is the cause.

1947 June 2 Beech Aircraft Corporation announces the new Model 34 *Beechcraft* as a short-haul transport.

1947 June 17 Princeton University begins construction of a 4,000-mph wind tunnel. This indicates the need to investigate the phenomenon of hypersonic flight, or anticipated flight that is five or more times the speed of sound.

1947 June 17

Construction of 4000-mph wind tunnel begins

1947 July 1 MX-774 contract with Convair to develop ballistic missiles is cancelled by the U.S. Army Air Force which feels that new strategic bombers are superior to an untested missile. Convair continues some phases of the work with its own funds, and pioneers new design concepts that lead ultimately to the Atlas launch vehicle.

1947 July 2 First Soviet swept-wing jet-fighter flies. Combining known results of German research as well as Soviet research and a British-designed engine, the Mikoyan-Gurevich *MiG-15* appears crude but performs excellently as evidenced during the Korean War when it is used by North Korea.

1947 July 16 First flight of the first jet-powered seaplane is made as the Saunders-Roe *S.R.A.1* flies successfully. This elegant-looking British aircraft is cancelled before it enters service because there does not appear to be a market for it. From this point on, seaplane use steadily decreases.

1947 September 6 First firing of a large rocket from a ship at sea occurs as a German V-2 rocket is fired from the deck of aircraft carrier U.S.S. *Midway* near Bermuda. The launch is successful but the rocket explodes about 5,000 feet in the air. The Navy becomes justifiably concerned about the dangers of liquid-fuel rockets aboard ships.

1947 September 18 The U.S. Air Force becomes an independent service within the new unified U.S. armed forces. Although each service branch will still have its own air component, this change means that the Air Force has emerged as the dominant branch and that air power is recognized to be the nation's first line of defense.

1947 September 25 First successful firing of an Aerobee sounding or research rocket is made at White Sands Proving Ground, New Mexico. Built by the Aerojet Engineering Company and the Applied Physics Laboratory, it proves that rockets can be valuable scientific tools to study the upper atmosphere.

1947 October 1 First flight of North American's *F-86 Sabre* swept-wing jet-fighter is made. As the first fighter able to exceed Mach 1 in a shallow dive, this aircraft features an advanced avionics package that makes it an all-weather airplane. It distinguishes itself with the United Nations forces in the Korean War.

1947 October 9 Engineers from General Electric Co. obtain the first carefully instrumented heat-transfer data from the supersonic flight of a V-2 rocket which travels 3,400 mph. Travel in outer space will require knowledge of what occurs at these high speeds.

1947 October 11 British Interplanetary Society opens its lecture season with a remarkably prescient talk by A. V. Cleaver who forecasts that the conquest of space will be in stages, from unmanned rockets through short, man-carrying flights in space, to circumnavigation of the moon and finally a landing on its surface. This is exactly the course of events will follow.

1947 October 14 First piloted airplane to exceed the speed of sound in level flight is the Bell *X-1* flown by Capt. Charles E. Yeager (b. 1925). This rocket-powered aircraft is launched or released from a parent aircraft and reaches a speed of 670 mph (1,078 km/h) or Mach 1.015. Mach speed is relative to an airplane's altitude, so that Mach 1.0 at sea level at 15 degrees Celsius is 760.98 mph. In the stratosphere (above 36,089 feet or 11,000 kilometers), Mach 1.0 is 659.78 mph.

1947 October 21 First flight of Northrop *YB-49* flying wing jet bomber is made in Hawthorne, California. This jet-powered aircraft consists entirely of a single large, V-shaped airfoil or wing which contains the crew, engines, and all systems. It performs successfully enough as a long-range bomber for the U.S. Air Force to order 30 to be built. This order is later cancelled.

1947 October 30 Soviets begin test launches of V-2 type missiles under the direction of Sergei P. Korolev (1906—1966).

1947 November 2 Howard Hughes (1905—1976) flies his Hughes *H4 Hercules* or "Spruce Goose," making it the largest airplane ever flown. Powered by eight 3,000-hp Pratt & Whitney piston engines, this huge wooden seaplane also has the greatest wing span ever built, 320 feet (97.54 meters) and an overall length of 219 feet. It is large enough to accommodate 700 passengers, but is intended as a freighter and has no cabin windows. It flies only this one time, covering about a mile over the Los Angeles harbor and never going higher than 33 feet. It is one of a kind and never gets to production.

1947 November 24 First complete Aerobee sounding rocket is launched to a height of 37 miles at White Sands Proving Ground, New Mexico.

1947 December 10 Lt. Col. John P. Stapp (b. 1910), USAF, makes his first rocket-propelled research sled ride. This rapid acceleration/deceleration experiment tests human endurance with an eye toward future manned space missions.

1947 December 15 A space biological research program begins under the National Institutes of Health at Holloman Air Force Base, New Mexico.

1947 December 17 First flight of the Boeing *B-47* swept-wing jet-bomber is made. It inaugurates a new configuration, with its six engines hanging in wing-pods below its very thin wings. This elegant design, with wings swept back at 35 degrees, is widely adopted for

| 1947 ■ Howard Hughes flies the *Spruce Goose* in Long Beach, California.

large American jet aircraft. It carries only a crew of three and serves the United States until replaced by the *B-52.*

1948 Elevators become more automated as the Otis Company installs its Autotronic system in several buildings in the United States. Electronic systems now count, register, and combine information to determine the elevator schedule. But operators are still needed to start the elevator.

1948 Jaguar XK 120 sports car is first introduced in England and creates a sensation. Equipped with a new, very high performance six-cylinder engine, this now-classic design can reach 172 mph in its standard production model. Its aerodynamic design is the first real innovative idea of the post-war period, and it remains in production for over 25 years.

1948 First torque converter-type automatic transmission offered on an American car is introduced by Buick. Now a standard feature of many automatic transmissions, this hydraulic or fluid system is the means by which engine torque (a turning or twisting shaft) can be transmitted, multiplied, and controlled. Buick calls the new system Dynaflow and puts it in its Roadmaster models.

1948 Reliable tubeless tires are first made available in the United States by B. F. Goodrich. These new tires require no inner tube and are built to maintain air pressure by forming an airtight seal with a tire bead or edge and the wheel rim. Nearly all auto tires are tubeless today.

1948 First radial-ply automobile tire is marketed by Michelin of France. Called the Michelin X, it is first fitted on a Citroen. Radials have their plies or inner cord material running at right angles to the beads or sides of a tire. They prove to be a strong tire that give good fuel economy and better road traction.

1948 First Land Rover is introduced in England as a four-wheel drive cross-country vehicle. Built originally as an interim, off-road design after the war and open like a Jeep, it becomes very popular and continues in production today.

1948 First fiberglass reinforced plastic row boats and dinghies are exhibited at the U.S. National Motor Boat Show. This new material combines hardness with lightness—ideal for a boat.

1948 First bathyscaphe, the *FNRS 2,* built by Swiss scientist Auguste Piccard (1884—1963), makes underwater trials in the Cape Verde Islands. This navigable diving vessel is designed to reach great depths in the ocean, and an improved version carries out a series of successful descents, including one of 13,000 feet (4,000 meters) on February 15, 1954. It consists of two main components, a steel crew cabin heavier than water and resistant to sea pressure, and a light container called a float, filled with gasoline which, lighter than water, provides the necessary lifting power. (See January 23, 1960)

1948 First Honda motorcycle appears on the market. In ten years, this Japanese company will be the world's leading producer of motorcycles and motorbikes.

1948 A.D.

Land Rover introduced

1948 First fishing vessel to be fitted with full radio, radar, and echometer equipment, the British *Rinovia III*, makes its first fishing trip. This 28-man crew fishing trawler is equipped with the latest post-war instruments which will eventually become standard equipment.

1948 January Wright Field and Patterson Field, both in Dayton, Ohio, are merged into a single installation called the Wright-Patterson Air Force Base.

1948 January 1 British railways are nationalized per the Transport Act. This Act provides for the government takeover of British rail, road, and canal transport. The Transport Act of 1981 allows the British Railways Board to divest itself of many railway and subsidiary interests in an attempt to involve more private capital.

1948 February 6 V-2 rocket is successfully guided and controlled electronically by General Electric technicians during a 70 mile high launch at White Sands Proving Ground, New Mexico.

1948 March 4 First American civilian to fly at supersonic speeds is Herbert H. Hoover in a Bell *X-1* in Muroc, California.

1948 April 23 The first helicopter violation on record is filed by the Civil Aeronautics Authority (CAA) against Roland Roelofs, of Riverdale, Maryland for buzzing (flying low and fast) the White House, the Capitol Building, and other restricted areas of Washington, D.C. at 200 feet.

1948 May 13 First Project Bumper (two-stage vehicle with a WAC Corporal atop a V-2) is launched at White Sands Proving Ground, New Mexico. The V-2 first stage rises 70 miles and the WAC goes another nine miles up. The launch provides valuable experience about staging rockets.

1948 June 2 President Harry S. Truman (1884—1972) signs a bill authorizing the construction of an $8 million international airport near Anchorage, Alaska and a $5 million public airport near Fairbanks.

1948 June 26 The Berlin Airlift begins as American and British aircraft bring food and supplies to the blockaded city of Berlin, Germany. Air power alone keeps the city alive for nearly a year until the Soviet Union ends their blockade.

1948 June 29 The Air Parcel Post Bill becomes U.S. law, establishing domestic air parcel post and raising first class postage rates for air mail from five cents to six cents.

1948 July 13 First Convair MX-774 test rocket built under the U.S. ballistic missile program is launched at White Sands Proving Ground, New Mexico. Its motor shuts off after 60 seconds of a planned 75 second burn, and the rocket falls back to earth.

1948 July 14 First Atlantic crossing by jet-aircraft is made by six British De Havilland *Vampires*, flying from Iceland and Greenland.

1948 July 26 Aerobee sounding rocket is launched to 70 miles, carrying cameras which photograph the actual curvature of the earth. Man begins to observe his planet from a distance for the first time.

1948 July 31 New York's Idlewild International Airport is dedicated. It becomes the world's largest airport and speeds travel into New York despite its distance from midtown Manhattan. (See 1963)

1948 August U.S. Air Force announces it has developed a remote control mechanism for its pulse jet flying bomb called the "Loon." Based on the German V-1 "Buzz Bomb," the Navy's flying bomb has a range of 150 miles.

1948 August 11 The Corporation Aircraft Owners Association announces that there are now 800 U.S. businesses flying more than 1,000 executive-type aircraft for business purposes.

1948 August 23 First jet-powered fighter to be designed specifically as a parasite aircraft is successfully launched from its parent bomber. The McDonnell *XF-85 Goblin* is carried by a Boeing *B-29* and launched by a retractable "skyhook." The ugly, stubby little *Goblin* is less than 15 feet long and is intended to protect the bomber if necessary. Further tests reveal that a hook-on or reattachment is difficult and dangerous, and the experiment is cancelled after only two *Goblins* are built. (See October 1950)

1948 September 18 First flight of a delta-wing jet airplane is made as the Convair *XF-92A* flies. Like the German *DM-1* which inspired it, the American Convair has a swept-back angle of 60 degrees. Powered by a 4,500-pound thrust Allison J-33A engine, its success leads to the development of the Convair *F-102 Delta Dagger*, an all-weather interceptor fighter. (See October 24, 1953)

1948 September 27 The second Convair MX-774 test rocket is launched and reaches a height of 47 km before it falls back to earth. Excessive pressure in the propellant tanks cause the rocket to explode.

1948 October 7 The California Aeronautics Commission denies a petition by the City of Los Angeles to ban skywriting over the city, stating that "neatly executed signs in the sky are no more a desecration of nature than a roadside billboard."

1948 November 4 U.S. Air Force announces the formation of the RAND Corporation. As a successor to Project RAND, originally begun by Douglas Aircraft, the new corporation will gather advanced scientific, technical, and military information pertinent to Air Force decision-making.

1948 November 6 Dr. H. Tsien at California Institute of Technology describes his plans for a nuclear powered space ship. The advantages of nuclear power for extended manned space travel are obvious, but the problems prove even greater. He returns to China in 1955 as a result of the U.S. Congress investigations into Un-American actvities, and plays a leading role in establishing China's missile and space programs.

1948 November 10 First symposium on the medical aspects of space travel is held at the U.S. Air Force School of Aviation Medicine in San Antonio, Texas.

1948 November 15 Track tests begin on the first gas turbine-electric locomotive to be built and operated in the United States. Tests are conducted in Erie, Pennsylvania by General Electric and American Locomotive Companies.

1948 November 30 Curtiss-Wright demonstrates its new reversible-pitch propellers which enable a *C-54* to make a controlled descent from 15,000 feet to 1,000 feet in one minute, 22 seconds.

1948 December 2 Third and final Convair MX-774 test rocket is launched at White Sands Proving Ground, New Mexico and explodes in flight due to vibrations in the liquid oxygen delivery system. Despite these failures, a great deal is learned.

1948 December 14 Increased U.S. emphasis on space is evidenced by the establishment of Jet Propulsion Centers at both Princeton University and California Institute of Technology. Funded by the Daniel and Florence Guggenheim Foundation, they provide research facililtes and graduate training for qualified young scientists and engineers in rocketry and astronautics. The Foundation extends its philanthropy to space as well as to aeronautics.

1948 December 16 First flight of Northrop *X-4 Bantam*, a tailless research airplane designed to investigate the subsonic flight characteristics of an aircraft with swept-back wings and no tail. Two X-4's are built and some 60 test flights are made in Muroc, California before the program ends in April 1954.

1949 Starting a car with a key instead of the old method of pushing a button is pioneered by Chrysler.

1949 Spartan, functional, and very popular Citroen 2 CV is introduced in France. Designed originally as a "peasant's car," this legendary but ugly little car has achieved something of a cult status today and still thrives.

1949 Very successful Morris Minor automobile first appears in England. Designed by Alec Issigonis (1906—1988), this four-cylinder, 37-hp car provides a surprising amount of room, and its torsion bar suspension (a rod in the suspension that functions like a spring when twisted) gives it excellent road-holding qualities. It remains in production until 1971 with no modifications.

1949 Pirelli in Italy develops the two-piece "dry suit" for divers. The diver enters the suit at the waist and is then sealed in with a waist ring and a rubber band.

1949 Chicago's O'Hare Airport is named for the late Edward H. "Butch" O'Hare (1914—1943) who earned a Congressional Medal of Honor during World War II, but who died at 29. Formerly called Orchard Place, the airport will become the world's busiest air travel facility.

1949 Several major U.S. transportation-related companies (General Motors, Standard Oil, Firestone Tire, and others) are convicted of criminally conspiring to replace existing electric transit lines with gasoline or diesel-powered buses. Despite the court action, the phase-out of trolleys continues and the companies are eventually successful.

1949 A.D.

Saab-Scania formed

1949 Saab-Scania AB is formed in Sweden to compete with Volvo. The company will become a major aerospace manufacturer as well as a car maker.

1949 January 15 First non-stop trans-Canada flight is made by the crew of a Royal Candian Air Force Douglas *DC-4M*. It flies from Vancouver, British Columbia to Halifax, Nova Scotia in 8 hours, 32 minutes, and averages a speed of 329 mph during the 2,785-mile flight.

1949 February

"Parachute" brake tested on jet

1949 February U.S. Air Force conducts tests of a special 30-foot parachute on a Boeing *XB-47* to act as a brake and shorten the landing distance of jet airplanes. This system proves most useful for aircraft carriers.

1949 February 26—March 2 First non-stop refuelled flight around the world is made by a Boeing *B-50*. American Capt. James Gallagher and *Luck Lady II* crew cover 23,452 miles (37,742 kilometers) in 94 hours, one minute and are refuelled in flight four times.

1949 April German rocket group in the Soviet Union prepares a design study of the R.14 rocket which can launch a 6,600-pound (2,994-kilogram) payload 1,800 miles (2,897 kilograms).

1949 April 21 First flight of the first successful ramjet airplane is made as the Leduc *0.10* flies in France. Ramjets cannot function at subsonic speeds since they do not have compressors like turbojet engines. They begin to operate at about twice the speed of sound (Mach 2) where the speed itself performs the function of compressing the air. The Leduc *0.10* is therefore carried atop a conventional transport plane from which it is launched at high speed.

1949 April 26 World endurance record for a flight-refuelled aircraft is completed in the United States by Dick Reidel and Bill Barris. They fly continuously in their Aeronca *Chief* light aircraft for 1,008 hours, one minute (over six weeks). They receive food and fuel handed up from a speeding vehicle four times a day.

1949 May According to *Tass* newspaper, a Soviet rocket climbs to a height of 68 miles carrying between 264 and 286 pounds of instruments.

1949 May 3 U.S. Naval Research Laboratory launches Viking rocket No. 1 at White Sands Proving Grounds, New Mexico. Built by Glenn L. Martin Co., it is America's most advanced liquid-fuel rocket and its first real research rocket. It reaches an altitude of 51.5 miles and a speed of 2,250 mph.

1949 May 9 First flight of Republic *XF-91* hybrid jet/rocket experimental interceptor aircraft is made in Muroc, California. The wings of this unusual aircraft are inversely tapered—wider and thicker at the tips than at the roots—for better low-speed handling. This is only a slight improvement on other jet designs, and it never enters production.

1949 May 11 U.S. President Harry S. Truman (1884—1972) signs a bill authorizing a 5,000-mile guided missile test range at Cape Canaveral, Florida.

1949 May 18 First helioport in New York officially opens at Pier 41 on the East River.

1949 June German Association for Space Research (Gesselschaft für Weltraumforschung), the successor to the Verein für Raumschiffahrt, passes a resolution calling for an international meeting of all astronautical societies to further the possibility of practical space flight. This leads eventually to the First International Astronautical Congress held in Paris, France in 1950.

1949 June 1 A survey conducted by a firm of New York aviation consultants shows that for the first time in history, air travel volume is greater than first class rail travel. In May of this year, revenue passenger-miles for domestic airlines totals 603 million compared to 582 million for Pullman trains.

1949 June 14 United States launches a V-2 rocket carrying an Air Force Aero Medical Laboratory monkey, Albert II, at White Sands Proving Ground, New Mexico. The monkey survives the 63-mile-high flight but is killed during reentry impact.

1949 July 27 First flight of the prototype De Havilland *D.H. 106 Comet* is made. It will become the world's first jet-powered airliner when it enters service in 1952.

1949 July 30 British South American Airways corporation is absorbed into British Overseas Airways Corporation (BOAC).

1949 August 9 First operational use in the United States of a pilot ejection seat is made by Lt. J. L. Fruin, who ejects from his *F-2H-1 Banshee* at 500 knots near Waterboro, South Carolina. This automatic emergency escape system with parachute landing requires only that a pilot pull a handle mounted on his seat. It provides a safe escape at all speeds and altitudes, even from a stationary aircraft on the ground.

1949 August 10 First Canadian jet aircraft, the Avro Canada C-102 transport, is flown in Ontario by J. H. Orrell and crew.

1949 September U.S. Air Force creates the Department of Space Medicine at its School of Aviation Medicine, Randolph Field, Texas. It is led by three German scientists: Hubertus Strughold (b. 1898), Heinz Haber, and Konrad J. K. Buettner (b. 1903). They will study the effects of acceleration and weightlessness. Their work on centrifuges and simulators contributes significantly to the U.S. manned space program.

1949 October 17 First scheduled U.S. airline to serve alcoholic beverages in flight within the United States is Northwest Airlines.

1949 November 2 First "double-decked" train in England goes into service on the Southern Region of British Railways. With seats on two levels, its larger passenger capacity makes station stops longer, and the train finally sees its last on October 1, 1971.

1949 November 3 First manned flight in a polyethylene balloon is made by Charles B. Moore over Minneapolis, Minnesota. Moore demonstrates that this new light-weight, low-cost plastic material works well for high-altitude balloon flight.

1949 November 4 U.S. Army's rocket team of German scientists plans a move from Fort Bliss, Texas, to Huntsville, Alabama. The growing missile program will shift 130 members of the original von Braun team to the larger facilities of the Redstone Arsenal in Huntsville. (See April 1, 1950)

1949 November 10 First flight is made of the first practical, tandem helicopter, the Piasecki *HRP-2*, a passenger transport helicopter. It is the heaviest helicopter built to date. It has tandem (two) rotors at each end, and its long, slightly curved profile inspires the name "Flying Banana."

1949
Nov. 10

First tandem helicopter flies

1949 November 11 First long-range rockets are fired from the testing ground of the British Commonwealth at Woomera, Australia. The range covers about 1,200 miles.

1949 November 21 First flight of the Sikorsky *H-19* helicopter is made. This is a large transport vehicle capable of carrying 10 men or nearly one ton of cargo.

1949 December 1 California Institute of Technology dedicates a hypersonic wind tunnel that can generate continuous speeds greater than ten times the speed of sound. It is designed specifically for rocket and guided missile research. The previous highest speed tunnel could reach only Mach 7 (seven times the speed of sound).

1950 First practical helicopter with a torqueless, ramjet-propelled rotor, the Hiller *Hornet,* makes its first flight. This two-seat helicopter is extremely small and can be used for observation only.

1950 First elevators to be run without an operator are installed by the Otis Company in the Atlantic Refining Building in Dallas, Texas. These new elevators are quickly accepted by the public and by 1956, most major commercial building owners decide to switch and eventually do away with operators. The elevator operator job becomes a dinosaur like the locomotive fireman who stoked the engine.

1950 Modern, efficient road-racing bicycle weighing only 24 pounds is produced. The Claud Butler bicycle, made in England, is made of steel and aluminum, combining strength and light weight.

1950 Tinted glass automobile windows first become available on Buick models. Designed initially to reduce glare and aid vision, they have evolved into today's sometimes totally darkened car windows that prevent anyone from seeing inside the car.

1950 First use of a MacPherson strut front suspension is on a British Ford. Designed by Earle S. MacPherson, this system has the shock absorber, suspension spring, and wheel spindle (shaft) assembly mounted on each front wheel. It is very popular on today's cars.

1950 First gas-turbine-powered car is the Jet 1, a two-seater built in England by Rover. It has a rear-mounted engine built for high speed. Turbines are rotary engines that use a fan-like device or vanes that rotate

c. 1950 ■ Electric bus on wheels, not tracks.

when subjected to pressure. Although fine for jet aircraft, they are still experimental on cars and must resolve problems such as those associated with high temperatures before they can compete with traditional gas engines.

c. 1950 Motorscooters made by Vespa and Lambretta are quickly adopted and become widely used. These handy, light, and small-engine two-wheelers are very economical to operate and prove popular as a baggage-carrying two-seater.

1950 British science writer Arthur C. Clarke (b. 1917) publishes his book *Interplanetary Flight: An Introduction to Astronautics*. Clarke begins a long and successful career as a popularizer of space.

1950 Subway in Stockholm, Sweden opens to passengers. This line in the shape of a T will grow to have 94 stations on 60 miles of track.

1950 New luxury electric passenger train, *Le Mistral*, begins service between Paris and Nice, France. The track seams on the 676-mile route are all welded and polished, and the train covers the distance in nine hours, eight minutes.

c. 1950 New roller skates in the United States feature smooth-riding clay wheels attached to double-action (pivoting) axles. These swiveling axles are later to become an important part of the modern skateboard. (See 1958)

1950 February The North American Aviation rocket engine facility at Santa Susana, California becomes operational. This company will become a major aerospace contractor.

1950 March 2 The first full-thrust test of the 75,000-pound thrust liquid rocket engine in the Navaho missile program is conducted. Although this missile program is soon cancelled, the technological fallout from it nearly justifies the program, since uprated versions of its engines are later applied to the Atlas and other missiles.

1950 March 3 Symposium on space medicine is held by the University of Illinois at its Professional Colleges in Chicago.

1950 April 1 U.S. Army begins move of Wernher von Braun (1912—1977) and his rocket staff from Fort Bliss, Texas to Huntsville, Alabama. The team will develop the Redstone missile at the Redstone Arsenal and later build the Jupiter C, the first missile to fly at an intercontinental range.

1950 April 12 First English Channel crossing in a sailplane is made by Englishman Lorne Welch who crosses from London, England to Brussels, Belgium in a Weihe sailplane. Welch catches the thermals (rising body

1950 ■ Interior of the Brooklyn Battery Tunnel, connecting lower Manhattan with Brooklyn in New York City.

of warm air) which form well inland and soars for a total of 210 miles.

1950 May U.S. Air Force scientists deliver a paper suggesting the use of aircraft flying aerodynamic parabolas (fast, bowl-shaped flight paths) to obtain up to 30 seconds of relative weightlessness. This proves to be an effective technique to familiarize future astronauts with this space phenomenon.

1950 May 19 First U.S. Army Hermes A-1 test rocket is fired at White Sands Proving Ground, New Mexico. As the United States begins to run out of captured German V-2 rockets, it develops the similarly-designed Hermes.

1950 June First serious and realistic science fiction film depicting flight to the moon is released. Called *Destination Moon*, it is written by Robert Heinlein and directed by George Pal. Well-known space artist Chesley Bonestell designs the sets.

1950 June 25 The Korean War begins as North Korea invades South Korea. Two days later President Truman orders the U.S. Air Force to assist South

1951 ■ Piasechi HRP-1 ``Flying Banana'' helicopter.

Korea and the United Nations calls on members to aid South Korea.

1950 July 24 First rocket launch from Cape Canaveral, Florida is made as Bumper No. 8 (WAC atop a V-2) climbs a total of 25 miles.

1950 July 28 First scheduled passenger service flown by a gas-turbine powered airliner (turboprop) is British European Airways's (BEA) Vickers *V.630 Viscount*. It carries 26 passengers from London to Paris, France.

1950 September 25 Pan American Airways acquires American Overseas Airlines.

1950 September 30 First International Astronautical Congress is held in Paris, France and proposes the creation of a permanent federation of national astronautical societies. This international convention indicates that space flight is becoming a serious topic of interest and concern to all nations. (See September 3, 1951)

1950 October U.S. Air Force cancels the *XF-85 Goblin* parasite fighter plane, citing it as an impractical concept.

1950 October U.S. Air Force announces its plans to replace all its conventional piston-engine aircraft with jet aircraft.

1950 October 22 First non-stop jet flight across the Atlantic is made by two Republic *F-84E* fighters. Flown by Col. David C. Schilling and Lt. Col. William Ritchie, the fighters are refuelled three times in flight. Schilling completes the London, England to Limestone, Maine flight, while Ritchie is forced to bail out safely over Newfoundland.

1950 November 8 First jet aircraft to be shot down by another occurs as U.S. Lt. Russel J. Brown, Jr. flying a Lockheed *F-80C*, shoots down a Soviet *MiG-15* jet fighter of the Chinese People's Republic Air Force over the Yalu River, Korea.

1951 Automobile power steering is first offered on the Chrysler Imperial models. This system uses hydraulic (fluid) pressure to minimize the effort required to turn the steering wheel. Developed during World War II for use on military vehicles, it becomes very popular and is used on nearly all cars today.

1951 A tunnel for bicyclists and pedestrians opens under the Tyne River in northeastern England.

1951 British science writer Arthur C. Clarke (b. 1917) publishes his book *The Exploration of Space*. This further popularizes the notion that manned space flight is feasible.

1951 During this year, the U.S. National Advisory Committee for Aeronautics (NACA) completes the first rocket combustion tests using fluorine.

1951 January 16 U.S. Air Force establishes Project MX-1593 (Project Atlas) as a study phase for a boost-glide vehicle as well as for an intercontinental ballistic missile. It contracts with Convair as a follow-on to

1951 A.D.

Car power steering offered

1951 A.D.

Idea of manned space flight popularized

the terminated MX-774 project. (See September 1951 and December 17, 1957)

*1951
January 26*

*First
supersonic
research
aircraft
made*

1951 January 26 First flight of Douglas *D-558-2 Skyrocket* supersonic research aircraft is made. This swept-wing, rocket and turbojet version of the jet-powered Douglas *D-558-1 Skystreak* transonic research aircraft, is launched from underneath its *B-29* mother-ship and exceeds Mach 1 (the speed of sound) in a dive. It later sets new speed and altitude records. On November 20, 1953, A. Scott Crossfield (b. 1921) becomes the first man to fly at twice the speed of sound while piloting his *Skyrocket*. It is retired in 1956 after providing much useful research data on supersonic flight.

1951 February Hiller Helicopters builds a small, two-seat helicopter powered by a 38-pound ramjet engine mounted on the tip of each rotor blade. Although it flies well, its extremely short range makes it impractical.

1951 February 5 The United States and Canada announce the establishment of the Distant Early Warning (DEW). This air defense system uses more than 30 radar stations located across the northern portion of the continent.

1951 February 21 First jet aircraft to make a nonstop, unrefuelled flight across the North Atlantic is English Electric *Canberra B.Mk 2* jet bomber. It flies from England to Baltimore, Maryland and is purchased by the U.S. Air Force, becoming the first non-U.S. designed aircraft to enter operational service with the United States.

1951 February 23 First flight of the prototype Dassault *Mystere* jet fighter is made in France. This advanced fighter with swept-back wings is the first French aircraft to exceed the speed of sound.

1951 March 15 First flight across the South Pacific, from Sydney, Australia, to Valparaiso, Chile, is made by American P. G. Taylor in the Consolidated Catalina seaplane *Frigate Bird II*.

1951 April 18 The first Aerobee sounding rocket with a biomedical experiment is launched at Holloman Air Force Base, New Mexico.

1951 May U.S. Air Force initiates the first research program on weightlessness. It is led by Hubertus Strughold (b. 1898) and Heinz Haber at the School of Aviation Medicine at Randolph Field, Texas.

1951 May 14 The U.S. Air Force Missile Test Center is established at Cape Canaveral, Florida and is assigned to the Air Research and Development Command (ARDC). This will become the launch site of many an historic space mission.

1951 May 29 First solo trans-Polar flight in a single engine aircraft is made by American Charles F. Blair. He flies from Bardufoss, Norway to Fairbanks, Alaska in a North American *P-51 Mustang*.

1951 June 17 U.S. Navy issues a contract to Convair for the development of a delta-wing (sweptback), hydro-ski-equipped seaplane with fighter ability. This is built and known as the *XF2Y-1 Sea Dart*. (See April 9, 1951)

1951 June 20 First flight of an aircraft with variable-sweep wings is made as the Bell *X-5* flies for 30 minutes at Edwards, California. This research aircraft has moveable wings which allow it to vary its configuration from straight wings for lower speeds to swept-back wings for high speeds.

1951 July 20 First flight of the prototype Hawker *Hunter* is made. This swept-wing jet fighter, one of the best transonic fighters and ground-support aircraft of its kind, becomes one of the most successful British military aircraft of the 1950s.

1951 August 17 First flight of the Douglas *AD-5 Skyraider* is made. This successful attack bomber sees action in the early 1970s in Vietnam.

1951 September U.S. Air Force decides to make Project MX-1593 (Atlas) only a ballistic missile and not a hypersonic boost-glide weapon.

1951 September 3 The International Astronautical Federation is formed by scientists of ten nations at the second International Congress on Astronautics.

1951 September 20 First U.S. successful recovery of animals from a rocket launch is made by the U.S. Air Force at Holloman Air Force Base, New Mexico. An instrumented monkey and 11 mice are flown to 236,000 feet by an Aerobee rocket and recovered alive.

1951 October 10 First U.S. operational guided ballistic missile is launched at White Sands Proving Ground, New Mexico. The Corporal missile has a range of 50—90 miles with a warhead and takes between six to seven hours to prepare for launch.

1951 October 29 U.S. testing of captured German V-2 rockets comes to an end with the firing of V-2 #66 at White Sands Proving Ground, New Mexico. The test program began on March 15, 1946 with a static firing and progressed from the first launch on April 16, 1946. The availability of these German rockets gave the United States invaluable experience in rocket design, propulsion, and handling.

1951 November 5 New Jersey Turnpike opens to traffic. This 118-mile-long toll road between New York and Philadelphia, Pennsylvania becomes an integral link for truck and car traffic on the eastern seaboard.

1951 December American aeronautical engineer Richard T. Whitcomb (b. 1921) verifies what becomes known as the "area rule." This broadly states that at the junction of an aircraft's body and wings there should be no abrupt changes in shape. This results in the "waisting" of the fuselage or body, making for a characteristic modern, high-speed "coke bottle" or "wasp waist" shape.

1951 December 16 First helicopter powered by a gas-turbine engine flies successfully. The Kaman *K-225* has a twin-rotor, meshing configuration that allows the two sets of blades or rotors to be placed close together or side-by-side atop the cabin. The use of a turbine makes for a lighter, simpler, more powerful engine compared to a conventional piston engine.

1952 Modern-type disc brakes, of Dunlop design, are fitted to Jaguar entries in a European auto race. As distinct from drum brakes, they are designed to operate by pressing friction pads against a rotating steel disc. One piston brake cylinder is mounted on each side of a disc to press the pads against it. Disc brakes are now common on a car's front wheels and are much less prone to brake fading.

1952 First manned weightless experiments are conducted in aircraft flights at Wright-Patterson Air Force Base, Dayton, Ohio. At the same time, the first weightless experiments with animals launched by rockets are conducted at Holloman Air Force Base, New Mexico.

1952 The Soviet Union sends 12 animals in 18 launchings on flights up to 100 kilometers. It then parachutes them safely from heights of 30 or 40 km. The Soviets have been conducting systematic research on the effects of space on living organisms since 1949.

1952 Volga-Don Canal, connecting the cities of Stalingrad on the Volga River with Kalach on the Don River, is completed. This north-to-south waterway runs 63 miles and has 13 locks.

1952 January 5 First all-cargo air service across the North Atlantic is offered by Pan American Airways using Douglas *DC-6*'s.

1952 March *Colliers* magazine publishes an article by Wernher von Braun (1912—1977) called "Crossing the Last Frontier" which proposes a spinning, wheel-shaped space station that could be placed in earth orbit.

1952 March 19 U.S. Air Force reveals that mammals (monkeys and mice) have been recovered alive and well after being launched by Aerobee sounding rockets to altitudes of some 200,000 feet (60,960 meters). Four of the monkeys died as a result of parachute failure, but tests indicate that "weightlessness does not appear to affect the animals' heart rates, blood pressure or respiration systems."

1952 April U.S. National Advisory Committee for Aeronautics (NACA) directs its laboratories to begin the study of problems associated with flight beyond the atmosphere.

1952 April 15 First flight of the first all-jet-propelled heavy bomber, the Boeing *YB-52*. This prototype for the *B-52 Stratfortress* was designed in the mid-1940s and has proven to be one of the most long-lived and useful military aircraft ever built. The first *B-52s* became operational in 1955 and were soon "on alert," which meant that a number were kept airborne, armed and fuelled at all times. They were used for U.S. strategic bombing during the Vietnam War (1964—1975) and as recently as the January—February 1991 Persian Gulf War. They have been regularly modified to improve and update their different systems, and many think they will be suitable for operation to the end of this century.

1952 A.D.

Soviet Union launches animals into space

1952 March

Space station proposed

1952 April 21 First jet airliner to enter commercial passenger service is the De Havilland *D.H. 106 Comet.* British Overseas Airways Corporation (BOAC) offers service between London, England and Rome, Italy.

1952 ■ First jet airliner, the De Haviland *Comet,* flies over England.

1952 May Number of diesel locomotives in the United States exceeds the number of steam locomotives for the first time. There are 19,082 diesel and 18,489 steam.

1952 May 3 First landing at the North Pole is made by Americans Lt. Col. William P. Benedict and Lt. Col. J. O. Fletcher on a ski-and-wheel equipped Air Force Douglas *C-47.*

1952 May 26

First stunt plane flies

1952 May 26 First flight of a tiny stunt plane (seven feet, two inches long) is made in Palm Springs, California. It is designed and built by Ray Stits and Bob Starr. (See 1987)

1952 May 29 First operational inflight refuelling of a combat aircraft is made during the Korean War, as 12 U.S. Republic *F-84E Thunderjets* are refuelled by *KB-29* tankers following an attack mission.

1952 June

Goodyear delivers new blimps

1952 June Goodyear delivers the new *ZPN-1* nonrigid airship to the U.S. Navy at Lakehurst, New Jersey. This very large blimp begins a new series of huge, long-range airships, indicating that despite the beginnings of space age thinking, the Navy feels there may still be a role for the airship.

1952 June 17 Aviation Medical Acceleration Laboratory is dedicated in Johnsville, Pennsylvania featuring a human centrifuge capable of producing accelerations up to 40 g's or 40 times the force of gravity. Such facilities and equipment are needed to determine the limits of human stress and endurance, since American pilots are constantly going higher, faster, and farther.

1952 June 18 "Blunt nose principle," which is later applied to design of both manned space capsules and ICBMs (inter-continental ballistic missiles), is first conceived by U.S. National Advisory Committee for Aeronautics scientist H. Julian Allen. He argues that a blunt shape absorbs only one-half percent of the heat generated by the reentry of a body into the earth's atmosphere. (See 1953)

1952 July 3 Last liner to hold the transatlantic speed record, the *United States,* leaves New York on its record-setting maiden voyage. It makes the eastbound voyage in three days, ten hours, and 40 minutes, averaging a speed of 35.59 knots. Despite this amazing time, the era of the scheduled transatlantic passenger liner will soon be over, as air travel improves in comfort and speed. (See 1958)

1952 July 14 U.S. National Advisory Committee for Aeronautics (NACA) Executive Committee directs its laboratories to begin the study of problems likely to be encountered in flight beyond the atmosphere. NACA is both responding to and seeking to promote advanced thinking about the future of aviation and space.

1952 July 26 Two monkeys and two mice are successfully launched and recovered after being sent to 200,000 feet by a U.S. Aerobee sounding rocket at Holloman Air Force Base, New Mexico.

1952 July 13—31 First Atlantic crossing by helicopter is made by two Sikorsky *S-55s.* The flight is not non-stop but is made in stages over a two week period.

1952 August 11 A civil agreement is signed in Tokyo for air services between the United States and Japan. Regular transportation links is one of the many important steps in the post-war revival of Japan.

1952 August 30 First large bomber to have a delta-wing (swept-back) design makes its first flight. Britain's Avro *Vulcan B.1* is the second of Britain's trio of V-bombers and sees more than 25 years of service with the R.A.F.

1952 October 18 *Colliers* publishes Wernher von Braun's (1912—1977) article, "Man on the Moon." It later becomes a book.

1952 November 19 The first liquid rocket engine with a thrust of over 100,000 pounds is test fired in the Santa Susana Mountains, California, in connection with the U.S. Air Force Navaho rocket program.

1952 November 19—20 First commercial flights to fly directly over the Polar regions, between Europe and North America, are made by Scandinavian Airlines System (SAS) using Douglas *DC-6B* airliners. Regularly scheduled services over the North Pole start in 1954. (See November 15-16, 1954)

1953 Edward Halton of Dallas, Texas conceives of the idea of an overhead monorail system in which small, automated vehicles would carry passengers directly between stations. (See 1970)

1953 First true American sports car is the Chevrolet Corvette. It is also the first series-production car with a reinforced fiberglass body fitted on a conventional steel frame. Like a true sports car, it seats only two, and has a six-cylinder engine with three carburetors and an automatic transmission. Only 300 are built this year. In 1969, a record 38,762 are built.

1953 ■ America's first sports car, the Corvette.

1953 Financial success and popularity of turnpikes in Pennsylvania, Maine, New Hampshire, and New Jersey demonstrate that the U.S. public is fed up with obsolete, congested roads and is willing to pay for these modern freeways.

1954 ■ Partially completed Hollywood-Santa Ana Freeway in California.

1953 U.S. National Advisory Committee for Aeronautics releases H. Julian Allen's "blunt nose principle" in the form of an offical report, NACA TN4047. (See June 18, 1952)

1953 Hubertus Strughold (b. 1898) of the U.S. Air Force School of Aviation Medicine publishes his book *The Green and Red Planet*, which is a physiological study of the possibility of life on Mars.

1953 Japanese rocket work begins with the establishment of two research groups from within the Institute of the Industrial Sciences of Tokyo University. One concentrates on supersonic aerodynamics and the other on aeronautical electronic equipment. (See 1956)

1953 First automobile air bag patent is registered to American John Hetrick of Pennsylvania. (See 1958)

1953 First submarine designed as a result of hydrodynamic research, the U.S. *Albacore*, is launched. This 210-foot vessel is given a more stream-lined hull shape for high underwater speeds. Overall, it has a rounded bow shape tapering to the tail, giving it the look of a blimp or whale.

1953 February American Medical Association authorizes the American Board of Preventive Medicine to establish aviation medicine as a distinct specialty and to grant certification for those properly qualified.

1953 February 1 Chance Vought delivers the last propeller-driven fighter, the *F4U Corsair*, to the U.S. Navy. Since the first *Corsair* flew in 1940, 12,571 have been built.

1953 March U.S. Lt. Col. John P. Stapp (b. 1910) travels 421 mph on a rocket-powered sled. This rapid acceleration and deceleration tolerance test is conducted on a 3,500-foot track. (See December 10, 1954)

1953 March Boeing delivers the last propeller-driven bomber, a *B-50*, to the U.S. Air Force. More than 4,250 *B-29* and *B-50 Superforts* were delivered to the U.S. Air Force in the past 10 years. More than 17,000 four-engine bombers were made since the first *B-17* in 1935.

1953 April 9 First delta-wing (swept-back), jet-propelled seaplane, Convair *XF2Y-1 Sea Dart*, makes its first flight in San Diego, California. Equipped with hydroskis to gain hydrodynamic lift, it becomes the first seaplane to exceed the speed of sound. The U.S. Navy eventually decides to abandon the whole seaplane fighter concept, probably because of advances in aircraft carrier/fighter systems.

1953 May

First underwater crossing of Atlantic

1953 May First underwater crossing of the Atlantic Ocean is made by the British submarine *Andrew*. It "snorkels" from Bermuda to the English Channel. (See 1933)

1953 May 16 First scheduled hydrofoil boat service begins passenger service between the Swiss and the Italian parts of Lake Maggiore. Today, over 100 hydrofoil passenger vessels are operating throughout the world.

1953 May 18 American Jacqueline Cochrane (d. 1980) becomes the first woman to fly faster than the speed of sound while flying a Canadian-built North American *F-86 Sabre*. On the same day, she sets the world speed record for women at 652 mph (1,049 km/h).

1953 May 23 Fritz von Opel (1899—1971) makes the first "official" demonstration of the Opel Rak II rocket car before an invited crowd of 2,000 in Germany. His black-powder rockets work well, propelling the car to 125 mph. Opel later predicts that rocket power will one day send man to other planets.

1953 May 25 First fighter aircraft capable of sustained supersonic speed in level flight, the North American *YF-100A*, makes its first flight at Edwards Air Force Base, California. When it enters service, it becomes known as the *F-100 Super Sabre*. With its thin, highly swept wings and beautifully streamlined fuselage, this supersonic fighter sees well over 20 years of active service.

1953 August 20 Redstone missile No. 1 is fired by U.S. Army Redstone Arsenal personnel at Cape Canaveral, Florida. This 63-foot-tall, single-stage, liquid-fuel rocket is basically an enlarged V-2 with a range of about 200 miles. It provides the basis for later Jupiter rockets used to launch the first U.S. astronauts.

1953 September 1 First scheduled international helicopter services begin between Brussels, Belgium to Lille, France, and from Rotterdam to Maastrich in Holland. It is operated by Belgian airline Sabena.

1953 September 1 First aerial refuelling of a jet aircraft by a jet tanker is made with a *B-47 Stratojet* by a *KB-47B* tanker.

1953 October American Astronautical Society (AAS) is founded at a meeting in New York of 35 individuals. A scientific organization dedicated to the development of the astronautical sciences, it still exists today. (See February 17, 1954)

1953 October 23 The Daniel and Florence Guggenheim Institute for Flight Structures is established at Columbia University in New York, for research and graduate training in flight structures, including structures intended for space flight.

1953 October 24 First flight of Convair *F-102A* delta-wing fighter is made. This swept-wing, super-sonic fighter features the "wasp waist" design of Whitcomb's "area rule." It becomes the U.S. Air Force's first operational delta-wing aircraft. (See December 1951)

1953 November 20 First man to exceed Mach 2 (twice the speed of sound) is American test pilot A. Scott Crossfield (b. 1921) in a Douglas *D-558-2 Skyrocket.* This supersonic research aircraft is dropped from a *B-29* mothership and reaches Mach 2.0005 (1,291 mph) in a dive from 70,000 feet.

1953 November 27 An official of the U.S.S.R. Academy of Sciences announces in Vienna, Austria that "science has reached such a stage that the launching of a stratoplane to the Moon, the creation of an artificial satellite of the Earth, is a real possibility."

1953 December 12 Mach 2.5 (a speed of two-and-one-half times the speed of sound) is achieved by Maj. Charles E. "Chuck" Yeager (b. 1923) in the Bell *X-1A.* Dropped from a cruising *B-29*, the rocket-propelled experimental aircraft reaches 1,650 mph (2,655 km/h) at 70,000 feet (21,330 meters).

1954 First gas-powered private car with direct fuel injection as standard feature is the "gullwing"-doored Mercedes-Benz 300 SL from Germany. This six-cylinder, large sports car can reach 160 mph. Its new fuel delivery system eliminates the need for a carburetor by spraying a specified amount of fuel into the cylinder.

1954 Toronto, Canada subway system first opens.

1954 First use of television in railroad communications is made.

1954 Cadillac becomes the first car manufacturer to adopt power steering as a standard feature on all its cars.

1954 First large fiberglass motorboat, the *Perpetua,* is built in England. The frame of this 48-foot (14-meter) yacht proves capable of withstanding the vibrations caused by its twin diesel engines, and is especially suited to deep water conditions.

1954 Kharmann-Ghia two-seat sportscar is introduced by Volkswagen. Although its small, air-cooled, rear engine is the same as the famous "Bug," its body by Kharmann of Osnabruck, Germany and designed by Ghia of Turin, Italy makes this a flashy, popular, and affordable sports car.

1954 American Motors Corporation is formed as a result of the merger of the Hudson Motor Car Company and Nash-Kelvinator.

1954 February 7 First flight of the prototype Lockheed *XF-104 Starfighter,* a jet-fighter which is to be widely used by the United States and other Western countries. It is a small aircraft, featuring very slim lines and small, thin, straight wings.

1954 February 17 The American Astronautical Society (AAS) is incorporated in the state of New York.

1954 March 1 The ban on the production of military aircraft in Japan, imposed after World War II, is lifted. An agreement is signed between the United States and Japan——the Lockheed Aircraft Corporation and the Kawasaki Aircraft Company——which allows Japan to manufacture Lockheed *F-94C Starfire* jet-fighters and *T-33A* jet trainers.

1954 April 29 United States launches for the first time a three stage rocket at Wallops Island, Virginia. It consists of two Nike sounding rockets in tandem and a small Deacon rocket as a third stage.

1954 May 13 St. Lawrence Seaway bill, authorizing construction of U.S.-Canadian artificial waterway connecting the Great Lakes and the Atlantic Ocean, is signed by President Dwight D. Eisenhower (1890—1969).

1954 May 13

St. Lawrence Seaway bill signed

1954 June 2 The tail-sitting Convair *XFY-1 Pogo* makes its first free vertical take-off and landing at Moffett Naval Air Station, Mountain View, California. This VTOL (vertical take-off and landing) aircraft resembles a fixed-wing aircraft sitting on its tail and pointing up, with four swept-back wings and contra-rotating propellers on its nose. It flies several times, taking off vertically and landing, tail-down, nose-up, on four small castors, but altogether proves an ungainly concept and is finally abandoned. (See November 2, 1954)

1954 June 24 New York Thruway opens to traffic. This 559-mile-long toll road connects New York City to Buffalo and becomes a very heavily-used road.

1954 June 25 Following a meeting of U.S. Army and Navy representatives, Project Orbiter is outlined as a plan to launch a 2.27-kilogram satellite into low earth orbit using a Redstone missile and Loki solid fuel rockets as a second stage.

1954 July 15 First U.S. jet-powered transport aircraft, Boeing *367-80*, makes its first flight as a prototype refuelling tanker/transport for the Air Force. It is developed simultaneously by Boeing as the Boeing *707* airliner and becomes the first of a superlative and long-lasting family of aircraft. The *707* is the most widely used subsonic jet airliner of the 1960s and its success would come at the expense of the new De Havilland *Comet*.

1954 August 3 First free flight of the Rolls-Royce TMR (thrust measuring rig) jet-lift vehicle is made in England. Called the "Flying Bedstead," it is an experimental vehicle built to test one concept—-whether deflected jet thrust can raise an aircraft vertically. This rig, made of functional, tubular steel pylons, leads to the development of the Short *SC.1* VTOL (vertical take-off and landing) aircraft. (See April 2, 1957)

1954 August 4 First flight of the prototype English Electric *P. 1* is made in England. It is from this swept-wing, research aircraft that the RAF's first supersonic fighter, *Lightning*, will be developed.

1954 August 5 First glide flight is made by Bell *X-2* experimental rocket plane. This is a swept-wing advance on the *X-1* and is built to achieve the demanding goal of reaching Mach 3 or three times the speed of sound.

1954 November 2 First full transition of an airplane from vertical to horizontal flight and back again is made by Convair's experimental tail-sitter VTOL (vertical take-off and landing) turbo-prop fighter, *XFY-1 Pogo*, in San Diego, California.

1954 November 15—16 Initial flights of the first regularly scheduled trans-Arctic air route are made by Scandinavian Airlines System (SAS) between Copenhagen, Denmark and Los Angeles, California with Douglas *DC-6Bs*.

1954 November 18 First inertial guidance system for a missile is tested by North American Aviation technicians. The Air Force X-10/Navaho missile uses the new system which guides it by means of a self-contained, automatically-controlling device that responds to changes in acceleration.

1954 December Walt Disney Films produces a film titled *Man in Space*.

1954 December 10 Tests are conducted to determine the ability of a pilot to eject from an aircraft at supersonic speeds. U.S. Lt. Col. John Paul Stapp rides a rocket sled which decelerates from 632 mph to zero in 125 seconds. He survives more than 40 G's (40 times the force of gravity).

1954 December 23 U.S. Government Memorandum of Understanding titled "Joint Project for a New High Speed Research Airplane" initiates what becomes the *X-15* program. (See March 19, 1959)

1955 First production car with self-levelling air suspension system as well as front disc brakes is the Citroen DS of France. Its aerodynamic body is also the first with detachable panels. The suspension system of this very advanced car uses pressurized air rather than springs for support.

1955 Worst accident in the history of auto racing occurs at the Le Mans 24 Hour Race (France) when a Mercedes 300 SLR harmlessly collides with an Austin-Healy. The Mercedes, however, veers off course and goes over a "safety" bank into the crowd. The driver and 83 spectators are killed.

1955 Canadian Avro VZ-9Z *Avrocar* is built on an experimental contract for the U.S. Army and Air Force. This large saucer or disk-shaped aircraft gets its direct lift from three internal jet engines that allow it to rise straight up. It then flies forward using vectored thrust. At 18 feet in diameter and weighing 5,650 pounds, it proves to have too many stability problems and is never developed.

1955 First subway in Rome, Italy opens. Linking the central railroad station to a convention center and government building complex, this line was planned originally by Italy's Fascist dictator, Benito Mussolini (1883—1945).

1955 Thunderbird (T-Bird) sports car is unveiled by Ford Motor Company. Built as a response to the

1955 ■ NASA's stable of "X" research aircraft.

very popular Chevrolet Corvette, this small, two-passenger sports car is produced for only three years before it changes radically, becoming a large car that stresses luxury over sportiness.

 1955 January 10 Pakistan International Airlines Corporation is established following the nationalization of commercial air transport in Pakistan.

1955 January 17 First nuclear-powered submarine, the U.S.S. *Nautilus*, is launched. Resembling a conventional submarine, this 320-foot- (98-meter-) long vessel has an underwater range that is nearly unlimited, being measured in years rather than miles. This can be considered the first true submarine, since all of its predecessors were really surface ships capable of brief underwater operations. The steam to run its two turbine engines is provided by a nuclear reactor.

1955 February 26 First known survivor of an ejection from an aircraft at supersonic speed is George Smith. Flying a *F-100 Super Sabre* which suddenly goes into an uncontrollable dive, Smith ejects at Mach 1.05, slightly past the speed of sound. He is immediately hit by 64 G's for a fraction of a second, which rip off his helmet and oxygen mask and knock him unconscious,

although his parachute opens automatically. Smith suffers severe internal injuries and takes six months to recover. This accident sends U.S. engineers back to work designing better suits, helmets, and masks.

1955 March The feasibility of an F-1 rocket engine developing one million pounds of thrust in a single chamber is established by Rocketdyne Division. The Saturn V, which launches all the later Apollo moon missions, will have five of these liquid-oxygen/kerosene motors in its first stage.

1955 April 1 First regular service begins by postwar Lufthansa, the reborn airline of West Germany. It offers flights within Germany, from Hamburg to Dusseldorf and Frankfurt, using a twin-engine Convair *340*. (See May 16, 1955)

1955 April 10 Final ratification of the Treaty of Paris lifts the 1945 ban on the building of powered aircraft in Germany and permits the formation of defense forces.

1955 April 26 Moscow radio reports U.S.S.R. plans to explore the moon with a remote-control tank and tells of plans for manned visits to the moon in near future.

1955 April 29 First flight of the McDonnell *XV-1* compound helicopter or convertaplane. Combining characteristics of both an airplane and a helicopter, this vehicle makes a vertical takeoff like a helicopter and then uses a pusher propeller for forward propulsion.

1955 May 16 Lufthansa, the West German airline, begins to operate air services throughout Europe.

1955 May 27 First short-haul jet airliner to go into widespread service, the Sud-Aviation *SE 210 Caravelle*, makes its first flight at Toulouse, France. This first French jet-powered airliner also creates a new design trend by adopting a rear mounted engine configuration.

1955 May 31 Soviet Union begins construction of the Baikonur Cosmodrome, a large launch facility on the steppes of Kazakhstan.

1955 July 8 First rocket sled test run is made on the new, 12,000-foot-long Supersonic Military Air Research Track (SMART) at Hurricane Mesa, Utah. The U.S. Air Force begins serious study of physiological behavior during rapid deceleration.

1955 July 29 President Dwight D. Eisenhower (1890—1969) announces that U.S. participation in the International Geophysical Year (July 1957—December 1958) will involve a satellite launch by the United States during that time period.

1955 August 15 Soviets to construct satellite

1955 August 15 Soviet official A. G. Karpenko reports that construction of a Soviet satellite would begin soon. The first satellite was to orbit between 125 and 625 miles, and later ones between 935 and 1,250 miles.

1955 September 3 First successful demonstration of the use of an ejection seat from a moving aircraft while still on the ground is made by British Sqn. Ldr. J. S. Fifield in England. He ejects from a modified Gloster *Meteor 7* that is travelling 120 mph (194 km/h).

1955 September 9 U.S. Department of Defense's Policy Council adopts the majority recommendation of the Stewart Committee which recommends that the Navy proceed with the development of the Vanguard launch vehicle to place a satellite in orbit as part of the U.S. contribution to the International Geophysical Year (IGY).

1955 October 13 Pan American Airways orders both the Douglas *DC-8* and Boeing *707* airliners for its fleet. This forces its competition to modernize as well and starts the jet-buying spree that heralds the subsonic jet age for airlines.

1955 October 22 First supersonic tactical fighter-bomber to be designed as such, Republic *F-105A*, exceeds the speed of sound on its first flight. Later known as *Thunderchief*, this all-weather aircraft serves during the Vietnam War.

1955 October 25 First flight of the prototype Saab *35 Draken* "double-delta" Mach 2 Swedish fighter. This is a highly original, multi-purpose aircraft that serves into the 1970s, performing interceptor, reconnaissance, and tactical strike roles.

1955 November 8 U.S. secretary of defense approves the Jupiter and Thor IRBM (intermediate range ballistic missile) programs. Jupiter is based on the V-2/Redstone missile, and Thor is based on the experience gained from building the Atlas missile.

1955 November 18 First powered flight of Bell *X-2* research aircraft is made. It is powered by the first throttleable rocket engine, the Curtiss Wright XLR25-CW-1. Two aircraft are built for transonic and supersonic speed research, but both are destroyed in accidents within a year.

1955 December 1 Remote control of a multiple-unit railroad car is demonstrated between New Rochelle and Rye, New York from a control panel in Larchmont, New York.

1955 December 10 First flight of the Ryan *X-13* VTOL (vertical take-off and landing) jet aircraft is made at Edwards Air Force Base, California. This flight is a conventional rolling take-off and landing using its bolt-on tricycle landing gear. (See November 28, 1956 and April 11, 1957)

1956 Renault's Dauphine model introduced this year is the first French car to sell over two million units (from 1956 to 1962). This small car has a rear-mounted, four cylinder engine and gives a top speed of 75 mph.

1956 United States enacts the Federal-Aid Highway Act of 1956 and actually begins its interstate highway program known formally as the National System of Interstate and Defense Highways. It is intended to be a 41,000-mile network of modern freeways, spanning the United States, and linking together and serving more than 90% of all the cities of over 50,000 population, and joining the main International Highway Routes connecting with Mexico and Canada. The Act authorizes expenditure of $25 billion for the 1957—1969 fiscal years.

1956 Japan launches its first small sounding rocket called Kappa 3. It is the first generation in the Kappa series. (See July 1, 1958)

1956 Egypt nationalizes the Suez Canal and temporarily closes it to shipping. This gives rise to the spectacular growth in the size of oil tankers. (See January 31, 1959)

1956 First regular hydrofoil service begins between Sicily and the Italian continent, operating at a speed of some 50 knots.

1956 Last trolley car in New York City is withdrawn from service across the Queensboro Bridge. Diesel buses replace the trolley service.

1956 First use of glass-fiber reinforced plastic (fiberglass) as shroud material for an outboard motor is made by Scott-Attwater Company of the United States.

1956 January 10 First static firing of a U.S. rocket engine having a thrust greater than 400,000 pounds occurs at Santa Susana, California and is conducted by the U.S. Air Force.

1956 January 26—27 A symposium held at the University of Michigan called "The Scientific Uses of Earth Satellites" reflects the growing American interest and concern with space and earth satellites in particular.

1956 February 1 Army Ballistic Missile Agency (ABMA) at Redstone Arsenal, Huntsville, Alabama is activated by the U.S. Army. Composed of Wernher von Braun's (1912—1977) rocket team, it is charged with developing the operational Redstone missile and the Jupiter IRBM (intermediate range ballistic missile).

1956 ■ Rocket pioneers Hermann Oberth (foreground) and Wernher von Braun to his left

1956 March First large-scale electronic data-processing computer is introduced to U.S. railroad operations. It is used to process stockholder dividend checks and for company payrolls.

1956 March U.S. Air Force begins studies of Project 7969 known as the Manned Ballistic Rocket Research System. The goal of this project is to put man in space but, as late as January 1958, the project had not received official sanction and is still restricted to limited design study.

1956 March 10 First aircraft to exceed 1,000 mph (1,609 km/h) is an English Fairey *Delta* 2. Piloted by Lt. Cdr. Peter Twiss, it reaches a speed of 1,132 mph (1,822 km/h).

1956 March 14 First Jupiter A is launched by the U.S. Army Ballistic Missile Agency (ABMA) at Cape Canaveral, Florida. Jupiter is a modified Redstone.

1956 March 28 U.S. Airman D. F. Smith remains in a sealed space cabin simulator for 24 hours.

1956 March 10 Aircraft exceeds 1,000 mph

1956 April 23 U.S. Army Ballistic Missile Agency (ABMA) informs the secretary of defense that it could launch a satellite with a Jupiter vehicle by January 1957. The United States is committed to the International Geophysical Year (IGY) Vanguard project and thus does not give ABMA the go-ahead.

1956 May 21

First U.S. H-bomb dropped

1956 May 21 First U.S. hydrogen bomb to be released from an aircraft is dropped by a Boeing *B-52B*, and explodes over Bikini atoll in the Pacific Ocean.

1956 June 1 The Douglas *DC-7C* long-range, piston-engine airliner enters service. This is the last of the famous *DC-4* family and the first airliner capable of non-stop crossings of both the Atlantic and the Pacific. Although it is to provide the most advanced standards of airline operation, it will be outmoded by airliners with jet engines.

1956 June 25

Two liners collide

1956 June 25 Collision at sea occurs in a thick fog south of Nantucket between the Swedish-American Lines's *Stockholm* and Italian liner *Andrea Doria*. The reinforced icebreaker prow of the Stockholm hits the *Andrea Doria* broadside and smashes 30 feet into its side, rupturing its watertight compartments. The *Stockholm* and an arriving French liner, *Ile de France*, rescue most of the survivors, and only 50 people die in the disaster. *Andrea Doria* sinks the next morning.

1956 June 30 Two airliners collide in midair over the Grand Canyon, killing 128 people. The TWA *Constellation* and United *DC-7* collide despite clear daylight skies, no turbulence, and little air traffic.

1956 July 4 First operational overflight is made by a Lockheed *U-2* reconnaissance aircraft. Taking off from Wiesbaden, Germany, the American spy plane flies over Moscow, Leningrad, and the Soviet Baltic Sea coast. It is designed to fly at supersonic speeds and photograph the earth from 60,000 feet. (See May 1, 1960)

1956 August 10 First manned flight into the stratosphere (the upper portion of the atmosphere above seven miles) in a polyethylene balloon is made by Lt. Cmdrs. Malcolm Ross (b. 1919) and Lee Lewis. Their open gondola flight is part of U.S. Office of Naval Research Project Strato-Lab and reaches 40,000 feet.

1956 August 23 First nonstop transcontinental helicopter flight is made by Vertol *H-21*, flying from San Diego, California to Washington, D.C. in 31 hours, 40 minutes. This twin-rotor transport sees service later in Vietnam, can fly about 75 mph, and can carry 15 passengers.

1956 September 12 First swept-wing jet airliner, the Tupolev *Tu-104*, enters service with Russian airline Aeroflot. Evolved from the *Tu-16* twin-jet bomber, its first flight was made in early 1955 and greatly surprised the West.

1956 September 20 First Jupiter C is launched by the U.S. Army Ballistic Missile Agency (ABMA) at Cape Canaveral, Florida. This modified Redstone is a three-stage version with greater lifting power. It reaches an impressive altitude of 682 miles and flies 3,400 miles downrange. It will be used to launch America's first satellite, *Explorer 1*, on January 31, 1958.

1956 September 27 First piloted airplane to exceed Mach 3 (three times the speed of sound) is the rocket-powered Bell *X-2*. It tumbles out of control and crashes after reaching 2,100 mph (3,380 km/h), killing U.S. Air Force pilot Capt. Milburn G. Apt.

1956 October U.S. National Advisory Committee for Aeronautics (NACA) initiates examination of the need for a manned rocket research vehicle as a follow-up to the *X-15* program. This is stimulated by a proposal by the Air Force's Air Research and Development Command (ARDC) which is proposing a future boost-glide type of manned vehicle.

1956 November 8 Trains with pneumatic (air-filled) tires are introduced into regular service on the Paris Metro (Chemin de Fer Metropolitan).

1956 November 11 First flight of U.S. Air Force's first supersonic bomber, Convair *B-58 Hustler*, is made in Fort Worth, Texas. Incorporating the "wasp waist" or "coke bottle" shape, this bomber is intended to fly very high and very fast. It does not prove to be entirely successful. (See December 1952)

1956 November 17 First flight of the French-built Dassault *Mirage III-C* jet fighter, which becomes the most successful European aircraft in this category since World War II and serves into the 1970s.

1956 November 25 First successful parachute jump in Antarctica is made by U.S. Air Force Sgt. Richard J. Patton. He jumps from 1,500 feet as a test to determine the cause of parachute malfunction in sub-zero weather conditions.

1956 November 28 First transition from horizontal flight to vertical flight and back again by a jet-powered aircraft is made by Ryan *X-13 Vertijet*, a VTOL (vertical take-off and landing) aircraft. (See April 11, 1957)

1957 First U.S. car fitted with air suspension is the Cadillac Eldorado Brougham. (See 1955)

1957 New method for fastening rail to ties is invented by Norwegian engineer Per Pande-Rolfsen. Called the "Pandrol," a contraction of his name, it is a spring-steel clip that is quickly driven into place with a hammer. It is unaffected by vibration and thus prevents "rail creep." It also simplifies rail-changing and the clips can be reused.

1957 In Japan, the first monorail train opens in Ueno, Tokyo.

1957 First cars fitted with twin double headlights (four headlights) are the Lincoln and Cadillac models.

1957 Landmark Technical Note titled "A Comparative Analysis of Long-Range Hypervelocity Vehicles" is issued by U.S. National Advisory Committee for Aeronautics (NACA). Written by H. Julian Allen, Alfred J. Eggers and fellow scientist Niece, it develops new avenues of scientific thought on manned reentry by using Allen's concepts of how a blunt body distributes reentry heat more evenly than does a pointed shape which is prone to very hot spots.

1957 First true container ship, the American *Gateway City*, begins operations. Its platforms are designed to carry 35-foot (10.7-meter) trailer vans which can be removed from the chassis of a truck and loaded directly onto the ship. (See 1969)

1957 Longest simple box girder bridge, the Sava Bridge in Belgrade, Yugoslavia, is built. This new design employs the principle of a simple box girder (a hollow rectangular or trapezoidal bridge structure designed to act as a beam) instead of a truss. It has two anchor spans of 246 feet and a center span 856 feet long.

1957 January 16—18 First nonstop jet flight around the world is made by three U.S. Air Force *B-52* jet bombers which complete a total distance of 24,325 miles (39,147 kilometers) in 45 hours, 19 minutes, averaging 537 mph (864 km/h). The flight is commanded by Maj. Gen. Archie J. Old, Jr.

1957 February 14 U.S. National Advisory Committee for Aeronautics (NACA) establishes "Round Three" Steering Committee to study the feasibility of a hypersonic boost-glide research airplane. This is considered the third stage of U.S. rocket-propelled supersonic research, the first being the X-series (*X-1 Rom X-5*), and the second is the *X-15* research aircraft. This boost-glide third stage will become known as *Dyna-Soar*, a planned outer space manned vehicle that would reach speeds of Mach 20 (20 times the speed of sound), and would represent a marriage of a ballistic missile and a winged aircraft.

1957 February 19 First flight by the *Bell X-14*, a deflected-jet, flat-ring VTOL (vertical take-off and landing) aircraft, is made in the United States. An experimental aircraft built to investigate the potential of direct jet-lift, it makes a hovering flight.

1957 March 3 First scheduled international helicopter service between capital cities (Brussels and Paris) is offered by Belgian airline Sabena using Sikorsky *S-58* helicopters.

1957 March 4—15 U.S. Navy airship ZPG-2 *Snowbird*, captained by Commander J. R. Hunt, completes a double crossing of the North Atlantic and establishes an endurance record for unrefuelled flight of 264 hours, 14 minutes, 18 seconds. It leaves from Massachusetts, goes south around the Canary and Cape Verde Islands, then returns via the Virgin Islands to Key West, Florida.

1957 April 2 First transition from vertical to horizontal flight and back again with the airplane always remaining in a flat, horizontal attitude is made in England by a Short *SC.1* VTOL (vertical take-off and landing) aircraft.

1957 April 8 First flight of McDonnell *F-101B Voodoo* is made. A reconnaissance version of this

1957
March 3
International helicopter service offered

fighter, with cameras housed in its nose, is heavily involved in surveillance of Cuba during the 1962 missile crisis, and makes many low-level runs over that island.

1957 April 11 First full transition by a jet-powered aircraft from vertical to horizontal flight and back again for a vertical descent is made by the tail-sitting Ryan *X-13 Vertijet.*

1957 May

First Toyota Corona built

1957 May First Toyota Corona is built. Intended as a small family car or a taxi, it launches one of the more successful Japanese automobiles.

1957 June 2 First solo balloon flight into the stratosphere (the upper portion of the atmosphere above seven miles) is made by U.S. Capt. Joseph W. Kittinger, Jr. (b. 1928). In his plastic balloon *Manhigh 1*, he stays aloft for six hours, 34 minutes and reaches an altitude of 96,000 feet.

1957 June 2 Trans-Europe Express (TEE) services are introduced in the first major effort to create a modern inter-city rail system that caters to first class travelers. It is the successful result of cooperation among the Belgian, French, West German, Italian, Luxembourg, Netherlands, and Swiss railway authorities.

1957 July 1 Largest demonstration of mail transportation by rocket is successfully conducted by the U.S. Rocket Research Institute. Five 14-foot-long by three-inch diameter solid-fuel rockets fly from Douglas County, Nevada to Topaz, Mono County, California and carry 5,000 letters. All land within a 500-foot circle. The Institute is a non-profit, educational institution.

1957 July 16

John Glenn sets Calif.–N.Y. speed record

1957 July 16 Maj. John H. Glenn, Jr. (b. 1921) sets a new California to New York speed record, flying from Los Alamitos Naval Air Station to Floyd Bennett Field in three hours, 23 minutes. Glenn's aircraft, a Chance Vought *F8U-1 Crusader*, is refuelled three times and averages a speed of 725 mph. He is one of the seven original Mercury astronauts, all of whom are test pilots, chosen on April 2, 1959. He becomes the first American to orbit the earth. (See February 20, 1962)

1957 August 7 United States solves its atmospheric reentry problem when a scale model nose cone using a protective ablative coating is launched 600 miles high and 1,200 miles downrange and recovered in good shape. A nose cone covered with ablating material

(material which itself burns up and does not transfer the heat to the surface it is covering) will be used on all manned space capsules until the space shuttle switches to a tile system of thermal protection. (See November 7, 1957)

1957 August 23—24 First nonstop transcontinental flight by a rotary-wing aircraft is made by a specially prepared Vertol *H-21C* twin-rotor helicopter. It flies from San Diego, California to Washington, D.C. in 31 hours, 40 minutes. It is refuelled in flight six times.

1957 August 26 Soviet Union announces the launching of its first ICBM (inter-continental ballistic missile) took place "a few days ago." This means to the West that the U.S.S.R. has both the capability to reach the United States with a warhead and the ability to place an object into low earth orbit.

1957 September 30—October 5 Scientists from 12 countries, including the Soviet Union, attend an International Rocket and Satellite Conference at the National Academy of Sciences, Washington, D.C. It is during this meeting that the Soviet Union launches *Sputnik 1*, the world's first earth satellite. (See October 4, 1957)

1957 October U.S. Air Force Aerospace Medical Center continues its experimental studies with space cabin simulation, using 20 Strategic Air Command volunteers, each of whom is confined from seven to eight days in a simulated space cabin environment.

1957 October 4 First man-made earth satellite is launched by the Soviet Union. Named *Sputnik 1*, it weighs 184 pounds, contains a battery-powered transmitter, and ressembles an aluminum globe. The easily-identified "beep" signals are monitored and replayed around the world, giving the Soviet Union a huge propaganda victory. They also remind the world that the U.S.S.R. has achieved an unrealized degree of technological sophistication and possesses launch vehicles with large lifting power.

1957 October 14 U.S. Air Force and the National Advisory Committee for Aeronautics (NACA) review studies of the past three years concerning *X-15* follow-up programs for manned research vehicles and decide to combine all studies into a single plan which is later designated as Dyna-Soar.

1957 November 1 Mackinac Straits Bridge between Michigan's upper and lower peninsulas, opens for traffic. Designed by David B. Steinman (1886—1960), it has a main span of 3,800 feet (1,158 meters) flanked by side spans of 1,800 feet (549 meters), making it, at the time of its completion, the longest continuous suspended length in the world. The level of aerodynamic stability achieved by this bridge indicates that the science of bridge-building has reached a new plateau.

1957 November 3 Second man-made earth satellite is launched by the Soviet Union. *Sputnik 2* weighs 1,120 pounds (six times *Sputnik 1*) and carries a dog named Laika as a passenger. This is the first vehicle to carry a living organism into orbit. Laika died on November 10. The Soviets do not yet have the ability to recover a satellite from orbit.

1957 November 7 U.S. President Dwight D. Eisenhower (1890—1969) announces that the problem of ballistic missile reentry has been solved, and displays the nose cone of an Army Jupiter C missile which survived intact its reentry from space. This is an important accomplishment, since man cannot go into space unless assured of a safe reentry through the atmosphere to earth.

1957 November 25 As a response to what it considers the Soviet space challenge and as a result of the shock to the American public that the Soviet *Sputnik 1* caused, the Preparedness Subcommittee of the Senate Committee on Armed Services begins a series of lengthy hearings on the state of the U.S. satellite and missile programs.

1957 December Maxime A. Faget (b. 1921), U.S. engineer at National Advisory Committee for Aeronautics (NACA) Langley Laboratory, first proposes the ballistic shape to be used for the manned Mercury space capsule. He envisages a high-drag, conical-shaped capsule with the pilot lying prone for re-entry and recovery.

1957 December 6 First U.S. attempt to launch a satellite fails as Vanguard TV-3 explodes only seconds after ignition at Cape Canaveral, Florida. Vanguard is the U.S. Navy project and the U.S. contribution to the IGY (International Geophysical Year). This failure, seen throughout the world on a televised broadcast, adds to the U.S. frustration and embarrassment in the face of continued Soviet success in space.

1957 December 17 First successful test firing of a U.S. Air Force Atlas ICBM (inter-continental ballistic missile) at Cape Canaveral, Florida. It lands within the target area after a flight of some 500 miles. The Atlas is not like the Army's V-2-based Redstone whose engineering is relatively unsophisticated and which uses massive force to boost its own great weight. Rather, the Atlas is a revolutionary launch vehicle with very thin, collapsible walls that require internal pressurization. For the lightweight Atlas, the shell of the missile is itself the wall of the propellant tanks. It also has a nose cone that can separate from the main body of the missile. These novel features are attributed to Belgian designer Karel J. Bossart, who works in the United States.

1957 December 19 First long-haul turbo-prop airline enters transatlantic service with British Overseas Airways Corporation (BOAC). The Bristol *Brittania 312* flies from from London to New York. Although it meets its long-haul design requirements very well, the jet airliners begin to take over within a year.

1958 This is the first year in which the total number of transatlantic air passengers exceeds the number of passengers crossing by sea.

1958 Between 1900 and 1958, 1,250,000 people have died as a result of road accidents.

1958 In Japan, the Kanmon national highway tunnel connecting Honshu and Kyushu opens.

1958 First production car with unitary body/chassis construction made of fiberglass is the Lotus Elite from England. Making the body and chassis one unit results in a lighter, more rigid structure. Its construction proves so expensive, however, that the Lotus Company nearly goes bankrupt.

1958 Aluminum automobile engines are developed in the United States. They are more resistant to wear and 30% lighter than traditional cast-iron engines.

1958 Ford Motor Company introduces a new car line, the Edsel, named in honor of Edsel Ford (son of Henry) who died in 1943. Despite incorporating many new features and being an essentially well-built car, the Edsel is swiftly rejected by the public and Ford suffers an enormous financial loss. Criticized as being over-designed and ugly to the point of vulgarity, it goes out of produc-

1958 A.D.

Ford introduces Edsel

tion in two years and the name Edsel becomes synonymous with massive failure or at least gross miscalculation.

1958 ■ Ford Edsel station wagon

1958 Longest road tunnel in the world, either under water or through rock, is begun. The Mont Blanc Tunnel is cut through granite 8,000 feet below the peak of snow-capped Mont Blanc, the highest mountain in the Alps. One opening is begun in Italy and the other in France, with the two crews meeting in August 1962. This seven-mile- (11-kilometer-) long tunnel provides a year-round automobile and truck route, cutting nearly 200 miles off the distance between Paris, France and Milan, Italy.

1958 A.D.

Crash-sensitive air bag patented

1958 Patent is granted to American inventor Harry Bertrand of Flint, Michigan for an automobile air bag system that uses a crash sensor. With this system, the bag inflates nearly coincidentally with the auto's impact, cushioning the driver's collision with the steering wheel and dashboard. In 1972, Ford Motor Company produces about 1,000 cars with air bags, but soon drops this demonstration project. (See 1973)

1958 Final configuration of a diver's "wet suit" is made, as designers realize that such a suit need not be completely watertight, for all that is required is to prevent the circulation of water inside the suit.

1958 Two small U.S. companies are formed to manufacture skateboards. The Logan Brothers attach skates to plywood boards and begin selling them. Bill and Mark Richards also begin producing square wooden boards with wheels in California.

1958 January 14 Qantas, Australia's international airline, begins the world's first scheduled round-the-world service, using Lockheed *L-1049 Super Constellations.*

1958 January 29 A three-day conference begins at Wright-Patterson Air Force Base, Ohio, at which Air Force and NACA (National Advisory Committee for Aeronautics) officials discuss various ideas on the prospect of a manned orbital spacecraft. (See October 7, 1958)

1958 January 31 First U.S. satellite is launched into earth orbit by an Army Jupiter C launch vehicle. Named *Explorer 1*, it weighs 30.8 pounds and carries a scientific instrument designed to measure and count electrically charged atoms in space. Unexpectedly, it discovers an unknown thick belt of radiation around the earth that is later named the Van Allen Belt after the scientist conducting the experiment. The United States has finally responded to the Soviet satellite challenge.

1958 February 3 Scientists at the California Institute of Technology report that initial data from the first U.S. satellite, *Explorer 1*, showed that cosmic radiation in the area of its orbit did not exceed 13 times the amount on earth. This would appear to pose no threat to human travel in this region.

1958 February 4 President Dwight D. Eisenhower (1890–1969) directs his new science advisor, James R. Killian, Jr. (b. 1904), to head a committee to study and recommend governmental organization of the U.S. space and missile program.

1958 February 6 U.S. Senate passes Senate Resolution 256, creating a Special Committee on Space and Astronautics to frame legislation pertinent to U.S. efforts in space. Congress realizes that it, like the Executive Branch, must begin to organize and educate itself about the new domain of outer space.

1958 February 7 United States establishes the Advanced Research Projects Agency (ARPA) within the Department of Defense as the single organization in charge of the nation's space program. Congress agrees to ARPA, but only for one year, while it studies the need for a new, civilian controlled agency.

1958 March 10 U.S. Air Force Ballistic Missile Division holds a conference to discuss a request by ARPA (Advanced Research Projects Agency) that the Air Force prepare a plan for "Man In Space Soonest." Because of the Air Force's Atlas launch vehicle, ARPA wanted it to conduct the necessary developments for an early launch of a manned space capsule. It further expected that it would lead to an orbital space station or a flight to the moon. With the creation of National Aeronautics and Space Administration (NASA) later in the year, this project and all others are absorbed into the new agency. (See October 7, 1958)

1958 March 17 U.S. Navy Vanguard rocket finally succeeds in placing a satellite in earth orbit. Named *Vanguard 1*, it is launched from Cape Canaveral, Florida and weighs 3.5 pounds.

1958 April 1 U.S. Saturn launch vehicle that eventually lifts man to the moon has its origins in a project announced as Juno V. The von Braun team decides that the only way of catching up to the Soviet's weight lifting capability is to build very large vehicles with large, clustered engines. (See August 15, 1958)

1958 April 2 President Dwight D. Eisenhower (1890—1969) addresses Congress and proposes the establishment of a National Aeronautics and Space Agency which would have responsibility for civilian space science and aeronautical research. It would perform this work in its own facilities and also do research for the military.

1958 April 9 Greatest altitude from which a successful emergency escape has been made occurs when a British bomber explodes at 56,000 feet (17,070 meters), expelling its crew of two. Both pilots free-fall to an altitude of 10,000 feet (3,050 meters), at which height their parachutes deploy automatically.

1958 April 14 U.S. Bureau of the Budget drafts a proposal for a National Aeronautics and Space Agency and submits it to Congress.

1958 April 17 Simulated seven-day trip to the moon is made by six U.S. Navy sailors in a space chamber at the Philadelphia Naval Base. Scientists are concerned about the psychological as well as physiological aspects of long-duration, manned flights in space.

1958 April 18 First Canadian aircraft to exceed Mach 1 (supersonic flight or faster than the speed of sound) in level flight, Avro CF-105 *Arrow*, is flown at Malton, Ontario by J. Zurakowski.

1958 May First submarine to incorporate nuclear propulsion and advanced hydrodynamic design, the U.S.S. *Skipjack*, is launched. Resembling the *Albacore*'s design and having its single propeller, while also having the nuclear power given the *Nautilus*, this is the fastest submarine built to date.

1958 May 1 Scientific findings from the two U.S. Explorer satellites disclose an unexpected band of high-intensity radiation extending from 600 miles above the earth to possibly an 8,000-mile altitude. This level of radiation is totally unexpected, and raises many questions about manned flight into space because of the heavy shielding that might be required. This does not prove to be a major problem in the long run.

1958 May 11 U.S. Lt. Cmdr. Jack Nieman completes 44 hours of a simulated high-altitude flight between 80,000 and 100,000 feet in a pressure chamber in Norfolk, Virginia.

1958 May 13 First U.S. air carrier to hire a black stewardess is Trans World Airlines (TWA).

1958 May 15 *Sputnik* 3 is launched into earth orbit by the Soviet Union. Called a "flying laboratory" because of the numerous and diverse scientific instrumentation aboard, the large satellite weighs 2,925 pounds. Compared to the first U.S. satellite which weighed about 30 pounds, this heavy orbital payload indicates just how powerful the Soviet launch vehicles are compared to those in the present U.S. stable.

1958 May 15
Sputnik 3
launched

1958 May 16 First aircraft to exceed 2,000 km/h (1,403 mph) is Lockheed *F-104A Starfighter*. It is flown over Southern California by U.S. Capt. W. W. Irvin.

1958 May 24 A gravity load of 83 G's (83 times the force exerted by gravity on a body at rest) is withstood for a fraction of a second by U.S. Capt. E. L. Breeding in a deceleration of a rocket sled at Holloman Air Force Base, New Mexico.

1958 May 27 First flight of the McDonnell *F-4 Phantom II* jet-fighter, recognized as the best all around aircraft developed in the United States since the end of World War II, and the most successful western fighter of the next decade. Five thousand will be built in twenty years.

1958 May 30 First flight of Douglas *DC-8* long-haul jet airliner. This U.S. aircraft, along with the Boeing *707*, would dominate the competition for some time on the prestigious, high-density routes.

1958 June 16 A Phase I development contract for the planned Dyna-Soar boost-glide orbital spacecraft is awarded by the U.S. Air Force to two teams of contractors led by the Martin Co. and Boeing Co.

1958 July 1 Japan launches a Kappa 6 two-stage rocket to an altitude of 30 miles from its Michikawa Rocket Center. The Japanese are still not anywhere close to orbiting a satellite and must develop a new series of rockets.

1958 July 17 The nose cone of a Jupiter missile is successfully recovered after an intermediate range flight. Nose cone reentry survival is imperative for both successful warhead delivery and safe manned space flights.

1958 July 23 Boeing Vertol *VZ-2A*, U.S. tilt-wing research aircraft, makes a successful transition from horizontal to vertical flight and back again for the first time.

1958 July 29 President Dwight D. Eisenhower (1890—1969) signs H. R. 12575, making it the National Aeronautics and Space Act of 1958 (Public Law 85-568). This is the formative legislation necessary if the planned civilian space agency is to come into existence.

1958 July 30 Successful tests are conducted at a U.S. Navy facility in Johnsville, Pennsylvania that subject humans to over 20 times the force of gravity. The subjects sit in a contour couch designed by National Advisory Committee for Aeronautics (NACA) scientist Maxime Faget (b. 1921), which is itself part of a cen-

trifuge. This couch eventually becomes an integral part of the Mercury capsule design.

1958 August 2 First full-power flight of a U.S. Air Force Atlas ICBM (inter-continental ballistic missile) using both its sustainer and booster engines. The new Atlas is nearing its readiness point and will prove a useful and dependable booster for the beginnings of the U.S. manned space program.

1958 August 3 First submarine to travel under the polar ice cap from the Pacific to the Atlantic is the U.S.S. *Nautilus*. It begins this journey on July 23 at Pearl Harbor, Hawaii.

1958 August 8 President Dwight D. Eisenhower (1890—1969) nominates T. Keith Glennan (b. 1905) to be administrator of the emerging new space agency and Hugh L. Dryden (1898—1965) as its deputy administrator.

1958 August 15 U.S. Federal Aviation Agency is created with the passage by Congress of the Federal Aviation Act of 1958 (U.S.C. 106). Later named the Federal Aviation Administration (FAA), this government agency regulates air commerce, including enforcement of safety regulations, construction and maintenance of airports, and use of navigable air space. It becomes part of the Department of Transportation in 1967.

1958 August 15 U.S. Saturn launch vehicle project that places men on the moon 11 years later is formally initiated by an ARPA (Advanced Research Projects Agency) order to the AOMC (Army Ordnance Missile Command) to "provide a large space vehicle booster of approximately 680 tons thrust based on a cluster of available rocket engines." The project is still called Juno V and not yet Saturn.

1958 August 31 First colloquium on space law is held in connection with the International Astronautical Federation (IAF) at The Hague, Netherlands. Societies from Japan, Bulgaria, Greece, Israel, and Nationalist China join the IAF, and observer status is granted to societies from India, Belgium, Czechoslovakia, Iran, and Canada.

1958 September Juno V (soon to be named Saturn) launch vehicle design studies are authorized to proceed at the Redstone Arsenal for the development of a 1.5 million-pound-thrust clustered first stage.

1958 September 7 Great Britain's first large-scale liquid rocket, the *Black Knight*, is launched at the Woomera Test Range, Australia. The 35-foot-tall, 3-foot-diameter rocket reaches 300 miles high.

1958 September 8 A joint NASA-ARPA (National Aeronautics and Space Administration-Advanced Research Projects Agency) Manned Satellite Panel is established to make final recommendations for a manned space flight program. The role of man in space has not yet been defined, but it is obvious that all concerned believe he should be there.

1958 September 24 First flight is made by an aircraft designed and built in the Chinese People's Republic. *Beijing No. 1* is a 10-seat, twin-engine transport, designed at the Aeronautical Engineering College in Beijing, China.

1958 October 1 The National Aeronautics and Space Administration (NASA) begins its first official day as the new U.S. agency responsible for aeronautics and space research. All existing National Advisory Committee for Aeronautics (NACA) facilities, personnel, policies, and advisory committees are transferred to NASA.

1958 October 1 First long-range jet airliner, De Havilland *D.H. 106 Comet 4*, enters transatlantic service with British Overseas Airways Corporation (BOAC). It is followed shortly afterwards by the Pan American Boeing *707*.

1958 October 7 During the first week of its existence, National Aeronautics and Space Administration (NASA) formally organizes Project Mercury. Its three objectives are: to place a manned space capsule in orbital flight around the earth; to investigate man's reactions to and capabilities in this environment; and to recover the capsule and pilot safely. It also forms a NASA Space Task Group organized at the Langley Research Center which draws up specifications for the Mercury capsule which, in turn, are based on earlier NACA and Air Force studies.

1958 October 11 U.S. space probe *Pioneer 1* is launched from Cape Canaveral, Florida and makes the first observations of the earth's magnetic field as well as the first measurements of micrometeorite density in interplanetary space. The spacecraft takes readings to a distance about one-third to the moon.

1958 October 26 Pan American World Airways begins regular daily service between New York and Paris, France using Boeing *707* jet airliners.

1958 November National Aeronautics and Space Administration (NASA) requests that a DX priority be given to both Project Mercury and to the development of a 1.5 million-pound-thrust F-1 engine for the Saturn launch vehicle. A DX priority rating would give these projects first call on material and supplies from government contractors. (See April 27, 1959 and January 18, 1960)

1958 November 7 National Aeronautics and Space Administration (NASA) holds the first bidders conference for a proposed manned space capsule for Project Mercury.

1958 November 21 National Aeronautics and Space Administration (NASA) forms a new Special Committee on Life Sciences to advise the agency on human factors, medical, and any related problems of NASA's planned manned space program.

1958 November 26 Project Mercury, the U.S. manned satellite program, is officially named by National Aeronautics and Space Administration (NASA). The name is announced publicly on December 17, 1958.

1958 Nov. 26

NASA announces manned satellite program

1958 November 28 U.S. Air Force Atlas rocket makes its first successful operational test launch in a flight of 6,325 statute miles and lands close to its target. The good performance and increased reliability of Atlas make it a candidate for launching a man into space.

1958 December Jawahar Tunnel, joining India and Kashmir, opens to traffic. This road tunnel bores through the Himalayas Mountains at 7,250 feet and is 8,120 feet long. It provides year-round access under Banihal Pass which was always closed by snow part of the year. It also has a four-foot wide pedestrian path.

1958 December 3 President Dwight D. Eisenhower (1890—1969) transfers the Jet Propulsion Laboratory of the California Institute of Technology from the U.S. Army to National Aeronautics and Space Administration (NASA). NASA continues to grow.

1958 December 10 First domestic jet airline passenger service is offered by National Airlines, between New York and Miami, Florida.

1958 December 12 Hydrogen balloon named *Small World*, with four English passengers, makes the first modern attempt to cross the Atlantic in a balloon. Taking off from Tenerife, Canary Islands, in an effort to sail east to west, it is forced down in the ocean after covering 1,200 miles in 94½ hours. Since the crew is made up of seamen, their gondola is sail-equipped and designed to function as a boat, which it does and takes them to safety in Barbados.

*1958
December 13*

*U.S. Army
launches
monkey
into space*

1958 December 13 U.S. Army Jupiter launch vehicle boosts a squirrel monkey named Gordo on a 1,500-mile flight in a nose cone. Although the monkey registers no known adverse effects from the launch and flight, a float mechanism fails and the water recovery of the nose cone is not possible.

1958 December 18 The era of active satellite communications begins as the United States launches *SCORE* (Signal Communications by Orbiting Relay Equipment) into earth orbit. The 8,750-pound communications relay satellite beams a Christmas message from President Dwight D. Eisenhower (1890—1969) in the first voice broadcast from space on December 19, 1958.

1959 Extremely popular and affordable Morris Mini Minor is built by Austin in Great Britain. Designed by Alec Issigonis (1906—1988), this boxy subcompact is the first transverse-engine (the engine is placed perpendicular to the car's length), front-wheel drive small car, which despite its size, provides surprising interior space. It is small enough to negotiate city traffic, easy to park, and cheap to run.

1959 A.D.

*Longest
railroad
tunnel opens*

1959 Longest railroad tunnel in Spain, the Padornelo Tunnel, opens. Over three miles (5,949 meters) long, it is in northeastern Spain near Portugal. This mountainous country has well over 1,000 tunnels.

1959 Alaska Department of Highways is first organized.

1959 First American compact car is the Chevrolet Corvair. Built to compete with the increasing number of small imports, it is the first U.S. rear-engine, air-cooled car. It later becomes a controversial vehicle when criticized by consumer advocate Ralph Nader (b. 1934) as being "unsafe at any speed," since it suffers an abnormally high number of incidents where it flips over. It goes out of production in 1970. Nader's campaign ultimately results in the introduction of federal safety standards for U.S. cars.

1959 U.S. Aeromedical Field Laboratory at Holloman Air Force Base, New Mexico begins the training of chimpanzees for the ballistic (up-and-down) and orbital test flights of Project Mercury. Since the problems of launching a man and those of how he will react in space are unknown, scientists begin their studies with trainable primates.

1959 First Soviet nuclear-powered submarine, the *Leninsky Komsomol,* is launched. Designated as the November class, this vessel is 360 feet (110 meters) long and has an underwater speed of 25 to 30 knots.

1959 St. Lawrence Seaway opens. Following a joint United States-Canada agreement in 1954, a deep waterway navigable by ocean-going ships is built from the mouth of the St. Lawrence River at the Atlantic Ocean to the far end of Lake Superior—a run of about 2,300 miles (3,830 kilometers). The most complex waterway ever undertaken, it uses a succession of 15 locks to raise ships to the extreme height of Lake Erie and then more locks at St. Mary's river to get them into Lake Superior. The key to this efficient waterway system is that it provides a steady 27-foot navigation depth its entire length.

1959 Longest bridle-chord bridge, the Severin Bridge in Cologne, Germany, is built. A bridle-chord or stayed box-girder bridge combines the principle of the simple box girder (a hollow rectangular or trapezoidal bridge structure designed to act as a beam) with that of the suspension bridge. It spans 297 meters and is extraordinarily light.

1959 January 2 First man-made object to escape earth's influence is launched. Soviet Union's *Lunik 1* speeds within about 3,500 miles of the moon and goes into orbit around the sun. The Soviets again demonstrate enormous launching power by sending a 297-pound (361-kilogram) instrumented satellite, accompanied by the

2,449-pound (1,110-kilogram) third stage, to escape velocity (at least 25,000 mph).

1959 January 8 National Aeronautics and Space Administration (NASA) requests eight Redstone-type launch vehicles from the Army to be used in early developmental flights in Project Mercury.

1959 January 12 National Aeronautics and Space Administration (NASA) announces its selection of McDonnell Aircraft Corp. as the source for the design, development, and construction of the Mercury manned space capsule. It is projected that the work will take two years to complete and cost about $15 million.

1959 January 28 National Aeronautics and Space Administration (NASA) selects 110 candidates in its first screening for Project Mercury astronauts. Most candidates come from the Air Force, Navy, and Marine test pilot schools.

1959 January 29 First jet passenger service across the United States is begun by American Airlines using Boeing *707* jet airliners.

1959 January 31 First ship over 100,000 tons, the *Universe Apollo*, goes into service. When Egypt closes the Suez Canal forcing all Middle East oil tankers bound for Europe to go around the Cape of Good Hope, South Africa, it becomes necessary to build larger tankers to carry as much oil as possible and keep costs down.

1959 February 3 The U.S. Air Force employs a newly-coined word, "aerospace," which it uses to describe activities that involve both air and space.

1959 March 10 First captive flight of the North American *X-15* supersonic rocket-propelled research aircraft is made under the body of a modified *B-52*. This very large aircraft is planned to be dropped at some 35,000 feet before igniting its rocket engines and climbing into the upper reaches of the atmosphere.

1959 April 2 Seven astronauts are selected for Project Mercury by National Aeronautics and Space Administration (NASA). Chosen from a field of 110 candidates after a series of rigorous physical and psychological tests are: Capts. Leroy G. Cooper, Jr. (b. 1927), Virgil I. Grissom (1926-1967), and Donald K. Slayton (USAF) (b. 1924); Lt. M. Scott Carpenter (b. 1925), Lt. Cmdr. Alan B.

Shepard, Jr. (b. 1923), and Lt. Comdr. Walter M. Schirra, Jr. (USN) (b. 1923); and Lt. Col. John H. Glenn (USMC) (b. 1921). All are test pilots.

1959 ■ Project Mercury astronauts upon selection.

1959 April 5 First jet aircraft designed and built in Czechoslovakia, Aero *L-29 Delfin*, makes its first flight. Over 3,000 of these two-seater jet trainers are produced for the Soviet Union and other Warsaw Pact air forces.

1959 April 22 Audoin Dollfus (b. 1925), French astronomer and son of early balloonist Charles Dollfus (1898—1981), reaches 42,000 feet using a large cluster of weather balloons. Dollfus ascends from Villacoublay, France in order to better study the planet Venus. His flight shows how a comparatively small telescope can yield better results or information than a larger, more powerful ground-based telescope, since it functions in the clearer regions of the upper air.

1959 April 22

Balloonist reaches 42,000 feet

 1959 April 27 Project Mercury is given a DX rating (highest national priority). (See November 1958)

 1959 May 1 National Aeronautics and Space Administration (NASA) announces its new facility

1959 April 27

Project Mercury given highest priority

under construction in Greenbelt, Maryland will be named Goddard Space Flight Center in honor of American rocket pioneer Robert H. Goddard (1888—1945).

1959 May 12

NASA begins training seven astronauts

1959 May 12 National Aeronautics and Space Administration (NASA) begins a training program for the seven Mercury astronauts to provide them with the technical knowledge and skills required to fly in a manned orbital capsule.

1959 May 15 Last operational flight by the British Royal Air Force (RAF) Short *Sunderland* flying-boat marks the end of the use of seaplanes by the RAF.

1959 May 28 Two monkeys are launched by a U.S. Army Jupiter C to an altitude of 300 miles and both are recovered alive. In this medical space experiment, the two monkeys—Able, a rhesus monkey and Baker, a squirrel monkey—survive a suborbital ride in the Jupiter nose cone.

1959 June First nuclear-powered submarine to carry ballistic missiles, the U.S.S. *George Washington,* is launched. This 380-foot- (115.8-meter-) long submarine carries 16 vertical tubes for firing Polaris missiles. It can fire them either submerged or at the surface.

1959 June 5

Construction begins at Cape Canaveral

1959 June 5 Construction begins at Cape Canaveral, Florida for the Saturn launch vehicle project. The enormous size of this planned moon-launch vehicle dictates that new construction be on a very large scale.

1959 June 7 First practical air-cushion vehicle, the *SR.N1* hovercraft, makes its first successful trip over water. Designed by British engineer Christopher Cockerell (b. 1910), it is an oval craft, with a diameter of 20 feet (6.1 meters) and weighing four tons. It features a flexible skirt that holds the cushion in place as it rides on a layer of air despite the unevenness of the surface. (See July 25, 1959)

1959 June 17 First flight of the Dassault *Mirage IV* is made in France. The first European supersonic jet bomber, this advanced, high-performance combat aircraft proves a capable Mach 2 (twice the speed of sound) performer.

1959 July Project Mercury astronauts complete their disorientation flights on a three-axis space flight simulator called MASTIF (multiple axis space test

inertia facility). This complex flight simulator has three degrees of freedom (roll, pitch, and yaw) in which the pilot tries to maintain a predetermined position by continuously correcting all its programmed movements.

1959 July 25 First crossing of the English Channel by hovercraft is made by British engineer Christopher Cockerell's (b. 1910) *SR.N1.*

1959 July 26 Longest duration parachute descent recorded is made by U.S. Lt. Col. William H. Rankin. After ejecting from his jet fighter at 47,000 feet (14,326 meters), he falls through a violent thunderstorm whose vertical currents repeatedly carry him upwards. Instead of an expected 11-minute descent, his time to the ground is 40 minutes.

1959 July 29 First jetway in United States is installed at the International Airport in San Francisco, California. Designed to protect passengers from the weather when they board or leave the jet plane, it is a powered telescopic or collapsible corridor that extends to the aircraft and connects the plane to the terminal. They are commonplace in all airports today.

1959 August 29 In a space-related test that measures human endurance, a U.S. Navy technician withstands a massive 31 G's (31 times the force exerted by gravity on a body at rest) in a centrifuge in Johnsville, Pennsylvania.

1959 September 1 Atlas ICBM (inter-continental ballistic missile) is declared operational by the U.S. Air Force Strategic Air Command. The Atlas is now ready for a manned space mission as well as a military mission.

1959 September 2 Theodore von Karman (1881—1963) is named chairman of a committee to establish an International Academy of Astronautics.

1959 September 9 Atlas vehicle named "Big Joe" successfully launches an unmanned Mercury capsule that is recovered in the South Atlantic after surviving reentry heat of more than 10,000 degrees Fahrenheit.

1959 September 12 Soviet Union's *Lunik 2* becomes the first man-made object to impact the moon. It impacts about 270 miles from the center of the moon at approximately 7,500 mph. The Soviets state that the 858-pound capsule was sterilized so as to not contaminate the moon.

1959 September 15 First nuclear-powered surface ship, the Soviet ice-breaker *Lenin*, makes it maiden voyage. Designed to work in ice up to six feet (1.8 meters) thick, it carries enough fuel to cruise for a year.

1959 September 17 First powered flight of North American *X-15* research aircraft is made. It is released from its *B-52* mothership and flown by A. Scott Crossfield (b. 1921) at Mach 2.3 (over twice the speed of sound). It later passes Mach 6 and altitudes of over 67 miles (107 km). (See October 24, 1968)

1959 September 18 The Douglas *DC-8* four-jet airliner enters service with United and Delta Air Lines. Next to the very popular Boeing *707*, it becomes the second most successful of the first-generation subsonic jet transports.

1959 October First round-the-world passenger service by jet airliner is offered by Pan American World Airways using a Boeing *707*.

1959 October 12 For the first time, the Soviet Union publicly reveals in print that it has a training program for manned space flight.

1959 October 21 U.S. President Dwight D. Eisenhower (1890—1969) announces that he is transferring, subject to Congressional approval, the Army's rocket team and facilities in Huntsville, Alabama, headed by Wernher von Braun (1912—1977), to the control of National Aeronautics and Space Administration (NASA). The work being conducted by the Army in Huntsville on the Saturn moon rocket is also transferred to NASA. This decision effectively takes the Army out of space work, except for a supporting role.

1959 November First prototype Goodrich full-pressure astronaut suits are delivered to National Aeronautics and Space Administration (NASA) for Project Mercury. The Navy Air Crew Equipment Laboratory (NACEL) of Philadelphia fit the suits to the seven astronauts and instruct them in their use.

1959 November 4 Astronaut escape system designed for the manned Mercury program is tested successfully at Wallops Island, Virginia. Escape rockets carry an unmanned capsule model safely away from the launch vehicle to a height of 35,000 feet.

1959 November 10 U.S. Air Force places contracts with both the Boeing and Martin companies for the development of the Dyna-Soar reusable spacecraft project.

1959 December U.S. Air Force Test Pilot School at Edwards Air Force Base proposes the curriculum for a space research pilot course for 1960—1965.

1959 December National Aeronautics and Space Administration (NASA) study team completes its study design of the upper stages of the Saturn launch vehicle.

1959 December 4 Unmanned test launches of the Mercury escape rocket system continue as National Aeronautics and Space Administration (NASA) successfully launches and safely recovers a monkey. The small monkey named Sam is launched 55 miles into space by a Little Joe solid-propellant rocket and travels 200 miles downrange.

1959 December 30 Preliminary findings from the U.S. scientific satellite *Explorer 7* are announced by scientists who indicate that a sporadic burst of radiation from the sun could influence manned space flight. Scientists are justifiably concerned about the short- and long-term effects of radiation on astronauts, since they have very little data so far to use.

1959 December 31 U.S. Mercury astronauts complete the basic and theoretical studies part of their training program and begin their practical engineering studies.

1960 In Japan, an underground parking lot is built in Hibiya, Tokyo.

1960 Britain's Daimler Motor Company merges into Jaguar Cars, Ltd.

1960 January 18 U.S. Saturn launch vehicle development program is assigned a DX rating (highest national priority). (See November 1958)

1960 January 20 National Aeronautics and Space Administration (NASA) presents its 10-year

1959
Dec. 30

Effects of
sun's
radiation
considered

c. 1960 ■ Modern short-distance city bus.

plan of space activities to the U.S. Congress. It calls for the launching of some 260 satellites and major probes, with a manned landing on the moon some time after 1970.

1960 January 21 In a test launch of the Mercury emergency escape system, a rhesus monkey named Miss Sam is launched and safely recovered after a nine-mile-high flight. Miss Sam seems to tolerate the 20-G load (20 times the force of gravity on a body at rest) in good shape.

1960 January 23 Record manned underwater descent is made by Swiss Jacques Piccard (b. 1922) and American Don Walsh in the bathyscaphe, *Trieste*. They descend to 35,810 feet (10,916 meters) in the Mariana Trench in the Pacific Ocean.

1960 February 3 In a simulated weightlessness experiment at the U.S. Air Force Medical Laboratory, a subject who is submerged in a liquid centrifuge with a 5-G spin (five times the force of gravity on a body at rest) demonstrates the beginnings of muscle deterioration when he does not exercise.

1960 February 26 Australia gives the United States permission via a joint agreement to establish

*1960
January 23

Record-
setting
manned
underwater
descent
made*

Mercury tracking stations across Australia. Since a manned orbital flight will circle the entire globe, National Aeronautics and Space Administration (NASA) begins the creation of a global network of land tracking stations so as to be able to maintain constant contact during flight.

1960 March 1 National Aeronautics and Space Administration (NASA) announces the establishment of the Office of Life Sciences. Headed by Dr. Clark T. Randt, it will emphasize a broad-based scientific study of life processes provided by manned exploration of space.

1960 March 15 Saturn launch vehicle development program is officially transferred to National Aeronautics and Space Administration (NASA) from ABMA (Army Ballistic Missile Agency).

1960 March 19 Spain reaches agreement with the United States permitting it to establish a tracking station for Project Mercury on the Canary Islands. (See February 26, 1960)

1960 April Seven Mercury astronauts complete a special training session at the Navy Aviation Medical Acceleration Laboratory, Johnsville, Pennsylvania.

c. 1960 ■ American *U-2* spy plane on the ground in California.

1960 April 1 First observation weather satellite, *Tiros 1*, is launched by the United States from Cape Canaveral, Florida. The 270-pound "eye-in-the-sky," called *Tiros* (television & infra-red observation satellite), carries wide-angle and narrow-angle TV cameras that transmit photos of the earth's weather systems from 450 miles high. Satellite weather begins today.

1960 April 13 First restart of an engine in space is accomplished by U.S. Navy's *Transit 1-B* navigational satellite. Restarting an engine offers the important ability to move a satellite while in orbit.

1960 April 14 C. A. Metzgen concludes one week in a self-sustained simulated space capsule environment at the U.S. Air Force Aerospace Laboratory.

1960 April 25 The last steam locomotive is withdrawn from Canadian National Railways. Ten years before, there were about 2,500 steam locomotives in Canada.

1960 May 1 A Lockheed *U-2* reconnaissance aircraft, piloted by U.S. Air Force Col. Francis Gary Powers (b. 1929), is shot down over the Soviet Union by a surface-to-air missile (SAM). This international incident not only results in the collapse of a planned United States-Soviet Summit Conference in Paris, but forces the United States to reconsider its entire mode of deployment of strategic aircraft, since they are obviously no longer safe from Soviet missiles.

1960 May 9 National Aeronautics and Space Administration (NASA) launches its first production model of the Mercury capsule to test the escape, landing, and recovery systems. The unmanned capsule reaches 2,540 feet before it is recovered.

1960 May 10 First undersea, around-the-world voyage is completed by U.S. nuclear submarine *Triton*. Following under water the route taken over 400 years earlier by Ferdinand Magellan (1480—1521), it travels 41,519 miles (66,804 kilometers) in 84 days.

1960 May 14 Founding of the International Academy of Astronautics is announced by the International Astronautical Federation and the Daniel and Florence Guggenheim Foundation.

1960 May 15 U.S.S.R. launches a 10,000-pound spacecraft into orbit and reveals few details. This is the first successful orbit of a spacecraft large enough to contain a man. Efforts to recover the capsule are not successful.

1960 May 15

U.S.S.R. launches 10,000-lb. spacecraft

1960 July 1 George C. Marshall Space Flight Center officially opens in Huntsville, Alabama as a National Aeronautics and Space Administration (NASA) center. Wernher von Braun (1912—1977) is named director of this launch vehicle development facility.

1960 July 2 The U.S. House Committee on Science and Astronautics calls for a revision of the National Space Program timetable so as to put a manned expedition on the moon during this decade rather than "after 1970," as provided in the NASA ten-year program. This shows that there is considerable sentiment in Congress for the crash program that John F. Kennedy (1917—1963) will soon suggest.

1960 July 29 Project Apollo is first announced at a National Aeronautics and Space Administration (NASA) Industry Conference. It is conceived as a program that would succeed Project Mercury and provide the capability for long duration manned flights in earth orbit, culminating in manned flights to the moon and back.

1960 August 11 First man-made object recovered after being in orbit is U.S. Air Force *Discoverer 13.* The instrumented satellite is recovered in the ocean near Hawaii.

1960 August 12 First passive communications satellite, *Echo 1,* is launched by National Aeronautics and Space Administration (NASA). The 100-foot diameter spherical balloon inflates after being placed in earth orbit and is visible from earth under good conditions. Made of aluminized Mylar plastic, it reflects a radio message from President John F. Kennedy (1917—1963) across the United States and demonstrates not only the feasibility of global communications by satellite but the benefits of the applications of space-based research.

1960 August 15 Two Air Force pilots are sealed in a model space cabin for a 17-day simulated trip to the moon at Brooks Air Force Base, Texas.

1960
August 16

Fastest
free-fall
takes place

1960 August 16 Highest altitude from which a man has fallen is Capt. Joseph W. Kittinger's (b. 1928) "highest step in the world." Stepping out of his *Excelsior III* balloon gondola at 102,500 feet (31,150 meters), Kittinger free-falls 84,700 feet (25,816 meters) for four minutes, 38 seconds before deploying a stabilizing drogue parachute. His main parachute deploys at 17,500 feet (5,334 meters). During his free-fall, he attains a speed of 614 mph (Mach 0.93 in the stratosphere, or nearly the speed of sound), and this must certainly be the greatest speed ever survived by a human body that was not contained within some type of vehicle.

1960
August 18

Aircraft
snares
satellite

1960 August 18 First mid-air recovery of an object returning to earth from space is made by the U.S. Air Force. Intelligence-gathering satellite *Discoverer 14* is snared by a *C-119* aircraft at 10,000 feet during its parachute descent.

1960 August 21 First successful recovery of living animals from earth orbit is made as the Soviet Union announces it recovered two dogs (Belka and Strelka) in excellent condition after they made 17 orbits around the earth.

1960 September 15 Two U.S. Air Force pilots, Capt. W. D. Habluetzel and Lt. J. S. Hargreaves, complete a 30-day, eight-hour, 24-minute simulated round trip to the moon in the space cabin simulator at the School of Aviation Medicine, Brooks Air Force Base, Texas. This is the longest simulation to date.

1960 September 24 First nuclear-powered aircraft carrier, the 1,123-foot- (342-meter-) long *Enterprise,* is launched by the United States. Its 4.5 acres (18,211 square meters) of flight deck can carry about 200 aircraft. It is designed to reach 35 knots.

1960 October 7 Aware that man will soon be flying in space, the Federation Aéronautique Internationale accepts the first rules to govern the establishment of official records for manned space flight. They hold their meeting in Barcelona, Spain.

1960 October 13 U.S. Air Force Atlas launch vehicle boosts a nose cone containing three black mice 650 miles into space at 17,000 mph. They land 5,000 miles downrange and are recovered near Ascension Island in good condition.

1960 October 21 First British nuclear-powered submarine, the *Dreadnought,* is launched. This advanced submarine has an American propulsion system, although later British submarines will have British-built systems.

1960 October 25 National Aeronautics and Space Administration (NASA) selects Convair, General Electric, and the Martin Company to conduct individual feasibility studies of an advanced manned spacecraft as part of Project Apollo.

1960 October 27 Institute of the Aeronautical Sciences changes its name to the Institute of Aerospace Sciences. This reflects man's entry into space.

1960 November 18 DeSoto automobiles will no longer be manufactured as one of the cars offered by Chrysler Corporation. This announcement discontinues a line of cars it had made since 1928.

1960 November 19 First free flight by a swivel-jet fixed-wing V/STOL (vertical/short take-off and landing) aircraft is made by the British Hawker *P.1127*. Designed by Sidney Camm, it has swivelling jet pipes to deflect the engine's thrust downward for vertical flight or straight backward for horizontal flight. It is later developed into the Hawker Siddeley *Harrier* strike aircraft still in use today. (See March 13, 1961)

1960 December 2 U.S. Air Force exposes human tissues to heavy radiation during the 50-hour orbital flight of *Discoverer 17*. The capsule containing bone marrow, gamma globulin, and other human specimens is recovered by an aircraft fitted with nets and hooks that snares the capsule as it descends by parachute.

1960 December 6 First flight of the Sikorsky *S-61L* helicopter is made in the United States. It serves as a transport craft as well as patrol, rescue, and even anti-submarine duty.

1960 December 16 Two airliners, both bound for New York during a snowstorm, collide over Staten Island. The TWA *Constellation* disintegrates immediately, and the United airliner flies a few miles before crashing into houses in the Park Slope section of Brooklyn, New York. All 128 people aboard the two planes are killed as well as five people on the ground.

1960 December 19 Modified Redstone booster (MR-1) launches an unmanned Mercury spacecraft in a suborbital trajectory. It impacts the ocean 235 miles downrange after reaching an altitude of 135 miles and a speed of 4,200 mph. The capsule is recovered less than one hour after launch. Alan B. Shepard, Jr.'s 1961 sub-orbital flight of May 5, 1961 will closely match this test flight.

1961 Small electric car called the Henney Killowatt is built on a converted Renault Dauphine chassis. Powered by a 36-volt battery system and a 7.1-hp motor, it has a range of 40 miles and reaches 35 mph. It is expensive, ahead of its time, and does not go into production.

1961 Jaguar introduces its legendary E-type sports car. This sleek sports car with aerodynamic lines, independent rear suspension, and front disc brakes is the first 150 mph production car.

1961 First private car built in Israel is the Sabra, later known as the Rom Carmel. This Haifa company is in partnership with Triumph of Coventry, England.

1961 Rocket belt is exhibited by Bell Aerosystem Company. Invented by American Wendell F. Moore, it consists of two vertical nozzles and a fuel tank strapped to the user's back. It is controlled by motorcylce-type handlebars and allows vertical take-offs and stationary flight. It does not prove practical and is used only for stunts and exhibitions.

1961 United States builds the first of its four-legged, unmanned offshore lighthouses to replace lightships in Buzzards Bay, Massachusetts and Brenton Reef, Rhode Island. It will continue to replace the uneconomic lightships with these small structures.

1961 Dulles International Airport opens in Virginia. It is the first civil airport designed to handle jet aircraft, and features innovative design and services like mobile passenger lounges which take passengers to their waiting planes instead of having the planes taxi in close to the hub. Planned to supplement Washington's National Airport and Baltimore's Friendship Airport, it is hardly used until the late 1980s when it finally becomes a full-fledged and heavily-used facility.

1961 A.D.

Dulles Airport opens

1961 January Internal studies of a manned lunar landing program are completed by National Aeronautics and Space Administration (NASA). Two methods of lunar landing are considered: the direct ascent based on a very large, Nova-type launch vehicle and the rendezvous method based on assembly in earth orbit using a number of Saturn launch vehicles. (See July 11, 1962)

1961 January 3 National Aeronautics and Space Administration's (NASA) Space Task Group officially becomes a separate NASA field office. It is charged with carrying out Project Mercury and other planned manned space flight programs.

1961 January 12 Italy launches its first scientific sounding rocket from a range in Sardinia. It sends its instruments to a height of 100 miles using a U.S. Nike-Cajun rocket.

1961 January 16 In a message accompanying his budget submission, President Dwight D. Eisenhower (1890—1969) hopefully predicts a U.S. manned orbital flight in 1961, but says he is not sure "if there are any valid scientific reasons for extending manned space flight beyond the Mercury program." President Eisenhower will never be an enthusiastic supporter of an expensive, crash program.

**1961
January 19

JFK supports
manned
space flight**

1961 January 19 National Aeronautics and Space Administration's (NASA) Marshall Space Flight Center awards a contract to both the Douglas and the Chance Vought companies to study the launching of a manned exploratory expedition into lunar and interplanetary space from earth orbit. John F. Kennedy's (1917—1963) presidential election victory the previous November has placed a vigorous supporter of manned space flight in the White House, and NASA begins to plan accordingly.

1961 January 29 U.S. Air Force selects the Titan II solid-propellant rocket as the launch vehicle for its Dyna-Soar boost-glide reuseable manned spacecraft.

**1961
January 31

Chimp
survives
ballistic
space flight**

1961 January 31 Unmanned Mercury capsule test launches continue as National Aeronautics and Space Administration (NASA) launches a 37-pound chimpanzee named Ham on a ballistic (up and down) flight of 18 minutes. The Mercury capsule weighs 2,400 pounds and is boosted by a Redstone rocket. Ham is recovered safely 418 miles downrange of Cape Canaveral, Florida in the ocean.

1961 February 12 First spacecraft launched from an orbiting platform is U.S.S.R.'s *Venera 1* interplanetary space probe. Soviets accomplish this first staged launching by putting a spacecraft containing the probe into a parking orbit and then firing *Venera 1*'s engine to launch it on a flyby course toward Venus.

1961 February 15 Sabena Airlines Boeing *707* crashes into a farm near Berg, Belgium, killing 72 people aboard and the farm's owner. Among the dead are 18 members of the U.S. figure skating team who are flying to Prague for the World Championship.

1961 February 16 First satellite to be placed in orbit by a solid-fuel rocket is National Aeronautics and Space Administration's (NASA) *Explorer 9*. A four-stage Scout vehicle launches it from Wallops Island, Virginia.

1961 February 18 U.S. Air Force launches *Discoverer 21* into orbit and restarts its Agena engine while in orbit. The manueverability this restart capability

implies is especially desirable for a military or intelligence-gathering satellite.

1961 February 21 National Aeronautics and Space Administration (NASA) Space Task Group selects John H. Glenn, Jr. (b. 1921), Virgil I. Grissom (1926—1967), and Alan B. Shepard, Jr. (b. 1923) to begin special training for the first suborbital manned Mercury flight. One of the three will be chosen shortly before the launch.

1961 February 22 France launches a small capsule containing a laboratory rat with its Veronique rocket.

1961 March U.S. Marine helicopter crews conduct extensive tests at Langley Air Force Base, Virginia to perfect the techniques of recovering a manned Mercury capsule from the sea after splashdown.

1961 March 9 Soviet Union launches a dog named Chernushka into earth orbit and recovers her safely. This is an important preliminary test for Yuri Gagarin's (1934—1968) later flight, as it checks out both structural and biological systems.

1961 March 13 First vertical flight of the British Hawker *P.1127* swivel-jet V/STOL (vertical/short take-off and landing) fighter. Later developed as the *Harrier*, it proves to have far greater tactical flexibility and survivability than conventional aircraft.

1961 March 28 U.S.S.R. announces that puppies delivered by the dog Strelka who flew in orbit August 21, 1960 were developing normally. This development, they say, "has an important bearing on our preparations for man's orbiting."

1961 April 6 A thrust of 1,640,000 pounds is achieved in a static firing of an F-1 rocket engine at Edwards Air Force Base, California. National Aeronautics and Space Administration (NASA) will use five F-1's to power the first stage of the huge, moon-launching Saturn V vehicle.

1961 April 12 Manned flight in space begins as Soviet cosmonaut Yuri Gagarin (1934—1968) is launched into earth orbit on a trajectory that takes him once around the earth. The 27-year-old Gagarin circles the earth in his *Vostok 1* spacecraft whose orbital apogee

1961 ■ *X-15* research aircraft lands at Edwards Air Force Base, California.

is 187 miles above the earth. During its entire flight, the spacecraft is controlled from the ground. *Vostok 1* makes a hard landing in a cowfield after its flight of one hour, 48 minutes, but Gagarin ejects at 22,000 feet and parachutes down separately. The Soviets stun and amaze the world once more with their space accomplishments.

1961 April 14 In response to questions from the U.S. House Science and Astronautics Committee, National Aeronautics and Space Administration (NASA) estimates the total cost of a manned lunar landing to be in the $20 to 40 billion range.

1961 April 20 U.S. National Academy of Sciences issues a report by its Space Science Board which likens astronauts to explorers of old, and says that the nation should be aware that, "Men will perish in space as they have on the high seas, in the Antarctic, in the heart of Africa, and wherever they have ventured into unknown regions."

1961 April 25 Mercury capsule carrying equipment equal to the weight of a man is launched by National Aeronautics and Space Administration (NASA) from Cape Canaveral, Florida. Although the Atlas launch vehicle malfunctions and is destroyed at 15,000 feet, the capsule is boosted away by the escape tower rockets and is recovered intact. This is an unintentional and successful real-time test of the astronaut launch escape system.

1961 May 5 First American in space is Alan B. Shepard, Jr. (b. 1923) who is launched on a suborbital trajectory by a Redstone booster from Cape Canaveral, Florida. The National Aeronautics and Space

Administration (NASA) astronaut rides in the Mercury capsule, *Freedom 7*, to a height of 116 miles and lands 297 miles downrange in the Atlantic. During his flight, which lasts 15 minutes, 22 seconds, Shepard is weightless for nearly five minutes. He is recovered safely by helicopter after emerging from his floating Mercury capsule. The United States still has not put a man in orbit, but at least has begun to respond to the Soviet challenge.

1961 May 12 U.S. Air Force announces plans to institute a special course at Edwards Air Force Base, California for the instruction of space pilots.

1961 May 25 In his second state of the Union address to Congress and the nation, President John F. Kennedy (1917—1963) commits the United States to a timetable for space accomplishment, saying, "I believe that this nation should commit itself to achieving the goal, before the decade is out, of landing a man on the moon and returning him safely to earth."

1961 May 25

JFK commits to moon landing

1961 May 26—27 First national Conference on the Peaceful Uses of Outer Space is held at Tulsa, Oklahoma. Leading American space scientists and technologists appraise the current and future applications of space science and technology for human welfare.

1961 May 27 First crossing of the English Channel by a VTOL (vertical take-off and landing) aircraft is made by the Short *SC.1*, which is flown by A. Roberts from England to Paris for the Paris Air Show.

1961 May 27 Arlberg-Orient Express train service goes out of business after nearly 79 years of operation between Paris, France and Istanbul, Turkey.

The Simplon-Orient ends service in 1961 as well. Both are unable to compete with air travel.

1961 June 5 The immense Saturn launch vehicle complex at Cape Canaveral, Florida is dedicated at a brief ceremony. The giant gantry (platform, crane, and tower) is the largest movable land structure in North America, weighing 2,800 tons and standing 310 feet high.

1961 June 16 Ad Hoc Task Group established by National Aeronautics and Space Administration (NASA) to determine the main problems as well as the major decisions required to accomplish a manned lunar landing by the end of the decade, reports its findings. At this point, the direct ascent to the moon method is favored over the rendezvous method.

1961 July 12 First static firing of the Rocketdyne F-1 engine is made by National Aeronautics and Space Administration (NASA). Five of these liquid-oxygen/kerosene motors will power the first stage of the Saturn V Apollo moon launch rocket.

1961 July 21 Second American flies in space as Virgil I. "Gus" Grissom (1926—1967) is launched in the *Liberty Bell 7* on a successful 15-minute-long, 118-mile-high suborbital flight. The flight is a repeat of Shepard's May mission until splashdown, when the Mercury capsule unexpectedly fills with seawater and sinks just after Grissom is hauled to safety by a helicopter.

1961 July 28 National Aeronautics and Space Administration (NASA) invites 12 companies to submit prime contractor proposals for the manned lunar Apollo spacecraft.

1961 August 7—25 Two U.S. Air Force officers are sealed in a space simulator for 17 days to test their reaction to almost pure oxygen at a 35,000-foot altitude. They emerge in good condition.

**1961
August 6

Man sleeps
in space**

1961 August 6 Soviet cosmonaut Gherman S. Titov (b. 1935) becomes the second man to orbit the earth in his *Vostok* 2 spacecraft. He also is the first to spend one complete day in space (25 hours, 18 minutes), the first to sleep in space (he tucks his floating arms under his harness, fearing they may touch some switches while he sleeps), and the first to be sick in space. He ejects from his capsule following reentry and parachutes safely to earth.

1961 August 9 First major contract of the Apollo program is awarded to Massachusetts Institute of Technology's (MIT) Instrumentation Laboratory to develop the guidance-navigation system for the Apollo spacecraft.

1961 August 24 National Aeronautics and Space Administration (NASA) announces three major steps required to meet President John Kennedy's manned lunar landing goal. They are: expansion of Cape Canaveral facilities to accommodate the large Saturn vehicle; create a manned space flight research center; and create a large booster fabrication and test facility. These will all be accomplished.

1961 September 8 United States and South Africa dedicate a deep space tracking antenna located 40 miles from Johannesburg, South Africa. It will operate in collaboration with deep space facilities at Goldstone, California and Woomera, Australia. These powerful facilities are needed to track both the interplanetary satellites and the planned Apollo missions.

1961 September 13 Unmanned Mercury capsule is launched into orbit by an Atlas vehicle from Cape Canaveral, Florida. It makes one orbit, reenters, and is recovered, thus proving the suitability of all its systems, including National Aeronautics and Space Administration's (NASA) worldwide tracking system.

1961 September 19 Houston, Texas is named by National Aeronautics and Space Administration (NASA) as the location for its new Manned Spacecraft Center. This new center will be the command center (following launch) for all manned missions leading to the manned lunar landing mission.

1961 September 19 U.S. Air Force forms a new Bioastronautics Division to consolidate all its applied research in this area into a single organization.

1961 September 29 U.S. Air Force awards three contracts intended to speed up development of its Dyna-Soar manned orbital space glider. Boeing will build the spacecraft, RCA its communications and tracking, and Honeywell its guidance system.

1961 October 27 First Saturn moon rocket launch is made by National Aeronautics and Space Administration (NASA) at Cape Canaveral, Florida. Test-launching only the first stage of its planned three stages, the eight clustered engines in the first stage propel the dummy upper stages to an altitude of 85 miles and 215 miles downrange.

1961 November 28 North American Aviation is selected by National Aeronautics and Space Administration (NASA) to design and build a three-man Apollo spacecraft leading to a manned landing on the moon. Two hundred NASA and Department of Defense (DOD) specialists evaluate each company's proposal.

1961 November 29 A U.S. Atlas launch vehicle places a chimpanzee, Enos, into orbit from Cape Canaveral, Florida in a full-stage dress rehearsal for a manned orbital flight. Retro rockets fire after the second orbit, and Enos is recovered from the Atlantic in good condition.

1961 November 29 John H. Glenn, Jr. (b. 1921) is named by National Aeronautics and Space Administration (NASA) as the prime astronaut for the first manned orbital flight. M. Scott Carpenter (b. 1925) is the backup.

1961 December 7 Plans for a two-man space capsule, called Mercury Mark II, to follow Project Mercury are announced by National Aeronautics and Space Administration (NASA). Later called Gemini, the capsule will be similar to that of Mercury but will be launched by a Titan II. One of its major objectives would be a test of orbital rendezvous (when two spacecraft meet in space) techniques necessary for an Apollo moon mission. (See January 3, 1962)

1961 December 26 Dyna-Soar project (U.S. Air Force's manned orbital space glider) has its development schedule compressed with the elimination of planned suborbital flights. It will now proceed from *B-52* drop tests to orbital flights. The Air Force senses it is losing support in its competition with National Aeronautics and Space Administration (NASA) for the role of man in space, and attempts to catch up quickly.

1962 First ever "million year" for a European car manufacturer is achieved by Volkswagen of Germany. Its popular Beetle is the largest selling import to the United States.

1962 U.S. Federal-Aid Highway Act passes and provides a major stimulus to urban transportation

1961 ■ *B-52* bomber at Edwards Air Force Base, California.

planning. It declares it to be in the national interest to encourage and promote the development of transportation systems embracing various modes of transport.

1962 Longest passenger ship ever built, the *France*, enters service. This 1,035-foot (315.5-meter) liner is probably the last transatlantic ship built in the grand tradition. It proves unable to make money on this run and eventually is taken off and converted into a Caribbean cruise ship.

1962 First person to swim the English Channel underwater, American frogman Fred Baldasare, successfully completes his attempt. During the crossing, he remains in a submerged cage that is monitored by closed circuit TV cameras.

1962 January 3 Two-man Mercury Mark II will be renamed Gemini, National Aeronautics and Space Administration (NASA) announces. It is named after the third constellation of the zodiac that features the twin stars Castor and Pollux.

1962 January 9 First flight of the Hawker Siddeley *Trident* medium-range airliner is made in England. This aircraft pioneers a new design that features three jet engines mounted on its tail.

1962 February 20 First American to orbit the earth is John H. Glenn, Jr. (b. 1921) in his Mercury capsule, *Friendship 7*. Launched by an Atlas booster from Cape Canaveral, Florida, Glenn completes three orbits spanning four hours, 55 minutes before splashing down

1962 A.D.

Underwater swimmer crosses English Channel

1962 February 20

First American orbits earth

safely in the Atlantic. It is estimated that over 60 million Americans witness the launch live on TV, and Glenn becomes an instant American hero. The United States begins to show real progress in its catch-up race with the Soviet Union.

1962 ■ Atlas launches John H. Glenn, Jr. into space.

1962 March 7 Launch Operations Center is established by National Aeronautics and Space Administration (NASA) at Cape Canaveral, Florida. The new center will serve all NASA space projects that are to be launched from the Cape.

1962 March 9 Titan II launch vehicle, chosen as the booster for the two-man Gemini space capsule, undergoes a successful full-power captive firing. Developed by the U.S. Air Force, the two-stage launch vehicle is more powerful than the Atlas and burns storable fuels that emit a stream of hot, clear gases instead of flames. (See March 16, 1962)

1962 March 14 Neil A. Armstrong (b. 1930), who will become the first man to walk on the moon, is among the six candidates selected by the U.S. Air Force as pilots for the Dyna-Soar program (manned orbital space glider). Four are Air Force pilots and two are National Aeronautics and Space Administration (NASA) test pilots. The Dyna-Soar is designed to be launched into orbit by a Titan III.

1962 March 15 Astronaut Donald K. Slayton (b. 1924), orginally scheduled for the next Mercury orbital flight, is disqualified because of an "erratic heart rate." Slayton will remain grounded by National Aeronautics and Space Administration (NASA) until 13 years later when he finally is cleared to fly an Apollo mission. (See July 15, 1975)

1962 March 16 Titan II makes its first successful launch as an ICBM (inter-continental ballistic missile). It is ready to launch the two-man Gemini spacecraft.

1962 April U.S. President John F. Kennedy (1917—1963) delivers a message to Congress on the subject of transportation. This speech regards transportation as one of the key factors in shaping U.S. cities and stresses the need for planning. It opens a new era in urban transportation and leads to needed legislation. (See 1962)

1962 April 4 Soviet newspaper reports that cosmonauts have had their training altered to include special exercise in an attempt to offset the nausea they experienced during prolonged weightlessness.

1962 April 18 Applications will be received, National Aeronautics and Space Administration (NASA) announces, for additional astronauts and will continue until June 1, 1962. Qualifications are slightly less demanding than those for Mercury, especially in terms of test-pilot time required. But they are more demanding in other ways, since the age limit is lowered to 35 and a college degree in science or engineering is required.

1962 April 18 National Aeronautics and Space Administration (NASA) approves the highest national priority for the Apollo manned lunar landing program.

1962 April 20 U.S. Air Force selects eight officers for the second class of its space pilot school. None of these pilots will ever fly in space.

1962 April 25 Saturn booster first stage makes its second successful launch test, sending its dummy second and third stages 65 miles high.

1962 April 26 First international satellite, *Ariel 1*, is launched by National Aeronautics and Space Administration (NASA) from Cape Canaveral, Florida. The scientific satellite, built by the United States, carries six British experiments.

1962 April 28 First details of a U.S. orbital space station that is under a feasibility study by National Aeronautics and Space Administration (NASA) are revealed. It is shaped like a doughnut and is inflated once in orbit. Space station designs that can hold from four to thirty people have been under study by NASA since November 1960. None has yet been built.

1962 May 2 First man-powered airplane to make an authenticated straight flight of over one-half mile is the Hatfield Man-Powered Aircraft Club's *Puffin*, flown in England by John C. Wimpenny. This record will stand for 10 years.

1962 May 24 Second manned U.S. orbital flight is made by M. Scott Carpenter (b. 1925) in the Mercury capsule, *Aurora 7*. Launched by an Atlas from a fog-bound Cape Canaveral, Florida, the three-orbit, nearly five-hour flight goes well until Carpenter, through either carelessness or distraction, wastes precious maneuvering fuel needed during reentry and consequently makes a late retro fire. This makes his capsule land at least 125 miles off the ocean area target. He is found three hours later sitting safely in his life raft. The human factor in space sometimes means the unpredictable.

1962 June Analysis of results obtained from the U.S. Air Force's *Discoverer 18* satellite indicates that dangerous radiation increases exponentially in higher earth orbits. This implies that regular manned space flights should probably occur in low earth orbit.

1962 June 1 National Aeronautics and Space Administration (NASA) begins screening over 250 applications for new astronaut positions. Fifty-three applications come from the armed services, while over 200 are submitted by civilians.

1962 June 7 Pakistan conducts its first space experiment in a joint program with the United States. A Nike-Cajun sounding rocket launches a Pakistan payload into the upper atmosphere.

1962 June 26 Dyna-Soar name is changed by the U.S. Air Force to the X-20. The proposed manned orbital space glider program still seeks a mission and an identity separate from National Aeronautics and Space Administration's NASA manned programs.

1962 July 3 First U.S. silicon rectifier locomotive is delivered to an eastern railroad. A rectifier is a device for converting alternating electric current to direct current.

1962 July 6 U.S. Civil Service Commission rules that National Aeronautics and Space Administration (NASA) is authorized to hire at maximum salaries for government service grades (GS 13—15), what it calls an "aerospace engineer and pilot." NASA calls them astronauts.

1962 July 10 First commercial transmission of live TV via satellite and the first transatlantic TV transmission takes place as National Aeronautics and Space Administration (NASA) launches *Telstar 1* communications satellite into orbit from Cape Canaveral, Florida. It is a joint program between American Telegraph & Telephone Co. (AT&T) and NASA.

1962 July 10

Telstar 1 satellite launched

1962 July 11 Decision on how to go to the moon is announced by National Aeronautics and Space Administration (NASA) which chooses the lunar orbit rendezvous (LOR) method. In this mode, a Saturn V vehicle launches a manned payload to the moon consisting of three modules. Once in lunar orbit, they separate with only one descending to its surface. When the surface mission is finished, they dock together, head back to earth, and only one module reenters and lands. NASA chooses LOR because it is the cheapest, technically easiest, quickest, and most likely to succeed.

1962 July 17 Women in space is the subject of Congressional hearings before the Subcommittee of the U.S. House Committee on Science and Astronautics. Jane B. Hart and Jerrie Cobb, representing the 13 women who completed unofficial space qualification tests at the Lovelace Foundation, testify that women are qualified and can contribute. Famous aviation pilot Jacqueline Cochran says that "there is no doubt in the world that women will go into space."

1962 July 17

Women in space discussed

1962 July 18 In testimony before the U.S. House Subcommittee of the Committee on Science and

Astronautics, astronaut John H. Glenn, Jr. (b. 1921) says, "I couldn't care less who's over there [in the next seat] as long as it's the most qualified person.... I wouldn't oppose a women's astronaut training program; I just see no requirement for it." Officially, National Aeronautics and Space Administration (NASA) says it has not found one woman who meets all the requirements: American citizenship, excellent physical condition, degree in physical or biological sciences or engineering, and experimental jet flight-test experience.

1962 July 20 First regular, passenger-carrying hovercraft service begins. Twenty-four paying passengers take the first ride from Rhyl in North Wales to Wallasey, England aboard a Vickers Armstrong *VAJ*.

1962 July 25 Manned Spacecraft Center at Houston, Texas invites 11 companies to submit research and development proposals for the Lunar Excursion Module (LEM) that will descend and land on the moon during the lunar orbit rendezvous (LOR) segment of the Apollo moon mission. (See November 7, 1962)

1962 August

Apollo details publicized

1962 August First details of the Apollo command module spacecraft are made available by National Aeronautics and Space Administration (NASA) to the public. The three-man crew will sit in adjacent couches during launch and reentry, and one couch will be stowed during flight for more room. It will be 365 cubic feet in volume, with 22 cubic feet of free area available to the crew. It will also have an airlock, permitting a pressure-suited astronaut to exit and enter.

1962 August 11

First pictures from space broadcast

1962 August 11 Soviet cosmonaut Andrian G. Nikolayev (b. 1929) is launched into earth orbit in *Vostok 3*. He broadcasts the first TV pictures from space, which show a spacecraft interior quite spacious compared to Mercury's tight quarters. The Soviets continue to surprise the world as he is joined in orbit the next day by a comrade in *Vostok 4*. Nikolayev remains in space over 94 hours, landing back on earth on August 15, 1962. (See August 12, 1962)

1962 August 12 Soviet cosmonaut Pavel R. Popovich (b. 1930) is launched in *Vostok 4* into earth orbit within three miles of his comrade Nikolayev who is in *Vostok 3*. The Soviets tout the rendezvous aspects of this mission, but in fact the Vostok spacecraft have no maneuvering ability in space. Popovich stays in orbit

nearly three full days and reenters on August 15, 1962. (See August 11, 1962)

1962 August 13 Ten U.S. Air Force pilots emerge from a simulated space cabin in which they had spent one month participating in a psychological test to determine how long a team of astronauts could work together efficiently on a prolonged mission in space. The project director felt that the experiment had exceeded his expectations.

1962 August 18 Norway, in cooperation with Denmark and the United States, launches its first rocket into the ionosphere (that part of the earth's atmosphere from about 25 to 250 miles high) from Andoeya, Norway.

1962 August 20 First nuclear-powered cargo ship, the U.S. Maritime Administration's *Savannah*, makes its maiden voyage from Yorktown, Virginia to Savannah, Georgia. It is able to carry 60 passengers and 10,000 tons of cargo at 20 knots without having to refuel for 3.5 years.

1962 September 3 U.S. Senate Committee on Aeronautical and Space Sciences report tells of National Aeronautics and Space Administration's (NASA) plans after Mercury. Gemini's two-man flights will be aimed at orbital rendezvous and the following Apollo three-man flights will be circumlunar missions followed by lunar landing flights.

1962 September 5 As many as nine different companies submit proposals to National Aeronautics and Space Administration (NASA) to design and build the lunar excursion modules, one of three modules comprising the Apollo spacecraft. NASA will award the contract in six to eight weeks time.

1962 September 8 RL-10 rocket engine is successfully static-fired at Marshall Space Flight Center, Huntsville, Alabama. A cluster of these engines will power the Saturn S-IV stage.

1962 September 9 The Martin Co. announces that a three-man crew "survived" a simulated, week-long round trip to the moon in a simulation chamber at their Baltimore, Maryland plant.

⟲ 1962 September 10 Fire in a simulated space cabin at the U.S. Air Force School of Aviation Medicine (SAM), Brooks Air Force Base, Texas causes serious smoke-inhalation injuries to one of two men spending their 13th consecutive day in the cabin. Atmosphere in the cabin is almost pure oxygen when the fire occurs. Its cause is unknown. In a similar flash fire on the ground, three Apollo astronauts are killed nearly five years later, prompting the switch to oxygen and nitrogen. (See January 27, 1967)

⟲ 1962 September 13 First paraglider research vehicle (Parasev) is flown by National Aeronautics and Space Administration (NASA) pilot Milton O. Thompson (b. 1926) after being towed to an altitude of 6,000 feet. Basically a Rogallo wing, it is tested as a replacement for parachutes in the Gemini program. Other possible uses of the paraglider concept include recovery of future spacecraft and rocket boosters.

⟲ 1962 September 17 National Aeronautics and Space Administration (NASA) reports that during John H. Glenn's (b. 1921) four-and-one-half-hour February 1962 orbital flight, he received less than half the heavy primary cosmic radiation dosage expected. The Mercury spacecraft walls and capsule instrumentation are credited with absorbing much of the rays.

⟲ 1962 September 17 M. G. O'Neil, president of General Tire & Rubber Co., tells a national convention of tire dealers that in ten years the astronautics industry may exceed the size of the combined automotive industries of the world. He then compares the impact of the space age to that of the discovery of America in 1492.

⟲ 1962 September 17 Nine new astronauts are named by National Aeronautics and Space Administration (NASA). Chosen from 253 applicants, the nine are: civilians Neil A. Armstrong (b. 1930) and Elliot M. See (1927—1966); Air Force officers Maj. Frank Borman (b. 1928), Capt. James A. McDivitt (b. 1929), Capt. Thomas P. Stafford (b. 1930), and Capt. Edward H. White (1930—1967); Naval officers Lt. Cmdr. John W. Young (b. 1930), James A. Lovell, Jr. (b. 1928) and Lt. Charles Conrad, Jr. (b. 1930). All are test pilots.

⟲ 1962 September 19 First flight of the Aero Space Lines Corporation "Pregnant Guppy" cargo-plane is made. This radically modified Boeing *377 Stra-*

tocruiser has an extremely enlarged upper fuselage to allow it to handle oversize cargo. These strange-looking aircraft are used to carry spacecraft components from the factory to the assembly site. (See March 13, 1970)

⟲ 1962 September 24 General Electric Company's Space Technology Center reveals its design for an astronaut escape system that is used if the reentry capsule malfunctions and cannot return to earth. Called "MOOSE" (man out of space easiest), the system uses a prepackaged spacecraft consisting of a plastic sack, folding heat shield, retrorocket pack, containers of foaming plastic, and a parachute. To use the system, the stranded astronaut would zip into the sack, step out of the faulty capsule, aim himself with a special scope, and fire his retrorocket. At this point, the heat shield would unfold and the sack would fill with rapid-hardening foam, protecting him from reentry heat. At 30,000 feet, the parachute would open. The effectiveness of this "cocoon" life-saving system is never tested.

⟲ 1962 September 28 First satellite placed in orbit that was designed and built by a nation other than the United States or the U.S.S.R. is Canada's *Alouette*. The scientific satellite is launched by National Aeronautics and Space Administration (NASA) for Canada.

⟲ 1962 October First full-duration static firing of the J-2 liquid-hydrogen rocket engine is successfully completed at Rocketdyne Division of North American Aviation. Inc. The J-2 engines will be clustered to power the S-II stage of the Saturn V moon launch vehicle.

⟲ 1962 October New program to test astronaut tolerance to space flight conditions begins as a new motion-simulator platform is ordered by National Aeronautics and Space Administration (NASA). It will move in six directions—pitch, roll, yaw, up-and-down, side-to-side, and back-to-forward.

1962 October

***New motion
simulator
tested***

⟲ 1962 October 3 Fifth manned Mercury flight is made as astronaut Walter M. Schirra, Jr. (b. 1923) is launched by an Atlas vehicle from Cape Canaveral, Florida. His spacecraft, *Sigma 7*, orbits the earth six times during the nine-hour, 13-minute mission and achieves all its flight objectives. It splashes down in the Pacific, and Schirra is recovered 40 minutes later.

⟲ 1962 October 5 $1.55 million contract is given to two companies for the development of spacesuits for the Apollo crew. The prime contractor, Hamilton Standard Division of United Aircraft Corp., will develop life-support and back-pack systems for lunar excursions. The Latex Corp. will fabricate the suits with Republic Aviation Corp. The new suits will provide the crew with greater mobility which will be needed if they are to move about freely on the moon.

1962 October 22 U.S. Air Force announces its selection of ten officers to be trained as space pilots, engineers, and program managers for the X-20 (Dyna-Soar) manned orbital space glider. One of those selected is Michael Collins (b. 1930) who will pilot the Apollo moon-orbiting command module for the first manned lunar landing. (See July 16, 1969)

1962 October 26 First railroad train information transmitted via satellite takes place from St. Louis, Missouri to Dallas, Texas via *Telstar* communications satellite.

1962 November 5 Apollo astronauts will only need special shielding devices for their eyes, since the Apollo spacecraft will provide most of the radiation shielding required, National Aeronautics and Space Administration (NASA) announces.

1962 November 7

Grumman selected as lunar module builder

1962 November 7 Grumman Aircraft Engineering Corp. is selected by National Aeronautics and Space Administration (NASA) to build the lunar excursion module (LEM) for the three man Apollo spacecraft. (See March 11, 1963)

1962 November 9 First stage of Saturn I launch vehicle is static-fired for full duration at full thrust (1.5 million pounds) for the first time. The Saturn I is the two-stage booster that will be used on all earth-orbiting Apollo missions.

1962 November 15 American aviator Jerrie Cobb tells the Women's Advertising Club of Washington, D.C. that, "We're bypassing the one scientific space feat we could accomplish now—putting the first woman in orbit...." Only seven months later, the Soviet Union does exactly what she calls for. (See June 16, 1963)

1962 November 16 Saturn I launch vehicle reaches 104-mile altitude in a ballistic (up and down) launch test at Cape Canaveral, Florida. Its dummy upper stage is filled with water which is released into the ionosphere and forms a massive cloud of ice particles for an experiment in atmospheric physics called Project Highwater.

1962 November 30 First tethered hovering flight of Lockheed *XV-4A Hummingbird* two-seat VTOL (vertical take-off and landing) research aircraft is made in the United States. This jet-lift fighter has two engines mounted horizontally on either side of the fuselage which divert their ducts downward for vertical lift and backward for horizontal flight. This project is not continued.

1962 December 9 U.S. Air Force Chief of Staff Gen. Curtis LeMay (b. 1906) describes what he sees as a follow-on to the planned X-20 (Dyna-Soar) manned orbital space glider, saying, "Eventually I see the development of a manned vehicle that can take off from existing runways, go into orbit, maneuver while re-entering the earth's atmosphere, and land at any air base in the conventional manner." Despite the eventual creation of the space shuttle, LeMay's criteria have not been met 30 years later.

1962 December 26 Homer E. Newell, director of Space Sciences at National Aeronautics and Space Administration (NASA) states a refreshingly different opinion about what an astronaut's qualifications should be, saying in a speech, "I have a complete and utter conviction that we should take a scientist and make a flyer out of him rather than the other way around."

1963 In Japan, the highway between Ritto and Amagasaki opens as the first in a series of National Land Development Highways that run vertically through the nation. (See 1965)

1963 First people mover is introduced by Westinghouse in Pittsburgh, Pennsylvania's South Park area. This demonstration program is a driverless vehicle called "Skybus" that is used as a suburb-to-city transport link. Running on a guideway, this automated people mover (APM) is controlled by a central system.

1963 British-French committee studies the revived idea of a tunnel linking the two countries and recommends that private enterprise offer the best means of both financing and executing the ambitious project. Technology has advanced to the point where *it* is not as much of a factor as political will and financial considerations. Both countries agree to build the tunnel. (See 1974)

1963 First company to market a car with a Wankel rotary engine is NSU of West Germany. It is a two-seater called the Sports Spyder. The Wankel is a radical departure from traditional piston gas engines, for instead of pistons and cylinders, it has a pair of triangular-shaped rotors that rotate inside an elliptical chamber, drawing in fuel, squeezing it until it is ignited, and expelling the burned gases, all in one continuous movement. Although rotary engines run very smoothly, they are less fuel efficient and have reliability problems. NSU (Neckarsulmer Strickmaschinen Union) eventually becomes part of a four-company group now known as Audi. (See 1967)

1963 Japanese bullet train, the Tokaido Shinkansen, runs at its highest speed of 256 km/h on a model line in Kanagawa.

1963 Longest prestressed concrete cantilever bridge at the time, the Medway Bridge near Chatham in England, is built. Bridging the Medway River in three connected spans, this very economical design spans 500 feet (152 meters). It is surpassed in length by the 682-foot (209-meter) span of the Bendorf Bridge in Koblenz, Germany. Prestressed concrete is concrete strengthened by having been allowed to set around tautly drawn steel wires (tensioned) or steel bars that extend through it.

1963 First rigid inflatable boat for use in rough seas, the *Atlanta*, is built. Designed by British Rear Admiral D. J. Hoare, it proves especially seaworthy in rough weather.

1963 Longest floating bridge, the Lacey V. Murrow Bridge, is completed. This pontoon bridge crosses Lake Washington on Interstate 90 in Seattle, Washington. The lake is very deep but has no currents and does not freeze, so a pontoon is built. The bridge is 12,596 feet overall, with a 7,518-foot floating section. Each of the 25 reinforced concrete pontoons measures 350 feet long and 60 feet wide.

1963 State of New York renames Idlewild Airport the John F. Kennedy (JFK) Airport in honor of the assassinated president.

1963 January Simplified Saturn launch vehicle terminology is announced by National Aeronautics and Space Administration (NASA). There will be three different Saturn boosters: Saturn I, Saturn IB, and the massive three-stage Saturn V that will send Apollo to the moon.

1963 January 14 Cooperative United States-India space program is announced by National Aeronautics and Space Administration (NASA) that will conduct joint scientific experiments in space. NASA will launch Indian payloads.

1963 January 21 Warnings are made by Geophysics Corp. of America that huge rockets "may cause modifications over large local areas or on a worldwide basis in the upper atmosphere." Twenty-five years later, evidence is found that tears or holes are made in the earth's protective ozone layer by such flights.

1963 January 21 Soviet scientist Anatoli A. Blagonravov says in an *Izvestia* article that recent Soviet manned flights prove that man can go to the moon. Man is not harmed by prolonged flights and he can avoid dangerous radiation and perform work in space, he says.

1963 January 23 In realistic tests at Langley Research Center, Virginia, National Aeronautics and Space Administration (NASA) reports that their research pilots demonstrated an ability to complete precise maneuvers of flight, despite seven days in very cramped quarters.

1963 January 28 New tracking system is installed on Eleuthera Island in the Bahamas by National Aeronautics and Space Administration (NASA). It will provide the necessary tracking accuracy for controlling space rendezvous manuever in Project Gemini and for tracking the return of the Apollo spacecraft.

1963 February Four men spend 14 days in a room simulating a slowly-rotating space station. National Aeronautics and Space Administration (NASA) reports that no mental or physical changes or problems were encountered during the experiment.

1963 February 1 American Institute of Aeronautics and Astronautics (AIAA) comes into existence. It is the result of a merger of the American Rocket Society (ARS) and the Institute of the Aeronautical Sciences

*1963
January 21
Soviets say
man can go
to moon*

(IAS). Still in existence today, it is the leading American technical society keyed to the dynamic developments of the space age.

1963 February 4   Astronaut M. Scott Carpenter (b. 1925) says in a speech that all three U.S. astronauts who had made orbital flights found weightlessness to be no problem and actually enjoyed it. It could even become addictive, he says.

1963 February 9   First flight of the three-jet Boeing 727 is made in the United States. Boeing adopts the tail-engine formula for this medium-range jet transport, and it soon outsells any and all rivals. Built in large numbers, it is used in both passenger and cargo versions.

1963
February 13

Meteoroids
puncture
satellite

1963 February 13   Meteoroid detector satellite *Explorer 16* records 16 punctures by meteoroids during its first 29 days in orbit. National Aeronautics and Space Administration (NASA) is attempting to gather data on the hazards of meteoroids to manned space flights.

1963 February 25   Largest contract signed to date by National Aeronautics and Space Administration (NASA) is with Boeing Co. for $418,820,967. For this amount, Boeing will design, develop, and manufacture 11 Saturn V first stage boosters. Saturn V will launch Apollo to the moon.

1963 March   U.S. Secretary of Defense Robert S. McNamara (b. 1916) testifies before Congress that there exists only an "ill-defined military requirement" for man in space, but that the United States should still place men in orbit. The question is, should we search for that military role with the X-20 (Dyna-Soar) manned orbital space glider or in cooperation with the Gemini two-man program?

1963 March 7

Moon's
composition
argued

1963 March 7   National Aeronautics and Space Administration (NASA) reports it has contradictory scientific theories about the composition of the surface of the moon. Some say it is made of finely powdered sand covering caverns and empty spaces, unable to support weight. Others argue directly opposite. NASA states: "This means we have to go there and find out." NASA has plans for unmanned spacecraft (Ranger and Surveyor) to do this dangerous work.

1963 March 8   First transatlantic satellite transmission of photographs is made from New York to Paris, France, Rome, Italy, and London, England via the U.S. communications satellite *Relay 1*. The photos are returned within 11 minutes by transatlantic cable.

1963 March 11   U.S. Air Force manned orbital space glider program, X-20 (formerly Dyna-Soar), is cut back to only a research and development level. This means the Air Force has not yet persuaded policy-makers that there is a need for a military manned space program.

1963 March 11   Grumman Aircraft Engineering Corp. signs a $387.9 million contract with National Aeronautics and Space Administration (NASA) to design, fabricate, and deliver 20 lunar excursion modules (LEM).

1963 March 28   Fourth and last test launch of the Saturn I launch vehicle confirms its engines' capability.

1963 March 29   Former President Dwight D. Eisenhower (1890—1969) again speaks out against what he considers overspending on space, especially on Apollo. He says, "I have never believed that a spectacular dash to the moon, vastly deepening our debt, is worth the added tax burden it will eventually impose upon our citizens."

1963 April 2   *Lunik 4* is successfully launched by the Soviet Union on a flight toward the moon. The large, unmanned spacecraft (3,135 pounds) passes by the moon on April 6, after about 90 hours of flying, and returns considerable scientific information to the Soviets about a moon voyage.

1963 April 9   First U.S. college program to train astronauts is established at Purdue University for the Air Force. A new Master's degree program in astronautics is also created.

1963 April 10   First nuclear submarine is lost and the worst submarine disaster in peacetime occurs as U.S. nuclear-powered submarine *Thresher* fails to surface. After carrying out deep diving tests in the Atlantic about 220 miles (354 kilometers) off the coast of Cape Cod, Massachusetts, the submarine disappears with a crew of 129. During October 1964, the bathyscaphe *Trieste II* takes photos of the *Thresher*'s hull lying at a depth of

6,400 feet (2,560 meters). No cause for the disaster has ever been determined.

1963 April 17 First British nuclear-powered submarine, the *Dreadnought,* is commissioned. The hull is British-built and the reactors are U.S.-built.

1963 April 22 *Aviation Week and Space Technology* reports in all seriousness the invention of an edible structural material by Sydney Schwartz, a Grumman Corporation physiologist. It quotes him saying that the edible structure, which is harder than tempered masonite, could "reduce the need for backup food in space flights."

1963 April 25 New biological tape recorders are announced by Cook Electric Co. designed for use in the Gemini program. Each recorder will receive and record six kinds of simultaneous biomedical signals from sensors within the astronaut's spacesuit. Monitoring the crew's state is a major goal for National Aeronautics and Space Administration (NASA).

1963 June American Larry Stevenson and his Makaha Company begin production of double-action (swiveling) skateboards shaped like surfboards. By this time, skateboarding is on its way to becoming a popular sport.

1963 June 3 Sixteen National Aeronautics and Space Administration (NASA) astronauts begin three days of jungle survival training at the U.S. Air Force Caribbean Air Command Tropic Survival School, Albrook Air Force Base, Canal Zone. NASA feels that astronauts must be prepared to survive on their own should their reentry from space accidently place them in a hostile environment.

1963 June 12 Project Mercury officially ends after achieving the U.S. goal of putting a man in orbit. Two suborbital and four orbital flights logged 52 hours, 23 minutes of flight time and 34 orbits of earth.

1963 June 14 Soviet Union launches its fifth man into space, as cosmonaut Valery F. Bykovsky (b. 1934) flies in *Vostok 5.* His four-day, 23-hour, six-minute flight in earth orbit is completely upstaged by the Soviet launch into space of the first woman to orbit the earth. He reenters on June 19, 1963 after 82 orbits. (See June 16, 1963)

1963 June 16 First woman in space is U.S.S.R.'s Valentina V. Tereshkova (b. 1937) who flies in *Vostok 6.* As a cotton-mill worker and an amateur parachutist, Tereshkova is even more of a passenger than most of the Soviet cosmonauts in the ground-controlled spacecraft. She has some difficult moments but reenters safely after nearly three full days in orbit. The Soviet Union captures another major space first.

1963 June 18 Recruitment of astronauts is broadened by National Aeronautics and Space Administration (NASA) which eliminates the requirement of a test pilot certificate.

1963 July 13 Whirlpool Corp. wins a National Aeronautics and Space Administration (NASA) contract for the development of food supply, personal hygiene items, and waste disposal system for Project Gemini manned space flights. As NASA projects much longer manned flights in space, it must plan for these very ordinary but essential services.

1963 August 5 Desert survival training begins for nine Gemini/Apollo astronauts. This contingency training is accomplished at Staed Air Force Base and Carson Sink, Nevada.

1963 August 8 "The Great Train Robbery" occurs on the rail line from Glasgow, Scotland to London, England. Nearly three million British pounds are stolen from the train in the 22 minutes it is brought to a standstill by a faked red signal. Four years later, Paramount Pictures spends 2.6 million pounds to reconstruct the event for a motion picture.

1963 September 13 Sixteen NASA astronauts begin training in the techniques of water and land parachute landings. This training is geared to what they could experience if a launch were aborted and they were ejected at a low altitude.

1963 September 23 First child is born to a parent who has travelled in space. Tayna Titov, daughter of Soviet cosmonaut Gherman Titov (b. 1935) who flew in *Vostok 2* on August 6, 1961, and his wife, Tamara.

1963 October 1 First direct flight to Antarctica from another continent is made by a U.S. Navy Lockheed *C-130 Hercules* transport. Piloted by Comdr. G. R. Kelley, the *Hercules* is a very large aircraft with excellent short takeoff and landing characteristics, and can operate well on rough landing strips.

1963 October 7 First flight of the Gates *Learjet* is made in the United States. This attractive-looking executive jet aircraft dominates its jet competition. It becomes standard for most large American companies to keep one of these comfortable flying boardrooms available for its executives.

1963 October 9 Work begins at North American Aviation on the fabrication of the Apollo command module's stainless steel skin and the molding of its honeycomb aluminum inner walls. This design will shield the astronauts from most harmful radiation during their flight to and from the moon.

1963
October 9

"Flying
carpet"
proposed

1963 October 9 Douglas Aircraft Co. continues advanced planning proposing a "flying carpet" astronaut escape system from orbital space stations. It would be a saucer-shaped vehicle that would expand into a blunt-nosed, cone-shaped craft that would survive reentry by using fabrics woven with filaments of nickel-based alloys that could withstand 1,600 degree temperatures. It is never developed.

1963 October 18 Fourteen new astronauts are selected by National Aeronautics and Space Administration (NASA) from a final field of 30. The new astronauts are: Edwin E. Aldrin, Jr. (b. 1930), William A. Anders (b. 1933), Charles A. Bassett II (1931—1966), Michael Collins (b. 1930), Donn F. Eisele (1930—1987), Theodore C. Freeman (1930—1964), and David R. Scott (b. 1932) (all Air Force officers); Alan L. Bean (b. 1932), Eugene A. Cernan (b. 1934), Roger B. Chaffee (1935—1967), Richard F. Gordon (b. 1929) (all Navy officers); Clifton C. Williams (1932—1967) (Marine officer); and R. Walter Cunningham (b. 1932) and Russell L. Schweickart (b. 1935), civilians. All qualify for Gemini and Apollo, bringing the total number of NASA astronauts to 30. Another contingent of astronauts will be named in late 1965.

1963
October 26

U.S.S.R.
won't land
on moon

1963 October 26 Soviet Premier Nikita S. Khrushchev (1894—1971) announces in *Izvestia* that the U.S.S.R. will not attempt to land a man on the moon. His statement is regarded by the United States as an attempt to undermine American support for the upcoming Apollo program. Whatever his motives, and whether truthful at the time or not, the Soviet Union does not put a man on the moon.

1963 October 30 National Aeronautics and Space Administration (NASA) announces it is compressing the Apollo flight schedule by eliminating four manned earth orbital flights that were scheduled to be made before any lunar flights. Studies have shown that running all-systems checks from the beginning is a quicker and more certain method of checkout than adding additional systems flight-by-flight. This "all-up" concept will prove successful as well as cheaper in the long run.

1963 November 3 Soviet cosmonauts Valentina V. Tereshkova (b. 1937) and Andrian G. Nikolayev (b. 1929) are married in a civil ceremony in Moscow. Soviet Premier Nikita S. Khrushchev (1894—1971) is present at the reception.

1963 November 4 Electric trolley car service ends in Baltimore, Maryland where it was first introduced 88 years earlier, and is replaced by diesel buses.

1963 November 7 Full scale test of the Apollo escape rocket system is successful at White Sands, New Mexico. Four rockets installed in the escape tower above the unmanned Apollo command module lift it to 5,000 feet and it drifts down with parachutes. As with Mercury, there must be a dependable astronaut escape system in case of launch vehicle malfunction.

1963 November 21 First rocket launched from India is the result of a cooperative India-France-United States project.

1963 November 26 Arbitration board set up by U.S. Congress to resolve a railroad and union dispute rules that 90% of all the diesel firemen's jobs are unnecessary and should be eliminated, but gradually. Railroads had intended to eliminate all 40,000 firemen's jobs at once. The fireman or stoker was in earlier times the member of the steam locomotive crew who fed the fire grate with fuel.

1963 November 27 J-2 liquid-hydrogen engine designed to power the upper stages of Saturn IB and Saturn V launch vehicles undergoes its first extended duration ground test firing.

1963 November 29 By executive order of President Lyndon B. Johnson (1908—1973), the National Aeronautics and Space Administration (NASA) launch operations center in Florida is renamed the John F. Kennedy Space Flight Center. In cooperation with the State of Florida, Cape Canaveral is renamed Cape Kennedy in honor of the assassinated president's dedication to the space program.

1963 December 10 Cancellation of X-20, the U.S. Air Force manned orbital space glider program previously called Dyna-Soar, is announced by Secretary of Defense Robert S. McNamara (b. 1916). Funds for this never-flown aerospace project are now directed to another proposed Air Force man-in-space project called the Manned Orbiting Laboratory (MOL). This is to be developed in conjunction with National Aeronautics and Space Administration's (NASA) forthcoming Gemini program.

1963 December 17 First flight of Lockheed C-141A *Starlifter* is made in Marietta, Georgia. This four turbo-fan, long-range military transport becomes one of the U.S. Air Force's main heavy transport aircraft.

1964 Longest tunnel of any kind in the world, the Seikan Tunnel in Japan, begins construction. Connecting the islands of Honshu and Hokkaido, it is 33.4 miles (53.8 kilometers) long when completed in 1988. Although a major engineering feat—14.3 miles (23.3 kilometers) lie under the Tsugaru Strait—this railroad line sees limited use upon opening because of the competition of air travel between the islands which is quicker and almost as cheap as rail travel. It seems fated to carry far fewer passengers than aircraft.

1964 First fully automatic automobile air conditioning system is Cadillac's "climate control" system.

1964 Urban Mass Transportation Act goes into effect in the United States. This first real effort to provide federal assistance for urban mass transportation development falls short of most of its goals as Congress does not authorize much money to carry it out.

1964 Longest reinforced concrete arch bridge, the Gladesville Bridge over the Parramatta River in Sydney Harbor, Australia, is completed. During the construction of its four connected arched ribs, the entire structure is supported by steel columns until the precast elements can support themselves. It spans 1,000 feet (305 meters) and carries six lanes of traffic.

1964 Seat belts are made standard equipment on cars produced by Studebaker-Packard Corporation. Although this decision marks a radical break with other major American automakers, the company goes out of business by year's end.

1964 January 1 Position paper is issued by National Aeronautics and Space Administration (NASA) on the Air Force Manned Orbiting Laboratory (MOL), stating that the "MOL should not be construed as the national space station," but rather a single experimental military project within the overall national program. The Air Force has shifted its emphasis from reentry technology (cancelled X-20) to in-orbit experiments, and NASA wants to make sure that the Air Force scope is strictly limited to military concerns.

1964 January 7 First power tool built specifically for use in space is demonstrated by Martin Co. and Black & Decker Manufacturing Co. Ressembling a home power drill in size and shape, the battery-powered "electric minimum reaction space tool" has 99.97% less reactive torque (rotating or twisting force) than ordinary utility drills.

1964 January 7 Request for proposal is issued by National Aeronautics and Space Administration (NASA) for deep space laser acquisition and tracking techniques in manned space missions. The Apollo moon mission must have two-way telemetry and voice communications as well as spacecraft-to-ground TV.

1964 January 28 Spain and the United States agree to construct and operate a space data and tracking acquisition station about 30 miles west of Madrid, Spain. It will be used primarily in National Aeronautics and Space Administration's (NASA) Deep Space Network.

1964 January 29 First successful test launch of both stages of the Saturn I launch vehicle is made from Cape Kennedy, Florida. It launches a dummy payload weighing 38,000 pounds into orbit.

1964 February 3 Wernher von Braun (1912—1977) tells of National Aeronautics and Space Administration's (NASA) plans to have the two Apollo

*1964
January 7
First
space-only
power tool
built*

astronauts standing in the Lunar Module during the moon landing. They will wear support gear, like elasticized parachute harnesses, to cushion the landing. Elimination of chairs and rearranging gear will result in an important weight reduction of 1,000 pounds.

**1964
February 22

Concerns
about ozone
layer raised**

1964 February 22 In a remarkable example of foresight and insight, Sir Bernard Lovell (b. 1913), director of Britain's Jodrell Bank Experimental Station, warns against the destruction of the earth's protective ozone layer, saying, "that zone is rather easy to destroy. And if it is intentionally or accidentally removed, then the ultraviolet radiation would penetrate to earth." Lovell uses the ozone layer as but one example of how the lack of any international controls on space activity could result in permanent ecological damage.

**1964
March 6—7

Astronauts
train at
Grand
Canyon**

1964 March 6—7 In a field exercise at the bottom of the Grand Canyon, National Aeronautics and Space Administration (NASA) astronauts are trained to be "competent observers" of rock and mineral formations in preparation for their trip to the moon.

1964 March 10 Soviet Union submits a draft treaty to the Legal Subcommittee of the United Nations Committee on the Peaceful Uses of Outer Space. It proposes aid to astronauts in distress and for the return of downed spacecraft. It differs slightly from a similar U.S. version. Both major space powers realize that there should be some mechanisms and rules in place to assist astronauts in trouble.

1964 March 20 European Space Research Organization (ESRO) is created for the purpose of promoting collaboration among European states in space research. Its first satellites were launched by the United States. It is replaced by the European Space Agency (ESA) ten years later. (See April 1, 1974)

**1964 April

Ford
Mustang
introduced**

1964 April Ford Mustang is first introduced and achieves instant success. As Ford's biggest postwar success, it is not especially distinguished mechanically, but succeeds rather on its appealing sporty design. It sells over one million in three years and much credit is given to the Lee Iacocca-designed sales package. (See March 2, 1966)

1964 April Longest bridge-tunnel, the Chesapeake Bay Bridge-Tunnel, opens to traffic. Linking Norfolk, Virginia to the tip of Cape Charles, this 17.5-mile

stretch is a combination of trestles, bridges, and tunnels. Two concrete-lined tunnels a mile long and 24 feet in diameter keep the Chesapeake Bay clear for ships to pass over. The main part of the structure is 12.5 miles of precast concrete trestles, 31 feet wide and capable of withstanding 20-foot waves.

1964 April 8 First Project Gemini test flight is made as an unmanned Gemini spacecraft is launched into orbit by a Titan II launch vehicle at Cape Kennedy, Florida.

1964 April 11 Capital Beltway around Washington, D.C. opens to traffic. This circular highway running through Maryland and Virginia totals 66 miles. Designed to handle 49,000 vehicles per day, it exceeds that total in the first year, and requires constant widening and repairs.

1964 April 22 National Aeronautics and Space Administration (NASA) announces it is cooperating fully with the U.S. Department of Defense (DOD) in exploring four different types of manned orbital systems. NASA's unstated goal is to find a post-Apollo mission for its manned space flight program, while DOD's goal is to simply get its military man-in-space program in operation.

1964 May 6 Dr. Charles A. Berry (b. 1923), chief of Medical Programs at the National Aeronautics and Space Administration (NASA) Manned Spacecraft Center, Houston, Texas, says that Apollo astronauts will be kept in isolation, prior to flight, longer than earlier space crews. Their families will also be given more attention to ensure the astronauts' health. If one member of the three-man crew becomes ill prior to a mission, the entire crew will be replaced by their backups.

1964 May 8 In a formal statement on long-duration manned space flights, National Aeronautics and Space Administration (NASA) states in all seriousness that its scientists are investigating the use of chewing gum for their astronauts, "to stimulate dental tissues and freshen the astronaut's mouth...."

1964 May 13 First flight test of the Apollo emergency escape system is made at White Sands, New Mexico. When National Aeronautics and Space Administration (NASA) deliberately explodes at 17,000 feet a Little Joe II rocket that is boosting an Apollo model, the escape tower rockets instantly ignite and carry the Apollo spacecraft safely away to a height of 24,000 feet where it then descends via parachutes.

1964 May 20 First nuclear-powered lighthouse, the Baltimore Light, goes into operation in Chesapeake Bay, Baltimore Harbor, Maryland. This 60-watt radioisotope nuclear generator can produce a continuous supply of electricity for ten years without refueling.

1964 May 22 Dr. W. Randolph Lovelace II, director of Space Medicine for National Aeronautics and Space Administration (NASA), states that "physiologically, women would make excellent astronauts." He adds that all they lack is "the experience in flying high-speed planes and handling the complicated equipment used in the program."

1964 June Future interplanetary space travelers should be no taller than five feet, seven inches and no heavier than 145 pounds, says Douglas Missile & Space Systems Division in its manned Mars exploration study. Six of these "20 percentile" men—men who are smaller than 80 percent of American men—who make a manned Mars flight would require one-and-one-third pounds less food per day than larger men. This would save nearly 500 pounds of food-cargo weight on a one-year trip.

1964 June 6 Silver City Airways (British) announces that on this day it has recorded the one millionth car it has flown between the U.K. and Europe. It first began its U.K. cross-Channel car ferry by air in 1948.

1964 June 8 First "space child" is born to Valentina V. Tereshkova (b. 1937) and Andrian G. Nikolayev (b. 1929), both Soviet cosmonauts who had flown in space. The Soviets make much of the healthy baby boy, citing him as evidence of the harmlessness of space travel. The famous couple eventually divorces.

1964 June 9 U.S. Air Force Manned Orbiting Laboratory (MOL) astronauts will not be trained by National Aeronautics and Space Administration (NASA). The space agency says it will train only its own Gemini and Apollo astronauts. This is a setback for the military which now will have to either train its own astronauts or launch them without any previous space flight experience.

1964 June 23 U.S. Army Map Service completes its topographic study of the moon. Prepared under contract to National Aeronautics and Space Administration (NASA), the lunar map is the most complete map to date and the first to show variations in heights over all the visible surface of the moon. It covers an area of about eight million square miles and identifies more than 5,000 surface features by name. If man is to walk on the moon, he must know in advance where he is going.

1964 June 24 A radio astronomer at the University of California, Berkeley puts forth his theory that the moon's surface resembles cotton candy and is only about 19% solid. This and many other ideas about the nature of the moon's surface can be neither disproven nor discounted until the surface can be actually or directly tested. Many feel that it is covered with a large layer of dust that will simply swallow up anything that tries to land on it.

1964 June 24
Moon-like-cotton-candy theory raised

1964 June 24 Fifteen National Aeronautics and Space Administration (NASA) astronauts begin a three-day jungle survival training course in the Panama Canal Zone under the supervision of the U.S. Air Force Tropic Survival School.

1964 June 24
Astronauts train in jungle

1964 June 29 Report is made by Dr. Bernard M. Wagner (b. 1928), chairman of New York Medical College's pathology department, that the Soviets have decided not to send any more women into space, as Soviet doctors were dismayed at Valentina V. Tereshkova's (b. 1937) performance. She was much too agitated during her flight, as evidenced by wide variations in her pulse rate, and she was not able to recover from the effects of the flight as quickly as her male counterparts.

1964 July 14 Dr. Charles A. Berry (b. 1923), chief of medical programs at National Aeronautics and Space Administration's (NASA) Manned Spacecraft Center, says that some communicable diseases could develop during 14-day-or-longer space missions if astronauts were exposed during preflight preparation. NASA would turn the spacecraft around and return it to earth if the condition were serious enough. Spacecraft will also be equipped with emergency medical supplies.

1964 July 16 Methods for astronauts to explore and get around on the moon are still being considered by National Aeronautics and Space Administration (NASA). Two devices are among the top candidates: a mobile laboratory in which men could work and also go out in spacesuits to gather samples, and a lunar hopper that resembles a helicopter for short flights to distant sites. Neither candidate is ever built, as NASA eventually goes with a simple lunar rover or car.

1964 July 28

Lunar probe impacts moon

1964 July 28 After six failures, the seventh lunar probe launched by National Aeronautics and Space Administration (NASA) finally succeeds. *Ranger 7* is launched from Cape Kennedy, Florida by an Atlas-Agena rocket, on a perfect trajectory to impact the moon. During the final 13 minutes before it crashes on the moon, its six cameras transmit 4,316 increasingly closer photographs back to earth. This one mission results in a gain factor of 2,000 in terms of the effective magnification of the lunar image.

1964 July 29 In its continuing evaluation of the paraglider system as a means of landing and recovering manned spacecraft, National Aeronautics and Space Administration (NASA) conducts a test flight in which a model Gemini capsule is towed to 6,000 feet by a helicopter, released, and maneuvers to a landing.

1964 July 31 First soaring flight to exceed 1,000 kilometers is made by Alvin H. Parker. Using thermals over the Great Plains, his elegant Sisu *1A* sailplane soars 1,040 meters (646 miles) from Odessa, Texas to Kimball, Nebraska.

1964 August 7 First manned free-flight test of the Gemini paraglider landing system is made at Edwards Air Force Base, California. When the Gemini mockup slung beneath the paraglider is released at 13,000 feet, the pilot loses control and is forced to bail out. The paraglider and capsule crash.

1964 August 10 Following the near-disastrous first free flight of the Gemini paraglider landing system on August 7, 1964, National Aeronautics and Space Administration (NASA) announces that the system will not be used for any scheduled Gemini flights. Water landings will be employed as they were in Project Mercury. NASA says that the paraglider system is simply too far behind in its development to be ready for the 12 scheduled Gemini flights.

1964 August 10 Fourteen newest National Aeronautics and Space Administration (NASA) astronauts begin a week-long desert survival course in Nevada under U.S. Air Force direction.

1964 August 25 Mobility tests of an astronaut wearing a pressurized suit while working in the rough, lava terrain of Oregon's Cascade Mountains are conducted by National Aeronautics and Space Administration (NASA).

1964 September 4 Forth Bridge, a new road suspension bridge located near the old Forth Railway Bridge in Scotland, opens to traffic. With a span of 3,300 feet (1,006 meters), it is the first 1,000-meter suspension bridge not designed and built by an American.

1964 September 8 Dr. Eugene B. Konecci (b. 1925), director of Biotechnology and Human Research for National Aeronautics and Space Administration (NASA), says that man in space has both pluses and minuses. As a transmitter, receiver, or control mechanism, man's capacity is limited compared to a machine's greater speed and capacity. But man, he says, "is the only available computer which can solve problems by logical induction, although unfortunately he cannot keep his emotions out of this thought process. He can make sense of fragmentary information."

1964 September 8 Statements by Soviet scientist A. G. Kuznetsov indicate that the Soviets have not yet determined which mixture of gases is best for manned space flight. The Vostok uses a mixture of nitrogen and oxygen.

1964 September 10 Jet-propelled back pack for Gemini astronauts is shown by Air Force Systems Command. It is part of the modular maneuvering unit (MMU) that Gemini crew will use during a planned space walk.

1964 September 10 U.S. Air Force Col. John M. Stapp tells an international gathering that pigs and bears had been used in tests to determine the best position for astronauts during the stress period of reentry. Human volunteers were used in 146 test runs, but anaesthetized bears and pigs were used for dangerous tests. The results indicate the safest position is landing backwards at a 45 degree angle to the line of impact.

1964 September 21 First flight of North American *XB-70 Valkyrie* is made. Originally planned as a manned U.S. strategic bomber that could fly at Mach 3 (three times the speed of sound) at altitudes above 70,000 feet, this aircraft does not go into production but is used only for research and testing. As such, it is the largest research aircraft ever built. Only two are built, one of which is destroyed in a mid-air collision with an *F-104* chase plane.

1964 October 1 Modern high-speed railroad line opens in Japan between Tokyo and Osaka. Run by the New Tokaido Line, this is the first of Japan's Shinkansen ("new railways"), which become widely known in the West as "bullet trains" because of their projectile-like styling. Its electric passenger trains will hit top speeds of 132 mph.

1964 October 12 First three-man space flight is achieved by the U.S.S.R. which launches *Voskhod 1* into orbit carrying Vladimir M. Komarov (1927—1967), Boris B. Yegorov (b. 1937) (a physician), and Konstantin P. Feoktistov (b. 1926) (a scientist). The Soviet Union captures another space first, although the brief mission (17 orbits in 24 hours, 17 minutes) and the extremely cramped quarters indicate a rush to fly. The spacecraft is basically a stripped-down, one-man Vostok. It has no ejection seats and the crew does not even wear spacesuits. The crew survives a hard landing in a field.

1964 October 19 Recruiting begins by National Aeronautics and Space Administration (NASA) for another 10 to 20 scientist-astronauts. Qualified applicants need a doctoral degree or its equivalent in the natural sciences, medicine, or engineering, and do not have to be qualified pilots, although those selected will be trained to fly.

1964 October 30 Former *X-15* test pilot Joseph Walker completes the first flight of the experimental Lunar Landing Research Vehicle for National Aeronautics and Space Administration (NASA). This four-legged vehicle that looks like it is made from an erector set is designed to simulate moon landing conditions and give Apollo astronauts some experience before they fly the lunar module.

1964 November 11 The world will be able to watch the first astronauts land on the moon, National Aeronautics and Space Administration (NASA) announces. Once on the surface, astronauts will also take transmit images back to earth as they walk along.

1964 November 21 Verrazano-Narrows Bridge between Brooklyn and Staten Island, New York for-

mally opens. Designed by Othmar H. Ammann (1879—1965), it is the longest suspension bridge when completed. With a main span of 4,260 feet (1,298 meters), it is so long that its designer has to factor in the curvature of the earth. Its two 690-foot (210-meter) towers are exactly perpendicular to the earth's surface, in that they are one-and-five-eighths inches farther apart at their tops than at their bases. Despite its size and grandeur, it offers no design breakthroughs and is really an elaboration of Roebling's Brooklyn Bridge.

1964 December 15 *San Marco 1*, a scientific satellite, is launched from Wallops Station, Virginia by an Italian crew trained by National Aeronautics and Space Administration (NASA). This is the first time a foreign country has designed, built, and launched a satellite into orbit as part of NASA's international program.

1964 December 18 More than 900 individuals apply to National Aeronautics and Space Administration (NASA) for the 10 to 20 scientist-astronaut positions. Altogether, NASA receives 1,351 applications or letters of interest.

1964 December 21 First major combat aircraft with variable geometry wings, General Dynamics *F-111*, makes its first flight. Flown by both the U.S. Air Force and Navy, the advanced fighter's wings can sweep fully forward during takeoff or back to more than 70 degrees for combat or high speeds.

1964 December 22 First flight of the Lockheed *SR-71 Blackbird* is made. This long-range reconnaissance Mach 3 (three times the speed of sound) aircraft uses its speed at great heights to evade interception. It is built in great secrecy in California and becomes the world's most reliable and capable aircraft for strategic reconnaissance. It sets a New York to London (3,470 miles or 5,584 kilometers) record of one hour, 55 minutes, 32 seconds. (See 1990)

1965 In Japan, the highway between Ritto and Amagasaki becomes part of the Meishin Highway, connecting Nagoya and Kobe. The stretch of newly-completed road which takes two hours to drive, is the first full-fledged highway in Japan.

1965 Brake lights and flashing directional light indicators finally become compulsory in Great Britain.

1964 Dec. 22

Mach 3 reconnaissance aircraft built

1965 First compulsory automobile exhaust emission controls are introduced in California. By 1968, every state has some form of emission control standards in force. Fuel shortages and anti-pollution legislation will force automakers to make major engine design changes in the coming years.

1965 A.D.

Largest front-wheel drive car built

1965 Largest front-wheel drive American production car, the Oldsmobile Toronado, is first introduced. This huge but sporty car is 17 feet, 7 inches long and 6 feet, 7 inches wide. It has a fastback body and retractable headlights, and an eight-cylinder engine producing 385 hp. General Motors produces a Cadillac version called the Eldorado.

1965 New diver propulsion vehicle is developed by the U.S. Navy. Called the Mark IV SDV (Swimmer Delivery Vehicle), it has a hydrodynamic design which both propels a diver and protects him as it reaches an underwater speed of five knots. It is electrically-powered.

1965 Zeeland Bridge in The Netherlands opens. One of the longest bridges in Europe, it connects North Beveland with Schouwen-Duiveland and cuts 20 miles from Rotterdam to Flushing.

1965 A.D.

Car-transporter ship built

1965 First ship built specifically to transport new automobiles to overseas dealers, the *Opama Maru*, is built in Japan. It can carry 1,200 cars.

1965 January 13 First transition flight, from vertical to horizontal flight, of the Hiller-Ryan-Vought *XC-142A* experimental V/STOL (vertical/short take-off and landing) aircraft. Resembling a conventional transport airplane, with four turbo-prop engines, the craft's entire wings and props rotate from normal horizontal to a full vertical position during transition flight. Although it works well, economic factors keep it from production.

1965 January 27 First use of an orbiting satellite is made as a radio link between a ground station and an aircraft in flight. U.S. communications satellite *Syncom 3* connects by radio a Pan American Boeing *707* and a remote ground control station. This successful test suggests the potential use of geostationary satellites (those whose orbit is synchronous with the earth and therefore stay fixed over one spot) for communication with aircraft.

1965 February 10 Four women are among the applicants being considered for the new scientist-astronaut positions, says National Aeronautics and Space Administration (NASA).

1965 February 12 First hovering flight of the French Dassault *Mirage III-V* VTOL (vertical take-off and landing) aircraft is made in France. Designed as a prototype for a Mach 2 (twice the speed of sound) VTOL fighter-bomber, this vectored-thrust system aircraft does not go into production because of a rash of accidents.

1965 February 16 Saturn I two-stage launch vehicle orbits a 33,000-pound payload from Cape Kennedy, Florida containing a model of the Apollo spacecraft and a *Pegasus* micrometeorite detection satellite. The Saturn/Apollo systems are tested and a satellite is orbited.

1965 February 17 *Ranger 7*, the second U.S. unmanned lunar photographic mission, is launched from Cape Kennedy, Florida. It returns 7,137 photos of the moon back to earth before crashing only 15 miles off target on the moon's Sea of Tranquility on February 20. The Sea of Tranquility is where men first land in 1969.

1965 February 25 First flight of the Douglas *DC-9* short-haul twin-jet airliner is made. This proves one of the most popular in its range and is produced in quantities for many airlines.

1965 March 6 First non-stop coast-to-coast helicopter flight across the North American continent is made by a Sikorsky *SH-3A Sea King*. Piloted by J. R. Williford, it flies 2,116 miles (3,405 kilometers) from the deck of the carrier *USS Hornet* in San Francisco, California to the deck of the carrier *USS Franklin D. Roosevelt* in Jacksonville, Florida.

1965 March 18 First man to walk in space is Soviet cosmonaut Aleksey Leonov (b. 1934), who is launched into orbit with Pavel Belyayev (1925—1970) in *Voskhod 2*. During the second orbit, Leonov floats outside the spacecraft, tethered by a cord providing him with oxygen and suit pressurization. The craft makes 18 orbits in 26 hours, two minutes, and lands well off target after making a forced and manually-controlled reentry and hard landing in a forest. The crew must contend with deep snow and wolves before being rescued. Once again, the Soviets do in space what has not yet been done.

1965 March 23 United States launches its first two-man spacecraft as *Gemini 3* is orbited by a two-stage Titan II from Cape Kennedy, Florida. Astronauts Virgil I. Grissom (1926—1967) and John W. Young (b. 1930) complete three orbits in a nearly five-hour flight. Their mission is the first to change its orbit (they make three trajectory changes) as well as the first to use an on-board computer. They land 52 miles off target in the Atlantic and Grissom gets badly seasick.

1965 March 24 Last spacecraft in the Ranger series is launched to the moon by National Aeronautics and Space Administration (NASA). As with its predecessors, it photographs potential landing sites until it crashes on the lunar surface. Of the nine Rangers launched, only the last three function properly and, together, return a total of 17,267 photographs of the moon's surface back to earth.

1965 April 6 First satellite intended for public telephone communications, *Early Bird 1*, is launched from Cape Kennedy, Florida by National Aeronautics and Space Administration (NASA). Designed and built by Hughes Aircraft, it is placed in geosynchronous orbit, approximately 35,900 kilometers above the earth. At this altitude, it makes one revolution in 24 hours, synchronous with the earth's rotation, and basically remains fixed above the same spot.

1965 May 5 Soviets announce that cosmonaut Aleksey Leonov (b. 1934), the first man to walk in space, received 1/230th of the permissable dose of radiation, showing that extra-vehicular activity is safe if done properly.

1965 May 6 Brazilian Space Commission (CNAE) and National Aeronautics and Space Administration (NASA) agree to cooperate in the launching of a scientific sounding rocket program to investigate lower regions of the atmosphere.

1965 June 3 First U.S. walk in space is conducted during mission of *Gemini 4* which is launched by a Titan II booster from Cape Kennedy, Florida. Astronauts James A. McDivitt (b. 1929) and Edward H. White II (1930—1967) make 62 orbits of the earth during their four-day, one-hour, 56-minute flight. White spends 20 minutes floating outside the capsule while tethered by a 25-foot-long cord that provides air and ventilation. He also uses a

hand-held maneuvering unit to move about in space. Europe gets its first live look at a launch via the Early Bird communications satellite. With this successful and spectacular flight, the United States begins to finally match the Soviets in space.

1965 June 12 First launch of the Canadian Black Brant 5B single-stage sounding rocket is made from Fort Churchill, Manitoba. It is designed to carry a scientific payload weighing 300 pounds as high as 300 miles.

1965 June 27 Six scientist-astronauts are selected by National Aeronautics and Space Administration (NASA) for the Apollo program. They are: Owen K. Garriott (b. 1930), Edward G. Gibson (b. 1936), Duane E. Graveline (b. 1931), Joseph P. Kerwin (b. 1932), Frank Curtis Michel (b. 1934), and Harrison Schmitt (b. 1935).

1965 July 12 Soviet cosmonaut Pavel Belyayev (1925—1970) writes in a Soviet newspaper that when his automatic landing system failed during reentry, he took manual control—something never done during any previous Soviet flight. The heat was so intense, he writes, that drops of molten metal ran down the portholes.

1965 July 12
Cosmonaut takes manual control of landing

1965 August 2 Prototype of a portable life support system (PLSS) is delivered by Hamilton Standard to National Aeronautics and Space Administration (NASA). Designed to be worn during a moon walk, it is a 60-pound back unit connected to a water-cooled undergarment the astronaut wears. It cools the astronaut by conducting his body heat into the water which would circulate through a web of plastic tubing in contact with his skin. The water would carry this heat into the portable unit which would recool and recirculate it. This system is used during all moon missions.

1965 August 2
Portable life support system built for moon walks

1965 August 5 First full-duration test firing of the Saturn V first stage is made at Marshall Space Flight Center, Huntsville, Alabama. During the two-and-one-half-minute static test, seven-and-one-half million pounds of thrust are generated by the five F-1 engines, each of which consumes liquid oxygen and kerosene at the rate of three tons a second.

1965 August 21 Two-man *Gemini 5* spacecraft is launched by a Titan II booster at Cape Kennedy, Florida. Astronauts L. Gordon Cooper (b. 1927) and Charles Conrad (b. 1930) make the longest U.S. flight to date and orbit the earth 120 times during their seven-day,

22-hour, 55-minute flight. The duration is significant since it matches the mission time of a moon flight.

1965 August 25 U.S. President Lyndon B. Johnson (1908—1973) announces he has approved development of the Manned Orbiting Laboratory (MOL) by the Department of Defense. Saying it will cost $1.5 billion, he states the program, "will bring us new knowledge about what man is able to do in space. It will enable us to relate that ability to the defense of America." Despite these moderate goals, the program will never put a man in space and will be cancelled in 1969.

1965 September 3 Paraglider makes its first successful manned free flight when a test pilot guides the spacecraft below to a preselected landing site at Edwards Air Force Base, California. Although scrubbed from the Gemini program, the paraglider or hang-glider concept is still being researched as a system by which a spacecraft can glide to earth after reentry.

c. 1965 ■ Paraglider used for the sport of hang-gliding.

1965
September 7

First combat
helicopter
flies

1965 September 7 First flight is made of Bell *209 Huey Cobra*, the first specially designed combat helicopter to go into large-scale service. Carrying guns, grenade launchers, missiles and rockets, this small attack helicopter is given considerable service by the United States in Vietnam.

1965 September 10 Astronaut recruiting is begun again by National Aeronautics and Space Administration (NASA) which feels it needs additional pilot/astronauts for its manned space flight missions. In a short time, NASA will have a surplus of men ready to fly and not enough missions to satisfy them all.

1965 September 30 U.S. President Lyndon B. Johnson (1908—1973) signs legislation authorizing a joint private-public high-speed transportation project along the Northeast Corridor between Washington, D.C., New York City, and Boston, Massachusetts. (See January 16, 1969)

1965 October Walter Dornberger (1895—1980), former chief of the German V-2 missile program and then-vice president for research at Bell Aerosystems Co., speaks on the eve of his retirement of what he believes the space future holds. His remarks include references to a permanent space station or military base in space which will be serviced by "a recoverable, reusable space transporter." This is an exact description of the space shuttle which first flies in 1981. The United States still has no permanent space station however.

1965 November 1 First regularly-scheduled rail service to run over 100 mph (161 km) is the Shinkansen or "bullet train" in Japan.

1965 November 15 First flight around the world overflying both Poles is made by U.S. airline Flying Tiger Line. Capt. J. L. Martin commands this flight using a Boeing *707*.

1965 November 26 France launches its first satellite, called *A-1*, with a three-stage Diamant booster from Hammaguir Range, Algeria. The 88-pound satellite carries a radio and radar transmitter but no scientific equipment.

1965 December 4 *Gemini 7* is launched by a Titan II booster from Cape Kennedy, Florida with astronauts Frank Borman (b. 1928) and James A. Lovell, Jr. (b. 1928) aboard. The spacecraft acts as a manned target for *Gemini 6* which is launched on December 15. Borman and Lovell spend nearly 14 days in their tiny Gemini cabin, testing their reactions to long duration Zero G. After splashdown in the Atlantic, the bearded men emerge in good condition but, as Borman says, "a little crummy." (See December 15, 1965)

1965 December 14 Longest simulated space voyage to date ends as four U.S. Air Force officers emerge from a simulated space capsule after 56 days.

They function in an oxygen-helium atmosphere and eat dehydrated foods. They are also able to exercise, watch TV, and wash. They complete their mission in obviously good condition.

1965 December 15 *Gemini 6* is launched by a Titan II booster from Cape Kennedy, Florida with astronauts Walter Schirra, Jr. (b. 1923) and Thomas P. Stafford (b. 1930) aboard. The purpose of this one-day mission is to rendezvous in space with the manned *Gemini 7* as its target. Schirra maneuvers his spacecraft to within one foot of *Gemini 7* and the two later fly together in formation 20 to 100 feet apart for over five hours. Reentry is near perfect as the craft splashes down in the Atlantic only 14 miles off target.

1966 *Unsafe at Any Speed* is written by American consumer activist Ralph Nader (b. 1934). This exposé of many of the faults of the U.S. automobile industry spurs Congressional interest and legislation. It is partly responsible for the enactment of the National Traffic and Motor Vehicle Safety Act which goes into law. **(See 1959)**

1966 U.S. Department of Transportation is created at Cabinet level to provide leadership in the identification of transportation problems and solutions, stimulate new technological advances, encourage cooperation among all interested parties, and recommend national policies and programs to accomplish these objectives.

1966 First electronic fuel-injection system for automobiles is developed by the British. A small computer checks engine operations, then injects or sprays an appropriate amount of fuel into each cylinder.

1966 Turkey builds it first passenger car. Called the Anadol, it is built in Istanbul by Otosan in conjunction with British Reliant Motors.

1966 Modern lighthouse is built at Dungeness in Kent, England using an entirely new method. The 130-foot-high tower is constructed from 21 pre-cast concrete rings which interlock with each other. The rings are stressed vertically with cables that run top-to-bottom. It has a foghorn and the xenon high-pressure arc lamp light is unattended.

1966 January 1 First "official" transit strike in New York City history occurs. With all forms of mass transit shut down, the city is engulfed in automobiles as people try to use their cars to get to work. Morning and evening gridlock occurs and just as many people crowd the sidewalks, as walking is the only alternative. The strike ends on January 13.

1966 January 6 In its most recent call for astronaut applicants, National Aeronautics and Space Administration (NASA) receives 351 responses. Of these, 192 (including all six female candidates) do not meet the minimum requirements. Of the remainder, 15 will be chosen.

1966 February 3 First soft-landing on the moon is made by the Soviet unmanned spacecraft *Lunik 9* which touches down in the Ocean of Storms. It carries an instrument package which begins relaying data back to earth.

1966 February 26 First U.S. launch of the Saturn IB (uprated Saturn) booster and the unmanned Apollo spacecraft. This successful test proves Apollo's worthiness during a reentry of about 4000 degrees Fahrenheit.

1966 February 28 Gemini astronauts Charles A. Bassett II (1931—1966) and Elliot M. See, Jr. (1927—1966) are killed when their *T-38* aircraft crashes into a building at St. Louis Municipal Airport while attempting to land in rain and fog. They were flying to McDonnell Aircraft Corp. for two weeks of training on a space simulator for their upcoming spaceflight.

1966 March 1 First spacecraft to land on another planet is the Soviet Union's *Venus 3* which reaches the surface of Venus. Launched on November 16, 1965, it carries instrumentation which relays data back to earth until it crashes on the surface.

1966 March 2 One millionth Ford Mustang is produced since this highly popular car was first introduced less than two years before. **(See April 1964)**

1966 March 14 First flight of the "stretched" Douglas *DC-8-61* airliner, with a capacity for 251 passengers, is made in the United States.

1966 March 16 First docking in space occurs as National Aeronautics and Space Administration (NASA) launches *Gemini 8* from Cape Kennedy, Florida on a Titan II booster. Manned by astronauts Neil A. Arm-

1966 February 3

Soviet spacecraft soft-lands on moon

1966 March 1

Soviet spacecraft crash-lands on Venus

strong (b. 1930) and David R. Scott (b. 1932), Gemini maneuvers toward the unmanned Agena target rocket already in orbit and easily achieves docking with it. After less than one-half hour of docking, a short-circuited thruster suddenly turns on, causing the joined spacecraft to roll and yaw violently. Armstrong quickly undocks, but the Gemini stays out of control, spinning one complete revolution every second. Armstrong turns off the automatic system and uses his reentry rockets to stop the spin. They then reenter safely but much earlier than planned.

1966 April 4 Selection of 19 astronauts is announced by National Aeronautics and Space Administration (NASA). They are civilians Vance D. Brand (b. 1931), Fred W. Haise, Jr. (b. 1933), Don L. Lind (b. 1930), and John L. Swigert, Jr. (1931—1982); Air Force officers Charles M. Duke, Jr. (b. 1935), Joe H. Engle (b. 1932), Edward G. Givens, Jr. (1930—1967), James B. Irwin (b. 1930), William R. Pogue (b. 1930), Stuart A. Roosa (b. 1933), and Alfred M. Worden (b. 1932); Navy officers John S. Bull (b. 1935), Ronald E. Evans (b. 1933), Thomas K. Mattingly (b. 1936), Bruce McCandless II (b. 1937), Edgar D. Mitchell (b. 1930), and Paul J. Weitz (b. 1932); and Marine officers Gerald P. Carr (b. 1932) and Jack R. Lousma (b. 1936).

1966 April 6 First regular passenger service across the English Channel by hovercraft is begun by Hoverlloyd Ltd.

1966 April 29 One of the world's largest and most sensitive automatic space tracking and telemetry antennas is officially dedicated at Goldstone, California. This 210-foot dish antenna is the newest in National Aeronautics and Space Administration's (NASA) Deep Space Network and is fully steerable.

1966 May 18—June 20 First round-the-world solo flight by a woman is made by British pilot Sheila Scott. She flies 29,000 miles (46,670 kilometers) in stages in her Piper Comanche *Myth Too.*

1966 May 30 First U.S. spacecraft to soft-land on the moon, *Surveyor 1,* is launched by an Atlas-Centaur booster. The first in a series of seven spacecraft designed to measure the bearing strength of the lunar surface, it lands on the moon June 2, 1966 and begins transmitting the first of its more than 10,000 clear, detailed TV images to earth. It is a three-legged arrangement of cameras, antennas, and instruments.

1966 June 3 *Gemini 9* is launched by a Titan II from Cape Kennedy, Florida carrying astronauts Thomas P. Stafford (b. 1930) and Eugene A. Cernan (b. 1934). When its Agena target rocket fails to deploy properly, docking exercises become impossible. After practicing rendezvous techniques, astronaut Cernan exits Gemini and walks in space but is not able to use the astronaut maneuvering unit with which he was supposed to fly freely about the spacecraft. Reentry is remarkably precise, landing within one mile of the recovery ship.

1966 June 24 Air India Boeing *707* airliner crashes into Mont Blanc, 45 feet below its peak, while trying to land in Geneva, Switzerland. All 117 people aboard are killed.

1966 July 12 First unpowered flight of Northrop *M2-F2* lifting body reentry research vehicle is made. Built with a body shape resembling the letter "D" flying on its side (flat side up), this small aircraft is dropped from a *B-52* at 45,000 feet (13,710 meters) to test its reentry characteristics in anticipation of National Aeronautics and Space Administration's (NASA) future space shuttle design. It makes its first powered reentry flight on November 25, 1970. The program ends in December 1972, having provided NASA with a wealth of powered reentry information. (See March 19, 1970)

1966 July 18 *Gemini 10* rendezvous and docking mission is launched by a Titan II booster from Cape Kennedy, Florida with astronauts John W. Young (b. 1930) and Michael Collins (b. 1930) aboard. After docking with the Agena target rocket, it uses that vehicle's engine to boost the joined craft to a higher orbit. Collins performs a tethered spacewalk and maneuvers back and forth between the two orbiting spacecraft. The mission demonstrates the excellent mobility of both astronauts and their spacecraft.

1966 July 18 U.S. Air Force announces its Manned Orbiting Laboratory (MOL) is progressing toward an October launch. An operational MOL would consist of a modified Gemini spacecraft connected to a "can-shaped" laboratory. The launch never occurs.

1966 August "First disaster in space will occur in 1967" is among the predictions for the coming year that are made by *Old Moore's Almanack*. This is the newest edition of a journal published in England for 270 years. (See January 27, 1967 and April 27, 1967)

1966 August 10 First of five lunar photographic missions begins with the launch of *Surveyor 1* by an Atlas-Agena D booster. This unmanned spacecraft becomes the first U.S. spacecraft to orbit the moon after a 92-hour flight crossing 236,319 miles of space. It returns 211 dual frames of film showing potential Surveyor and Apollo landing sites.

1966 August 16 George E. Mueller (b. 1918), associate administrator for Manned Space Flight at National Aeronautics and Space Administration (NASA), says NASA's principal consideration regarding men in space is safety. He states, however, that the cost, complexities, and uncertainties involving the rescue of astronauts in space makes it appear that it is better to spend the time and money on making flights safer in the first place.

1966 August 31 First hovering flight of British Hawker Siddeley *Harrier* fighter aircraft is made. Three years later it becomes the first jet-powered V/STOL (vertical/short take-off and landing) combat aircraft to gain operational status.

1966 September 8 Severn Bridge, connecting England and Wales, officially opens. This suspension bridge achieves a major breakthrough in design, resulting also in a substantial reduced cost breakthrough. The major advance, attributable to English engineer Gilbert Roberts, is its deck design which is streamlined so that it lessens wind resistance. This does away with the need for stiffening girders. By reducing the amount of steel used throughout, the cost of this innovative bridge is one-tenth that of Verrazano.

1966 September 12 *Gemini 11* is launched into earth orbit by a Titan II booster with astronauts Charles Conrad, Jr. (b. 1930) and Richard F. Gordon (b. 1929) aboard. During their three-day mission, the crew achieves docking with the Agena rocket target during their first orbit. They then use its engine to fly 700 miles higher in orbit. The walk in space still poses some problems. After a fully automatic retrofire and reentry, Gemini splashes down within one-and-one-half miles of its recovery ship.

1966 November 11 In the tenth and final mission in the two-man Gemini program, *Gemini 12* is launched by a Titan II booster with astronauts James A. Lovell, Jr. (b. 1928) and Edwin E. Aldrin, Jr. (b. 1930) aboard. This flight is a final tune-up and preparation for the Apollo series to come, and it goes very well. The crew docks with the Agena rocket target vehicle and Aldrin has no problems with his space walk, staying outside his spacecraft for two hours, eight minutes. They reenter on target, about three miles from the recovery ship and are picked up in 20 minutes.

1966 November 15 Project Gemini is officially ended by National Aeronautics and Space Administration (NASA). It achieves all its pre-Apollo space flight goals, and its crews spend 1,993 hours, 34 minutes in space.

1966
Nov. 15

Project
Gemini ends

1966 December 23 First flight of the French Dassault *Mirage F-1* is made in France. This high-performance multi-mission fighter incorporates many new changes, including the use of swept wings.

1967 Longest and heaviest train ever assembled and run is the U.S. freight train comprising 500 coal cars. Weighing 43,000 tons and extending four miles (6.5 kilometers), this record train is pulled by three 3,600-hp diesel locomotives. Its run is between Iager, Virginia and Portsmouth, Ohio.

1967 A.D.

500-car train
runs

1967 First rotary-engine Mazda, a model 110S, is produced. (See 1963)

1967 Sweden changes its rules of the road, requiring drivers to switch from driving on the left and to begin driving on the right. This matches the rest of continental Europe, and only Britain remains driving on the left.

1967 Mass transit in the United States continues its downward spiral, as the year-end totals equal only eight billion. This is down from a 1945 high of 23 billion. More Americans are using automobiles to get around.

1967 New subway system opens in Montreal, Quebec, Canada. The cars on this underground rail system have rubber tires.

1967 January 27 Representatives of 62 nations sign the Outer Space Treaty at separate ceremonies in Washington, D.C., London, England, and in Moscow, U.S.S.R. This first real application of law to space activities, among its several clauses, prevents all nations from claiming any celestial body and prohibits the orbiting of weapons of mass destruction.

1967 January 27

Three astronauts die in spacecraft fire

1967 January 27 Three U.S. astronauts die, apparently instantly, when a flash fire sweeps through their Apollo spacecraft during a launch countdown demonstration test being conducted on the ground. Killed are Virgil I. Grissom (1926—1967), one of the original seven Mercury astronauts; Edward H. White II (1930—1967), first American to walk in space; and Roger B. Chaffee (1935—1967), preparing for his first space flight. Fire is caused by an electrical short circuit which sparks and turns the 100% oxygen atmosphere into an instant inferno. Accident investigation will cause a year's delay, but many feel that it resulted in the discovery and correction of many faults, without which men would have never have reached the moon.

1967 January 28 James E. Webb (b. 1906), administrator of National Aeronautics and Space Administration (NASA), comments on tragic Apollo fire of the previous day, saying, "We've always known that something like this would happen sooner or later, but it's not going to be permitted to stop the program…. Although everyone realized that some day space pilots would die, who would have thought the first tragedy would be on the ground?"

1967 January 31

Pure oxygen fire occurs again

1967 January 31 In a bizarre replay of the Apollo tragedy of four days earlier, two U.S. Air Force officers die at Brooks Air Force Base, Texas when they enter a pure oxygen chamber to take blood samples from rabbits who are under observation to determine the effects of pure oxygen on the blood. Both airmen die within hours of burns from the flash fire. Pure oxygen is proving to be a highly dangerous environment.

1967 February 3 Three Apollo astronauts who died January 27, 1967 were killed by "asphyxiation due to smoke inhalation," National Aeronautics and Space Administration (NASA) reports. Fire cause is unknown at this time.

1967 February 6 U.S. Air Force announces it will not use a pure oxygen atmosphere on its manned flights. The planned Manned Orbiting Laboratory (MOL) program will use a mixture of oxygen and helium. It is less of a fire hazard, is lightweight, and conducts heat away from the spacecraft.

1967 February 25 In its third interim report, the Review Board created to investigate all aspects of the fatal fire of January 27, 1967, indicates a number of items related to the design and performance of Apollo's environmental control unit that will require careful examination and probable redesign.

1967 March 6 Using measurements verified by two Lunar Orbiter spacecraft, two Jet Propulsion Laboratory scientists now can calculate lunar distances with an accuracy of less than 50 feet compared to a previous discrepancy of one mile. They calculate the distance between the earth and the moon at 250,000 miles with a variation of 20,500 miles.

1967 March 18 First major oil pollution disaster at sea occurs off Land's End, England as supertanker *Torrey Canyon* runs aground and rips a 650-foot- (198-meter-) long hole in its hull. From this, it spills about 833,000 barrels of crude oil that soils the coasts of England and France. This is the first of several increasingly disastrous oil spills to occur since the introduction of VLCCs (very large crude carriers) over 100,000 tons.

1967 March 29 First flight of the Hindustan Aeronautics *HAL HF-24 Marut* is made in Bangalore, India. This single-seat supersonic jet-fighter is the first India-designed fighter.

1967 April 6 Trans World Airlines becomes the first American airline to have a fleet composed entirely of jet aircraft.

1967 April 9 Final report of Apollo Review Board which investigated the fatal fire of January 27, 1967 indicates that the probable cause was a sparking short circuit in worn, defective, or poorly insulated wire. It also said the following contributed to the disaster: a sealed cabin with an oxygen atmosphere; combustible materials throughout the cabin; vulnerable wiring; inadequate crew escape procedures; and inadequate rescue provisions. This is an almost across-the-board condemnation of the way things were done. The Board offers 21 specific recommendations that must be implemented.

1967 April 23—24 First Soviet cosmonaut to die in space is veteran Vladimir M. Komarov (1927—1967). After the successful launch of the *Soyuz 1* spacecraft, trouble occurs after about one full day in space. Komarov was to have been a target for a second Soyuz with a crew of three, but several system malfunctions cause him to attempt an emergency reentry. Soviets announce that the tumbling spacecraft caused the parachute to fail, resulting in a high-speed impact. But many observers feel that Komarov may have already died during a high-temperature reentry, again caused by a tumbling spacecraft. Like the United States after its Apollo fire, the Soviets will spend a year reassessing and correcting.

1967 April 26 First satellite launched into orbit from a platform at sea is Italy's *San Marco 2*. It is launched by National Aeronautics and Space Administration (NASA) in cooperation with the Italian Space Commission (ISC).

1967 May 28 British sailor Francis Chichester (1901—1972) reaches Plymouth, England having completed the fastest circumnavigation of the world in a small boat. His *Gipsy Moth* travels 15,517 miles in 119 days, averaging 130 miles a day. It is 54 feet long, weighs 11.5 tons, and has over 2,400 square feet of sail.

1967 May 31—June 1967 First non-stop helicopter crossing of the North Atlantic is made by two Sikorsky *HH-3E*'s. They fly from New York to Paris, France in 30 hours, 46 minutes. Each helicopter refuels nine times while covering the 4,270 miles (6,872 kilometers).

1967 June Suez Canal is closed to all shipping because of the Arab-Israeli War. Fourteen ships are trapped in the Bitter Lakes and one in Lake Timsah. The war leaves mines as well as wrecks behind, and these must be removed before the Canal can reopen. (See 1974)

1967 June 6 First U.S. astronaut to die off-duty is Edward G. Givens (1930—1967), who is killed when the car he is driving misses a curve and crashes into an embankment. Givens had been selected on April 4, 1966.

1967 June 9 Two scientists from the National Center for Air Pollution suggest that the decrease in the worldwide air temperature since the 1940s might be caused by man-made pollutants in the atmosphere. The scientists note that rather than causing a temperature drop, prolonged coal and oil burning should have made temperatures rise. The latter phenomenon is now recognized as the debated and controversial "greenhouse effect."

1967 June 29 Eight U.S. Apollo astronauts fly to Iceland for an eight-day expedition to gather geological data from an area believed to be similar to the moon's surface. Fifteen astronauts will join them later.

1967 June 30 U.S. Air Force names four of its pilots to the Manned Orbiting Laboratory (MOL) program. Among the names is Robert H. Lawrence, Jr. (1935—1967), the nation's first black man to be selected for a space mission.

1967 June 30

First black selected as astronaut

1967 July 8 First Soviet variable-geometry (moveable wings offering a range of sweep) fighters, *MiG-23* and *Su-7B*, are revealed publicly for the first time, at an air display at Moscow's Domodedovo airport. The MiG-2324 is later used during the Soviet conflict in Afganistan.

1967 August 4 Eleven civilian scientist-astronauts are selected by National Aeronautics and Space Administration (NASA). They are: Joseph P. Allen (b. 1937), Philip K. Chapman (b. 1935), Anthony W. England (b. 1942), Karl G. Henize (b. 1926), Donald L. Holmquest (b. 1939), William B. Lenoir (b. 1939), John A. Llewellyn (b. 1933), Franklin S. Musgrave (b. 1935), Brian T. O'Leary (b. 1940), Robert A. Parker (b. 1936), and William E. Thornton (b. 1929). All have either a Ph.D or an M.D. degree.

1967 August 8 World's longest non-stop air route is inaugurated jointly by Aerolineas Argentinas and Iberia. Flying between Buenos Aires, Argentina and Madrid, Spain, the route covers 6,462 miles (10,400 kilometers).

1967 August 18 First two Apollo spacesuits incorporating changes recommended by the Apollo Review Board arrive at the Manned Spacecraft Center, Houston, Texas. Most of the changes involve replacement of flammable with non-flammable materials and overall greater fire-resistance properties.

1967 August 18

Safer spacesuits introduced

1967 September Sweden changes to driving on the right side of the road, leaving only England and a few Commonwealth or ex-Commonwealth countries driving on the left side.

1967 October U.S. railroads announce plans for an Automatic Car Identification (ACI) system to promptly locate freight cars. It will work in conjunction with TeleRail Automated Information Network (TRAIN), with its central computer in Washington, D.C.

1967 October 5 U.S. astronaut Clifton C. Williams, Jr. (1932—1967) is killed when his *T-38* jet aircraft crashes and disintegrates near Tallahasee, Florida. He apparently blacked out from an oxygen deficiency.

1967 November 9 First all-up test of the three-stage Saturn V launch vehicle is made at Kennedy Space Center, Florida. Its S-IVB third stage is placed in orbit and restarts there for the first time. The unmanned Apollo command module reenters on target with no problems. As the most powerful launch vehicle yet developed by the United States, the Saturn V stands 363 feet tall with Apollo sitting on top.

1967 December 8

First black astronaut killed

1967 December 8 U.S. astronaut Robert H. Lawrence, Jr. (1935—1967), the first black man selected for a mission in the nation's space program, is killed during a routine training flight when his *F-104* aircraft crashes on landing at Edwards Air Force Base, California. Counting one Soviet, he is the sixth astronaut to die during 1967.

1967 December 16 First transition from vertical to horizontal flight is made by the German Dornier *Do 31E*. This experimental VTOL (vertical take-off and landing) has two engines—one for vertical lift and the other for horizontal flight. Although it is a simple system, it is also a considerably heavy arrangement.

1968 Lincoln Continental is specially built as the U.S. president's limousine. It weighs 5.5 tons, including 2 tons of steel plate. It is just as fast as a regular limo and is designed to travel 50 mph even with all its tires shot out.

1968 United States requires antipollution devices on all cars to control hydrocarbon emissions.

1968 Belgium completes the upgrading of the Canal de Charleroi à Bruxelles, begun in 1957. Engineer Gustave Willems builds a mile-long inclined plane which covers a rise of 223 feet and eliminates 28 old locks and a 3,500-foot tunnel. Vessels are transported individually overland from one body of water to another while floating in a barge that is essentially a rail car and runs on steel rails.

1968 Diver's Unisuit is introduced in Sweden. This underwater suit can be used for most diving operations under any climatic conditions. It is a completely dry suit and has an air or gas layer around the diver's body providing insulation.

1968 January 7 *Surveyor 7*, the seventh and last spacecraft in National Aeronautics and Space Administration's (NASA) program to analyze the lunar surface is launched. It soft lands on the moon on January 9, becoming the fifth U.S. spacecraft to do so, and transmits photos of the lunar surface back to earth. Besides the valuable photos, Surveyor has demonstrated that the bearing strength of the moon's surface is adequate for a spacecraft of its size and weight.

1968 January 31 *Lunar Orbiter 5*, the fifth and last of National Aeronautics and Space Administration's (NASA) project to photograph potential landing sites, is crashed onto the moon. Launched August 1, 1967, it is sent into the moon after making 1,200 orbits and nearly exhausting its supply of altitude control gas. NASA does not want any wildly-acting or uncontrollable bodies orbiting the moon for its upcoming manned missions. The entire Lunar Orbiter project photographed 99% of the lunar surface during 6,034 orbits.

1968 February 8 Apollo Site Selection Board formed by National Aeronautics and Space Administration (NASA) chooses five ellipse-shaped, three-by-five-mile lunar landing areas. Criteria for selection are area smoothness, approach path, propellant conservation, countdown recycling time, free-return trajectory, optimum lighting, and slope. The first two sites are in the Sea of Tranquility where man will first touch down. The Board used Lunar Orbiter and Surveyor photos during its work.

1968 February 29 Iowa State University scientist James A. Van Allen (b. 1914) says that the dominance of manned flight in national funding is detrimental to unmanned, scientific missions. Although he is not an outright opponent of manned space flight, he says that so far man has done nothing in space but survive.

1968 March 14 First manned Apollo mission will use 60% oxygen and 40% nitrogen in the cabin atmosphere while on the launch pad, National Aeronau-

1968 ■ Dulles International Airport, Washington, D.C.

tics and Space Administration (NASA) announces. In orbit, Apollo will use pure oxygen. NASA states that pure oxygen can be used in space with assurance, since it had made proper safety changes.

1968 March 27 First man in space, Soviet cosmonaut Yuri A. Gagarin (1934—1968), is killed with a comrade when their *MiG-15* jet aircraft crashes northwest of Moscow during a training flight.

1968 April 21 Soviet Union reports that its unmanned spacecraft, *Cosmos 112* and *Cosmos 113*, achieved an automatic docking on April 15. The spacecraft were also able to change orbits, reorient, and maneuver in space. The Soviet's unmanned spacecraft duplicate what the United States achieved in the manned Gemini program.

1968 April 22 Space rescue treaty is signed in three different cities by representatives of 43 nations. The treaty provides for assistance to astronauts in an emergency and for the safe return of the crews and the space hardware. After the past year's accidents, both major powers realize such a treaty is in everyone's interest.

1968 May 5 First non-stop Atlantic crossing by an executive jet aircraft is made as a Grumman *Gulfstream II* lands in London, England after completing a 3,500-mile (5,633 kilometers) flight from Teterboro, New Jersey.

1968 May 6 U.S. astronaut Neil A. Armstrong ejects from National Aeronautics and Space Administration's (NASA) Lunar Landing Research Vehicle (LLRV) and parachutes safely at Ellington Air Force Base, Texas. Armstrong had reached 500 feet during a simulated lunar landing when his test craft suddenly malfunctioned, crashed, and burned on impact. Armstrong survives to be the first man on the moon next year.

1968 May 22 First flight of a Spanish-built *SF-5B* is made. This is a two-seat trainer version of the Northrop *F-5* fighter.

1968 May 27 U.S. nuclear-powered attack submarine *Scorpion* is lost in the Atlantic Ocean off the Azores. It had a crew of 99 men aboard.

1968 June 20 Romanian airline Tarom begins its Bucharest-Frankfurt service using a British Aircraft Corporation *One-Eleven* (YR-BCA) aircraft.

1968 June 30 First flight of the Lockheed *C-5A Galaxy* is made at Dobbins Air Force Base, Georgia. Intended for use as a heavy logistics transport, it is at this time the world's largest airplane.

1968 July 15 First direct flights between the United States and the Soviet Union begin as commercial jets from each country (Pan American and Aeroflot) fly between New York and Moscow.

1968 July 15

U.S.—U.S.S.R. direct flights begin

1968 August 5 A special airstrip for STOL (short take-off and landing) operations is put into use at La Guardia Airport, New York.

1968 August 6 U.S. Air Force experiments on human reactions to extreme heat indicate that astronauts could possibly survive reentry through the earth's atmosphere if the cabin cooling system fails. In tests at Wright-Patterson Air Force Base, Ohio, subjects were subjected to 300—400 degrees heat in a four-foot-high oven three times a day. Some could stand up to 15 minutes at 300 degrees. The upper limit was two to three minutes at 400 degrees.

1968 August 6

Extreme heat experiments conducted

1968 September 8 First flight of the British-French SEPECAT *Jaguar E-01* is made in France. This single-seat fighter performs well at low altitudes and has a range of sensors in its nose for night operations.

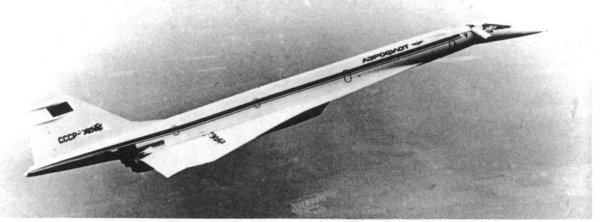

1968 ■ Soviet Tupolev *Tu-144* supersonic transport.

1968 October 11 *Apollo 7*, first manned mission in the U.S. Apollo lunar landing program, is launched successfully by a Saturn IB booster from the Kennedy Space Center, Florida. This nearly 11-day mission in earth orbit goes perfectly as the crew, astronauts Walter M. Schirra, Jr. (b. 1923), Donn F. Eisele (b. 1930), and R. Walter Cunningham (b. 1932), fully tests the command and service modules. The Service Propulsion System (SYS) engine is fired eight times, once for 66 seconds to simulate lunar orbit insertion and de-orbit burns. They splash down in the Atlantic after 163 revolutions of the earth.

1968 October 24 Final flight of North American *X-15* is made. This is the 199th flight of this U.S. rocket research aircraft that often flew over Mach 6 (six times the speed of sound) and into the upper reaches of the atmosphere (350,000 feet).

1968 October 26 Soviet Union launches *Soyuz 3* with cosmonaut Georgy T. Beregovoy (b. 1942) on board. The mission lasts three days, 22 hours, 51 minutes and includes a rendezvous with the unmanned *Soyuz 2* that was launched a day earlier. This flight marks no real progress in the Soviet manned space flight program.

1968 December 3 International space treaty, Agreement on the Rescue of Astronauts, the Return of Astronauts, and the Return of Space Objects, is proclaimed in effect by U.S. President Lyndon B. Johnson (1908—1973). This humanitarian agreement is recognized as being in the interests of all parties.

1968 December 21 First manned mission to orbit the moon is successfully conducted by the crew of *Apollo 8*. The huge Saturn V launch vehicle propels a manned mission into space for the first time, as astronauts Frank Borman (b. 1928), James A. Lovell, Jr. (b. 1928), and William A. Anders (b. 1933) enter lunar orbit on Christmas Eve. Their readings from the Book of Genesis as they circle the moon on Christmas Day makes this one of the most memorable space flights in history. They reenter and splash down safely after a six-day, three-hour flight.

1968 December 31 First flight of the Tupolev *Tu-144*, the world's first supersonic jet transport. This flight is the first time that its Kuznetsov NK-144 turbofan engines are tested in the air. It soon begins regular service. It later becomes the first commercial transport to exceed Mach 2 (twice the speed of sound).

1969 This is the worst year for road fatalities in the United States, as 54,895 people are killed. In this century, more than 25 million people have been killed on the world's roads. At this rate, the year 2000 could see the automobile claiming more victims than World Wars I and II combined.

1969 First stage of a combined underground and surface subway system (patterned after the Paris Metro Chemin de Fer Metropolitan) opens in Mexico City, Mexico.

1969 Federal safety standards for automobiles are introduced nationally by the U.S. government.

1969 First French nuclear-powered submarine *Redoutable* is completed. (See 1971)

1969 First LASH ship, the Japanese-built *Acadia Forest,* is launched. This specialized LASH container ship (Lighter Aboard SHip) carries very large floating containers called lighters. It is equipped with a massive gantry crane that straddles the deck and is used to load and unload lighters. Each lighter has a 400-ton capacity and is stowed in the holds on deck. Loading and discharging is rapid (15 minutes per lighter), and no port or dock facilities are necessary, since a group of lighters can be towed by tugs onto inland waterways.

1969 First ship to use a special air-bubble system for moving through ice, the *Finncarrier,* is built by Finland. This cargo ferry uses compressed air, which is forced through holes in the lower hull and combines with water, to form a kind of slippery film that reduces friction.

1969 January 14 *Soyuz 4* is launched into earth orbit by the Soviet Union with cosmonaut Vladimir Shatalov (b. 1927) aboard. This spacecraft is the target for *Soyuz 5* which is launched the following day with a crew of three cosmonauts. The two spacecraft dock and Shatalov receives two cosmonauts from *Soyuz 5.* His craft, *Soyuz 4,* reenters and lands safely with a crew of three on January 17. (See January 15, 1969)

1969 January 15 An underwater test program begins at Marshall Space Flight Center, Huntsville, Alabama as National Aeronautics and Space Administration (NASA) plans for the first U.S. space station. Since weightlessness is impossible to duplicate for more than a fraction of a minute, NASA puts subjects in spacesuits underwater to approximate working conditions in an orbiting space workshop.

1969 January 15 *Soyuz 5* is launched into earth orbit by the Soviet Union with cosmonauts Yevegeny Khrunov (b. 1933), Boris Volnyov (b. 1934), and Aleksey Yeliseyev (b. 1943) aboard. After docking with *Soyuz 4,* which contains cosmonaut Vladimir Shatalov (b. 1927), cosmonauts Khrunov and Yeliseyev conduct the first two-man walk in space (for one hour) before they enter *Soyuz 4* and eventually land safely on earth with Shatalov on January 17. Volynov reenters alone in *Soyuz 5* on January 18. This is the first time men have switched spacecraft in space.

1969 January 16 "Metroliner" first enters service on the Penn Central, running between New York and Washington, D.C. This six-coach electric train covers the 224 miles (360 kilometers) in 179 minutes. This time is soon reduced to 150 minutes.

1969 February 9 First flight of the Boeing 747 "Jumbo Jet" airliner is made near Seattle, Washington. This wide-bodied, long-range transport is capable of carrying 347 passengers, and is the largest aircraft in commercial airline service in the world. In addition to standard passenger versions, this popular aircraft allows for many easily-made changes, including a nose-loading door for special cargo.

*1969
February 9

First "Jumbo Jet" flies*

1969 ■ Boeing 747 airliner.

1969 February 12 First flight of the Soviet Mil *Mi-12* is made. This twin-rotor aircraft is the world's largest helicopter, with an overall span over the rotor tips of 219 feet, 10 inches (67 meters), and a fuselage length of 121 feet, 4½ inches (37 meters). It later sets a payload-lifting record of 88,636 pounds (40,204 kilograms), lifted to a height of 7,398 feet (2255 meters).

1969 March 2 First flight of the British Aircraft Corporation/Aérospatiale *Concorde 001* supersonic transport is made in Toulouse, France. Although the product of joint British-French collaboration, *Concorde 001* is assembled in France. It becomes the first supersonic commercial transport to operate regularly scheduled passenger service. Both British Airways and Air France offer service to New York.

*1969
March 2

First SST flies*

1969 March 3 *Apollo 9,* third manned Apollo mission, is launched by a Saturn V from Cape Kennedy,

1969 ■ *Concorde* supersonic transport takes off.

Florida with astronauts James A. McDivitt (b. 1929), David R. Scott (b. 1932), and Russell L. Schweickart (b. 1935) aboard. During this in-space simulation of a lunar landing mission, the lunar module is flown as a separate spacecraft for the first time, and the first crew transfer is made via an internal docking connection. Schweickart performs a space walk, holding on to spacecraft handrails, and tests the new Apollo space suit and its unique portable life-support system back-pack. Splashdown occurs after a space mission of ten days and one hour.

1969 March 10

Why machine won't replace man in space

1969 March 10 Explaining why man cannot be replaced in space by a machine, George E. Mueller (b. 1918), National Aeronautics and Space Administration (NASA) associate administrator for manned space flight, says man has three unique capabilities: "he has a very wide-band set of sensors for acquiring information; he has in his head a built-in memory and computer that cannot yet be matched by our largest and fastest machines; and finally he has a remarkably versatile capability for action, and physical operations with his body, hands, and tools."

1969 March 19 First scheduled jet air service inside the Arctic Circle begins as Nordair inaugurates a weekly return service between Montreal, Canada and Resolution Bay, Cornwallis Island, Canada.

1969 April 8 High-speed TurboTrains service begins between New York and Boston, and Montreal and Toronto. These experimental trains are powered by aircraft turbines.

1969 April 9 First U.K.-assembled supersonic transport, *Concorde 002*, makes a successful first flight in England.

1969 April 14 Astronaut Neil A. Armstrong (b. 1930) will be the first man to step on the moon, announces National Aeronautics and Space Administration (NASA). He will be followed by astronaut Edwin E. Aldrin, Jr. (b. 1930) during *Apollo 11*.

1969 April 28 First transatlantic flight by a vectored-thrust VTOL (vertical take-off and landing) aircraft is made. A British Hawker Siddeley *Harrier GR.1* flies from Middlesex, England to Floyd Bennett Field, New York.

1969 April 30 First woman airline pilot in the West, Turi Widerose of Norway, makes her first scheduled flight as a first officer for Scandinavian Airlines.

1969 May 2 Cunard Line's *Queen Elizabeth II* leaves Southampton, England for New York on its maiden voyage. It has only three main boilers but can achieve 28.5 knots with the most powerful twin-propeller machinery ever installed in a passenger liner. It crosses the Atlantic only during the summer months, and earns its keep by worldwide cruising. During the British-Argentina conflict of 1982, it is used as a troop ship to the Falkland Islands.

1969 May 16 Revised quarantine procedures are announced by National Aeronautics and Space Administration (NASA) for the upcoming Apollo manned moon mission. To prevent bringing back contamination from the moon, astronauts will dispose on the moon, under containment conditions, exposed equipment; they will brush, vacuum clean, and bag clothing and other equipment for return; and they will prevent lunar dust from being transferred from the lunar module to the command module and continuously filter the command module during the return trip.

1969 May 18 *Apollo 10* moon landing rehearsal mission is launched by a Saturn V carrying astronauts Thomas P. Stafford (b. 1930), John W. Young (b. 1930), and Eugene A. Cernan (b. 1934). This flight is made primarily to fully test the lunar module which Stafford and Cernan fly, simulating a moon landing. They descend to 14 kilometers (8.7 miles) of the lunar surface while Young travels alone in the command module in lunar orbit. A safe return to earth after a mission of eight days, three minutes gives the green light to the first moon landing later this year.

1969 May 26 Fastest speed ever reached by humans is attained during the U.S. *Apollo 10* manned lunar orbital flight. Crew members Thomas Stafford (b. 1930), John Young (b. 1930), and Eugene Cernan (b. 1934) reach 24,791 mph (39,897 km/h) in their *Apollo 10* command module as they return to earth from the moon.

1969 June 10 Manned Orbiting Laboratory (MOL) is cancelled, U.S. Department of Defense (DOD) announces. It offers the "continuing urgency of reducing Federal defense spending" and "advances in automated techniques for unmanned satellite systems" as major reasons. An unstated reason is the inability to demonstrate a military need for a separate manned space program.

1969 June 21 Cancellation of U.S. Air Force Manned Orbiting Laboratory (MOL) program leaves the Air Force with $1 billion in space hardware and 14 highly trained astronauts. Most of the money was spent on launch vehicles which can be used to launch unmanned satellites. MOL astronauts will be offered to National Aeronautics and Space Administration (NASA).

1969 July 20 First book taken from the earth to the moon is a miniature copy of *Robert Hutchings Goddard—Father of the Space Age* taken on the *Apollo 11* mission by astronaut Edward E. Aldrin, Jr. (b. 1930). Upon return, the book was given to Mrs. Esther Goddard who donated it to the Goddard Library at Clark University, Massachusetts.

1969 July 20 Man first walks on the moon. The *Apollo 11* crew of Neil A. Armstrong (b. 1930), Edwin E. Aldrin, Jr. (b. 1930) and Michael Collins (b. 1930), launched by a Saturn V from Cape Kennedy, Florida on July 16, achieves the eight-year national goal set by President John F. Kennedy (1917—1963) on May 25, 1961. Neil Armstrong steps from the lunar module onto the moon, proclaiming: "That's one small step for man, one giant leap for mankind." Aldrin joins Armstrong minutes later. Both gather lunar samples and conduct and set up experiments during their two hours outside the lunar module. The landing and moon walk is watched live on TV by millions of people worldwide. The entire mission takes eight days, three hours, 19 minutes.

1969 July 20

Man walks on moon

1969 ■ Edwin E. "Buzz" Aldrin, Jr. stands on the Moon during *Apollo 11* mission.

1969 August 14 With cancellation of the U.S. Air Force's Manned Orbiting Laboratory (MOL), National Aeronautics and Space Administration (NASA) announces that seven of the fourteen MOL aerospace research pilots will become NASA astronauts. They are: (Air Force) Karol J. Bobko (b. 1937), Charles G. Fullerton (b. 1936), Henry W. Hartsfield, Jr. (b. 1933), and Donald H. Peterson (b. 1933); (Navy) Robert L. Crippen (b. 1937) and Richard H. Truly (b. 1937); and (Marines) Robert F.

Overmyer (b. 1936). This brings the total of active NASA astronauts to 54.

1969 September 15 First flight of Cessna *Citation* is made in Wichita, Kansas. This is the first of a new family of turbofan-powered executive business jets. Its engines are mounted just behind and above the wings.

1969 September 15 — Mars mission recommended

1969 September 15 A long-range U.S. goal of a manned Mars mission before the end of the century is among the recommendations included in the Space Task Group's report to President Richard M. Nixon (b. 1913). Nixon defers a decision on this plan, stating that budgetary considerations would be a factor. No decision is made and the Group's recommendation is ignored.

1969 October 11 — Three Soviet launches occur three days in a row

1969 October 11 Soviet Union launches *Soyuz 6*, the first of three manned spacecraft in three days. Carrying cosmonauts Georgy S. Shonin (b. 1935) and Valery N. Kubasov (b. 1935), the spacecraft stays in earth orbit to rendezvous but not dock with *Soyuz 7* and *Soyuz 8*. This puzzling three-spacecraft mission consists of little more than maneuvers about one another. No docking occurs and no crews transfer. *Soyuz 6* reenters safely after four days, 22 hours, 42 minutes. (See October 12 and 13, 1969)

1969 October 12 *Soyuz 7* is launched one day after the Soviet Union launches *Soyuz 6* and one day before *Soyuz 8*. The three-man crew of cosmonauts Anatoly V. Filipchenko (b. 1928), Vladislav N. Volkov (1935—1971), and Viktor V. Gorbatko (b. 1934) maneuvers its craft close to the two other orbiting spacecraft but does not dock with either. There is speculation that a crew transfer was intended. *Soyuz 7* reenters safely after four days, 22 hours, 41 minutes. (See October 11 and October 13, 1969)

1969 October 13 *Soyuz 8* is launched by the Soviet Union carrying cosmonauts Vladimir A. Shatalov (b. 1927) and Aleksey S. Yeliseyev (b. 1943). This is the third manned spacecraft launched by the Soviets in three days, indicating that some major accomplishment was intended. When nothing but a rendezvous of the three craft is achieved, *Soyuz 8* reenters safely after four days, 22 hours, 51 minutes. All three spacecraft touch down within ten minutes of each other. (See October 11 and 12, 1969)

1969 October 20 Finnair (Finland) becomes the first airline to operate aircraft with an inertial guidance system on scheduled passenger services. This system uses a computer to integrate information from three accelerometers so as to pinpoint the position of the aircraft at all times. The requirement for a navigator as a crew member can now be dropped.

1969 October 31 New post-flight quarantine procedures are announced by National Aeronautics and Space Administration (NASA) for upcoming *Apollo 12* manned moon mission. Some strict procedures used in *Apollo 11* are eliminated, but the crew will still be kept in a mobile quarantine facility for three weeks.

1969 November 7 Moon scientists confirm the dating of *Apollo 11* moon rocks at four-and-one-half billion years or more, indicating that the lunar surface is far older than any material originating on the earth's surface.

1969 November 10 Report titled *The Biomedical Foundations of Manned Space Flight* is submitted to the President's Science Advisor. Written by the Space Science and Technology Panel of the President's Science Advisory Committee, it states that National Aeronautics and Space Administration (NASA) should now begin a biomedical program to "qualify man for space flight." The report states that the next stages of manned space flight will be much more demanding, and that NASA should not continue without sound and thorough biomedical understanding.

1969 November 14 Second manned lunar landing mission is launched by a Saturn V from Cape Kennedy, Florida with astronauts Charles (Pete) Conrad, Jr. (b. 1930), Richard F. Gordon, Jr. (b. 1929), and Alan L. Bean (b. 1932) aboard. Thirty-six seconds after blast-off, the launch vehicle is struck by lightning and the spacecraft loses electrical power temporarily but with no ill effect. *Apollo 12* lunar module lands accurately on the moon, 553 feet from the unmanned *Surveyor 3*, and Conrad and Bean make two excursions totaling seven-and-one-half hours walking on the surface. The crew splashes down safely in the mid-Pacific after a mission of ten days, four hours, 36 minutes.

1969 November 29 Trans-Australian Railway is officially completed as a golden spike is driven at Broken Hill in New South Wales. (See March 1970)

1969 December An article in *Air Force and Space Digest* touts the future space shuttle as key to the opening of space, "much as the railroads opened a stream of travel into the American West." Also in prospect, says the writer, is the day when astronauts are as numerous as airline pilots and space flights would be scheduled daily. However, ten years after the first space shuttle flight, the medium of space is as difficult, hostile, and expensive as it ever was, and man in space is still an exceptional event.

1969 December 1 First legislation to limit aircraft noise levels at airports is introduced in U.S. Federal Air Regulation, Part 36.

1970 Urban Mass Transportation Assistance Act passes in the United States. This landmark act implies a long-term federal commitment to finance mass transportation. This permits local planners to work with some assurance of support.

1970 Head restraints fitted to the back of front car seats become compulsory in the United States. These reduce the extent of neck injuries when a car is hit from behind.

1970 Solid state circuitry begins to replace the older electronic systems used in elevator control systems. This results in a weight and size reduction as well as in greater reliability and easier maintenance.

1970 Clean Air Act is passed in the United States as an amendment to the Environmental Quality Improvement Act of 1970. Both state that the federal government has the final say in decisions affecting the environment. Clean Air Act creates the Environmental Protection Agency (EPA) and requires it to set new automobile emissions standards.

1970 First of the twin towers of the New York World Trade Center is completed and has the highest rise elevator. With a height of 1,350 feet and 110 floors, the towers and their related buildings use more than 244 elevators and 70 escalators to transport 50,000 employees daily.

1970 Federal-Aid Highway Act passes in the United States. This law provides for a change in the long-standing 50-50 matching ratio for the regular federal-aid highways and urban streets. After July 1, 1963, the federal government will pay 70% of these highway costs.

1970 Personal Rapid Transit (PRT) system begins full-scale testing in West Germany. This is an automated guideway transit system using 12 passenger vehicles that travel on hard rubber wheels along five-foot-wide steel guideways. They are propelled by a linear electric motor. It does not become operational.

1970 Super-cavity propellers are first introduced by the U.S. Navy. The new propellers use a depression around the blades and benefit from the vapor pocket created by the turbulence to obtain higher speeds.

1970 Between this year and 1985, fatalities caused by transportation accidents in the United States account for about half of the total accidental fatalities from all causes. Motor vehicle accidents account for approximately 93% of the total transportation deaths.

1970 Comparative transportation survey reports that rail travel is 2.5 times as safe as air travel, 1.5 as safe as bus travel, and 23 times safer than automobile travel.

c. 1970 Surfboard riding is again transformed with the change to shorter boards and the addition of twin fins. With these innovations, the rider no longer needs simple physical strength to accomplish turns.

c. 1970 A.D.

Surfboards get shorter

c. 1970 Regular hydrofoil service is offered by the Soviet Union up and down its main rivers. One of its hydrofoils, the *Meteor*, has a capacity of 150. Since propulsion is by jet engines, the heavy fuel consumption of hydrofoils prevent them being used for fast ocean voyages.

1970 January 12 First Boeing 747 wide-body transport (Pan American) to make a transatlantic proving flight lands at London Heathrow Airport from New York.

1970 February 11 Japan becomes the fourth nation to orbit an earth satellite using its own launch vehicle. The 10.9-kilogram (24-pound) satellite, called *Ohsumi,* is launched by a Japanese four-stage Lambda 4S rocket.

1970 February 13 National Aeronautics and Space Administration's (NASA) Manned Spacecraft Center, Houston, Texas, announces the creation of the Space Shuttle Program Office. NASA begins the organizational transition to accommodate its planned new space transportation system.

1970 February 18 Request for Proposals (RFP) are issued by National Aeronautics and Space Administration (NASA) for preliminary definition and planning studies for the main propulsion system of a reusable space shuttle.

1970 February 18 Dr. Charles A. Berry (b. 1923), director of medical research and operations for National Aeronautics and Space Administration (NASA), states that the only medical side effect thus far from prologed manned space flights was "some cardiovascular deterioration" which was normal and attributed to the less demanding environment (no gravity) of space. He stresses, however, that medical knowledge is inadequate to risk a two-year manned mission to Mars.

1970 March Trans-Australian Railway begins service between Sydney and Perth as the Indian-Pacific Express makes twice-a-week runs 2,460 miles through forests, deserts, mountains, farmland.

1970 March 13 First flight of Aero Space Lines *Guppy-101* is made. This is a larger version of the Boeing *Stratocruiser* modified in 1962.

1970 March 19 First powered flight of Martin Marietta *X-24A* lifting body research aircraft is made. A follow-up to the Northrop *M2-F2* program, it conducts additional reentry and landing tests for the coming National Aeronautics and Space Administration (NASA) space shuttle. It is rebuilt later as the *X-24B* which makes its first flight on August 1, 1973.

**1970
March 31**

**Skylab
program
planned**

1970 March 31 Wernher von Braun (1912—1977), now deputy associate administrator for planning at National Aeronautics and Space Administration (NASA) Headquarters, describes the planned Skylab program as "this country's first orbital space station." The Skylab program will basically put to use the leftover Saturn launch vehicle and Apollo spacecraft components.

1970 April 11

**Drama in
space**

1970 April 11 Most dramatic space mission occurs when a now-routine manned flight to the moon is transformed by an explosion into a life-and-death struggle to return safely to earth. *Apollo 13* astronauts James A. Lovell, Jr. (b. 1928), John L. Swigert, Jr. (b. 1931), and Fred W. Haise, Jr. (b. 1933) must improvise and use the lunar module as a lifeboat during the emergency return trip. If the command module oxygen tank had exploded after the moon landing instead of before it, the astronauts would not have survived, since they would have discarded the lunar module (and its propulsion and life-support systems) prior to their return, and would have had no backups. They return safely after a harrowing trip of five days, 22 hours, 54 minutes.

1970 April 17 A Sikorsky *CH-53D* helicopter flies between London, England and Paris, France to demonstrate that modern helicopters can provide reliable inter-city services.

1970 April 24 People's Republic of China launches its first satellite into earth orbit using its own booster rocket. The research satellite, identified by the West as *Chicom 1*, weighs 173 kilograms (381 pounds).

1970 June 1 Soviet Union's *Soyuz 9* spacecraft is launched into earth orbit carrying cosmonauts Andrian G. Nikolayev (b. 1929) and Vitaly I. Sevastyanov (b. 1935). This long-duration mission proves valuable by underscoring the post-flight readaptation problems that occur if astronauts do not rigorously exercise while in space. Both astronauts suffer major adaptation problems for two weeks following their flight of 17 days, 16 hours, 58 minutes. Both the Soviets and the United States learn the value of exercise.

1970 May 29 U.S. National Academy of Sciences (NAS) releases a report, *Infectious Disease in Manned Spaceflight: Probabilities and Countermeasures*, which recommends that preflight quarantine precautions be taken before manned moon flights as well as after them.

1970 June 13 Four U.S. crewmen are sealed into a space station ground simulator to test regenerative life support systems. During the 90-day experiment, the crew will drink reclaimed water and breathe regenerated oxygen.

1970 June 16 Final critical-design review of a manned lunar roving vehicle is held by National Aeronautics and Space Administration (NASA) which will decide the configuration of the moon vehicle astronauts will drive during the last two Apollo moon missions.

1970 July 1 The Melbourne International Airport opens at Tullamarine, Australia.

c. 1970 ■ Modern airport terminal design makes air transportation more efficient.

1970 July 1 Chengtu-Kunming railroad opens in China. In its entire run of 674 miles (1,085 kilometers), it has 427 tunnels and 653 bridges.

1970 July 2 First flight of Saab *37 Viggen* multi-purpose combat aircraft is made in Sweden. This attack aircraft proves to be a high-quality performer.

1970 July 18 First flight of Italy's Aeritalia *G.222* is made at Torino-Caselle Airport. This general-purpose military transport prototype can carry up to 44 troops.

1970 August First all-paper man-carrying aircraft flies on three occasions. Built from paper, glue, and masking tape as part of a class project at Ohio State University, the paper glider achieves a maximum airspeed of about 60 mph (96 km/h) after being pulled into the air by a car.

1970 August 15 World's largest known rotational machine is tested by North American Rockwell Corp. The 12-meter- (40-foot-) long, bullet-shaped crew module was built to evaluate human performance in a rotating environment and can rotate at 4 rpm.

1970 August 22 First nonstop transpacific flight by a rotary aircraft is made by two Sikorsky *HH-3C* helicopters. Refuelled in flight, they cover 9,000 miles (14,484 kilometers).

1970 August 29 A first flight is made by the Britten-Norman "stretched" three-engine Islander business jet, later named *Trislander*. This is one of the few executive jets made in England that competes with those of the United States.

1970 August 29 First flight of the McDonnell Douglas *DC-10* wide-bodied medium-haul airliner is made in Long Beach, California. This large capacity, three-engine aircraft can seat as many as 345 in economy class. After a crash kills 346 people near Paris, an imperfectly designed baggage door is found in the fuselage. (See March 3, 1974)

1970 October 24 The last flight in the North American *X-15* research aircraft program is made by National Aeronautics and Space Administration (NASA) pilot William H. Dana. Powered by a liquid oxygen and ammonia rocket engine and released in flight from a Boeing *B-52*, this ultra-high speed, high-altitude craft flew during its many flights as fast as 4,534 mph (7,297 km/h) and as high as 354,200 feet.

1970 November 4 The French-built *Concorde 001* prototype attains its design cruising speed of Mach 2 (twice the speed of sound) for the first time. The U.K.-built *002* achieves its supersonic cruising speed nine days later.

1970 November 7 Second longest tunnel in the United States, the Flathead Tunnel in northwest Montana, opens. Part of the Great Northern Railroad, it is built because the federal government's Libby Dam project flooded much of the main line beneath Lake Koocanusa. Workers use new laser beam technology to guide drilling. It is just under seven miles long.

1970 November 12 First flight is made of the first Japanese designed and built military jet transport. The *XC-1* is built by Nihon Aeroplane Manufacturing Company (NAMC) of Japan.

1970 November 16 First flight of the Lockheed *L-1011 TriStar* wide-body jet-airliner is made in the United States. This three-engine aircraft can hold as many as 400 passengers and competes with the Boeing *747*, McDonnell *DC-10*, and Airbus Industrie *A300*. Wide-body aircraft will soon become the norm for high density routes where speed is not essential. Passengers sit in long

1970
August 29

*First DC-10
flies*

1970
November 4

*French
Concorde
001 cruises
at Mach 2*

rows separated by two aisles, giving easy access to aircraft exits and facilities.

1970 November 17 Lunar roving training vehicle is delivered by Boeing Co. to National Aeronautics and Space Administration (NASA). This four-wheel, battery-operated, two-man trainer is 3.2 meters (ten feet, seven inches) long and has an aircraft-like stick hand controller instead of a steering wheel. It will be used by Apollo astronauts to practice driving on the moon.

1970 December 21 First flight of the Grumman *F-14 Tomcat* variable-geometry (moveable wings offering a range of sweep) jet-fighter is made in the United States. Following a successful flight, the aircraft is lost due to a complete hydraulic failure. This carrier-based Navy aircraft is one of the world's most advanced fighters, seeing action into the 1990s.

1971 First automobile to have a headlight washer-wiper system is Sweden's Saab 99.

1971 A.D.

Canal conservation begins

1971 Chesapeake and Ohio Canal National Historical Park is established by the United States. This precedent-setting creation is administered by the National Park Service. The park runs the entire length of the canal, which has a mule-drawn barge service near Washington, D.C., and its towpath is open throughout as a footpath. It marks the beginning of an awareness of canal conservation.

1971 First French nuclear-powered submarine, the *Redoutable*, is commissioned.

1971 January 31

"Fore!"

1971 January 31 Third manned moon landing mission begins as *Apollo 14* is launched by a Saturn V from Cape Kennedy, Florida with astronauts Alan B. Shepard, Jr. (b. 1923), Stuart A. Roosa (b. 1933), and Edgar D. Mitchell (b. 1930) aboard. Shepard and Roosa perform two moonwalks totaling nine hours. The most memorable point of this routine mission is Shepard's hitting a golf ball while on the moon. Reentry occurs safely in the Pacific after a flight of nine days, two minutes.

1971 March Report issued by National Aeronautics and Space Administration (NASA), *Manned Space Program Accident/Incident Summaries*, indicates that of some 10,000 case documents reviewed concerning all types of accidents during the Apollo program, 74% had human error as a contributing factor.

1971 March 24 The U.S. Senate decides, by a single vote, not to provide financial backing for prototypes of an American supersonic transport aircraft. President Lyndon B. Johnson (1908—1973) had previously selected the Boeing design over Lockheed. The Boeing *2707-300* had a movable wing and could carry 300 passengers at a top speed of 1,800 mph. Congress terminates the project officially on May 20, 1971 for several reasons, such as concern for high costs, environmental and sonic boom effects, and congestion at airports.

1971 April 14 First round-the-world cargo services are offered by Trans-Mediterranean Airways of Lebanon, formed in 1953 to provide non-scheduled freight services from Beirut.

1971 April 19 Soviet Union launches the *Salyut 1* space station into earth orbit. It will be occupied by cosmonauts later in the year and become the first manned space station. (See June 6, 1971)

1971 April 23 *Soyuz 10* is launched by the Soviet Union carrying cosmonauts Vladimir A. Shatalov (b. 1927), Aleksey S. Yeliseyev (b. 1943), and Nikolay N. Rukavishnikov (b. 1932). This planned 30-day mission is cut short when something goes wrong after *Soyuz 10* docks with the unmanned orbiting workshop, *Salyut 1*. This is the first manned spacecraft to be launched and to land at night. The crew returns to earth safely after a flight of only one day, 23 hours, 45 minutes.

1971 April 28 Quarantine of astronauts after moon missions is no longer necessary, National Aeronautics and Space Administration (NASA) announces. It also states that "there is no hazard to man, animal, or plants in the lunar material."

1971 May 1 National Railroad Passenger Corporation, known as Amtrak and formed under the Rail Passenger Service Act of 1970, takes over the passenger services of 22 leading U.S. railroads. In a move to improve deteriorating passenger service, it assumes responsibility for long-distance passenger trains in the United States.

1971 May 8 First flight of the Dassault *Mirage G8* variable-geometry (moveable wings offering a range of sweep) fighter aircraft is made in France. This advanced version is based on the well-tested *Mirage III* fighter.

1971 ■ Drawing of a Soviet spacecraft about to dock with *Salyut* station.

1971 June Planned Skylab space station is described by National Aeronautics and Space Administration (NASA) as being the largest manned spacecraft ever built. It will be 36 meters (118 feet) long and weigh 82,238 kilograms (181,304 pounds). It will carry about 50 scientific, medical, applications, and solar astronomy experiments.

1971 June 6 Soviet Union launches *Soyuz 11* into earth orbit with cosmonauts Georgy T. Dobrovolsky (1928—1971), Vladislav N. Volkov (1935—1971), and Viktor I. Patsayev (1933—1971) aboard. They dock with the orbiting unmanned space station *Salyut 1* and stay aboard three weeks, conducting experiments. After undocking, the normal explosive separation from the docking mechanism shakes open an exhaust valve. The cabin depressurizes and in 45 seconds the cosmonauts are dead. After a routine, remote-controlled landing, the dead cosmonauts are found in their seats. Had they been wearing spacesuits inside the cabin, they would have survived.

1971 June 11—August 4 First flight by a light plane from equator to equator via the North Pole is made by British pilot Shelia Scott. Flying in a Piper *Aztec D*, she covers 34,000 miles (54,718 kilometers).

1971 July 14 First flight of the German VFW-Fokker *VFW 614* jet transport is made in Bremen, West Germany. Designed for low-density traffic, short-haul routes, and operation from shorter runways, this aircraft is also the first to mount its engines on pylons above the wing.

1971 July 20 First flight of the Mitsubishi *XT-2* jet trainer is made. It is the first supersonic aircraft designed and built in Japan.

1971 July 26 United States launches *Apollo 15*, on its fourth successful manned lunar landing mission. Astronauts David R. Scott (b. 1932), Alfred M. Worden (b. 1932), and James B. Irwin (b. 1930) are launched by a Saturn V from Cape Kennedy, Florida. This successful mission is the first to use the manned lunar roving vehicle to explore the moon's surface. This is also the first time an operational satellite is deployed from a manned spacecraft. Scott and Irwin spend three days on the moon, including 21 hours in moonwalks and driving. On the return to earth, Worden makes a 38-minute spacewalk. The crew returns safely to earth after a 12-day, 7-hour, 53-minute mission.

1971 July 26
Lunar roving vehicle used on moon

1971 ■ Lunar Rover sits in front of the Moon's Mount Hadley during *Apollo 15* mission.

1971 July 30 Japanese *F-86 Sabrejet* collides with an All-Nippon Airways *727*, killing all 162 aboard the airliner. The student pilot of the military jet parachutes to safety but is convicted for knowingly flying into a commercial air route.

1971 September 3 First jet aircraft built by the Brazilian aircraft industry, the EMBRAER/Aermacchi *EMB-326GB Xavante* jet trainer, makes its first flight near Sao Paulo.

1971 October 1 Astronaut food taste tests for upcoming Skylab missions are conducted to evaluate astronauts' preferences and energy requirements.

1971 October 20 A new international air terminal opens at Brasilia Airport in Brazil.

1971 November 24

D.B. Cooper hijacks plane

1971 November 24 Infamous American hijacker D. B. Cooper takes over a Northwest Airlines *727*, allows passengers to leave after obtaining 10,000 $20 bills, forces plane to take off again, and parachutes into a storm above the wild, snowy Cascade Mountains near Ariel, Washington. He is never found.

1972 Washington, D.C.'s Metro subway line opens its first station, beginning a planned system of 75 miles, connecting Virginia and Maryland with the District of Columbia. Nearly 20 years later, the system is a success, and despite its heavy use, is one of the cleanest and safest underground systems in the United States. It is not yet completely built.

1972 American Canal Society is founded. Among its activities is a listing of all known North American navigation works.

1972 January 5 James C. Fletcher (b. 1919), administrator of National Aeronautics and Space Administration (NASA), describes the future shuttle as an "airplane-like orbiter, about the size of a *DC-9* ... capable of carrying into orbit and back again to earth useful payloads up to 15 feet [4.6 meters] in diameter by 60 feet [18 meters] long, and weighing up to 65,000 pounds [29,500 kilograms]." Since the shuttle is intended to launch all U.S. satellites, its payload size and capabilities are influenced greatly by Department of Defense (DOD) requirements.

1972 January 5 U.S. President Richard M. Nixon (b. 1913) announces the decision to develop a space shuttle system. He says the new system "will revolutionize transportation into space, by routinizing it. It will take the astronomical costs out of astronautics." These goals of regular, routine flights and low costs have not yet been achieved by the shuttle.

1972 February 24 Dr. Charles A. Berry (b. 1923), director for life sciences for National Aeronautics and Space Administration (NASA), says that there are no findings to date which would prevent a manned space mission of 28 days.

1972 March 15 United States decides that the space shuttle booster stage will be powered by recoverable, solid-fueled rocket motors in parallel burn configuration, rather than by a pressure-fed liquid-fueled rocket motor. This decision is based on the assumption that solid-fuel rockets have lower development costs and present lower technical risks. Twenty years from now, many scientists will argue that solid rockets are doing severe damage to the earth's protective ozone layer.

1972 April New high-speed Japanese rail line, the San-Yo Shin Kansen, opens and links Osaka with Okayama. The new line can handle trains that travel up to 155 mph.

1972 April 1 The Civil Aviation Authority (CAA), England's first independent body for regulating civil aviation and providing air traffic control and navigation services, begins its functions. The U.S. equivalent was formed in 1938.

1972 April 16 Fifth U.S. manned moon mission, *Apollo 16,* is launched by a Saturn V from Cape Kennedy, Florida. Astronauts John W. Young (b. 1930), Thomas K. Mattingly II (b. 1936), and Charles M. Duke, Jr. (b. 1935) conduct a chatty mission in which Young and Duke enthusiastically drive the lunar rover over considerable distances. They spend a total of 20 hours, 15 minutes walking on the moon during three separate excursions. The crew returns safely after an 11-day, one-hour, 51-minute mission.

1972 April 25 World straight-line distance record for single-seat sailplanes is set by German Hans Werner Grosse, who sails 907 miles (1,460 kilometers) in a Schleicher *AS-W12* sailplane.

1972 April 29 A specially equipped McDonnell Douglas *F-4 Phantom II* becomes the first aircraft to be flown in the United States with a "fly-by-wire" control system. This new system links the pilot to his control surfaces by means of computer-connected electrical impulses rather than the old mechanical or hydraulic means. The modern pilot's control inputs are correlated by the computer with all other factors to give him optimum control.

1972 May 10 First flight of the prototype Fairchild *A-10A Warthog* is made. This slow-flying, close-support, anti-armor aircraft carries a devastating load of missiles and bombs as well as a 25-mm gun and proves itself as a valuable and lethal aircraft for the United States during the January—February 1991 Persian Gulf War.

1972 May 19 Skylab orbital workshop is described by National Aeronautics and Space Administration (NASA). Basically it is the third stage of a Saturn V launch vehicle, called the S-IVB, which has been converted into a habitable workshop for astronauts. Among its 1,300 individual items are 2,000 pounds (910 kilograms) of food, 6,000 pounds (2,700 kilograms) of water, 60 changes of astronaut clothes, 210 pairs of shorts, 55 bars of soap, 1,800 urine and fecal bags, 108 pens and pencils, and a vacuum cleaner.

1972 May 24 U.S. President Richard M. Nixon (b. 1913) and Soviet Premier Aleksey N. Kosygin (1904—1980) sign an agreement that includes a project to rendezvous and dock an American and a Soviet spacecraft in earth orbit and to exchange crews sometime during 1975. After years of hostility, suspicion, and competition, this agreement to cooperate in space, even for this one mission, is a major accomplishment.

1972 May 26 Cessna Aircraft Corporation announces completion of the company's 100,000th aircraft, becoming the first company in the world to achieve such a production figure.

1972 May 27 Comparing its planned missions in space with its large astronaut corps, National Aeronautics and Space Administration (NASA) officials state that there are three times as many people as are needed, and that many astronauts may never fly in the near future.

1972 July 17 First major joint U.S.-U.S.S.R. press conference is held concerning planned Apollo-Soyuz Test Project. A great deal of technical discussion and planning must be conducted to assure that the two manned space systems can be functionally compatible in space.

1972 July 26 National Aeronautics and Space Administration (NASA) announces that North American Rockwell Corp. has been selected as the prime contractor to build the space shuttle orbiter. It is awarded a six-year, $2.6 billion contract, and will receive an initial $540 million to cover the first two years of development.

1972 July 26
Rockwell selected as prime space shuttle manufacturer

1972 July 27 First flight of the McDonnell Douglas *F-15A Eagle* fighter is made at Edwards Air Force Base, California. Although primarily a fighter, this aircraft can carry an enormous bomb load of 12,000 pounds (5,450 kilograms).

1972 August 11 First flight of Northrop *F-5E Tiger II* is made at Edwards Air Force Base, California. This light, aggressive fighter is yet another version of the *F-5* family.

1972 September 7 Skylab Orbital Workshop is delivered to the Marshall Space Flight Center, Huntsville, Alabama from whence it will be moved to Cape Kennedy, Florida. The finished workshop weighs 55,000 pounds (25,000 kilograms).

1972 September 20 Three U.S. astronauts emerge from a Skylab simulator in which they had been confined since July 26. They experienced no major problems that would affect the plans for the Skylab mission.

1972 October 13 F-27 turbo-prop airliner carrying members and fans of an Uruguayan rugby team crashes on the Chilean side of a 12,000-foot peak in the Andes Mountains. Twenty people die in the crash and subsequent avalanche, but 16 escape and manage to survive the next 69 days by eating parts of the dead. When finally rescued after two survivors hike for ten days to a village, the group eventually admits to cannibalism for survival. Their story is written by Piers Paul Read, and *Alive* becomes a best seller.

1972

October 28

First Airbus flies

1972 October 28 First flight of the Airbus Industrie *A300B Airbus* is made in Toulouse, France. A twin-engine, short-haul, wide-bodied airliner, it is built by France, Germany, and Britain.

1972 December 7 Final manned moon mission, *Apollo 17*, is launched by a Saturn V from Cape Kennedy, Florida. The crew of Eugene A. Cernan (b. 1934), Ronald E. Evans (b. 1933), and Harrison H. Schmitt (b. 1935) contains the only astronaut-geologist (Schmitt) to go to the moon. After a spectacular night launch and lunar landing, Cernan and Schmitt spend three days exploring the moon, driving their lunar rover for a total of 21 miles. Following a one-hour, seven-minute space walk by Evans on their return trip, they land safely in the Pacific after the longest moon mission, 12 days, 13 hours, 52 minutes.

1972 December 23 First human-powered aircraft to have a two-man crew, Hertfordshire Pedal Aeronaut's *Toucan*, makes its first flight. Propelled by pedalers Bryan Bowman and Derek May, it has a wing span of 142.7 feet (37.5 meters), exactly that of a Boeing *707-320*. It flies for 204 feet (62 meters) and never gets above two feet (0.6 meters) off the ground. On July 3, 1973, with the same crew, it covers 2,100 feet (640 meters).

1972 December 29 First major air disaster involving the new jumbo jets occurs in the Florida Everglades as an Eastern Airlines *L-1011* crashes and kills 101 of the 176 people aboard.

1973 A.D.

GM offers air bag

1973 First automobile air bag is offered by General Motors. This is an inflatable cushion restraint installed in a car's steering wheel or dashboard that inflates in a fraction of a second, usually with nitrogen, upon collision and protects the driver or front passengers. The auto industry resists adopting this safety system, and nearly 20 years later, it is still not standard equipment on most cars.

1973 Sears Tower (1,454 feet high) in Chicago, Illinois is completed and includes new, space-saving design for elevators. Instead of elevators running from the first floor to the top, there are lobbies at two points between to change for cars to the higher floors. This saves space since fewer elevators are needed for the upper floors and the elevator shafts can be stacked one on top of the other.

1973 Federal-Aid Highway Act passes in the United States and opens up the highway trust fund for urban mass transportation. This is a significant step toward integrating and balancing the highway and mass transportation programs.

1973 Germany's Volkswagen Beetle exceeds the all-time, same model sales record held by the Ford Model T of 16,536,075.

1973 American Frank Nasworthy of California introduces the first polyurethane wheel designed specifically for skateboards. This major innovation makes for a quieter, more maneuverable ride since the softer wheels have a better grip. This revolutionizes skateboarding, making it accessible to most people.

1973 Third London Bridge officially opens. Consisting of three prestressed concrete arches, it is 104 feet (31 meters) wide and is built on the same spot as the old Rennie bridge, but road traffic is never interrupted. Prestressed concrete is concrete strengthened by being allowed to set around tautly drawn steel wires or bars (tensioned) that extend through it.

1973 First permanent land link between Europe and Asia, the Bosporus Bridge at Istanbul, opens. Built by the Turkish Government, this suspension bridge of 3,524 feet (1,074 meters) connects east and west Turkey. The form of this bridge is similar to that of the Severn Bridge and thus is aerodynamically designed.

1973 January 7 First hot-air airship, the *Cameron D96*, makes its first flight. Developed in England by Cameron Balloons of Bristol, it is crewed by Don Cameron and E. T. Hall.

1973 February 17 U.S. President Richard M. Nixon (b. 1913) signs Public Law 93-8 and designates National Aeronautics and Space Administration's (NASA) Manned Spacecraft Center at Houston, Texas the Lyndon B. Johnson Space Center in honor of the recently deceased president who had helped create NASA and pushed strongly for the Apollo program.

1973 February 23 U.S.S.R. announces that it has abandoned its women's cosmonaut training program, saying "We train only young men, not women." This change is only temporary as the Soviets launch the second woman in space nearly 20 years later. (See August 19, 1982)

1973 February 28 First flight of the McDonnell Douglas *DC-10-30CF* is made, a version of the wide-body jet that can be converted overnight from passenger to full cargo configuration or vice versa.

1973 April 3 Soviet Union launches its second orbiting workshop, *Salyut 2*, into earth orbit. It never receives cosmonauts however, as it begins tumbling wildly on April 25, due to either an explosion or misfiring thrusters. After its solar panels are torn off, it is damaged beyond use.

1973 May 14 United States launches its first-generation space station, *Skylab 1* Orbital Workshop, into earth orbit from Cape Kennedy, Florida using its last Saturn V booster. During launch, the meteoroid shield is torn off and its solar array system is damaged. Eleven days later, the workshop is visited by astronauts who save the entire Skylab mission with their repairs. (See May 25, 1973)

1973 May 25 *Skylab 2* is launched into earth orbit by a Saturn IB booster carrying astronauts Charles Conrad, Jr. (b. 1930), Paul J. Weitz (b. 1933), and Joseph P. Kerwin (b. 1932). The crew improvises and builds an effective sun shield while also prying loose a jammed solar panel. All of this is done outside the station, demonstrating how much effective work astronauts can accomplish during a space walk. Following repairs, the mission settles down to one of experiment and testing, and concludes after 28 days, 50 minutes.

1973 June 3 First crash of a supersonic transport aircraft occurs as a Tupolev *Tu-144* goes down during a demonstration flight at the Paris Air Show.

1973 June 3 Longest railroad tunnel in Norway, the Lierasen Tunnel, opens. Over six miles (10,700 meters) long, it runs between Oslo and Drammen.

1973 June 29 *Skylab 2* crew tells how easy it was to adapt to zero gravity in space, and that exercise was essential to their physical well-being. They say that even more exercise should be done on later flights.

1973 July 25 The highest altitude attained by an air-breathing aircraft is achieved by the Soviet's Mikoyan *Ye-266M* specially modified aircraft. Piloted by Alexander Fedotov, this flight also sets the current world absolute altitude record of 123,524 feet (37,650 meters).

1973 July 26 First flight of Sikorsky *S-69* ABC (advancing blade concept) helicopter is made. This new blade design makes it possible to eliminate the need for an anti-torque rotor found at the tail of most helicopters. Following a crash and other problems, this concept is not developed further.

1973 July 28 *Skylab 3* is launched by a Saturn IB booster carrying astronauts Alan L. Bean (b. 1932), Jack R. Lousma (b. 1936), and Owen K. Garriott (b. 1930). Entire crew feels severe motion sickness for the first three days, after which they adapt. Temporary problem with the command module prompts ground control to begin rescue plans, but they are not needed. Crew performs its duties, space walks, and experiments very well and return after a mission of 59 days, 11 hours, nine minutes.

1973 July 28

59-day Skylab 3 mission takes place

1973 August 1 First unpowered flight of Martin Marietta *X-24B* lifting-body research aircraft is made following its launch from a *B-52*. Lifting bodies are small, wingless airplanes in which the entire craft itself acts as an airfoil or wing. They were used to test reentry technology. The information gained from these vehicles enabled the National Aeronautics and Space Administration (NASA) to design the space shuttle, which is capable of orbiting the earth, reentering the atmosphere, and landing on a runway.

1973 September Aerospace journal *Interavia* tells of Soviet plans for a reusable space shuttle which would consist of two vehicles, one atop the other— one a booster, the other an orbiter—that would take off horizontally from a runway. After separation, each

1973 ■ *Skylab 3* crew demonstrates weightlessness.

would glide and land following their respective missions. The Soviets do build a shuttle that looks very much like the U.S. version, but it still has not flown.

1973 September 27 Soviet Union launches *Soyuz 12* into earth orbit carrying cosmonauts Vasily G. Lazarev (b. 1928) and Oleg G. Makarov (b. 1933). This is the first flight since the fatal *Soyuz 11*, and it tests a redesigned Soyuz. No longer a three-man craft, it has maneuvering capabilities and is intended to be a space-ferry and dock with an orbiting station. The crew wears spacesuits in flight for the first time since 1965. They return safely after a successful test flight of one day, 23 hours, 16 minutes.

1973 October

OPEC oil embargoes begin

1973 October Oil shortages begin in the United States as the Organization of Petroleum Exporting Countries (OPEC) embargoes oil shipments to the United States. It is immediately recognized that oil is of paramount importance to the U.S. economy in general and to the transportation sector in particular. Gas shortages and subsequent steep price increases soon become a major factor in all transportation planning.

1973 October 9 Original name of Cape Canaveral is restored to Cape Kennedy by the U.S.

Department of the Interior, acting on a unanimous recommendation by an interagency committee of the Board on Geographic Names. Historians believe the Cape was named by Spanish explorer Ponce de Leon more than 400 years ago. The action does not change the name of National Aeronautics and Space Administration's (NASA) Kennedy Space Center, named after U.S. President John F. Kennedy (1917—1963).

1973 October 21 First electrically powered manned aircraft to fly is Austrian-built Militky *MB-E1* (Militky Brditschka Electric). Flown in Linz, Austria, it is a modified sailplane powered by a Bosch electric motor driven by rechargeable batteries.

1973 October 26 First flight of Dassault-Bréguet/Dornier *Alpha Jet* is made in Istres, France. This jet trainer and attack aircraft becomes a successful part of the French and West German air forces.

1973 November 16 Longest U.S. space mission begins with the launch of *Skylab 4* into earth orbit by a Saturn IB. Astronauts Gerald P. Carr (b. 1932), Edward G. Gibson (b. 1936), and William R. Pogue (b. 1930) perform 56 experiments and 26 science demonstrations, as well as 22 hours, 24 minutes walking in space. This final Skylab mission totals 84 days, one hour, 15 minutes when completed. The astronauts actually grow one to two inches taller from their stretched spinal columns in space and lose some muscle mass, but they are back to normal after a few days on earth.

1973 November 23 First aircraft designed and built by the Republic of China (Taiwan) makes it first flight. The *XH-C-1A* trainer is built by Aero Industry Development Centre (AIDC).

1973 December 18 Soviets launch *Soyuz 13* into earth orbit with cosmonauts Pyotr Klimuk (b. 1942) and Valentin Lebedev (b. 1942) aboard. Placed into orbit while the U.S. *Skylab 4* mission is on-going, it marks the first time that Soviets and Americans are in space at the same time. The mission ends safely after seven days, 20 hours, 55 minutes.

1974 National Mass Transportation Assistance Act passes in the United States. It authorizes for the first time the use of federal funds for local transit projects.

1973 ■ Air Force *SR-71* reconnaissance plane takes off.

1974 Joint English-French tunnel project is begun. British Prime Minister Harold Wilson (b. 1916), begins the English Channel tunnel project (now called the "Chunnel") with public funds but is forced to halt in January 1975 because of economic problems. The British are forced to choose between a competing British-French project—the supersonic transport, Concorde—and the tunnel, and instead select the airliner. Digging stops after 1,200 feet have been drilled. (See 1986)

1974 Work begins clearing the Suez Canal of war-caused debris and explosive mines. (See June 1967)

1974 January 2 Emergency Highway Energy Conservation Act goes into effect in the United States. This law establishes a national speed limit of 55 mph in order to reduce gasoline consumption following the oil embargo of October 1973.

1974 February 2 First flight is made of General Dynamics *YF-16* lightweight fighter at Edwards Air Force Base, California. Called the *Fighting Falcon,* this extremely agile American fighter sees action in the Persian Gulf War of January—February 1991.

1974 February 21 Dr. Charles A. Berry (b. 1923), director of life sciences for National Aeronautics and Space Administration (NASA), says that during the last two Skylab missions, astronauts had experienced initial reductions in blood cell mass which was then compensated for by their bodies' speeding up its blood-forming elements. He states that there is much to learn about the mechanisms of adaptive changes that occur while living in space.

1974 March First passenger hydrofoil to use water-jet propulsion, the American *Jetfoil 010,* is launched. Two Rocketdyne R-20 water-jet pumps allow it to cruise at 52 mph (84 km/ph) and still give its 250—400 passengers a smooth ride. Jetfoils soon go in service throughout the world.

1974 ■ Boeing *Jetfoil One* hydrofoil in Puget Sound.

1974 March 1 First flight of Sikorsky *YCH-53E Super Stallion* is made. This tactical transport helicopter is a three-turboshaft development of the Sikorsky *S-65A* and provides the U.S. Navy and Marine Corps with a heavy-lift, multi-purpose helicopter. It carries 55 troops and a crew of three.

1974 March 3 Worst air disaster to date involving a single aircraft occurs as a Turkish Airlines *DC-10* crashes near Paris after take-off from Orly Airport, killing all 346 people on board. An investigation reveals that failure of a cargo door caused decompression and loss of control. (See August 12, 1985)

1974 March 8 Charles de Gaulle Airport at Roissy-en-France is officially opened. This new international airport is 15½ miles (25 kilometers) from the center of Paris. Besides such advanced systems as its see-through tubes containing escalators, it also seeks architecturally to make a statement of national pride.

c. 1974 ■ Specially-built liquefied natural gas (LNG) tankers are potentially hazardous.

1974 April 21 Design work begins on a rescue system for space shuttle passengers called a "beach ball." Each would be large enough for one person to crawl into, zip up, and pressurize. It would allow non-astronaut passengers to survive in space for up to one hour should they have to abandon the shuttle and wait for a rescue shuttle.

1974 May 6

Turbotrains

introduced

1974 May 6 French Railways introduces a series of turbotrains between Bordeaux, Limoges, and Lyons.

1974 June 9 First flight of Northrop *YF-17* experimental lightweight fighter is made. This aircraft is built to test what might be called the aerodynamics of agility, with all of the factors of weight, materials, and design geared to making it as agile as possible.

1974 June 25 *Salyut 3* orbiting research station is launched by the Soviet Union. This first successful

Soviet space station is occupied by cosmonauts eight days later. (See July 3, 1974)

1974 July 3 Soviets launch *Soyuz 14* into earth orbit carrying cosmonauts Pavel R. Popovich (b. 1930) and Yuri P. Artyukhin (b. 1940). They dock with and enter orbiting *Salyut 3* and conduct the first manned spy mission. Using a 33-foot focal length optical telescope trained on the earth, they turn Salyut into a military research station. The crew returns safely after a mission of 15 days, 17 hours, 30 minutes.

1974 August 14 Fastest speed ever attained by a flanged rail vehicle is 255 mph (410 km/h) by the Linear Induction Motor Test Vehicle. Jet engines provide the initial thrust for this test run by the U.S. Department of Transportation's High Speed Ground Test Center in Pueblo, Colorado.

1974 August 26 *Soyuz 15* is launched by the Soviet Union with cosmonauts Gennady V. Serafanov (b. 1942) and Lev S. Demin (b. 1926) aboard. This mission was to have spent one month in the *Salyut 3* orbiting station, but a failure in its guidance system forced excessive fuel consumption and the crew makes an emergency reentry at night. The 47-year-old Demin is the first grandfather to fly in space. The mission lasts only two days, 12 minutes.

1974 September Amtrak and Greyhound Bus Lines agree to allow either to write interconnecting train-bus tickets.

1974 September 11 First flight of Bell *206L Long Ranger* is made. This modified, turbine-powered, general-purpose light helicopter has a longer fuselage and carries five passengers and a crew of two.

1974 September 14 Longest underwater tunnel in the United States, the Bay Area Rapid Transit (BART) Trans Bay Tube, opens. Carrying rapid transit trains beneath the bay between San Francisco and Oakland, California, it is 3.6 miles (5.8 kilometers) long.

1974 October 17 First flight of Sikorsky *YUH-60A Black Hawk* utility transport helicopter (Utility Tactical Transport Aircraft System) is made in Connecticut. It is adopted by the U.S. Army for air support, airmobile cavalry, and air ambulance purposes. It carries 11 troops.

1974 December 2 Soviets launch *Soyuz 16* with cosmonauts Anatoly V. Filipchenko (b. 1928) and Nikolay N. Rukavishnikov (b. 1932) on board. This mission is a dress rehearsal to test the special docking adaptor to be used in the upcoming joint Apollo-Soyuz mission. It also is conducted to demonstrate to the United States the Soviet's confidence and competence in space, following a series of mission failures. It checks out the new device and returns safely to earth after five days, 22 hours, 24 minutes.

1974 December 23 First flight of the Rockwell International *B-1* high-altitude supersonic bomber is made. Originally designed as a manned strategic bomber to replace the *B-52* fleet, it features variable-geometry wings (moveable wings offering a range of sweep). Although its original production total was a planned 244 aircraft, only four are produced before U.S. President Jimmy Carter (b. 1924) cancels the program. (See June 30, 1977)

1974 December 26 First flight of Airbus Industrie *A300B4*, the long-range version of Europe's wide-body jetliner, is made.

1974 December 26 Soviet Union launches *Salyut 4* orbital work station. It will be occupied by a two-man crew in two weeks. (See January 11, 1975)

1975 Annual races begin as sponsored by International Human Powered Vehicle Association. Entrants have no restrictions on design and the races are intended to serve as labs for new technology and new designs. Many bicycle entries are powered by riders who are in a reclining or recumbent position rather than the traditional upright, sitting position.

c. 1975 Sail is added to a surfboard to create sailboarding or windsurfing. The sail allows surfers to experience wave swells on the open ocean, and liberates them from having to wait on shore for a wave.

1975 January 11 First extended Soviet manned space mission begins as *Soyuz 17* is launched into earth orbit with cosmonauts Aleksey A. Gubarev (b. 1931) and Georgy M. Grechko (b. 1931) aboard. They dock with orbiting space station *Salyut 4*, enter, and conduct a series of important exercises to ease their adaptation to space. They return safely after 29 days, 13 hours, 20 minutes.

1975 February 7 Report issued jointly by the National Cancer Institute and the U.S. Department of Transportation states that a decrease in the amount of ozone in the stratosphere would cause an increase in skin cancer.

1975 February 7 Eight Soviet cosmonauts composing the prime and backup crews for the upcoming Apollo-Soyuz joint space flight arrive in Washington, D.C. to join their U.S. counterparts. All will begin a two-week training period that includes mission simulation and briefings on all aspects of the joint flight.

1975
February 7

Joint Apollo-Soyuz flight planned

c. 1975 ■ One type of mobile lounge that brings passengers to the plane and jacks itself up to allow them to board.

1975 March 10 Longest double-track railroad tunnel, the Shin Kanmon Tunnel in Japan, opens. This 11-mile-long (18,713 meters) underwater tunnel connects Honshu and Kyushu.

1975 March 31 First large aircraft to employ an air cushion landing system (ACLS) is De Havilland Canada *XC-8A Buffalo*. This specially-modified transport is used to evaluate the applicability of hovering or air cushion systems to aircraft for use in especially difficult landing areas.

1975 April 5 First manned launch abort occurs as a Soyuz spacecraft carrying cosmonauts Vasily Lazarev (b. 1928) and Oleg Makarov (b. 1933) fails to gain orbit. During launch, when the A2 rocket second stage ignites, the vehicle begins to veer out of control since its first stage had not separated completely. Soyuz is then ejected and makes an emergency landing from a sub-orbital altitude of 90 miles. The crew not only endures a high load of 14 G's (14 times the force exerted by gravity on a body at rest), but lands on the side of a mountain and is saved by their parachute getting snarled in a tree.

1975 May Science journal *Physics Today* reports that the Saturn V launch of the orbital station *Skylab 1* tore a temporary "hole" in the ionosphere. The molecular hydrogen and water vapor from the exhaust caused the oxygen atoms in the ionosphere to recombine, losing one electron each, thus causing a hole, it says. The sun replaced the electrons within three hours, patching the hole. Fifteen years later, scientists are concerned by the ozone-destroying properties of solid-fuel rockets whose exhausts contain large amounts of hydrochloric acid.

1975 May 22 Soviet Union launches the highly successful *Soyuz 18* into earth orbit with cosmonauts Pyotr Klimuk (b. 1942) and Vitaly Sevastyanov (b. 1935) aboard. They dock with and enter orbiting *Salyut 4* where they spend the next two months. Among their experiments and observations is the discovery of a black hole in the constellation Cygnus. After a mission of 62 days, 23 hours, 20 minutes, they return safely.

1975 May 31 European Space Agency (ESA) officially comes into existence. It is composed of the ten member-countries that formed the old European Space Research Organization (Belgium, Denmark, France, West Germany, Italy, The Netherlands, Spain, Sweden, Switzerland, and the United Kingdom). The new agency plans to develop, with the lead of France, a new heavy launch vehicle called Ariane.

1975 June 5 Suez Canal is finally opened to ships eight years after it is closed due to the Arab-Israeli War. British, French, and Americans clear the canal of wrecked vessels and over 600,000 explosive devices of all kinds. (See June 1967)

1975 July 1 First electrified trunk railroad in China opens between Chengtu and Paochi in the Province of Szechwan. A trunk is a main route or line from which branch or feeder lines diverge.

1975 July 15 United States launches *ASTP* (*Apollo-Soyuz Test Project*) seven-and-one-half hours after *Soyuz 19* goes into orbit, to participate with Soviets in first international manned space flight. The U.S. crew is made up of Thomas P. Stafford (b. 1930), Vance D. Brand (b. 1931), and 51-year-old Donald K. Slayton (b. 1924), who was an original Mercury astronaut but who never flew in space because of a now-resolved heart problem. Following docking, joint experiments, and crew transfers, a fuel leak during reentry causes Brand to lose consciousness and the others to experience eye and lung discomfort. None suffers permanent injury. The mission lasts nine days, one hour, 28 minutes.

1975 July 15 First international manned space flight begins with the Soviet launch of *Soyuz 19* carrying cosmonauts Aleksey A. Leonov (b. 1934) and Valery N. Kubasov (b. 1935). They are soon joined in space by an Apollo spacecraft carrying three astronauts. After a successful docking, there are joint experiments and even crew transfers. The spacecraft remained linked for two days. *Soyuz 19* reenters safely after a flight of five days, 22 hours, 54 minutes. (See July 15, 1975 ASTP)

1975 August 21 Future U.S. space shuttle is called "the ultimate recycling program" by a Rockwell International Corp. official in a speech at Transportation Day at the Canadian National Exhibition in Toronto. Describing it as the first economical and effective use of space, he says further that, "the job of transportation is not just to move people and goods from point to point—it is to also move history forward by enabling society to capitalize on their discoveries."

1975 August 26 First flight of the McDonnell Douglas *YC-15* STOL (short take-off and landing) transport is made. Designed to meet U.S. military requirements, it is eventually abandoned for economic reasons.

1975 September 1 First aircraft to make two return transatlantic flights (or four transatlantic crossings in one day) is Aérospatiale/BAC *Concorde*. This supersonic transport flies from London, England to Gander, Newfoundland, Canada twice.

1975 September 30 First flight of Hughes Model *77* (*YAH-64*) two-seat, attack helicopter is made. Designed to be an all-weather, day/night helicopter, it becomes part of the U.S. Army fleet.

1975 October 1 Rockwell International Corp. and National Aeronautics and Space Administration (NASA) sign a $1.8 billion supplemental agreement for the follow-on development of the space shuttle orbiter. It calls for the construction of Orbiters 101 and 102 and six orbital flight tests.

1975 November 12 All expendable launch vehicles except the small Scout will be eliminated after the space shuttle becomes operational, National Aeronautics and Space Administration (NASA) tells a U.S. House Subcommittee. The Air Force however, wants extra vehicles on hand after the shuttle in case problems develop. NASA makes a risky decision which proves costly after the shuttle does indeed develop major reliability problems.

1975 December 6 First airmail flight by a supersonic aircraft is made by the Tupolev *Tu-144*, carrying mail between Moscow and Alma Ata, within the U.S.S.R.

1975 December 6 Longest tunnel in the Southern Hemisphere opens on the long industrial mining line between Toquepala and Cuajone, Peru. It is 18.6 miles (30 kilometers) long.

1975 December 30 Largest ship ever shipwrecked at sea, the Norwegian supertanker *Berge Istra*, explodes en route from Brazil to Japan and sinks. Only two survivors of the 227,556-ton vessel are found. The two men, who are rescued on January 18, 1976, report that the ship is blown apart by three explosions. Thirty other crewmen are lost.

1976 First inflatable boats to be constructed of woven Kevlar 29 are tested on wild rivers in California, Idaho, and West Virginia. Developed by the U.S. Dupont Company, Kevlar is half lighter than its nylon counterpart and has exceptional tensile strength and stiffness. It proves capable of surviving sharp rocks and boulders.

1976 January 21 First passenger services by a supersonic airliner are made, as British Airways and Air France *Concorde* supersonic transports take off simultaneously for Bahrain and Rio de Janeiro.

1976 February 22 Steam may power the rockets of tomorrow, says Freeman Dyson (b. 1923) of the Princeton Institute for Advanced Study. Speaking at the annual meeting of the American Association for the Advancement of Science, he says that these steam engines would be powered by laser beams so powerful they could instantly turn water into superheated, high-velocity steam that could carry a one-ton spacecraft into earth orbit. He mentions the work of Arthur Kantrowitz (b. 1913) of the Avco Everett Research Laboratory who has done research on laser propulsion.

1976 March 3 National Aeronautics and Space Administration (NASA) formally announces that women will definitely be admitted to the U.S. space program. Although the exact number is not determined, they will form a part of the 15 mission specialists chosen to fly on the space shuttle once it becomes operational. NASA fulfills this pledge.

*1976
March 3
**NASA admits
women to
space
program***

1976 March 9 Worst cable car disaster ever occurs at Cavalese, Italy as 42 people are killed when the cable snaps and sends the gondola crashing into the valley below.

1976 March 24 First flight of General Dynamics *YF-16* following its conversion to a control-configured vehicle (CCV) experimental aircraft. CCV is an active control system that uses a sensor and a computer to enhance a fighter's maneuverability. For a transport, it offers improved fuel savings and a smoother ride. It becomes an integral part of all modern aircraft.

1976 May 7 *The Washington Post* newspaper reports that National Aeronautics and Space Administration (NASA) "quietly" removed a launch abort system for the shuttle three years ago. This system would function during the first two-and-one-half minutes of the launch. NASA says that the pilot and co-pilot will have ejection seats during test flights but once operational, "There is no way to install seven ejection seats in the shuttle."

1976 June 22 Soviet Union launches the orbiting station *Salyut 5* into earth orbit. It will be occupied by Soviet cosmonauts in two weeks. (See July 6, 1976)

1976 July 6 *Soyuz 21* is launched into earth orbit by the Soviet Union with cosmonauts Boris Volnyov (b. 1934) and Vitaly Zholobov (b. 1937) aboard.

They link up with *Salyut 5* and enter the station for a series of military reconnaissance and space manufacturing experiments. A problem with the station atmosphere forces them to return early. They total 49 days, six hours, 24 minutes.

1976 July 14 Tanzam line opens and links the Zambian terminal of Kapiri Mposhi with the Tanzanian port of Dar es Salaam. This line, which runs over 1,155 miles (1,859 kilometers), is one of the most important new transportation developments in Africa.

*1976
August 1–
Sept. 30*

*First home-
built aircraft
flies around
the world*

1976 August 1–September 30 First home-built or amateur-constructed aircraft to fly around the world is Don Taylor's Thorp *T-18*. This two-seat, all-metal sporting aircraft completes a distance of 24,627 miles (39,633 kilometers) in 171.5 actual flying hours. More than 1,300 sets of plans for this aircraft are sold.

1976 September 8 U.S. President Gerald R. Ford (b. 1913) names Shuttle Orbiter 101 the *Enterprise* over the objections of National Aeronautics and Space Administration (NASA) officials who had chosen the name *Constitution*. The White House responded to nearly 100,000 fans of the TV series "Star Trek" who signed letters and petitions to have the shuttle named after the spaceship in that series.

1976 September 15 Soviet Union launches *Soyuz 22* with cosmonauts Valery Bykovsky (b. 1934) and Vladimir Aksenov (b. 1935) aboard. This week-long mission is devoted primarily to earth observations and photography. Two thousand four hundred photos are taken covering thirty specific targets. The crew returns safely after seven days, 21 hours, 52 minutes.

*1976
September 17*

*First space
shuttle man-
ufactured*

1976 September 17 U.S. space shuttle orbiter named *Enterprise* is rolled out of Rockwell International's assembly facility at Palmdale, California. It is hailed by National Aeronautics and Space Administration (NASA) officials as inaugurating "the new era of space transportation."

1976 October 10—16 More than 1,000 of the world's top government and industry space experts gather at Anaheim, California at the week-long 27th Congress of the International Astronautical Federation whose meeting theme is "The New Era of Space Transportation." The discussions and papers are dominated by talk of the U.S. space shuttle.

1976 ■ *Argo Merchant* aground and spilling oil off Nantucket Island.

1976 October 14 *Soyuz 23* is launched by the Soviet Union and proves to be a short but dramatic mission. The crew of Vyacheslav Zudov (b. 1942) and Valery Rozhdestvensky (b. 1939) intend to enter the orbiting station *Salyut 5*, but when their rendezvous approach electronics fail while approaching the station, they are forced to make an emergency reentry. *Soyuz 23* makes the first Soviet "splashdown," landing in the icy Lake Tengiz at night, with high winds and a temperature of -20 degrees Celsius. The cosmonauts are rescued in a dramatic fashion.

1976 December 2 First flight of Boeing *747-123* following its modification by Boeing to become the National Aeronautics and Space Administration's (NASA) space shuttle carrier. It is intended to carry the space shuttle orbiter *Enterprise* "piggy-back" on top of its fuselage, since NASA plans to launch the shuttle in the east and land it in the west.

1976 December 22 First flight of the Soviet Union's first wide-body jet, Ilyushin *Il-86*, is made in Moscow. This airliner carries its four engine pods under the wings, the way Boeing and Douglas aircraft do.

1977 "Ladies Only" compartments on British trains are abolished under the Sex Discrimination Act of 1976. They could be retained only if an equal number of "Men Only" compartments were set aside.

1977 Fiat of Italy produces a two-passenger prototype electric city automobile that is powered by nickel-zinc batteries. It has a top speed of 47 mph and a range of 70 miles at a constant 37 mph.

1977 February 1 One thousand, one hundred and forty-seven applications for the space shuttle astronaut candidate program are initially received by National Aeronautics and Space Administration (NASA). There are openings for at least 15 pilot and 15 mission specialist candidates. Most of the applications were for the less skilled mission specialist jobs. Pilots will control the shuttle during launch, orbit, and landing. Specialists will be primarily responsible for experiment operations. (See July 15, 1977)

1977 February 7 Soviet Union launches *Soyuz 24* with cosmonauts Viktor V. Gorbatko (b. 1934) and Yuri Glazkov (b. 1939) on board. This strictly military reconnaissance mission is conducted from the orbiting *Salyut 5* station, which the crew is able to enter with no problems. The crew cuts its mission short when an "acrid odor" in the station forces them to reenter. The mission lasts 17 days, 17 hours, 26 minutes.

1977 February 18 First modern aircraft to be used for piggy-back transportation is the Boeing space shuttle carrier, with the National Aeronautics and Space Administration (NASA) space shuttle *Enterprise* mounted above it. The test flight is made successfully at NASA's Dryden Flight Research Center and five are planned to follow. In all five flights, the *Enterprise* is unmanned.

1977 March 24 First flight of Lockheed *YC-141B Starlifter* is made. This very large aircraft has a lengthened fuselage and becomes one of the U.S. Air Force's two main heavy transport models.

1977 March 27 World's greatest air tragedy (579 people killed) occurs as two Boeing 747s collide on the runway at Los Rodeos Airport, Tenerife, Canary Islands. In conditions of dense fog, a KLM Royal Dutch Airlines 747 mistakenly rushes down the runway at full power for a takeoff and slams nearly head-on into a Pan American World Airways 747 taxiing up the runway in preparation for its own takeoff. Los Rodeos is handling twice its normal volume because of temporary rerouting. It also has no ground radar and controllers must watch aircraft on the ground.

1977 May 3 First hovering flight of Bell *XV-15* tilt-rotor research aircraft is made. This converta-plane has rotors (and engines) that tilt on the ends of its short, fixed wings. It makes its first full transition to full airplane flight on July 24, 1979.

1977 June 17 Only two major, new construction efforts were made at the Kennedy Space Center, Florida to accommodate the space shuttle, National Aeronautics and Space Administration (NASA) announces. One was an orbiter landing facility that is now one of the largest runways in the world. The other was a very large hangar, the "orbiter processing facility," with two high bays for servicing the orbiter before and after landing.

1977 June 30 U.S. President Jimmy Carter (b. 1924) announces cancellation of the Rockwell International *B-1* supersonic strategic bomber program, explaining that the United States will rely instead on unmanned cruise missiles for strategic attack. Although only four are built and production stops, research continues, and in 1981, President Ronald Reagan (b. 1911) revives the program as the *B-1B*. (See October 2, 1981)

1977 July 15 Over 8,000 individuals had applied for the 30 to 40 space shuttle astronaut positions, National Aeronautics and Space Administration (NASA) announces at the close of the recruiting period.

1977 August 12 U.S. space shuttle orbiter *Enterprise* makes its first free gliding flight at Edwards Air Force Base, California. Following its launch or release from atop the Boeing 747 plane that takes it to 27,000 feet (8,100 meters), it makes an unpowered glide and a flawless landing in the Mojave Desert. Astronauts Fred W. Haise (b. 1933) and Charles G. Fullerton (b. 1936) pilot the shuttle in this test of its subsonic airworthiness and landing capabilities.

1977 August 12

First space shuttle takes test flight

1977 August 23 First human-powered aircraft to fly a figure-eight mile is American Paul Mac-Cready's (b. 1925) *Gossamer Condor*. Designed by Mac-Cready and piloted by racing cyclist Bryan Allen, the pioneer ultra-light aircraft wins the £50,000 Kremer International Competition Award posted by the Royal Aeronautical Society of Great Britain. Weighing 70 pounds and spanning 96 feet (29.26 meters), the aircraft covers the required distance in seven-and-one-half minutes. Computing power and new, ultra-light materials are used brilliantly by MacCready in building this aircraft. This breakthrough design leads to its successor, *Gossamer Albatross*. (See June 12, 1979)

**1977
September 29**

*U.S.S.R.
launches
orbiting
station*

1977 September 29 Soviet Union launches a new orbiting space station, *Salyut 6*, amid uncharacteristic pre-flight publicity which cites its opening of a "new era." It is to be occupied by cosmonauts. (See October 9 and December 10, 1977)

1977 October 9 Soviet Union's *Soyuz 25*, carrying cosmonauts Vladimir Kovalenok (b. 1942) and Valery Ryumin (b. 1939), is launched for a long-term mission with the new *Salyut 6* space station. Once again a docking mechanism failure forces the early termination of this publicized and ambitious mission. The crew reenters safely after only two days, 46 minutes.

**1977
December 10**

*Untethered
cosmonaut
saved*

1977 December 10 Highly successful *Soyuz 26* is launched by the Soviet Union with cosmonauts Yuri Romanenko (b. 1944) and Georgy Grechko (b. 1931) aboard. During their three-month-long flight, they are resupplied by a robot tanker and conduct the first Soviet space walk since 1969. It is during this walk that the tethered Grechko saves Romanenko's life when the latter eagerly leans out too far, loses his grip, and untethered, starts to float away. The cosmonauts return after a record mission of 96 days, ten hours.

1977 December 22 First flight of the Soviet Union's Antonov *An-72 Coaler* light tactical transport STOL (short take-off and landing) aircraft is made. Produced to replace its aging prop-driven STOLs, it has a new and unusual twin-turboprop layout with its two large engines mounted above its wings. This design allows the outpouring air to blow over the wing surface and down the flaps, increasing the plane's lift.

1978 First American compact cars with front-wheel drive are the Dodge Omni and Plymouth Horizon. The U.S. auto industry is slow to respond to the public's acceptance of smaller (mostly imported) cars.

1978 January 10 Soviet Union's *Soyuz 27* is launched with cosmonauts Vladimir Dzhanibekov (b. 1942) and Oleg Makarov (b. 1933) aboard. They dock with the orbiting station *Salyut 6*, which the *Soyuz 26* cosmonauts have been in for one month, and bring them supplies and mail. After a short stay, they switch space-

craft and return safely to earth in *Soyuz 26* after a mission of five days, 22 hours, 59 minutes.

1978 January 16 Selection of 15 space shuttle pilot-astronauts and 20 mission-specialists is announced by National Aeronautics and Space Administration (NASA). In this eighth group of astronauts, the pilot-astronauts are: (Air Force) Richard Covey (b. 1946), Frederick Gregory (b. 1941), Stanley Griggs (1939—1989), Steven Nagel (b. 1946), Francis Scobee (1939—1986), Brewster Shaw (b. 1945), and Loren Shriver (b. 1944); and (Navy) Daniel Brandenstein (b. 1943), Michael Coats (b. 1946), John Creighton (b. 1943), Robert Gibson (b. 1946), Frederick Hauck (b. 1941), Jon McBride (b. 1943), David Walker (b. 1944), and Donald Williams (b. 1942). The mission-specialists are: (civilians) Anna Fisher (b. 1949), Shannon Lucid (b. 1943), Judith Resnik (1949—1986), Sally Ride (b. 1951), Margaret Seddon (b. 1947), and Kathryn Sullivan (b. 1951); (Air Force) Guion Bluford (b. 1942), John Fabian (b. 1939), Richard Mullane (b. 1945), George Nelson (b. 1950), and Ellison Onizuka (1946—1986); (Navy) Dale Gardner (b. 1948), Terry Hart (b. 1946), Steven Hawley (b. 1951), Jeffrey Hoffman (b. 1944), and Ronald McNair (1950—1986); (Army) Robert Stewart (b. 1942), Norman Thagard (b. 1943), and James Van Hoften (b. 1944); and (Marines) James Buchli (b. 1945). This group of 35 includes six women, three blacks, and an American of Japanese descent. NASA broadens all of its selection criteria.

1978 March 2 First non-Soviet or non-American is launched into space by the Soviet Union in *Soyuz 28*. Czechoslovakian cosmonaut Vladimir Remek (b. 1948) is carried as a crew member along with Soviet cosmonaut Aleksey Gubarev (b. 1931). They dock with orbiting station *Salyut 6*, and join two cosmonauts who have been there since December 10. After a week of experiments, *Soyuz 28* returns safely, totaling seven days, 20 hours, 16 minutes.

1978 March 6 Major oil spill occurs as supertanker *Amoco Cadiz* breaks in two in heavy seas off the coast of Brittany, France. En route from the Persian Gulf to Lyme, England, the fully-loaded vessel (1.6 million barrels of crude oil) suffers a failure in its steering mechanism. A tugboat attempts to save it from going aground on the rocks but fails when its tow line snaps. The crew is removed by helicopter and nearly all the cargo spills out, creating an oil slick that covers 110 miles of coastline. Human error following the grounding appears to compound the catastrophe.

1978 March 10 First flight of Dassault *Mirage 2000*, a single-seat interceptor and air superiority fighter, is made in Istres, France. With its redesigned wing and advanced systems, it becomes the next-generation multi-role fighter for the French Air Force.

1978 May 9 First crossing of the English Channel by a powered hang-glider is made by David Cook. He installs a piston engine on a Volmer *VJ-23 Swingwing* and crosses in one hour, 15 minutes.

1978 May 21 Narita International Airport, Tokyo, Japan, becomes operational.

1978 June 27 Soviet Union launches *Soyuz 30* carrying the first Polish cosmonaut, Miroslaw Hermaszewski (b. 1941), and Soviet cosmonaut Pyotr Klimuk (b. 1942). They join *Soyuz 29* cosmonauts in the orbiting station, *Salyut 6*, and conduct experiments to study the manufacture of semiconductor materials in space. Both the Soviet Union and the United States strive to determine how the special conditions of weightlessness can be used to an advantage for the manufacture of special materials. The crew returns safely after seven days, 22 hours, four minutes.

1978 July First truly open-water passenger/car ferry capable of year-round service, the British *SR.N4*, goes into service. Able to carry 254 passengers and 30 cars, this 165-ton hovercraft can cope with wave heights between 8 and 12 feet (2.5—3.5 meters).

1978 July 15 *Soyuz 29* is launched by the Soviet Union with cosmonauts Vladimir Kovalyonok (b. 1942) and Alexander Ivanchenkov (b. 1940) aboard. After docking with and entering the orbiting station *Salyut 6*, the crew conducts earth resource and space manufacturing experiments during its long stay. After 139 days, 14 hours, 48 minutes, they reenter safely.

1978 July 26 Sixteen of the thirty-five new National Aeronautics and Space Administration (NASA) astronaut candidates begin water survival school in Florida. Since the shuttle is launched over water, it is important for these new recruits to be trained in water survival techniques. Among the 16 are the six female candidates.

1978 August 12—17 First transatlantic crossing by a gas balloon is made by *Double Eagle II*, crewed by Ben L. Abruzzo (b. 1930), Maxie L. Anderson and Larry M. Newman (b. 1947). This flight also establishes new endurance and distance records for gas balloons of 3,107 miles (5,001 kilometers) and 137 hours, 5 minutes, 60 seconds.

1978 August 20 First flight of British Aerospace *Sea Harrier* is made in Surrey, England. This aircraft carrier-based VTOL (vertical take-off and landing) fighter goes into service the next year with the Royal Navy and is first used in combat during the Falklands Islands conflict with Argentina (April—June 1982). It is very successful in air-to-air battles and none is downed by another aircraft.

1978 August 26 First cosmonaut from East Germany, Sigmund Jahn (b. 1937), is launched into space along with Soviet cosmonaut Valery Bykovsky (b. 1934), in *Soyuz 31*. After a now-routine docking and entry mission to orbiting station *Salyut 6*, cosmonuat Jahn conducts a military photographic exercise. They return safely after seven days, 20 hours, 49 minutes.

1978 September 12 Longest tunnel in New Zealand opens between Apata and Waharoa in the North Island. This single-track railroad tunnel is 5.5 miles (8.8 kilometers) long.

1978 September 19 National Aeronautics and Space Administration (NASA) conducts final successful airdrop test which demonstrates that the shuttle solid-rocket strap-on boosters can be retrieved by parachute and thus can be reused. Each empty booster will weigh about 172,000 pounds (78,000 kilograms).

1978 October Sixty-five percent of the food on future shuttle missions will be cooked and packaged before the flight and then reheated on board. Twenty percent would be off-the-shelf items like peanut butter, snap-top puddings, and chewing gum. Food technologists strive to prepare and present astronauts with food they are accustomed to eating on earth.

1978 November 2 Soviet Union reports that after the 139-day space flight of cosmonauts Vladimir Kovalyonok (b. 1942) and Alexander Ivanchenkov (b. 1940) in orbiting station, *Salyut 6*, the crew readjusted quicker than most to the gravity condi-

1978
Sept. 19

NASA concludes shuttle boosters can be reused

tions of earth, mainly because they had exercised more than most previous crews.

1978 November 9　First flight of McDonnell Douglas *YAV-8B Advanced Harrier* is made. This VTOL (vertical take-off and landing) combat aircraft is an American development of the British Aerospace *Harrier.*

1978 November 18　First flight of joint McDonnell Douglas and Northrop *F/A-18 Hornet* is made. This single-seat, carrier-based fighter is extremely agile and performs well for the United States during the Persian Gulf War of January—February 1991.

1978 December 19　First solar-powered aircraft, *Solar One,* makes a successful but brief hop-flight in England. Britons David Williams and Fred To later fly the aircraft for almost three-quarters of a mile (1,200 meters) on June 13, 1979. Since it uses batteries to store the electricity generated by its 750 solar cells, some argue that this is an electric, rather than solar, aircraft.

1979 A.D.

Trains tested using magnetic levitation

1979　Railroad trains using the principle of magnetic levitation are tested by the Japanese whose test model reaches a record speed of 321.2 mph.

1979 January　General Dynamics *F-16 Fighting Falcon* enters operational service with U.S. Air Force. Perhaps the best and most cost effective tactical combat aircraft of the 1980s, this multirole fighter continues to be the backbone of the U.S. tactical fleet into the 1990s.

1979 January 25

First four shuttles named

1979 January 25　Names for the first four space shuttle orbiters are in honor of famous U.S. explorer ships, National Aeronautics and Space Administration (NASA) announces. *Columbia* is named after the ship that located the Columbia River in 1792; *Challenger* is named after the ship that gathered 50 volumes worth of data on the earth's oceans during 1872—1876; *Discovery* was the name of the ship that sought the northwest passage and explored Hudson's Bay during 1610—1611; and *Atlantis* was a two-masted ocean research vessel that logged a half million miles from 1930 to 1966. *Enterprise,* the first orbiter built for atmospheric tests only, was named after both the spacecraft in TV's popular "Star Trek" series and the vessel that explored the Arctic from 1851 to 1854.

1979 January 29　First flight of Northrop *RF-5E* is made at Edwards Air Force Base, California. This specialized reconnaissance version of the *F-5E* fighter/bomber has nose-mounted sensors.

1979 February 25　Soviet Union launches *Soyuz 32* with cosmonauts Vladimir Lyakhov (b. 1941) and Valery Ryumin (b. 1939) aboard. They dock and enter the orbiting station *Salyut 6* and conduct a very long-duration mission. Plans included visits by later manned flights, but these were not successful. They conduct astronomical experiments as well as an unscheduled space walk. The crew concludes a 175-day, 36-minute mission with a safe return to earth.

1979 March 9　First flight of French Dassault *Super Mirage 4000* is made. This single-seat multi-role combat aircraft is very advanced, with a delta wing and a fly-by-wire (computer-based) active control system. A delta wing is triangular-shaped and swept back. It became a new design concept with the achievement of supersonic speed. It reduces the amount of wing surface that is hit by the forward velocity of air. Despite this, buyers are not interested and it is not developed.

1979 April 10　*Soyuz 33* is launched by the Soviet Union and suffers a primary engine failure in orbit. Crewed by Nikolay N. Rukavishnikov (b. 1932) and Bulgarian cosmonaut Georgy Ivanov (b. 1940), the spacecraft was planned to link up with orbiting station *Salyut 6,* but is forced to use a back-up engine and make an emergency return to earth. This forced reentry may have generated as much as 15+ G's (15 times the force of gravity on a body at rest) on the cosmonauts who probably endure the highest G's of any men in space. They return safely after one day, 23 hours, one minute.

1979 June 1　As the orbiting U.S. station *Skylab 1* begins to lose its orbital speed and threatens to reenter the earth's atmosphere, National Aeronautics and Space Administration (NASA) plans to alter its orbital path if this is necessary to ensure it falling to earth over less populated areas. (See June 20, 1979)

1979 June 12　First man-powered aircraft to cross the English Channel is the *Gossamer Albatross,* designed and built under the leadership of Paul MacCready (b. 1925). Flown by bicyclist Bryan Allen, it crosses from Folkestone, England to the French coast in two hours, 49 minutes and wins the £100,000 Kremer Prize. It is calculated that this ultra-light craft actually flies about 35 miles. While an improvement on the *Gossamer Condor,* its wire bracing has high aerodynamic drag, and the tail-first design makes it difficult to fly, especially at higher speeds. Although a breakthrough, such disadvantages prove it to be an evolutionary dead-end.

◢ 1979 June 20 Most of *Skylab 1* will be destroyed by atmospheric friction when it falls to earth, says National Aeronautics and Space Administration (NASA), although there may be two heavy pieces (an airlock shroud and a lead-lined film vault) that may survive reentry and hit the earth. (See July 11, 1979)

◢ 1979 July 11 *Skylab 1* deorbits and reenters over the Indian Ocean, with pieces falling over parts of the Australian outback. There are no reports of damage or injury, for which the U.S. government was prepared to compensate. The mayor of Kalgoorlie, Australia later squeezes in its town hall lobby the largest, recovered fragment, a six-and-one-half foot by three-and-one-quarter foot cylindrical piece of metal.

◢ 1979 July 19 Largest oil spill at sea occurs as two fully-loaded supertankers collide off the coast of Tobago, causing huge amounts of oil to pour into the Caribbean Sea. Although there is a thunderstorm in progress, there is no apparent reason why the *Atlantic Empress* (carrying 2 million barrels of crude oil) and the *Aegean Captain* (carrying 1.5 million barrels) should have collided. *Atlantic Empress* is engulfed in flames and is a total loss, with 26 of its crew of 40 missing. Between the two vessels, 2.1 million barrels of oil spills out, most of it drifting onto the open sea.

◢ 1979 August 11 India's first attempt to orbit its own spacecraft using its own launcher from its own site is unsuccessful as the seven-story-tall booster crashes five minutes after lift-off. (See July 18, 1980)

◢ 1979 September 10 Martin Marietta delivers to National Aeronautics and Space Administration (NASA) a manned maneuvering unit (MMU) designed for astronauts to use moving about and working outside the space shuttle. It is worn on the astronaut's back and allows movement in the weightlessness of space by using nitrogen gas jets to control direction.

◢ 1979 October 9 New program office called Space Transportation System Operations is created in National Aeronautics and Space Administration

(NASA) Headquarters. Responsible not only for shuttle operations but scheduling, pricing, and launch-service agreements as well, this new office reflects NASA`s ambitious plans to operate the shuttle as a real user-oriented program. NASA expects a heavy response and a heavy shuttle schedule.

✕ 1979 October 18 First flight of McDonnell Douglas *DC-9 Super 81* is made. This is an increased wing-span/lengthened fuselage version of the *DC-9-50,* altered to provide increased capacity on short/medium-range routes. It can carry 172 passengers, which is 33 more than the older *DC-9* series.

✕ 1979 November 16 First flight of Lockheed *L-1011 TriStar* is made. This wide-body, "airbus" type of airliner contains advances such as extended wingtips to reduce drag, and active controls for automatic correction of any sudden gust loads on the wings. It competes with Boeing's *747* and McDonnell Douglas's *DC-10* for the same long-range, international passenger air routes.

🚀 1979 December 17 Soviet Union launches an improved, new-style *Soyuz T* spacecraft into earth orbit. This unmanned, rehearsal flight includes a remote-control docking with orbiting station *Salyut 6.*

1980 Otis Elevators introduces the glass-walled "observation elevator." Unlike traditional elevators which run inside an enclosed shaft, this shaft is placed on the outside of the building where passengers can view the surroundings. These prove very popular, especially for hotels.

1980 A.D.

Glass-walled observation elevators introduced

1980 Six years after the U.S. speed limit is set at 55 mph, 470,000 radar detectors are sold in one year. In 1985, some 1.7 million are sold, indicating widespread belief that this speed is unrealistically slow for highways. A radar detector "listens" for radar waves generated by police speed traps and signals the speeding driver when it "hears" them.

1980 Trishaw taxis become a cheap form of transport in Malaysia. These are simply two-wheeled trailers attached to the front of a bicycle. These three-wheel cycle-trailers provide an inexpensive means of adapting a bicycle to carry more passengers or heavy loads.

c. 1980 ■ Typical huge oil supertanker.

c. 1980 MagLev (magnetic levitation) research begins in the United States, Germany, and Japan with small, tracked vehicles using linear electric motors for propulsion and reverse magnetic force for levitation. These very high-speed cars may have a practical future as an economical system for airport "people movers." They cannot compete economically with the longer-range, new high-speed trains like the French TGV.

1980 Japan National Railways runs an experimental "maglev" train at 320 mph on a four-mile test track. Based on the fact that like poles of a magnet repel each other, the same magnets that lift the train off the track also help propel it. Because the energy that drives a magnetic levitation (maglev) vehicle comes from the current in the track coils, the train does not have to carry any fuel or generating equipment. It is light- and energy-efficient.

1980 Japanese automobile production surpasses that of the United States for the first time.

1980 General Motors announces plans to introduce small electric cars in 1984. It will be a hybrid vehicle that couples a small heat engine with a battery. Any real, all-purpose electric passenger car still awaits a breakthrough in battery development.

1980 Daimler-Benz automakers of West Germany begin installing air bags in their Mercedes-Benz automobiles upon special order. It will still be another ten years before U.S. auto companies make them easily available to consumers. (See 1990)

1980 First sail-assisted commercial ship to be built in past 50 years, Japan's *Shin-Aitoku-Maru*, is launched. This 1,750-ton tanker uses new materials and computer technology to build a sail system that supplements its engines. The entire mast and sail can be rotated mechanically on their own axes from a central control room. The sails are not hoisted or lowered but rather rolled out mechanically from the mast, and the system is thus able to respond to weather changes and obtain the most favorable angle to the wind.

1980 March 18 New National Aeronautics and Space Administration (NASA) regulation covers a situation "when a barroom brawl breaks out in space." The new rule would permit a shuttle commander to "use any reasonable and necessary means, including physical force" to maintain order on board. The police power would also include the authority to arrest a person in space and charge him or her with a crime punishable by a $5,000 fine, a year in prison, or both.

1980 April 9 *Soyuz 35* is launched by the Soviet Union with cosmonauts Leonid I. Popov (b. 1945) and Valery V. Ryumin (b. 1939) aboard. They dock with orbiting station *Salyut 6* and stay long enough to host three separate flight crews. Ryumin is a last-minute replacement, having spent 175 days of the previous year in space aboard the *Salyut* station. On this flight with Popov, he breaks his own record, returning safely after a mission of 184 days, 20 hours, 12 minutes.

1980 May 15 National Aeronautics and Space Administration (NASA) announces that shuttle flights will be substantially delayed due to the removal and treatment of as many as 10,000 of the shuttle's 30,922 heat-protection tiles. Tests have shown that many of the

1980 A.D.

Japanese car production surpasses U.S.

tiles need to be made more dense as well as have their sticking power increased. Unlike Apollo which was protected during the extreme heat of reentry by an ablative coating which absorbs heat as it burns away, the tile system must maintain its structural integrity or a hole could produce a dangerous hot spot.

1980 May 26 Soviet Union launches *Soyuz 36* with cosmonauts Valery N. Kubasov (b. 1935) and Bertalan Farkas (b. 1949) of Hungary aboard. They dock with the occupied *Salyut 6* station, and cosmonaut Farkas brings the crew a meal of goulash, pâté de fois gras, fried pork, and jellied tongue, besides some experiments to perform. He and Kubasov stay one week and return safely after seven days, 20 hours, 46 minutes using the *Soyuz 35* spacecraft.

1980 May 30 Nineteen new candidates are chosen by National Aeronautics and Space Administration (NASA) for space shuttle training. The eight new pilot candidates are: (Air Force) John E. Blaha (b. 1942), Roy D. Bridges (b. 1943), Guy S. Gardner (b. 1948), and Ronald J. Grabe (b. 1945); (Navy) Richard N. Richards (b. 1946) and Michael J. Smith (1945—1986); and (Marines) Charles F. Bolden, Jr. (b. 1946) and Brian D. O'Connor (b. 1946). The 11 new mission-specialist selections are: (civilians) James P. Bagian (b. 1952), Franklin R. Chang-Diaz (b. 1950), Mary L. Cleave (b. 1947), Bonnie J. Dunbar (b. 1949), and William F. Fisher (b. 1946); (Marines) David C. Hilmers (b. 1950) and Robert C. Springer (b. 1942); (Navy) David C. Leestma (b. 1949); and (Army) Sherwood C. Spring (b. 1944). William Fisher is married to Anna Fisher (b. 1949), a NASA astronaut selected two years earlier.

1980 June 5 First manned flight test of the improved Soyuz spacecraft is made as *Soyuz T-2* is launched with cosmonauts Yuri V. Malyshev (b. 1941) and Vladimir V. Aksenov (b. 1935) aboard. Although it looks the same externally, the new, uprated craft has an onboard computer and new guidance system. After launch, it is this system that fails and the crew performs a manual docking. They spend three days in the already-manned *Salyut 6* and wear new-style spacesuits. They return safely after a mission of three days, 22 hours, 19 minutes.

1980 July 8 Despite being flooded with requests, National Aeronautics and Space Administration (NASA) announces it has no plans to carry tourists or paying passengers into space aboard the shuttle.

1980 July 18 India becomes the sixth country to build and launch its own satellite as it puts the 771-pound satellite, *Rohini*, into earth orbit. It is launched from Sriharikota Island, near Madras, on a four-stage SLV-3 solid-rocket launch vehicle.

1980 July 23 Soviet Union launches *Soyuz 37* carrying Vietnamese pilot Pham Tuan (b. 1947), the first Asian in space, and veteran cosmonaut Viktor V. Gorbatko (b. 1934). They dock with orbiting station *Salyut 6*, and join the crew already there. The Soviets make much of the fact that Pham Tuan is the only pilot said to have shot down a U.S. *B-52* during the Vietnam War. After seven days, 20 hours, 42 minutes, they reenter safely.

1980 July 30 An era ends as the last of the original 118-man "von Braun team" retires from National Aeronautics and Space Administration's (NASA) Marshall Space Flight Center, Huntsville, Alabama. Gustav A. Kroll came to the United States from Germany in 1945 with Wernher von Braun (1912—1977) and other Peenemünde crew members as part of Operation Paperclip.

1980 August 29 Space shuttle crew will use "personal rescue enclosures" in an emergency evacuation situation in space, National Aeronautics and Space Administration (NASA) announces. These 34-inch diameter balls are fitted with life support and communications gear for one person and would protect a crew member during an in-space transfer to another spacecraft.

1980 September Longest road tunnel, the St. Gotthard Tunnel, opens to motor traffic. Like the railway tunnel under the St. Gotthard Pass in Switzerland built a century before, this modern tunnel for cars takes ten years to complete. Along with the 25-foot-wide tunnel for cars, four ventilation tunnels are built as well as a safety or escape tunnel which parallels it. Designed for safety, it has redundant lighting systems, signalling systems, shelters, fire equipment, telephones, radio, and TV for communications. It is built as a gentle curve, since designers feel it is less tiring for drivers who will not have to hold a perfectly straight course for ten miles.

1980 September 18 Soviet Union launches *Soyuz 38* carrying the first black man to fly in space, Cuban Arnaldo Tamayo Mendez (b. 1942). He and Soviet cosmonaut Yuri V. Romanenko (b. 1944) dock with orbiting station *Salyut 6* and join cosmonauts Leonid I. Popov

1980
Sept. 18

First black flies in space

(b. 1945) and Valery V. Ryumin (b. 1939). They conduct experiments and return safely after a mission of seven days, 20 hours, 43 minutes.

1980 November 20

Solar plane flies

1980 November 20 The MacCready *Solar Challenger* makes its first short-duration test flight solely on solar power. This one-man aircraft has 2,540 square feet of solar cell surface which can produce up to 2,676 watts of power in reasonable sunlight. It weighs 194 pounds. (See July 7, 1981)

1980 November 27 First Soviet three-man space crew since 1971 is launched as *Soyuz T-3* enters orbit carrying cosmonauts Leonid D. Kizim (b. 1941), Oleg G. Makarov (b. 1933), and Gennady M. Strekalov (b. 1940). They dock with orbiting station *Salyut 6* and for the next 12 days perform repairs and maintenance work on the well-used space station. They overhaul its hydraulic control, refuelling, and communications systems and return safely after 12 days, 19 hours, eight minutes.

1981 A.D.

Computer introduced on BMW

1981 Germany's BMW introduces a new on-board computer which tells the driver when it needs to be serviced. In ten years, nearly every non-economy car will have computer chips to control and monitor its systems.

1981 "Planetran," an advanced magnetic levitation (maglev) concept which suggests that 6,000 mph underground travel is possible, is seriously considered by engineers. First proposed by Robert M. Salter of the Rand Corporation in 1957, this underground vacuum tube system would eliminate not only the friction of wheels running on a steel rail but air resistance as well. Passengers would ride in an airplane-shaped levitated car through a guideway. One proposed system would have 7,800 miles of tunnels with a primary route stretching from New York to Dallas and Los Angeles. A Transcontinental trip on this futuristic system would take 54 minutes.

1981 British Rail's Advanced Passenger Train (APT) makes its first run with a revenue-earning passenger. This radical, tilt-body design is powered electrically from the middle rather than the front. It achieves rapid acceleration and a top speed of 125 mph as an inter-city passenger train.

1981 Humber Bridge, new suspension bridge over the estuary of the Humber River on the east coast of England, opens. This extremely long (4,626 feet or 1,410 meters) suspension bridge takes advantage of the aerodynamic advances of the Severn Bridge and resembles it in design—being light and economical. Its reinforced concrete towers each consist of two hollow legs braced horizontally. It is the longest single-span suspension bridge yet built.

1981 November 12 U.S. space shuttle *Columbia* (STS-2) makes a successful lift-off from Kennedy Space Center, Florida with astronauts Joe H. Engle (b. 1932) and Richard H. Truly (b. 1937) aboard. The planned five-day mission is cut to two days, six hours, 13 minutes by a faulty fuel cell. Despite this, the crew manages to test out the necessary systems. This is the first time a spacecraft that has already flown once in space is used to fly again.

1981 January 28 Pan American Airlines begins a regular, twice-a-week United States to China air service (New York to Beijing).

1981 February 12 U.S. balloonists Max Anderson (1934—1983) and Don Ida (1933—1983) lift off from Luxor, Egypt in the helium-filled balloon *Jules Verne*. Their round-the-world flight attempt is aborted on February 14 after travelling some 4,667 kilometers (2,900 miles) to Mirchpur, India. The balloon envelope is made of translucent polyethylene.

1981 February 20 U.S. space shuttle engines work perfectly during 20-second test at National Aeronautics and Space Administration's (NASA) Kennedy Space Center, Florida. The three engines at the base of the delta-wing spacecraft generate 1.1 million pounds of thrust for 20 seconds while it remains bolted to the launch pad.

1981 March 12 *Soyuz T-4* is launched by the Soviet Union carrying cosmonauts Vladimir V. Kovalenok (b. 1942) and Viktor P. Savinykh (b. 1940). They dock with and enter orbiting station *Salyut 6*, now on its last legs, and remain aboard conducting experiments during a mission that lasts 74 days, 17 hours, 38 minutes. Cosmonaut Savinykh is the one hundredth person to fly in space.

1981 March 22 Soviet Union launches another foreign-born cosmonaut into space as *Soyuz 39* enters orbit carrying Mongolia's Jugderdemidyin Gurragcha (b. 1947) and Soviet cosmonaut Vladimir A. Dzhanibekov (b. 1942). They dock with orbiting station

1981 ■ Space shuttle *Columbia* lands after its first space mission.

Salyut 6 already carrying the *Soyuz T-4* crew, conduct some experiments, and reenter after a seven-day, 20-hour, 43-minute mission.

1981 April 12 First winged, reusable spacecraft is launched into space as the U.S. space shuttle *Columbia* (STS-1) enters earth orbit. Carrying astronauts John W. Young (b. 1930) and Robert L. Crippen (b. 1937), the revolutionary craft is launched on the 20th anniversary of Yuri Gagarin's first flight in space. The shuttle's solid-fuel rocket boosters are jettisoned after burning out, and they splash down in the Atlantic using parachutes. This is the first time solid rockets are used to put a man in space. The large external tank separates nearly nine minutes into the launch and breaks up as planned. After two days of in-orbit tests, the crew pilots the shuttle to a perfect landing on the lake bed at Edwards Air Force Base, California. Mission time is two days, six hours, 21 minutes. Despite the loss of some tiles with no effect, the long-delayed flight is a total success.

1981 May 14 Soviet Union launches a Rumanian cosmonaut, Dumitru D. Prunariu (b. 1952), along with Soviet veteran Leonid I. Popov (b. 1945), in *Soyuz 40*. This is the final manned mission to the orbiting station *Salyut 6* which the crew occupies. They return safely after a mission of seven days, 20 hours, 38 minutes.

1981 June 6 Worst rail disaster on record occurs in India as a passenger train goes off the tracks while crossing a bridge, killing as many as 1,000 people. The heavily-loaded train plunges off the 150-foot-(45-meter-) high bridge into the Bagnati River.

1981 June 18 First flight of Lockheed *F-117A* stealth attack aircraft is made. All design and system details of this aircraft will be kept absolutely secret for the next nine years. (See April 21, 1990)

1981 June 18

First secret flight of stealth made

1981 June 26 First flight of Grumman/General Dynamics *EF-111A Raven* is made. This is an unarmed, variable-geometry (movable wings offering a range of sweep) aircraft specially developed to be a tactical jamming aircraft. During the January—February 1991 Persian Gulf War, the United States uses the *Raven* to jam ground-based radars and confuse ground control intercept sites, thereby clearing the way for ensuing waves of attack aircraft.

1981 July 7 First solar-powered aircraft flight across the English Channel is made by the Mac-Cready *Solar Challenger*. The 180-mile (290 kilometers) flight takes five hours, 23 minutes, during which time it reaches an altitude of 11,000 feet and maintains an average speed of 35 mph. Pilot Steve Ptacek takes off near Paris, France and lands in Manston, England. Power to the *Solar Challenger* is provided by at least 16,128 solar cells on the upper surfaces of the wing and tailplane. These provide maximum power of 3 hp to its electric motor.

1981 July 29 Professional Air Traffic Controllers Organization (PATCO) membership overwhelmingly rejects a tentative contract reached with the U.S. government. The vote is 13,495 to 616. (See August 3, 1981)

1981 August 3 Some 13,000 U.S. Professional Air Traffic Controllers Organization (PATCO) members walk out, effectively beginning a union strike and a shutdown of the nation's air transportation system. President Ronald Reagan (b. 1911) orders all air controllers back to work within 48 hours or threatens firing. About 1,500 return during this time under the government's pledge of amnesty, but Reagan fires the rest. Government supervisors and military personnel fill in temporarily as controllers. (See October 22, 1981)

1981 September 26 First flight of Boeing *767* wide-body transport is made. This medium-range, new generation aircraft has two aisles between seat rows. Besides computerized control, this new aircraft is best described by its very economical operating characteristics.

1981 October 2

B-1 bomber reinstituted

1981 October 2 President Ronald Reagan reinstitutes the *B-1* bomber program cancelled by the Carter administration in 1977. Now called the *B-1B*, it is expected to operate into the next century. (See 1984)

1981 October 9 First non-stop transcontinental flight in a balloon is made by the helium-filled balloon *Superchicken III*. Flown by Fred Gorrell and John Shoecroft, the balloon is launched from Costa Mesa, near Los Angeles, California and lands on Blackbeard's Island, Georgia, covering 2,515 miles (4,048 kilometers) in 55 hours, 25 minutes.

1981 October 19 Flight delays of U.S. scheduled commercial airlines are running about six times the rate they were before the Professional Air Traffic Controllers Organization (PATCO) strike.

1981 October 22

Air traffic controllers lose union representation

1981 October 22 AFL-CIO Professional Air Traffic Controllers Organization (PATCO) is decertified, losing its right to represent its members. The U.S. Federal Labor Relations Authority finds that the union had called, condoned, and was party to a strike. As employees of the Federal Aviation Administration, PATCO members are prohibited from striking against the federal government.

1981 November 5 First flight of McDonnell Douglas *AV-8B* VTOL (vertical take-off and landing) fighter is made. This single-seat version of the British *Harrier* is used by the U.S. Marines as well as the Royal Air Force (RAF) and the Spanish Navy.

1981 November 9—12 First manned crossing of the Pacific in a gas balloon is made by Ben L.

Abruzzo (b. 1930), Larry M. Newman (b. 1947), Ron Clarke and Rocky Aoki (b. 1938) in the helium-filled balloon *Double Eagle V*. They cover 5,208.68 miles (8,382.54 kilometers) during their flight from Nagashima, Japan to the U.S. west coast. They crash-land in severe weather in Covello, California, some 170 miles (274 kilometers) north of San Francisco.

1981 December 17 First flight of a modified Hughes *OH-6A* helicopter is made. It is altered to a NOTAR (no tail rotor) configuration which, instead of having a conventional tail rotor, uses pressurized air ejected through a controllable slot to offset torque effect.

1982 First compact car produced by German large-car manufacturer Daimler-Benz is its 190 model. These scaled-down versions of their bigger cars are a steady seller ten years later.

1982 Antilocking braking system for automobiles is developed by the German company Bosch. Fitted initially on high-priced cars, it allows the vehicle to be brought to a complete standstill in a very short time without skidding or blocking. It performs well on all road surfaces, but this safety feature is still not standard equipment on most cars.

1982 February 1 Flight version of Spacelab is unveiled by National Aeronautics and Space Administration (NASA). The result of a joint venture between NASA and the European Space Agency (ESA), Spacelab is a cylindrical module built to fit into the shuttle cargo bay where the crew would work in a shirtsleeve environment conducting experiments. More than 50 European firms and ten member nations helped to build Spacelab which is planned to fly in the shuttle next year.

1982 February 19 First flight of Boeing *757* is made in Renton, Washington. This is a new, narrow-body sister-ship to Boeing's wide-body *767*. It is a short to medium range transport and carries 223 passengers, compared to the *767*'s 289. Both reflect the current concern for economical operating characteristics.

1982 March 22 U.S. space shuttle *Columbia* is launched on mission STS-3, with astronauts Jack R. Lousma (b. 1936) and C. Gordon Fullerton (b. 1936) on board. Despite being plagued by many small technical problems, the mission goes well and is extended an extra day because of a storm in the landing area.

1982 April 19 Soviet Union launches improved and modernized orbiting space station, *Salyut 7*. It can accommodate up to five people and will soon be occupied.

1982 May 13 *Soyuz T-5* is launched successfully by the Soviet Union carrying cosmonauts Anatoli N. Berezovoy (b. 1921) and Valentin V. Lebedev (b. 1942). They dock with the new *Salyut 7* orbiting station and play host to two later manned flights. They also conduct a space walk, hand-launch two small satellites via the station airlock, and conduct many experiments during their very long mission which totals 211 days, eight hours, five minutes.

1982 June 24 Soviet Union launches the first French national into space aboard *Soyuz T-6*. French cosmonaut Jean-Loup Chretien (b. 1938) is accompanied by Soviets Vladimir A. Dzhanibekov (b. 1942) and Alexander S. Ivanchenkov (b. 1940), and the crew docks with the manned *Salyut 7* orbiting station. They conduct a mission that lasts seven days, 22 hours, 42 minutes, and space novice Chretien later says the reentry and landing is more dramatic than the launch.

1982 June 25 Longest tunnel entirely in Switzerland, the Furka Base Tunnel, opens. This railroad tunnel over nine miles (15,381 meters) long is part of the Furka-Oberlap Railway and provides a year round link between the Cantons of Wallis and Graubunden.

1982 June 27 U.S. space shuttle *Columbia* lifts off on STS-4 mission, its last proving flight. The crew of Thomas K. Mattingly (b. 1936) and Henry W. Hartsfield (b. 1933) launch a military payload for the Department of Defense (DOD) as well as other, smaller satellites. The mission lasts seven days, one hour, nine minutes.

1982 August 19 Second woman to fly in space, Svetlana Y. Savitskaya (b. 1948), is launched into orbit on *Soyuz T-7* along with cosmonauts Leonid I. Popov (b. 1945) and Alexandr A. Serebrov (b. 1944). They dock with *Salyut 7* orbiting station and conduct a mission lasting seven days, 21 hours, 52 minutes. This flight shows that Soviets are still very much concerned with their image as a leader in space "firsts," or, in this case, seconds, since the United States has plans to launch its first woman in space, Sally K. Ride. The Soviets long ago captured the prize of orbiting the first woman on June 16,

1963, but they apparently did not want to be scooped on this mission nearly 20 years later.

1982 September 1–30 First round-the-world flight in a helicopter (in stages) is made by Bell *Long Ranger II*. Flown by Americans H. Ross Perot, Jr. and Jay W. Coburn, it makes 29 stops.

1982 September 9 First privately funded U.S. rocket is launched from an island off the Texas coast by Space Services Inc. (SSI) of America. The booster successfully launched a mock payload to 196 miles and then dropped into the Gulf of Mexico. The firm hopes to offer relatively inexpensive space transportation to those wanting to put up private satellites without government assistance. They purchased the booster from National Aeronautics and Space Administration (NASA).

1982 October 1 U.S. Federal Aviation Administration (FAA) establishes operating regulations for ultra-light aircraft, in FAR Part 103.

1982 November 11 First operational flight of the U.S. space shuttle is made as *Columbia* goes into orbit on mission STS-5. This is also the first spacecraft to fly with four crew members, astronauts Vance D. Brand (b. 1931), Robert F. Overmyer (b. 1936), Joseph P. Allen (b. 1937), and William B. Lenoir (b. 1939). They launch two communications satellites but cancel a space walk due to Portable Life Support System problems. They return safely at Edwards Air Force Base, California after a mission of five days, two hours, 14 minutes.

1982 Nov. 11 First space shuttle operation occurs

1983 One of the first automobiles with a "talking dashboard" is the Austin Rover Maestro. This electronic system alerts the driver to engine problems.

1983 Fort McHenry Tunnel, largest U.S. tunnel project in terms of cost and scope, opens. Passing beneath Baltimore Harbor, this immersed tube type tunnel consists of twin sections, each carrying double bore tunnels, and providing a total of eight automobile lanes. The entire tunnel is 180 feet wide and the immersed tube section is 5,300 feet long. This new tunnel provides an alternative to the congested and slow Baltimore Harbor Tunnel in Maryland that opened in 1957.

1983 A.D. Largest U.S. tunnel opens

1983 Japanese engineers claim a breakthrough in making a workable engine out of pottery. Developed by Asahi Glass Company, it is made from carbon silicon and nitrogen silicon ceramics that are nearly as strong as steel but conduct much less heat. Operating at high temperatures, these new engines would be efficient, cut pollution, and use almost any kind of fuel.

1983 A.D.

Intermittent windshield wiper developed

1983 Windshield wiper that adjusts its speed automatically to the intensity of falling rain is developed by Japanese automobile company Nissan.

1983 January First subway system in Venezuela opens in Caracas.

1983 January 10 U.S. space shuttle *Challenger* flight is postponed due to leak in engine compartment. Checks eventually reveal hairline cracks in fuel coolant lines and all three main engines must be removed.

1983 April 4

First Challenger flight takes place

1983 April 4 First flight of U.S. space shuttle *Challenger* goes well as STS-6 mission astronauts Paul J. Weitz (b. 1932), Karol J. Bobko (b. 1937), F. Story Musgrave (b. 1935), and Donald H. Peterson (b. 1933) are launched into earth orbit. Crew deploys a communications satellite and astronauts Musgrave and Peterson perform the first space walk from a shuttle. The mission lasts five days, 23 minutes.

1983 April 20 Soviet Union launches *Soyuz T-8* on an intended link-up mission and stay aboard orbiting station *Salyut 7*. However, cosmonauts Vladimir G. Titov (b. 1937), Gennady M. Strekalov (b. 1940), and Alexandr A. Serebrov (b. 1944) are forced to cancel a docking maneuver when their rendezvous radar fails and they are moving toward the station at too great a speed. The mission ends after two days, 20 minutes.

1983 May 1

Man flies on lawn chair

1983 May 1 Lawrence R. Walters is fined $4,000 by the Federal Aviation Administration for operating an aircraft without an Airworthiness Certificate. On July 3, 1982, Walters took off from his driveway in San Pedro, California in a lawn chair supported by 42 weather balloons, and reached an altitude of 16,000 feet.

1983 May 9 First all-woman flight crew to fly a round trip across the Atlantic is the Air Force *C-141* crew from the 18th Military Airlift Squadron, McGuire Air Force Base, New Jersey.

1983 June 18 First U.S. woman astronaut, Sally K. Ride (b. 1951), is launched into space aboard the space shuttle *Challenger* on mission STS-7. She is accompanied by astronauts Robert L. Crippen (b. 1937), Frederick H. Hauck (b. 1941), John M. Fabian (b. 1939), and Norman E. Thagard (b. 1943) who, with her, comprise the first five-person crew to be launched into space. They deploy three satellites and demonstrate the shuttle's remote manipulator system by retrieving one of them from space. This is the first time a satellite is retrieved by a manned spacecraft. The mission ends successfully after six days, two hours, 24 minutes.

1983 ■ Sally K. Ride, first American woman in space, during shuttle mission *STS-7*.

1983 June 27 *Soyuz T-9* is launched by Soviet Union with cosmonauts Vladimir A. Lyakhov (b. 1941) and Alexandr P. Alexandrov (b. 1943) aboard. They dock with orbiting station *Salyut 7* and remain aboard despite mounting technical problems. A leaking propulsion system is the most serious and they are forced to make two walks in space to make repairs. They finally are forced to return after a mission of 149 days, nine hours, 46 minutes.

1983 July 22—August 5 First solo helicopter flight around the world in stages is made by Australian pilot Dick Smith. Flying a Bell *JetRanger III*, he covers 35,258 miles (56,742 kilometers).

1983 August 6 Major oil spill occurs as Spanish supertanker *Castillo de Bellever* catches fire as it rounds the Cape of Good Hope, off South Africa, and breaks in two. Both parts of the vessel sink, and its entire cargo of 1.75 million barrels of crude oil is lost at sea. Three crewmen also die in the fire.

1983 August 30 U.S. space shuttle *Challenger* is launched with astronauts Richard H. Truly (b. 1937), Daniel C. Brandenstein (b. 1943), Guion S. Bluford (b. 1942), Dale A. Gardner (b. 1948), and William E. Thornton (b. 1929) aboard. This mission STS-8 accomplishes several firsts, carrying the first black American, Bluford, into space and also being the first to be launched and to land at night. The crew deploys a communications satellite for India and tests the remote manipulator system. The mission ends after six days, one hour, eight minutes.

1983 September 27 Two Soviet cosmonauts escape death when the escape rocket atop their capsule carries them away from an exploding launch vehicle that is about to launch them into space. Cosmonauts Vladimir G. Titov (b. 1947) and Gennady M. Strekalov (b. 1940) land safely two miles away. This is the first time that a launch escape system is used to save lives.

1983 October France's modern, high-speed electric, inter-city train, the TGV (Train à Grande Vitesse), goes into full service. Its major run, from Paris to Lyon, is cut to a flat two hours. This and other successful lines around the world prove that this is the real age of the electric train.

1983 October 4 Englishman Richard Noble drives his jet-engine powered car just over 650 mph, breaking the land speed record. Designed by John Ackroyd, the *Thrust 2* has a huge, circular air inlet at its front, a lightweight, aerodynamically-shaped frame, and solid wheels.

1983 November 28 First flight of the European Space Agency's (ESA) Spacelab is made aboard the U.S. space shuttle *Columbia*. This mission STS-9 is the first time a crew of six is sent aloft. Along with the astronauts—John W. Young (b. 1930), Brewster H. Shaw (b. 1945), Owen K. Garriott (b. 1930), Robert A. R. Parker (b. 1936)—is a new type of astronaut-passenger, the payload specialist. There are two on this flight, Byron K. Lichtenberg (b. 1948) and ESA's Ulf Merbold (b. 1941). They conduct 70 detailed experiments as part of Spacelab and reenter safely after a mission of ten days, seven hours, 47 minutes.

1983 November 30 Experimental Aircraft Association (EAA), a U.S. organization devoted to sport flying and home-built aircraft, announces it has obtained supplemental type certificates (STCs) that allow the use of unleaded automobile gasoline in Cessna *120, 140, 180,* and *182* aircraft. Additional aircraft are added to this list later.

1984 Soviet Union's Antonov *An-124* transport aircraft makes its first appearance in the West at the Paris Air Show, although it first flew in the Soviet Union on December 26, 1982. This huge new heavy transport is similar to the Lockheed *C-5* although it is able to lift a considerably larger payload than the *C-5.* Its 24-wheel landing gear enables it to operate from unprepared fields, hard-packed snow, and ice-covered swampland. It can carry up to 88 passengers on an upper deck.

1984 Rogers Pass rail tunnel is begun for the Canadian Pacific Railway. When completed, this will be the longest transportation tunnel in North America. It is planned as a nine-mile-long tunnel through the Selkirk Mountains. It is actually two tunnels in tandem.

1984 Platinum auto spark plugs are developed by West German company Bosch. Benefits claimed are: lower spark voltage needed, improved starting, minimal missing on acceleration, as well as being relatively maintenance free.

1984 Mississippi cable car crossing the Mississippi River at New Orleans, Louisiana opens. Built on the occasion of the Louisiana World's Fair, it has the world's longest monocable span (700 meters) and costs $5 million to build. After the Fair, it becomes another means of urban transport.

1984 A.D.

Mississippi River cable car opens

1984 Michelin Bib-foam tire is developed for cross-country motorcycle racing. Its inner tube is replaced by a plastic foam, thus eliminating any chance of going flat.

1984 New type of dirigible is developed in Europe by Jurgen Bothe. Intended to transport cargo and passengers over short distances, it has a mixed lift capability obtained from helium and helicopter-type rotors.

1984 Largest tidal river barrier, the Thames Barrier at Woolrich in London, England, opens. Designed to protect vulnerable sea areas along the Thames River from flooding by the North Sea, it consists of ten movable steel gates, nine piers, and two abutments and is 1,706 feet long and 105 feet high. It has four hydraulically powered gates that are 200 feet wide that

1984 A.D.

Largest tidal river barrier opens

open to facilitate shipping and rotate 90 degrees to lie flat with the river bottom.

1984 January 25 U.S. President Ronald W. Reagan (b. 1911) says in his State of the Union address that the United States should build a permanently manned space station "within a decade." National Aeronautics and Space Administration (NASA) seeks to build a station that would function as a science laboratory, astronomical observatory, space manufacturing center, servicing facility for spacecraft, and an assembly site for larger orbiting structures. A long-range program is eventually decided upon and becomes an international cooperative project, involving the United States, Canada, Japan, and nine member-nations of the European Space Agency (ESA). (See December 1, 1987)

1984 February 3 First untethered space walk in history is made during this shuttle mission. U.S. space shuttle *Challenger* is launched carrying astronauts Vance D. Brand (b. 1931), Robert L. Gibson (b. 1946), Ronald E. McNair (1950—1986), Robert L. Stewart (b. 1942), and Bruce McCandless II (b. 1937). McCandless first uses the manned maneuvering unit (MMU), a self-contained, propulsive backpack, that enables him to move freely in space without having to be tethered to a spacecraft. Stewart also uses the MMU. National Aeronautics and Space Administration (NASA) begins new flight numbering system, now calling this mission 41-B instead of continuing the STS system. The mission concludes after seven days, 23 hours, 15 minutes with the first Cape Canaveral, Florida landing—the first time a spacecraft had landed at its launch site.

1984 February 8 Soviet Union launches *Soyuz T-10* which becomes the longest manned flight to date. The crew of Leonid D. Kizim (b. 1941), Vladimir A. Solovyov (b. 1946), and Oleg Y. Atkov (b. 1949) dock with orbiting station *Salyut 7*, and occupy it for about eight months. During that time they conduct experiments, make six separate space walks, and host two other manned missions. The mission ends safely after 236 days, 22 hours, 50 minutes.

1984 March 11 Fifth group of space shuttle candidates is selected by National Aeronautics and Space Administration (NASA). The 22 two candidates are: (civilians) David T. Allen, William M. Decampli, Jan D. Dozier, Wendy S. Hale, Rosario M. Izquierdo, G. David

1984 February 3 First untethered space walk occurs

Low (b. 1956), Kenneth J. Myers, William S. O'Keefe, Donald R. Pettit, Lonnie Sharpe, Kathryn C. Thornton (b. 1952), and C. Lacy Veach (b. 1944); (Air Force) Larry D. Autry, Joseph A. Carretto, and William A. Flanagan; and (Navy) Dennis N. Bostich, Keith E. Crawford, Fred D. Knox, Michael J. McCulley (b. 1943), William F. Readdy (b. 1952), Gregory J. Rose, and James B. Waddell.

1984 April 3 Soviet Union launches *Soyuz T-11* with cosmonauts Yuri V. Malyshev (b. 1941), Gennady M. Strekalov (b. 1940), and India's first space man, Rakesh Sharma (b. 1949). They dock with the occupied station *Salyut 7* and spend a week conducting experiments. The mission lasts seven days, 21 hours, 41 minutes.

1984 April 6 U.S. space shuttle *Challenger* is launched on mission 41-C with astronauts Robert L. Crippen (b. 1937), Francis R. Scobee (1939—1986), George D. Nelson (b. 1950), Terry J. Hart (b. 1946), and James D. A. Van Hoften (b. 1944). Crew launches one satellite and performs the first capture, repair, and redeployment of another satellite. Their mission lasts six days, 23 hours, 40 minutes.

1984 July 12 New York becomes the first U.S. state to require drivers, front-seat passengers, and children under 10 to wear seat belts.

1984 July 17 *Soyuz T-12* is launched by the Soviet Union carrying cosmonauts Vladimir A. Dzhanibekov (b. 1942), Svetlana Y. Savitskaya (b. 1948), and Igor P. Volk (b. 1937). Soviets again scoop the United States when Savitskaya becomes the first woman to walk in space. The crew docks with orbiting station *Salyut 7* and performs experiments, one of which is Savitskaya's cutting, welding, and soldering tests outside the station. The mission lasts 11 days, 19 hours, 14 minutes.

1984 August 30 First flight of the U.S. space shuttle *Discovery* is made carrying astronauts Henry W. Hartsfield (b. 1933), Michael L. Coats (b. 1946), Richard M. Mullane (b. 1945), Steven A. Hawley (b. 1951), Judith A. Resnik (1949—1986), and Charles D. Walker (b. 1948). Mission 41-D is delayed several months and undergoes a launch pad abort, but once in space, its crew deploys three communications satellites. Walker is the first fare-paying passenger in space as his company, McDonnell Douglas, pays National Aeronautics and Space Administration (NASA) to take him along so he can operate their electrophoresis experiment. The mission lasts six days, 56 minutes and the new shuttle performs well.

⊿ 1984 October 5 First crew of seven is launched into space aboard U.S. space shuttle *Challenger* on mission 41-G. The crew consists of Robert L. Crippen (b. 1937), Jon A. McBride (b. 1943), David C. Leestma (b. 1949), Paul D. Scully-Power (b. 1944), and Canadian Marc Garneau (b. 1949), as well as two women, Sally K. Ride (b. 1951), making her second space flight, and Kathryn D. Sullivan (b. 1951), on her first. This is the first space flight to have two women aboard. Sullivan becomes the first American woman to walk in space and is accompanied by Leestma. The mission lasts eight days, five hours, 23 minutes.

1984 October 18 First flight of Rockwell International *B-1B* bomber is made in Palmdale, California. This controversial, intercontinental-range bomber is intended to fly at very low levels at near-supersonic speeds to avoid radar detection. It has variable-geometry wings (moveable wings that provide a range of sweep) and a four-man crew. Ninety-seven are eventually built. (See April 30, 1988)

⊿ 1984 November 8 U.S. space shuttle *Discovery* is launched with astronauts Frederick H. Hauck (b. 1941), David M. Walker (b. 1944), Anna L. Fisher (b. 1949), Dale A. Gardner (b. 1948), and Joseph P. Allen (b. 1937) aboard. Besides deploying two communications satellites, the crew of mission 51-A was able to retrieve and return to earth two satellites that were stranded in useless orbits. This is the first time a manned spacecraft brings a satellite back to earth. Astronauts Gardner and Allen use their manned maneuvering units (MMU) to make spectacular space walks to retrieve the satellites. When robot devices cannot do the job of getting the satellites into the shuttle's cargo bay, the two astronauts literally manhandle them in themselves. This gives some indication of the advantages of man-in-space. Astronaut Fisher is the first mother to fly in space. The mission lasts seven days, 23 hours, 45 minutes.

⊿ 1984 December 19 Reports suggest that the Soviet Union has launched a small, scale-model of a reusable, winged spaceplane or shuttle. It makes one orbit of the earth, glides back into the atmosphere, and splashes down in the Black Sea. It is thought this unmanned mission is the fourth model flight in a new Soviet shuttle program.

1985 First automobile to have antilock brakes as a standard feature is the Ford Granada. These brakes which prevent skids, are designed to maintain their braking power in a pulsing manner just below the point where the wheel loses traction. A wheel speed sensor sends information to a microprocessor which controls fluid pressure to each brake cylinder.

1985 Employment in the general field of transportation reaches a U.S. high of 10.9 million workers. As a percentage of total U.S. employment however, this figure is 10.2%—down from a 1955 high of 14.1%.

1985 Anti-skid braking system for automobiles is introduced by Swedish company Volvo. This electronic system intervenes if a car skids during acceleration and assures that all four wheels are turning at the same speed. This sophisticated safety feature considerably reduces the loss of control due to a slippery road surface.

1985 A.D.
Automobile anti-skid brakes introduced

1985 United States has nearly four times the yearly number of road accidents involving persons than the second highest nation. Its accident total for this year is 2,257,668, compared to the next highest (Japan has 579,190). This is attributed to the United States having the largest number of cars on the road, but it also is a result of Americans being able to drive at a younger age and with fewer restrictions than many other countries, and having greater distances to cover.

1985 January 15 National Transportation Safety Board reports that since 1947, a total of 235 airplanes have disappeared during flights over the United States. Of these, 56 occurred over Alaska.

1985 January 17 U.S. Senator Jake Garn (R-Utah) (b. 1932) will fly in space next month aboard the space shuttle, National Aeronautics and Space Administration (NASA) announces. Garn is chairman of the Senate subcommittee that oversees NASA's budget. NASA has decided to promote itself by taking ordinary people—like a congressman, teacher, and a journalist—into space. After the *Challenger* disaster which kills the schoolteacher, Sharon Christa McAuliffe (1948—1986), NASA stops these promotions.

1985 January 24 First classified military mission of the space shuttle, mission 51-C, is launched from the Kennedy Space Center, Florida. Aboard the *Discovery* are Thomas K. Mattingly (b. 1936), Loren J. Shriver (b.

1944), Ellison S. Onizuka (1946—1986), James F. Buchli (b. 1945), and Gary E. Payton (b. 1948). They reach earth orbit and deploy an electronic intelligence satellite for the Department of Defense (DOD). The mission is shortened one day because of weather conditions in Florida, and the crew lands after a mission of three days, one hour, 33 minutes.

**1985
February 21**

**NASA seeks
teacher for
shuttle flight**

1985 February 21 Ten thousand, six hundred and ninety school teachers respond to a National Aeronautics and Space Administration (NASA) call for applications for a space shuttle flight. Two teachers per state will be chosen by NASA, with ten semifinalists chosen from that group. Of the ten, NASA will chose one primary and one backup candidate to undergo flight training. (See July 19, 1985)

1985 April 2 In testimony before U.S. House committee, a Department of Defense (DOD) official states that there is a national need for a "transatmospheric vehicle" that would be able to quickly reach space and return like an ordinary aircraft. Unlike the lengthy and complicated vertical rocket launch of the shuttle, this ideal plane would take off from a runway, reach Mach 25 (25 times the speed of sound), and enter space. DOD argues that none of the technical problems of such a plane are insurmountable.

1985 April 12

**U.S. Senator
flies on
shuttle**

1985 April 12 U.S. space shuttle *Discovery* is launched on mission 51-D with astronauts Karol J. Bobko (b. 1937), Donald E. Williams (b. 1942), M. Rhea Seddon (b. 1947), S. David Griggs (b. 1939), Jeffrey A. Hoffman (b. 1944), Charles D. Walker (b. 1948), and U.S. Senator Jake Garn (b. 1932). This flight was unremarkable except for the controversial presence of a U.S. senator. The mission lasts six days, 23 hours, 56 minutes.

1985 April 15 Contract for definition and preliminary design of a permanent manned space station is given to McDonnell Douglas Astronautics Co. and Rockwell International's Space Station Systems Division by National Aeronautics and Space Administration (NASA). NASA must have plans ready if it ever gets approval and funding to build a permanent station.

1985 April 29 U.S. space shuttle *Challenger* is launched into space with Robert F. Overmyer (b. 1936), Frederick D. Gregory (b. 1941), William E. Thornton (b. 1929), Norman E. Thagard (b. 1943), Don L. Lind (b. 1930), Lodewijk van den Berg (b. 1932), and Taylor G.

Wang (b. 1940) aboard. Mission 51-B carries the first operational European Space Agency (ESA) Spacelab which includes 24 rats and two monkeys. The flight also includes three men over 50 years old. The mission lasts seven days, eight minutes.

1985 June 4 New group of 12 astronauts is chosen by National Aeronautics and Space Administration (NASA), with five pilots and seven mission specialists. They are: (civilians) Jerome Apt (b. 1949), Tamara Jernigan (b. 1959), Linda Godwin (b. 1952), Richard Hieb (b. 1955), and Stephen Oswald (b. 1951); (Air Force) Brian Duffy (b. 1953) and Carl Meade (b. 1950); (Navy) Michael Baker (b. 1953), Stephen Thorne (1953—1986), and Pierre Thuot (b. 1955); (Army) Charles Gemar (b. 1955); and (Marines) Robert Cabana (b. 1949).

1985 June 6 Soviet Union launches *Soyuz T-13* with cosmonauts Vladimir A. Dzhanibekov (b. 1942) and Viktor P. Savinykh (b. 1940) aboard. They dock with the unpowered *Salyut 7* orbiting station and restore it to usefulness after making repairs. During their near four month stay, they are resupplied twice by unmanned spacecraft and visited by the crew of *Soyuz T-14*. After a mission of 112 days, three hours, 12 minutes, they return safely to earth.

1985 June 17 U.S. space shuttle *Discovery* is launched with a crew of seven, two of whom are non-Americans. Patrick Baudry (b. 1949) (France) and Sultan Salman Al-Saud (b. 1956) (Saudi Arabia) join astronauts Daniel C. Brandenstein (b. 1943), John O. Creighton (b. 1943), Shannon W. Lucid (b. 1943), Steven R. Nagel (b. 1946), and John M. Fabian (b. 1939) and deploy three communications satellites. Mission 51-G lasts seven days, one hour, 39 minutes.

1985 July 19 Sharon Christa McAuliffe (1948—1986), a social studies teacher at Concord High School, Concord, New Hampshire, is chosen by National Aeronautics and Space Administration (NASA) to go into space in January 1986 aboard the space shuttle. As part of NASA's civilian-in-space program, she will become the first private citizen passenger in the history of space flight.

1985 July 29 U.S. space shuttle *Challenger* launches another European Space Agency (ESA) Spacelab which carries experiments in life sciences, plasma physics, astronomy, and solar physics. The crew of mission

c. 1985 ■ Typical take-off waiting line at most major airports.

51-F consists of C. Gordon Fullerton (b. 1936), Roy D. Bridges, Jr. (b. 1943), F. Story Musgrave (b. 1935), Anthony W. England (b. 1942), Karl G. Henize (b. 1926), Loren W. Acton (b. 1936), and John-David F. Bartoe (b. 1944). The 58-year-old Henize is the oldest person to date to fly in space. The mission lasts seven days, 22 hours, 45 minutes.

1985 August 12 Worst single aircraft disaster in aviation history occurs as a Japan Air Lines crash kills 520 people.

1985 August 27 U.S. space shuttle *Discovery* is launched carrying astronauts Joe H. Engle (b. 1932), Richard O. Covey (b. 1946), James D. A. van Hoften (b. 1944), John M. Lounge (b. 1946), and William F. Fisher (b. 1946). The crew deploys three communications satellites and space walks by van Hoften and Fisher retrieve the failed *Leasat 3*. It is repaired and put back in space. Mission 51-I lasts seven days, two hours, 18 minutes.

1985 September 17 *Soyuz T-14* is launched by the Soviet Union with cosmonauts Vladimir V. Vasyutin (b. 1952), Georgy M. Grechko (b. 1931), and Alexandr A. Volkov (b. 1948) aboard. They dock with the orbiting station *Salyut 7* and join the crew of *Soyuz T-13* there. After *T-13* returns to earth, the mission continues until it is forced to return because of cosmonaut's Vasyutin's illness. This is the first time a flight in space is curtailed by a sick crew member. Vasyutin developed an infection and a very high fever. The mission lasts 64 days, 21 hours, 52 minutes.

1985 October 3 First flight of U.S. space shuttle *Atlantis* is made as the crew of Karol J. Bobko (b.

1939), Ronald J. Grabe (b. 1945), David C. Hilmers (b. 1950), Robert L. Stewart (b. 1942), and William A. Pailes (b. 1952) is launched into earth orbit. This is the second classified mission conducted for the Department of Defense (DOD), and the crew deploys a pair of military communications satellites. Mission 51-J lasts only four days, one hour, 46 minutes.

1985 October 15 Boeing receives the largest order in its history, as United Airlines orders 110 Boeing *737-300*s and six *747-200*s, worth $3.1 billion. Within days, Northwest Airlines orders ten *747-400*s, ten *757-200*s, and three *747-400*s, worth $2 billion.

1985 October 30 U.S. space shuttle *Challenger* is launched with a European Space Agency (ESA) Spacelab aboard. The crew consists of Henry W. Hartsfield (b. 1933), Steven R. Nagel (b. 1946), Guion S. Bluford, Jr. (b. 1942), James F. Buchli (b. 1945), Bonnie J. Dunbar (b. 1949), Rheinhard Furrer (b. 1940), Ernst Messerschmid (b. 1945), and Wubbo Ockels (b. 1946). West Germany manages and controls the Spacelab experiments. This is the first time an eight-person crew is sent into space. Mission 61-A lasts seven days, 45 minutes.

1985 November 26 U.S. space shuttle *Atlantis* is launched carrying astronauts Brewster H. Shaw, Jr. (b. 1945), Bryan D. O'Connor (b. 1946), Jerry L. Ross (b. 1948), Mary L. Cleave (b. 1947), Sherwood C. Spring (b. 1944), Charles D. Walker (b. 1948), and Rudolfo Neri Vela (b. 1952) of Mexico. The crew deploys three communications satellites and Ross and Spring conduct spacewalks testing space construction techniques. Mission 61-B lasts six days, 21 hours, four minutes.

1985
October 30

First eight-person crew sent into space

1985 ■ Japanese National Railways' Tokaido Line can reach 155 mph.

1985 December First supersonic flight of Grumman *X-29* forward swept-wing (FSW) demonstrator aircraft is made. The newest in the U.S. X-series of experimental research aircraft, it makes 200 test flights by June 1988, providing extensive new aerodynamic data and information on computerized aircraft flight control.

1986 Engine technology reaches a new milestone when a General Electric/NASA unducted fan engine flies for the first time on a Boeing 727. This engine uses two counter-rotating, eight-blade fans at the rear. Called the propfan concept, it promises enhanced economy, although its maintenance costs are high.

1986 A.D.

OPEC unity falls apart

1986 Oil prices collapse as the Organization of Oil Producing Countries (OPEC) unity falls apart. Gasoline prices plummet and energy efficiency becomes less important to many people. American car buyers move toward larger, more luxurious cars again.

1986 Fully automated highways, in which computers rather than the driver control an automobile's speed, braking, and spacing, are being studied by the Southern California Association of Governments (SCAG). Many believe that automation and highway electrification—in which vehicles would pick up electric power from cables buried beneath the road—are inevitable in the future.

1986 English Channel tunnel idea is revived once again as a joint British-French project. A rail tunnel is selected over proposals for a suspension bridge, a bridge-and-tunnel link, and a combined rail-and-road link. The venture will be privately financed by a consortium of British and French firms with stock sales and bank loans and is now called Eurotunnel instead of Chunnel. (See October 30, 1990)

1986 Japan and the United States account for nearly 50 percent of the world's passenger car production. Although Japan produces slightly more passenger cars than the United States, the United States produces nearly 42 percent of the world's total for commercial vehicles.

1986 January Largest urban automated people mover (APM) in operation is the Vancouver Skytrain. It has a 13-mile double track and 15 station stops. APMs operate on a guideway and get their propulsion from a variety of electric motors, magnetic fields, or cables.

1986 January 12 U.S. space shuttle *Columbia* is launched with Robert L. Gibson (b. 1946), Charles F. Bolden, Jr. (b. 1946), Franklin Chang-Diaz (1950—1986), Steven A. Hawley (b. 1951), George D. Nelson (b. 1950), Robert J. Cenker (b. 1948), and U.S. Congressman Bill Nelson (b. 1942). Mission 61-C seemed nagged by many, small technical problems as well as bad weather before the flight and during planned landing. The mission lasts six days, two hours, six minutes.

1986 January 28 U.S. space shuttle *Challenger* disintegrates in mid-air explosion 73 seconds after lifting off from the pad. Crew of seven, Francis R. Scobee (1939—1986), Michael J. Smith (1945—1986), Ellison S. Onizuka (1946—1986), Judith A. Resnik (1949—1986),

1986 ■ Goodyear blimp *Columbia* in Pasadena, California.

Ronald E. McNair (1950—1986), Gregory K. Jarvis (1944—1986), and schoolteacher Sharon Christa McAuliffe (1948—1986), are killed. Explosion is later found to be due to the burning through of a seal at a joint (the O-ring) between the segments of one of the solid rocket boosters. It is further determined that there existed a combination of deficiencies of design, misunderstandings, the behavior of the insulating putty and joint dynamics, and low air temperatures. Crew compartment is later recovered with crew remains from 72,200 feet (22,000 meters) of water.

1986 February 19 Soviet Union launches core of permanent new space station called *Mir* or Peace. It is about 42.5 feet (13 meters) long, 13.5 feet (four meters) maximum diameter, and weighs about 21 tons. It contains several ports which will accept docking units that can be added on. All of its systems are improved over the older Salyut versions and, when fully utilized, it can accommodate a crew of 12.

1986 March U.S. National Commission on Space, which was tasked by President Ronald Reagan (b. 1911) to formulate space policy for the next 50 years, recommends the establishment of a permanent moon base by 2017 and a base on Mars by 2027. The total estimated cost of both is $7 trillion. Since Apollo ended, economics has come to dominate all aspects of the U.S. space program, and the Commission's enormously expensive agenda cannot find much support.

1986 March 13 Soviet Union launches *Soyuz T-15* with cosmonauts Leonid D. Kizim (b. 1941) and Vladimir A. Solovyov (b. 1946) aboard. In this ambitious mission, the crew docks with the new orbiting station, *Mir*, and activates all its systems. During May, they undock and link up with the old *Salyut 7*, which they enter to retrieve some experiments. They perform spacewalks from both *Salyut 7* and *Mir*, which they return to before ending the mission. During eight spacewalks, they are outside the spacecraft for 31 hours, 40 minutes. The mission ends on July 16, after 125 days, four hours, one minute.

1986 April Automated people mover (APM) system opens in Miami, Florida. This $148 million dual-track loop system called the "Metromover" connects with the downtown stop on the Miami rail system to deliver passengers to various points downtown.

1986 April

People mover opens in Miami

1986 May 21 Soviet Union launches unmanned *Soyuz TM* to test a new generation of manned spacecraft. It docks with the unmanned *Mir* station, uses its propulsion system to adjust the orbit of the linked vehicles, and then undocks and reenters on May 30. The improved *Soyuz TM* has all new systems, from communications, rendezvous and docking, to propulsion.

1986 June Futuristic Beechcraft *Starship* business jet is certified by the U.S. Federal Aviation Administration (FAA). This highly advanced executive transport conceived by *Voyager* designer Burt Rutan (b. 1943), is fabricated almost wholly out of extremely strong but untraditional materials or composites. Its basic structure consists of layers of graphite fabric around a core of honeycombed Nomex bonded by high-pressures and temperatures. The 1989 list price for one is $3.8 million. In terms of economy, a new competitor like the Italian Piaggio *P.180 Avanti* has about 50 percent better fuel mileage at 300 knots, can fly faster, and operate from shorter airstrips as well.

1986 June 2 Greatest distance achieved by a hang-glider is made by American Randy Haney who flies an unpowered hang-glider 199.75 miles (321.47 kilometers) from his takeoff point.

1986 July West Germany announces it is considering the design of a two-stage reusable spaceplane called the *Sanger 2*. It would be a two-stage vehicle that takes off horizontally and which could put payloads into earth orbit at one-fifth the cost of the U.S. space shuttle.

1986 August

Challenger accident investigation continues

1986 August Cockpit voice recording released by National Aeronautics and Space Administration (NASA) indicates that *Challenger* astronauts were unaware of the impending disaster until pilot Michael J. Smith's (1945—1986) last words, "Uh-oh!" at the moment of explosion. After the crew compartment was torn away from the orbiter by aerodynamic forces, it depressurized and crew members were probably rendered unconscious. After climbing to 63,320 feet (19,300 meters), it fell back and impacted the water at about 207 mph (334 km/h).

1986 September Ground is broken for the planned Los Angeles Metro Rail. This controversial and very expensive project is planned to be a 150-mile (240-kilometer) light rail transit system that will aid the area's traffic problems. Estimates are that by the year 2000, Los Angeles County's population will have grown by 25%, the number of licensed drivers by 32%, and the number of automobile trips by 32%. (See August 16, 1990)

1986 December 14—23 First aircraft to fly around the world non-stop and unrefuelled is specially-built Voyager Aircraft Inc. *Voyager*. Designed by Burt Rutan (b. 1943) and flown by Dick Rutan and Jeana Yeager (b. 1952), it is a trimaran monoplane constructed of composite materials that include Magnamite graphite and Hexcel honeycomb. It has two British-built, high-efficiency engines, one of which is water-cooled. Its takeoff weight is 9,750 pounds. It covers nearly 24,987 miles (40.212 kilometers) flying westbound from Edwards Air Force Base, California in nine days, three minutes, 44 seconds. At landing, it has only 14 gallons of fuel left. This flight more than doubles all unrefueled non-stop records and demonstrates the possibilities of all-composite structures.

1987 World's smallest airplane, the *Baby Bird*, makes its first flight. A high-wing monoplane with a wood and welded steel tube frame covered with fabric, it has a wing span of six feet, three inches (1.91 meters), is 11 feet (3.35 meters) long, and weighs 252 pounds (114 kilograms) empty. It is flown by Harold Nemer.

1987 Three Japanese automobile makers, Honda, Mazda, and Nissan, announce they are planning to introduce an automobile with four-wheel steering into the American market. This new technology permits the rear wheels to change direction as the front are turned, offering better control at high speeds and more maneuverability when parking.

1987 New General Motors test automobile, the Pontiac Pursuit, is equipped with electronic four-wheel drive and "steer-by-wire" systems. The latter eliminates the shaft that connects the steering wheel to the axle in conventional cars. It uses instead electronic wiring linked to sensors that relay the car's speed and the steering wheel movements to an electronic control unit.

1987 Automated people mover (APM) system opens in Detroit, Michigan. The cars on this 2.9-mile long single guideway loop system have steel wheels that ride on steel tracks. They are propelled by linear induction motors (electric). It is a primary means for tourists to travel between Detroit's exhibit hall, conven-

1986 ■ Dick Rutan and Jeana Yeager fly *Voyager* during its record around-the-world flight.

tion center, and hotel circuit. It averages about 13,000 passengers a day. The system cost $201 million.

1987 Automotive statistics reveal that 10,000 teenagers die on the road each year in automobile accidents, more than from any other single cause. $1 billion is also spent each year to treat and rehabilitate another 130,000 teens who are injured but who survive. Drinking is the biggest cause of teenager automobile accidents.

1987 First black female astronaut is selected by NASA (National Aeronautics and Space Administration). Mae C. Jemison (b. 1956), a 1981 Ph.D. graduate in medicine from Cornell University, is among a group of 15 chosen as astronauts for future space shuttle flights. Others in the group are Thomas D. Akers (b. 1931), Andrew M. Allen, James S. Boss, Kenneth D. Bowersox, Curtis L. Brown, Jr., Kevin P. Clinton, Jan D. Dozier, C. Michael Foale, Gregory J. Harbaugh (b. 1956), Donald R. McMonagle (b. 1952), Bruce E. Melnick (b. 1949), William F. Readdy, Kenneth S. Reightler, Jr. (b. 1951), and Mario Runco, Jr.

1987 In a worldwide ranking of rail systems, the United States has the most trackage or total miles of track, registering twice as much as the second-ranked Soviet Union. The Soviet Union, however, has the highest total of passenger miles, as well as by far the most tons of freight moved by rail.

1987 In a worldwide ranking of national civil aviation systems, the United States dominates, ranking first in tons of air cargo; first (by nearly three times) in the total of passenger miles by air; and first in the number of airports with scheduled flights (its 824 airports are followed by Australia's 441).

1987 In a worldwide ranking of national road and highway systems, the United States has the highest total of miles of paved roads. Its 3,891,781 miles (6,263,043 kilometers) of roads is nearly four times as much as the second-ranked nation which, surprisingly, is India.

1987 February 5 Soviet Union launches *Soyuz TM-2* with cosmonauts Yuri V. Romanenko (b. 1944) and Alexandr Leveykin (b. 1951) aboard. The improved Soyuz spacecraft docks with the new *Mir* orbiting station and crew conducts tests of all-new systems. After a successful mission, the crew reenters safely on July 30, with a mission total of 174 days, three hours, 26 minutes.

1987 March 6 Worst peacetime disaster in the history of the English Channel occurs as British ferry *Herald of Free Enterprise* capsizes after leaving the Belgian port of Zeebruge for Dover, England. This large ferry is designed to carry up to 1,300 passengers and 350 vehicles, but is carrying only 543 people when it suddenly rolls over on its side and becomes three-quarters submerged. An investigation reveals that human error or carelessness which leaves its bow doors open causes the catastrophe which kills 188 people. No one checks the doors to assure they are closed, and water rushes in, tipping it over. A multinational rescue operation prevents further loss of human life.

1987 March 10 U.S. Senate Commerce Committee votes to give the secretary of transportation 12 months to establish mandatory drug and alcohol testing of rail, aviation, and motor carrier industry employees.

1987 April 18

Mid-air parachute rescue occurs

1987 April 18 Unique parachute rescue occurs when Debbie William is knocked unconscious during a multiple free-fall. Gregory Robertson maneuvers his own free-fall close to her and is able to pull her ripcord at 3,500 feet (1,065 meters). He saves her life by only ten seconds.

1987 June Office of Exploration is created by National Aeronautics and Space Administration (NASA) with astronaut Sally K. Ride (b. 1951) as acting associate administrator. Its object is to coordinate an effort that could "expand the human presence beyond Earth." By this, NASA has in mind things like robotic exploration of the moon and planets, a permanent moon base, and a manned expedition to Mars. NASA keeps trying to capture the public's and Congress's imagination.

1987 July 2 Hot-air balloon *Atlantic Flyer* is launched from Sugarloaf, Maine carrying Richard Branson and Per Lindstrand to begin the first hot-air balloon crossing of the Atlantic Ocean. Despite crash-landing in the Irish Sea, they get very close to the coast of England, and complete their flight after 31 hours, 41 minutes. (See January 15, 1991)

1987 July 22 *Soyuz TM-3* is launched by the Soviet Union carrying cosmonauts Alexandr Viktorenko (b. 1947), Alexandr Alexandrov (b. 1943), and Syrian passenger Mohammed Faris (b. 1951). The crew docks with the now-enlarged *Mir* orbiting complex and

joins crew of *TM-2* already there. *TM-3* returns to earth with a different crew member, Laveykin from *TM-2*, whose electrocardiogram shows irregularities. Alexandrov, from *TM-3*, stays aboard the station and later returns with *TM-2*. The mission lasts 160 days, seven hours, 16 minutes.

1987 August Cost of a new shuttle to replace the destroyed *Challenger* is estimated by manufacturer Rockwell International to be $2.12 billion.

1987 December 1 Prime contractors for the U.S. contribution to the International Space Station are announced by National Aeronautics and Space Administration (NASA). They are Boeing Aerospace Company, McDonnell Douglas Astronautics Co., General Electric, and Rocketdyne.

1987 December 20 Worst peacetime maritime disaster in the 20th century occurs as Philippine inter-island ferry *Dona Paz* collides with Philippine oil tanker *Victor* in the waters of the Tablas Strait, some 110 miles (175 kilometers) south of Manila. The ferry is overloaded with passengers travelling to Manila for Christmas, and it is engulfed in flames when the tanker catches fire. It is believed that as many as 3,000 people are killed, since the ferry is carrying twice as many as it is legally authorized. Between the two vessels, only 26 survive.

1987 December 21 Soviet Union launches *Soyuz TM-4* carrying cosmonauts Vladimir Titov (b. 1947), Musa Manarov (b. 1951), and Anatoliy Levchenko (1941—1988). After docking with the orbiting *Mir* complex, the crew enters and joins the already-manned station. Cosmonaut Levchenko returns to earth with the *TM-3* crew and Titov and Manarov stay aboard *Mir* for nearly six months. Their mission ends after 180 days, five hours.

1988 Government of West Germany commits itself to building the first commercial, high-speed maglev line in the world. Called Transrapid, it will run between Hamburg and Hanover, about 90 miles. It runs on a steel guideway and operates via magnetic attraction. This system is the opposite of the Japanese maglev that levitates its cars via magnetic repulsion. (See 1980)

1988 Report released by the Motor Vehicle Manufacturers Association reveals that: the number of automobiles in use in the world is 386 million; the number of registered automobiles in the United States is 135

1988 ■ Europe's Airbus Industrie's *A320* airliner.

million; the average American automobile gets 18 mpg, drives 10,300 miles a year, and costs $13,581; and Americans devote 20% of their annual household expenses to owning and operating an automobile.

1988 Work begins on Akashi Bridge, spanning the Inland Sea and connecting mainland Japan to the major island of Shikoku. When finished, it will be the longest suspension bridge ever built. It will have three spans totalling 12,828 feet, with a record-setting center span of 6,527 feet, and will be supported by main towers that are 1,092 feet above sea level. Construction has been made difficult by the very deep water, strong currents, and the hazards of typhoons. The bridge will be so large that it must be covered by sheets of rubber and ferrite—a magnetic ceramic—to absorb radar and minimize clutter on ships' radar screens. Its planned completion date is 1998.

1988 April Emergency escape from the U.S. space shuttle orbiter is approved by National Aeronautics and Space Administration (NASA). New system uses a telescopic pole which, when needed, extends from an opened hatch and allows each astronaut to slide out on a ring attachment and then use a conventional parachute. The new system is for use when the shuttle is gliding down from 24,000 to 11,000 feet (7,315 to 3,353 meters).

1988 April 23 Human-powered aircraft *Daedalus* flies 72 miles from Crete and lands off the coast of Greek island of Santorini. Piloted by Greek cycling champion Kanellos Kanellopoulos, the fragile aircraft weighs 70 pounds and has diaphanous wings (of paper-thin fineness) spanning 112 feet. Research for such ultra-light, composite aircraft could eventually lead to new types of aircraft that

can fly very high in the earth's atmosphere. Such HA/LE (high altitude, long endurance) vehicles would seek to combine low cost, mobility, and staying power.

1988 April 29 First flight of Boeing *747-400* is made. This Advanced Superjet has a crew of two and can carry between 412 and 509 passengers over 8,000 miles. Sales in 1990 of 170 of these wide-body transports broke all records.

1988 April 30 Final Rockwell International *B-1B* bomber is delivered to the U.S. Air Force. Strategic Air Command now has 97 of these manned penetrating bombers in service. Its complex swing-wing design, which allows it to fly in a wide variety of subsonic to supersonic modes, accounts for much of the aircraft's high price. At a cost of $250 million per aircraft, the United States can afford only a small number. During World War II, when the United States was mass-producing *B-17* bombers, they cost $187,742 per aircraft.

1988 June 7 Soviet Union launches *Soyuz TM-5* with cosmonauts Viktor Savinykh (b. 1940), Anatoly Solovyev (b. 1948), and Alexandr Alexandrov (b. 1943) aboard. The crew docks with new orbiting station *Mir* and enters the occupied station to perform experiments. They return using *Soyuz TM-4* and leave their spacecraft for the other crew. Total mission time is nine days, 20 hours, 13 minutes.

1988 July 18 U.S. President Ronald Reagan (b. 1911) names the planned U.S.-International Space Station "Freedom." At this point in its development however, only $900 million of National Aeronautics and

1988 April 30

Final B-1B bomber delivered to USAF

Space Administration's (NASA) $10.6 billion budget is for the planned station.

1988 August 29 *Soyuz TM-6* is launched by the Soviet Union carrying cosmonauts Vladimir Lyakhov (b. 1941), Valeriy Polyakov (b. 1942), and Afghan passenger Abdul Mohmand (b. 1959). Crew docks with the manned *Mir* station and enters to perform experiments. They return using former mission's *TM-5* spacecraft and leave theirs behind. The mission lasts eight days, 19 hours, 27 minutes.

**1988
September 19

Israel
launches
satellite**

1988 September 19 Israel becomes the eighth nation to launch a satellite on its own. It orbits a 344-pound (156-kilogram) satellite named *Offeq* from a site in the Negev desert using a Shavit launcher.

1988 September 29 U.S. space shuttle *Discovery* is launched on first U.S. manned space flight since the 1986 *Challenger* disaster. Aboard are Frederick H. Hauck (b. 1941), Richard O. Covey (b. 1946), John M. Lounge (b. 1946), David C. Hilmers (b. 1950), and George D. Nelson (b. 1950). This shuttle incorporates many major modifications made following the *Challenger* investigation. This redesign costs nearly $2.5 billion and shuttle launch costs are now averaging about $500 million, many times the original estimates. Crew deploys a satellite and conducts shake-down of new systems. Mission STS-26 lasts four days, one hour.

1988 October Canadian government announces that three finalists have been chosen to build a bridge linking Prince Edward Island with New Brunswick, Canada. A tunnel is rejected as too expensive and a causeway is considered environmentally risky. The proposed bridge would span the Northumberland Strait at its narrowest point, between Borden, P.E.I. and Jourimain Island, New Brunswick, making it (in wintertime) the longest bridge over ice-covered waters. It is expected to be a two-lane, high-level structure with piers about 200 meters apart. There will be a wider opening in the middle for large ships to pass through. In January 1988, a P.E.I. plebiscite was held, and Islanders voted 60 to 40 percent in favor of a bridge link.

1988 October 29 Soviet Union makes its first attempt to launch its space shuttle called *Buran* or Snowstorm. This full-size vehicle very much resembles the U.S. version. It does not have its own launch system

and must always be mated to the Energiya booster. It can fly unmanned or have a crew. This unmanned launch is aborted 51 seconds before liftoff. (See November 15, 1988)

1988 November 15 Soviet Union launches its first reusable space shuttle called *Buran*. The unmanned vehicle is launched by an Energiya booster into orbit and makes a three hour, 25 minute flight of two orbits. It reenters and lands like an airplane on a 2.8-mile- (4.5-kilometer-) long runway. Like the U.S. shuttle, it uses protective tiles during reentry. A second unmanned flight is scheduled for late 1991 and its first manned mission is planned for 1992 or later.

1988 November 22 Rollout of Northrop *B-2* stealth bomber gives the world its first glimpse of one of the most closely guarded secret projects since World War II. An ultra-modern version of the old flying wing, everything about this aircraft is designed to minimize its detectability. Besides overall compound curved configuration which scatters incoming radar beams, each of its twin-engine exhaust ducts is designed and located to reduce the aircraft's infrared (heat) signature. Even fuel additives minimize the size of exhaust particles to make its contrails invisible in white light. (See July 1989)

1988 November 26 Soviet Union launches *Soyuz TM-7* carrying cosmonauts Alexandr Volkov (b. 1948), Sergey Krikalev (b. 1958), and French passenger Jean-Loup Chretien (b. 1938). After docking with the orbiting, occupied *Mir* station, the crew performs experiments and Chretien and Volkov take a walk in space to perform experiments outside the spacecraft. Chretien returns on December 21 in *Soyuz TM-6* with cosmonauts Titov and Manarov who complete a record 366 days in space. *Soyuz TM-7* returns with crew of Krikalev, Volkov, and Polyyakov on April 27, 1989 completing a mission that lasts 151 days, 11 hours.

1988 December 2 U.S. space shuttle *Atlantis* is launched with astronauts Robert L. Gibson (b. 1946), Guy S. Gardner (b. 1948), Richard M. Mullane (b. 1945), Jerry L. Ross (b. 1948), and William M. Shepherd (b. 1949) aboard. This classified mission places a radar imaging reconnaissance satellite in orbit for the Department of Defense (DOD) and conducts other ground observations. Mission STS-27 last four days, nine hours, six minutes.

1988 December 21 First flight of Soviet *An-225* heavy transport aircraft is made. Currently the world's largest plane, it is a 50 percent scale-up of the Soviet *An-124*, with a redesigned, twin-fin tail unit and six turbofan engines. Its 141-foot-long cabin can accommodate 16 large freight containers or 80 automobiles. There are also plans to carry the Soviet *Buran* space shuttle orbiter and sections of the giant *Energiya* rocket launch vehicle.

1989 Automated people mover (APM) system that operates on magnetic levitation is installed in Las Vegas, Nevada to connect the convention center with a new downtown transportation center. These driverless, usually elevated cars on guideways already exist in several airports and figure in the plans of other U.S. cities (New York, Houston, and Phoenix). The planned system for Phoenix will have 62 miles and therefore exceed the longest system now in Vancouver. (See January 1986)

1989 Work begins on twin elevated highways for a two-mile section of Interstate 310 in Louisiana between I-10 and U.S. Route 90. As this section goes through protected wetlands, the contractor is not allowed to put any heavy equipment on the ground during construction. As a result, the expensive "end-on" method is being used, in which each section of the elevated highway is built from the top of the last completed section which, in turn, sits atop piles driven in the ground.

1989 January Oleg Borisov of the Academy of Soviet Sciences discusses Soviet plans for putting men on Mars between 2005 and 2010. He describes nuclear-powered spacecraft that is assembled in earth orbit, travels to Mars, and from which two men will descend to Mars to explore its surface.

1989 March 13 U.S. space shuttle *Discovery* is launched carrying astronauts Michael L. Coats (b. 1946), John E. Blaha (b. 1942), James P. Bagian (b. 1952), James F. Buchli (b. 1945), and Robert C. Springer (b. 1942). The crew launches three satellites and conducts several experiments. STS-29 mission lasts four days, 23 hours, 39 minutes.

1989 March 24 Largest tanker oil spill in U.S. history occurs as the *Exxon Valdez*, loaded with 1.26 million barrels of crude oil, runs aground on a reef in the Gulf of Alaska, 25 miles (40 kilometers) from Valdez. The resultant spill of some 240,000 barrels (about 11 million gallons) extends over 2,600 square miles (6,700 square kilometers)—an area larger than the state of Delaware—and over thousands of miles of Prince William Sound and into the Gulf of Alaska. The occurrence of such a disaster despite favorable conditions (fine weather, good radio contact, absence of traffic, and clear visibility of ten miles) underscores the inability of sophisticated technology to correct simple human error.

1989 April 1 Power depletion aboard Soviet space station *Mir* forces a temporary "mothballing" of the laboratory for several months. Soviets must scrub next manned *Soyuz TM-8* flight which will not fly until late summer. (See September 5, 1989)

1989 May 4 U.S. space shuttle *Atlantis* flies with astronauts David M. Walker (b. 1944), Ronald J. Grabe (b. 1945), Norman E. Thagard (b. 1943), Mary L. Cleave (b. 1947), and Mark C. Lee (b. 1952) aboard. The crew deploys the Venus probe *Magellan* as well as the two-stage booster that will propel it to that planet. They also perform fluid research and earth observation experiments. STS-30 mission lasts four days, 57 minutes.

1989 June 3 Worst rail disaster in Soviet history occurs as a gas pipeline explodes, engulfing two passing passenger trains in flames near the town of Ufa in the Ural Mountains of the Soviet Union. It is estimated that over 650 people are killed in the inferno, most of them children.

1989 June 3
Worst Soviet rail disaster kills 650

1989 July First flight of Northrop *B-2* stealth bomber is made.

1989 August 8 U.S. space shuttle *Columbia* is launched carrying astronauts Brewster H. Shaw, Jr. (b. 1945), Richard N. Richards (b. 1946), James C. Adamson (b. 1946), David C. Leestma (b. 1949) and Mark N. Brown (b. 1951). The crew deploys Department of Defense (DOD) maneuverable reconnaissance satellite and conducts other military-oriented experiments. STS-28 mission lasts five days, one hour.

1989 September 5 Soviet Union launches *Soyuz TM-8* with cosmonauts Aleksandr Viktorenko (b. 1947) and Alexandr Serebrov (b. 1944) aboard. They dock with the orbiting station *Mir* and set about getting it ready to receive its first large, specialized module called *Kvant-2*. This newly-added unmanned segment is nearly as large as the *Mir* itself and adds considerable room and capability to the station. Both cosmonauts test manned maneuvering units (MMU) that are similar to those of the United States in separate space walks. This mission lasts 166 days, six hours.

1989 October 17

California earthquake damages freeway and bridge

1989 October 17 Earthquake in California collapses a one-mile- (1.5-kilometer-) long section of the double-decker Nimitz Freeway (Interstate Highway 880) in Oakland. Thirty-nine dead are later found in cars crushed between layers of concrete and asphalt. Same (7.1 Richter scale) quake causes a 50-foot (15-meter) section of the upper level of the Bay Bridge, connecting San Francisco to Oakland, to fall onto its lower roadway, killing two people. (See October 25, 1989)

1989 October 18 U.S. space shuttle *Atlantis* is launched with astronauts Donald E. Williams (b. 1942), Michael J. McCulley (b. 1943), Shannon W. Lucid (b. 1943), Franklin R. Chang-Diaz (b. 1950), and Ellen S. Baker (b. 1953) aboard. The crew launches a Jupiter probe and the Jupiter orbiter *Galileo*. STS-34 mission lasts four days, 23 hours, 39 minutes.

1989 October 25 Engineers from the University of California investigating the Nimitz Freeway collapse find that the columns supporting the upper roadway were of adequate strength, but had not been effectively secured with reinforced steel to the main structure.

1989 October 26 U.S. Congressional legislation for California earthquake disaster relief is signed by President George Bush (b. 1924). Part of the relief package is $1 billion for Federal Highway Administration repairs to damaged roads and bridges.

1989 November 18 Section of the San Francisco-Oakland Bay Bridge damaged by the October 17 earthquake reopens to traffic.

1989 November 23 U.S. space shuttle *Discovery* is launched with astronauts Frederick D. Gregory (b. 1941), John E. Blaha (b. 1942), Kathryn C. Thornton (b. 1952), F. Story Musgrave (b. 1935), and Manley L. Carter (b. 1947) aboard. This classified mission deploys a Department of Defense (DOD) satellite and conducts other military-related experiments. STS-33 mission lasts five days, seven minutes.

1990 U.S. Air Force announces that Lockheed *SR-71 Blackbird* will be phased out from operational duty. The victim of tight budgets, it will remain as a research aircraft. During 25 years of service, it was able to provide reconnaissance coverage of up to 100,000 square miles of territory in one hour, day or night, in all weather. At the time of its retirement, it still remains the fastest and highest-flying operational aircraft in the world, holding absolute records for speed over 2,000 mph.

1990 For the first time in U.S. automotive history, air bags are installed in a sizeable (three million) number of automobiles. This number will increase in the following years, since passenger- as well as driver-side air bags will be required by the mid-1990s.

1990 General Motors introduces an electrically-powered test car. Called the Impact, it accelerates from 0 to 60 mph in eight seconds and can travel 120 miles before its batteries need recharging.

1990 World Solar Challenge auto races are held in Darwin, Australia. First held in 1987, this race has 36 entries ranging from experimental vehicles built by major U.S. companies to those entered by various university teams. They are all radically-designed vehicles, emphasizing streamlining and lightness while incorporating solar array panels. These panels convert sunlight into electricity. The five-and-one-half-day race is won by a Swiss entry whose average 40.74 mph results in an energy efficiency equal to running the 1,900-mile course on less than 1.5 gallons of gasoline.

1990 January Fastest Atlantic passenger ship crossing is achieved by the *Hoverspeed Great Britain*. This 242-foot-long ship is the world's largest catamaran (a vessel with two side-by-side hulls). Its twin hulls are linked by a bridging structure that acts like a third, middle hull that provides extra buoyancy in high seas or extreme weather. Powered by four 16-cylinder diesel engines which drive its huge water-jets, it can reach a top speed of 42 knots. It makes its first trip from England to New York in three days, seven hours, 54 minutes.

1990 January 9 U.S. space shuttle *Columbia* is launched carrying astronauts Daniel C. Brandenstein (b. 1943), James D. Wetherbee (b. 1952), Bonnie J. Dunbar (b. 1949), Marsha S. Ivins (b. 1951), and G. David Low (b. 1956). The crew deploys the *Syncom IV-5* (a

1990 ■ High speed Metroliner makes Washington-New York in about 2½ hours.

Hughes geosynchronous communications satellite) and retrieves the long duration exposure facility (LDEF). Placed in orbit by the space shuttle in 1984, this structure tested the effects of long-term exposure to the space environment and is studied closely upon its return to earth. STS-32 mission lasts ten days, 21 hours.

1990 February 11 Soviet Union launches *Soyuz TM-9* with cosmonauts Anatoly Solovyev (b. 1948) and Aleksandr Balandin aboard. Crew docks with and enters orbiting station *Mir.* Both cosmonauts perform space walks to effect repairs and also conduct many biological experiments with baby chicks and quails aboard the station. Mission returns August 9, 1990 with total mission time of 178 days, 22 hours, 19 minutes.

1990 February 28 U.S. space shuttle *Atlantis* is launched with astronauts John O. Creighton (b. 1943), John H. Casper (b. 1943), David C. Hilmers (b. 1950), Richard M. Mullane (b. 1945), and Pierre J. Thuot (b. 1955) aboard. This classified mission is conducted for the Department of Defense (DOD). Mission STS-36 lasts four days, ten hours, 19 minutes.

1990 April 21 First public viewing of Lockheed *F-117A* stealth attack aircraft is conducted. Development of this unique aircraft started as early as 1978 and was kept secret for years. It incorporates low-observable (stealth) characteristics such as a faceted design with surfaces set at unusual angles to scatter incoming radar beams. Also, its engines are "buried" in the fuselage to reduce its infrared (heat) signature. It has one mission only: to fly at night and destroy high-priority targets with pinpoint accuracy. It sees considerable action during the

Persian Gulf War of January—February 1991. Altogether, 59 are built, although three are lost in test flight accidents.

1990 April 24 U.S. space shuttle *Discovery* is launched with astronauts Loren J. Shriver (b. 1944), Charles F. Bolden, Jr. (b. 1946), Steven A. Hawley (b. 1951), Bruce McCandless II (b. 1937), and Kathryn D. Sullivan (b. 1951) aboard. Crew deploys the Hubble Space Telescope (HST) into earth orbit. This large, very sensitive astronomical observatory (it weighs 11 tons and is over 13 meters long) finally achieves the goal of astronomers who sought to use a telescope from above the distorting atmosphere surrounding earth and to view the universe from the absolute clarity of space. Mission STS-31 lasts five days, one hour, 16 minutes.

1990 June 22 First roll-out of Northrop/McDonnell Douglas *YF-23* is made. It is one of two prototypes (the other is the Lockheed/Boeing/General Dynamics *YF-22A*) competing to become the next U.S. Air Force advanced tactical fighter (AFT). During its flight evaluation phase, it reaches Mach 1.8 (nearly twice the speed of sound) and a maximum altitude of 50,000 feet. It is designed to incorporate low-observable (stealth) characteristics while preserving a high degree of maneuverability.

1990 August 1 Soviet Union launches *Soyuz TM-10* with cosmonauts Gennadiy Manakov and Gennady Strekalov (b. 1940) aboard. Crew docks with and enters the orbiting *Mir* station. They conduct several experiments and training exercises but are unable to make a walk in space because of a faulty airlock hatch. They return to earth with Japanese journalist Toyohiro

1990 April 24

Hubble
Space
Telescope
deploys
into orbit

Akiyama from *TM-11*, on December 10, 1990 completing a mission of 130 days, 20 hours, 36 minutes.

1990 August 16 First commuter rail system in Los Angeles, California begins operations. Running from the city's financial district to the town of Long Beach, this 19-mile (30-kilometer) line is the first segment of a planned 150-mile (240-kilometer) rail system planned over the next 20 years.

1990 October 6

Shuttle astronauts explore Sun's polar regions

1990 October 6 U.S. space shuttle *Discovery* is launched carrying astronauts Richard N. Richards (b. 1946), Robert D. Cabana (b. 1949), Thomas D. Akers (b. 1931), Bruce E. Melnick (b. 1949), and William M. Shepherd (b. 1949). The crew deploys a European Space Agency (ESA) satellite, *Ulysses*, to explore polar regions of the Sun. The crew also measures atmospheric ozone. Mission STS-41 lasts four days, two hours, ten minutes.

1990 October 30 First of three of the world's longest undersea tunnels joining England and France for the first time is dug as British and French tunnelling crews on opposite sides break through and link up. Scheduled for a May 1993 opening, Eurotunnel will consist of two one-way rail tunnels whose trains will carry both passengers and vehicles. A third, narrower service tunnel will run between and connect them every 1,240 feet. The rail tubes are 24 feet in diameter and will be 31 miles long—24 miles of which is underwater. The tunnelling machines used are 700 feet long caterpillars at the working end of which is an 8.4 meter digging head.

1990 November 15 U.S. space shuttle *Atlantis* is launched with astronauts Richard O. Covey (b. 1946), Frank L. Culbertson (b. 1949), Charles D. Gemar (b. 1955), Carl J. Meade (b. 1950), and Robert C. Springer (b. 1942) aboard. The crew deploys a Department of Defense (DOD) satellite on this classified flight. Mission STS-38 lasts four days, 21 hours, 55 minutes.

1990 December 2 Soviet Union launches *Soyuz TM-11* carrying cosmonauts Viktor Afanasyev and Musa Manarov (b. 1951), as well as a Japanese journalist, Toyohiro Akiyama. They dock with the manned orbiting station, *Mir*, and Akiyama returns to earth on December 10, 1990 with the crew of *TM-10*. Both crew members perform several space walks in which they perform a great deal of structural work on the station. They return to earth with British passenger Sharman from *TM-12*, on May 20, 1991, completing a mission of 167 days.

1990 December 2 U.S. space shuttle *Columbia* is launched with astronauts Vance D. Brand (b. 1931), Guy S. Gardner (b. 1948), Jeffrey A. Hoffman (b. 1944), John M. Lounge (b. 1946), Robert A. R. Parker (b. 1936), Samuel T. Durrance (b. 1943), and Ronald A. Parise (b. 1951). On this first shuttle mission dedicated to astrophysics and the first *Spacelab* mission since the *Challenger* accident, the crew uses a group of astronomical telescopes kept in its cargo bay. Mission STS-35 lasts eight days, 23 hours, five minutes.

1991 U.S. Federal Highway Administration (FHWA) indicates that American highway infrastructure is badly showing its age. It estimates that bridges are the nation's worst problem in this area, and that of the country's 576,665 bridges, 225,826 are classified as deficient. About three-fourths of these are "functionally obsolete" and the remainder are "structurally deficient."

1991 U.S. government is spending $20 million this year to help develop a cluster of technologies known collectively as Intelligent Vehicle-Highway Systems (IVHS). These "smart highways" of the future are projected to cut the average commute as much as 50 percent in dense urban areas and to save between $24 to $32 million annually in time and gas.

1991 Hampton Roads Tunnel scheduled to open this year, is delayed until 1992. This twin-tube, four-lane road tunnel will be 4,454 feet long and will travel beneath the Newport News, Virginia ship channel. A sunken tube tunnel, it is constructed of large, closed tubes that are first sunk and then joined together underwater.

1991 January 15 First hot-air balloon to cross the Pacific Ocean takes off from Miyakonojo, Japan with Richard Branson and Per Lindstrand aboard. They touch down on a frozen lake in the North West Territories of Canada on January 17, 1991, and are rescued by helicopter.

1991 March 3 First jet crash in U.S. history to be judged as "no known cause" by the National Transportation Safety Board (NTSB) occurs at Denver, Colorado's Stapleton International Airport. United Airlines Flight 505, with a crew of 6 and 20 passengers, unaccountably pitches up, yawes to the right, and nose-dives

1991 ■ Northrop Corporation *B-2* Advanced Technology Bomber (Stealth).

into the ground, killing everyone aboard. NTSB rules out any mechanical failure on the Boeing 737-200, as well as human error. Weather is not considered a factor. This is the first unsolved case in the 25-year history of NTSB, and it keeps its files open as both it and Boeing continue to reevaluate the evidence.

1991 March 28 Near disaster in space is announced by the Soviet Union which says that its manned space station, *Mir*, came within 40 feet of colliding on March 23, 1991 with an unmanned cargo module. Soviet ground controllers noticed only seconds before impact that computers which should have been docking the module with *Mir* were in fact steering it on a collision course which would surely have killed the two cosmonauts aboard the station. A controller immediately overrode the computer.

1991 April Mobil Oil Company opens the first of ten planned methanol filling stations in Pasadena, California. As a result of the 1990 Clean Air Act, U.S. energy producers, utilities, and automakers are beginning to develop and test alternative-fuel powered vehicles, and methanol may be one of those future fuels.

1991 April Solar and Electric 500 automobile races are held in Phoenix, Arizona. These alternative fuel cars are experimental and emit 90 percent fewer pollutants than gas-fuelled cars. A model built by Swiss watchmaker Swatch averages 52 mph as it moves almost silently around its 186-mile (300-kilometer) course. A battery-powered Honda CRX wins its 200-kilometer race averaging 54 mph.

1991 April 3 *The Washington Post* writes of a classified Department of Defense (DOD) program called "Timberwind" which seeks to develop a nuclear reactor-powered rocket capable of lifting great weights into space on short notice. The concept is supposed to operate by generating sufficient heat to vaporize liquid hydrogen fuel, which would produce much more thrust than standard chemical rocket propulsion. This system would incorporate small, specially coated fuel elements capable of transferring heat with great efficiency. Besides its military potential, this new form of nuclear propulsion has potential for long-duration manned flights to planets such as Mars.

1991 April 5 U.S. space shuttle *Atlantis* is launched with astronauts Steven Nagel (b. 1946),

Kenneth Cameron (b. 1949), Linda Godwin (b. 1952), Jay Apt (b. 1949), and Jerry Ross (b. 1948). During the flight, astronauts test three different space station transport systems which could be used in building a space station in orbit. Each experimental system is a variation of the rail and cart system where an astronaut travels along the outside of the shuttle on a single or double set of rails or tracks using either an electric motor, a mechanical or pumping lever, or a manual or hand-pulled system. Astronaut Ross reports that the manual system is by far the best to get around. Astronaut Apt makes an unscheduled spacewalk to repair an antenna. STS-37 lasts six days, 32 minutes.

1991 April 28 U.S. space shuttle *Discovery* is launched with astronauts Michael Coats (b. 1946), Blaine Hammond (b. 1952), Gregory Harbaugh (b. 1956), Guion Bluford (b. 1942), Richard Hieb (b. 1955), Donald McMonagle (b. 1952), and Charles Lacy Veach (b. 1944) aboard. This classified Department of Defense (DOD) mission conducts experiments on detecting enemy missiles from space against a variety of natural backdrops. STS-39 lasts eight days, seven hours, 22 minutes.

1990 May 15

Space station plans threatened

1991 May 15 Planned U.S. space station "Freedom" is threatened by a House Appropriations Subcommittee vote to terminate funding for the international space effort. If the United States does stop development, it would also back out of agreements it has made with the European Space Agency (ESA), Japan, and Canada which have spent some $5 billion on their parts of the manned space station.

1991 May 18 Soviet Union launches *Soyuz TM-12* with cosmonauts Anatoly Artsebarsky and Sergei Krikalev (b. 1958) and British food technologist Helen Sharman aboard. Sharman is the first U.K. subject to fly in space, and returns to earth on May 20, 1991 with cosmonauts Viktor Afanasyev and Musa Manarov from *TM-11*. Artsebarsky returns on October 10, 1991 with cosmonaut Kazakh Takhtar Aubarkirov and Austrian Franz Viehboeck from *TM-13*. Krikalev remains in space.

1991 May 22 Launch of U.S. space shuttle *Columbia* is delayed by National Aeronautics and Space Administration (NASA) after discovery of badly cracked temperature sensors in the fuel line. If the pencil-shaped sensor had broken off, pieces would have been carried with the fuel into the Shuttle's high-pressure turbopump

causing at least engine failure and possibly the loss of the entire spacecraft.

1991 June 5 U.S. space shuttle *Columbia* is launched with astronauts Bryan D. O'Connor (b. 1946), Sidney M. Gutierrez (b. 1951), James P. Bagian (b. 1952), Tamara E. Jernigan (b. 1959), M. Rhea Seddon (b. 1947), Francis A. Gaffney (b. 1949), and Millie Hughes-Fulford (b. 1945). On this first mission dedicated entirely to understanding the physiological effects of space flight, the crew conducts an extensive series of biomedical experiments on human subjects, rodents, and jellyfish. Mission STS-40 lasts nine days, two hours, 15 minutes.

1991 June 13 U.S. Senate votes to create a 185,000-mile "national highway system." In addition to the existing 44,000-mile interstate system, 141,000 miles of primary highways that feed into it would be built to form an integrated national system. Individual states would be required to spend at least 17.5% of their discretionary surface transportation funds on the new system. This $123 billion bill has not yet become law. (See July 19, 1991)

1991 July 19 U.S. House of Representatives votes to expand the interstate highway system by creating 15 coast-to-coast "corridors of national significance." The House's plan will cost $153.5 billion and would build or upgrade older roads to create thousands of miles of four-lane highways. This plan, like the Senate's, is designed to set national surface transportation policy in the post-interstate era. It has not yet become law.

1991 August United States and Soviet Union announce a space swap, agreeing to fly each other's astronauts on a future mission. The United States will take a Soviet cosmonaut aboard its space shuttle and the Soviets will place an American astronaut aboard its *Mir* space station. Later political developments in the Soviet Union will cause this and other agreements to be placed on hold. Nonetheless, the agreement is a signal that cooperation in space is once again viewed as a positive tool of foreign policy by both countries.

1991 August 2 U.S. space shuttle *Atlantis* is launched with astronauts John E. Blaha (b. 1942), Michael A. Baker (b. 1953), Shannon W. Lucid (b. 1943), G. David Low (b. 1956), and James C. Adamson (b. 1946) aboard. The crew launches the fourth Tracking and Data

Relay Satellite (TDRS-5). Mission STS-43 lasts eight days, 21 hours, 21 minutes.

1991 September 12 U.S. space shuttle *Discovery* is launched with astronauts John Creighton (b. 1943), Kenneth Reightler, Jr. (b. 1951), Charles D. Gemar (b. 1955), James F. Buchli (b. 1945), and Mark N. Brown (b. 1951) aboard. The crew launches an Upper Atmosphere Research Satellite (UARS). Mission STS-48 lasts five days, eight hours, 28 minutes.

1991 October 2 Soviet Union launches Soyuz *TM-13* with cosmonauts Alexsandr Volkov (b. 1948), Kazakh Takhtar Aubarkirov, and Austrian Franz Viehboeck aboard. Crew docks with and enters orbiting *Mir* station. Cosmonauts Aubarkirov and Viehboeck return to earth on October 10, 1991 with cosmonaut Anatoly Artsebarsky from *TM-12*. Volkov remains in space with *TM-12's* Sergei Krikalev.

1991 November 21 Tilt-train technology will be tested on the Washington-New York-Boston corridor, Amtrak announces. During 1992, Amtrak will use the 150-mph Swedish X2000 to gauge its effectiveness and popularity. The new train is designed to allow higher speeds on existing tracks, for it automatically tilts as it enters curves and counters the centrifugal force passengers normally feel. Its computer automatically turns the wheel and axle assembly to follow the curve, making for an unusually smooth and comfortable ride—as well as a faster one.

1991 November 21 First person to row a boat across the North Pacific Ocean lands in Ilwaco, Washington. Forty-six-year-old Frenchman Gerard d'Aboville, ends his 133-day solo voyage which covers 5,500 miles. He left Chosi, Japan in his 26-foot boat, the *Sector*, on July 11, and rowed at an average speed of two knots or 41 nautical miles a day in his kayak-like vessel. He claims to have capsized "35 or 36 times in incredibly violent storms."

1991 November 24 U.S. space shuttle *Atlantis* is launched with astronauts Frederick D. Gregory (b. 1941), Terrence T. Henricks (b. 1952), F. Story Musgrave (b. 1935), Mario Runco, Jr. (b. 1952), James S. Voss (b. 1949), and Thomas J. Hennen aboard. Crew launches a Department of Defense (DOD) defense support program (DSP) satellite into geosynchronous orbit and conducts several experiments concerning radiation measurements. Navigation module problems cut the planned ten-day flight to six days, and mission STS-44 returns on December 1, 1991.

1991 November 29 Worst highway pileup in U.S. history occurs on California's Interstate 5, as a sudden daytime dust storm induced by a long drought reduces visibility to zero. The resultant rear-end collisions are scattered over a one-and-one-half-mile stretch of highway and involve 93 cars and 11 tractor-trailers, leaving 17 dead and 150 injured. This desolate stretch of highway, about 15 miles north of Coalinga, is especially dry due to the long drought, and the suddenness of the 60 mph wind gusts obliterating all visibility, combined with heavy post-Thanksgiving traffic, make for a transportation catastrophe.

1991 December Alamillo cable-stayed bridge is completed in Seville, Spain in preparation for the Universal Exhibition, Expo '92. Linking the Isla de La Cartuja with Seville, it is one of seven new bridges being built there (as well as many other buildings) for what has been called an "architectural Olympics." Designed by Santiago Calatrava, it is a unique 453-foot-high pylon which supports a 656-foot deck and leans a dramatic 58 degrees to the horizontal. Built of steel and concrete, it is as much of a work of art as it is a functional bridge.

1991 December 4 Pan American World Airways goes out of business after 64 years of service. The sudden shutdown of this aviation pioneer strands many passengers and leaves about 9,000 employees out of work. Its troubles began in 1978 with airline deregulation and were followed by its very expensive acquisition of National Airlines in 1980. This is the third airline to cease operations in 1991, with Eastern Airlines stopping in January and Midway in November.

1991 December 5 "Smart card" electronic highway toll collection system is announced by AT&T and Vapor Canada Inc. This new system would allow drivers to drive by toll booths and have their tolls calculated electronically. Drivers would insert a card into a device about the size of a hand-held calculator mounted on the dashboard. The toll charge could then be billed to a credit card or deducted from a cash account. AT&T says many highway authorities have expressed serious interest in the system, which could help them to ease traffic delays.

1991 Nov. 29 Worst highway pileup kills 17

1991 December 4 Pan Am goes out of business

1991 December 19 Agreement is reached by local jurisdictions that assures the completion of the remaining 13.5 miles of the Washington D.C.-area Metrorail system. Completion of the planned 103-mile subway system is projected for as early as 2001. When finished, the system which serves Washington, D.C., Maryland, and Virginia, is expected to have cost $2.2 billion.

Adult Bibliography

General

Carpenter, Reginald, Peter Kall-Bishop, Kenneth Munson, and Robert Wyatt. *Powered Vehicles: A Historical Review.* New York: Crown Publishers, 1974. 240 pp. *Interesting book. Ambitiously deals with the history of ships, rail, autos, aircraft, and space travel. Very detailed index; many line drawings.*

Glazebrook, George P. *A History of Transportation in Canada.* New York: Greenwood Press, 1969. 475 pp. *Originally published in 1938. Excellent history from earliest transportation beginnings in Canada to pre-World War II. Covers all aspects of water, rail, and roads.*

Hawkes, Nigel. *Structures: The Way Things Are Built.* New York: Macmillan Publishing Company, 1990. 240 pp. *Among the major architectural achievements surveyed are several significant tunnels and bridges. Up-to-date with excellent illustrations.*

Miller, John A. *Fares, Please! From Horse-Cars to Streamliners.* New York: D. Appleton-Century Company, 1941. 204 pp. *Dated but excellent history of public transportation from the horse-drawn omnibus to the electric trolley.*

Sandstrom, Gosta E. *Man the Builder.* New York: McGraw-Hill Book Company, 1970. 280 pp. *Large, solid work that contains major sections on construction of historic railways, canals, and bridges.*

Schodek, Daniel L. *Landmarks in American Civil Engineering.* Cambridge, MA: The MIT Press, 1987. 383 pp. *Among its 14 sections are separate chapters on American canals, roads, bridges, tunnels, railroads, and airports of historical significance. Solid, well-written survey.*

Stephens, John H. *The Guinness Book of Structures: Bridges, Towers, Tunnels, Dams.* Middlesex: Guinness Superlatives Ltd., 1976. 288 pp. *Excellent, highly-detailed source contains all manner of tables; offers some history as well as specifications and quantitative details.*

Tuma, Inz J. *The Pictorial Encyclopedia of Transport.* London: Hamlyn, 1979. 495 pp. *Densely illustrated (634 images) with enough text to provide some historical context.*

AIR

General

Allen, Oliver E. *The Airline Builders.* Alexandria, VA: Time-Life Books, 1981. 176 pp. *Solid, focused history of airlines from the mouths of the history-makers themselves; well-illustrated.*

The Almanac of Airpower. New York: Arco, 1989. 256 pp. *Contains up-to-date almanac-type data and information on entire stable of U.S. Air Force aircraft and aeronautical systems.*

American Heritage History of Flight. New York: Simon & Schuster, 1962. 416 pp. *Dated source but excellent general history of early flight. Later segments emphasize American World War II air experience.*

Bowers, Peter M. *Unconventional Aircraft.* Blue Ridge Summit, PA: Tab Books, 1990. 323 pp. *Excellent book; very broad coverage; up-to-date and one of a kind.*

A Chronology of American Aerospace Events. Washington, DC: Department of the Air Force, 1961. 153 pp. *Covers period from 1903—1960 with two chronologies, by day and by year. Emphasizes U.S. Air Force.*

Ege, Lennart. *Balloons and Airships: 1783—1973.* London: Blandford Press, 1973. 234 pp. *Small book (pocket encyclopedia), but contains many details.*

FAA Historical Fact Book: A Chronology, 1926—1971. Washington, DC: Federal Aviation Administration, 1974. 315 pp. *Good organizational history of FAA told chronologically.*

Fuller, G. A., J. A. Griffin, and K. M. Molson. *125 Years of Canadian Aeronautics.* Willowdale, Ont.: Canadian Aviation Historical Society, 1983. 328 pp. *Chronology covers 1840—1965 with later emphasis on Canadian military achievements.*

Gablehouse, Charles. *Helicopters and Autogiros.* Philadelphia: J. B. Lippincott, 1969. 254 pp. *Good standard history, although now dated.*

Gerken, Louis C. *Airships: History and Technology.* Chula Vista, CA: American Scientific Corp., 1990. 464 pp. *Thorough, comprehensive history; up-to-date.*

Gibbs-Smith, Charles H. *The Aeroplane.* London: H. M. Stationery Office, 1960. 375 pp. *Extremely broad-ranging, authoritative, and ambitious history; has become a classic in the field.*

Gibbs-Smith, Charles H. *Aviation: An Historical Survey from Its Origins to the End of World War II.* London: H. M. Stationery Office, 1985. 320 pp. *Most recent edition of this classic work.*

Gibbs-Smith, Charles H. *Flight Through the Ages.* London: Thomas Y. Crowell Company, Inc., 1974. 240 pp. *Excellent, complete chronology of air and space exploration, from myths to satellites; has many good line drawings.*

Gibbs-Smith, Charles H. *A History of Flying*. London: B. T. Batsford Ltd., 1953. 304 pp. *First of his classic, authoritative histories; one of the best.*

Gurney, Gene. *A Chronology of World Aviation*. New York: Franklin Watts, Inc., 1965. 254 pp. *Straight-forward chronology covering 1783—1965. Contains many post-Sputnik entries on space events.*

Hallion, Richard P. *Designers and Test Pilots*. Alexandria, VA: Time-Life Books, 1983. 176 pp. *Well-written and thorough. Solid history of often-neglected individuals, the creative designers and courageous pilots.*

Hart, Clive. *The Prehistory of Flight*. Berkeley: University of California Press, 1985. 279 pp. *Unique book. Extremely detailed and best yet on this neglected subject. Could be the definitive work to date.*

Heinmuller, John P. V. *Man's Fight to Fly*. New York: Aero Print Co., 1945. 370 pp. *Chronology covering the period 1783—1939. Both personality and record-oriented.*

Jackson, Donald D. *The Aeronauts*. Alexandria, VA: Time-Life Books, 1980. 176 pp. *Solid, well-written history of balloons that focuses on the men and women whose deeds made history.*

Kane, Robert M. *Air Transportation*. Dubuque, IA: Kendall/Hunt Publishing Company, 1990. *Popular textbook that focuses on the regulatory and administrative aspects of air transport; oddly-paged, big book.*

King, H. F. *Milestones of the Air: Jane's 100 Significant Aircraft*. New York: McGraw-Hill Book Co., 1969. 157 pp. *Beginning with the Wright Flyer to today's Concorde, specifications and accomplishments are given for each aircraft.*

Lambermont, Paul M., and Anthony Pirie. *Helicopters and Autogyros of the World*. New York: A. S. Barnes and Company, 1970. 446 pp. *Brief chronological survey. Bulk of the book is organized by country, with details on each craft.*

McFarland, Marvin. *The Papers of Wilbur and Orville Wright*. New York: Arno Press, 1972. 1,278 pp. *This two-volume reprint of the 1953 work chronologically presents the edited papers, letters, and diary entries of the Wrights, offering an invaluable record of their historic accomplishments.*

Miller, Francis T. *The World in the Air*. New York: G. P. Putnam's Sons, 1930. 556 pp. (2 volumes). *Chronologically arranged; very dated and short on details but heavily illustrated.*

Nayler, J. L. *Aviation: Its Technical Development*. Philadelphia: Dufour Editions, 1965. 290 pp. *Excellent survey and explanatory text on the science of aeronautics and its historical development.*

Payne, L. G. S. *Air Dates*. London: Heinemann, 1957. 565 pp. *Typical chronology, from 1783—1956, with heavy emphasis on military aspects.*

Reay, David A. *The History of Man-Powered Flight*. New York: Pergamon Press, 1977. 355 pp. *Good, solid history. Attempts international coverage. Excellent on technical details.*

Rolt, L. T. C. *The Aeronauts*. New York: Walker, 1966. 267 pp. *Good survey of the early history of ballooning, 1783—1903.*

Sherwin, K. *Man-Powered Flight*. Kings Lanfgley: Argus Books Ltd., 1975. 193 pp. *Detailed technical treatment; not historical.*

Shrader, Welman A. *Fifty Years of Flight*. Cleveland, OH: Eaton Manufacturing Company, 1954. 178 pp. *Very detailed, year-by-year account of the accomplishments of the American aviation industry.*

Taylor, Michael J. H., and John W. R. Taylor. *Encyclopedia of Air-* craft. New York: G. P. Putnam's Sons, 1978. 253 pp. *Typical encyclopedic or alphabetical treatment by aircraft name; good on details.*

Other

Hart, Clive. *Kites: An Historical Survey*. New York: Paul P. Appel, 1982. 210 pp. *Best single source history of kites available. Begins survey with China and goes to present day; understandable technical explanations.*

Welch, Ann, and Lorne Welch. *The Story of Gliding*. London: John Murray, 1980. 262 pp. *Solid although dated comprehensive history of gliding.*

LAND

General

Bird, Anthony. *Roads and Vehicles*. London: Arrow Books, 1973. 246 pp. *Good historical treatment of roads and vehicles stops at turn-of-the-century; has a basically British focus.*

Burtt, *Philip*. *The History and Development of Road Transport*. New York: I. Pitman & Sons, Ltd., 1927. *Dated source but contains useful, chronologically-organized facts about roads and early automobiles.*

Paterson, James. *The History and Development of Road Transport*. London: Sir Isaac Pitman & Sons, Ltd., 1927. 118 pp. *Very dated but touches briefly on most major forms of land transport. More of a survey than a real history.*

Automobiles

Bird, Anthony. *The Motor Car: 1765—1914*. London: B. T. Batsford Ltd., 1960. 256 pp. *Excellent level of detail on early historical development; ends with Model T and Rolls Silver Ghost.*

Cummins, C. Lyle, Jr. *Internal Fire*. Warrendale, PA: Society of Automotive Engineers, Inc., 1989. 357 pp. *Excellent source. May be the definitive history of the development of the internal combustion engine.*

Davis, G. J. *Automotive Reference*. Boise, ID: Whitehorse, 1987. 460 pp. *Excellent reference work. Combines usefulness of a glossary with that of a solid, technical book. Easy-to-understand entries.*

Diesel, Eugen, Gustav Goldbeck, and Friedrich Schildberger. *From Engines to Autos*. Chicago: Henry Regnery Company, 1960. 302 pp. *History of automobile told via the stories of five German pioneers: Otto, Daimler, Benz, Diesel, and Bosch.*

Electric Vehicles at a Glance. New York: McGraw-Hill, 1978. 32 pp. *Very brief chronology of the development of electric vehicles, from 1837 to 1978.*

Flink, James J. *America Adopts the Automobile: 1895—1910*. Cambridge, MA: The MIT Press, 1970. 343 pp. *Excellent scholarly history; very focused, detailed, and ambitious.*

Georgano, G. N. *The New Encyclopedia of Motorcars: 1885 to the Present*. New York: E. P. Dutton: 688 pp. *Exhaustive and complete A to Z treatment of all car and manufacturer names.*

Karslake, Kent, and Laurence Pomery. *From Veteran to Vintage: A History of Motoring and Motorcars from 1884 to 1914*. London: Temple Press Ltd., 1956. 353 pp. *Good background details with European and racing emphasis.*

Lewis, Albert L., and Walter A. Musciano. *Automobiles of the World*. New York: Simon and Schuster, 1977. 731 pp. *Brief but excellent historical summaries by year and by car; contains drawings of each automobile discussed.*

Nixon, St. John C. *The Antique Automobile.* London: Cassell & Company Ltd., 1956. 236 pp. *Straight-forward history with European emphasis.*

Ruiz, Marco. *One Hundred Years of the Motor Car: 1886 to 1986.* London: Willow Books, 1985. 280 pp. *Good historical, car-by-car approach. Very detailed with photos of many major model changes.*

Stein, Ralph. *The Treasury of the Automobile.* New York: Golden Press, 1961. 248 pp. *Generally good work but difficult to use. Lack of an index is a problem. Interesting emphasis on author's personal experiences.*

Wherry, Joseph H. *Automobiles of the World.* Philadelphia: Chilton Book Company, 1968. 713 pp. *Very large, comprehensive book. Broadly international in scope.*

Young, A. B. Filson. *The Complete Motorist.* Wakefield, Eng.: EP Publishing Ltd., 1973. 338 pp. *First published in 1904. Some history, containing information on hard-to-find autos, but mostly a detailed, technical, how-to book.*

Bicycles and Motorcycles

Caunter, Cyril F. *Motor Cycles: A Technical History.* London: Her Majesty's Stationery Office, 1982. 164 pp. *Scholarly, comprehensive, and definitive work now updated.*

Hough, Richard A., and L. J. K. Setright. *A History of the World's Motorcycles.* New York: Harper & Row, 1973. 208 pp. *Solidly-researched and excellent international history from 1900 to 1972.*

Sheldon, James. *Veteran and Vintage Motor Cycles.* London: B. T. Batsford, 1961. 208 pp. *Good early history but strictly English and European focus.*

Horses

Barclay, Harold B. *The Role of the Horse in Man's Culture.* New York: J. A. Allen, 1980. 398 pp. *Scholarly, readable survey of all aspects of the horse and its relationship to man.*

Dent, Anthony A. *The Horse: Through Fifty Years of Civilization.* London: Phaidon Press, 1974. 288 pp. *Well illustrated, broad international survey of the horse and its use by man.*

Rail

Ellis, C. Hamilton. *The Lore of the Train.* London: George Allen & Unwin Ltd., 1971. 240 pp. *Very thorough, heavily detailed history; contains many line drawings.*

Hastings, Paul. *Railroads: An International History.* London: Ernest Benn Ltd., 1972. 144 pp. *Brief historical survey of high points. Includes information on railroads in Africa, Australia, and the Andes.*

History of Railways. Hamlyn: New English Library, 1976. 512 pp. *Very large historical work with broadest possible scope; excellent source.*

McPherson, James A. (ed.). *Railroad: Trains and Train People in American Culture.* New York: Random House, 1976. 185 pp. *Series of brief essays that place the history of American trains in a large context. Contains brief "railroad timetable" covering 1804 to 1974.*

Marshall, John. *Rail: The Records.* Middlesex: Guinness Superlatives Ltd., 1985. 192 pp. *Current and very broad in scope with information also on bridges and tunnels.*

Nock, Oswald S. *Encyclopedia of Railways.* London: Octopus Books, 1977. 480 pp. *Excellent one-book source; broadly historical and international in scope.*

Phillips, Lance. *Yonder Comes the Train.* New York: A. S. Barnes, 1965. 395 pp. *Very detailed historical survey to 1965 of development of the American rail system.*

Roads

America's Highways, 1776—1976: A History of the Federal-Aid Program. Washington, D.C.: Federal Highway Administration, 1977. 553 pp. *Excellent, large administrative and organizational history of U.S. highway programs from earliest times.*

The First Fifty Years: 1914—1964. Washington, D.C.: American Association of State Highway Officials, 1964. *Good background information on organizational development of the U.S. road system, with detailed state-by-state treatment.*

Gregory, J. W. *The Story of the Road.* London: Adam & Charles Black, 1938. 306 pp. *Very dated but has good sections on ancient and medieval roads, especially good on China and Inca roads.*

Labatutt, Jean, and Wheaton J. Lane (eds). *Highways in Our National Life.* New York: Arno Press, 1972. 506 pp. *Forty-six separate essays by scholars who survey the social as well as technical aspects of highways in the life of the United States.*

Rose, Albert C. *Historic American Highways.* Washington, D.C.: Association of State Highway Officials, 1953. 183 pp. *Contains 109 separate essays (1539—1945) that cover many historical aspects of the development of U.S. roads and highways. Reprinted in 1976 as Historic American Roads.*

Rose, Albert C. *Public Roads of the Past: 3500 B.C. to 1800 A.D.* Washington, D.C.: American Association of State Highway Officials, 1952. 101 pp. *Twenty-one essays that chronologically tell the history of early public roads (to 1800). Sometimes difficult to use but full of information; no index.*

Schreiber, Hermann. *Merchants, Pilgrims and Highwaymen.* New York: G. P. Putnam's Sons, 1962. 236 pp. *Very good, detailed history of roads through the ages that has rich contextual information as well. Stops at the turn-of-the-century.*

Wixom, Charles W. *Pictorial History of Roadbuilding.* Washington, D.C.: American Road Builders' Association, 1975. 207 pp. *Brief technical history of road building in the U.S., with many excellent illustrations.*

Tunnels

Black, Archibald. *The Story of Tunnels.* New York: Whittlesey House, 1937. 245 pp. *Very dated although good on much older material.*

Davidson, Frank P. *Tunneling and Underground Transport.* New York: Elsevier, 1987. 236 pp. *Brief historical section; heavy on technical aspects; very current.*

Dean, Frederick E. *Tunnels and Tunnelling.* London: Frederick Muller Ltd., 1962. 144 pp. *Brief historical survey with emphasis on technical aspects.*

Sandstrom, Gosta E. *Tunnels.* New York: Rinehart & Winston, 1963. 427 pp. *Excellent, broadly historical work.*

Other

American Roller Skates: 1860—1910. Lincoln, NE: National Museum of Roller Skating, 1983. 64 pp. *Brief but good history of skates, with the bulk of the book devoted to photos of old skates.*

Bobrick, Benson. *Labyrinths of Iron: A History of the World's Sub-*

ways. New York: Newsweek Books, 1981. 352 pp. *Excellent, readable, and solid history; international in scope.*

Butler, J. S. *Lifts and Elevators.* London: Imperial College of Science and Technology, 1968. 60 pp. *Hard-to-find but good brief technical history.*

Davidson, Ben. *The Skate-Board Book.* New York: Grosset & Dunlap, 1976. 109 pp. *Brief attempt at history but mostly a how-to book.*

Hilton, George W. *The Cable Car in America.* San Diego, CA: Howell-North, 1982. 484 pp. *Best available survey of all aspects of cable traction in the United States.*

Lunn, Arnold. *A History of Ski-ing.* London: Oxford University Press, 1927. 492 pp. *Dated but heavy on early details; mostly British focus.*

Lunn, Arnold. *The Story of Ski-ing.* London: Eyre & Spottiswoode, 1952. 224 pp. *More of a real history than his first book.*

Macksey, Kenneth. *The Guinness History of Land Warfare.* Middlesex: Guinness Superlatives Ltd., 1973. 248 pp. *Transport plays a major role in land warfare, and as such, it is touched upon and placed in context.*

Rayner, Ranulf. *The Story of Skiing.* David & Charles, 1989. 96 pp. *Large format, heavily-illustrated with brief historical texts.*

Richardson, E. C. *The Ski-Runner.* Cecil Palmer, 1924. 234 pp. *Basically an early how-to, technical book, but contains valuable historical details.*

Scharff, Robert (ed.). *Encyclopedia of Skiing.* New York: Harper & Row, Publishers, 1970. 427 pp. *Contains good, 51-page section on the history of skiing, with a chronological list of some highlights.*

Strakosch, George R. *Elevators and Escalators.* New York: John Wiley & Sons, 1983. 365 pp. *Large, major technical survey with little history.*

Stratton, Ezra M. *The World on Wheels: or, Carriages, with Their Historical Associations from the Earliest to the Present Time.* New York: B. Blom, 1972. 489 pp. *Reprint of 1878 exhaustive treatment of carriages from early sleds to last quarter of 19th century. Well-illustrated.*

Tarr, Lazlo. *The History of the Carriage.* London: Vision, 1969. 331 pp. *Definitive source in English; comprehensive in scope and detail.*

Yoshida, Mitsukuni. *The Wheel: A Japanese History.* Tokyo: Tokyo Kogyo, 1981. 109 pp. *Brief but unique survey of the history of the wheel in Japanese transport; many illustrations and high-point chronology.*

SPACE

General

Baker, David. *The History of Manned Space Flight.* New York: Crown Publishers, Inc., 1982. 544 pp. *This very large book is the most comprehensive treatment of the history of manned spaceflight available. Should be updated.*

Baker, David. *The Rocket: The History and Development of Rocket & Missile Technology.* London: New Cavendish Books, 1978. 276 pp. *Large format book is the best available work on the development of rocketry; a comprehensive, major source.*

Braun, Wernher von, and Frederick I. Ordway III. *The Rockets' Red Glare.* New York: Anchor Press: 1976. 212 pp. *Good short history of rocketry co-authored by one of its pioneers.*

Braun, Wernher von, and Frederick I. Ordway III. *Space Travel: A*

History. New York: Harper & Row, 1985. 308 pp. *Solid history with extra emphasis on early, military development of rocketry.*

Cambridge Encyclopedia of Space. Cambridge, Eng.: Cambridge University Press, 1990. 386 pp. *Largest, best, most comprehensive and current single book on space flight.*

Cassutt, Michael. *Who's Who in Space: The First 25 Years.* Boston: G. K. Hall, 1987. 311 pp. *Major source for biographical information on all U.S., Soviet, and international "space travelers." Also contains flight logs and chronology.*

Gurney, Gene, and Jeff Forte. *Space Shuttle Log: The First 25 Flights.* Blue Ridge Summit, PA: Tab Books Inc., 1988. 293 pp. *Focuses on the first shuttle era and gives crew, launch, operations, and landing information on each flight. Well-illustrated.*

Newkirk, Dennis. *Almanac of Soviet Manned Space Flight.* Houston: Gulf Publishing Company, 1990. 391 pp. *Very detailed treatment of all major Soviet manned space flights as well as a historical explanation of related Soviet space efforts.*

Smith, Melvyn. *Space Shuttle.* Newbury Park, CA: Haynes Publications, Inc., 1989. 304 pp. *Excellent, broad-ranging source that begins with early "X aircraft" flights and ends with Challenger accident. Contains logs of all research aircraft and space flights. Well illustrated.*

Winter, Frank H. *The First Golden Age of Rocketry.* Washington, D.C.: Smithsonian Institution Press, 1990. *Exhaustive, comprehensive examination of the history of rocketry from its practical beginnings in India through the 19th century.*

Winter, Frank H. *Rockets into Space.* Cambridge, MA: Harvard University Press, 1990. 165 pp. *Excellent, solid history of the evolution of modern rocketry. Good bibliography.*

WATER

Bridges

Beckett, Derek. *Bridges.* New York: Paul Hamlyn, 1969. 191 pp. *Focuses on 12 famous bridges. Offers good technical history of each.*

Edwards, Llewellyn N. *A Record of History and Evolution of Early American Bridges.* Orono, ME: University Press, 1959. 204 pp. *Good treatment focused on American bridges to 1900.*

Gies, Joseph. *Bridges and Men.* New York: Doubleday, 1963. 343 pp. *Well-written, broad history. Interweaves personal stories with history.*

Hopkins, Henry J. *A Span of Bridges: An Illustrated History.* New York: Praeger, 1970. 288 pp. *Not traditionally organized but well-written and detailed.*

Plowden, David. *Bridges: The Spans of North America.* New York: W. W. Norton & Company, 1984. 328 pp. *Excellent, detailed treatment of the major North American bridges.*

Robins, Frederick W. *Story of the Bridge.* Birmingham, Eng.: Cornish Bros., 1948. 278 pp. *Dated but good history, although index very thin.*

Tyrrell, Henry G. *History of Bridge Engineering.* Chicago: Published by the Author, 1911. 479 pp. *Extremely detailed, bridge-by-bridge treatment. Very old work but often includes bridges seldom mentioned by anyone else.*

Whitney, Charles S. *Bridges: Their Art, Science and Evolution.* New York: Greenwich House, 1983. 360 pp. *Very broad based, sophisticated,* well-written book that offers a unique treatment of the history of bridges. First published in 1929. Heavily illustrated.

Canals

Drago, Harry S. *Canal Days in America*. New York: Clarkson N. Potter, Inc., 1972. 311 pp. *Focuses on short period in the 19th century when the canal system was a vital part of U.S. transportation. Very detailed with many good illustrations.*

Hadfield, Charles. *World Canals: Inland Navigation Past and Present*. New York: Facts on File, 1986. 432 pp. *Excellent, fact-filled historical survey; international in scope. A major source.*

Harlow, Alvin F. *Old Towpaths: The Story of the American Canal Era*. Port Washington, NY: Kennikat Press, Inc., 1964. 403 pp. *Excellent historical treatment, canal by canal.*

Harris, Robert. *Canals and Their Architecture*. New York: Frederick A. Praeger, 1969. 223 pp. *Not a typical history; rather, deals with the integral parts or sub-systems of a canal system; heavily illustrated.*

Shaw, Ronald E. *Canals for a Nation: The Canal Era in the United States, 1790—1860*. Lexington, KY: The University Press of Kentucky, 1990. 284 pp. *Scholarly work that surveys all aspects of the U.S. canal system.*

Instruments and Lighthouses

Hague, Douglas B., and Rosemary Christie. *Lighthouses: Their Architecture, History and Archaeology*. Llandysul: Gomer Press, 1975. 307 pp.

Hewson, J. B. *A History of the Practice of Navigation*. Glasgow: Brown, Son, & Ferguson, Ltd., 1983. 295 pp. *Excellent detailed history. Covers development of all major sea-going navigational instruments.*

Hitchins, Henry L. *From Lodestone to Gyro-Compass*. New York: Hutchinson's Scientific and Technical Publications, 1952. 219 pp. *Although not current, contains solid historical treatment of the development and uses of the compass.*

Holland, Francis R., Jr. *America's Lighthouses: Their Illustrated History Since 1716*. Brattleboro, VT: The Stephen Greene Press, 1972. 226 pp. *Well illustrated, heavily detailed and documented work organized lighthouse by lighthouse.*

Naish, John. *Seamarks: Their History and Development*. London: Stanford Maritime, 1985. 192 pp. *Up-to-date work with good historical sections.*

Putnam, George R. *Lighthouses and Lightships of the United States*. Boston: Houghton Mifflin Company, 1933. 324 pp. *Dated source but very detailed on older U.S. lighthouses and ships; organized by geographical region.*

Stevenson, D. Alan. *The World's Lighthouses Before 1820*. London: Oxford University Press, 1959. 310 pp. *Major, authoritative work. Organized chronologically with later sections devoted to fuller treatment of major lighthouses.*

Strobridge, Truman R. *Chronology of Aids to Navigation and the Old Lighthouse Service: 1716—1939*. Washington, D.C.: United States Coast Guard, 1974. 39 pp. *Brief but thorough chronology that notes all the major events and accomplishments of the U.S. Coast Guard's involvement with lighthouses.*

Taylor, E. G. R. *The Haven-Finding Art: A History of Navigation from Odysseus to Captain Cook*. London: Hollis & Carter, 1971. 310 pp. *Very thorough treatment. Highlights major voyages of exploration.*

Ships

Angelucci, Enzo, and Attilio Cucari. *Ships*. New York: Greenwich House, 1983. 336 pp. *Extremely heavy on technical details; contains over 60 pages of technical specifications by vessel.*

Bathe, Basil W. *Seven Centuries of Sea Travel*. New York: Tudor Publishing Company, 1973. 298 pp. *Very large book with emphasis on illustrations, not historical detail. Ranges from Crusades to present.*

Bauer, K. Jack. *A Maritime History of the United States: The Role of America's Seas and Waterway*. Columbia, SC: University of South Carolina Press, 1988. 359 pp. *Definitive history of all aspects of U.S. water-related activities.*

Field, Cyril. *The Story of the Submarine*. London: Sampson, Low, Marston & Company, Ltd., 1908. 304 pp. *Very dated source but is especially useful for its broad yet detailed treatment of older material.*

Frere-Cook, Gervis, and Kenneth Macksey. *The Guinness History of Sea Warfare*. Middlesex: Guinness Superlatives Ltd., 1975. 245 pp. *Expected emphasis on firsts, but surprisingly good historical treatment of large subject.*

Gilfillan, S. C. *Inventing the Ship*. Chicago: Follett Publishing Company, 1935. 294 pp. *Good study of the development of all major inventions or sub-systems, from power to sail; dated.*

Greenhill, Basil. *Evolution of the Wooden Ship*. New York: Facts on File, 1989. 239 pp. *Immensely detailed history of a building tradition, with excellent accompanying drawings. Contains large sections on the actual construction of several types of wooden boats and ships.*

Haws, Duncan. *Ships and the Sea: A Chronological Review*. New York: Crowell, 1975. 240 pp. *Detailed chronological treatment of the evolution and development of ships. Earliest entry is 5000 B.C. Good line drawings.*

Hornell, James. *Water Transport: Origins & Early Evolution*. Newton Abbot: David & Charles, 1970. 307 pp. *Comprehensive, definitive work on all major forms of boats and small craft. A major source.*

Kemp, Peter. *Encyclopedia of Ships and Seafaring*. London: Stanford Maritime, 1980. 256 pp. *Excellent and very useful historical encyclopedia. As comprehensive as any one-volume encyclopedia can be.*

Kemp, Peter. *The History of Ships*. London: Orbis Publishing, 1978. 288 pp. *Well-written, interesting, good history. Excellent source.*

Marx, Robert F. *The History of Underwater Exploration*. New York: Dover Publications, Inc., 1990. 198 pp. *Good, standard historical work on all underwater activities, with very interesting anecdotes. Especially good on recent developments.*

Preble, George H. *A Chronological History of the Origin and Development of Steam Navigation*. Philadelphia: L. R. Hamersly & Co., 1895. 418 pp. *Exhaustively detailed history of the progress of steam navigation from 1543 to 1882. Organization is strictly chronological. Excellent unknown and under-used source.*

Ransome-Wallis, P. *North Atlantic Panorama: 1900—1976*. London: I. Allan, 1977. 192 pp. *Year-by-year, ship-by-ship history of transatlantic liners.*

Sailing Ships: Their History and Development. London: Science Museum, 1959. 95 pp. *A major, authoritative work on sailing ships that contains exhaustive detail. Concludes with clipper ships.*

Sweeney, James B. *A Pictorial History of Oceanographic Submersibles.* New York: Crown Publishers, Inc., 1970. 310 pp. *Organized chronologically. Excellent, thorough historical survey as well as well-illustrated source.*

Other

Gardiner, Frederic M. *Wings on the Ice: A Comprehensive View of the Sport of Ice Boating.* New York: Yachting Publishing Corp., 1938.

160 pp. *Brief historical chapter on the development of ice boating, followed by treatment of technique and design.*

Margan, Frank, and Ben R. Finney. *Pictorial History of Surfing.* New York: Paul Hamlyn, 1970. 319 pp. *Oddly-organized and difficult to use; heavily illustrated.*

Oppenheim, François. *The History of Swimming.* North Hollywood, CA: Swimming World, 1970. 149 pp. *More of a fact book than any real historical treatment.*

Young Adult Bibliography

General

Asimov, Isaac. *Asimov's Chronology of Science and Discovery.* New York: Harper & Row, 1989. 707 pp. *Transportation entries are scattered throughout. Has good, brief explanatory essays.*

Brown, Barbara. *Transport Through the Ages.* London: Arthur Barker Ltd., 1971. 128 pp. *Only four pages of text with remainder of book being a real picture history. Author provides 412 drawings of all manner of transportation modes.*

De Old, Alan, Everett Sheets, and William Alexander. *Transportation: The Technology of Moving People and Products.* Worcester, MA: Davis Publications, Inc., 1986. 534 pp. *Excellent textbook on the fundamentals of transportation technology.*

Firestone, Harvey S., Jr. *Man on the Move: The Story of Transportation.* New York: G. P. Putnam's Sons, 1967. 318 pp. *Dated but readable historical survey of transportation advances in air, land, sea, and space.*

Georgano, G. N. *A History of Transport.* London: J. M. Dent & Sons Ltd., 1972. 311 pp. *Well-illustrated popular history organized by road, rail, water, and air transport. Does not cover space flight.*

Giscard d'Estaing, Valerie-Anne. *The Second World Almanac of Inventions.* New York: World Almanac, 1986. 352 pp. *Transportation items account for little over one tenth of the book, but is still very useful. A popular and interesting brief treatment of who invented what.*

Gregory, Malcolm S. *History and Development of Engineering.* London: Longman, 1971. 190 pp. *Very brief but good history of engineering that stresses major historical accomplishments.*

Lee, Laurie, and David Lambert. *The Wonderful World of Transportation.* New York: Doubleday and Company, Inc., 1969. 96 pp. *Briefest of high-point summaries.*

Mount, Ellis, and Barbara A. List. *Milestones in Science and Technology.* Phoenix, AZ: Oryx Press, 1987. 141 pp. *Very useful reference book organized alphabetically by name of invention, discovery, or fact. Entries are brief historical summaries. Contains several terms pertinent to transportation.*

Pannell, J. P. M. *Man the Builder: An Illustrated History of Engineering.* London: Thames and Hudson, 1977. 256 pp. *Very good, brief engineering history of roads, bridges, canals, and railways.*

Rand McNally Encyclopedia of Transportation. Chicago: Rand McNally & Company, 1976. 256 pp. *Good one-book source. Attempts to be as broad as possible, covering biographies, industries, components, and related topics.*

Ridley, Anthony. *An Illustrated History of Transportation.* New York: The John Day Company, 1969. 186 pp. *Brief, high-point survey; small-format book.*

Robertson, Patrick. *The Shell Book of Firsts.* London: Eboury Press, 1983. 264 pp. *Interesting and fun reference book. Offers a chronological list of "firsts" arranged alphabetically, and contains many transport-related entries.*

St. Clair, Labert. *Transportation: Land, Air, Water.* New York: Dodd, Mead & Company, 1942. 349 pp. *Dated but very good, broad historical survey. Easy to read. Stops before World War II.*

Sommerfield, Vernon. *Speed, Space and Time.* London: Thomas Nelson and Sons, Ltd., 1935. 299 pp. *Dated but good general historical survey of the ship, road, railway, car, balloon, and airplane.*

Sommerfield, Vernon. *The Wheel.* London: Nicholson & Watson, Ltd., 1938. 248 pp. *Dated but good general survey of public, not private, transportation. Complements his earlier work, Speed, Space and Time.*

Starr, Edward A. *From Trail Dust to Star Dust.* Dallas, TX: Transportation Press, 1945. 260 pp. *Brief, easy historical survey of all major forms of transportation in the United States.*

Throm, Edward L. *Popular Mechanics' Picture History of American Transportation.* New York: Simon and Schuster, 1952. 312 pp. *Very dated and difficult to use for history, but contains many interesting period drawings and photographs.*

Upton, Neil. *An Illustrated History of Civil Engineering.* London: Heinemann, 1975. 192 pp. *Major emphasis on bridges but also much on canals and tunnels.*

AIR

General

Anderson, E. W. *Man the Aviator.* London: Priory Press Ltd., 1975. 96 pp. *Brief, general survey touches only on high spots.*

Beaubois, Henry. *Airships: An Illustrated History.* London: Macdonald and Jane's, 1974. 235 pp. *Standard, broad history with excellent illustrations.*

Christy, Joe. *1001 Flying Facts and Firsts.* Blue Ridge Summit, PA: Tab Books Inc., 1989. 220 pp. *Typical chronology with emphasis on firsts; popular treatment.*

De Leeuw, Hendrik. *From Flying Horse to Man in the Moon.* New York: St. Martin's Press, 1963. 310 pp. *Popular history of flight with emphasis on individual accomplishments.*

Dwiggins, Don. *Man-Powered Aircraft.* Blue Ridge Summit, PA: Tab Books, 1979. 192 pp. *Brief, popular treatment; now dated.*

Dwiggins, Don. *On Silent Wings: Adventures in Motorless Flight.* New York: Grosset & Dunlap, Inc., 1970. 151 pp. *Good popular treatment of the history of gliding.*

Flight: A Pictorial History of Aviation. New York: Year, 1958. 192 pp. *Anecdotal treatment of high points but very well illustrated.*

Friedlander, Mark P., Jr., and Gene Gurney. *Higher, Faster, and Farther.* New York: William Morrow & Co., 1973. 349 pp. *Record-oriented history; narrow in scope.*

Kirschner, Edwin J. *Aerospace Balloons: From Montgolfière to Space.* Fallbrook, CA: Aero Publishers, Inc., 1985. 120 pp. *Brief, popular history with emphasis on modern aspects.*

Macknight, Nigel, and Nicola Macknight. *The Colour Encyclopedia of Aircraft.* London: Octopus, 1980. 224 pp. *Organized by aircraft type; emphasis on military aircraft.*

Mondey, David. *The International Encyclopedia of Aviation.* New York: Crown Publishers, 1977. 480 pp. *Excellent, large reference work that is a superb one-book source.*

Mondey, David, and Michael J. H. Taylor. *The Guinness Book of Aircraft.* London: Guinness, 1988. 256 pp. *Highly detailed chronology with emphasis on firsts and records. Usefully organized by type of aeronautical activity.*

Taylor, John W. R. *A Picture History of Flight.* London: Edward Hulton, 1950. 192 pp. *Standard picture history with few details.*

Taylor, Michael J. H., and David Mondey. *Milestones of Flight.* London: Jane's, 1983. 288 pp. *Totally chronological text, beginning with 863 B.C. and ending in 1982. Includes major space accomplishments along with excellent chronology of aeronautics.*

Other

Dean, Anabel. *Up, Up, and Away: The Story of Ballooning.* Philadelphia: Westminster Press, 1980. 192 pp. *Popular, easy-to-read historical treatment.*

Haining, Peter. *The Dream Machines.* London: New English Library, 1972. 180 pp. *Anecdotal, brief histories of ballooning's high points; many interesting illustrations.*

Pelham, David. *The Penguin Book of Kites.* New York: Penguin Books, 1976. 227 pp. *Brief popular historical treatment with details on all major types of kites.*

LAND

General

Benson, D. S. *Man and the Wheel.* London: Priory Press Ltd., 1973. 128 pp. *Easy to read high-point historical survey of the transport use of the wheel.*

Tunis, Edward. *Wheels: A Pictorial Survey.* New York: Thomas Y. Crowell Company, 1977. 96 pp. *Brief historical survey from beginnings of the wheel to post-World War II. More illustrative than historical; no index.*

Automobiles

Clymer, Floyd. *Treasury of Early American Automobiles: 1877—1925.* New York: McGraw-Hill Book Company, Inc., 1950. 213 pp. *Eccentrically organized and difficult to use but still very interesting. Catches spirit of the times by using period photos and advertisements.*

Harding, Anthony, Warren Allport, David Hodges, and John Davenport. *The Guinness Book of the Car.* London: Guinness Books, 1987. 256 pp. *Excellent reference with good, high-point chronology; also good manufacturer histories and biographies.*

Macbeth, Graham. *The Centenary Encyclopedia of Automobiles.* Middlesex: Temple Press, 1984. 576 pp. *Very heavily illustrated source organized by subject area. Especially good on older subjects.*

Rolt, L. T. C. *Motoring History.* London: Dutton Vista, 1964. 159 pp. *Very brief work that covers 1769—1964 period. Has many interesting photos.*

Shacket, Sheldon R. *The Complete Book of Electric Vehicles.* Chicago: Domus Books, 1979. 168 pp. *Short history plus sections on various subsystems and types of electric vehicles. Simple, explanatory technical sections.*

Stern, Philip Van Doren. *A Pictorial History of the Automobile: 1903—1953.* New York: The Viking Press, 1953. 256 pp. *Nostalgic but thorough; captures feeling of earlier times. Organized chronologically with emphasis totally on the United States.*

Sutton, Richard. *Car.* New York: Alfred A. Knopf, 1990. 63 pp. *Simple, easy-to-understand technical explanations; extremely brief but covers important large areas.*

Wise, David B. *The Illustrated Encyclopedia of the World's Automobiles.* New York: A&W Publishers, Inc., 1979. 352 pp. *Excellent general history, international in scope. Heavily illustrated.*

Bicycles and Motorcycles

Calif, Ruth. *World on Wheels.* New York: Cornwall Books, 1983. 176 pp. *Very good history of the bicycle and its relatives. Comprehensively covers period up to World War I. Many old, interesting illustrations.*

Durry, Jean. *The Guinness Guide to Bicycling.* Enfield, Eng.: Guinness Superlatives, 1977. 218 pp. *Very brief section on historical development; good on technical aspects as well as racing competition.*

McGurn, James. *On Your Bicycle.* New York: Facts on File Publications, 1987. 208 pp. *Easy-to-read, solid history with many good illustrations.*

Setright, L. J. K. *The Guinness Book of Motorcycling Facts and Feats.* Middlesex: Guinness Superlatives Ltd., 1979. 257 pp. *Good chronological treatment of historical and technical development of motorcycles; includes racing information.*

Horses

Edwards, Elwyn H. *The Howell Book of Saddlery and Tack.* New York: Howell Book House, Inc., 1988. 256 pp. *Encyclopedic approach to all particulars of horse-related equipment. Easy-to-use and well-illustrated.*

Edwards, Lionel. *Thy Servant the Horse.* London: Country Life Ltd., 1952. *Easy-to-read, brief historical survey.*

Popescu, Charlotte. *Horses at Work.* London: Batsford Academic and Educational Ltd., 1983. 72 pp. *Very brief high-point survey.*

Rail

Allen, G. Freeman. *Railways: Past, Present & Future.* New York: William Morrow and Company, Inc., 1987. 303 pp. *Excellent study that combines historical fact with technical information.*

Ellis, C. Hamilton. *Railway History.* New York: Dutton Vista Paperback, 1966. 160 pp. *Good, brief historical survey with many illustrations.*

Nock, Oswald S. *The Dawn of World Railways: 1800—1850.* New York: Macmillan, 1972. 179 pp. *Contains 84 brief entries touching on the high points of rail history during its first 50 years. Half of the book is composed of color drawings of all aspects of railways.*

Profiles of American Railroading. Schenectady, NY: General Electric Co., 1965. 48 pp. *Brief chronological survey of some of the more significant U.S. railroad accomplishments.*

Webb, Robert N. *The Illustrated True Book of American Railroads.* New York: Grosset & Dunlap, 1957. 154 pp. *Brief, popular history of American railroads. Dated but useful for U.S. history.*

Roads

Borth, Christy. *Mankind on the Move: The Story of Highways.* Washington, DC: Automotive Safety Foundation, 1969. 314 pp. *Popular history of roads with most of the book devoted to a treatment of U.S. roads and highways.*

Carter, Ernest F. *Famous Roads of the World.* London: Frederick Muller Ltd., 1962. 143 pp. *Brief historical summary. Emphasis on Europe and England.*

Hindley, Geoffrey. *A History of Roads.* London: Peter Davies, 1971. 158 pp. *Good, brief general history from ancient times to 1970.*

Tunnels

Beaver, Patrick. *History of Tunnels.* London: P. Davies, 1972. 155 pp. *Fairly brief but very well done. Excellent explanatory text.*

Bloch, Marie H. *Tunnels.* New York: Coward-McCann, Inc., 1954. 95 pp. *Very brief historical survey but catches most major accomplishments.*

Doherty, Charles H. *Science and the Tunneller.* Leicester: Brockhampton Press, 1967. 96 pp. *Very brief, popular treatment. Simple, easy-to-read.*

Other

Anderson, Paul. *Tell Me About Elevators.* New York: Otis Elevator Company, 1976. 40 pp. *Brief survey with emphasis on Otis contributions.*

Arnold, Peter. *The Hamlyn Book of Skateboarding.* New York: Hamlyn, 1977. 61 pp. *How-to, technical book with briefest of historical references; well-illustrated.*

Cassorla, Anthony. *The Ultimate Skateboard Book.* Philadelphia: Running Press, 1988. 128 pp. *Minimal history; mostly focuses on equipment and technique.*

Ford, Barbara. *The Elevator.* New York: Walker and Company, 1982. 64 pp. *Brief, easy-to-read, general survey.*

Lunn, Peter. *The Guinness Book of Skiing.* Middlesex: Guinness Superlatives Ltd., 1983. 185 pp. *Excellent information source on all aspects; good historical section.*

SPACE

Bali, Mrinal. *Space Exploration: A Reference Handbook.* Santa Barbara, CA: ABC-CLIO, 1990. 240 pp. *Up-to-date factbook with chronological, biographical, and other basic information.*

Furniss, Tim. *Space Flight: The Records.* Middlesex: Guinness Books, 1985. 168 pp. *Excellent "Manned Space Flight Diary" up to 1985. Also has detailed sections on manned firsts, biographical information, and flight logs.*

Gatland, Kenneth (ed.). *The Illustrated Encyclopedia of Space Technology.* New York: Orion Books, 1989. 303 pp. *Excellent explanatory sections on all aspects of space technology with detailed, 46-page "Space Diary."*

McAleer, Neil. *The Omni Space Almanac: A Complete Guide to the Space Age.* New York: World Almanac, 1987. 382 pp. *Good popular, easy-to-use survey of all aspects of space flight; fact-filled.*

The McGraw-Hill Encyclopedia of Space. New York: McGraw-Hill Book Company, 1967. 831 pp. *Good early effort at a one-book encyclopedia. Dated but contains some early details not found in later, similar works.*

Spangenburg, Ray, and Diane Moser. *Opening the Space Frontier.* New York: Facts on File, 1989. 111 pp. *Fact-filled, flight-by-flight treatment of manned space flight; also has sectional chronologies.*

Spangenburg, Ray, and Diane Moser. *Space People From A-Z.* New York: Facts on File, 1990. 100 pp. *Brief biographies of all those who have flown in space through 1989.*

WATER

Bridges

Shirley-Smith, H. *The World's Great Bridges.* London: Phoenix House, 1964. 250 pp. *Standard, broad-scope history; very easy to use.*

Steinman, David B., and Sara Ruth Watson. *Bridges and Their Builders.* New York: Dover Publications, 1957. 401 pp. *Enjoyable to read and very useful. Emphasis on individual designers.*

Canals

Boardman, Fon W., Jr. *Canals.* New York: Henry Z. Walck, Inc., 1959. 139 pp. *Brief, easy-to-read treatment of history's major canals.*

McKnight, Hugh. *The Guinness Guide to Waterways of Western Europe.* Middlesex: Guinness Superlatives Ltd., 1978. 240 pp. *Informational guide with the briefest of historical sections.*

Payne, Robert. *The Canal Builders.* New York: Macmillan, 1959. 278 pp. *Dated but especially good on ancient and Renaissance periods. Focuses primarily on the engineers who built the canals.*

Instruments & Lighthouses

Anderson, E. W. *Man the Navigator.* London: Priory Press Ltd., 1973. 128 pp. *Very brief survey. Touches lightly on only major developments.*

Beaver, Patrick. *A History of Lighthouses.* London: Peter Davies, 1971. 158 pp. *Well-written historical survey touching all major developments.*

Chase, Mary Ellen. *The Story of Lighthouses.* New York: W. W. Norton & Company, Inc., 1965. 169 pp. *Easy-to-read brief treatment. Although not a real history, it is interesting and useful.*

Holland, Francis R., Jr. *Great American Lighthouses.* Washington,

DC: The Preservation Press, 1989. 346 pp. *Excellent guide to existing lighthouses; little real history.*

Hutson, A. B. A. *The Navigator's Art.* London: Mills & Boon Ltd., 1974. 192 pp. *Popular standard history.*

Smith, Arthur. *Lighthouses.* Boston: Houghton Mifflin Company, 1971. 146 pp. *Popular history with general information on over 50 lighthouses; major emphasis is on the United States.*

Ships

Casson, Lionel. *Illustrated History of Ships & Boats.* New York: Doubleday, 1964. 272 pp. *Adequate general survey with excellent illustrations.*

Culver, Henry B. *The Book of Old Ships.* New York: Garden City Publishing Company, Inc., 1935. 306 pp. *Captures the spirit rather than the details of these great ships; easy to read and useful.*

Culver, Henry B. *Forty Famous Ships.* New York: Garden City Publishing Company, Inc., 1938. 320 pp. *More romantic and anecdotal than historical, but interesting and stimulating fun.*

Desmond, Kevin. *The Guinness Book of Motorboating Facts and Feats.* Middlesex: Guinness Superlatives Ltd., 1979. 257 pp. *Standard Guinness emphasis on firsts; also contains very good historical details on origins and development.*

Dunn, Lawrence. *The Book of Ships.* New York: Time-Life Books, 1968. 128 pp. *Extremely brief, small book that treats over 75 individual famous ships and gives illustrations of each.*

Gibson, Charles E. *The Story of the Ship.* New York: Henry Schuman, 1948. 272 pp. *Dated source but a useful, popular historical survey.*

Griffiths, Maurice. *Man the Shipbuilder.* Priory Press Ltd., 1973. 128 pp. *Brief, general historical survey; catches major construction developments.*

Horton, Edward. *The Illustrated History of the Submarine.* New York: Doubleday & Company, Inc., 1974. 160 pp. *Fairly brief, standard history. Very good illustrations.*

Landstrom, Bjorn. *The Ship.* London: Allen & Unwin, 1961. 309 pp. *Chronological, vessel-by-vessel historical treatment offers much information. Has many illustrations and is easy to read.*

Lewis, Edward V., and Robert O'Brien. *Ships.* New York: Time-Life Books, 1970. 200 pp. *Typically solid Time-Life publication. Good survey with excellent explanatory sections.*

Lobley, Douglas. *Ships Through the Ages.* New York: Octopus Books, 1972. 144 pp. *Brief, popular history with emphasis on large ships.*

Tryckare, Tre. *The Book of Ships.* New York: Time-Life Books, 1968. *Extremely brief, ship-by-ship treatment of over 75 ships. This very small book gives an illustration of each but has no connecting history to offer.*

Other

Nations, David, and Kevin Desmond. *The Guinness Guide to Water Skiing.* Middlesex: Guinness Superlatives, 1977. 240 pp. *Brief historical survey with the bulk of book devoted to techniques and equipment.*

Young, Nat. *The History of Surfing.* Tucson, AZ: The Body Press, 1987. 200 pp. *Best available, although short on details. Up-to-date and well illustrated.*

on the
MOVE
Index

Index